STUDENT SOLUTIONS MANUAL

Nancy S. Boudreau

Bowling Green State University

STATISTICS

for
business
and
economics
10e

McClave   Benson   Sincich

PEARSON

Prentice
Hall

D1366939

Upper Saddle River, NJ 07458

Vice President and Editorial Director, Mathematics: Christine Hoag
Executive Editor: Petra Recter
Supplement Editor: Joanne Wendelken
Senior Managing Editor: Linda Behrens
Assistant Managing Editor: Lynn Savino Wendel
Production Editor: Ashley M. Booth
Supplement Cover Manager: Paul Gourhan
Supplement Cover Designer: Victoria Colotta
Manufacturing Buyer: Ilene Kahn
Associate Director of Operations: Alexis Heydt-Long

© 2008 Pearson Education, Inc.
Pearson Prentice Hall
Pearson Education, Inc.
Upper Saddle River, NJ 07458

Printed in the United States of America

10 9 8 7 6 5 4 3 2 1

ISBN 13: 978-0-13-240937-7
ISBN 10: 0-13-240937-2

Pearson Education Ltd., *London*
Pearson Education Australia Pty. Ltd., *Sydney*
Pearson Education Singapore, Pte. Ltd.
Pearson Education North Asia Ltd., *Hong Kong*
Pearson Education Canada, Inc., *Toronto*
Pearson Educación de Mexico, S.A. de C.V.
Pearson Education—Japan, *Tokyo*
Pearson Education Malaysia, Pte. Ltd.

Contents

Preface

This solutions manual is designed to accompany the text, *Statistics for Business and Economics*, Tenth Edition, by James T. McClave, P. George Benson, and Terry Sincich. It provides answers to most odd-numbered exercises for each chapter in the text. Other methods of solution may also be appropriate; however, the author has presented one that she believes to be most instructive to the beginning Statistics student. The student should first attempt to solve the assigned exercises without help from this manual. Then, if unsuccessful, the solution in the manual will clarify points necessary to the solution. The student who successfully solves an exercise should still refer to the manual's solution. Many points are clarified and expanded upon to provide maximum insight into and benefit from each exercise.

Instructors will also benefit from the use of this manual. It will save time in preparing presentations of the solutions and possibly provide another point of view regarding their meaning.

Some of the exercises are subjective in nature and thus omitted from the Answer Key at the end of *Statistics for Business and Economics*, Tenth Edition. The subjective decisions regarding these exercises have been made and are explained by the author. Solutions based on these decisions are presented; the solution to this type of exercise is often most instructive. When an alternative interpretation of an exercise may occur, the author has often addressed it and given justification for the approach taken.

I would like to thank Kelly Barber for creating the art work and for typing this work.

Nancy S. Boudreau
Bowling Green State University
Bowling Green, Ohio

Statistics, Data, and Statistical Thinking　Chapter 1

1.1　Statistics is a science that deals with the collection, classification, analysis, and interpretation of information or data. It is a meaningful, useful science with a broad, almost limitless scope of applications to business, government, and the physical and social sciences.

1.3　The four elements of a descriptive statistics problem are:

1.　The population or sample of interest. This is the collection of all the units upon which the variable is measured.
2.　One or more variables that are to be investigated. These are the types of data that are to be collected.
3.　Tables, graphs, or numerical summary tools. These are tools used to display the characteristic of the sample or population.
4.　Conclusions about the data based on the patterns revealed. These are summaries of what the summary tools revealed about the population or sample.

1.5　The first major method of collecting data is from a published source. These data have already been collected by someone else and is available in a published source. The second method of collecting data is from a designed experiment. These data are collected by a researcher who exerts strict control over the experimental units in a study. These data are measured directly from the experimental units. The third method of collecting data is from a survey. These data are collected by a researcher asking a group of people one or more questions. Again, these data are collected directly from the experimental units or people. The final method of collecting data is observationally. These data are collected directly from experimental units by simply observing the experimental units in their natural environment and recording the values of the desired characteristics.

1.7　A population is a set of existing units such as people, objects, transactions, or events. A variable is a characteristic or property of an individual population unit such as height of a person, time of a reflex, amount of a transaction, etc.

1.9　A representative sample is a sample that exhibits characteristics similar to those possessed by the target population. A representative sample is essential if inferential statistics is to be applied. If a sample does not possess the same characteristics as the target population, then any inferences made using the sample will be unreliable.

1.11　A population is a set of existing units such as people, objects, transactions, or events. A process is a series of actions or operations that transform inputs to outputs. A process produces or generates output over time. Examples of processes are assembly lines, oil refineries, and stock prices.

1.13   The data consisting of the classifications A, B, C, and D are qualitative. These data are nominal and thus are qualitative. After the data are input as 1, 2, 3, and 4, they are still nominal and thus qualitative. The only differences between the two data sets are the names of the categories. The numbers associated with the four groups are meaningless.

1.15   a.   The population of interest is all citizens of the United States.

      b.   The variable of interest is the view of each citizen as to whether the president is doing a good or bad job. It is qualitative.

      c.   The sample is the 2000 individuals selected for the poll.

      d.   The inference of interest is to estimate the proportion of all citizens who believe the president is doing a good job.

      e.   The method of data collection is a survey.

      f.   It is not very likely that the sample will be representative of the population of all citizens of the United States. By selecting phone numbers at random, the sample will be limited to only those people who have telephones. Also, many people share the same phone number, so each person would not have an equal chance of being contacted. Another possible problem is the time of day the calls are made. If the calls are made in the evening, those people who work in the evening would not be represented.

1.17   I.   Qualitative; the possible responses are "yes" or "no," which are nonnumerical.

      II.   Quantitative; age is measured on a numerical scale, such as 15, 32, etc.

      III.   Qualitative; the possible responses are "yes" or "no," which are nonnmerical.

      IV.   Qualitative; the possible responses are "laser printer" or "another type of printer," which are nonnumerical.

      V.   Qualitative; the speeds can be classified as "slower," "unchanged," or "faster," which are nonnumerical.

      VI.   Quantitative; the number of people in a household who have used Windows 95 at least once is measured on a numerical scale, such as 0, 1, 2, etc.

1.19   a.   Whether the data collected on the chief executive officers at the 500 largest U. S. companies is a population or a sample depends on what one is interested in. If one is only interested in the information from the CEO's of the 500 largest U.S. companies, then this data form a population. If one is interested in the information on CEO's from all U.S. firms, then this data would form a sample.

      b.   1.   The industry type of the CEO's company is a qualitative variable. The industry type is a name.

          2.   The CEO's total compensation is a meaningful number. Thus, it is a quantitative variable.

3.   The CEO's total compensation over the previous five years is quantitative.

4.   The number of company stock shares (millions) held is a meaningful number. Thus, it is a quantitative variable.

5.   The CEO's age is a meaningful number. Thus, it is a quantitative variable.

6.   The CEO's efficiency rating is a meaningful number. Thus, it is a quantitative variable.

1.21   a.   The population of interest is all employees in the U.S.

       b.   The variable of interest is whether an employee is likely to remain in his/her job in the next five years if he/she is provided with mentoring.

       c.   Since the answer to the question would be either 'yes' or 'no', the variable is qualitative.

       d.   The sample is the 1000 employees in the U.S. who were actually surveyed.

       e.   Since 62% of those surveyed indicated that they would remain in their jobs for the next five years if they received mentoring, we could infer that the majority of all workers would remain in their jobs for the next five years if they receive mentoring.

1.23   a.   Length of maximum span can take on values such as 15 feet, 50 feet, 75 feet, etc. Therefore, it is quantitative.

       b.   The number of vehicle lanes can take on values such as 2, 4, etc. Therefore, it is quantitative.

       c.   The answer to this item is "yes" or "no," which are not numeric. Therefore, it is qualitative.

       d.   Average daily traffic could take on values such as 150 vehicles, 3,579 vehicles, 53,295 vehicles, etc. Therefore, it is quantitative.

       e.   Condition can take on values "good," "fair," or "poor," which are not numeric. Therefore, it is qualitative.

       f.   The length of the bypass or detour could take on values such as 1 mile, 4 miles, etc. Therefore, it is quantitative.

       g.   Route type can take on values "interstate," U.S.," "state," "county," or "city," which are not numeric. Therefore, it is qualitative.

1.25   a.   The process being studied is the distribution of pipes, valves, and fittings to the refining, chemical, and petrochemical industries by Wallace Company of Houston.

       b.   The variables of interest are the speed of the deliveries, the accuracy of the invoices, and the quality of the packaging of the products.

c.   The sampling plan was to monitor a subset of current customers by sending out a questionnaire twice a year and asking the customers to rate the speed of the deliveries, the accuracy of the invoices, and the quality of the packaging minutes. The sample is the total numbers of questionnaires received.

d.   The Wallace Company's immediate interest is learning about the delivery process of its distribution of pipes, valves, and fittings. To do this, it is measuring the speed of deliveries, the accuracy of the invoices, and the quality of its packaging from the sample of its customers to make an inference about the delivery process to all customers. In particular, it might use the mean speed of its deliveries to the sampled customers to estimate the mean speed of its deliveries to all its customers. It might use the mean accuracy of its invoices to the sampled customers to estimate the mean accuracy of its deliveries to all its customers. It might use the mean rating of the quality of its packaging to the sampled customers to estimate the mean rating of the quality of its packaging to all its customers.

e.   Several factors might affect the reliability of the inferences. One factor is the set of customers selected to receive the survey. If this set is not representative of all the customers, the wrong inferences could be made. Also, the set of customers returning the surveys may not be representative of all its customers. Again, this could influence the reliability of the inferences made.

1.27   a.   The population from which the sample was selected is the set of all department store executives.

b.   There are two variables measured by the authors. They are job-satisfaction and Machiavellian rating for each of the executives.

c.   The sample is the set of 218 department store executives who completed the questionnaire.

d.   The method of data collection is a survey.

e.   The inference made by the authors is that those executives with higher job-satisfaction scores are likely to have a lower 'mach' rating.

1.29   a.   Some possible questions are:

1.   In your opinion, why has the banking industry consolidated in the past few years? Check all that apply.

a.   Too many small banks with not enough capital.
b.   A result of the Savings and Loan scandals.
c.   To eliminate duplicated resources in the upper management positions.
d.   To provide more efficient service to the customers.
e.   To provide a more complete list of financial opportunities for the customers.
f.   Other. Please list.

2. Using a scale from 1 to 5, where 1 means strongly disagree and 5 means strongly agree, indicate your agreement to the following statement: "The trend of consolidation in the banking industry will continue in the next five years."

   1 strongly disagree   2 disagree   3 no opinion   4 agree   5 strongly agree

b. The population of interest is the set of all bank presidents in the United States.

c. It would be extremely difficult and costly to obtain information from all 10,000 bank presidents. Thus, it would be more efficient to sample just 200 bank presidents. However, by sending the questionnaires to only 200 bank presidents, one risks getting the results from a sample which is not representative of the population. The sample must be chosen in such a way that the results will be representative of the entire population of bank presidents in order to be of any use.

1.31 a. The population of interest is the set of all people in the United States over 14 years of age.

b. The variable being measured is the employment status of each person. This variable is qualitative. Each person is either employed or not.

c. The problem of interest to the Census Bureau is inferential. Based on the information contained in the sample, the Census Bureau wants to estimate the percentage of all people in the labor force who are unemployed.

2.1   First, we find the frequency of the grade A. The sum of the frequencies for all five grades must be 200. Therefore, subtract the sum of the frequencies of the other four grades from 200. The frequency for grade A is:

$$200 - (36 + 90 + 30 + 28) = 200 - 184 = 16$$

To find the relative frequency for each grade, divide the frequency by the total sample size, 200. The relative frequency for the grade B is 36/200 = .18. The rest of the relative frequencies are found in a similar manner and appear in the table:

Grade on Statistics Exam	Frequency	Relative Frequency
A: 90 –100	16	.08
B: 80 – 89	36	.18
C: 65 – 79	90	.45
D: 50 – 64	30	.15
F: Below 50	28	.14
Total	200	1.00

2.3   a.   The type of graph is a pie chart.

        b.   The variable measured on each of the industrial robots is task category.

        c.   From the graph, the task that uses the highest percentage of industrial robots is Material Handling with 34.0%.

        d.   Thirty-two percent or .32 * 144,000 = 46,080. Thus, 46,080 industrial robots were used for spot welding. The percentage of industrial robots used for either spot welding or arc welding is 32.0% + 20.0% = 52.0%.

2.5   a.   Using MINITAB, a Pareto diagram for the data is:

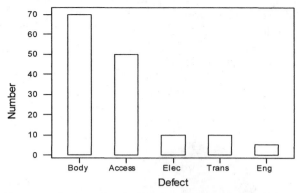

The most frequently observed defect is a body defect.

b.   Using MINITAB, a Pareto diagram for the Body Defect data is:

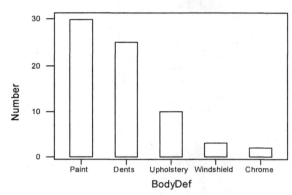

Most body defects are either paint or dents. These two categories account for (30 + 25) / 70 = 55 / 70 = .786 of all body defects. Since these two categories account for so much of the body defects, it would seem appropriate to target these two types of body defects for special attention.

2.7   a.   Using MINITAB the side-by-side relative frequency bar charts are:

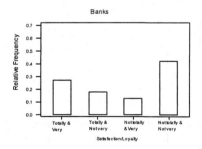
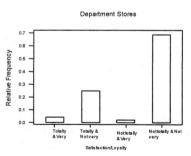

b.   Since the data are qualitative, we could have described them using pie charts.

c. For the banking industry, a little over a quarter of those who are totally satisfied are very loyal. This is a relatively small percentage. However, in the department stores, only 4% of those who are totally satisfied are very loyal. This indicates that very few department store customers are very loyal.

2.9 Using MINITAB, a pie chart of the data is:

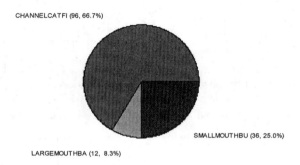

Pie Chart of Species

2.11 Using MINITAB, the pie charts are:

Color

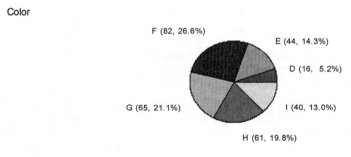

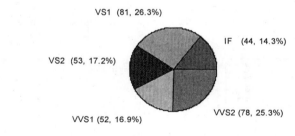

Clarity

The F color occurs the most often with 26.6%. The clarity that occurs the most is VS1 with 26.3%. The D color occurs the least often with 5.2%. The clarity that occurs the least is IF with 14.3%.

2.13   a.   The variable measured by Performark is the length of time it took for each advertiser to respond back.

b.   The pie chart is:

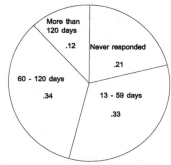

c.   Twenty-one percent of .21 × 17,000 = 3,570 of the advertisers never respond to the sales lead.

d.   The information from the pie chart does not indicate how effective the "bingo cards" are. It just indicates how long it takes advertisers to respond, if at all.

2.15   a.   The Pareto diagram is:

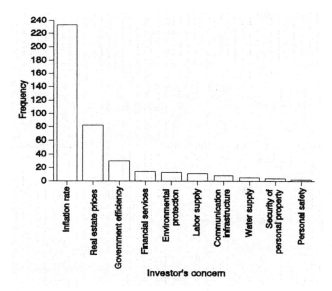

b.   The environmental factor of most concern is "Inflation rate" with 233/402 = .58 or 58% of the investors indicating this as their most serious concern. The second most serious concern was "Real Estate prices." Over 20% ((82/402) × 100% = 20.4%) of the investors chose this concern. Each of the other categories were chosen by less than 10% of the investors.

c.   Two factors out of 10 represent 20% of the factors. The two factors are "Inflation rate" and "Real estate prices." These two factors represent ((233 + 82)/402 = .78) 78% of the investors. This is very close to 80%.

2.17 To find the number of measurements for each measurement class, multiply the relative frequency by the total number of observations, $n = 500$. The frequency table is:

Measurement Class	Relative Frequency	Frequency
.5 – 2.5	.10	500(.10) = 50
2.5 – 4.5	.15	500(.15) = 75
4.5 – 6.5	.25	500(.25) = 125
6.5 – 8.5	.20	500(.20) = 100
8.5 – 10.5	.05	500(.05) = 25
10.5 – 12.5	.10	500(.10) = 50
12.5 – 14.5	.10	500(.10) = 50
14.5 – 16.5	.05	500(.05) = 25
		500

The frequency histogram is:

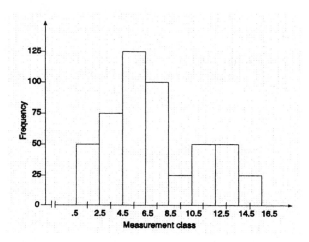

2.19 a. This is a frequency histogram because the number of observations is graphed for each interval rather than the relative frequency.

b. There are 14 measurement classes.

c. There are 49 measurements in the data set.

2.21 a. For male USGA golfers, there are about 28.5% with handicaps greater than 20.

b. For female USGA golfers, there are about 82% with handicaps greater than 20.

2.23   a.   The stem-and-leaf display for the runs scored by St. Louis is:

```
Stem-and-leaf of St. Louis      N = 58
Leaf Unit = 0.10
     2     1   00
     7     2   00000
    15     3   00000000
    20     4   Ⓞ0000
    26     5   000000
   (11)    6   ⓄⓄⓄ00000000
    21     7   Ⓞ000
    17     8   Ⓞ0000000
     9     9   00
     7    10   Ⓞ0
     5    11   Ⓞ0
     3    12
     3    13   0
     2    14   Ⓞ
     1    15   Ⓞ
```

b.   The games where McGuire hit multiple home runs are circled above. The number of runs scored when McGuire hit multiple home runs tends to be at or above the median. Thus, the Cardinals tend to score more runs when McGuire hit multiple home runs.

2.25   a.   Using MINITAB, the relative frequency (percent) histogram is:

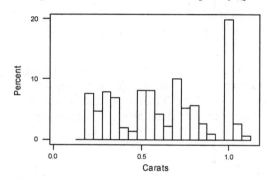

b.   Using MINITAB, the relative frequency (percent) histogram for the GIA group is:

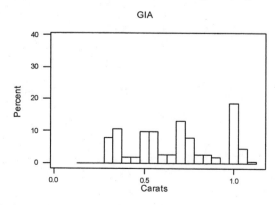

c. Using MINITAB, the relative frequency (percent) histograms for the HRD and IGI groups are:

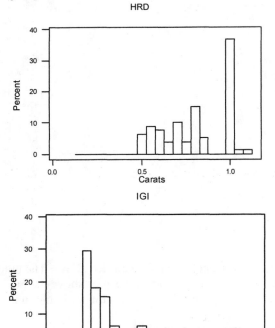

d. The HRD group does not assess any diamonds less than .5 carats and almost 40% of the diamonds they assess are 1.0 carats or higher. The IGI group does not assess very many diamonds over .5 carats and more than half are .3 carats or less. More than half of the diamonds assessed by the GIA group are more than .5 carats, but the sizes are less than those of the HRD group.

2.27 a. Using MINITAB, the stem-and-leaf display is:

```
Stem-and-Leaf of PENALTY          N = 38
Leaf Unit = 10000

 (28)    ⓪ 0 0①① 111②② 222222③③ 33334444899
  10     1⓪ 0239
   5     2
   5     3 0
   4     4 0
   3     5
   3     6
   3     7
   3     8 5
   2     9 3
   1    10 0
```

b. See the circled leaves in part **a**.

c.   Most of the penalties imposed for Clean Air Act violations are relatively small compared to the penalties imposed for other violations. All but one of the penalties for Clean Air Act violations are below the median penalty imposed.

2.29   a.   Using MINITAB, the frequency histograms for the 2 years of SAT scores are:

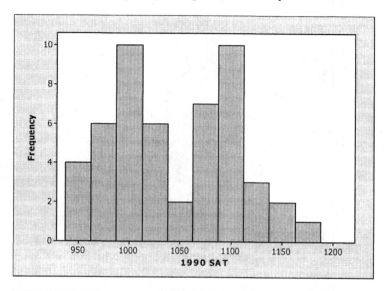

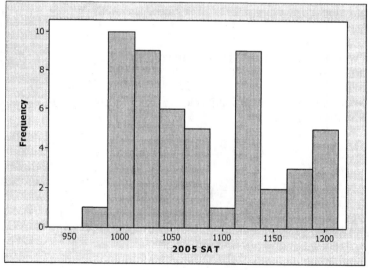

The data from 2005 are shifted to the right of those for 1990.

b.   Using MINITAB, the frequency histogram of the differences is:

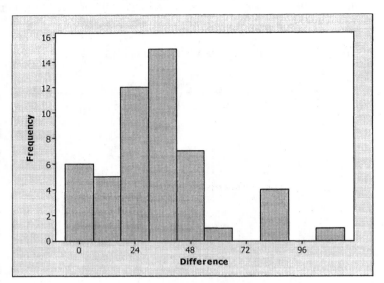

c.   Very few, if any, of the observations of differences are negative. This implies that the SAT scores for 2005 are bigger than the SAT scores for 1990 for the most part.

d.   Based on the graph, the largest improvement is around 100 points. From the actual data, the real value of the point is 111. The state associated with this large difference is Illinois.

2.31   a.   The percentage of realizations of V with values ranging from .425 to .675 is approximately $13.5 + 11.5 + 8 + 6 + 5.75 = 44.75\%$.

        b.   The norm constraint level V that has approximately 10% of the realizations less than it is approximately .325.

2.33   a. $\sum x = 5 + 1 + 3 + 2 + 1 = 12$

        b. $\sum x^2 = 5^2 + 1^2 + 3^2 + 2^2 + 1^2 = 40$

        c. $\sum (x-1) = (5-1) + (1-1) + (3-1) + (2-1) + (1-1) = 7$

        d. $\sum (x-1)^2 = (5-1)^2 + (1-1)^2 + (3-1)^2 + (2-1)^2 + (1-1)^2 = 21$

        e. $\left(\sum x\right)^2 = (5 + 1 + 3 + 2 + 1)^2 = 12^2 = 144$

2.35   Using the results from Exercise 2.33:

a. $\sum x^2 - \dfrac{\left(\sum x\right)^2}{5} = 40 - \dfrac{144}{5} = 40 - 28.8 = 11.2$

b. $\sum(x-2)^2 = (5-2)^2 + (1-2)^2 + (3-2)^2 + (2-2)^2 + (1-2)^2 = 12$

c. $\sum x^2 - 10 = 40 - 10 = 30$

2.37   Assume the data are a sample. The sample mean is:

$$\bar{x} = \frac{\sum x}{n} = \frac{3.2 + 2.5 + 2.1 + 3.7 + 2.8 + 2.0}{6} = \frac{16.3}{6} = 2.717$$

The median is the average of the middle two numbers when the data are arranged in order (since $n = 6$ is even). The data arranged in order are: 2.0, 2.1, 2.5, 2.8, 3.2, 3.7. The middle two numbers are 2.5 and 2.8. The median is:

$$\frac{2.5 + 2.8}{2} = \frac{5.3}{2} = 2.65$$

2.39   The mean and median of a symmetric data set are equal to each other. The mean is larger than the median when the data set is skewed to the right. The mean is less than the median when the data set is skewed to the left. Thus, by comparing the mean and median, one can determine whether the data set is symmetric, skewed right, or skewed left.

2.41   Assume the data are a sample. The mode is the observation that occurs most frequently. For this sample, the mode is 15, which occurs three times.

The sample mean is:

$$\bar{x} = \frac{\sum x}{n} = \frac{18 + 10 + 15 + 13 + 17 + 15 + 12 + 15 + 18 + 16 + 11}{11} = \frac{160}{11} = 14.545$$

The median is the middle number when the data are arranged in order. The data arranged in order are: 10, 11, 12, 13, 15, 15, 15, 16, 17, 18, 18. The middle number is the 6th number, which is 15.

2.43   a.   For a distribution that is skewed to the left, the mean is less than the median.

b.   For a distribution that is skewed to the right, the mean is greater than the median.

c.   For a symmetric distribution, the mean and median are equal.

2.45   a.   The sample mean is:

$$\bar{x} = \frac{\sum_{i=1}^{n} x_i}{n} = \frac{49 + 52 + 51 + \cdots + 51}{50} = \frac{2494}{50} = 49.88$$

The sample median is found by finding the average of the 25th and 26th observations once the data are arranged in order. The 25th and 26th observations are 49 and 50. The average of 49 & 50 is 49.5. Thus, the sample median is 49.5.

The mode is the observation that occurs the most. It is 51, which occurs 8 times.

b.   Since the mean is slightly greater than the median, the data are skewed to the right a little.

c.

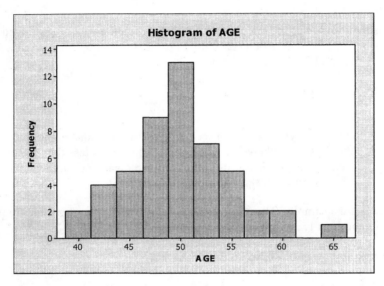

The modal class is the interval with the largest frequency. From the histogram the modal class is 48.75 to 51.25.

2.47   a.   The sample mean is:

$$\bar{x} = \frac{\sum_{i=1}^{n} x_i}{n} = \frac{.30 + .30 + .30 + \ldots + 1.09}{308} = \frac{194.32}{308} = .631$$

The average number of carats for the 308 diamonds is .631

b.   The median is the average of the middle two observations once they have been ordered. The 154th and 155th observations are .62 and .62. The average of these two observations is .62.

Half of the diamonds weigh less than .62 carats and half weigh more.

c.   The mode is 1.0. This observation occurred 32 times.

d. Since the mean and median are close in value, either could be a good descriptor of central tendency.

2.49 The mean is 141.31 hours. This means that the average number of semester hours per candidate for the CPA exam is 141.31 hours. The median is 140 hours. This means that 50% of the candidates had more than 140 semester hours of credit and 50% had less than 140 semester hours of credit. Since the mean and median are so close in value, the data are probably not skewed, but close to symmetric.

2.53 a. For the "Joint exchange offer with prepack" firms, the mean time is 2.6545 months, and the median is 1.5 months. Thus, the average time spent in bankruptcy for "Joint" firms is 2.6545 months, while half of the firms spend 1.5 months or less in bankruptcy.

For the "No prefiling vote held" firms, the mean time is 4.2364 months, and the median is 3.2 months. Thus, the average time spent in bankruptcy for "No prefiling vote held" firms is 4.2364 months, while half of the firms spend 3.2 months or less in bankruptcy.

For the "Prepack solicitation only" firms, the mean time is 1.8185 months, and the median is 1.4 months. Thus, the average time spent in bankruptcy for "Prepack solicitation only" firms is 1.8185 months, while half of the firms spend 1.4 months or less in bankruptcy.

b. Since the means and medians for the three groups of firms differ quite a bit, it would be unreasonable to use a single number to locate the center of the time in bankruptcy. Three different "centers" should be used.

2.55 a. The primary disadvantage of using the range to compare variability of data sets is that the two data sets can have the same range and be vastly different with respect to data variation. Also, the range is greatly affected by extreme measures.

b. The sample variance is the sum of the squared deviations from the sample mean divided by the sample size minus 1. The population variance is the sum of the squared deviations from the population mean divided by the population size.

c. The variance of a data set can never be negative. The variance of a sample is the sum of the *squared* deviations from the mean divided by $n - 1$. The square of any number, positive or negative, is always positive. Thus, the variance will be positive.

The variance is usually greater than the standard deviation. However, it is possible for the variance to be smaller than the standard deviation. If the data are between 0 and 1, the variance will be smaller than the standard deviation. For example, suppose the data set is .8, .7, .9, .5, and .3. The sample mean is:

$$\bar{x} = \frac{\sum x}{n} = \frac{.8 + .7 + .9 + .5 + .3}{.5} = \frac{3.2}{5} = .64$$

The sample variance is:

$$s^2 = \frac{\sum x^2 - \frac{\left(\sum x\right)^2}{n}}{n-1} = \frac{2.28 - \frac{3.2^2}{5}}{5-1} = \frac{2.28 - 2.048}{4} = \frac{.325}{4} = .058$$

The standard deviation is $s = \sqrt{.058} = .241$

2.57   a.   Range = 4 − 0 = 4

$$s^2 = \frac{\sum x^2 - \frac{\left(\sum x\right)^2}{n}}{n-1} = \frac{22 - \frac{8^2}{5}}{4-1} = 2.3 \qquad\qquad s = \sqrt{2.3} = 1.52$$

b.   Range = 6 − 0 = 6

$$s^2 = \frac{\sum x^2 - \frac{\left(\sum x\right)^2}{n}}{n-1} = \frac{63 - \frac{17^2}{7}}{7-1} = 3.619 \qquad\qquad s = \sqrt{3.619} = 1.90$$

c.   Range = 8 − (−2) = 10

$$s^2 = \frac{\sum x^2 - \frac{\left(\sum x\right)^2}{n}}{n-1} = \frac{154 - \frac{30^2}{10}}{10-1} = 7.111 \qquad\qquad s = \sqrt{7.111} = 2.67$$

d.   Range = 2 − (−3) = 5

$$s^2 = \frac{\sum x^2 - \frac{\left(\sum x\right)^2}{n}}{n-1} = \frac{29 - \frac{(-5)^2}{18}}{18-1} = 1.624 \qquad\qquad s = \sqrt{1.624} = 1.274$$

2.59   a. $\sum x = 3 + 1 + 10 + 10 + 4 = 28$

$\sum x^2 = 3^2 + 1^2 + 10^2 + 10^2 + 4^2 = 226$

$$\bar{x} = \frac{\sum x}{n} = \frac{28}{5} = 5.6$$

$$s^2 = \frac{\sum x^2 - \frac{\left(\sum x\right)^2}{n}}{n-1} = \frac{226 - \frac{28^2}{5}}{5-1} = \frac{69.2}{4} = 17.3 \qquad\qquad s = \sqrt{17.3} = 4.1593$$

b. $\sum x = 8 + 10 + 32 + 5 = 55$

$\sum x^2 = 8^2 + 10^2 + 32^2 + 5^2 = 1213$

$$\bar{x} = \frac{\sum x}{n} = \frac{55}{4} = 13.75 \text{ feet}$$

$$s^2 = \frac{\sum x^2 - \frac{\left(\sum x\right)^2}{n}}{n-1} = \frac{1213 - \frac{55^2}{4}}{4-1} = \frac{456.75}{3} = 152.25 \text{ square feet}$$

$$s = \sqrt{152.25} = 12.339 \text{ feet}$$

c. $\sum x = -1 + (-4) + (-3) + 1 + (-4) + (-4) = -15$

$\sum x^2 = (-1)^2 + (-4)^2 + (-3)^2 + 1^2 + (-4)^2 + (-4)^2 = 59$

$\bar{x} = \dfrac{\sum x}{n} = \dfrac{-15}{6} = -2.5$

$s^2 = \dfrac{\sum x^2 - \dfrac{\left(\sum x\right)^2}{n}}{n-1} = \dfrac{59 - \dfrac{(-15)^2}{6}}{6-1} = \dfrac{21.5}{5} = 4.3 \qquad s = \sqrt{4.3} = 2.0736$

d. $\sum x = \dfrac{1}{5} + \dfrac{1}{5} + \dfrac{1}{5} + \dfrac{2}{5} + \dfrac{1}{5} + \dfrac{4}{5} = \dfrac{10}{5} = 2$

$\sum x^2 = \left(\dfrac{1}{5}\right)^2 + \left(\dfrac{1}{5}\right)^2 + \left(\dfrac{1}{5}\right)^2 + \left(\dfrac{2}{5}\right)^2 + \left(\dfrac{1}{5}\right)^2 + \left(\dfrac{4}{5}\right)^2 = \dfrac{24}{25} = .96$

$\bar{x} = \dfrac{\sum x}{n} = \dfrac{2}{6} = \dfrac{1}{3} = .33$ ounce

$s^2 = \dfrac{\sum x^2 - \dfrac{\left(\sum x\right)^2}{n}}{n-1} = \dfrac{\dfrac{24}{25} - \dfrac{2^2}{6}}{6-1} = \dfrac{.2933}{5} = .0587$ square ounce

$s = \sqrt{.0587} = .2422$ ounce

2.61   This is one possibility for the two data sets.

Data Set 1: 0, 1, 2, 3, 4, 5, 6, 7, 8, 9
Data Set 2: 0, 0, 1, 1, 2, 2, 3, 3, 9, 9

The two sets of data above have the same range = largest measurement – smallest measurement = 9 – 0 = 9.

The means for the two data sets are:

$\bar{x}_1 = \dfrac{\sum x}{n} = \dfrac{0+1+2+3+4+5+6+7+8+9}{10} = \dfrac{45}{10} = 4.5$

$\bar{x}_2 = \dfrac{\sum x}{n} = \dfrac{0+0+1+1+2+2+3+3+9+9}{10} = \dfrac{30}{10} = 3$

The dot diagrams for the two data sets are shown below.

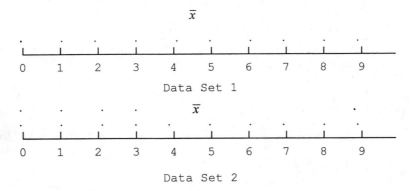

2.63   a.   The numbers of lawyers at the top-ranked firms with headquarters in Orlando are:

355 159 158 150 100 70 63 63

The range is the largest observation minus the smallest or $355 - 63 = 292$.

b.   The numbers of lawyers at the top-ranked firms with headquarters in Miami are:

301 144 141 105 85 85 70 70 64

The range is the largest observation minus the smallest or $301 - 64 = 237$.

c.   No. The range gives us no information about the values of the data, only the difference between the largest and the smallest observations.

2.65   a.   For the length data, the maximum length is 52 cm and the minimum length is 17.5 cm. The range is $52 - 17.5 = 34.5$ cm. The variance is:

$$s^2 = \frac{\sum_i x_i^2 - \frac{\left(\sum_i x_i\right)^2}{n}}{n-1} = \frac{270,712 - \frac{6,165^2}{144}}{144-1} = 47.363 \text{ square cm}$$

The standard deviation is:

$$s = \sqrt{s^2} = \sqrt{47.363} = 6.882 \text{ cm}$$

b. For the weight data, the maximum weight is 2,302 grams and the minimum weight is 173 grams. The range is $2,302 - 173 = 2,129$ grams. The variance is:

$$s^2 = \frac{\sum_i x_i^2 - \frac{\left(\sum_i x_i\right)^2}{n}}{n-1} = \frac{178,949,449 - \frac{151,159^2}{144}}{144-1} = 141,786.9741 \text{ square grams}$$

The standard deviation is:

$$s = \sqrt{s^2} = \sqrt{141,786.9741} = 376.55 \text{ grams}$$

c. For the DDT data, the maximum DDT level is 1,100 parts per million and the minimum DDT level is .11 parts per million. The range is $1,100 - .11 = 1,099.89$ parts per million. The variance is:

$$s^2 = \frac{\sum_i x_i^2 - \frac{\left(\sum_i x_i\right)^2}{n}}{n-1} = \frac{1,469,419 - \frac{3,507.1^2}{144}}{144-1} = 9,678.350 \text{ square parts per million}$$

The standard deviation is:

$$s = \sqrt{s^2} = \sqrt{9,678.350} = 98.379 \text{ parts per million}$$

2.67 a. The range is the largest observation minus the smallest observation or $13 - 1 = 12$
The variance is:

$$s^2 = \frac{\sum_i x_i^2 - \frac{\left(\sum_i x_i\right)^2}{n}}{n-1} = \frac{498 - \frac{80^2}{20}}{20-1} = 9.368$$

The standard deviation is:

$$s = \sqrt{s^2} = \sqrt{9.368} = 3.061$$

b. The largest observation is 13. It is deleted from the data set. The new range is:

$9 - 1 = 8.$

The variance is:

$$s^2 = \dfrac{\sum_i x_i^2 - \dfrac{\left(\sum_i x_i\right)^2}{n}}{n-1} = \dfrac{329 - \dfrac{67^2}{19}}{19-1} = 5.152$$

The standard deviation is:

$$s = \sqrt{s^2} = \sqrt{5.152} = 2.270$$

When the largest observation is deleted, the range, variance and standard deviation decrease.

c. The largest observation is 13 and the smallest is 1. When these two observations are deleted from the data set, the new range is:
9 − 1 = 8.

The variance is:

$$s^2 = \dfrac{\sum_i x_i^2 - \dfrac{\left(\sum_i x_i\right)^2}{n}}{n-1} = \dfrac{328 - \dfrac{66^2}{18}}{18-1} = 5.059$$

The standard deviation is:

$$s = \sqrt{s^2} = \sqrt{5.059} = 2.249$$

When the largest and smallest observations are deleted, the range, variance and standard deviation decrease.

2.69 a. The unit of measurement of the variable of interest is dollars (the same as the mean and standard deviation). Based on this, the data are quantitative.

b. Since no information is given about the shape of the data set, we can only use Chebyshev's Rule.

$900 is 2 standard deviations below the mean, and $2100 is 2 standard deviations above the mean. Using Chebyshev's Rule, at least 3/4 of the measurements (or 3/4 × 200 = 150 measurements) will fall between $900 and $2100.

$600 is 3 standard deviations below the mean and $2400 is 3 standard deviations above the mean. Using Chebyshev's Rule, at least 8/9 of the measurements (or 8/9 × 200 ≈ 178 measurements) will fall between $600 and $2400.

$1200 is 1 standard deviation below the mean and $1800 is 1 standard deviation above the mean. Using Chebyshev's Rule, nothing can be said about the number of measurements that will fall between $1200 and $1800.

$1500 is equal to the mean and $2100 is 2 standard deviations above the mean. Using Chebyshev's Rule, at least 3/4 of the measurements (or $3/4 \times 200 = 150$ measurements) will fall between $900 and $2100. It is possible that all of the 150 measurements will be between $900 and $1500. Thus, nothing can be said about the number of measurements between $1500 and $2100.

2.71   According to the Empirical Rule:

a.   Approximately 68% of the measurements will be contained in the interval $\bar{x} - s$ to $\bar{x} + s$.

b.   Approximately 95% of the measurements will be contained in the interval $\bar{x} - 2s$ to $\bar{x} + 2s$.

c.   Essentially all the measurements will be contained in the interval $\bar{x} - 3s$ to $\bar{x} + 3s$.

2.73   Using Chebyshev's Rule, at least 8/9 of the measurements will fall within 3 standard deviations of the mean. Thus, the range of the data would be around 6 standard deviations. Using the Empirical Rule, approximately 95% of the observations are within 2 standard deviations of the mean. Thus, the range of the data would be around 4 standard deviations. We would expect the standard deviation to be somewhere between Range/6 and Range/4.

For our data, the range $= 760 - 135 = 625$.

The Range/6 $= 625/6 = 104.17$ and Range/4 $= 625/4 = 156.25$.

Therefore, I would estimate that the standard deviation of the data set is between 104.17 and 156.25.

It would not be feasible to have a standard deviation of 25. If the standard deviation were 25, the data would span $625/25 = 25$ standard deviations. This would be extremely unlikely.

2.75   a.   The 2 standard deviation interval around the mean is:

$\bar{x} \pm 2s \Rightarrow 141.31 \pm 2(17.77) \Rightarrow 141.31 \pm 35.54 \Rightarrow (105.77, \ 176.85)$

b.   Using Chebyshev's Theorem, at least ¾ of the observations will fall within 2 standard deviations of the mean. Thus, at least ¾ of first-time candidates for the CPA exam have total credit hours between 105.77 and 176.85.

c.   In order for the above statement to be true, nothing needs to be known about the shape of the distribution of total semester hours.

2.77   a.   The sample mean is:

$$\bar{x} = \frac{\sum\limits_{i=1}^{n} x_i}{n} = \frac{16,040}{169} = 94.91$$

The sample variance is:

$$s^2 = \frac{\sum\limits_{i=1}^{n} x^2 - \frac{\left(\sum\limits_{i=1}^{n} x_i\right)^2}{n}}{n-1} = \frac{1,526,288 - \frac{16,040^2}{169}}{169-1} = 23.2837$$

The standard deviation is:

$$s = \sqrt{s^2} = \sqrt{23.2837} = 4.83$$

b. $\bar{x} \pm s \Rightarrow 94.91 \pm 4.83 \Rightarrow (90.08, \quad 99.74)$

$\bar{x} \pm 2s \Rightarrow 94.91 \pm 2(4.83) \Rightarrow 94.91 \pm 9.66 \Rightarrow (85.25, \quad 104.57)$

$\bar{x} \pm 3s \Rightarrow 94.91 \pm 3(4.83) \Rightarrow 94.91 \pm 14.49 \Rightarrow (80.42, \quad 109.40)$

c.   There are 137 out of 169 observations in the first interval. This is (137/169)*100% = 81.1%. There are 165 out of 169 observations in the second interval. This is (165/169)*100% = 97.6%. There are 166 out of 169 observations in the second interval. This is (166/169)*100% = 98.2%.

The percentages for the first 2 intervals are somewhat larger than we would expect using the Empirical Rule. The Empirical Rule indicates that approximately 68% of the observations will fall within 1 standard deviation of the mean. It also indicates that approximately 95% of the observations will fall within 2 standard deviations of the mean. Chebyshev's Theorem says that at least ¾ or 75% of the observations will fall within 2 standard deviations of the mean and at least 8/9 or 88.9% of the observations will fall within 3 standard deviations of the mean. It appears that our observed percentages agree with Chebyshev's Theorem better than the Empirical Rule.

2.79   The sample mean is:

$$\bar{x} = \frac{\sum\limits_{i=1}^{n} x_i}{n} = \frac{240.9 + 248.8 + 215.7 + \cdots + 238.0}{10} = \frac{2347.4}{10} = 234.74$$

The sample variance deviation is:

$$s^2 = \frac{\sum\limits_{i=1}^{n} x_i^2 - \frac{\left(\sum\limits_{i=1}^{n} x_i\right)^2}{n}}{n-1} = \frac{551,912.1 - \frac{2347.4^2}{10}}{9} = \frac{883.424}{9} = 98.1582$$

The sample standard deviation is:

$$\sqrt{s^2} = \sqrt{98.1582} = 9.91$$

The data are fairly symmetric, so we can use the Empirical Rule. We know from the Empirical Rule that almost all of the observations will fall within 3 standard deviations of the mean. This interval would be:

$$\bar{x} \pm 3s \Rightarrow 234.74 \pm 3(9.91) \Rightarrow 234.74 \pm 29.73 \Rightarrow (205.01, \ 264.47)$$

2.81   a.   Since no information is given about the distribution of the velocities of the Winchester bullets, we can only use Chebyshev's Rule to describe the data. We know that at least 3/4 of the velocities will fall within the interval:

$$\bar{x} \pm 2s \Rightarrow 936 \pm 2(10) \Rightarrow 936 \pm 20 \Rightarrow (916, 956)$$

Also, at least 8/9 of the velocities will fall within the interval:

$$\bar{x} \pm 3s \Rightarrow 936 \pm 3(10) \Rightarrow 936 \pm 30 \Rightarrow (906, 966)$$

      b.   Since a velocity of 1,000 is much larger than the largest value in the second interval in part **a**, it is very unlikely that the bullet was manufactured by Winchester.

2.83   Since we do not know if the distribution of the heights of the trees is mound-shaped, we need to apply Chebyshev's Rule. We know $\mu = 30$ and $\sigma = 3$. Therefore,

$$\mu \pm 3\sigma \Rightarrow 30 \pm 3(3) \Rightarrow 30 \pm 9 \Rightarrow (21, 39)$$

According to Chebyshev's Rule, at least 8/9 or .89 of the tree heights on this piece of land fall within this interval and at most $\frac{1}{9}$ or .11 of the tree heights will fall above the interval.

However, the buyer will only purchase the land if at least $\frac{1000}{5000}$ or .20 of the tree heights are at least 40 feet tall. Therefore, the buyer should not buy the piece of land.

2.85   We know $\mu = 25$ and $\sigma = .1$. Therefore,

$$\mu \pm 2\sigma \Rightarrow 25 \pm 2(.1) \Rightarrow 25 \pm .2 \Rightarrow (24.8, 25.2)$$

The machine is shut down for adjustment if the contents of two consecutive bags fall more than 2 standard deviations from the mean (i.e., outside the interval (24.8, 25.2)). Therefore, the machine was shut down yesterday at 11:30 (25.23 and 25.25 are outside the interval) and again at 4:00 (24.71 and 25.31 are outside the interval).

2.87   Using the definition of a percentile:

	Percentile	Percentage Above	Percentage Below
a.	75th	25%	75%
b.	50th	50%	50%
c.	20th	80%	20%
d.	84th	16%	84%

2.89   We first compute z-scores for each x value.

a. $z = \dfrac{x - \mu}{\sigma} = \dfrac{100 - 50}{25} = 2$

b. $z = \dfrac{x - \mu}{\sigma} = \dfrac{1 - 4}{1} = -3$

c. $z = \dfrac{x - \mu}{\sigma} = \dfrac{0 - 200}{100} = -2$

d. $z = \dfrac{x - \mu}{\sigma} = \dfrac{10 - 5}{3} = 1.67$

The above z-scores indicate that the x value in part **a** lies the greatest distance above the mean and the x value of part **b** lies the greatest distance below the mean.

2.91   The mean score of U.S. eighth-graders on a mathematics assessment test is 279. This is the average score. The 10th percentile score is 231. This means that 10% of the U.S. eighth-graders score below 231 on the test and 90% score higher. The 25th percentile is 255. This means that 25% of the U.S. eighth-graders score below 255 on the test and 75% score higher. The 75th percentile is 304. This means that 75% of the U.S. eighth-graders score below 304 on the test and 25% score higher. The 90th percentile is 324. This means that 90% of the U.S. eighth-graders score below 324 on the test and 10% score higher.

2.93   a.   The sample mean is:

$$\overline{x} = \frac{\sum_{i=1}^{n} x_i}{n} = \frac{5,432.34}{497} = 10.930$$

Note: There are 3 observations that have missing values for total 2005 pay.

The sample variance is:

$$s^2 = \frac{\sum_{i=1}^{n} x^2 - \frac{\left(\sum_{i=1}^{n} x_i\right)^2}{n}}{n-1} = \frac{272,909 - \frac{5,432.34^2}{497}}{497-1} = 430.5083$$

The standard deviation is:

$$s = \sqrt{s^2} = \sqrt{430.5083} = 20.749$$

b.   The z-score would be:

$$z = \frac{x - \overline{x}}{s} = \frac{75.33 - 10.930}{20.749} = 3.10$$

c.   The z-score would be:

$$z = \frac{x - \overline{x}}{s} = \frac{1.1 - 10.930}{20.749} = -0.47$$

d.   The z-score associated with Oracle CEO Lawrence Ellison is 3.10. This is a very large value for a z-score. Most of the observations will be within 3 standard deviations of the mean. This person made more money than most of the other CEO's in the survey. The z-score associated with Microsoft CEO S. A. Ballmer is −0.47. This value is very close to 0. A z-score of 0 would indicate that the observation was equal to the mean. Since this z-score is negative and close to 0, this person had a 2005 pay of less than 1 standard deviation below the mean. The distribution of 2005 pays is skewed to the right. Thus, the Empirical Rule does not apply. Chebyshev's Rule can also not be applied since the pay for this last CEO is less than 1 standard deviation from the mean.

2.95   Since the 90th percentile of the study sample in the subdivision was .00372 mg/L, which is less than the USEPA level of .015 mg/L, the water customers in the subdivision are not at risk of drinking water with unhealthy lead levels.

2.97   a.   The 10th percentile is the score that has at least 10% of the observations less than it. If we arrange the data in order from the smallest to the largest, the 10th percentile score will be the .10(75) = 7.5 or 8th observation. When the data are arranged in order, the 8th observation is 0. Thus, the 10th percentile is 0.

b.   The 95th percentile is the score that has at least 95% of the observations less than it. If we arrange the data in order from the smallest to the largest, the 95th percentile score will be the .95(75) = 71.25 or 72nd observation. When the data are arranged in order, the 72nd observation is 21. Thus, the 95th percentile is 21.

c. The sample mean is:

$$\bar{x} = \frac{\sum_{i=1}^{n} x_i}{n} = \frac{393}{75} = 5.24$$

The sample variance is:

$$s^2 = \frac{\sum_i x_i^2 - \frac{\left(\sum_i x_i\right)^2}{n}}{n-1} = \frac{5943 - \frac{393^2}{75}}{75-1} = 52.482$$

The standard deviation is:

$$s = \sqrt{s^2} = \sqrt{52.482} = 7.244$$

The z-score for a county with 48 Superfund sites is:

$$z = \frac{x - \bar{x}}{s} = \frac{48 - 5.24}{7.244} = 5.90$$

d. Yes. A score of 48 is almost 6 standard deviations from the mean. We know that for any data set almost all (at least 8/9 using Chebyshev's Theorem) of the observations are within 3 standard deviations of the mean. To be almost 6 standard deviations from the mean is very unusual.

2.99 To determine if the measurements are outliers, compute the z-score.

a. $z = \frac{x - \bar{x}}{s} = \frac{65 - 57}{11} = .727$ Since this z-score is less than 3 in magnitude, 65 is not an outlier.

b. $z = \frac{x - \bar{x}}{s} = \frac{21 - 57}{11} = -3.273$ Since this z-score is more than 3 in magnitude, 21 is an outlier.

c. $z = \frac{x - \bar{x}}{s} = \frac{72 - 57}{11} = 1.364$ Since this z-score is less than 3 in magnitude, 72 is not an outlier.

d. $z = \frac{x - \bar{x}}{s} = \frac{98 - 57}{11} = 3.727$ Since this z-score is more than 3 in magnitude, 98 is an outlier.

2.101   The interquartile range is IQR = $Q_U - Q_L = 85 - 60 = 25$.

The lower inner fence = $Q_L - 1.5(IQR) = 60 - 1.5(25) = 22.5$.

The upper inner fence = $Q_U + 1.5(IQR) = 85 + 1.5(25) = 122.5$.

The lower outer fence = $Q_L - 3(IQR) = 60 - 3(25) = -15$.

The upper outer fence = $Q_U + 3(IQR) = 85 + 3(25) = 160$.

With only this information, the box plot would look something like the following:

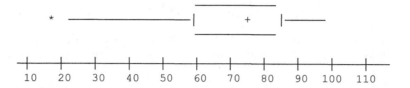

The whiskers extend to the inner fences unless no data points are that small or that large. The upper inner fence is 122.5. However, the largest data point is 100, so the whisker stops at 100. The lower inner fence is 22.5. The smallest data point is 18, so the whisker extends to 22.5. Since 18 is between the inner and outer fences, it is designated with a *. We do not know if there is any more than one data point below 22.5, so we cannot be sure that the box plot is entirely correct.

2.103   a.   The z-score is:

$$z = \frac{x - \bar{x}}{s} = \frac{160 - 141.31}{17.77} = 1.05$$

Since the z-score is not large, it is not considered an outlier.

b.   Z-scores with values greater than 3 in absolute value are considered outliers. An observation with a z-score of 3 would have the value:

$$z = \frac{x - \bar{x}}{s} \Rightarrow 3 = \frac{x - 141.31}{17.77} \Rightarrow 3(17.77) = x - 141.31 \Rightarrow 53.31 = x - 141.31 \Rightarrow x = 194.62$$

An observation with a z-score of -3 would have the value:

$$z = \frac{x - \bar{x}}{s} \Rightarrow -3 = \frac{x - 141.31}{17.77} \Rightarrow -3(17.77) = x - 141.31 \Rightarrow -53.31 = x - 141.31 \Rightarrow x = 88.00$$

Thus any observation of semester hours that is greater than or equal to 194.62 or less than or equal to 88 would be considered an outlier.

2.105   a.   Using MINITAB, the boxplots for each type of firm are:

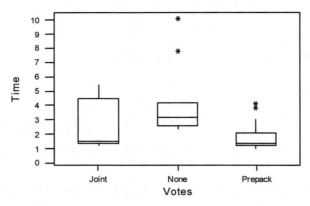

b.   The median bankruptcy time for Joint firms is about 1.5. The median bankruptcy time for None firms is about 3.2. The median bankruptcy time for Prepack firms is about 1.5.

c.   The range of the "Prepack" firms is less than the other two, while the range of the "None" firms is the largest. The interquartile range of the "Prepack" firms is less than the other two, while the interquartile range of the "Joint" firms is larger than the other two.

d.   No. The interquartile range for the "Prepack" firms is the smallest which corresponds to the smallest standard deviation. However, the second smallest interquartile range corresponds to the "none" firms. The second smallest standard deviation corresponds to the "Joint" firms.

e.   Yes. There is evidence of two outliers in the "Prepack" firms. These are indicated by the two *'s. There is also evidence of two outliers in the "None" firms. These are indicated by the two *'s.

2.107   a.   Using MINITAB, the boxplot is:

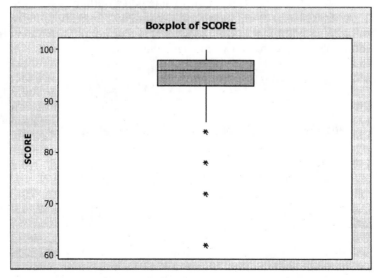

From the boxplot, there appears to be 4 outliers: 62, 72, 78, and 84.

b. From Exercise 2.77, $\bar{x} = 94.91$ and $s = 4.83$. Since the data are skewed to the left, we will consider observations more than 3 standard deviations from the mean to be outliers. An observation with a z-score of 3 would have the value:

$$z = \frac{x - \bar{x}}{s} \Rightarrow 3 = \frac{x - 94.91}{4.83} \Rightarrow 3(4.83) = x - 94.91 \Rightarrow 14.49 = x - 94.91 \Rightarrow x = 109.4$$

An observation with a z-score of -3 would have the value:

$$z = \frac{x - \bar{x}}{s} \Rightarrow -3 = \frac{x - 94.91}{4.83} \Rightarrow -3(4.83) = x - 94.91 \Rightarrow -14.49 = x - 94.91 \Rightarrow x = 80.42$$

Observations greater than 109.40 or less than 80.42 would be considered outliers. Using this criterion, the following observations would be outliers: 62, 72, and 78.

c. No, these methods do not agree. Using the boxplot, 4 observations were identified as outliers. Using the z-score method, only 3 observations were identified as outliers. Since the data are very highly skewed to the left, the z-score method may not be appropriate.

2.109 a. Using MINITAB, the box plot is:

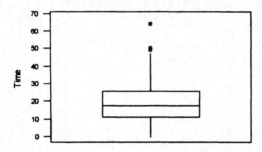

The median is about 18. The data appear to be skewed to the right since there are 3 suspect outliers to the right and none to the left. The variability of the data is fairly small because the IQR is fairly small, approximately $26 - 10 = 16$.

b. The customers associated with the suspected outliers are customers 268, 269, and 264.

c. In order to find the z-scores, we must first find the mean and standard deviation.

$$\bar{x} = \frac{\sum x}{n} = \frac{815}{40} = 20.375$$

$$s^2 = \frac{\sum x^2 - \frac{\left(\sum x\right)^2}{n}}{n-1} = \frac{24129 - \frac{815^2}{40}}{40-1} = 192.90705$$

$$s = \sqrt{192.90705} = 13.89$$

The z-scores associated with the suspected outliers are:

Customer 268 $z = \dfrac{49 - 20.375}{13.89} = 2.06$

Customer 269 $z = \dfrac{50 - 20.375}{13.89} = 2.13$

Customer 264 $z = \dfrac{64 - 20.375}{13.89} = 3.14$

All the z-scores are greater than 2. These are very unusual values.

2.111 Using MINITAB, the scatterplot is:

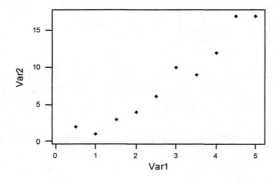

2.113   Using MINITAB, the scatterplot of the data is:

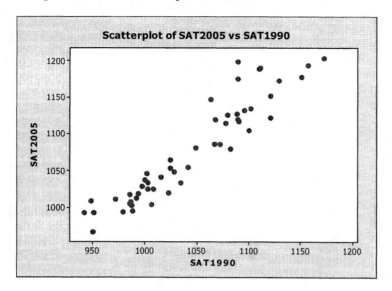

As the 1990 SAT increases, the 2005 SAT scores also tend to increase.

2.115   Using MINITAB, the scatterplot is:

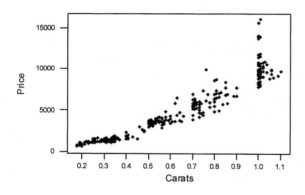

As the number of carats increases the price of the diamond tends to increase.

2.117 Using MINITAB, the scatterplot of Length and Weight is:

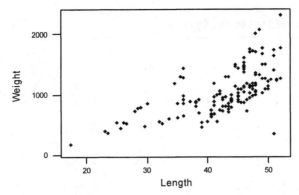

There appears to be a positive linear relationship. As length increases, weight also tends to increase.

Using MINITAB, the scatterplot of Length and DDT level is:

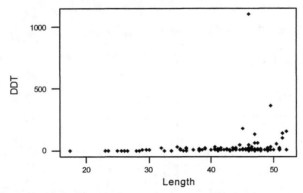

There appears to be a slight positive linear relationship between Length and DDT levels. As Length increases, DDT levels also tend to increase. There appears to be an outlying value for DDT level.

Using MINITAB, the scatterplot of Weight and DDT level is:

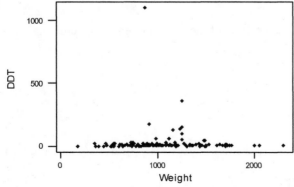

There does not appear to be a relationship between weight and DDT level. There does appear to be an outlying value for DDT level.

2.119 The relative frequency histogram is:

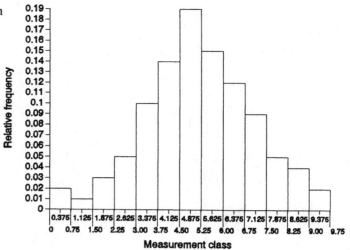

2.121 a. $z = \dfrac{x - \mu}{\sigma} = \dfrac{50 - 60}{10} = -1$

$z = \dfrac{70 - 60}{10} = 1$

$z = \dfrac{80 - 60}{10} = 2$

b. $z = \dfrac{x - \mu}{\sigma} = \dfrac{50 - 60}{5} = -2$

$z = \dfrac{70 - 60}{5} = 2$

$z = \dfrac{80 - 60}{5} = 4$

c $z = \dfrac{x - \mu}{\sigma} = \dfrac{50 - 40}{10} = 1$

$z = \dfrac{70 - 40}{10} = 3$

$z = \dfrac{80 - 40}{10} = 4$

d. $z = \dfrac{x - \mu}{\sigma} = \dfrac{50 - 40}{100} = .1$

$z = \dfrac{70 - 40}{100} = .3$

$z = \dfrac{80 - 40}{100} = .4$

2.123   a. $\sum x = 13 + 1 + 10 + 3 + 3 = 30$

$\sum x^2 = 13^2 + 1^2 + 10^2 + 3^2 + 3^2 = 288$

$\bar{x} = \dfrac{\sum x}{} = \dfrac{30}{5} = 6$

$s^2 = \dfrac{\sum x^2 - \dfrac{\left(\sum x\right)^2}{n}}{n-1} = \dfrac{288 - \dfrac{30^2}{5}}{5-1} = \dfrac{108}{4} = 27$ $s = \sqrt{27} = 5.20$

b. $\sum x = 13 + 6 + 6 + 0 = 25$

$\sum x^2 = 13^2 + 6^2 + 6^2 + 0^2 = 241$

$\bar{x} = \dfrac{\sum x}{} = \dfrac{25}{4} = 6.25$

$s^2 = \dfrac{\sum x^2 - \dfrac{\left(\sum x\right)^2}{n}}{n-1} = \dfrac{241 - \dfrac{25^2}{4}}{4-1} = \dfrac{84.75}{3} = 28.25$ $s = \sqrt{28.25} = 5.32$

c. $\sum x = 1 + 0 + 1 + 10 + 11 + 11 + 15 = 49$

$\sum x^2 = 1^2 + 0^2 + 1^2 + 10^2 + 11^2 + 11^2 + 15^2 = 569$

$\bar{x} = \dfrac{\sum x}{} = \dfrac{49}{7} = 7$

$s^2 = \dfrac{\sum x^2 - \dfrac{\left(\sum x\right)^2}{n}}{n-1} = \dfrac{569 - \dfrac{49^2}{7}}{7-1} = \dfrac{226}{6} = 37.67$ $s = \sqrt{37.67} = 6.14$

d. $\sum x = 3 + 3 + 3 + 3 = 12$

$\sum x^2 = 3^2 + 3^2 + 3^2 + 3^2 = 36$

$\bar{x} = \dfrac{\sum x}{} = \dfrac{12}{4} = 3$

$s^2 = \dfrac{\sum x^2 - \dfrac{\left(\sum x\right)^2}{n}}{n-1} = \dfrac{36 - \dfrac{12^2}{4}}{4-1} = \dfrac{0}{3} = 0$ $s = \sqrt{0} = 0$

2.125   The range is found by taking the largest measurement in the data set and subtracting the smallest measurement. Therefore, it only uses two measurements from the whole data set. The standard deviation uses every measurement in the data set. Therefore, it takes every measurement into account—not just two. The range is affected by extreme values more than the standard deviation.

2.127   Using MINITAB, the scatterplot is:

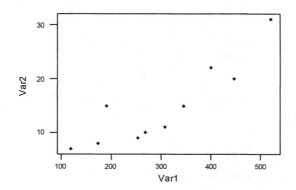

2.129   Using MINITAB, the pie chart is:

Pie Chart of DrivStar

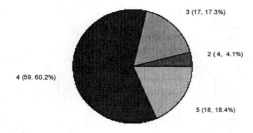

3 (17, 17.3%)

2 (4, 4.1%)

4 (59, 60.2%)

5 (18, 18.4%)

2.131   The sample mean is:

$$\bar{x} = \frac{\sum\limits_{i=1}^{n} x_i}{n} = \frac{185.00 + 56.70 + 56.70 + \cdots + 63.00}{14} = \frac{728.59}{14} = 52.042$$

The median is found as the average of the 7th and 8th observations, once the data have been ordered. The ordered data are:

9.00 11.95 20.95 21.95 29.99 35.00 56.70 56.70 56.70 56.70 61.95 63.00 63.00 185.00

The 7th and 8th observations are 56.70 and 56.70. The median is:

$$\frac{56.70 + 56.70}{2} = \frac{113.40}{2} = 56.70$$

The mode is the number which occurs the most. In this case, the mode is 56.70, which occurs 4 times.

Since the data are somewhat skewed to the right, the mode and median are better measures of central tendency than the mean.

2.133   a.   Frequency bar chart.

b.   It presents the number of napkins (out of 1000) that fall into each of four categories.

c.   Of the 1000 napkins printed, 700 were successful. Another way of saying this is 700/1000 × 100% = 70% of the imprints were successful.

2.135   a.   Using MINITAB, a bar chart of the data is:

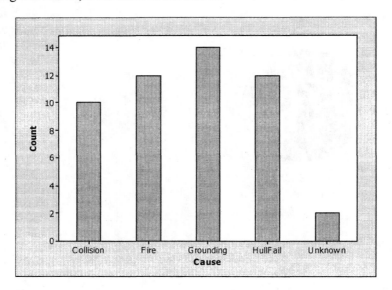

Since the bars are of very similar in size, there is no one cause that is much more likely to occur than the others.

b.   Using MINITAB, the descriptive statistics are:

Descriptive Statistics: Spillage

Variable	N	N*	Mean	SE Mean	StDev	Minimum	Q1	Median	Q3	Maximum
Spillage	50	0	59.82	7.55	53.36	21.00	31.00	39.50	63.50	257.00

The mean spillage amount is 59.82 thousand metric tons, while the median is 39.50. Since the median is so much smaller than the mean, it indicates that the data are skewed to the right. The standard deviation is 53.36. Again, since this value is so close to the mean, it indicates that the data are skewed to the right.

Since the data are skewed to the right, we cannot use the Empirical Rule to describe the data. Chebyshev's Rule can be used. Using Chebyshev's Rule, we know that at least 8/9 of the observations will be within 3 standard deviations from the mean.

$$\bar{x} \pm 3s \Rightarrow 59.82 \pm 3(53.36) \Rightarrow 59.82 \pm 160.08 \Rightarrow (-100.26, \ 219.90)$$

Thus, at least 8/9 of all oil spills will be between -100.26 and 219.90 thousand metric tons. Since a spill cannot be less than 0, the actual interval will be from 0 to 219.90 thousand metric tons.

2.137   a.   First, we must compute the total processing times by adding the processing times of the three departments. The total processing times are as follows:

Request	Total Processing Time	Request	Total Processing Time	Request	Total Processing Time
1	13.3	17	19.4*	33	23.4*
2	5.7	18	4.7	34	14.2
3	7.6	19	9.4	35	14.3
4	20.0*	20	30.2	36	24.0*
5	6.1	21	14.9	37	6.1
6	1.8	22	10.7	38	7.4
7	13.5	23	36.2*	39	17.7*
8	13.0	24	6.5	40	15.4
9	15.6	25	10.4	41	16.4
10	10.9	26	3.3	42	9.5
11	8.7	27	8.0	43	8.1
12	14.9	28	6.9	44	18.2*
13	3.4	29	17.2*	45	15.3
14	13.6	30	10.2	46	13.9
15	14.6	31	16.0	47	19.9*
16	14.4	32	11.5	48	15.4
				49	14.3*
				50	19.0

The stem-and-leaf displays with the appropriate leaves circled are as follows:

```
   Stem-and-leaf of Mkt          Stem-and-leaf of Engr
     Leaf Unit = 0.10              Leaf Unit = 0.10

    6   0   0 112446            7    0   4466699
    7   1   3                  14    1   333378 ⑧
   14   2   ⓪ 024699          19    2   ① 22 ④ 6
   16   3   2 ⑤               23    3   1568
   22   4   ⓪⓪① 577          (5)   4   24688
  (10)   5   0344556889        22    5   233
   18   6   000 ② 2247 ⑨⑨     19    6   ⓪ 12 ③ 9
    8   7   003 ⑧             14    7   ②② 379
    4   8   ⓪ 7               9    8
    2   9                      9    9   66
    2  10   0                  7   10   0
    1  11   0                  6   11   3
                               5   12   02 ③
                               2   13   ⓪
                               1   14   ④
```

```
   Stem-and-leaf of Accnt              Stem-and-leaf of Total
      Leaf Unit = 0.10                    Leaf Unit = 1.00

   19   0   11111111111 ② 2333444      1    0   1
   (8)   0   55556 ⑧ 88                3    0   33
   23   1   00                          5    0   45
   21   1   7 ⑨                        11    0   666677
   19   2   00 ② 3                     17    0   888999
   15   2                              21    1   0000
   15   3   23                         (5)   1   33333
   13   3   78                         24    1   4 ④ 44445555
   11   4                              14    1   66 ⑦⑦
   11   4                              10    1   ⑧ 9 ⑨⑨
   11   5                               6    2   ⓪
   11   5   8                           5    2   ③
   10   6   2                           4    2   ④ 4
    9   6                              HI    30, ㊱
    9   7   ⓪
    8   7
    8   8   4
 HI    ㊴, ⑩⑤ ⑬⑤ 144,
        ⑱②, 220, ㉚⓪
```

Of the 50 requests, 10 were lost. For each of the three departments, the processing times for the lost requests are scattered throughout the distributions. The processing times for the departments do not appear to be related to whether the request was lost or not. However, the total processing times for the lost requests appear to be clustered towards the high side of the distribution. It appears that if the total processing time could be kept under 17 days, 76% of the data could be maintained, while reducing the number of lost requests to 1.

b.   For the Marketing department, if the maximum processing time was set at 6.5 days, 78% of the requests would be processed, while reducing the number of lost requests by 4. For the Engineering department, if the maximum processing time was set at 7.0 days, 72% of the requests would be processed, while reducing the number of lost requests by 5. For the Accounting department, if the maximum processing time was set at 8.5 days, 86% of the requests would be processed, while reducing the number of lost requests by 5.

2.139 a.   One reason the plot may be interpreted differently is that no scale is given on the vertical axis. Also, since the plot almost reaches the horizontal axis at 3 years, it is obvious that the bottom of the plot has been cut off. Another important factor omitted is who responded to the survey.

b.   A scale should be added to the vertical axis. Also, that scale should start at 0.

2.141 a.   Since the mean is greater than the median, the distribution of the radiation levels is skewed to the right.

b. $\bar{x} \pm s \Rightarrow 10 \pm 3 \Rightarrow (7, 13)$; $\bar{x} \pm 2s \Rightarrow 10 \pm 2(3) \Rightarrow (4, 16)$; $\bar{x} \pm 3s \Rightarrow 10 \pm 3(3) \Rightarrow (1, 19)$

Interval	Chebyshev's	Empirical
(7, 13)	At least 0	≈68%
(4, 16)	At least 75%	≈95%
(1, 19)	At least 88.9%	≈100%

Since the data are skewed to the right, Chebyshev's Rule is probably more appropriate in this case.

c.   The background level is 4. Using Chebyshev's Rule, at least 75% or .75(50) ≈ 38 homes are above the background level. Using the Empirical Rule, ≈ 97.5% or .975(50) ≈ 49 homes are above the background level.

d. $z = \dfrac{x - \bar{x}}{s} = \dfrac{20 - 10}{3} = 3.333$

It is unlikely that this new measurement came from the same distribution as the other 50. Using either Chebyshev's Rule or the Empirical Rule, it is very unlikely to see any observations more than 3 standard deviations from the mean.

2.143 a.   Using MINITAB, the stem-and-leaf plot for an NFL team's current value is:

Stem-and-Leaf Display: Value

```
Stem-and-leaf of Value   N  = 32
Leaf Unit = 10

    7    6   5777999
   12    7   01113
   15    7   568
   (5)   8   02234
   12    8   567779
    6    9   04
    4    9   5
    3   10   4
    2   10   6
    1   11
    1   11
    1   12
    1   12   6
```

b.   Yes. Most of the values are in the neighborhood of $600 to $900 million. However, there are a few teams with very large values. The distribution is skewed to the right.

c.   From the stem-and-leaf display above, the median is the average of the 16th and 17th values. The values from the plot are 800 and 820, giving a median of 810. The actual values are 806 and 820. The average of 806 and 820 is 813. Thus, the median is 813.

d.   Using MINITAB, the descriptive statistics are:

Descriptive Statistics: Value, Income

Variable	N	N*	Mean	SE Mean	StDev	Minimum	Q1	Median	Q3	Maximum
Value	32	0	819.0	23.8	134.6	658.0	709.8	813.0	877.8	1264.0
Income	32	0	32.43	2.32	13.14	7.80	18.38	34.85	42.28	54.30

The z-score for the Pittsburgh Steelers for current value is:

$$z = \frac{x - \bar{x}}{s} = \frac{820 - 819}{134.6} = .007$$

The z-score for the Pittsburgh Steelers for operating income is:

$$z = \frac{x - \bar{x}}{s} = \frac{36.5 - 32.43}{13.14} = .310$$

e.   The z-score for the current value is 0.007. The Pittsburgh Steelers' current value is 0.007 standard deviations above the mean current value of all NFL teams. The z-score for operating income is 0.31. The Pittsburgh Steelers' operating income is 0.31 standard deviations above the mean operating income of all NFL teams.

f.   There are 4 teams that have a positive current value z-score (value above the mean of 819.0) and a negative operating income z-score (value below the mean of 32.43). These teams are:

Philadelphia Eagles
Carolina Panthers
Miami Dolphins
Seattle Seahawks

g.   Using MINITAB, the box plot is:

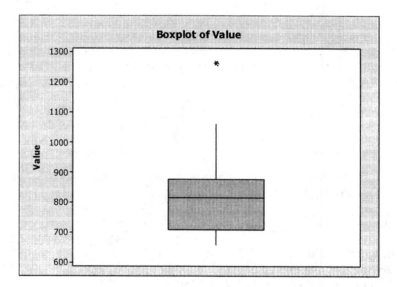

From the box plot, there is one potential outlier. This point lies inside the outer fences but outside the inner fences. This potential outlier is associated with the Washington Redskins (1,264). The z-score associated with the potential outlier is:

$$z = \frac{x - \bar{x}}{s} = \frac{1264 - 819.0}{134.6} = 3.31$$

Using the z-score, the current value associated with the Washington Redskins is an outlier.

h.   To investigate the trend between an NFL team's current value and its operating income, we will construct a plot of the current value against the operating income.

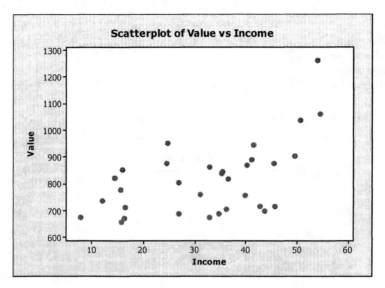

From the plot, it appears that as a team's operating income tends to increase, the current value also tends to increase.

2.145   The time series plot for the data is:

Of the 25 observations, only 7 are less than the claimed number of 12 minutes. Thus, the claim that "your hood will be open less than 12 minutes when we service your car" is probably not true.

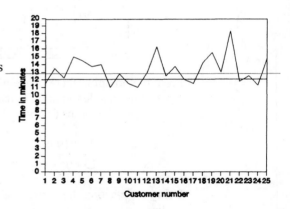

2.147   First we make some preliminary calculations.

Of the 20 engineers at the time of the layoffs, 14 are 40 or older. Thus, the probability that a randomly selected engineer will be 40 or older is 14/20 = .70. A very high proportion of the engineers is 40 or over.

In order to determine if the company is vulnerable to a disparate impact claim, we will first find the median age of all the engineers. Ordering all the ages, we get:

$$\underline{29}, \underline{32}, \underline{34}, 35, \underline{38}, 39, 40, 40, 40, \underline{40}, \underline{40}, 41, \underline{42}, \underline{42}, 44, \underline{46}, 47, 52, \underline{55}, 64$$

The median of all 20 engineers is $\dfrac{40+40}{2} = \dfrac{80}{2} = 40$

Now, we will compute the median age of those engineers who were not laid off. The ages underlined above correspond to the engineers who were not laid off. The median of these is $\dfrac{40+40}{2} = \dfrac{80}{2} = 40$.

The median age of all engineers is the same as the median age of those who were not laid off. The median age of those laid off is $\dfrac{40+41}{2} = \dfrac{81}{2} = 40.5$, which is not that much different from the median age of those not laid off. In addition, 70% of all the engineers are 40 or older. Thus, it appears that the company would not be vulnerable to a disparate impact claim.

2.149   There is evidence to support this claim. The graph peaks at the interval above 1.002. The heights of the bars decrease in order as the intervals get further and further from the peak interval. This is true for all bars except the one above 1.000. This bar is greater than the bar to its right. This would indicate that there are more observations in this interval than one would expect, suggesting that some inspectors might be passing rods with diameters that were barely below the lower specification limit.

3.1 a. Since the probabilities must sum to 1,

$$P(E_3) = 1 - P(E_1) - P(E_2) - P(E_4) - P(E_5) = 1 - .1 - .2 - .1 - .1 = .5$$

   b. $P(E_3) = 1 - P(E_3) - P(E_2) - P(E_4) - P(E_5)$
      $\Rightarrow 2P(E_3) = 1 - .1 - .2 - .1 \Rightarrow 2P(E_3) = .6 \Rightarrow P(E_3) = .3$

   c. $P(E_3) = 1 - P(E_1) - P(E_2) - P(E_4) - P(E_5) = 1 - .1 - .1 - .1 - .1 = .6$

3.3 $P(A) = P(1) + P(2) + P(3) = .05 + .20 + .30 = .55$
   $P(B) = P(1) + P(3) + P(5) = .05 + .30 + .15 = .50$
   $P(C) = P(1) + P(2) + P(3) + P(5) = .05 + .20 + .30 + .15 = .70$

3.5 a. $\dbinom{N}{n} = \dbinom{5}{2} = \dfrac{5!}{2!(5-2)!} = \dfrac{5 \cdot 4 \cdot 3 \cdot 2 \cdot 1}{2 \cdot 1 \cdot 3 \cdot 2 \cdot 1} = \dfrac{120}{12} = 10$

   b. $\dbinom{N}{n} = \dbinom{6}{3} = \dfrac{6!}{3!(6-3)!} = \dfrac{6 \cdot 5 \cdot 4 \cdot 3 \cdot 2 \cdot 1}{3 \cdot 2 \cdot 1 \cdot 3 \cdot 2 \cdot 1} = \dfrac{720}{36} = 20$

   c. $\dbinom{N}{n} = \dbinom{20}{5} = \dfrac{20!}{5!(20-5)!} = \dfrac{20 \cdot 19 \cdot 18 \cdots 3 \cdot 2 \cdot 1}{5 \cdot 4 \cdot 3 \cdot 2 \cdot 1 \cdot 15 \cdot 14 \cdot 13 \cdots 3 \cdot 2 \cdot 1}$

   $$= \dfrac{2.432902008 \times 10^{18}}{1.569209242 \times 10^{14}} = 15,504$$

3.7 a. If we denote the marbles as B_1, B_2, R_1, R_2, and R_3, then the ten sample points are:

   (B_1, B_2) (B_1, R_1) (B_1, R_2) (B_1, R_3) (B_2, R_1) (B_2, R_2) (B_2, R_3) (R_1, R_2) (R_1, R_3) (R_2, R_3)

   b. Each of the sample points would be equally likely. Thus, each would have a probability of 1/10 of occurring.

   c. There is one sample point in A: (B_1, B_2). Thus, $P(A) = \dfrac{1}{10}$.

   There are 6 sample points in B: (B_1, R_1) (B_1, R_2) (B_1, R_3) (B_2, R_1) (B_2, R_2) (B_2, R_3).
   Thus, $P(B) = 6\left(\dfrac{1}{10}\right) = \dfrac{6}{10} = \dfrac{3}{5}$.

   There are 3 sample points in C: (R_1, R_2) (R_1, R_3) (R_2, R_3). Thus, $P(C) = 3\left(\dfrac{1}{10}\right) = \dfrac{3}{10}$.

3.9 a. Let J = Raise based on job performance, C = Raise based on cost of living, and U = Unsure.

The 3 sample points are: J, C, and U

b. We will base the probabilities on the proportions of the 10,000 U.S. workers surveyed who responded in each category. Thus,

$$P(J) = .35, \ P(C) = .50, \text{ and } P(U) = .15$$

c. P(Raise based on either job performance or cost of living) $= P(J) + P(C) = .35 + .50 = .85$

3.11 a. Define the following event:

C: {Slaughtered chicken passes inspection with fecal contamination}

$$P(C) = \frac{1}{100} = .01$$

b. Based on the data, $P(C) = \dfrac{306}{32,075} = .0095 \approx .01$

Yes. The probability of a slaughtered chicken passing inspection with fecal contamination rounded off to 2 decimal places is .01.

3.13 Define the following events:

E: {Industrial accident caused by faulty Engineering & Design}

P: {Industrial accident caused by faulty Procedures & Practices}

M = {Industrial accident caused by faulty Management & Oversight }

T = {Industrial accident caused by faulty Training & Communication}

a. $P(E) = 27 / 83 = .325$. Approximately 32.5% of all industrial accidents are caused by faulty Engineering and Design.

b. P(Industrial accident caused by something other than procedures & practices) $= (27 + 22 + 10) / 83 = 59 / 83 = .711$. Approximately 71.1% of all industrial accidents are caused by something other than faulty procedures & practices.

3.15   Since one would be selecting 3 stocks from 15 without replacement, the total number of ways to select the 3 stocks would be a combination of 15 things taken 3 at a time.

The number of ways would be

$$\binom{15}{3} = \frac{15!}{3!(15-3)!} = \frac{15 \cdot 14 \cdot 13 \cdots 3 \cdot 2 \cdot 1}{3 \cdot 2 \cdot 1 \cdot 12 \cdot 11 \cdot 10 \cdots 3 \cdot 2 \cdot 1} = \frac{1.307674368 \times 10^{12}}{2874009600} = 455$$

3.17   a.   Since we want to maximize the purchase of grill #2, grill #2 must be one of the 3 grills in the display. Thus, we have to pick 2 more grills from the 4 remaining grills. Since order does not matter, the number of different ways to select 2 grill displays from 4 would be a combination of 4 things taken 2 at a time. The number of ways is:

$$\binom{4}{2} = \frac{4!}{2!(4-2)!} = \frac{4 \cdot 3 \cdot 2 \cdot 1}{2 \cdot 1 \cdot 2 \cdot 1} = \frac{24}{4} = 6$$

Let Gi represent Grill i. The possibilities are:

$G_1G_2G_3$, $G_1G_2G_4$, $G_1G_2G_5$, $G_2G_3G_4$, $G_2G_3 G_5$, $G_2G_4G_5$

b.   To find reasonable probabilities for the 6 possibilities, we divide the frequencies by the total sample size of 124. The probabilities would be:

$P(G_1G_2G_3) = 35 / 124 = .282$

$P(G_1G_2G_4) = 8 / 124 = .065$

$P(G_1G_2G_5) = 42 / 124 = .339$

$P(G_2G_3G_4) = 4 / 124 = .032$

$P(G_2G_3G_5) = 1 / 124 = .008$

$P(G_2G_4G_5) = 34 / 124 = .274$

c. $P(\text{ display contained Grill \#1}) = P(G_1G_2G_3) + P(G_1G_2G_4) + P(G_1G_2G_5)$
$= .282 + .065 + .339 = .686$

3.19   a.   The odds in favor of an Oxford Shoes win are $\frac{1}{3}$ to $1 - \frac{1}{3} = \frac{2}{3}$ or 1 to 2.

b.   If the odds in favor of Oxford Shoes are 1 to 1, then the probability that Oxford Shoes wins is
$$\frac{1}{1+1} = \frac{1}{2}.$$

c.   If the odds against Oxford Shoes are 3 to 2, then the odds in favor of Oxford Shoes are 2 to 3. Therefore, the probability that Oxford Shoes wins is $\frac{2}{2+3} = \frac{2}{5}$.

3.21 a. Suppose we let the four positions in a sample point represent in order (1) Raise a broad mix of crops, (2) Raise livestock, (3) Use chemicals sparingly, and (4) Use techniques for regenerating the soil, such as crop rotation. A farmer is either likely (L) to engage in an activity or unlikely (U). The possible classifications are:

LLLL   LLLU   LLUL   LULL   ULLL   LLUU   LULU   LUUL   ULLU   ULUL
UULL   LUUU   ULUU   UULU   UUUL   UUUU

b. Since there are 16 classifications or sample points and all are equally likely, then each has a probability of 1/16.

$$P(UUUU) = \frac{1}{16}$$

The probability that a farmer will be classified as likely on at least three criteria is

$$P(LLLL) + P(LLLU) + P(LLUL) + P(LULL) + P(ULLL) = 5\left(\frac{1}{16}\right) = \frac{5}{16}.$$

3.23 a. *A*: {*HHH, HHT, HTH, THH, TTH, THT, HTT*}
B: {*HHH, TTH, THT, HTT*}
$A \cup B$: {*HHH, HHT, HTH, THH, TTH, THT, HTT*}
A^c: {*TTT*}
$A \cap B$: {*HHH, TTH, THT, HTT*}

b. $P(A) = \dfrac{7}{8}$ $P(B) = \dfrac{4}{8} = \dfrac{1}{2}$ $P(A \cup B) = \dfrac{7}{8}$

$P(A^c) = \dfrac{1}{8}$ $P(A \cap B) = \dfrac{4}{8} = \dfrac{1}{2}$

c. $P(A \cup B) = P(A) + P(B) - P(A \cap B) = \dfrac{7}{8} + \dfrac{1}{2} - \dfrac{1}{2} = \dfrac{7}{8}$

d. No. $P(A \cap B) = \dfrac{1}{2}$ which is not 0.

3.25 a. $P(A) = P(E_1) + P(E_2) + P(E_3) + P(E_5) + P(E_6) = \dfrac{1}{5} + \dfrac{1}{5} + \dfrac{1}{5} + \dfrac{1}{20} + \dfrac{1}{10} = \dfrac{15}{20} = \dfrac{3}{4}$

b. $P(B) = P(E_2) + P(E_3) + P(E_4) + P(E_7) = \dfrac{1}{5} + \dfrac{1}{5} + \dfrac{1}{20} + \dfrac{1}{5} = \dfrac{13}{20}$

c. $P(A \cup B) = P(E_1) + P(E_2) + P(E_3) + P(E_4) + P(E_5) + P(E_6) + P(E_7)$

$$= \dfrac{1}{5} + \dfrac{1}{5} + \dfrac{1}{5} + \dfrac{1}{20} + \dfrac{1}{20} + \dfrac{1}{10} + \dfrac{1}{5} = 1$$

d. $P(A \cap B) = P(E_2) + P(E_3) = \dfrac{1}{5} + \dfrac{1}{5} = \dfrac{2}{5}$

e. $P(A^c) = 1 - P(A) = 1 - \dfrac{3}{4} = \dfrac{1}{4}$

f. $P(B^c) = 1 - P(B) = 1 - \dfrac{13}{20} = \dfrac{7}{20}$

g. $P(A \cup A^c) = P(E_1) + P(E_2) + P(E_3) + P(E_4) + P(E_5) + P(E_6) + P(E_7)$
$$= \dfrac{1}{5} + \dfrac{1}{5} + \dfrac{1}{5} + \dfrac{1}{20} + \dfrac{1}{20} + \dfrac{1}{10} + \dfrac{1}{5} = 1$$

h. $P(A^c \cap B) = P(E_4) + P(E_7) = \dfrac{1}{20} + \dfrac{1}{5} = \dfrac{5}{20} = \dfrac{1}{4}$

3.27　a. $P(A) = .50 + .10 + .05 = .65$

b. $P(B) = .10 + .07 + .50 + .05 = .72$

c. $P(C) = .25$

d. $P(D) = .05 + .03 = .08$

e. $P(A^c) = .25 + .07 + .03 = .35$　(Note: $P(A^c) = 1 - P(A) = 1 - .65 = .35$)

f. $P(A \cup B) = P(B) = .10 + .07 + .50 + .05 = .72$

g. $P(A \cap C) = 0$

h. Two events are mutually exclusive if they have no sample points in common or if the probability of their intersection is 0.

$P(A \cap B) = P(A) = .50 + .10 + .05 = .65$. Since this is not 0, A and B are not mutually exclusive.

$P(A \cap C) = 0$. Since this is 0, A and C are mutually exclusive.

$P(A \cap D) = .05$. Since this is not 0, A and D are not mutually exclusive.

$P(B \cap C) = 0$. Since this is 0, B and C are mutually exclusive.

$P(B \cap D) = .05$. Since this is not 0, B and D are not mutually exclusive.

$P(C \cap D) = 0$. Since this is 0, C and D are mutually exclusive.

3.29   Define the event:

B: {Small business owned by non-Hispanic white female}

From the problem, $P(B) = .27$

The probability that a small business owned by a non-Hispanic white is male-owned is $P(B^c) = 1 - P(B) = 1 - .27 = .73$.

3.31   Define the following events:

IM: {18-to-34 year-old cell phone user uses instant messaging}

NA: {18-to-34 year-old cell phone user uses none of the featurees}

a. $P(IM) = .43$

b. P(18-to-34 year-old cell phone user uses at least one of the features)
$= 1 - P(NA) = 1 - .16 = .84$

3.33   Define the following events:

A: {oil structure is active}

I: {oil structure is inactive}

C: {oil structure is caisson}

W: {oil structure is well protector}

F: {oil structure is fixed platform}

a.   The simple events are all combinations of structure type and activity type. The simple events are:

AC, AW, AF, IC, IW, IF

b.   Reasonable probabilities would be the frequency divided by the sample size of 3,400. The probabilities are:

$P(AC) = 503 / 3,400 = .148$ $P(AW) = 225 / 3,400 = .066$

$P(AF) = 1,447 / 3,400 = .426$ $P(IC) = 598 / 3,400 = .176$

$P(IW) = 177 / 3,400 = .052$ $P(IF) = 450 / 3,400 = .132$

c. $P(A) = P(AC) + P(AW) + P(AF) = .148 + .066 + .426 = .640$

d. $P(W) = P(AW) + P(IW) = .066 + .052 = .118$

e. $P(IC) = .176$

f. $P(I \cup F) = P(IC) + P(IW) + P(IF) + P(AF) = .176 + .052 + .132 + .426 = .786$

g. $P(C)^c = 1 - P(C) = 1 - \{P(AC) + P(IC)\} = 1 - \{.148 + .176\} = 1 - .324 = .676$

3.35   a. $P(A) = \dfrac{1,465}{2,143} = .684$

b. $P(B) = \dfrac{265}{2,143} = .124$

c.   No. There is one sample point that they have in common: Plaintiff trial win – reversed, Jury

d. $P(A^c) = 1 - P(A) = 1 - .684 = .316$

e. $P(A \cup B) = \dfrac{194 + 71 + 429 + 111 + 731}{2,143} = \dfrac{1,536}{2,143} = .717$

f. $P(A \cap B) = \dfrac{194}{2,143} = .091$

3.37   a. $P(A) = 8/28.44 = .281$

$P(B) = 7.84/28.44 = .276$

$P(C) = 1.24/28.44 = .044$

$P(D) = (1.0 + 1.24)/28.44 = 2.24/28.44 = .079$

$P(E) = 1.24/28.44 = .044$

b. $P(A \cap B) = 0/28.44 = 0$

c. $P(A \cup B) = (7.84 + 8)/28.44 = 15.84/28.44 = .557$

d. $P(B^c \cap E) = 0$

e. $P(A \cup E) = 9.24/28.44 = .325$

f.   Two events are mutually exclusive if they have no sample points in common or if the probability of their intersection is 0.

$P(A \cap B) = 0$. Since this is 0, A and B are mutually exclusive.

$P(A \cap C) = 0$. Since this is 0, A and C are mutually exclusive.

$P(A \cap D) = 0$. Since this is 0, A and D are mutually exclusive.

$P(A \cap E) = 0$. Since this is 0, A and E are mutually exclusive.

$P(B \cap C) = 1.24/28.44 = .044$. Since this is not 0, B and C are not mutually exclusive.

$P(B \cap D) = 2.24/28.44 = .079$. Since this is not 0, B and D are not mutually exclusive.

$P(B \cap E) = 1.24/28.44 = .044$. Since this is not 0, B and E are not mutually exclusive.

$P(C \cap D) = 1.24/28.44 = .044$. Since this is not 0, C and D are not mutually exclusive.

$P(C \cap E) = 1.24/28.44 = .044$. Since this is not 0, C and E are not mutually exclusive.

$P(D \cap E) = 1.24/28.44 = .044$. Since this is not 0, D and E are not mutually exclusive.

3.39   Define the following events:

A: {Air pressure is over-reported by 4 psi or more}
B: {Air pressure is over-reported by 6 psi or more}
C: {Air pressure is over-reported by 8 psi or more

a.   For gas station air pressure gauges that read 35 psi, $P(B) = .09$.

b.   For gas station air pressure gauges that read 55 psi, $P(C) = .09$.

c.   For gas station air pressure gauges that read 25 psi, $P(A^c)$ $1 - P(A) = 1 - .16 = .84$.

d.   No. If air pressure is over-reported by 6 psi or more, then it is also over-reported by 4 psi or more. Thus, these 2 events are not mutually exclusive.

e.   The columns in the table are not mutually exclusive. All events in the last column (% Over-reported by 8 psi or more) are also part of the events in the first and second columns. All events in the second column are also part of the events in the first column. In addition, there is no column for the event 'Over-reported by less than 4 psi or not over-reported'.

3.41   a. $P(A|B) = \dfrac{P(A \cap B)}{P(B)} = \dfrac{.1}{.2} = .5$

       b. $P(B|A) = \dfrac{P(A \cap B)}{P(A)} = \dfrac{.1}{.4} = .25$

       c.   Events A and B are said to be independent if $P(A|B) = P(A)$. In this case, $P(A|B) = .5$ and $P(A) = .4$. Thus, A and B are not independent.

3.43   a.   If two events are independent, then $P(A \cap B) = P(A)P(B) = .4(.2) = .08$.

       b.   If two events are independent, then $P(A|B) = P(A) = .4$.

       c. $P(A \cup B) = P(A) + P(B) - P(A \cap B) = .4 + .2 - .08 = .52$

3.45   a. $P(A) = P(E_1) + P(E_2) + P(E_3)$
            $= .2 + .3 + .3$
            $= .8$

            $P(B) = P(E_2) + P(E_3) + P(E_5)$
            $= .3 + .3 + .1$
            $= .7$

            $P(A \cap B) = P(E_2) + P(E_3)$
            $= .3 + .3$
            $= .6$

       b. $P(E_1|A) = \dfrac{P(E_1 \cap A)}{P(A)} = \dfrac{P(E_1)}{P(A)} = \dfrac{.2}{.8} = .25$

            $P(E_2|A) = \dfrac{P(E_2 \cap A)}{P(A)} = \dfrac{P(E_2)}{P(A)} = \dfrac{.3}{.8} = .375$

            $P(E_3|A) = \dfrac{P(E_3 \cap A)}{P(A)} = \dfrac{P(E_3)}{P(A)} = \dfrac{.3}{.8} = .375$

            The original sample point probabilities are in the proportion .2 to .3 to .3 or 2 to 3 to 3.

            The conditional probabilities for these sample points are in the proportion .25 to .375 to .375 or 2 to 3 to 3.

       c.   (1) $P(B|A) = P(E_2|A) + P(E_3|A)$
                  $= .375 + .375$ (from part **b**)
                  $= .75$

(2) $P(B|A) = \dfrac{P(A \cap B)}{P(A)} = \dfrac{.6}{.8} = .75$ (from part **a**)

The two methods do yield the same result.

d. If A and B are independent events, $P(B|A) = P(B)$.

From part **c**, $P(B|A) = .75$. From part **a**, $P(B) = .7$.

Since $.75 \neq .7$, A and B are not independent events.

3.47 a. $P(A) = P(E_1) + P(E_3) = .22 + .15 = .37$

b. $P(B) = P(E_2) + P(E_3) + P(E_4) = .31 + .15 + .22 = .68$

c. $P(A \cap B) = P(E_3) = .15$

d. $P(A|B) = \dfrac{P(A \cap B)}{P(B)} = \dfrac{.15}{.68} = .2206$

e. $P(B \cap C) = 0$

f. $P(C|B) = \dfrac{P(C \cap B)}{P(B)} = \dfrac{0}{.68} = 0$

g. For pair A and B: A and B are not independent because $P(A|B) \neq P(A)$ or $.2206 \neq .37$.

For pair A and C:

$P(A \cap C) = P(E_1) = .22$
$P(C) = P(E_1) + P(E_5) = .22 + .1 = .32$
$P(A|C) = \dfrac{P(A \cap C)}{P(C)} = \dfrac{.22}{.32} = .6875$

A and C are not independent because $P(A|C) \neq P(A)$ or $.6875 \neq .37$.

For pair B and C: B and C are not independent because $P(C|B) \neq P(C)$ or $0 \neq .32$.

3.49 a. $P(A \cap C) = 0 \Rightarrow A$ and C are mutually exclusive.
$P(B \cap C) = 0 \Rightarrow B$ and C are mutually exclusive.

b. $P(A) = P(1) + P(2) + P(3) = .20 + .05 + .30 = .55$
$P(B) = P(3) + P(4) = .30 + .10 = .40$
$P(C) = P(5) + P(6) = .10 + .25 = .35$
$P(A \cap B) = P(3) = .30$
$P(A|B) = \dfrac{P(A \cap B)}{P(B)} = \dfrac{.30}{.40} = .75$

A and B are independent if $P(A \mid B) = P(A)$. Since $P(A \mid B) = .75$ and $P(A) = .55$, A and B are not independent.

Since A and C are mutually exclusive, they are not independent. Similarly, since B and C are mutually exclusive, they are not independent.

c. Using the probabilities of sample points,
$$P(A \cup B) = P(1) + P(2) + P(3) + P(4) = .20 + .05 + .30 + .10 = .65$$

Using the additive rule,
$$P(A \cup B) = P(A) + P(B) - P(A \cap B) = .55 + .40 - .30 = .65$$

Using the probabilities of sample points,
$$P(A \cup C) = P(1) + P(2) + P(3) + P(5) + P(6)$$
$$= .20 + .05 + .30 + .10 + .25 = .90$$

Using the additive rule,
$$P(A \cup C) = P(A) + P(C) - P(A \cap C) = .55 + .35 - 0 = .90$$

3.51 Define the following events:

A: {Company is a trading company}
B: {Company is based in Japan}

From the problem, we know that $P(A \cap B) = \dfrac{6}{20} = .3$ and $P(B) = \dfrac{11}{20} = .55$

$$P(A \mid B) = \frac{P(A \cap B)}{P(B)} = \frac{.3}{.55} = .545$$

3.53 Define the following events:

A: {Internet user owns at least one computer}
B: {Internet user logs on to the internet for more than 30 hours per week}

From the exercise, $P(A) = .80$, $P(B) = .25$ and $P(A \cap B) = .15$.

a. $P(B \mid A) = \dfrac{P(A \cap B)}{P(A)} = \dfrac{.15}{.80} = .1875$

b. $P(A \mid B) = \dfrac{P(A \cap B)}{P(B)} = \dfrac{.15}{.25} = .60$

3.55 Define the following events:

P: {Capital punishment case had serious, reversible error}
R: {Acquittal for defendant on retrial}

a. $P(P) = .68$

$P(R|P) = .07$

b. $P(R \cap P) = P(R \mid P)P(P) = .07(.68) = .04796$

3.57   Define the following events as in Exercise 3.38:

A: {Wheelchair user had an injurious fall}
B: {Wheelchair user had all five features installed in the home}
C: {Wheelchair user had no falls}
D: {Wheelchair user had none of the features installed in the home}

a. $P(A \mid B) = \dfrac{P(A \cap B)}{P(B)} = \dfrac{2/306}{9/306} = \dfrac{2}{9} = .222$

b. $P(A \mid D) = \dfrac{P(A \cap D)}{P(D)} = \dfrac{20/306}{109/306} = \dfrac{20}{109} = .183$

3.59   Define the following events:

A: {Alarm A sounds alarm}

B: {Alarm B sounds alarm}

I: {Intruder}

a.   From the problem:

$P(A \mid I) = .9$
$P(B \mid I) = .95$
$P(A \mid I^c) = .2$
$P(B \mid I^c) = .1$

b.   Since the two systems are operating independently of each other,

$P(A \cap B \mid I) = P(A \mid I)\,P(B \mid I) = .9(.95) = .855$

c. $P(A \cap B \mid I^c) = P(A \mid I^c)\,P(B \mid I^c) = .2(.1) = .02$

d. $P(A \cup B \mid I) = P(A \mid I) + P(B \mid I) - P(A \cap B \mid I) = .9 + .95 - .855 = .995$

3.61   Define the following events:

A: {Algorithm predicts defects}

B: {Module has defects}

C: {Algorithm is correct}

a. $Acccuracy = P(C)$

$$= P(A \cap B) + P(A^c \cap B^c) = \frac{a}{a+b+c+d} + \frac{d}{a+b+c+d} = \frac{a+d}{a+b+c+d}$$

b. $Detection\ rate = P(A \mid B) = \dfrac{d}{b+d}$

c. $False\ alarm = P(A \mid B^c) = \dfrac{c}{a+c}$

d. $Precision = P(B \mid A) = \dfrac{d}{c+d}$

e.   From the SWDEFECTS file the table is:

		Module has Defects	
		False	True
Algorithm Predicts Defects	No	400	29
	Yes	49	20

$Acccuracy = P(C) = P(A \cap B) + P(A^c \cap B^c)$

$$= \frac{a}{a+b+c+d} + \frac{d}{a+b+c+d} = \frac{a+d}{a+b+c+d} = \frac{400+20}{400+29+49+20} = \frac{420}{498} = .843$$

$Detection\ rate = P(A \mid B) = \dfrac{d}{b+d} = \dfrac{20}{29+20} = \dfrac{20}{49} = .408$

$False\ alarm = P(A \mid B^c) = \dfrac{c}{a+c} = \dfrac{49}{400+49} = \dfrac{49}{449} = .109$

$Precision = P(B \mid A) = \dfrac{d}{c+d} = \dfrac{20}{49+20} = \dfrac{20}{69} = .290$

3.63   Define the following events:

> A: {Selected firm implemented TQM}
> B: {Selected firm's sales increased}

From the information given, $P(A) = 30/100 = .3$, $P(B) = 60/100 = .6$, and $P(A|B) = 20/60$ $= 1/3$.

a. $P(A) = 30/100 = .3$
$P(B) = 60/100 = .6$

b.   If A and B are independent, $P(A|B) = P(A)$. However, $P(A|B) = 1/3 \neq P(A) = .3$. Thus, A and B are not independent.

c.   Now, $P(A|B) = 18/60 = .3$. Since $P(A|B) = .3 = P(A) = .3$, A and B are independent.

3.65   Define the following events:

> A: {Patient receives PMI sheet}
> B: {Patient was hospitalized}

$P(A) = .20$, $P(A \cap B) = .12$

$$P(B|A) = \frac{P(A \cap B)}{P(A)} = \frac{.12}{.20} = .60$$

3.67   a.   If the coin is balanced, then $P(H) = .5$ and $P(T) = .5$ on any trial. Also, we can assume that the results of any coin toss is independent of any other. Thus,

$$P(H \cap H \cap H \cap H \cap H \cap H \cap H \cap H \cap H \cap H)$$
$$= P(H)P(H)P(H)P(H)P(H)P(H)P(H)P(H)P(H)P(H)$$
$$= .5(.5)(.5)(.5)(.5)(.5)(.5)(.5)(.5) = .5^{10} = .0009766$$

$$P(H \cap H \cap T \cap T \cap H \cap T \cap T \cap H \cap H \cap H)$$
$$= P(H)P(H)P(T)P(T)P(H)P(T)P(T)P(H)P(H)P(H)$$
$$= .5(.5)(.5)(.5)(.5)(.5)(.5)(.5)(.5) = .5^{10} = .0009766$$

$$P(T \cap T \cap T \cap T \cap T \cap T \cap T \cap T \cap T \cap T)$$
$$= P(T)P(T)P(T)P(T)P(T)P(T)P(T)P(T)P(T)P(T)$$
$$= .5(.5)(.5)(.5)(.5)(.5)(.5)(.5)(.5) = .5^{10} = .0009766$$

b.   Define the following events:

A: {10 coin tosses result in all heads or all tails}
B: {10 coin tosses result in mix of heads and tails}

$$P(A) = P(H \cap H \cap H \cap H \cap H \cap H \cap H \cap H \cap H \cap H)$$
$$+ P(T \cap T \cap T \cap T \cap T \cap T \cap T \cap T \cap T \cap T)$$
$$= .0009766 + .0009766 = .0019532$$

c. $P(B) = 1 - P(A) = 1 - .0019532 = .9980468$

d.   From the above probabilities, the chances that either all heads or all tails occurred is extremely rare. Thus, if one of these sequences really occurred, it is most likely sequence #2.

3.69   a.   The number of samples of size $n = 3$ elements that can be selected from a population of $N = 600$ is:

$$\binom{N}{n} = \binom{600}{3} = \frac{600!}{3!597!} = \frac{600(599)(598)}{3(2)(1)} = 35,820,200$$

b.   If random sampling is employed, then each sample is equally likely. The probability that any sample is selected is 1/35,820,200.

c.   To draw a random sample of three elements from 600, we will number the elements from 1 to 600. Then, starting in an arbitrary position in Table I, Appendix B, we will select three numbers by going either down a column or across a row. Suppose that we start in the first three positions of column 8 and row 17. We will proceed down the column until we select three different numbers, skipping 000 and any numbers between 601 and 999. The first sample drawn will be 448, 298, and 136 (skip 987). The second sample drawn will be 47, 263, and 287. The 20 samples selected are:

Sample Number	Items Selected	Sample Number	Items Selected
1	448, 298, 136	11	345, 420, 152
2	47, 263, 287	12	144, 68, 485
3	153, 147, 222	13	490, 54, 178
4	360, 86, 357	14	428, 297, 549
5	205, 587, 254	15	186, 256, 261
6	563, 408, 258	16	90, 383, 232
7	428, 356, 543	17	438, 430, 352
8	248, 410, 197	18	129, 493, 496
9	542, 355, 208	19	440, 253, 81
10	399, 313, 563	20	521, 300, 15

None of the samples contain the same three elements. Because the probability in part **b** was so small, it would be very unlikely to have any two samples with the same elements.

3.71   a.   First, we need to define the area from which the telephone numbers are to be selected. If the area is the entire country, we will need to include area codes in our random numbers. Suppose we restrict ourselves to a single area code. Within a single area code, assuming that all "first three digits" are possible, we would select 7-digit numbers at random. We would start at a particular point in Table I, Appendix B, say row 7 and the beginning of column 3. We would use the five digits of column 3 plus the first two digits of column 4. We would proceed down the column until we selected the needed sample of different numbers.

        b.   Starting in row 7 and the beginning of column 3, the ten 7-digit numbers selected would be:

                5642069
                0546307
                6366110
                5334253
                8823133
                4823503
                5263692
                8752985
                7104808
                5182151

        c.   If the first three digits are to be 373, then we only need to use 4-digit numbers. Suppose we start in row 32, column 11, using the last four digits in the column, and proceeding down the column. The five numbers would be:

                3736038
                3739841
                3733611
                3734952
                3739080

3.73   a.   If we randomly select one account from the 5,382 accounts, the probability of selecting account 3,241 is $1/5,382 = .000186$.

        b.   To draw a random sample of 10 accounts from 5,382, we will number the accounts from 1 to 5,382. Then, starting in an arbitrary position in Table I, Appendix B, we will select 10 numbers by going either down a column or across a row. Suppose that we start in the first four positions of column 10 and row 5. We will proceed down the column until we select 10 different numbers, skipping 0000 and any numbers between 5,382 and 9,999. The sample drawn will be:

                1505, 4884, 1256, 1798, 3159, 2084, 0827, 2635, 4610, 2217

c.   No. If the samples are randomly selected, any sample of size 10 is equally likely. The
      total number of ways to select 10 accounts from 5,382 is:

$$\binom{N}{n} = \binom{5,382}{10} = \frac{5,382!}{10!5,372!} = \frac{5,382(5381)(5380)\ldots(5373)}{10(9)(8)\ldots(1)}$$
$$= 5.572377607 \times 10^{30}$$

The probability that any one sample is selected is $1/5.572377607 \times 10^{30}$. Each of the two
samples shown have the same probability of occurring.

3.75   Suppose we want to select 900 intersections by numbering the intersections from 1 to 500,000.
We would then use a random number table or a random number generator from a software
program to select 900 distinct intersection points. These would then be the sampled markets.

Now, suppose we want to select the 900 intersections by selecting a row from the 500 and a
column from the 1,000. We would first number the rows from 1 to 500 and number the
columns from 1 to 1,000. Using a random number generator, we would generate a sample of
900 from the 500 rows. Obviously, many rows will be selected more than once. At the same
time, we use a random number generator to select 900 columns from the 1,000 columns.
Again, some of the columns could be selected more than once. Placing these two sets of
random numbers side-by-side, we would use the row-column combinations to select the
intersections. For example, suppose the first row selected was 453 and the first column
selected was 731. The first intersection selected would be row 453, column 731. This process
would be continued until 900 unique intersections were selected.

3.77   First, we find the following probabilities:

$$P(A \cap B_1) = P(A|B_1)P(B_1) = .4(.2) = .08$$
$$P(A \cap B_2) = P(A|B_2)P(B_2) = .25(.15) = .0375$$
$$P(A \cap B_3) = P(A|B_3)P(B_3) = .6(.65) = .5075$$
$$P(A) = P(A \cap B_1) + P(A \cap B_2) + P(A \cap B_3) = .08 + .0375 + .39 = .5075$$

a. $$P(B_1 | A) = \frac{P(A \cap B_1)}{P(A)} = \frac{.08}{.5075} = .158$$

b. $$P(B_2 | A) = \frac{P(A \cap B_2)}{P(A)} = \frac{.0375}{.5075} = .074$$

c. $$P(B_3 | A) = \frac{P(A \cap B_3)}{P(A)} = \frac{.39}{.5075} = .768$$

3.79   a.   Converting the percentages to probabilities,

$$P(275 - 300) = .52, \ P(305 - 325) = .39, \text{ and } P(330 - 350) = .09.$$

b.   Using Bayes Theorem,

$$P(275-300\,|\,CC) = \frac{P(275-300 \cap CC)}{P(CC)}$$

$$= \frac{P(CC\,|\,275-300)P(275-300)}{P(CC\,|\,275-300)P(275-300) + P(CC\,|\,305-325)P(305-325) + P(CC\,|\,330-350)P(330-350)}$$

$$= \frac{.775(.52)}{.775(.52) + .77(.39) + .86(.09)} = \frac{.403}{.403 + .3003 + .0774} = \frac{.403}{.7807} = .516$$

3.81   Define the following events:

  U: {Athlete uses testosterone}

  P: {Test is positive}

a.   *Sensitivity* is $P(P\,|\,U) = \dfrac{50}{100} = .5$

b.   *Specificity* is $P(P^c\,|\,U^c) = 1 - \dfrac{9}{900} = 1 - .01 = .99$

c.   First, we need to find the probability that an athlete is a user: $P(U) = 100\,/\,1000 = .1$.

  Next, we need to find the probability of a positive test:

  $$P(P) = P(P\,|\,U)P(U) + P(P\,|\,U^c)P(U^c) = .5(.1) + .01(.9) = .05 + .009 = .059$$

  Positive predictive value is $P(U\,|\,P) = \dfrac{P(U \cap P)}{P(P)} = \dfrac{P(P\,|\,U)P(U)}{P(P)} = \dfrac{.5(.1)}{.059} = .847$

3.83   Define the following events:

  A_1: {Fuse made by line 1}
  A_2: {Fuse made by line 2}
  D: {Fuse is defective}

From the Exercise, we know $P(D|A_1) = .06$ and $P(D|A_2) = .025$. Also, $P(A_1) = P(A_2) = .5$.

Two fuses are going to be selected and we need to find the probability that one of the two is defective. We can get one defective fuse out of two by getting a defective on the first and non-defective on the second ($D \cap D^C$) or non-defective on the first and defective on the second ($D^C \cap D$). The probability of getting one defective out of two fuses given line 1 is:

$$P(D \cap D^C\,|\,A_1) + P(D^C \cap D\,|\,A_1) = P(D\,|\,A_1)P(D^C\,|\,A_1) + P(D^C\,|\,A_1)P(D\,|\,A_1)$$
$$= .06(1 - .06) + (1 - .06)(.06) = .06(.94) + .94(.06) = .1128 = P(1\ D\,|\,A_1)$$

The probability of getting one defective out of two fuses given line 2 is:

$$P(D \cap D^C \mid A_2) + P(D^C \cap D \mid A_2) = P(D \mid A_2)P(D^C \mid A_2) + P(D^C \mid A_2)P(D \mid A_2)$$
$$= .025(1 - .025) + (1 - .025)(.025) = .025(.975) + .975(.025) = .04875 = P(1 \, D \mid A_2)$$

The probability of getting one defective out of two fuses is:

$$P(1 \, D) = P(1 \, D \cap A_1) + P(1 \, D \cap A_2) = P(1 \, D \mid A_1)P(A_1) + P(1 \, D \mid A_2)P(A_2)$$
$$= .1128(.5) + .04875(.5) = .0564 + .024375 = .080775$$

Finally, we want to find:

$$P(A_1 \mid 1 \, D) = \frac{P(1 \, D \cap A_1)}{P(1 \, D)} = \frac{.0564}{.080775} = .6982$$

3.85   Define the following event:

D: {Chip is defective}

From the Exercise, $P(S_1) = .15$, $P(S_2) = .05$, $P(S_3) = .10$, $P(S_4) = .20$, $P(S_5) = .12$, $P(S_6) = .20$, and $P(S_7) = .18$. Also, $P(D|S_1) = .001$, $P(D|S_2) = .0003$, $P(D|S_3) = .0007$, $P(D|S_4) = .006$, $P(D|S_5) = .0002$, $P(D|S_6) = .0002$, and $P(D|S_7) = .001$.

a. We must find the probability of each supplier given a defective chip.

$$P(S_1 \mid D) = \frac{P(S_1 \cap D)}{P(D)} =$$

$$\frac{P(D \mid S_1)P(S_1)}{P(D \mid S_1)P(S_1) + P(D \mid S_2)P(S_2) + P(D \mid S_3)P(S_3) + P(D \mid S_4)P(S_4) + P(D \mid S_5)P(S_5) + P(D \mid S_6)P(S_6) + P(D \mid S_7)P(S_7)}$$

$$= \frac{.001(.15)}{.001(.15) + .0003(.05) + .0007(.10) + .006(.20) + .0002(.12) + .0002(.02) + .001(.18)}$$

$$= \frac{.00015}{.00015 + .000015 + .00007 + .0012 + .000024 + .00004 + .00018} = \frac{.00015}{.001679} = .0893$$

$$P(S_2 \mid D) = \frac{P(S_2 \cap D)}{P(D)} = \frac{P(D \mid S_2)P(S_2)}{P(D)} = \frac{.0003(.05)}{.001679} = \frac{.000015}{.001679} = .0089$$

$$P(S_3 \mid D) = \frac{P(S_3 \cap D)}{P(D)} = \frac{P(D \mid S_3)P(S_3)}{P(D)} = \frac{.0007(.10)}{.001679} = \frac{.00007}{.001679} = .0417$$

$$P(S_4 \mid D) = \frac{P(S_4 \cap D)}{P(D)} = \frac{P(D \mid S_4)P(S_4)}{P(D)} = \frac{.006(.20)}{.001679} = \frac{.0012}{.001679} = .7147$$

$$P(S_5 \mid D) = \frac{P(S_5 \cap D)}{P(D)} = \frac{P(D \mid S_5)P(S_5)}{P(D)} = \frac{.0002(.12)}{.001679} = \frac{.000024}{.001679} = .0143$$

$$P(S_6 \mid D) = \frac{P(S_6 \cap D)}{P(D)} = \frac{P(D \mid S_6)P(S_6)}{P(D)} = \frac{.0002(.20)}{.001679} = \frac{.00004}{.001679} = .0238$$

$$P(S_7 \mid D) = \frac{P(S_7 \cap D)}{P(D)} = \frac{P(D \mid S_7)P(S_7)}{P(D)} = \frac{.001(.18)}{.001679} = \frac{.00018}{.001679} = .1072$$

Of these probabilities, .7147 is the largest. This implies that if a failure is observed, supplier number 4 was most likely responsible.

b. If the seven suppliers all produce defective chips at the same rate of .0005, then $P(D|S_i)$ =.0005 for all i = 1, 2, 3, ... 7 and $P(D)$ = .0005.

For any supplier i, $P(S_i \cap D) = P(D \mid S_i)P(S_i) = .0005 P(S_i)$ and

$$P(S_i \mid D) = \frac{P(S_i \cap D)}{P(D)} = \frac{P(D \mid S_i)P(S_i)}{.0005} = \frac{.0005 P(S_i)}{.0005} = P(S_i)$$

Thus, if a defective is observed, then it most likely came from the supplier with the largest proportion of sales (probability). In this case, the most likely supplier would be either supplier 4 or supplier 6. Both of these have probabilities of .20.

3.87   a.   If events A and B are mutually exclusive, then $P(A \cap B) = 0$.

$$P(A \mid B) = \frac{P(A \cap B)}{P(B)} = \frac{0}{.3} = 0$$

b.   No. If events A and B are independent, then $P(A \mid B) = P(A)$. However, from the Exercise we know $P(A) = .2$ and from part a, we know $P(A \mid B) = 0$. Thus, events A and B are not independent.

3.89 $P(A \cap B) = .4, P(A \mid B) = .8$

Since the $P(A \mid B) = \dfrac{P(A \cap B)}{P(B)}$, substitute the given probabilities into the formula and solve for $P(B)$.

$$.8 = \frac{.4}{P(B)} \Rightarrow P(B) = \frac{.4}{.8} = .5$$

3.91   a. $P(A \cap B) = 0$

$P(B \cap C) = P(2) = .2$

$P(A \cup C) = P(1) + P(2) + P(3) + P(5) + P(6) = .3 + .2 + .1 + .1 + .2 = .9$

$P(A \cup B \cup C) = P(1) + P(2) + P(3) + P(4) + P(5) + P(6)$
$= .3 + .2 + .1 + .1 + .1 + .2 = 1$

$P(B^c) = P(1) + P(3) + P(5) + P(6) = .3 + .1 + .1 + .2 = .7$

$P(A^c \cap B) = P(2) + P(4) = .2 + .1 = .3$

$P(B \mid C) = \dfrac{P(B \cap C)}{P(C)} = \dfrac{P(2)}{P(2) + P(5) + P(6)} = \dfrac{.2}{.2 + .1 + .2} = \dfrac{.2}{.5} = .4$

$P(B \mid A) = \dfrac{P(B \cap A)}{P(A)} = \dfrac{0}{P(A)} = 0$

b.   Since $P(A \cap B) = 0$, and $P(A) \cdot P(B) > 0$, these two would not be equal, implying A and B are not independent. However, A and B are mutually exclusive, since $P(A \cap B) = 0$.

c. $P(B) = P(2) + P(4) = .2 + .1 = .3$. But $P(B \mid C)$, calculated above, is .4. Since these are not equal, B and C are not independent. Since $P(B \cap C) = .2$, B and C are not mutually exclusive.

3.93   a. $6! = 6 \cdot 5 \cdot 4 \cdot 3 \cdot 2 \cdot 1 = 720$

b. $\dbinom{10}{9} = \dfrac{10!}{9!(10-9)!} = \dfrac{10 \cdot 9 \cdot 8 \cdot \, \cdots \, \cdot 1}{9 \cdot 8 \cdot 7 \cdot \, \cdots \, \cdot 1 \cdot 1} = 10$

c. $\dbinom{10}{1} = \dfrac{10!}{1!(10-1)!} = \dfrac{10 \cdot 9 \cdot 8 \cdot \, \cdots \, \cdot 1}{1 \cdot 9 \cdot 8 \cdot \, \cdots \, \cdot 1} = 10$

d. $\dbinom{6}{3} = \dfrac{6!}{3!(6-3)!} = \dfrac{6 \cdot 5 \cdot 4 \cdot 3 \cdot 2 \cdot 1}{3 \cdot 2 \cdot 1 \cdot 3 \cdot 2 \cdot 1} = 20$

e. $0! = 1$

3.95   Define the following event:

A: {INA member is male}

$P(A) = \dfrac{3}{650} = .0046$

3.97   a.   This statement is false. All probabilities are between 0 and 1 inclusive. One cannot have a probability of 4.

b.   If we assume that the probabilities are the same as the percents (changed to proportions), then this is a true statement.

$$P(4 or 5) = P(4) + P(5) = .6020 + .1837 = .7857$$

c.   This statement is true. There were no observations with one star. Thus, $P(1) = 0$.

d.   This statement is false. $P(2) = .0408$ and $P(5) = .1837$. $P(5) > P(2)$.

3.99   a. $B \cap C$

b. A^c

c. $C \cup B$

d. $A \cap C^c$

3.101   Define the following events:

G: {regularly use the golf course}
T: {regularly use the tennis courts}

Given: $P(G) = .7$ and $P(T) = .5$

The event "uses neither facility" can be written as $G^c \cap T^c$ or $(G \cup T)^c$. We are given $P(G^c \cap T^c) = P[(G \cup T)^c] = .05$. The complement of the event "uses neither facility" is the event "uses at least one of the two facilities" which can be written as $G \cup T$.

$$P(G \cup T) = 1 - P[(G \cup T)^c] = 1 - .05 = .95$$

From the additive rule, $P(G \cup T) = P(G) + P(T) - P(G \cap T)$
$$\Rightarrow .95 = .7 + .5 - P(G \cap T)$$
$$\Rightarrow P(G \cap T) = .25$$

a.   The Venn Diagram is:

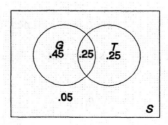

b. $P(G \cup T) = .95$ from above.

c. $P(G \cap T) = .25$ from above.

d. $P(G \mid T) = \dfrac{P(G \cap T)}{P(T)} = \dfrac{.25}{.5} = .5$

3.103   Define the following events:

A: {U.S. household does not own stock}
B: {U.S. household does own stock}
C: {U.S. household spends more and saves less}
D: {U.S. household spends less and saves more}
E: {No effect}

We are given that $P(B) = .50$. Since the figures in the table are only for stockholders, they are all conditional probabilities. $P(E|B) = .85$, $P(C|B) = .034$, and $P(D|B) = .116$

a. $P(A) = 1 - P(B) = 1 - .50 = .50$.

b. $P(C|B) = .034$

c. $P(B \cap D) = P(D \mid B)P(B) = .116(.50) = .058$

3.105   Define the following events:

A: {The watch is accurate}
N: {The watch is not accurate}

Assuming the manufacturer's claim is correct,

$P(N) = .05$ and $P(A) = 1 - P(N) = 1 - .05 = .95$

The sample space for the purchase of four of the manufacturer's watches is listed below.

(A, A, A, A)	(N, A, A, A)	(A, N, N, A)	(N, A, N, N)
(A, A, A, N)	(A, A, N, N)	(N, A, N, A)	(N, N, A, N)
(A, A, N, A)	(A, N, A, N)	(N, N, A, A)	(N, N, N, A)
(A, N, A, A)	(N, A, A, N)	(A, N, N, N)	(N, N, N, N)

a.   All four watches not being accurate as claimed is the sample point (N, N, N, N).

Assuming the watches purchased operate independently and the manufacturer's claim is correct,

$P(N, N, N, N) = P(N)P(N)P(N)P(N) = .05^4 = .00000625$

b.   The sample points in the sample space that consist of exactly two watches failing to meet the claim are listed below.

(A, A, N, N) (N, A, A, N)
(A, N, A, N) (N, A, N, A)
(A, N, N, A) (N, N, A, A)

The probability that exactly two of the four watches fail to meet the claim is the sum of the probabilities of these six sample points.

Assuming the watches purchased operate independently and the manufacturer's claim is correct,

$$P(A, A, N, N) = P(A)P(A)P(N)P(N) = (.95)(.95)(.05)(.05) = .00225625$$

All six of the sample points will have the same probability. Therefore, the probability that exactly two of the four watches fail to meet the claim when the manufacturer's claim is correct is

$$6(0.00225625) = .0135$$

c.   The sample points in the sample space that consist of three of the four watches failing to meet the claim are listed below.

(A, N, N, N) (N, N, A, N)
(N, A, N, N) (N, N, N, A)

The probability that three of the four watches fail to meet the claim is the sum of the probabilities of the four sample points.

Assuming the watches purchased operate independently and the manufacturer's claim is correct,

$$P(A, N, N, N) = P(A)P(N)P(N)P(N) = (.95)(.05)(.05)(.05) = .00011875$$

All four of the sample points will have the same probability. Therefore, the probability that three of the four watches fail to meet the claim when the manufacturer's claim is correct is

$$4(.00011875) = .000475$$

If this event occurred, we would tend to doubt the validity of the manufacturer's claim since its probability of occurring is so small.

d.   All four watches tested failing to meet the claim is the sample point (N, N, N, N).

Assuming the watches purchased operate independently and the manufacturer's claim is correct,

$$P(N, N, N, N) = P(N)P(N)P(N)P(N) = (.05)^4 = .00000625$$

Since the probability of observing this event is so small if the claim is true, we have strong evidence against the validity of the claim. However, we do not have conclusive proof that the claim is false. There is still a chance the event can occur (with probability .00000625) although it is extremely small.

3.107   Define the following events:

A: {Acupoll predicts the success of a particular product}
B: {Product is successful}

From the problem, we know

$P(A \mid B) = .89$ and $P(B) = .90$

Thus, $P(A \cap B) = P(A \mid B)P(B) = .89(.90) = .801$

3.109   Define the following events:

A: {Never smoked cigars}
B: {Former cigar smoker}
C: {Current cigar smoker}
D: {Died from cancer}
E: {Did not die from cancer}

a. $P(D \mid A) = \dfrac{P(D \cap A)}{P(A)} = \dfrac{782/137,243}{121,529/137,243} = \dfrac{782}{121,529} = .006$

b. $(D \mid B) = \dfrac{P(D \cap B)}{P(B)} = \dfrac{91/137,243}{7,848/137,243} = \dfrac{91}{7,848} = .012$

c. $P(D \mid C) = \dfrac{P(D \cap C)}{P(C)} = \dfrac{141/137,243}{7,866/137,243} = \dfrac{141}{7,866} = .018$

3.111 a. $P(B) = \dfrac{5{,}021}{833{,}303} = .0060$

b. $P(A \cap B) = \dfrac{1{,}808}{833{,}303} = .0022$

c. $P(A \cup B) = P(A) + P(B) - P(A \cap B)$
$$= \frac{341{,}180}{833{,}303} + \frac{5{,}021}{833{,}303} - \frac{1{,}808}{833{,}303} = \frac{344{,}393}{833{,}303} = .4133$$

d. $P(A \mid B) = \dfrac{(A \cap B)}{P(B)} = \dfrac{1{,}808/833{,}303}{5{,}021/833{,}303} = \dfrac{1{,}808}{5{,}021} = .3601$

e. No. If A and B are independent, then $P(A \mid B) = P(A)$. Here, $P(A \mid B) \neq P(A)$ or .3601 $\neq$ .4094. Thus, A and B are not independent.

3.113 Define the following events:

S_1: {Salesman makes sale on the first visit}
S_2: {Salesman makes a sale on the second visit}

$P(S_1) = .4 \quad P(S_2 \mid S_1^c) = .65$

The sample points of the experiment are:

$S_1 \cap S_2^c$
$S_1^c \cap S_2$
$S_1^c \cap S_2^c$

The probability the salesman will make a sale is:

$P(S_1 \cap S_2^c) + P(S_1^c \cap S_2) = P(S_1) + P(S_2 \mid S_1^c)P(S_1^c) = .4 + .65(1 - .4) = .4 + .39 = .79$

3.115 Define the following events:

O_1: {Component #1 operates properly}
O_2: {Component #2 operates properly}
O_3: {Component #3 operates properly}

$P(O_1) = 1 - P(O) = 1 - .12 = .88$
$P(O_2) = 1 - P(O) = 1 - .09 = .91$
$P(O_3) = 1 - P(O) = 1 - .11 = .89$

a. $P(\text{System operates properly}) = P(O_1 \cap O_2 \cap O_3)$
$$= P(O_1)P(O_2)P(O_3)$$
(since the three components operate independently)
$$= (.88)(.91)(.89) = .7127$$

b. $P(\text{System fails}) = 1 - P(\text{system operates properly})$
$$= 1 - .7127 \text{ (see part } \mathbf{a})$$
$$= .2873$$

3.117　We will denote the five successful utility companies as S_1, S_2, S_3, S_4, and S_5 and the two failing companies as F_1 and F_2. There are

$$\binom{7}{3} = \frac{7!}{3!4!} = \frac{7 \cdot 6 \cdot 5 \cdot 4 \cdot 3 \cdot 2 \cdot 1}{3 \cdot 2 \cdot 1 \cdot 4 \cdot 3 \cdot 2 \cdot 1} = 35$$

possible ways to choose three companies from the seven, as shown below:

(S_1, S_2, S_3)	(S_1, S_3, S_4)	(S_1, S_4, S_5)	(S_1, S_5, F_1)
(S_1, S_2, S_4)	(S_1, S_3, S_5)	(S_1, S_4, F_1)	(S_1, S_5, F_2)
(S_1, S_2, S_5)	(S_1, S_3, F_1)	(S_1, S_4, F_2)	
(S_1, S_2, F_1)	(S_1, S_3, F_2)		(S_1, F_1, F_2)
(S_1, S_2, F_2)			
(S_2, S_3, S_4)	(S_2, S_4, S_5)	(S_2, S_5, F_1)	(S_2, F_1, F_2)
(S_2, S_3, S_5)	(S_2, S_4, F_1)	(S_2, S_5, F_2)	
(S_2, S_3, F_1)	(S_2, S_4, F_2)		
(S_2, S_3, F_2)			
(S_3, S_4, S_5)	(S_3, S_5, F_1)	(S_3, F_1, F_2)	
(S_3, S_4, F_1)	(S_3, S_5, F_2)		
(S_3, S_4, F_2)			
(S_4, S_5, F_1)	(S_5, F_1, F_2)		
(S_4, S_5, F_2)			
(S_4, F_1, F_2)			

a. Each outcome is equally likely, so each sample point has probability 1/35. From the 35 events listed, 10 do not contain F_1 or F_2. Therefore, $P(\text{selecting none}) = 10/35$.

b. From the 35 events listed, 20 contain either F_1 or F_2, but not both. Therefore, $P(\text{selecting one}) = 20/35$.

c. From the 35 events listed, 5 contain both F_1 and F_2. Therefore, $P(\text{selecting both}) = 5/35$.

3.119   Define the following events:

A: {Press is correctly adjusted}
B: {Press is incorrectly adjusted}
D: {part is defective}

From the exercise, $P(A) = .90$, $P(D|A) = .05$, and $P(D|B) = .50$. We also know that event B is the complement of event A. Thus, $P(B) = 1 - P(A) = 1 - .90 = .10$.

$$P(B|D) = \frac{P(B \cap D)}{P(D)} = \frac{P(D|B)P(B)}{P(D|B)P(B) + P(D|A)P(A)}$$

$$= \frac{.50(.10)}{.50(.10) + .05(.90)} = \frac{.05}{.05 + .045} = \frac{.05}{.095} = .526$$

3.121   Define the flowing events:

A: {Dealer draws a blackjack}
B: {Player draws a blackjack}

a.   For the dealer to draw a blackjack, he needs to draw an ace and a face card. There are

$$\binom{4}{1} = \frac{4!}{1!(4-1)!} = \frac{4 \cdot 3 \cdot 2 \cdot 1}{1 \cdot 3 \cdot 2 \cdot 1} = 4 \text{ ways to draw an ace and}$$

$$\binom{12}{1} = \frac{12!}{1!(12-1)!} = \frac{12 \cdot 11 \cdot 10 \cdots 1}{1 \cdot 11 \cdot 10 \cdot 9 \cdots 1} = 12 \text{ ways to draw a face card (there are 12 face}$$

cards in the deck).

The total number of ways a dealer can draw a blackjack is $4 \cdot 12 = 48$.

The total number of ways a dealer can draw 2 cards is

$$\binom{52}{2} = \frac{52!}{2!(52-2)!} = \frac{52 \cdot 51 \cdot 50 \cdots 1}{2 \cdot 1 \cdot 50 \cdot 49 \cdot 48 \cdots 1} = 1326$$

Thus, the probability that the dealer draws a blackjack is $P(A) = \dfrac{48}{1326} = .0362$

b.   In order for the player to win with a blackjack, the player must draw a blackjack and the dealer does not. Using our notation, this is the event $B \cap A^C$. We need to find the probability that the player draws a blackjack ($P(B)$) and the probability that the dealer does not draw a blackjack given the player does ($P(A^C | B)$). Then, the probability that the player wins with a blackjack is $P(A^C|B)P(B)$.

The probability that the player draws a blackjack is the same as the probability that the dealer draws a blackjack, which is $P(B) = .0362$.

There are 5 scenarios where the dealer will not draw a blackjack given the player does. First, the dealer could draw an ace and not a face card. Next, the dealer could draw a face card and not an ace. Third, the dealer could draw two cards that are not aces or face cards. Fourth, the dealer could draw two aces, and finally, the dealer could draw two face cards.

The number of ways the dealer could draw an ace and not a face card given the player draws a blackjack is

$$\binom{3}{1}\binom{36}{1} = \frac{3!}{1!(3-1)!} \cdot \frac{36!}{1!(36-1)!} = \frac{3 \cdot 2 \cdot 1}{1 \cdot 2 \cdot 1} \cdot \frac{36 \cdot 35 \cdot 34 \cdots 1}{1 \cdot 35 \cdot 34 \cdot 33 \cdots 1} = 3(36) = 108$$

(Note: Given the player has drawn blackjack, there are only 3 aces left and 36 non-face cards.)

The number of ways the dealer could draw a face card and not an ace given the player draws a blackjack is

$$\binom{11}{1}\binom{36}{1} = \frac{11!}{1!(11-1)!} \cdot \frac{36!}{1!(36-1)!} = \frac{11 \cdot 10 \cdot 9 \cdots 1}{1 \cdot 10 \cdot 9 \cdot 8 \cdots 1} \cdot \frac{36 \cdot 35 \cdot 34 \cdots 1}{1 \cdot 35 \cdot 34 \cdot 33 \cdots 1} = 11(36) = 396$$

The number of ways the dealer could draw neither a face card nor an ace given the player draws a blackjack is

$$\binom{36}{2} = \frac{36!}{2!(36-2)!} = \frac{36 \cdot 35 \cdot 34 \cdots 1}{2 \cdot 1 \cdot 34 \cdot 33 \cdot 32 \cdots 1} = 630$$

The number of ways the dealer could draw two aces given the player draws a blackjack is

$$\binom{3}{2} = \frac{3!}{2!(3-2)!} = \frac{3 \cdot 2 \cdot 1}{2 \cdot 1 \cdot 1} = 3$$

The number of ways the dealer could draw two face cards given the player draws a blackjack is

$$\binom{11}{2} = \frac{11!}{2!(11-2)!} = \frac{11 \cdot 10 \cdot 9 \cdots 1}{2 \cdot 9 \cdot 8 \cdot 7 \cdots 1} = 55$$

The total number of ways the dealer can draw two cards given the player draws a blackjack is

$$\binom{50}{2} = \frac{50!}{2!(50-2)!} = \frac{50 \cdot 49 \cdot 48 \cdots 1}{2 \cdot 1 \cdot 48 \cdot 47 \cdot 46 \cdots 1} = 1225$$

The probability that the dealer does not draw a blackjack given the player draws a blackjack is

$$P(A^C \mid B) = \frac{108 + 396 + 630 + 3 + 55}{1225} = \frac{1192}{1225} = .9731$$

Finally, the probability that the player wins with a blackjack is

$$P(B \cap A^C) = P(A^C \mid B)P(B) = .9731(.0362) = .0352$$

3.123 First, we will list all possible sample points for placing a car (C) and 2 goats (G) behind doors #1, #2, and #3. If the first position corresponds to door #1, the second position corresponds to door #2, and the third position corresponds to door #3, the sample space is:

$(C\,G\,G)$ $(G\,C\,G)$ $(G\,G\,C)$

Now, suppose you pick door #1. Initially, the probability that you will win the car is 1/3 – only one of the sample points has a car behind door #1.

The host will now open a door behind which is a goat. If you pick door #1 in the first sample point $(C\,G\,G)$, the host will open either door #2 or door #3. Suppose he opens door #3 (it really does not matter). If you pick door #1 in the second sample point $(G\,C\,G)$, the host will open door #3. If you pick door #1 in the third sample point $(G\,G\,C)$, the host will open door #2. Now, the new sample space will be:

$(C\,G)$ $(G\,C)$ $(G\,C)$

where the first position corresponds to door #1 (the one you chose) and the second position corresponds to the door that was not opened by the host.

Now, if you keep door #1, the probability that you win the car is 1/3. However, if you switch to the remaining door, the probability that you win the car is now 2/3. Based on these probabilities, it is to your advantage to switch doors.

The above could be repeated by selecting door #2 initially or door #3 initially. In either of these cases, again, the probability of winning the car is 1/3 if you do not switch and 2/3 if you switch. Thus, Marilyn was correct.

Random Variables and Probability Distributions   *Chapter 4*

4.1   a.   The number of newspapers sold by New York Times each month can take on a countable number of values. Thus, this is a discrete random variable.

  b.   The amount of ink used in printing the Sunday edition of the New York Times can take on an infinite number of different values. Thus, this is a continuous random variable.

  c.   The actual number of ounces in a one gallon bottle of laundry detergent can take on an infinite number of different values. Thus, this is a continuous random variable.

  d.   The number of defective parts in a shipment of nuts and bolts can take on a countable number of values. Thus, this is a discrete random variable.

  e.   The number of people collecting unemployment insurance each month can take on a countable number of values. Thus, this is a discrete random variable.

4.3   Since there are only a fixed number of outcomes to the experiment, the random variable, x, the number of stars in the rating, is discrete.

4.5   The variable x, total compensation in 2005 (in $ millions), is reported in whole number dollars. Since there are a countable number of possible outcomes, this variable is discrete.

4.7   An economist might be interested in the percentage of the work force that is unemployed, or the current inflation rate, both of which are continuous random variables.

4.9   The manager of a clothing store might be concerned with the number of employees on duty at a specific time of day, or the number of articles of a particular type of clothing that are on hand.

4.11 a.   When a die is tossed, the number of spots observed on the upturned face can be 1, 2, 3, 4, 5, or 6. Since the six sample points are equally likely, each one has a probability of 1/6.

    The probability distribution of x may be summarized in tabular form:

x	1	2	3	4	5	6
$p(x)$	$\dfrac{1}{6}$	$\dfrac{1}{6}$	$\dfrac{1}{6}$	$\dfrac{1}{6}$	$\dfrac{1}{6}$	$\dfrac{1}{6}$

b. The probability distribution of x may also be presented in graphical form:

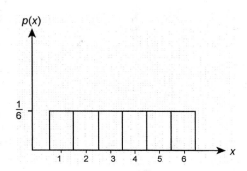

4.13   a. We know $\sum p(x) = 1$. Thus, $p(2) + p(3) + p(5) + p(8) + p(10) = 1$

$$\Rightarrow p(5) = 1 - p(2) - p(3) - p(8) - p(10) = 1 - .15 - .10 - .25 - .25 = .25$$

b. $P(x = 2 \text{ or } x = 10) = P(x = 2) + P(x = 10) = .15 + .25 = .40$

c. $P(x \le 8) = P(x = 2) + P(x = 3) + P(x = 5) + P(x = 8) = .15 + .10 + .25 + .25 = .75$

4.15   a. The sample points are (where H = head, T = tail):

	HHH	HHT	HTH	THH	HTT	THT	TTH	TTT
x = # heads	3	2	2	2	1	1	1	0

b. If each event is equally likely, then $P(\text{sample point}) = \dfrac{1}{n} = \dfrac{1}{8}$

$$p(3) = \frac{1}{8}, \; p(2) = \frac{1}{8} + \frac{1}{8} + \frac{1}{8} = \frac{3}{8}, \; p(1) = \frac{1}{8} + \frac{1}{8} + \frac{1}{8} = \frac{3}{8}, \text{ and } p(0) = \frac{1}{8}$$

c. Using Minitab, the graph of $p(x)$ is:

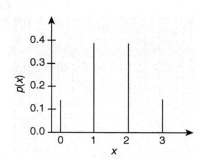

d. $P(x = 2 \text{ or } x = 3) = p(2) + p(3) = \dfrac{3}{8} + \dfrac{1}{8} = \dfrac{4}{8} = \dfrac{1}{2}$

4.17   a. $\mu = E(x) = \sum xp(x) = -4(.02) + (-3)(.07) + (-2)(.10) + (-1)(.15) + 0(.3)$
$$+ 1(.18) + 2(.10) + 3(.06) + 4(.02)$$
$$= -.08 - .21 - .2 - .15 + 0 + .18 + .2 + .18 + .08 = 0$$

$\sigma^2 = E[(x - \mu)^2] = \sum (x - \mu)^2 p(x)$
$$= (-4 - 0)^2(.02) + (-3 - 0)^2(.07) + (-2 - 0)^2(.10)$$
$$+ (-1 - 0)^2(.15) + (0 - 0)^2(.30) + (1 - 0)^2(.18)$$
$$+ (2 - 0)^2(.10) + (3 - 0)^2(.06) + (4 - 0)^2(.02)$$
$$= .32 + .63 + .4 + .15 + 0 + .18 + .4 + .54 + .32 = 2.94$$

$\sigma = \sqrt{2.94} = 1.715$

b.

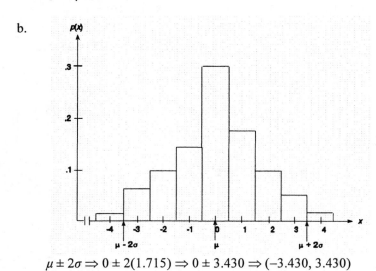

$\mu \pm 2\sigma \Rightarrow 0 \pm 2(1.715) \Rightarrow 0 \pm 3.430 \Rightarrow (-3.430, 3.430)$

c. $P(-3.430 < x < 3.430) = p(-3) + p(-2) + p(-1) + p(0) + p(1) + p(2) + p(3)$
$$= .07 + .10 + .15 + .30 + .18 + .10 + .06 = .96$$

4.19   a.   The probability distribution for x is found by converting the Percent column to a probability column by dividing the percents by 100. The probability distribution of x is:

x	$p(x)$
2	.0408
3	.1735
4	.6020
5	.1837

b. $P(x = 5) = p(5) = .1837.$

c. $P(x \le 2) = p(2) = .0408.$

d. $\mu = E(x) = \sum_{i=1}^{4} x_i p(x_i) = 2(.0408) + 3(.1735) + 4(.6020) + 5(.1837)$

$$= .0816 + .5205 + 2.4080 + .9185 = 3.9286$$

The average star rating for a car's drivers-side star rating is 3.9286.

4.21   a.   Yes. For all values of x, $0 \le p(x) \le 1$ and $\sum p(x) = .01 + .02 + .03 + .05 + .08 + .09 +$
.11 + .13 + .12 + .10 + .08 + .06 + .05 + .03 + .02 + .01 + .01 = 1.00.

   b. $P(x = 16) = .06$

   c. $P(x \le 10) = p(5) + p(6) + p(7) + p(8) + p(9) + p(10)$
   $= .01 + .02 + .03 + .05 + .08 + .09 = .28$

   d. $P(5 \le x \le 15) = p(5) + p(6) + p(7) + p(8) + p(9) + p(10) + p(11) + p(12) + p(13)$
   $+ p(14) + p(15)$
   $= .01 + .02 + .03 + .05 + .08 + .09 + .11 + .13 + .12 + .10 + .08$
   $= .82$

4.23   a. $p(0) = \dfrac{\binom{20}{0}\binom{100-20}{3-0}}{\binom{100}{3}} = \dfrac{\dfrac{20!}{0!(20-0)!}\dfrac{80!}{3!(80-3)!}}{\dfrac{100!}{3!(100-3)!}} = \dfrac{\dfrac{20!}{0!20!}\dfrac{80!}{3!77!}}{\dfrac{100!}{3!97!}} = \dfrac{1 \cdot \dfrac{80 \cdot 79 \cdot 78}{3 \cdot 2}}{\dfrac{100 \cdot 99 \cdot 98}{3 \cdot 2}}$

   $= \dfrac{82,160}{161,700} = .508$

   b. $p(1) = \dfrac{\binom{20}{1}\binom{100-20}{3-1}}{\binom{100}{3}} = \dfrac{\dfrac{20!}{1!(20-1)!}\dfrac{80!}{2!(80-2)!}}{\dfrac{100!}{3!(100-3)!}} = \dfrac{\dfrac{20!}{1!19!}\dfrac{80!}{2!78!}}{\dfrac{100!}{3!97!}} = \dfrac{20 \cdot \dfrac{80 \cdot 79}{2}}{\dfrac{100 \cdot 99 \cdot 98}{3 \cdot 2}}$

   $= \dfrac{63,200}{161,700} = .391$

   c. $p(2) = \dfrac{\binom{20}{2}\binom{100-20}{3-2}}{\binom{100}{3}} = \dfrac{\dfrac{20!}{2!(20-2)!}\dfrac{80!}{1!(80-1)!}}{\dfrac{100!}{3!(100-3)!}} = \dfrac{\dfrac{20!}{2!18!}\dfrac{80!}{1!79!}}{\dfrac{100!}{3!97!}} = \dfrac{\dfrac{20 \cdot 19}{2} \cdot 80}{\dfrac{100 \cdot 99 \cdot 98}{3 \cdot 2}}$

   $= \dfrac{15,200}{161,700} = .094$

   d. $p(3) = \dfrac{\binom{20}{3}\binom{100-20}{3-0}}{\binom{100}{3}} = \dfrac{\dfrac{20!}{3!(20-3)!}\dfrac{80!}{0!(80-0)!}}{\dfrac{100!}{3!(100-3)!}} = \dfrac{\dfrac{20!}{3!17!} \cdot 1}{\dfrac{100!}{3!97!}} = \dfrac{\dfrac{20 \cdot 19 \cdot 18}{3 \cdot 2} \cdot 1}{\dfrac{100 \cdot 99 \cdot 98}{3 \cdot 2}}$

   $= \dfrac{1,140}{161,700} = .007$

4.25　a.　$p(1) = (.23)(.77)^{1-1} = (.23)(.77)^0 = .23$. The probability that one would encounter a contaminated cartridge on the first trial is .23.

　　　b.　$p(5) = (.23)(.77)^{5-1} = (.23)(.77)^4 = .0809$. The probability that one would encounter a the first contaminated cartridge on the fifth trial is .0809.

　　　c.　$P(x \geq 2) = 1 - P(x \leq 1) = 1 - P(x = 1) = 1 - .23 = .77$. The probability that the first contaminated cartridge is found on the second trial or later is .77.

4.27　a.　The properties of valid probability distributions are:

$$\sum p(x) = 1 \text{ and } 0 \leq p(x) \leq 1 \text{ for all } x.$$

For ARC a_1:$0 \leq p(x) \leq 1$ for all x and $\sum p(x) = .6 + .25 + .1 + .05 = 1.00$
Thus, this is a valid probability distribution.

For ARC a_2:$0 \leq p(x) \leq 1$ for all x and $\sum p(x) = .6 + .3 + .1 = 1.00$
Thus, this is a valid probability distribution.

For ARC a_3:$0 \leq p(x) \leq 1$ for all x and $\sum p(x) = .9 + .1 = 1.00$
Thus, this is a valid probability distribution.

For ARC a_4:$0 \leq p(x) \leq 1$ for all x and $\sum p(x) = .9 + .1 = 1.00$
Thus, this is a valid probability distribution.

For ARC a_5:$0 \leq p(x) \leq 1$ for all x and $\sum p(x) = .9 + .1 = 1.00$
Thus, this is a valid probability distribution.

For ARC a_6:$0 \leq p(x) \leq 1$ for all x and $\sum p(x) = .7 + .25 + .05 = 1.00$
Thus, this is a valid probability distribution.

　　　b.　For Arc a_1, $P(x > 1) = P(x = 2) + P(x = 3) = .25 + .6 = .85$

　　　c.　For Arc a_2, $P(x > 1) = P(x = 2) = .6$
For Arc a_3, $P(x > 1) = 0$
For Arc a_4, $P(x > 1) = 0$
For Arc a_5, $P(x > 1) = 0$
For Arc a_6, $P(x > 1) = P(x = 2) = .7$

　　　d.　For Arc a_1,
$$E(x) = \sum xp(x) = 3(.60) + 2(.25) + 1(.10) + 0(.05) = 1.80 + .50 + .1 + 0 = 2.40$$

The average capacity of Arc a_1 is 2.40.

For Arc a_2,
$$E(x) = \sum xp(x) = 2(.60) + 1(.30) + 0(.10) = 1.20 + .30 + 0 = 1.50$$

The average capacity of Arc a_2 is 1.50.

For Arcs a_3, a_4, and a_5,
$$E(x) = \sum xp(x) = 1(.90) + 0(.10) = .90 + 0 = .90$$

The average capacity of Arc a_3 is 0.90. The average capacity of Arc a_4 is 0.90.
The average capacity of Arc a_5 is 0.90.

For Arc a_6,
$$E(x) = \sum xp(x) = 2(.70) + 1(.25) + 0(.10) = 1.40 + .25 + 0 = 1.65$$

The average capacity of Arc a_6 is 1.65.

e. For Arc a_1,
$$\sigma^2 = E[(x - \mu)]^2 = \sum (x - \mu)^2 p(x)$$
$$= (3 - 2.4)^2 (.60) + (2 - 2.4)^2 (.25) + (1 - 2.4)^2 (.10) + (0 - 2.4)^2 (.05)$$
$$= (.6)^2 (.60) + (-.4)^2 (.25) + (-1.4)^2 (.10) + (-2.4)^2 (.05)$$
$$= .216 + .04 + .196 + .288 = .74$$
$$\sigma = \sqrt{.74} = .860$$

For Arc a_2,
$$\sigma^2 = E[(x - \mu)]^2 = \sum (x - \mu)^2 p(x)$$
$$= (2 - 1.5)^2 (.60) + (1 - 1.5)^2 (.30) + (0 - 1.5)^2 (.10)$$
$$= (.5)^2 (.60) + (-.5)^2 (.30) + (-1.5)^2 (.10)$$
$$= .15 + .075 + .225 = .45$$
$$\sigma = \sqrt{.45} = .671$$

For Arcs a_3, a_4, and a_5,

$$\sigma^2 = E[(x - \mu)]^2 = \sum (x - \mu)^2 p(x)$$
$$= (1 - .9)^2 (.90) + (0 - .9)^2 (.10)$$
$$= (.1)^2 (.90) + (-.9)^2 (.10)$$
$$= .009 + .081 = .090$$
$$\sigma = \sqrt{.09} = .300$$

Random Variables and Probability Distributions

For Arc a_6,

$$\sigma^2 = E\left[(x - \mu)\right]^2 = \sum (x - \mu)^2 \, p(x)$$
$$= (2 - 1.65)^2 (.70) + (1 - 1.65)^2 (.25) + (0 - 1.65)^2 (.05)$$
$$= (.35)^2 (.70) + (-.65)^2 (.25) + (-1.65)^2 (.05)$$
$$= .08575 + .105625 + .136125 = .3275$$
$$\sigma = \sqrt{.3275} = .572$$

4.29   a.   Let x = the potential flood damages. Since we are assuming if it rains the business will incur damages and if it does not rain the business will not incur any damages, the probability distribution of x is:

x	0	300,000
$p(x)$	.7	.3

         b.   The expected loss due to flood damage is

$$E(x) = \sum_{\text{All } x} xp(x) = 0(.7) + 300,000(.3) = 0 + 90,000 = \$90,000$$

4.31   a.   Since there are 20 possible outcomes that are all equally likely, the probability of any of the 20 numbers is 1/20. The probability distribution of x is:

$$P(x = 5) = 1/20 = .05; \quad P(x = 10) = 1/20 = .05; \text{ etc.}$$

x	5	10	15	20	25	30	35	40	45	50	55	60	65	70	75	80	85	90	95	100
$p(x)$	.05	.05	.05	.05	.05	.05	.05	.05	.05	.05	.05	.05	.05	.05	.05	.05	.05	.05	.05	.05

         b. $E(x) = \sum xp(x) = 5(.05) + 10(.05) + 15(.05) + 20(.05) + 25(.05) + 30(.05) + 35(.05)$
             $+ 40(.05) + 45(.05) + 50(.05) + 55(.05) + 60(.05) + 65(.05) + 70(.05) + 75(.05)$
             $+ 80(.05) + 85(.05) + 90(.05) + 95(.05) + 100(.05) = 52.5$

         c. $\sigma^2 = E(x - \mu)^2 = \sum (x - \mu)^2 p(x) = (5 - 52.5)^2(.05) + (10 - 52.5)^2(.05)$
             $+ (15 - 52.5)^2(.05) + (20 - 52.5)^2(.05) + (25 - 52.5)^2(.05) + (30 - 52.5)^2(.05)$
             $+ (35 - 52.5)^2(.05) + (40 - 52.5)^2(.05) + (45 - 52.5)^2(.05) + (50 - 52.5)^2(.05)$
             $+ (55 - 52.5)^2(.05) + (60 - 52.5)^2(.05) + (65 - 52.5)^2(.05) + (70 - 52.5)^2(.05)$
             $+ (75 - 52.5)^2(.05) + (80 - 52.5)^2(.05) + (85 - 52.5)^2(.05) + (90 - 52.5)^2(.05)$
             $+ (95 - 52.5)^2(.05) + (100 - 52.5)^2(.05)$
             $= 831.25$

$$\sigma = \sqrt{\sigma^2} = \sqrt{831.25} = 28.83$$

Since the uniform distribution is not mound-shaped, we will use Chebyshev's theorem to describe the data. We know that at least 8/9 of the observations will fall with 3 standard deviations of the mean and at least 3/4 of the observations will fall within 2 standard deviations of the mean. For this problem,

$\mu \pm 2\sigma \Rightarrow 52.5 \pm 2(28.83) \Rightarrow 52.5 \pm 57.66 \Rightarrow (-5.16, 110.16)$. Thus, at least 3/4 of the data will fall between -5.16 and 110.16. For our problem, all of the observations will fall within 2 standard deviations of the mean. Thus, x is just as likely to fall within any interval of equal length.

d. If a player spins the wheel twice, the total number of outcomes will be $20(20) = 400$. The sample space is:

5, 5	10, 5	15, 5	20, 5	25, 5...	100, 5
5,10	10,10	15,10	20,10	25,10...	100,10
5,15	10,15	15,15	20,15	25,15...	100,15
.	.	.	.	.	.
.	.	.	.	.	.
.	.	.	.	.	.
5,100	10,100	15,100	20,100	25,100...	100,100

Each of these outcomes are equally likely, so each has a probability of $1/400 = .0025$.

Now, let x equal the sum of the two numbers in each sample. There is one sample with a sum of 10, two samples with a sum of 15, three samples with a sum of 20, etc. If the sum of the two numbers exceeds 100, then x is zero. The probability distribution of x is:

x	$p(x)$
0	.5250
10	.0025
15	.0050
20	.0075
25	.0100
30	.0125
35	.0150
40	.0175
45	.0200
50	.0225
55	.0250
60	.0275
65	.0300
70	.0325
75	.0350
80	.0375
85	.0400
90	.0425
95	.0450
100	.0475

e. We assumed that the wheel is fair, or that all outcomes are equally likely.

f. $\mu = E(x) = \sum xp(x) = 0(.5250) + 10(.0025) + 15(.0050) + 20(.0075) + ...+ 100(.0475)$

$= 33.25$

$\sigma^2 = E(x - \mu)^2 = \sum (x - \mu)^2 p(x) = (0 - 33.25)^2(.525) + (10 - 33.25)^2(.0025)$

$+ (15 - 33.25)^2(.0050) + (20 - 33.25)^2(.0075) + ...+ (100 - 33.25)^2(.0475)$

$= 1471.3125$

$\sigma = \sqrt{\sigma^2} = \sqrt{1471.3125} = 38.3577$

g. $P(x = 0) = .525$

h. Given that the player obtains a 20 on the first spin, the possible values for x (sum of the two spins) are 0 (player spins 85, 90, 95, or 100 on the second spin), 25, 30, ..., 100. In order to get an x of 25, the player would spin a 5 on the second spin. Similarly, the player would have to spin a 10 on the second spin order to get an x of 30, etc. Since all of the outcomes are equally likely on the second spin, the distribution of x is:

x	$p(x)$
0	.20
25	.05
30	.05
35	.05
40	.05
45	.05
50	.05
55	.05
60	.05
65	.05
70	.05
75	.05
80	.05
85	.05
90	.05
95	.05
100	.05

i. The probability that the players total score will exceed one dollar is the probability that x is zero. $P(x = 0) = .20$

j. Given that the player obtains a 65 on the first spin, the possible values for x (sum of the two spins) are 0 (player spins 40, 45, 50, up to 100 on second spin), 70, 75, 80,..., 100. In order to get an x of 70, the player would spin a 5 on the second spin. Similarly, the player would have to spin a 10 on the second spin in order to get an x of 75, etc. Since all of the outcomes are equally likely on the second spin, the distribution of x is:

x	$p(x)$
0	.65
70	.05
75	.05
80	.05
85	.05
90	.05
95	.05
100	.05

The probability that the players total score will exceed one dollar is the probability that x is zero. $P(x = 0) = .65$.

4.33 Let x = bookie's earnings per dollar wagered. Then x can take on values $1 (you lose) and $-5 (you win). The only way you win is if you pick 3 winners in 3 games. If the probability of picking 1 winner in 1 game is .5, then $P(www) = p(w)p(w)p(w) = .5(.5)(.5) = .125$ (assuming games are independent).

Thus, the probability distribution for x is:

x	$p(x)$
$1	.875
$-5	.125

$$E(x) = \sum xp(x) = 1(.875) - 5(.125) = .875 - .625 = \$.25$$

4.35 a. $\dfrac{6!}{2!(6-2)!} = \dfrac{6!}{2!4!} = \dfrac{6 \cdot 5 \cdot 4 \cdot 3 \cdot 2 \cdot 1}{(2 \cdot 1)(4 \cdot 3 \cdot 2 \cdot 1)} = 15$

b. $\dbinom{5}{2} = \dfrac{5!}{2!(5-2)!} = \dfrac{5!}{2!3!} = \dfrac{5 \cdot 4 \cdot 3 \cdot 2 \cdot 1}{(2 \cdot 1)(3 \cdot 2 \cdot 1)} = 10$

c. $\dbinom{7}{0} = \dfrac{7!}{0!(7-0)!} = \dfrac{7!}{0!7!} = \dfrac{7 \cdot 6 \cdot 5 \cdot 4 \cdot 3 \cdot 2 \cdot 1}{(1)(7 \cdot 6 \cdot 5 \cdot 4 \cdot 3 \cdot 2 \cdot 1)} = 1$

(Note: $0! = 1$)

d. $\dbinom{6}{6} = \dfrac{6!}{6!(6-6)!} = \dfrac{6!}{6!0!} = \dfrac{6 \cdot 5 \cdot 4 \cdot 3 \cdot 2 \cdot 1}{(6 \cdot 5 \cdot 4 \cdot 3 \cdot 2 \cdot 1)(1)} = 1$

e. $\dbinom{4}{3} = \dfrac{4!}{3!(4-3)!} = \dfrac{4!}{3!1!} = \dfrac{4 \cdot 3 \cdot 2 \cdot 1}{(3 \cdot 2 \cdot 1)(1)} = 4$

4.37   a. $P(x = 1) = \dfrac{5!}{1!4!}(.2)^1(.8)^4 = \dfrac{5 \cdot 4 \cdot 3 \cdot 2 \cdot 1}{(1)(4 \cdot 3 \cdot 2 \cdot 1)}(.2)^1(.8)^4 = 5(.2)^1(.8)^4 = .4096$

       b. $P(x = 2) = \dfrac{4!}{2!2!}(.6)^2(.4)^2 = \dfrac{4 \cdot 3 \cdot 2 \cdot 1}{(2 \cdot 1)(2 \cdot 1)}(.6)^2(.4)^2 = 6(.6)^2(.4)^2 = .3456$

       c. $P(x = 0) = \dfrac{3!}{0!3!}(.7)^0(.3)^3 = \dfrac{3 \cdot 2 \cdot 1}{(1)(3 \cdot 2 \cdot 1)}(.7)^0(.3)^3 = 1(.7)^0(.3)^3 = .027$

       d. $P(x = 3) = \dfrac{5!}{3!2!}(.1)^3(.9)^2 = \dfrac{5 \cdot 4 \cdot 3 \cdot 2 \cdot 1}{(3 \cdot 2 \cdot 1)(2 \cdot 1)}(.1)^3(.9)^2 = 10(.1)^3(.9)^2 = .0081$

       e. $P(x = 2) = \dfrac{4!}{2!2!}(.4)^2(.6)^2 = \dfrac{4 \cdot 3 \cdot 2 \cdot 1}{(2 \cdot 1)(2 \cdot 1)}(.4)^2(.6)^2 = 6(.4)^2(.6)^2 = .3456$

       f. $P(x = 1) = \dfrac{3!}{1!2!}(.9)^1(.1)^2 = \dfrac{3 \cdot 2 \cdot 1}{(1)(2 \cdot 1)}(.9)^1(.1)^2 = 3(.9)^1(.1)^2 = .027$

4.39   a. $\mu = np = 25(.5) = 12.5$

          $\sigma^2 = np(1 - p) = 25(.5)(.5) = 6.25$
          $\sigma = \sqrt{\sigma^2} = \sqrt{6.25} = 2.5$

       b. $\mu = np = 80(.2) = 16$

          $\sigma^2 = np(1 - p) = 80(.2)(.8) = 12.8$
          $\sigma = \sqrt{\sigma^2} = \sqrt{12.8} = 3.578$

       c. $\mu = np = 100(.6) = 60$

          $\sigma^2 = np(1 - p) = 100(.6)(.4) = 24$
          $\sigma = \sqrt{\sigma^2} = \sqrt{24} = 4.899$

       d. $\mu = np = 70(.9) = 63$

          $\sigma^2 = np(1 - p) = 70(.9)(.1) = 6.3$
          $\sigma = \sqrt{\sigma^2} = \sqrt{6.3} = 2.510$

       e. $\mu = np = 60(.8) = 48$
          $\sigma^2 = np(1 - p) = 60(.8)(.2) = 9.6$
          $\sigma = \sqrt{\sigma^2} = \sqrt{9.6} = 3.098$

f. $\mu = np = 1,000(.04) = 40$

$\sigma^2 = np(1-p) = 1,000(.04)(.96) = 38.4$
$\sigma = \sqrt{\sigma^2} = \sqrt{38.4} = 6.197$

4.41 x is a binomial random variable with $n = 4$.

a. If the probability distribution of x is symmetric, $p(0) = p(4)$ and $p(1) = p(3)$.

Since $p(x) = \binom{n}{x} p^x q^{n-x}$ $x = 0, 1, \dots, n$,

When $n = 4$,

$\binom{4}{0} p^0 q^4 = \binom{4}{4} p^4 q^0 \Rightarrow \dfrac{4!}{0!4!} p^0 q^4 = \dfrac{4!}{4!0!} p^4 q^0 \Rightarrow q^4 = p^4 \Rightarrow p = q$

Since $p + q = 1$, $p = .5$

Therefore, the probability distribution of x is symmetric when $p = .5$.

b. If the probability distribution of x is skewed to the right, then the mean is greater than the median. Therefore, there are more small values in the distribution (0, 1) than large values (3, 4). Therefore, p must be smaller than .5. Let $p = .2$ and the probability distribution of x will be skewed to the right.

c. If the probability distribution of x is skewed to the left, then the mean is smaller than the median. Therefore, there are more large values in the distribution (3, 4) than small values (0, 1). Therefore, p must be larger than .5. Let $p = .8$ and the probability distribution of x will be skewed to the left.

d. In part **a**, x is a binomial random variable with $n = 4$ and $p = .5$.

$p(x) = \binom{4}{x} .5^x .5^{4-x}$ $x = 0, 1, 2, 3, 4$

$p(0) = \binom{4}{0} .5^0 .5^4 = \dfrac{4!}{0!4!} .5^4 = 1(.5)^4 = .0625$

$p(1) = \binom{4}{1} .5^1 .5^3 = \dfrac{4!}{1!3!} .5^4 = 4(.5)^4 = .25$

$p(2) = \binom{4}{2} .5^2 .5^2 = \dfrac{4!}{2!2!} .5^4 = 6(.5)^4 = .375$

$p(3) = p(1) = .25$ (since the distribution is symmetric)

$p(4) = p(0) = .0625$

The probability distribution of x in tabular form is:

x	0	1	2	3	4
$p(x)$	.0625	.25	.375	.25	.0625

$$\mu = np = 4(.5) = 2$$

The graph of the probability distribution of x when $n = 4$ and $p = .5$ is as follows.

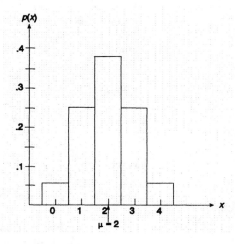

In part **b**, x is a binomial random variable with $n = 4$ and $p = .2$.

$$p(x) = \binom{4}{x} .2^x .8^{4-x} \quad x = 0, 1, 2, 3, 4$$

$$p(0) = \binom{4}{0} .2^0 .8^4 = 1(1).8^4 = .4096$$

$$p(1) = \binom{4}{1} .2^1 .8^3 = 4(.2)(.8)^3 = .4096$$

$$p(2) = \binom{4}{2} .2^2 .8^2 = 6(.2)^2(.8)^2 = .1536$$

$$p(3) = \binom{4}{3} .2^3 .8^1 = 4(.2)^3(.8) = .0256$$

$$p(4) = \binom{4}{4} .2^4 .8^0 = 1(.2)^4(1) = .0016$$

The probability distribution of x in tabular form is:

x	0	1	2	3	4
$p(x)$	.4096	.4096	.1536	.0256	.0016

$$\mu = np = 4(.2) = .8$$

The graph of the probability distribution of x when $n = 4$ and $p = .2$ is as follows:

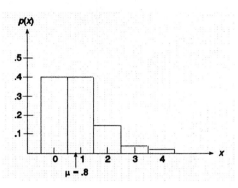

In part **c**, x is a binomial random variable with $n = 4$ and $p = .8$.

$$p(x) = \binom{4}{x} .8^x .2^{4-x} \quad x = 0, 1, 2, 3, 4$$

$$p(0) = \binom{4}{0} .8^0 .2^4 = 1(1).2^4 = .0016$$

$$p(1) = \binom{4}{1} .8^1 .2^3 = 4(.8)(.2)^3 = .0256$$

$$p(2) = \binom{4}{2} .8^2 .2^2 = 6(.8)^2(.2)^2 = .1536$$

$$p(3) = \binom{4}{3} .8^3 .2^1 = 4(.8)^3(.2) = .4096$$

$$p(4) = \binom{4}{4} .8^4 .2^0 = 1(.8)^4(1) = .4096$$

The probability distribution of x in tabular form is:

x	0	1	2	3	4
$p(x)$	.0016	.0256	.1536	.4096	.4096

Note: The distribution of x when $n = 4$ and $p = .2$ is the reverse of the distribution of x when $n = 4$ and $p = .8$.

$$\mu = np = 4(.8) = 3.2$$

The graph of the probability distribution of x when $n = 4$ and $p = .8$ is as follows:

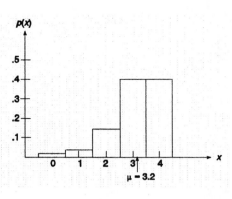

e. In general, when $p = .5$, a binomial distribution will be symmetric regardless of the value of n. When p is less than .5, the binomial distribution will be skewed to the right; and when p is greater than .5, it will be skewed to the left. (Refer to parts **a**, **b**, and **c**.)

4.43 a. Let x = number of small businesses owned by non-Hispanic whites that are female owned in 200 trials. Then x is a binomial random variable with $n = 200$ and $p = .27$.

$$\mu = E(x) = np = 200(.27) = 54$$

b. Let x = number of small businesses owned by non-Hispanic whites that are female owned in 8 trials. Then x is a binomial random variable with $n = 8$ and $p = .27$.

$$P(x = 0) = \binom{n}{x} p^x (1 - p)^{n-x} = \binom{8}{0} .27^0 (.73)^{8-0} = .73^8 = .0806$$

$$P(x = 4) = \binom{n}{x} p^x (1 - p)^{n-x} = \binom{8}{4} .27^4 (.73)^{8-4} = \frac{8!}{4!(8-4)!} .27^4 .73^4 = .1056$$

4.45 a. We will check the 5 characteristics of a binomial random variable.

1. The experiment consists of $n = 20$ identical trials.
2. There are only 2 possible outcomes for each trial. Let S = intruding object is detected and F = intruding object is not detected.
3. The probability of success (S) is the same from trial to trial. For each trial, $p = P(S) = .8$ and $q = 1 - p = 1 - .8 = .2$.
4. The trials are independent.
5. The binomial random variable x is the number of intruding objects in the 20 trials that are detected.

Thus, x is a binomial random variable.

b. For this experiment, $n = 20$ and $p = .8$.

c. Using Table II, Appendix B, with $n = 20$ and $p = .8$,

$$P(x = 15) = P(x \le 15) - P(x \le 14) = .370 - .196 = .174$$

d. Using Table II, Appendix B, with n = 20 and p = .8,

$$P(x \geq 15) = 1 - P(x \leq 14) = 1 - .196 = .804$$

e. $E(x) = np = 20(.8) = 16$. For every 20 intruding objects, SBIRS will detect an average of 16.

4.47 Let x = number of major bridges in Denver that will have a rating of 4 or below in 2020 in 10 trials. Then x has an approximate binomial distribution with $n = 10$ and $p = .09$.

a. $P(x \geq 3) = 1 - P(x \leq 2) = 1 - P(x = 0) - P(x = 1) - P(x = 2)$

$$= 1 - \binom{10}{0}.09^0 (.91)^{10-0} - \binom{10}{1}.09^1 (.91)^{10-1} - \binom{10}{2}.09^2 (.91)^{10-2}$$

$$= 1 - \frac{10!}{0!10!}.09^0 .91^{10} - \frac{10!}{1!9!}.09^1 .91^9 - \frac{10!}{2!8!}.09^2 .91^8 = 1 - .389 - .385 - .171 = .055$$

b. Since the probability of seeing at least 3 bridges out of 10 with ratings of 4 or less is so small, we can conclude that the forecast of 9% of all major Denver bridges will have ratings of 4 or less in 2020 is too small. There would probably be more than 9%.

4.49 Define the following events:

A: {Taxpayer is audited}
B: {Taxpayer has income less than $100,000)
C: {Taxpayer has income of $100,000 or higher}

a. From the information given in the problem,

$$P(A \mid B) = 15/1000 = .015$$
$$P(A \mid C) = 30/1000 = .030$$

b. Let x = number of taxpayers with incomes under $100,000 who are audited. Then x is a binomial random variable with $n = 5$ and $p = .015$.

$$P(x = 1) = \binom{5}{1}.015^1 .985^{(5-1)} \frac{5!}{1!4!}.015^1 .985^{(4)} = .0706$$

$$P(x > 1) = 1 - [P(x = 0) + P(x = 1)]$$

$$= 1 - \left[\binom{5}{0}.015^0 .985^{(5-0)} + .0706\right]$$

$$= 1 - \left[\frac{5!}{0!5!}.015^0 .985^5 + .0706\right]$$

$$= 1 - [.9272 + .0706] = 1 - .9978 = .0022$$

c. Let x = number of taxpayers with incomes of \$100,000 or more who are audited. Then x is a binomial random variable with $n = 5$ and $p = .030$.

$$P(x = 1) = \binom{5}{1}.03^1.97^{(5-1)} \frac{5!}{1!4!}.03^1.97^4 = .1328$$

$$
\begin{aligned}
P(x > 1) &= 1 - [P(x = 0) + P(x = 1)] \\
&= 1 - \left[\binom{5}{0}.03^0.97^{(5-0)} + .1328 \right] \\
&= 1 - \left[\frac{5!}{0!5!}.03^0.97^5 + .1328 \right] \\
&= 1 - [.8587 + .1328] = 1 - .9915 = .0085
\end{aligned}
$$

d. Let x = number of taxpayers with incomes under \$100,000 who are audited. Then x is a binomial random variable with $n = 2$ and $p = .015$.

Let y = number of taxpayers with incomes \$100,000 or more who are audited. Then y is a binomial random variable with $n = 2$ and $p = .030$.

$$P(x = 0) = \binom{2}{0}.015^0.985^{(2-0)} = \frac{2!}{0!2!}.015^0.985^2 = .9702$$

$$P(y = 0) = \binom{2}{0}.03^0.97^{(2-0)} = \frac{2!}{0!2!}.03^0.97^2 = .9409$$

$$P(x = 0)P(y = 0) = .9702(.9409) = .9129$$

e. We must assume that the variables defined as x and y are binomial random variables. We must assume that the trials are identical, the probability of success is the same from trial to trial, and that the trials are independent.

4.51 a. $\mu = E(x) = np = 800(.60) = 480$

$$\sigma = \sqrt{npq} = \sqrt{800(.60)(.40)} = \sqrt{192} = 13.856$$

b. Half of the 800 food items would be 400. A value of $x = 400$ would have a z-score of:

$$z = \frac{x - \mu}{\sigma} = \frac{400 - 480}{13.856} = -5.77$$

Since the z-score associated with 400 items is so small (-5.77), it would be virtually impossible to observe less than half with any pesticides if the 60% value was correct.

4.53   a.   We must assume that the probability that a specific type of ball meets the requirements is always the same from trial to trial and the trials are independent. To use the binomial probability distribution, we need to know the probability that a specific type of golf ball meets the requirements.

b.   For a binomial distribution,

$$\mu = np$$
$$\sigma = \sqrt{npq}$$

In this example, n = two dozen = $2 \cdot 12 = 24$.

$p = .10$ (Success here means the golf ball *does not* meet standards.)
$q = .90$
$\mu = np = 24(.10) = 2.4$
$\sigma = \sqrt{npq} = \sqrt{24(.10)(.90)} = 1.47$

c.   In this situation,

p = Probability of success
   = Probability golf ball *does* meet standards
   = .90
$q = 1 - .90 = .10$
$n = 24$
$E(x) = \mu = np = 24(.90) = 21.60$
$\sigma = \sqrt{npq} = \sqrt{24(.10)(.90)} = 1.47$ (Note that this is the same as in part **b**.)

4.55   a.   The random variable x is discrete since it can assume a countable number of values (0, 1, 2, ...).

b.   This is a Poisson probability distribution with $\lambda = 3$.

c.   In order to graph the probability distribution, we need to know the probabilities for the possible values of x. Using Table III of Appendix B with $\lambda = 3$:

$p(0) = .050$
$p(1) = P(x \leq 1) - P(x = 0) = .199 - .050 = .149$
$p(2) = P(x \leq 2) - P(x \leq 1) = .423 - .199 = .224$
$p(3) = P(x \leq 3) - P(x \leq 2) = .647 - .423 = .224$
$p(4) = P(x \leq 4) - P(x \leq 3) = .815 - .647 = .168$
$p(5) = P(x \leq 5) - P(x \leq 4) = .916 - .815 = .101$
$p(6) = P(x \leq 6) - P(x \leq 5) = .966 - .916 = .050$
$p(7) = P(x \leq 7) - P(x \leq 6) = .988 - .966 = .022$
$p(8) = P(x \leq 8) - P(x \leq 7) = .996 - .988 = .008$
$p(9) = P(x \leq 9) - P(x \leq 8) = .999 - .996 = .003$
$p(10) \approx .001$

The probability distribution of x in graphical form is:

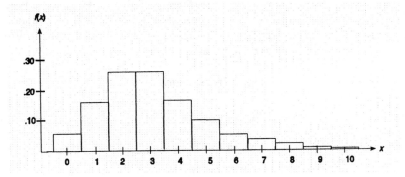

d. $\mu = \lambda = 3$
$\sigma^2 = \lambda = 3$
$\sigma = \sqrt{3} = 1.7321$

e. The mean of x is the same as the mean of the probability distribution, $\mu = \lambda = 3$.

The standard deviation of x is the same as the standard deviation of the probability distribution, $\sigma = 1.7321$.

4.57 a. For $\lambda = 1$, $P(x \leq 2) = .920$ (from Table III, Appendix B)

b. For $\lambda = 2$, $P(x \leq 2) = .677$

c. For $\lambda = 3$, $P(x \leq 2) = .423$

d. The probability decreases as λ increases. This is reasonable because λ is equal to the mean. As the mean increases, the probability that x is less than a particular value will decrease.

4.59 a. Using Table III, Appendix B, with $\lambda = 5$,

$$P(x < 3) = P(x \leq 2) = .125$$

b. $E(x) = \lambda = 5$. The average number of calls blocked during the peak hour of video conferencing call time is 5.

4.61 a. Using Table III, Appendix B, with $\lambda = 1.2$, $P(x = 0) = .301$

b. $P(x = 1) = P(x \leq 1) - P(x = 0) = .663 - .301 = .362$

c. $E(x) = \lambda = 1.2$

$$\sigma = \sqrt{\lambda} = \sqrt{1.2} = 1.095$$

4.63   a. $\sigma = \sqrt{\sigma^2} = \sqrt{\lambda} = \sqrt{4} = 2$

       b. $P(x > 10) = 1 - P(x \le 10)$
                      $= 1 - .977$ (Table III, Appendix B)
                      $= .003$

            No. The probability that a sample of air from the plant exceeds the EPA limit is only
            .003. Since this value is very small, it is not very likely that this will occur.

       c.   The experiment consists of counting the number of parts per million of vinyl chloride in
            air samples. We must assume the probability of a part of vinyl chloride appearing in a
            million parts of air is the same for each million parts of air. We must also assume the
            number of parts of vinyl chloride in one million parts of air is independent of the number
            in any other one million parts of air.

4.65   a.   From the problem, $\lambda = .37$. Thus, $\sigma = \sqrt{\lambda} = \sqrt{.37} = .6083$

       b.   In order to plot the distribution of x, we must first calculate the probabilities.

            $$P(x = 0) = \frac{\lambda^0 e^{-\lambda}}{0!} = \frac{.37^0 e^{-.37}}{0!} = .6907$$

            $$P(x = 1) = \frac{.37^1 e^{-.37}}{1!} = .2556$$

            $$P(x = 2) = \frac{.37^2 e^{-.37}}{2!} = .0473$$

            $$P(x = 3) = \frac{.37^3 e^{-.37}}{3!} = .0058$$

            $$P(x = 4) = \frac{.37^4 e^{-.37}}{4!} = .0005$$

            $$P(x = 5) = \frac{.37^5 e^{-.37}}{5!} = .00004$$

The plot of the distribution is:

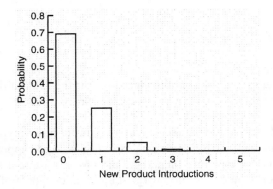

c. $P(x > 2) = 1 - P(x \le 2) = 1 - .6907 - .2556 - .0473 = .0064$

Since this probability is so small, it would be very unlikely that a mainframe manufacturer would introduce more than 2 new products per year.

$P(x < 1) = P(x = 0) = .6907$

Since this probability is not small, it would not be unusual for a mainframe manufacturer to introduce less than 1 new product per year.

4.67 $\mu = \lambda = 3$, using Table III, Appendix B:

$P(x = 0) = .050$

The probability that no bulbs fail in one hour is .050. If we let $y =$ number of one hour intervals out of 8 that have no bulbs fail, then y is a binomial random variable with $n = 8$ and $p = .05$. Then, the probability that no bulbs fail in an 8 hour shift is

$$P(y = 8) = \binom{8}{8}.05^8.95^{(8-8)} = \frac{8!}{8!(8-8)!}.05^8.95^0$$

$$= \frac{8 \cdot 7 \cdot 6 \cdot 5 \cdot 4 \cdot 3 \cdot 2 \cdot 1}{8 \cdot 7 \cdot 6 \cdot 5 \cdot 4 \cdot 3 \cdot 2 \cdot 1 \cdot 1}.05^8.95^0 = .05^8$$

We must assume that the 8 one-hour intervals are independent and identical, and that the probability that no bulbs fail is the same for each one-hour interval.

4.69   a. $f(x) = \dfrac{1}{d-c} \quad (c \le x \le d)$

$$\frac{1}{d-c} = \frac{1}{45-20} = \frac{1}{25} = .04$$

So, $f(x) = \begin{cases} .04 & (20 \le x \le 45) \\ 0 & \text{otherwise} \end{cases}$

b. $\mu = \dfrac{c+d}{2} = \dfrac{20+45}{2} = \dfrac{65}{2} = 32.5$

$\sigma = \dfrac{d-c}{\sqrt{12}} = \dfrac{45-20}{\sqrt{12}} = 7.2169$

$\sigma^2 = (7.2169)^2 = 52.0833$

c.

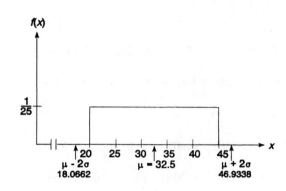

$\mu \pm 2\sigma \Rightarrow 32.5 \pm 2(7.2169) \Rightarrow (18.0662,\ 46.9338)$

$P(18.0662 < x < 46.9338) = P(20 < x < 45) = (45 - 20).04 = 1$

4.71 a. $f(x) = \dfrac{1}{d-c} \qquad (c \le x \le d)$

$\dfrac{1}{d-c} = \dfrac{1}{7-3} = \dfrac{1}{4}$

$f(x) = \begin{cases} \dfrac{1}{4} & (3 \le x \le 7) \\[2mm] 0 & \text{otherwise} \end{cases}$

b. $\mu = \dfrac{c+d}{2} = \dfrac{3+7}{2} = \dfrac{10}{2} = 5$

$\sigma = \dfrac{d-c}{\sqrt{12}} = \dfrac{7-3}{\sqrt{12}} = \dfrac{4}{\sqrt{12}} = 1.155$

c. $\mu \pm \sigma \Rightarrow 5 \pm 1.155 \Rightarrow (3.845,\ 6.155)$

$P(\mu - \sigma \le x \le \mu + \sigma) = P(3.845 \le x \le 6.155) = \dfrac{b-a}{d-c} = \dfrac{6.155 - 3.845}{7-3} = \dfrac{2.31}{4}$

$= .5775$

4.73 $f(x) = \dfrac{1}{d-c} = \dfrac{1}{200-100} = \dfrac{1}{100} = .01$

$f(x) = \begin{cases} .01 & (100 \le x \le 200) \\ 0 & otherwise \end{cases}$

$\mu = \dfrac{c+d}{2} = \dfrac{100+200}{2} = \dfrac{300}{2} = 150$

$\sigma = \dfrac{d-c}{\sqrt{12}} = \dfrac{200-100}{\sqrt{12}} = \dfrac{100}{\sqrt{12}} = 28.8675$

a. $\mu \pm 2\sigma \Rightarrow 150 \pm 2(28.8675) \Rightarrow 150 \pm 57.735 \Rightarrow (92.265, 207.735)$

$P(x < 92.265) + P(x > 207.735) = P(x < 100) + P(x > 200)$
$$= \quad 0 \quad + \quad 0$$
$$= 0$$

b. $\mu \pm 3\sigma \Rightarrow 150 \pm 3(28.8675) \Rightarrow 150 \pm 86.6025 \Rightarrow (63.3975, 236.6025)$

$P(63.3975 < x < 236.6025) = P(100 < x < 200) = (200 - 100)(.01) = 1$

c.   From **a**, $\mu \pm 2\sigma \Rightarrow (92.265, 207.735)$.

$P(92.265 < x < 207.735) = P(100 < x < 200) = (200 - 100)(.01) = 1$

4.75   a.   Let x = temperature with no bolt-on trace elements. Then x has a uniform distribution.

$$f(x) = \dfrac{1}{d-c} \quad (c \le x \le d)$$

$$\dfrac{1}{d-c} = \dfrac{1}{290-260} = \dfrac{1}{30}$$

Therefore, $f(x) = \begin{cases} \dfrac{1}{30} & (260 \le x \le 290) \\ 0 & otherwise \end{cases}$

$$P(280 < x < 284) = (284 - 280)\dfrac{1}{30} = 4\left(\dfrac{1}{30}\right) = .133$$

Let y = temperature with bolt-on trace elements. Then y has a uniform distribution.

$$f(y) = \dfrac{1}{d-c} \quad (c \le y \le d)$$

$$\dfrac{1}{d-c} = \dfrac{1}{285-278} = \dfrac{1}{7}$$

Therefore, $f(y) = \begin{cases} \dfrac{1}{7} & (278 \le y \le 285) \\ 0 & \text{otherwise} \end{cases}$

$$P(280 < y < 284) = (284 - 280)\frac{1}{7} = 4\left(\frac{1}{7}\right) = .571$$

b. $\quad P(x \le 268) = (268 - 260)\dfrac{1}{30} = 8\left(\dfrac{1}{30}\right) = .267$

$$P(y \le 268) = (268 - 260)(0) = 0$$

4.77   To construct a relative frequency histogram for the data, we can use 7 measurement classes.

$$\text{Interval width} = \frac{\text{Largest number - smallest number}}{\text{Number of classes}} = \frac{98.0716 - .7434}{7} = 13.9$$

We will use an interval width of 14 and a starting value of .74335.

The measurement classes, frequencies, and relative frequencies are given in the table below.

Class	Measurement Class	Class Frequency	Class Relative Frequency
1	.74335 – 14.74335	6	6/40 = .15
2	14.74335 – 28.74335	4	.10
3	28.74335 – 42.74335	6	.15
4	42.74335 – 56.74335	6	.15
5	56.74335 – 70.74335	5	.125
6	70.74335 – 84.74335	4	.10
7	84.74335 – 98.74335	9	.225
		40	1.000

The histogram looks like the data could be from a uniform distribution. The last class (84.74335 – 98.74335) has a few more observations in it than we would expect. However, we cannot expect a perfect graph from a sample of only 40 observations.

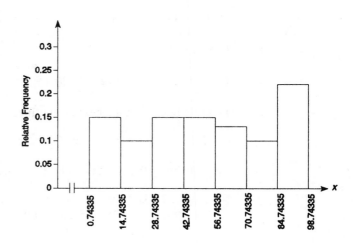

4.79   a.   The amount dispensed by the beverage machine is a continuous random variable since it can take on any value between 6.5 and 7.5 ounces.

b.   Since the amount dispensed is random between 6.5 and 7.5 ounces, x is a uniform random variable.

$$f(x) = \frac{1}{d-c} \quad (c \leq x \leq d)$$

$$\frac{1}{d-c} = \frac{1}{7.5 - 6.5} = \frac{1}{1} = 1$$

Therefore, $f(x) = \begin{cases} 1 & (6.5 \leq x \leq 7.5) \\ 0 & \text{otherwise} \end{cases}$

The graph is as follows:

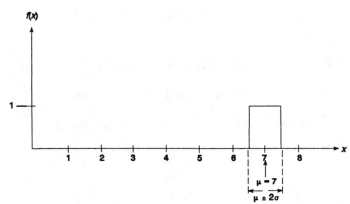

c. $\mu = \dfrac{c+d}{2} = \dfrac{6.5 + 7.5}{2} = \dfrac{14}{2} = 7$

$\sigma = \dfrac{d-c}{\sqrt{12}} = \dfrac{7.5 - 6.5}{\sqrt{12}} = .2887$

$\mu \pm 2\sigma \Rightarrow 7 \pm 2(.2887) \Rightarrow 7 \pm .5774 \Rightarrow (6.422, 7.577)$

d. $P(x \geq 7) = (7.5 - 7)(1) = .5$

e. $P(x < 6) = 0$

f. $P(6.5 \leq x \leq 7.25) = (7.25 - 6.5)(1) = .75$

g.   The probability that the next bottle filled will contain more than 7.25 ounces is:

$$P(x > 7.25) = (7.5 - 7.25)(1) = .25$$

The probability that the next 6 bottles filled will contain more than 7.25 ounces is:

$$P[(x > 7.25) \cap (x > 7.25) \cap (x > 7.25) \cap (x > 7.25) \cap (x > 7.25) \cap (x > 7.25)]$$
$$= [P(x > 7.25)]^6 = .25^6 = .0002$$

4.81   Let x = length of time a bus is late. Then x is a uniform random variable with probability
distribution:

$$f(x) = \begin{cases} \dfrac{1}{20} & (0 \leq x \leq 20) \\ 0 & \text{otherwise} \end{cases}$$

a. $\mu = \dfrac{0+20}{2} = 10$

b. $P(x \geq 19) = (20 - 19) \cdot \left(\dfrac{1}{20}\right) = \dfrac{1}{20} = .05$

c.   It would be doubtful that the director's claim is true, since the probability of the being
more than 19 minutes late is so small.

4.83   Let x = number of inches a gouge is from one end of the spindle. Then x has a uniform
distribution with $f(x)$ as follows:

$$f(x) = \begin{cases} \dfrac{1}{d-c} = \dfrac{1}{18-0} = \dfrac{1}{18} & 0 \leq x \leq 18 \\ 0 & \text{otherwise} \end{cases}$$

In order to get at least 14 consecutive inches without a gouge, the gouge must be within 4
inches of either end. Thus, we must find:

$$P(x < 4) + P(x > 14) = (4 - 0)(1/18) + (18 - 14)(1/18)$$
$$= 4/18 + 4/18 = 8/18 = .4444$$

4.85   Using Table IV, Appendix B:

a. $P(z > 1.46) = .5 - P(0 < z \leq 1.46)$
$= .5 - .4279 = .0721$

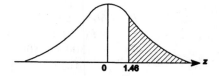

b. $P(x < -1.56) = .5 - P(-1.56 \leq z < 0)$
$= .5 - .4406 = .0594$

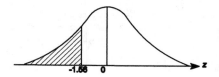

c. $P(.67 \leq z \leq 2.41)$
$= P(0 < z \leq 2.41) - P(0 < z < .67)$
$= .4920 - .2486 = .2434$

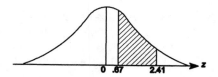

d. $P(-1.96 \le z < -.33)$
$= P(-1.96 \le z < 0) - P(-.33 \le z < 0)$
$= .4750 - .1293 = .3457$

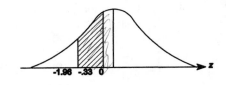

e. $P(z \ge 0) = .5$

$0.3707 \ge 0.0250 =$

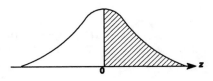

f. $P(-2.33 < z < 1.50)$
$= P(-2.33 < z < 0) + P(0 < z < 1.50)$
$= .4901 + .4332 = .9233$

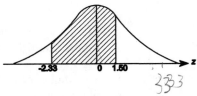

333

4.87 Using Table IV, Appendix B:

a. $P(-1 \le z \le 1)$
$= P(-1 \le z \le 0) + P(0 < z \le 1)$
$= .3413 + .3413 = .6826$

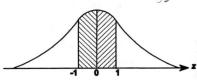

b. $P(-1.96 \le z \le 1.96)$
$= P(-1.96 \le z < 0) + P(0 \le z \le 1.96)$
$= .4750 + .4750 = .9500$

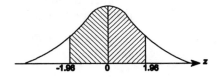

c. $P(-1.645 \le z \le 1.645)$
$= P(-1.645 \le z < 0) + P(0 \le z \le 1.645)$
$= .4500 + .4500 = .90$
(using interpolation)

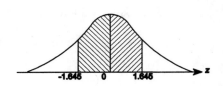

d. $P(-2 \le z \le 2)$
$= P(-2 \le z < 0) + P(0 \le z \le 2)$
$= .4772 + .4772 = .9544$

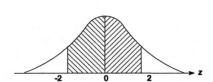

4.89 Using Table IV of Appendix B:

a. $P(z \le z_0) = .2090$
$A = .5000 - .2090 = .2910$

Look up the area .2910 in the body of Table IV; $z_0 = -.81$.

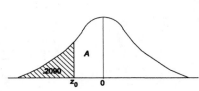

(z_0 is negative since the graph shows z_0 is on the left side of 0.)

b. $P(z \le z_0) = .7090$

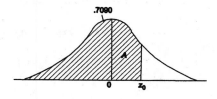

$P(z \le z_0) = P(z \le 0) + P(0 \le z \le z_0)$
$\qquad = .5 + P(0 \le z \le z) = .7090$

Therefore, $P(0 \le z \le z_0) = .7090 - .5 = .2090$

Look up the area .2090 in the body of Table IV; $z_0 \approx .55$.

c. $P(-z_0 \le z < z_0) = .8472$

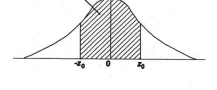

$P(-z_0 \le z < z_0) = 2P(0 \le z \le z_0)$
$2P(0 \le z \le z_0) = .8472$

Therefore, $P(0 \le z \le z_0) = .4236$.

Look up the area .4236 in the body of Table IV; $z_0 = 1.43$.

d. $P(-z_0 \le z < z_0) = .1664$

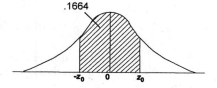

$P(-z_0 \le z \le z_0) = 2P(0 \le z \le z_0)$
$2P(0 \le z \le z_0) = .1664$

Therefore, $P(0 \le z \le z_0) = .0832$.

Look up the area .0832 in the body of Table IV; $z_0 = .21$.

e. $P(z_0 \le z \le 0) = .4798$

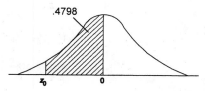

$P(z_0 \le z \le 0) = P(0 \le z \le -z_0)$

Look up the area .4798 in the body of Table IV;
$z_0 = -2.05$.

f. $P(-1 < z < z_0) = .5328$

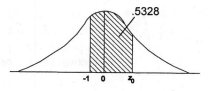

$P(-1 < z < z_0)$
$\qquad = P(-1 < z < 0) + P(0 < z < z_0)$
$\qquad = .5328$

$P(0 < z < 1) + P(0 < z < z_0) = .5328$

Thus, $P(0 < z < z_0) = .5328 - .3413 = .1915$

Look up the area .1915 in the body of Table IV; $z_0 = .50$.

4.91 The random variable x has a normal distribution with $\mu = 50$ and $\sigma = 3$.

a. $P(x \le x_0) = .8413$

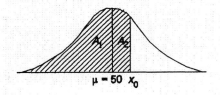

So, $A_1 + A_2 = .8413$

Since $A_1 = .5$, $A_2 = .8413 - .5 = .3413$.
Look up the area .3413 in the body of Table IV,
Appendix B; $z_0 = 1.0$.

To find x_0, substitute all the values into the z-score formula:

$$z = \frac{x - \mu}{\sigma}$$
$$1.0 = \frac{x_0 - 50}{3}$$
$$x_0 = 50 + 3(1.0) = 53$$

b. $P(x > x_0) = .025$
So, $A = .5000 - .025 = .4750$

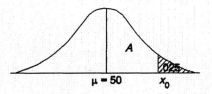

Look up the area .4750 in the body of Table IV,
Appendix B; $z_0 = 1.96$.

To find x_0, substitute all the values into the z-score formula:

$$z = \frac{x - \mu}{\sigma}$$
$$1.96 = \frac{x_0 - 50}{3}$$
$$x_0 = 50 + 3(1.96) = 55.88$$

c. $P(x > x_0) = .95$

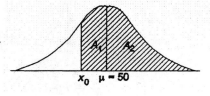

So, $A_1 + A_2 = .95$. Since $A_2 = .5$, $A_1 = .95 - .5 = .4500$.
Look up the area .4500 in the body of Table IV,
Appendix B; (since it is exactly between two values,
average the z-scores). $z_0 \approx -1.645$.

To find x_0, substitute into the z-score formula:

$$z = \frac{x - \mu}{\sigma}$$
$$-1.645 = \frac{x_0 - 50}{3}$$
$$x_0 = 50 - 3(1.645) = 45.065$$

d. $P(41 \leq x < x_0) = .8630$

$$z = \frac{x - \mu}{\sigma} = \frac{41 - 50}{3} = -3$$

$A_1 = P(41 \leq x \leq \mu) = P(-3 \leq z \leq 0)$
  $= P(0 \leq z \leq 3)$
  $= .4987$

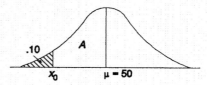

$A_1 + A_2 = .8630$, since $A_1 = .4987$, $A_2 = .8630 - .4987 = .3643$. Look up .3643 in the body of Table IV, Appendix B; $z_0 = 1.1$.

To find x_0, substitute into the z-score formula:

$$z = \frac{x - \mu}{\sigma}$$

$$1.1 = \frac{x_0 - 50}{3}$$
$$x_0 = 50 + 3(1.1) = 53.3$$

e. $P(x < x_0) = .10$

So $A = .5000 - .10 = .4000$

Look up area .4000 in the body of Table IV, Appendix B; $z_0 = 1.28$. Since z_0 is to the left of 0, $z_0 = -1.28$.

To find x_0, substitute all the values into the z-score formula:

$$z = \frac{x - \mu}{\sigma}$$

$$-1.28 = \frac{x_0 - 50}{3}$$
$$x_0 = 50 - 1.28(3) = 46.16$$

f. $P(x > x_0) = .01$

So $A = .5000 - .01 = .4900$

Look up area .4900 in the body of Table IV, Appendix B; $z_0 = 2.33$.
To find x_0, substitute all the values into the z-score formula:

$$z = \frac{x - \mu}{\sigma}$$

$$2.33 = \frac{x_0 - 50}{3}$$
$$x_0 = 50 + 2.33(3) = 56.99$$

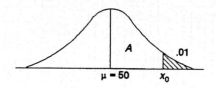

4.93   a. $P(10 \le x \le 12) = P\left(\dfrac{10-11}{2} \le z \le \dfrac{12-11}{2}\right)$

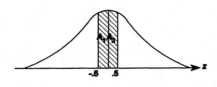

$= P(-0.50 \le z \le 0.50)$
$= A_1 + A_2$
$= .1915 + .1915 = .3830$

b. $P(6 \le x \le 10) = P\left(\dfrac{6-11}{2} \le z \le \dfrac{10-11}{2}\right)$

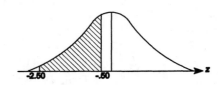

$= P(-2.50 \le z \le -0.50)$
$= P(-2.50 \le z \le 0) - P(-0.50 \le z \le 0)$
$= .4938 - .1915 = .3023$

c. $P(13 \le x \le 16) = P\left(\dfrac{13-11}{2} \le z \le \dfrac{16-11}{2}\right)$

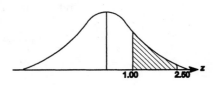

$= P(1.00 \le z \le 2.50)$
$= P(0 \le z \le 2.50) - P(0 \le x \le 1.00)$
$= .4938 - .3413 = .1525$

d. $P(7.8 \le x \le 12.6)$

$= P\left(\dfrac{7.8-11}{2} \le z \le \dfrac{12.6-11}{2}\right)$

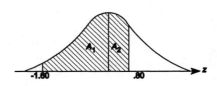

$= P(-1.60 \le z \le 0.80)$
$= A_1 + A_2$
$= .4452 + .2881 = .7333$

e. $P(x \ge 13.24) = P\left(z \ge \dfrac{13.24-11}{2}\right)$

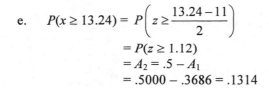
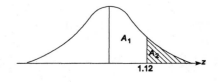

$= P(z \ge 1.12)$
$= A_2 = .5 - A_1$
$= .5000 - .3686 = .1314$

f. $P(x \ge 7.62) = P\left(z \ge \dfrac{7.62-11}{2}\right)$

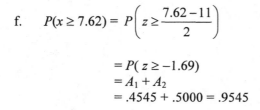
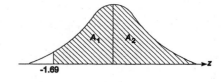

$= P(z \ge -1.69)$
$= A_1 + A_2$
$= .4545 + .5000 = .9545$

4.95

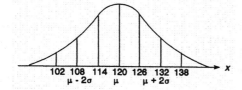

Using Table IV, Appendix B:

a. $P(\mu - 2\sigma \le x \le \mu + 2\sigma) = P(-2 \le z \le 2)$
$= P(-2 \le z \le 0) + P(0 \le z \le 2)$
$= .4772 + .4772 = .9544$

b. $P(x \ge 128) = P\left(z \ge \dfrac{128 - 120}{6}\right) = P(z \ge 1.33) = .5 - .4082 = .0918$

c. $P(x \le 108) = P\left(z \le \dfrac{108 - 120}{6}\right) = P(z \le -2) = .5 - .4772 = .0228$

d. $P(112 \le x \le 130) = P\left(\dfrac{112 - 120}{6} \le z \le \dfrac{130 - 120}{6}\right) = P(-1.33 \le z \le 1.67)$
$= P(-1.33 \le z \le 0) + P(0 \le z \le 1.67)$
$= .4082 + .4525 = .8607$

e. $P(114 \le x \le 116) = P\left(\dfrac{114 - 120}{6} \le z \le \dfrac{116 - 120}{6}\right) = P(-1 \le z \le -.67)$
$= P(-1 \le z \le 0) - P(-.67 \le z \le 0)$
$= .3413 - .2486 = .0927$

f. $P(115 \le x \le 128) = P\left(\dfrac{115 - 120}{6} \le z \le \dfrac{128 - 120}{6}\right) = P(-.83 \le z \le 1.33)$
$= P(-.83 \le z \le 0) + P(0 \le z \le 1.33)$
$= .2967 + .4082 = .7049$

4.97 Let x = age of a powerful woman. The random variable x has a normal distribution with $\mu =$ 50 and $\sigma = 5.3$. Using Table IV, Appendix B,

a. $P(55 < x < 60) = P\left(\dfrac{55 - 50}{5.3} < z < \dfrac{60 - 50}{5.3}\right) = P(.94 < z < 1.89)$
$= P(0 < z < 1.89) - P(0 < z < .94) = .4706 - .3264 = .1442$

b. $P(48 < x < 52) = P\left(\dfrac{48 - 50}{5.3} < z < \dfrac{52 - 50}{5.3}\right) = P(-.38 < z < .38)$
$= P(-.38 < z < 0) + P(0 < z < .38) = .1480 + .1480 = .2960$

c. $P(x < 35) = P\left(z < \dfrac{35 - 50}{5.3}\right) = P(z < -2.83)$

$$= .5 - P(-2.83 < z < 0) = .5 - .4977 = .0023$$

d. $P(x > 40) = P\left(z > \dfrac{40 - 50}{5.3}\right) = P(z > -1.89)$

$$= .5 + P(-1.89 < z < 0) = .5 + .4706 = .9706$$

4.99 Let x = weight of captured fish. The random variable x has a normal distribution with $\mu =$ 1,050 grams and $\sigma = 375$ grams. Using Table IV, Appendix B,

a. $P(1,000 < x < 1,400) = P\left(\dfrac{1,000 - 1,050}{375} < z < \dfrac{1,400 - 1,050}{375}\right) = P(-0.13 < z < 0.93)$

$$= P(-0.13 < z < 0) + P(0 < z < 0.93) = .0517 + .3238 = .3755$$

b. $P(800 < x < 1,000) = P\left(\dfrac{800 - 1,050}{375} < z < \dfrac{1,000 - 1,050}{375}\right) = P(-0.67 < z < -0.13)$

$$= P(-0.67 < z < 0) - P(-0.13 < z < 0) = .2486 - .0517 = .1969$$

c. $P(x < 1,750) = P\left(z < \dfrac{1,750 - 1,050}{375}\right) = P(z < 1.87) = .5 + P(0 < z < 1.87) = .5 + .4693 = .9693$

d. $P(x > 500) = P\left(z > \dfrac{500 - 1,050}{375}\right) = P(z > -1.47) = .5 + P(-1.47 < z < 0) = .5 + .4292 = .9292$

4.101 Let x = transmission delay. The random variable x has a normal distribution with $\mu = 48.5$ and $\sigma = 8.5$. Using Table IV, Appendix B,

a. $P(x < 57) = P\left(z < \dfrac{57 - 48.5}{8.5}\right) = P(z < 1.00)$

$$= .5 + P(0 < z < 1) = .5 + .3413 = .8413$$

b. $P(40 < x < 60) = P\left(\dfrac{40 - 48.5}{8.5} < z < \dfrac{60 - 48.5}{8.5}\right) = P(-1 < z < 1.35)$

$$= P(-1 < z < 0) + P(0 < z < 1.35) = .3413 + .4115 = .7528$$

4.103 a. Let x = passenger demand. The random variable x has a normal distribution with $\mu = 125$ and $\sigma = 45$.

For the Boeing 727, the probability that the passenger demand will exceed the capacity is:

$$P(x > 148) = P\left(z > \dfrac{148 - 125}{45}\right) = P(z > .51) = .5 - .1950 = .3050 \text{ (using Table IV)}$$

For the Boeing 757, the probability that the passenger demand will exceed the capacity is:

$$P(x > 182) = P\left(z > \frac{182 - 125}{45}\right) = P(z > 1.27) = .5 - .3890 = .1020$$

b. For the Boeing 727, the probability that the flight will depart with one or more empty seats is:

$$P(x \leq 147) = P\left(z \leq \frac{147 - 125}{45}\right) = P(z \leq .49) = .5 + .1879 = .6879$$

For the Boeing 757, the probability that the flight will depart with one or more empty seats is:

$$P(x \leq 181) = P\left(z \leq \frac{181 - 125}{45}\right) = P(z \leq 1.24) = .5 + .3925 = .8925$$

c. For the Boeing 727, the probability that the spill is more than 100 passengers is:

$$P(x > 248) = P\left(z > \frac{248 - 125}{45}\right) = P(z > 2.73) = .5 - .4968 = .0032$$

4.105 a. Using Table IV, Appendix B, and $\mu = 75$ and $\sigma = 7.5$,

$$P(x > 80) = P\left(z > \frac{80 - 75}{7.5}\right) = P(z > .67) = .5 - .2486 = .2514$$

Thus, 25.14% of the scores exceeded 80.

b. $P(x \leq x_0) = .98$. Find x_0.

$$P(x \leq x_0) = P\left(z \leq \frac{x_0 - 75}{7.5}\right) = P(z \leq z_0) = .98$$

$A_1 = .98 - .5 = .4800$
Looking up area .4800 in Table IV, $z_0 = 2.05$.

$$z_0 = \frac{x_0 - 75}{7.5} \Rightarrow 2.05 = \frac{x_0 - 75}{7.5} \Rightarrow x_0 = 90.375$$

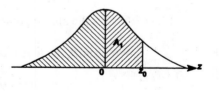

4.107 Let x = monthly rate of return to stock ABC and y = monthly rate of return to stock XYZ. The random variable x is normally distributed with $\mu = .05$ and $\sigma = .03$ and y is normally distributed with $\mu = .07$ and $\sigma = .05$. You have \$100 invested in each stock.

a. The average monthly rate of return for ABC stock is $\mu = .05$.
    The average monthly rate of return for XYZ stock is $\mu = .07$.
    Therefore, stock XYZ has the higher average monthly rate of return.

b.　$E(x) = .05$ for each $1.

Since we have $100 invested in stock ABC, the monthly rate of return would be $100(.05) = \$5$.

Therefore, the expected value of the investment in stock ABC at the end of 1 month is $100 + 5 = \$105$.

$E(y) = .07$ for each $1.

Since we have $100 invested in stock XYZ, the monthly rate of return would be $100(.07) = \$7$.

Therefore, the expected value of the investment in stock XYZ at the end of 1 month is $100 + 7 = \$107$.

c.　We need to find the probability of incurring a loss for each stock and compare them.

P(incurring a loss on stock ABC)　　P(incurring a loss on stock XYZ)
$= P$(monthly rate of return is　　　　$= P$(monthly rate of return is
　　negative on stock ABC)　　　　　　　negative on stock XYZ)
$= P(x < 0)$　　　　　　　　　　　　　　$= P(y < 0)$

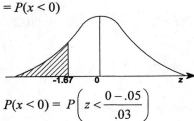

$$P(x < 0) = P\left(z < \frac{0 - .05}{.03}\right) \qquad P(y < 0) = P\left(z < \frac{0 - .07}{.05}\right)$$

$$
\begin{aligned}
&= P(z < -1.67) &&= P(z < -1.4)\\
&= .5000 - .4525 &&= .5000 - .4192\\
&= .0475 \text{ (Table IV, Appendix B)} &&= .0818 \text{ (Table IV, Appendix B)}
\end{aligned}
$$

Since the probability of incurring a loss is smaller for stock ABC, stock ABC would have a greater protection against occurring a loss next month.

4.109　Let $x =$ the amount of dye discharged. The random variable x is normally distributed with $\sigma = 4$.

We want P(shade is unacceptable) $\leq .01$

　　$\Rightarrow P(x > 6) \leq .01$

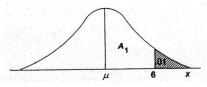

Then $A_1 = .50 - .01 = .49$. Look up the area .49 in the body of Table IV, Appendix B; (take the closest value) $z_0 = 2.33$.

To find μ, substitute into the z-score formula:

$$z = \frac{x - \mu}{\sigma}$$

$$2.33 = \frac{6 - \mu}{.4}$$

$$\mu = 6 - .4(2.33) = 5.068$$

4.111 a. The proportion of measurements that one would expect to fall in the interval $\mu \pm \sigma$ is about .68.

b. The proportion of measurements that one would expect to fall in the interval $\mu \pm 2\sigma$ is about .95.

c. The proportion of measurements that one would expect to fall in the interval $\mu \pm 3\sigma$ is about 1.00.

4.113 If the data are normally distributed, then the normal probability plot should be an approximate straight line. Of the three plots, only plot c implies that the data are normally distributed. The data points in plot c form an approximately straight line. In both plots **a** and **b**, the plots of the data points do not form a straight line.

4.115 a. $IQR = Q_U - Q_L = 53 - 47 = 6$

b. From the printout, s = 5.275

c. If the data are approximately normal, then $\frac{IQR}{s} \approx 1.3$. For this problem,

$$\frac{IQR}{s} = \frac{6}{5.275} = 1.137 \approx 1.3.$$ Thus, the distribution is approximately normal.

d. From Exercise 2.45 d, the histogram is:

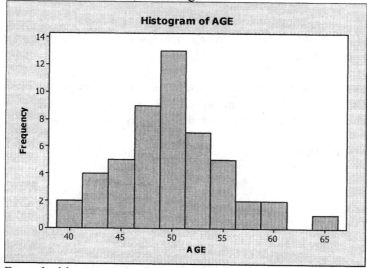

From the histogram, the data appear to be approximately mound-shaped. Thus, the data are approximately normal.

4.117　The information given in the problem states that $\bar{x} = 4.71$, $s = 6.09$, $Q_L = 1$, and $Q_U = 6$. To be normal, the data have to be symmetric. If the data are symmetric, then the mean would equal the median and would be half way between the lower and upper quartile. Half way between the upper and lower quartiles is 3.5. The sample mean is 4.71, which is much larger than 3.5. This implies that the data may not be normal. In addition, the interquartile range divided by the standard deviation will be approximately 1.3 if the data are normal. For this data,

$$\frac{IQR}{s} = \frac{Q_U - Q_L}{s} = \frac{6 - 1}{6.09} = .82$$

The value of .82 is much smaller than the necessary 1.3 to be normal. Again, this is an indication that the data are not normal. Finally, the standard deviation is larger than the mean. Since one cannot have values of the variable in this case less than 0, a standard deviation larger than the mean indicates that the data are skewed to the right. This implies that the data are not normal.

4.119　We will look at the 4 methods for determining if the data are normal. First, we will look at a histogram of the data. Using MINITAB, the histogram of the driver's head injury rating is:

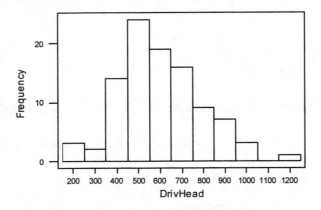

From the histogram, the data appear to be somewhat skewed to the right. This indicates that the data are normal.

Next, we look at the intervals $\bar{x} \pm s$, $\bar{x} \pm 2s$, $\bar{x} \pm 3s$. If the proportions of observations falling in each interval are approximately .68, .95, and 1.00, then the data are approximately normal. Using MINITAB, the summary statistics are:

Descriptive Statistics: DrivHead

Variable	N	Mean	Median	TrMean	StDev	SE Mean
DrivHead	98	603.7	605.0	600.3	185.4	18.7

Variable	Minimum	Maximum	Q1	Q3
DrivHead	216.0	1240.0	475.0	724.3

$\bar{x} \pm s \Rightarrow 603.7 \pm 185.4 \Rightarrow (418.3, \ 789.1)$　68 of the 98 values fall in this interval. The proportion is .69. This is very close to the .68 we would expect if the data were normal.

$\bar{x} \pm 2s \Rightarrow 603.7 \pm 2(185.4) \Rightarrow 603.7 \pm 370.8 \Rightarrow (232.9, \quad 974.5)$ 96 of the 98 values fall in this interval. The proportion is .98. This is a fair amount larger than the .95 we would expect if the data were normal.

$\bar{x} \pm 3s \Rightarrow 603.7 \pm 3(185.4) \Rightarrow 603.7 \pm 556.2 \Rightarrow (47.5, \quad 1,159.9)$ 97 of the 98 values fall in this interval. The proportion is .99. This is fairly close to the 1.00 we would expect if the data were normal.

From this method, it appears that the data may be normal.

Next, we look at the ratio of the IQR to s. IQR $= Q_U - Q_L = 724.3 - 475 = 249.3$.

$\dfrac{\text{IQR}}{s} = \dfrac{249.3}{185.4} = 1.3$ This is equal to the 1.3 we would expect if the data were normal. This method indicates the data may be normal.

Finally, using MINITAB, the normal probability plot is:

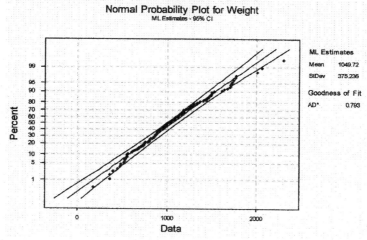

Since the data form a fairly straight line, the data may be normal.

From the 4 different methods, all indications are that the driver's head injury rating data are normal.

4.121 From Exercise 2.49, it states that the mean number of semester hours for those taking the CPA exam is 141.31 and the median is 140. It also states that most colleges only require 128 semester hours for an undergraduate degree. Thus, the minimum value for the total semester hours is around 128. From Exercise 2.75, it states that the standard deviation is 17.77. The z-score associated with 128 is:

$$z = \frac{x - \mu}{\sigma} = \frac{128 - 141.31}{17.77} = -.75$$

If the data are normal, we know that about .34 of the observations are between the mean and 1 standard deviation below the mean. Thus, .16 of the observations are more than 1 standard deviation below the mean. With this distribution, that is impossible. Thus, the data are not normal. The mean is greater than the median, so we know that the data are skewed to the right.

4.123   a. $\mu = np = 100(.01) = 1.0$, $\sigma = \sqrt{npq} = \sqrt{100(.01)(.99)} = .995$

$\mu \pm 3\sigma \Rightarrow 1 \pm 3(.995) \Rightarrow 1 \pm 2.985 \Rightarrow (-1.985, 3.985)$

Since this interval does not fall in the interval $(0, n = 100)$, the normal approximation is not appropriate.

b. $\mu = np = 20(.6) = 12$, $\sigma = \sqrt{npq} = \sqrt{20(.6)(.4)} = 2.191$

$\mu \pm 3\sigma \Rightarrow 12 \pm 3(2.191) \Rightarrow 12 \pm 6.573 \Rightarrow (5.427, 18.573)$

Since this interval falls in the interval $(0, n = 20)$, the normal approximation is appropriate.

c. $\mu = np = 10(.4) = 4$, $\sigma = \sqrt{npq} = \sqrt{10(.4)(.6)} = 1.549$

$\mu \pm 3\sigma \Rightarrow 4 \pm 3(1.549) \Rightarrow 4 \pm 4.647 \Rightarrow (-.647, 8.647)$

Since this interval does not fall within the interval $(0, n = 10)$, the normal approximation is not appropriate.

d. $\mu = np = 1000(.05) = 50$, $\sigma = \sqrt{npq} = \sqrt{1000(.05)(.95)} = 6.892$

$\mu \pm 3\sigma \Rightarrow 50 \pm 3(6.892) \Rightarrow 50 \pm 20.676 \Rightarrow (29.324, 70.676)$

Since this interval falls within the interval $(0, n = 1000)$, the normal approximation is appropriate.

e. $\mu = np = 100(.8) = 80$, $\sigma = \sqrt{npq} = \sqrt{100(.8)(.2)} = 4$

$\mu \pm 3\sigma \Rightarrow 80 \pm 3(4) \Rightarrow 80 \pm 12 \Rightarrow (68, 92)$

Since this interval falls within the interval $(0, n = 100)$, the normal approximation is appropriate.

f. $\mu = np = 35(.7) = 24.5$, $\sigma = \sqrt{npq} = \sqrt{35(.7)(.3)} = 2.711$

$\mu \pm 3\sigma \Rightarrow 24.5 \pm 3(2.711) \Rightarrow 24.5 \pm 8.133 \Rightarrow (16.367, 32.633)$

Since this interval falls within the interval $(0, n = 35)$, the normal approximation is appropriate.

4.125 x is a binomial random variable with $n = 100$ and $p = .4$.

$$\mu \pm 3\sigma \Rightarrow np \pm 3\sqrt{npq} \Rightarrow 100(.4) \pm 3\sqrt{100(.4)(1-.4)}$$
$$\Rightarrow 40 \pm 3(4.8990) \Rightarrow (25.303, 54.697)$$

Since the interval lies in the range 0 to 100, we can use the normal approximation to approximate the probabilities.

a. $P(x \le 35) \approx P\left(z \le \dfrac{(35+.5)-40}{4.899}\right)$

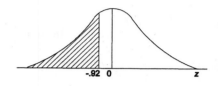

$= P(z \le -.92)$
$= .5000 - .3212 = .1788$
(Using Table IV in Appendix B.)

b. $P(40 \le x \le 50)$

$\approx P\left(\dfrac{(40-.5)-40}{4.899} \le z \le \dfrac{(50+.5)-40}{4.899}\right)$

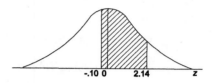

$= P(-.10 \le z \le 2.14)$
$= P(-.10 \le z \le 0) + P(0 \le z \le 2.14)$
$= .0398 + .4838 = .5236$
(Using Table IV in Appendix B.)

c. $P(x \ge 38) \approx P\left(z \ge \dfrac{(38-.5)-40}{4.899}\right)$

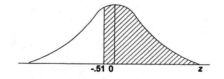

$= P(z \ge -.51)$
$= .5000 + .1950 = .6950$
(Using Table IV in Appendix B.)

4.127   a.   From Exercise 4.42, we demonstrated that x, the number of young adults in 200 that own a mobile phone with internet access, is a binomial random variable with $n = 200$ and $p = .20$.

$E(x) = \mu = np = 200(.20) = 40$.

b. $\sigma = \sqrt{\sigma^2} = \sqrt{npq} = \sqrt{200(.20)(.80)} = \sqrt{32} = 5.657$

c. $z = \dfrac{x-\mu}{\sigma} = \dfrac{50.5-40}{5.657} = 1.86$

d.   To see if the normal approximation is appropriate, we use:

$$\mu \pm 3\sigma \Rightarrow 40 \pm 3(5.657) \Rightarrow 40 \pm 16.971 \Rightarrow (23.029, \ 56.971)$$

Since the interval lies in the range of 0 to 200, the normal approximation is appropriate.

$P(x \le 50) \approx P(z \le 1.86) = .5 + .4686 = .9686$ (Using Table IV, Appendix B)

4.129   Let x = number of patients who undergo laser surgery who have serious post-laser vision problems in 100,000 trials. Then x is a binomial random variable with n = 100,000 and $p = .01$.

$E(x) = \mu = np = 100,000(.01) = 1,000$.

$$\sigma = \sqrt{\sigma^2} = \sqrt{npq} = \sqrt{100,000(.01)(.99)} = \sqrt{990} = 31.464$$

To see if the normal approximation is appropriate, we use:

$$\mu \pm 3\sigma \Rightarrow 1,000 \pm 3(31.464) \Rightarrow 1,000 \pm 94.392 \Rightarrow (905.608, \ 1,094.392)$$

Since the interval lies in the range of 0 to 100,000, the normal approximation is appropriate.

$$P(x < 950) \approx P\left(z < \frac{949.5 - 1000}{31.464}\right) = P(z < -1.61) = .5 - .4463 = .0537$$
(Using Table IV, Appendix B)

4.131   Let x = number of bottles (brands) selected in 65 trials that contain tap water. Then x is a binomial random variable with $n = 65$ and $p = .25$.

$E(x) = \mu = np = 65(.25) = 16.25$

$$\sigma = \sqrt{\sigma^2} = \sqrt{npq} = \sqrt{65(.25)(.75)} = \sqrt{12.1875} = 3.49$$

To see if the normal approximation is appropriate, we use:

$$\mu \pm 3\sigma \Rightarrow 16.25 \pm 3(3.49) \Rightarrow 16.25 \pm 10.47 \Rightarrow (5.78, \ 26.72)$$

Since this interval lies in the range from 0 to 65, the normal approximation is appropriate.

$$P(x \geq 20) = P\left(z \geq \frac{(20 - .5) - 16.25}{3.49}\right) = P(z \geq .93) = .5 - P(0 \leq z \leq .93) = .5 - .3238 = .1762$$
(Using Table IV, Appendix B)

4.133   Let x = number of defective CDs in n = 1,600 trials. Then x is a binomial random variable with $n = 1,600$ and $p = .006$.

$E(x) = \mu = np = 1,600(.006) = 9.6$.

$$\sigma = \sqrt{\sigma^2} = \sqrt{npq} = \sqrt{1,600(.006)(.994)} = \sqrt{9.5424} = 3.089$$

To see if the normal approximation is appropriate, we use:

$$\mu \pm 3\sigma \Rightarrow 9.6 \pm 3(3.089) \Rightarrow 9.6 \pm 9.267 \Rightarrow (0.333, \ 18.867)$$

Since the interval lies in the range of 0 to 1,600, the normal approximation is appropriate.

$$P(x \geq 12) \approx P\left(z \geq \frac{11.5 - 9.6}{3.089}\right) = P(z \geq 0.62) = .5 - .2324 = .2676$$

(Using Table IV, Appendix B)

Since this probability is fairly large, it would not be unusual to see 12 or more defectives in a sample of 1,600 if 99.4% were defect-free. Thus, there would be no evidence to cast doubt on the manufacturer's claim.

4.135   a.   There are well over a million college students in 4-year public and private institutions. In order to collect a truly random sample, each of the college students must have an equal chance of being selected. This would be extremely hard to do.

b.   Suppose your institution was a 4-year public institution. Let x = number of students receiving financial aid in 100 trials. The random variable x has a binomial distribution with $n = 100$ and $p = .45$. To determine if the normal approximation is appropriate, we check:

$$\mu \pm 3\sigma \Rightarrow np \pm 3\sqrt{npq} \Rightarrow 100(.45) \pm 3\sqrt{100(.45)(.55)}$$
$$\Rightarrow 45 \pm 3(4.9749) \Rightarrow 45 \pm 14.9247 \Rightarrow (30.0753, 59.9247)$$

Since the interval lies in the range 0 to 100, we can use the normal approximation to approximate the probabilities.

$$P(x \geq 50) \approx P\left(z \geq \frac{(50 - .5) - 45}{4.9749}\right) = P(z \geq .90) = .5 - .3159 = .1841$$

$$P(x < 25) \approx P\left(z < \frac{(25 - .5) - 45}{4.9749}\right) = P(z < -4.12) = .5 - .5 = 0$$

Suppose your institution was a 4-year private institution. Let x = number of students receiving financial aid in 100 trials. The random variable x has a binomial distribution with $n = 100$ and $p = .52$. To determine if the normal approximation is appropriate, we check:

$$\mu \pm 3\sigma \Rightarrow np \pm 3\sqrt{npq} \Rightarrow 100(.52) \pm 3\sqrt{100(.52)(.48)}$$
$$\Rightarrow 52 \pm 3(4.996) \Rightarrow 52 \pm 14.988 \Rightarrow (37.012, 66.988)$$

Since the interval lies in the range 0 to 100, we can use the normal approximation to approximate the probabilities.

$$P(x \geq 50) \approx P\left(z \geq \frac{(50 - .5) - 52}{4.996}\right) = P(z \geq -.50) = .5 + .1915 = .6915$$

$$P(x < 25) \approx P\left(z < \frac{(25 - .5) - 52}{4.996}\right) = P(z < -5.50) \approx .5 - .5 = 0$$

c. In order for the normal approximation to be appropriate, the interval $\mu \pm 3\sigma$ should lie in the interval 0 to n. This assumption was checked in part **b**.

4.137 a–b. The different samples of $n = 2$ with replacement and their means are:

Possible Samples	$\bar{x}$	Possible Samples	$\bar{x}$
0, 0	0	4, 0	2
0, 2	1	4, 2	3
0, 4	2	4, 4	4
0, 6	3	4, 6	5
2, 0	1	6, 0	3
2, 2	2	6, 2	4
2, 4	3	6, 4	5
2, 6	4	6, 6	6

c. Since each sample is equally likely, the probability of any 1 being selected is $\dfrac{1}{4}\left(\dfrac{1}{4}\right) = \dfrac{1}{16}$

d.
$$P(\bar{x} = 0) = \frac{1}{16}$$
$$P(\bar{x} = 1) = \frac{1}{16} + \frac{1}{16} = \frac{2}{16}$$
$$P(\bar{x} = 2) = \frac{1}{16} + \frac{1}{16} + \frac{1}{16} = \frac{3}{16}$$
$$P(\bar{x} = 3) = \frac{1}{16} + \frac{1}{16} + \frac{1}{16} + \frac{1}{16} = \frac{4}{16}$$
$$P(\bar{x} = 4) = \frac{1}{16} + \frac{1}{16} + \frac{1}{16} = \frac{3}{16}$$
$$P(\bar{x} = 5) = \frac{1}{16} + \frac{1}{16} = \frac{2}{16}$$
$$P(\bar{x} = 6) = \frac{1}{16}$$

$\bar{x}$	$p(\bar{x})$
0	1/16
1	2/16
2	3/16
3	4/16
4	3/16
5	2/16
6	1/16

e.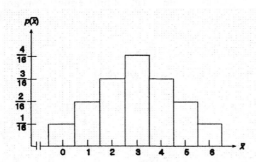

4.139 If the observations are independent of each other, then

$P(1, 1) = p(1)p(1) = .2(.2) = .04$
$P(1, 2) = p(1)p(2) = .2(.3) = .06$
$P(1, 3) = p(1)p(3) = .2(.2) = .04$
etc.

a.

Possible Sample	$\bar{x}$	$p(\bar{x})$	Possible Samples	$\bar{x}$	$p(\bar{x})$
1, 1	1	.04	3, 4	3.5	.04
1, 2	1.5	.06	3, 5	4	.02
1, 3	2	.04	4, 1	2.5	.04
1, 4	2.5	.04	4, 2	3	.06
1, 5	3	.02	4, 3	3.5	.04
2, 1	1.5	.06	4, 4	4	.04
2, 2	2	.09	4, 5	4.5	.02
2, 3	2.5	.06	5, 1	3	.02
2, 4	3	.06	5, 2	3.5	.03
2, 5	3.5	.03	5, 3	4	.02
3, 1	2	.04	5, 4	4.5	.02
3, 2	2.5	.06	5, 5	5	.01
3, 3	3	.04			

Summing the probabilities, the probability distribution of is:

$\bar{x}$	$p(\bar{x})$
1	.04
1.5	.12
2	.17
2.5	.20
3	.20
3.5	.14
4	.08
4.5	.04
5	.01

b.

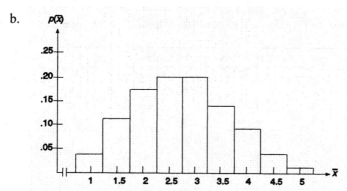

c. $P(\bar{x} \geq 4.5) = .04 + .01 = .05$

d. No. The probability of observing = 4.5 or larger is small (.05).

4.141 a. For a sample of size $n = 2$, the sample mean and sample median are exactly the same. Thus, the sampling distribution of the sample median is the same as that for the sample mean (see Exercise 4.139**a**).

  b. The probability histogram for the sample median is identical to that for the sample mean (see Exercise 4.139**b**).

4.145 a. $\mu_{\bar{x}} = \mu = 100, \sigma_{\bar{x}} = \dfrac{\sigma}{\sqrt{n}} = \dfrac{\sqrt{100}}{\sqrt{4}} = 5$

  b. $\mu_{\bar{x}} = \mu = 100, \sigma_{\bar{x}} = \dfrac{\sigma}{\sqrt{n}} = \dfrac{\sqrt{100}}{\sqrt{25}} = 2$

  c. $\mu_{\bar{x}} = \mu = 100, \sigma_{\bar{x}} = \dfrac{\sigma}{\sqrt{n}} = \dfrac{\sqrt{100}}{\sqrt{100}} = 1$

  d. $\mu_{\bar{x}} = \mu = 100, \sigma_{\bar{x}} = \dfrac{\sigma}{\sqrt{n}} = \dfrac{\sqrt{100}}{\sqrt{50}} = 1.414$

  e. $\mu_{\bar{x}} = \mu = 100, \sigma_{\bar{x}} = \dfrac{\sigma}{\sqrt{n}} = \dfrac{\sqrt{100}}{\sqrt{500}} = .447$

  f. $\mu_{\bar{x}} = \mu = 100, \sigma_{\bar{x}} = \dfrac{\sigma}{\sqrt{n}} = \dfrac{\sqrt{100}}{\sqrt{1000}} = .316$

4.147 a. $\mu = \sum xp(x) = 1(.1) + 2(.4) + 3(.4) + 8(.1) = 2.9$

  $\sigma^2 = \sum (x - \mu)^2 p(x) = (1 - 2.9)^2(.1) + (2 - 2.9)^2(.4) + (3 - 2.9)^2(.4) + (8 - 2.9)^2(.1)$
  $= .361 + .324 + .004 + 2.601 = 3.29$

  $\sigma = \sqrt{3.29} = 1.814$

  b. The possible samples, values of , and associated probabilities are listed:

Possible Samples	$\bar{x}$	$p(\bar{x})$	Possible Samples	$\bar{x}$	$p(\bar{x})$
1, 1	1	.01	3, 1	2	.04
1, 2	1.5	.04	3, 2	2.5	.16
1, 3	2	.04	3, 3	3	.16
1, 8	4.5	.01	3, 8	5.5	.04
2, 1	1.5	.04	8, 1	4.5	.01
2, 2	2	.16	8, 2	5	.04
2, 3	2.5	.16	8, 3	5.5	.04
2, 8	5	.04	8, 8	8	.01

$$P(1, 1) = p(1)p(1) = .1(.1) = .01$$
$$P(1, 2) = p(1)p(2) = .1(.4) = .04$$
$$P(1, 3) = p(1)p(3) = .1(.4) = .04$$
etc.

The sampling distribution of is:

$\bar{x}$	$p(\bar{x})$
1	.01
1.5	.08
2	.24
2.5	.32
3	.16
4.5	.02
5	.08
5.5	.08
8	.01
	1.00

c. $\mu_{\bar{x}} = E(\bar{x}) = \sum \bar{x}p(\bar{x}) = 1(.01) + 1.5(.08) + 2(.24) + 2.5(.32) + 3(.16) + 4.5(.02)$
$$+ 5(.08) + 5.5(.08) + 8(.01)$$
$$= 2.9 = \mu$$

$$\sigma_{\bar{x}}^2 = \sum (\bar{x} - \mu_{\bar{x}})^2 \, p(\bar{x}) = (1 - 2.9)^2(.01) + (1.5 - 2.9)^2(.08) + (2 - 2.9)^2(.24)$$
$$+ (2.5 - 2.9)^2(.32) + (3 - 2.9)^2(.16) + (4.5 - 2.9)^2(.02)$$
$$+ (5 - 2.9)^2(.08) + (5.5 - 2.9)^2(.08) + (8 - 2.9)^2(.01)$$
$$= .0361 + .1568 + .1944 + .0512 + .0016 + .0512 + .3528$$
$$+ .5408 + .2601$$
$$= 1.645$$

$$\sigma_{\bar{x}} = \sqrt{1.645} = 1.283$$
$$\sigma_{\bar{x}} = \sigma / \sqrt{n} = 1.814 / \sqrt{2} = 1.283$$

4.149   In Exercise 4.148, it was determined that the mean and standard deviation of the sampling distribution of the sample mean are 20 and 2 respectively. Using Table IV, Appendix B:

a. $P(\bar{x} < 16) = P\left(z < \dfrac{16 - 20}{2} \right) = P(z < -2) = .5 - .4772 = .0228$

b. $P(\bar{x} > 23) = P\left(z > \dfrac{23 - 20}{2} \right) = P(z > 1.50) = .5 - .4332 = .0668$

c. $P(\bar{x} > 25) = P\left(z > \dfrac{25 - 20}{2} \right) = P(z > 2.5) = .5 - .4938 = .0062$

d. $P(16 < \bar{x} < 22) = P\left(\dfrac{16-20}{2} < z < \dfrac{22-20}{2}\right) = P(-2 < z < 1)$

$$= .4772 + .3413 = .8185$$

e. $P(\bar{x} < 14) = P\left(z < \dfrac{14-20}{2}\right) = P(z < -3) = .5 - .4987 = .0013$

4.151 By the Central Limit Theorem, the sampling distribution of is approximately normal with
$\mu_{\bar{x}} = \mu = 30$ and $\sigma_{\bar{x}} = \sigma/\sqrt{n} = 16/\sqrt{100} = 1.6$. Using Table IV, Appendix B:

a. $P(\geq 28) = P\left(z \geq \dfrac{28-30}{1.6}\right) = P(z \geq -1.25) = .5 + .3944 = .8944$

b. $P(22.1 \leq \bar{x} \leq 26.8) = P\left(\dfrac{22.1-30}{1.6} \leq z \leq \dfrac{26.8-30}{1.6}\right) = P(-4.94 \leq z \leq -2)$

$$= .5 - .4772 = .0228$$

c. $P(\bar{x} \leq 28.2) = P\left(z \leq \dfrac{28.2-30}{1.6}\right) = P(z \leq -1.13) = .5 - .3708 = .1292$

d. $P(\bar{x} \geq 27.0) = P\left(z \geq \dfrac{27.0-30}{1.6}\right) = P(z \geq -1.88) = .5 + .4699 = .9699$

4.153 a. $\mu_{\bar{x}} = \mu = 141$

b. $\sigma_{\bar{x}} = \dfrac{\sigma}{\sqrt{n}} = \dfrac{18}{\sqrt{100}} = 1.8$

c. By the Central Limit Theorem, the sampling distribution of $\bar{x}$ is approximately normal.

d. $z = \dfrac{\bar{x} - \mu_{\bar{x}}}{\sigma_{\bar{x}}} = \dfrac{142 - 141}{1.8} = 0.56$

e. $P(\bar{x} > 142) = P(z > 0.56) = .5 - .2123 = .2877$ (Using Table IV, Appendix B)

4.155 By the Central Limit Theorem, the sampling distribution of $\bar{x}$ is approximately normal
with $\mu_{\bar{x}} = \mu = 19$ and $\sigma_{\bar{x}} = \dfrac{\sigma}{\sqrt{n}} = \dfrac{65}{\sqrt{100}} = 6.5$.

Using Table IV, Appendix B,

$$P(\bar{x} < 10) = P\left(z < \dfrac{10-19}{6.5}\right) = P(z < -1.38) = .5 - .4162 = .0838$$

4.157   a.   By the Central Limit Theorem, the sampling distribution of $\bar{x}$ is approximately normal with a mean $\mu_{\bar{x}} = \mu = .53$ and standard deviation $\sigma_{\bar{x}} = \dfrac{\sigma}{\sqrt{n}} = \dfrac{.193}{\sqrt{50}} = .0273$.

      b. $P(\bar{x} > .58) = P\left(z > \dfrac{.58 - .53}{.0273} \right) = P(z > 1.83) = .5 - .4664 = .0336$

      c.   If Before Tensioning: $\mu_{\bar{x}} = \mu = .53$

$$P(\bar{x} \geq .59) = P\left(z \geq \dfrac{.59 - .53}{.0273} \right) = P(z \geq 2.20) = .5 - .4861 = .0139$$

If After Tensioning: $\mu_{\bar{x}} = \mu = .58$

$$P(\bar{x} \geq .59) = P\left(z \geq \dfrac{.59 - .58}{.0273} \right) = P(z \geq 0.37) = .5 - .1443 = .3557$$

Since the probability of getting a maximum differential of .59 or more Before Tensioning is so small, it would be very unlikely that the measurements were obtained before tensioning. However, since the probability of getting a maximum differential of .59 or more After Tensioning is not small, it would not be unusual that the measurements were obtained after tensioning. Thus, most likely, the measurements were obtained After Tensioning.

4.159   a.   By the Central Limit Theorem, the sampling distribution of is approximately normal with

$$\mu_{\bar{x}} = \mu \text{ and } \sigma_{\bar{x}} = \sigma / \sqrt{n}.$$

      b.   Let $\mu = 18.5$. Since we do not know σ we will estimate it with $s = 6$.

$$P(\bar{x} \geq 19.1) \approx P\left(z \geq \dfrac{19.1 - 18.5}{6/\sqrt{344}} \right) = P(z \geq 1.85) = .5 - .4678 = .0322$$

      c.   Let $\mu = 19.5$. Since we do not know σ we will estimate it with $s = 6$.

$$P(\bar{x} \geq 19.1) \approx P\left(z \geq \dfrac{19.1 - 19.5}{6/\sqrt{344}} \right) = P(z \geq -1.24) = .5 + .3925 = .8925$$

      d.   If $P(\bar{x} \geq 19.1) = .5$, then the population mean must be equal to 19.1. (For a normal distribution, half of the distribution is above the mean and half is below the mean.)

      e.   If $P(\bar{x} \geq 19.1) = .2$, then the population mean is less than 19.1. We know the probability that is greater than the mean is .5. Since $P(x \geq 19.1) = .2$ which is less than .5, we know that 19.1 must be to the right of the mean. Thus, the population mean must be less than 19.1.

4.161   a.   By the Central Limit Theorem, the sampling distribution of is approximately normal with $\mu_{\bar{x}} = \mu$ and $\sigma_{\bar{x}} = \sigma / \sqrt{n} = \sigma / \sqrt{50}$.

   b. $\mu_{\bar{x}} = \mu = 40$ and $\sigma_{\bar{x}} = \sigma / \sqrt{50} = 12 / \sqrt{50} = 1.6971$.

$$P(\bar{x} \geq 44) = P\left(z \geq \frac{44 - 40}{1.6971}\right) = P(z \geq 2.36) = .5 - .4909 = .0091$$

(using Table IV, Appendix B)

   c. $\mu \pm 2\sigma / \sqrt{n} \Rightarrow 40 \pm 2(1.6971) \Rightarrow 40 \pm 3.3942 \Rightarrow (36.6058, 43.3942)$

$$P(36.6058 \leq \bar{x} \leq 43.3942) = P\left(\frac{36.6058 - 40}{1.6971} \leq z \leq \frac{43.3942 - 40}{1.6971}\right)$$
$$= P(-2 \leq z \leq 2) = 2(.4772) = .9544$$

(using Table IV, Appendix B)

4.163   For $n = 50$, we can use the Central Limit Theorem to decide the shape of the distribution of the sample mean bacterial counts. For the handrubbing sample, the sampling distribution of $\bar{x}$ is approximately normal with a mean of $\mu = 35$ and standard deviation $\frac{\sigma}{\sqrt{n}} = \frac{59}{\sqrt{50}} = 8.344$. For the handwashing sample, the sampling distribution of $\bar{x}$ is approximately normal with a mean of $\mu = 69$ and standard deviation

$$\frac{\sigma}{\sqrt{n}} = \frac{106}{\sqrt{50}} = 14.991.$$

For Handrubbing:

$$P(\bar{x} < 30 \mid \mu = 35) = P\left(z < \frac{30 - 35}{8.344}\right) = P(z < -.60) = .5 - .2257 = .2743$$

(using Table IV, Appendix B)

For Handwashing:

$$P(\bar{x} < 30 \mid \mu = 69) = P\left(z < \frac{30 - 69}{14.991}\right) = P(z < -2.60) = .5 - .4953 = .0047$$

(using Table IV, Appendix B)

Since the probability of getting a sample mean of less than 30 for the handrubbing is not small compared with that for the handwashing, the sample of workers probably came from the handrubbing group.

4.165 $p(x) = \binom{n}{x} p^x q^{n-x}$ $x = 0, 1, 2, \ldots, n$

a. $P(x = 3) = p(3) = \binom{7}{3} .5^3.5^4 = \dfrac{7!}{3!4!} .5^3.5^4 = 35(.125)(.0625) = .2734$

b. $P(x = 3) = p(3) = \binom{4}{3} .8^3.2^1 = \dfrac{4!}{3!1!} .8^3.2^1 = 4(.512)(.2) = .4096$

c. $P(x = 1) = p(1) = \binom{15}{1} .1^1.9^{14} = \dfrac{15!}{1!14!} .1^1.9^{14} = 15(.1)(.228768) = .3432$

4.167   From Table II, Appendix B:

a. $P(x = 14) = P(x \le 14) - P(x \le 13) = .584 - .392 = .192$

b. $P(x \le 12) = .228$

c. $P(x > 12) = 1 - P(x \le 12) = 1 - .228 = .772$

d. $P(9 \le x \le 18) = P(x \le 18) - P(x \le 8) = .992 - .005 = .987$

e. $P(8 < x < 18) = P(x \le 17) - P(x \le 8) = .965 - .005 = .960$

f. $\mu = np = 20(.7) = 14$

$\sigma^2 = npq = 20(.7)(.3) = 4.2, \sigma = \sqrt{4.2} = 2.049$

g. $\mu \pm 2\sigma \Rightarrow 14 \pm 2(2.049) \Rightarrow 14 \pm 4.098 \Rightarrow (9.902, 18.098)$

$$P(9.902 < x < 18.098) = P(10 \le x \le 18) = P(x \le 18) - P(x \le 9)$$
$$= .992 - .017 = .975$$

4.169   a.   Discrete - The number of damaged inventory items is countable.

b.   Continuous - The average monthly sales can take on any value within an acceptable limit.

c.   Continuous - The number of square feet can take on any positive value.

d.   Continuous - The length of time we must wait can take on any positive value.

4.171   a. $P(z \le 2.1) = A_1 + A_2$
$= .5 + .4821$
$= .9821$

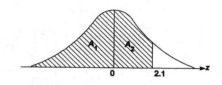

b. $P(z \geq 2.1) = A_2 = .5 - A_1$
    $= .5 - .4821$
    $= .0179$

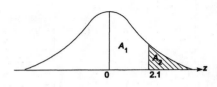

c. $P(z \geq -1.65) = A_1 + A_2$
    $= .4505 + .5000$
    $= .9505$

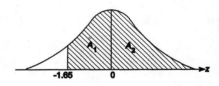

d. $P(-2.13 \leq z \leq -.41)$
    $= P(-2.13 \leq z \leq 0) - P(-.41 \leq z \leq 0)$
    $= .4834 - .1591$
    $= .3243$

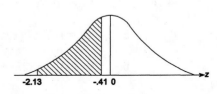

e. $P(-1.45 \leq z \leq 2.15) = A_1 + A_2$
    $= .4265 + .4842$
    $= .9107$

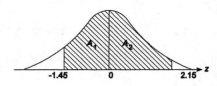

f. $P(z \leq -1.43) = A_1 = .5 - A_2$
    $= .5000 - .4236$
    $= .0764$

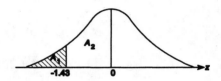

4.173 a. $P(x \leq 80) = P\left(z \leq \dfrac{80 - 75}{10}\right) = P(z \leq .5)$
        $= .5000 + .1915 = .6915$
        (Table IV, Appendix B)

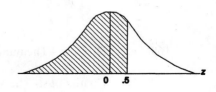

b. $P(x \geq 85) = P\left(z \geq \dfrac{85 - 75}{10}\right) = P(z \geq 1)$
    $= .5000 - .3413 = .1587$
    (Table IV, Appendix B)

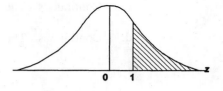

c. $P(70 \leq x \leq 75) = P\left(\dfrac{70 - 75}{10} \leq z \leq \dfrac{75 - 75}{10}\right)$
    $= P(-.5 \leq z \leq 0)$
    $= P(0 \leq z \leq .5) = .1915$

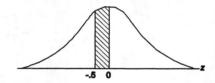

d. $P(x > 80) = 1 - P(x \le 80) = 1 - .6915 = .3085$ (Refer to part **a.**)

e. $P(x = 78) = 0$, since a single point does not have an area.

f. $P(x \le 110) = P\left(z \le \dfrac{110 - 75}{10}\right) = P(z \le 3.5)$

$\approx .5000 + .5000 = 1.0$

(Table IV, Appendix B)

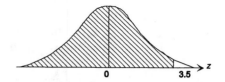

4.175 x is normal random variable with $\mu = 40$, $\sigma^2 = 36$, and $\sigma = 6$.

a. $P(x \ge x_0) = .10$

So, $A = .5000 - .1000 = .4000$.

$z_0 = 1.28$ (See part **a.**)

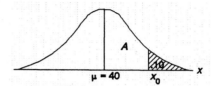

To find x_0, substitute the values into the z-score formula:

$$z_0 = \frac{x_0 - \mu}{\sigma} \Rightarrow 1.28 = \frac{x_0 - 40}{6} \Rightarrow x_0 = 1.28(6) + 40 = 47.68$$

b. $P(\mu \le x \le x_0) = .40$

Look up the area .4000 in the body of Table IV, Appendix B; (take the closest value) $z_0 = 1.28$.

To find x_0, substitute the values into the z-score formula:

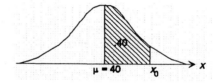

$$z_0 = \frac{x_0 - \mu}{\sigma} \Rightarrow 1.28 = \frac{x_0 - 40}{6} \Rightarrow x_0 = 40 + 6(1.28) = 47.68$$

c. $P(x < x_0) = .05$

So, $A = .5000 - .0500 = .4500$.

Look up the area .4500 in the body of Table IV, Appendix B; $z_0 = -1.645$. (.45 is halfway between .4495 and .4505; therefore, we average the z-scores

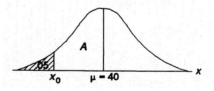

$$\frac{1.64 + 1.65}{2} = 1.645$$

z_0 is negative since the graph shows z_0 is on the left side of 0.

To find x_0, substitute the values into the z-score formula:

$$z_0 = \frac{x_0 - \mu}{\sigma} \Rightarrow -1.645 = \frac{x_0 - 40}{6} \Rightarrow x_0 = -1.645(6) + 40 = 30.13$$

d. $P(x > x_0) = .40$

So, $A = .5000 - .4000 = .1000$.

Look up the area .1000 in the body of Table IV, Appendix B; (take the closest value) $z_0 = .25$.

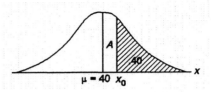

To find x_0, substitute the values into the z-score formula:

$$z_0 = \frac{x_0 - \mu}{\sigma} \Rightarrow .25 = \frac{x_0 - 40}{6} \Rightarrow x_0 = 40 + 6(.25) = 41.5$$

e. $P(x_0 \le x < \mu) = .45$

Look up the area .4500 in the body of Table IV, Appendix B; $z_0 = -1.645$. (.45 is halfway between .4495 and .4505; therefore, we average the z-scores

$$\frac{1.64 + 1.65}{2} = 1.645$$

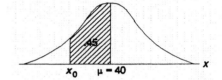

z_0 is negative since the graph shows z_0 is on the left side of 0.

To find x_0, substitute the values into the z-score formula:

$$z_0 = \frac{x_0 - \mu}{\sigma} \Rightarrow -1.645 = \frac{x_0 - 40}{6} \Rightarrow x_0 = 40 - 6(1.645) = 30.13$$

4.177 By the Central Limit Theorem, the sampling distribution of is approximately normal.

$$\mu_{\bar{x}} = \mu = 19.6, \ \sigma_{\bar{x}} = \frac{3.2}{\sqrt{68}} = .388$$

a. $P(\bar{x} \le 19.6) = P\left(z \le \frac{19.6 - 19.6}{.388}\right) = P(z \le 0) = .5$ (using Table IV, Appendix B)

b. $P(\bar{x} \le 19) = P\left(z \le \frac{19 - 19.6}{.388}\right) = P(z \le -1.55) = .5 - .4394 = .0606$

(using Table IV, Appendix B)

c. $P(\bar{x} \ge 20.1) = P\left(z \ge \frac{20.1 - 19.6}{.388}\right) = P(z \ge 1.29) = .5 - .4015 = .0985$

(using Table IV, Appendix B)

d. $P(19.2 \le \bar{x} \le 20.6) = P\left(\dfrac{19.2 - 19.6}{.388} \le z \le \dfrac{20.6 - 19.6}{.388} \right)$

$$= P(-1.03 \le z \le 2.58) = .3485 + .4951 = .8436$$

(using Table IV, Appendix B)

4.179   Given: $\mu = 100$ and $\sigma = 10$

n	1	5	10	20	30	40	50
$\dfrac{\sigma}{\sqrt{n}}$	10	4.472	3.162	2.236	1.826	1.581	1.414

The graph of $\sigma / \sqrt{n}$ against n is given here:

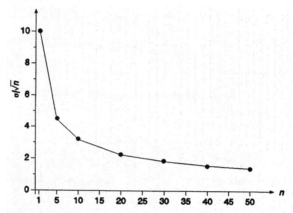

4.181   a. $\displaystyle\sum_{i=1}^{6} p(x_i) = p(0) + p(1) + p(2) + p(3) + p(4) + p(5)$

          $= .0102 + .0768 + .2304 + .3456 + .2592 + .0778 = 1.0000$

    b. $P(x = 4) = .2592$

    c. $P(x < 2) = P(x = 0) + P(x = 1) = .0102 + .0768 = .0870$

    d. $P(x \ge 3) = P(x = 3) + P(x = 4) + P(x = 5) = .3456 + .2592 + .0778 = .6826$

    e. $\mu = E(x) = \displaystyle\sum_{i=1}^{6} x_i p(x_i) = 0(.0102) + 1(.0768) + 2(.2304) + 3(.3456) + 4(.2592) + 5(.0778)$

          $= 0 + .0768 + .4608 + 1.0368 + 1.0368 + .3890 = 3.0002$

On the average, 3 out of every 5 dentists will use nitrous oxide.

4.183 a. If x is uniformly distributed over the interval \$10,000 to \$15,000, then $d = \$15,000$ and $c = \$10,000$.

$$E(x) = \frac{c+d}{2} = \frac{\$10,000 + \$15,000}{2} = \$12,500$$

The average monthly reimbursements to the employees is \$12,500.

b. $$f(x) = \begin{cases} \dfrac{1}{d-c} = \dfrac{1}{\$15,000 - \$10,000} = \dfrac{1}{\$5,000} = .0002 & (\$10,000 \leq x \leq \$15,000) \\ 0 & \text{otherwise} \end{cases}$$

$P(x > \$12,000) = (\$15,000 - \$12,000).0002 = .6$

c. $P(x > a) = .20 \Rightarrow (\$15,000 - a).0002 = .20$
$\Rightarrow 3 - .0002a = .2$
$\Rightarrow .0002a = 2.8$
$\Rightarrow a = \$14,000$

4.185 a. The distribution of x has a mean of $\mu = 26$ and a standard deviation of σ. There is no information given to indicate the shape of the distribution.

b. The distribution of $\bar{x}$ has a mean of $\mu_{\bar{x}} = \mu = 26$ and a standard deviation of $\sigma_{\bar{x}} = \sigma/\sqrt{n}$. Since $n = 200$ is sufficiently large, the Central Limit Theorem says that the sampling distribution of is approximately normal.

c. If $\sigma = 20$, then $\sigma_{\bar{x}} = \sigma/\sqrt{n} = 20/\sqrt{200} = 1.4142$.

$$P(\bar{x} > 26.8) = P\left(z > \frac{26.8 - 26}{1.4142}\right) = P(z > .57) = .5 - .2157 = .2843$$

d. If $\sigma = 10$, then $\sigma_{\bar{x}} = \sigma/\sqrt{n} = 10/\sqrt{200} = .7071$

$$P(\bar{x} > 26.8) = P\left(z > \frac{26.8 - 26}{.7071}\right) = P(z > 1.13) = .5 - .3708 = .1292$$

4.187 Let x = maximum number of years one expects to spend with any one employer. For this problem, $\mu = 18.2$ and $\sigma = 10.64$. The minimum value for x is 0, which has a z-score of:

$$z = \frac{x - \mu}{\sigma} = \frac{0 - 18.2}{10.64} = -1.71$$

Since the smallest possible value of x is only 1.71 standard deviations from the mean, it is very unlikely that the data are normal. A normal distribution will have about .0436 or 4.36% of the observations more than 1.71 standard deviations below the mean.

$(P(z < -1.71) = .5 - .4564 = .0436)$

For this data set, there are no observations more than 1.71 standard deviations below the mean.

4.189   a.   In order for the number of deaths to follow a Poisson distribution, we must assume that the probability of a death is the same for any week. We must also assume that the number of deaths in any week is independent of any other week.

The first assumption may not be valid. The probability of a death may not be the same for every week. The number of passengers varies from week to week, so the probability of a death may change. Also, things such as weather, which varies from week to week may increase or decrease the chance of derailment.

   b. $E(x) = \lambda = 20$
   $\sigma = \sqrt{\lambda} = \sqrt{20} = 4.4721$

   c.   The z-score corresponding to $x = 4$ is:
   $$z = \frac{4 - 20}{4.4721} = -3.55$$

Since this z-score is more than 3 standard deviations from the mean, it would be very unlikely that only 4 or fewer deaths occur next week.

   d.   Using Table III, Appendix B with $\lambda = 20$,

   $$P(x \le 4) = 0.000$$

This probability is consistent with the answer in part **c**. The probability of 4 or fewer deaths is essentially zero, which is very unlikely.

4.191   Using MINITAB, the stem-and-leaf display is:

```
Stem-and-leaf of Time      N  = 49
Leaf Unit = 0.10

  (26)    1  00001122222344444445555679
   23     2  11446799
   15     3  002899
    9     4  11125
    4     5  24
    2     6
    2     7 8
    1     8
    1     9
    1    10 1
```

The data are skewed to the right, and do not appear to be normally distributed.

Using MINITAB, the descriptive statistics are:

Variable	N	Mean	Median	TrMean	StDev	SE Mean
Time	49	2.549	1.700	2.333	1.828	0.261

Variable	Minimum	Maximum	Q1	Q3
Time	1.000	10.100	1.350	3.500

$\bar{x} \pm s \Rightarrow 2.549 \pm 1.828 \Rightarrow (0.721, 4.377)$

$\bar{x} \pm 2s \Rightarrow 2.549 \pm 2(1.828) \Rightarrow 2.549 \pm 3.656 \Rightarrow (\pm 1.107, 6.205)$

$\bar{x} \pm 3s \Rightarrow 2.549 \pm 3(1.828) \Rightarrow 2.549 \pm 5.484 \Rightarrow (-2.935, 8.033)$

Of the 49 measurements, 44 are in the interval (0.721, 4.377). The proportion is 44/49 = .898. This is much larger than the proportion (.68) stated by the Empirical Rule.

Of the 49 measurements, 47 are in the interval (−1.107, 6.205). The proportion is 47/49 = .959. This is close to the proportion (.95) stated by the Empirical Rule.

Of the 49 measurements, 48 are in the interval (−2.935, 8.033). The proportion is 48/49 = .980. This is smaller than the proportion (1.00) stated by the Empirical Rule.

This would imply that the data are not normal.

IQR = $Q_U − Q_L$ = 3.500 − 1.350 = 2.15. IQR/s = 2.15/1.828 = 1.176. If the data are normally distributed, this ratio should be close to 1.3. Since 1.176 is smaller than 1.3, this indicates that the data may not be normal.

Using MINITAB, the normal probability plot is:

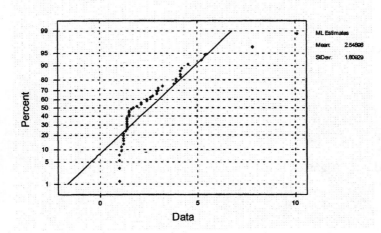

Since this plot is not a straight line, the data are not normal.

All four checks indicate that the data are not normal.

4.193   Let x equal the difference between the actual weight and recorded weight (the error of measurement). The random variable x is normally distributed with $\mu = 592$ and $\sigma = 628$.

a.   We want to find the probability that the weigh-in-motion equipment understates the actual weight of the truck. This would be true if the error of measurement is positive.

$$P(x > 0) = P\left(z > \frac{0 - 592}{628}\right)$$
$$= P(z > -.94)$$
$$= .5000 + .3264$$
$$= .8264$$

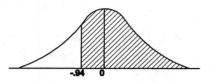

b. $P(\text{overstate the weight}) = 1 - P(\text{understate the weight})$
$$= 1 - .8264$$
$$= .1736 \quad \text{(Refer to part \textbf{a}.)}$$

For 100 measurements, approximately $100(.1736) = 17.36$ or 17 times the weight would be overstated.

c. $$P(x > 400) = P\left(z > \frac{400 - 592}{628}\right)$$
$$= P(z > -.31)$$
$$= .5000 + .1217$$
$$= .6217$$

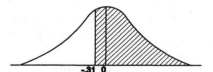

d.   We want $P(\text{understate the weight}) = .5$
To understate the weight, $x > 0$. Thus, we want to find μ so that $P(x > 0) = .5$

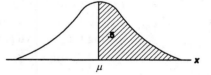

$$P(x > 0) = P\left(z > \frac{0 - \mu}{628}\right) = .5$$

From Table IV, Appendix B, $z_0 = 0$. To find μ, substitute into the z-score formula:

$$z_0 = \frac{x_0 - \mu}{\sigma} \Rightarrow 0 = \frac{0 - \mu}{628} \Rightarrow \mu = 0$$

Thus, the mean error should be set at 0.
We want $P(\text{understate the weight}) = .4$

To understate the weight, $x > 0$. Thus, we want to find μ so that $P(x > 0) = .4$

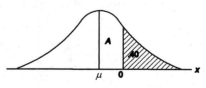

$A = .5 - .40 = .1$. Look up the area .1000 in the body of Table IV, Appendix B, $z_0 = .25$.

To find μ, substitute into the z-score formula:

$$z_0 = \frac{x_0 - \mu}{\sigma} \Rightarrow .25 = \frac{0 - \mu}{628} \Rightarrow \mu = 0 - (.25)628 = -157$$

Thus, the mean error should be set at -157.

4.195   a. $\mu = n \cdot p = 25(.05) = 1.25$
$\sigma = \sqrt{npq} = \sqrt{25(.05)(.95)} = 1.09$

Since μ is not an integer, x could not equal its mean.

b.   The event is $(x \geq 5)$. From Table II with $n = 25$ and $p = .05$:

$P(x \geq 5) = 1 - P(x \leq 4) = 1 - .993 = .007$

c.   Since the probability obtained in part **b** is so small, it is unlikely that 5% applies to this agency. The percentage is probably greater than 5%.

4.197   We know from the Empirical Rule that almost all the observations are larger than $\mu - 2\sigma$. ($\approx 95\%$ are between $\mu - 2\sigma$ and $\mu + 2\sigma$). Thus $\mu - 2\sigma > 100$.

For the binomial, $\mu = np = n(.4)$ and $\sigma = \sqrt{npq} = \sqrt{n(.4)(.6)} = \sqrt{.24n}$

$\mu - 2\sigma > 100 \Rightarrow .4n - 2\sqrt{.24n} > 100 \Rightarrow .4n - .98\sqrt{n} - 100 > 0$

Solving for $\sqrt{n}$, we get:

$$\sqrt{n} = \frac{.98 \pm \sqrt{.98^2 - 4(.4)(-100)}}{2(.4)} = \frac{.98 \pm 12.687}{.8}$$
$$\Rightarrow \sqrt{n} = 17.084 \Rightarrow n = 17.084^2 = 291.9 \approx 292$$

4.199   Even though the number of flaws per piece of siding has a Poisson distribution, the Central Limit Theorem implies that the distribution of the sample mean will be approximately normal with $\mu_{\bar{x}} = \mu = 2.5$ and $\sigma_{\bar{x}} = \frac{\sigma}{\sqrt{n}} = \frac{\sqrt{2.5}}{\sqrt{35}} = .2673$. Therefore,

$$P(\bar{x} > 2.1) + P\left(z > \frac{2.1 - 2.5}{\sqrt{2.5}/\sqrt{35}}\right) = P(z > -1.50) = .5 + .4332 = .9332$$

(using Table IV, Appendix B)

Inferences Based on a Single Sample: Estimation with Confidence Intervals

Chapter 5

5.1   a.   For $\alpha = .10$, $\alpha/2 = .10/2 = .05$. $z_{\alpha/2} = z_{.05}$ is the z–score with .05 of the area to the right of it. The area between 0 and $z_{.05}$ is $.5 - .05 = .4500$. Using Table IV, Appendix B, $z_{.05} = 1.645$.

      b.   For $\alpha = .01$, $\alpha/2 = .01/2 = .005$. $z_{\alpha/2} = z_{.005}$ is the z–score with .005 of the area to the right of it. The area between 0 and $z_{.005}$ is $.5 - .005 = .4950$. Using Table IV, Appendix B, $z_{.005} = 2.58$.

      c.   For $\alpha = .05$, $\alpha/2 = .05/2 = .025$. $z_{\alpha/2} = z_{.025}$ is the z–score with .025 of the area to the right of it. The area between 0 and $z_{.025}$ is $.5 - .025 = .4750$. Using Table IV, Appendix B, $z_{.025} = 1.96$.

      d.   For $\alpha = .20$, $\alpha/2 = .20/2 = .10$. $z_{\alpha/2} = z_{.10}$ is the z–score with .10 of the area to the right of it. The area between 0 and $z_{.10}$ is $.5 - .10 = .4000$. Using Table IV, Appendix B, $z_{.10} = 1.28$.

5.3   a.   For confidence coefficient .95, $\alpha = .05$ and $\alpha/2 = .05/2 = .025$. From Table IV, Appendix B, $z_{.025} = 1.96$. The confidence interval is:

$$\bar{x} \pm z_{.025}\frac{s}{\sqrt{n}} \Rightarrow 28 \pm 1.96\frac{\sqrt{12}}{\sqrt{75}} \Rightarrow 28 \pm .784 \Rightarrow (27.216, 28.784)$$

      b. $\bar{x} \pm z_{.025}\frac{s}{\sqrt{n}} \Rightarrow 102 \pm 1.96\frac{\sqrt{22}}{\sqrt{200}} \Rightarrow 102 \pm .65 \Rightarrow (101.35, 102.65)$

      c. $\bar{x} \pm z_{.025}\frac{s}{\sqrt{n}} \Rightarrow 15 \pm 1.96\frac{.3}{\sqrt{100}} \Rightarrow 15 \pm .0588 \Rightarrow (14.9412, 15.0588)$

      d. $\bar{x} \pm z_{.025}\frac{s}{\sqrt{n}} \Rightarrow 4.05 \pm 1.96\frac{.83}{\sqrt{100}} \Rightarrow 4.05 \pm .163 \Rightarrow (3.887, 4.213)$

      e.   No. Since the sample size in each part was large (n ranged from 75 to 200), the Central Limit Theorem indicates that the sampling distribution of is approximately normal.

5.5　**a.**　For confidence coefficient .95, $\alpha = .05$ and $\alpha/2 = .05/2 = .025$. From Table IV, Appendix B, $z_{.025} = 1.96$. The confidence interval is:

$$\bar{x} \pm z_{\alpha/2}\frac{s}{\sqrt{n}} \Rightarrow 26.2 \pm 1.96\frac{4.1}{\sqrt{70}} \Rightarrow 26.2 \pm .96 \Rightarrow (25.24, 27.16)$$

b.　The confidence coefficient of .95 means that in repeated sampling, 95% of all confidence intervals constructed will include μ.

c.　For confidence coefficient .99, $\alpha = .01$ and $\alpha/2 = .01/2 = .005$. From Table IV, Appendix B, $z_{.005} = 2.58$. The confidence interval is:

$$\bar{x} \pm z_{\alpha/2}\frac{s}{\sqrt{n}} \Rightarrow 26.2 \pm 2.58\frac{4.1}{\sqrt{70}} \Rightarrow 26.2 \pm 1.26 \Rightarrow (24.94, 27.46)$$

d.　As the confidence coefficient increases, the width of the confidence interval also increases.

e.　Yes. Since the sample size is 70, the Central Limit Theorem applies. This ensures the distribution of is normal, regardless of the original distribution.

5.7　A point estimator is a single value used to estimate the parameter, μ. An interval estimator is two values, an upper and lower bound, which define an interval with which we attempt to enclose the parameter, μ. An interval estimate also has a measure of confidence associated with it.

5.9　Yes. As long as the sample size is sufficiently large, the Central Limit Theorem says the distribution of is approximately normal regardless of the original distribution.

5.11　**a.**　The target population is the 500 CEOs who participated in the *Forbes'* survey.

b.　Using MINITAB, a sample of 50 CEOs was selected. The ranks of the 50 selected are:
9, 10, 14, 18, 19, 22, 25, 32, 38, 39, 45, 49, 50, 55, 60, 66, 69, 77, 96, 104, 106, 115, 147, 152, 192, 197, 209, 213, 229, 241, 245, 261, 268, 278, 283, 292, 305, 309, 325, 337, 342, 358, 364, 370, 376, 384, 405, 417, 433, 470.

c.　Using MINITAB, the descriptive statistics are:

Descriptive Statistics: PAY2005 ($mil)

```
Variable           N   N*   Mean  SE Mean  StDev  Minimum    Q1  Median     Q3
PAY2005 ($mil)    50    0  15.29     2.29  16.22     1.10  3.77    7.49  22.40

Variable        Maximum
PAY2005 ($mil)    69.66
```

The sample mean is $\bar{x} = 15.29$ and the sample standard deviation is $s = 16.22$.

d.　For confidence coefficient .99, $\alpha = .01$ and $\alpha/2 = .01/2 = .005$. From Table IV, Appendix B, $z_{.005} = 2.58$. The confidence interval is:

$$\bar{x} \pm z_{\alpha/2}\frac{s}{\sqrt{n}} \Rightarrow 15.29 \pm 2.58\frac{16.22}{\sqrt{50}} \Rightarrow 15.29 \pm 5.92 \Rightarrow (9.37,\ 21.21)$$

e. We are 99% confident that the true mean salary of all 500 CEOs in the *Forbes'* survey is between \$9.37 million and \$21.21 million.

f. Using MINITAB, the descriptive statistics for the entire data set are:

Descriptive Statistics: PAY2005 ($mil)

```
Variable            N   N*    Mean  SE Mean   StDev    Minimum     Q1  Median
PAY2005 ($mil)    497    3  10.930    0.931  20.749  0.000000000  2.838   5.540

Variable            Q3  Maximum
PAY2005 ($mil)  11.555  249.420
```

The true mean salary of all 500 CEOs is \$10.93 million. This value does fall within the 99% confidence interval that we found in part d.

5.13 a. For confidence coefficient .99, $\alpha = .01$ and $\alpha/2 = .01/2 = .005$. From Table IV, Appendix B, $z_{.005} = 2.58$. The 99% confidence interval is:

$$\bar{x} \pm z_{\alpha/2} \frac{s}{\sqrt{n}} \Rightarrow 141.31 \pm 2.58 \left(\frac{17.77}{\sqrt{100,000}} \right) \Rightarrow 141.31 \pm .145 \Rightarrow (141.165, \ 141.455)$$

b. We are 99% confident that the mean number of semester hours taken by all first–time candidates for the CPA exam is between 141.165 and 145.455.

c. Since the sample size was so large, no conditions must hold for the interpretation in part b to be valid.

5.15 a. For confidence coefficient .90, $\alpha = .10$ and $\alpha/2 = .10/2 = .05$. From Table IV, Appendix B, $z_{.05} = 1.645$. The confidence interval is:

$$\bar{x} \pm z_{\alpha/2} \frac{s}{\sqrt{n}} \Rightarrow 19 \pm 1.645 \frac{65}{\sqrt{265}} \Rightarrow 19 \pm 6.57$$
$$\Rightarrow (12.43, \ 25.57)$$

We are 90% confident that the mean change in SAT–Mathematics score is between 12.43 and 25.57 points.

b. For confidence coefficient .90, $\alpha = .10$ and $\alpha/2 = .10/2 = .05$. From Table IV, Appendix B, $z_{.05} = 1.645$. The confidence interval is:

$$\bar{x} \pm z_{\alpha/2} \frac{s}{\sqrt{n}} \Rightarrow 7 \pm 1.645 \frac{49}{\sqrt{265}} \Rightarrow 7 \pm 4.95$$
$$\Rightarrow (2.05, \ 11.95)$$

We are 90% confident that the mean change in SAT–Verbal score is between 2.05 and 11.95 points.

c. The SAT–Mathematics test would be the most likely of the two to have 15 as the mean change in score. This value of 15 is in the 90% confidence interval for the mean change in SAT–Mathematics score. However, 15 does not fall in the 90% confidence interval for the mean SAT–Verbal test.

5.17 a. Using MINITAB, the descriptive statistics are:

Descriptive Statistics: IQ25, IQ60

Variable	N	Mean	Median	TrMean	StDev	SE Mean
IQ25	36	66.83	66.50	66.69	14.36	2.39
IQ60	36	45.39	45.00	45.22	12.67	2.11

Variable	Minimum	Maximum	Q1	Q3
IQ25	41.00	94.00	54.25	80.00
IQ60	22.00	73.00	36.25	58.00

For confidence coefficient .99, $\alpha = .01$ and $\alpha/2 = .01/2 = .005$. From Table IV, Appendix B, $z_{.005} = 2.58$. The confidence interval is:

$$\bar{x} \pm z_{\alpha/2} \frac{s}{\sqrt{n}} \Rightarrow 66.83 \pm 2.58 \frac{14.36}{\sqrt{36}} \Rightarrow 66.83 \pm 6.17$$
$$\Rightarrow (60.66, \quad 73.00)$$

We are 99% confident that the mean raw IQ score for all 25–year–olds is between 60.66 and 73.00.

b. We must assume that the sample is random and that the observations are independent.

c. For confidence coefficient .95, $\alpha = .05$ and $\alpha/2 = .05/2 = .025$. From Table IV, Appendix B, $z_{.025} = 1.96$. The confidence interval is:

$$\bar{x} \pm z_{\alpha/2} \frac{s}{\sqrt{n}} \Rightarrow 45.39 \pm 1.96 \frac{12.67}{\sqrt{36}} \Rightarrow 45.39 \pm 4.14$$
$$\Rightarrow (41.25, \quad 49.53)$$

We are 95% confident that the mean raw IQ score for all 60–year–olds is between 41.25 and 49.53.

5.19 a. For confidence coefficient .95, $\alpha = .05$ and $\alpha/2 = .025$. From Table IV, Appendix B, $z_{.025} = 1.96$. The confidence interval is:

$$\bar{x} \pm z_{\alpha/2} \frac{s}{\sqrt{n}}$$

Younger: $4.17 \pm 1.96 \frac{.75}{\sqrt{241}} \Rightarrow 4.17 \pm .095 \Rightarrow (4.075, 4.265)$

We are 95% confident that the mean job satisfaction score for all adults in the younger age group is between 4.075 and 4.265.

Middle–Age: $4.04 \pm 1.96\dfrac{.81}{\sqrt{768}} \Rightarrow 4.04 \pm .057 \Rightarrow (3.983, 4.097)$

We are 95% confident that the mean job satisfaction score for all adults in the middle–age age group is between 3.983 and 4.097.

Older: $4.31 \pm 1.96\dfrac{.82}{\sqrt{677}} \Rightarrow 4.31 \pm .062 \Rightarrow (4.248, 4.372)$

We are 95% confident that the mean job satisfaction score for all adults in the older age group is between 4.248 and 4.372.

b. Let y = number of 95% confidence intervals that do not contain the population mean in 3 trials. Then y is a binomial random variable with $n = 3$ and $p = .05$.

$$P(y \geq 1) = 1 - P(y = 0) = 1 - \binom{3}{0}.05^0.95^3 = 1 - .857375 = .142625$$

Thus, it is more likely that at least one of three intervals will not contain the population mean than it is for a single confidence interval to miss the population mean.

The probability that a single confidence interval will not contain the population mean is .05.

5.21 a. For confidence coefficient .80, $\alpha = 1 - .80 = .20$ and $\alpha/2 = .20/2 = .10$. From Table IV, Appendix B, $z_{.10} = 1.28$. From Table VI, with df $= n - 1 = 5 - 1 = 4$, $t_{.10} = 1.533$.

b. For confidence coefficient .90, $\alpha = 1 - .90 = .05$ and $\alpha/2 = .10/2 = .05$. From Table IV, Appendix B, $z_{.05} = 1.645$. From Table VI, with df $= n - 1 = 5 - 1 = 4$, $t_{.05} = 2.132$.

c. For confidence coefficient .95, $\alpha = 1 - .95 = .05$ and $\alpha/2 = .05/2 = .025$. From Table IV, Appendix B, $z_{.025} = 1.96$. From Table VI, with df $= n - 1 = 5 - 1 = 4$, $t_{.025} = 2.776$.

d. For confidence coefficient .98, $\alpha = 1 - .98 = .02$ and $\alpha/2 = .02/2 = .01$. From Table IV, Appendix B, $z_{.01} = 2.33$. From Table VI, with df $= n - 1 = 5 - 1 = 4$, $t_{.01} = 3.747$.

e. For confidence coefficient .99, $\alpha = 1 - .99 = .02$ and $\alpha/2 = .02/2 = .005$. From Table IV, Appendix B, $z_{.005} = 2.575$. From Table VI, with df $= n - 1 = 5 - 1 = 4$, $t_{.005} = 4.604$.

f. Both the t- and z-distributions are symmetric around 0 and mound-shaped. The t–distribution is more spread out than the z-distribution.

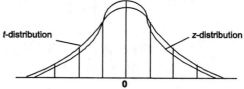

5.23 a. $P(-t_0 < t < t_0) = .95$ where df $= 10$
Because of symmetry, the statement can be written
$P(0 < t < t_0) = .475$ where df $= 10$
$\Rightarrow P(t \geq t_0) = .025$
$t_0 = 2.228$

b. $P(t \le -t_0 \text{ or } t \ge t_0) = .05$ where df = 10

$\Rightarrow 2P(t \ge t_0) = .05$

$\Rightarrow P(t \ge t_0) = .025$ where df = 10

$t_0 = 2.228$

c. $P(t \le t_0) = .05$ where df = 10

Because of symmetry, the statement can be written

$\Rightarrow P(t \ge -t_0) = .05$ where df = 10

$t_0 = -1.812$

d. $P(t < -t_0 \text{ or } t > t_0) = .10$ where df = 20

$\Rightarrow 2P(t > t_0) = .10$

$\Rightarrow P(t > t_0) = .05$ where df = 20

$t_0 = 1.725$

e. $P(t \le -t_0 \text{ or } t \ge t_0) = .01$ where df = 5

$\Rightarrow 2P(t \ge t_0) = .01$

$\Rightarrow P(t \ge t_0) = .005$ where df = 5

$t_0 = 4.032$

5.25 First, we must compute $\bar{x}$ and s.

$$\bar{x} = \frac{\sum x}{n} = \frac{30}{6} = 5$$

$$s^2 = \frac{\sum x^2 - \frac{\left(\sum x\right)^2}{n}}{n-1} = \frac{176 - \frac{(30)^2}{6}}{6-1} = \frac{26}{5} = 5.2$$

$$s = \sqrt{5.2} = 2.2804$$

a. For confidence coefficient .90, $\alpha = 1 - .90 = .10$ and $\alpha/2 = .10/2 = .05$. From Table VI, Appendix B, with df = $n - 1 = 6 - 1 = 5$, $t_{.05} = 2.015$. The 90% confidence interval is:

$$\bar{x} \pm t_{0.5} \frac{s}{\sqrt{n}} \Rightarrow 5 \pm 2.015 \frac{2.2804}{\sqrt{6}} \Rightarrow 5 \pm 1.876 \Rightarrow (3.124, 6.876)$$

b. For confidence coefficient .95, $\alpha = 1 - .95 = .05$ and $\alpha/2 = .05/2 = .025$. From Table VI, Appendix B, with df = $n - 1 = 6 - 1 = 5$, $t_{.025} = 2.571$. The 95% confidence interval is:

$$\bar{x} \pm t_{.025} \frac{s}{\sqrt{n}} \Rightarrow 5 \pm 2.571 \frac{2.2804}{\sqrt{6}} \Rightarrow 5 \pm 2.394 \Rightarrow (2.606, 7.394)$$

c. For confidence coefficient .99, $\alpha = 1 - .99 = .01$ and $\alpha/2 = .01/2 = .005$. From Table VI, Appendix B, with df $= n - 1 = 6 - 1 = 5$, $t_{.005} = 4.032$. The 99% confidence interval is:

$$\bar{x} \pm t_{.005} \frac{s}{\sqrt{n}} \Rightarrow 5 \pm 4.032 \frac{2.2804}{\sqrt{6}} \Rightarrow 5 \pm 3.754 \Rightarrow (1.246, 8.754)$$

d. a) For confidence coefficient .90, $\alpha = 1 - .90 = .10$ and $\alpha/2 = .10/2 = .05$. From Table VI, Appendix B, with df $= n - 1 = 25 - 1 = 24$, $t_{.05} = 1.711$. The 90% confidence interval is:

$$\bar{x} \pm t_{.05} \frac{s}{\sqrt{n}} \Rightarrow 5 \pm 1.711 \frac{2.2804}{\sqrt{25}} \Rightarrow 5 \pm .780 \Rightarrow (4.220, 5.780)$$

b) For confidence coefficient .95, $\alpha = 1 - .95 = .05$ and $\alpha/2 = .05/2 = .025$. From Table VI, Appendix B, with df $= n - 1 = 25 - 1 = 24$, $t_{.025} = 2.064$. The 95% confidence interval is:

$$\bar{x} \pm t_{.025} \frac{s}{\sqrt{n}} \Rightarrow 5 \pm 2.064 \frac{2.2804}{\sqrt{25}} \Rightarrow 5 \pm .941 \Rightarrow (4.059, 5.941)$$

c) For confidence coefficient .99, $\alpha = 1 - .99 = .01$ and $\alpha/2 = .01/2 = .005$. From Table VI, Appendix B, with df $= n - 1 = 25 - 1 = 24$, $t_{.005} = 2.797$. The 99% confidence interval is:

$$\bar{x} \pm t_{.005} \frac{s}{\sqrt{n}} \Rightarrow 5 \pm 2.797 \frac{2.2804}{\sqrt{25}} \Rightarrow 5 \pm 1.276 \Rightarrow (3.724, 6.276)$$

Increasing the sample size decreases the width of the confidence interval.

5.27 For confidence coefficient .90, $\alpha = .10$ and $\alpha/2 = .10/2 = .05$. From Table VI, Appendix B, with df $= n - 1 = 25 - 1 = 24$, $t_{.05} = 1.711$. The 90% confidence interval is:

$$\bar{x} \pm t_{.05} \frac{s}{\sqrt{n}} \Rightarrow 75.4 \pm 1.711 \frac{10.9}{\sqrt{25}} \Rightarrow 75.4 \pm 3.73 \Rightarrow (71.67, \ \ 79.13)$$

We are 90% confident that the mean breaking strength of the white wood is between 71.67 and 79.13.

5.29 a. First, we must compute some preliminary satistics:

$$\bar{x} = \frac{\sum x}{n} = \frac{28.856}{10} = 2.8856$$

$$s^2 = \frac{\sum x^2 - \frac{\left(\sum x\right)^2}{n}}{n-1} = \frac{221.90161 - \frac{(28.856)^2}{10}}{10-1} = 15.4039$$

$$s = \sqrt{s^2} = \sqrt{15.4039} = 3.925$$

For confidence coefficient .99, $\alpha = .01$ and $\alpha/2 = .01/2 = .005$. From Table VI, Appendix B, with df $= n - 1 = 10 - 1 = 9$, $t_{.005} = 3.250$. The confidence interval is:

$$\bar{x} \pm t_{.005}\frac{s}{\sqrt{n}} \Rightarrow 2.8856 \pm 3.250\frac{3.925}{\sqrt{10}} \Rightarrow 2.8856 \pm 4.034 \Rightarrow (-1.148, 6.919)$$

b.   First, we must compute some preliminary statistics:

$$\bar{x} = \frac{\sum x}{n} = \frac{4.083}{10} = .4083$$

$$s^2 = \frac{\sum x^2 - \dfrac{\left(\sum x\right)^2}{n}}{n-1} = \frac{2.227425 - \dfrac{(4.083)^2}{10}}{10-1} = .06226$$

$$s = \sqrt{s^2} = \sqrt{0.06226} = .2495$$

For confidence coefficient .99, $\alpha = .01$ and $\alpha/2 = .01/2 = .005$. From Table VI, Appendix B, with df $= n - 1 = 10 - 1 = 9$, $t_{.005} = 3.250$. The confidence interval is:

$$\bar{x} \pm t_{.005}\frac{s}{\sqrt{n}} \Rightarrow .4083 \pm 3.250\frac{.2495}{\sqrt{10}} \Rightarrow .4083 \pm .2564 \Rightarrow (.1519, .6647)$$

c.   We are 99% confident that the mean lead level in water specimens from Crystal Lake Manors is between -1.148 and 6.919 or 0 and 6.919 μ/L since no value can be less than 0.

We are 99% confident that the mean copper level in water specimens from Crystal Lake Manors is between .1519 and .6647 mg/L.

d.   The phrase "99% confident" means that if repeated samples of size n were selected and 99% confidence intervals constructed for the mean, 99% of all intervals constructed would contain the mean.

5.31   a.   From the printout, the 95% confidence interval is $(-2,237.61\%, 12,108.44\%)$. We are 95% confident that the true mean 5-year revenue growth rate for the 2005 Technology Fast 500 is between $-2,237.61\%$ and $12,108.44\%$.

b.   The population being sampled from must be normally distributed.

c.   From the stem-and-leaf display in the printout, the data appear to be skewed to the right. The data do not appear to have come from a normal distribution. Therefore, the 95% confidence interval in part **a** may not be valid.

5.33   a.   Using MINITAB, the descriptive statistics are:

Descriptive Statistics: Skid

Variable	N	N*	Mean	SE Mean	StDev	Minimum	Q1	Median	Q3	Maximum
Skid	20	0	358.5	26.3	117.8	141.0	276.0	367.5	438.0	574.0

For confidence coefficient .95, $\alpha = .05$ and $\alpha/2 = .05/2 = .025$. From Table VI, Appendix B, with df $= n - 1 = 20 - 1 = 19$, $t_{.025} = 2.093$. The 95% confidence interval is:

$$\bar{x} \pm t_{.05}\frac{s}{\sqrt{n}} \Rightarrow 358.5 \pm 2.093\frac{117.8}{\sqrt{20}} \Rightarrow 358.5 \pm 55.13 \Rightarrow (303.37,\ 413.63)$$

b.   We are 95% confident that the mean skidding distance is between 303.37 and 413.63 meters.

c.   In order for the inference to be valid, the skidding distances must be from a normal distribution. We will use the four methods to check for normality. First, we will look at a histogram of the data. Using MINITAB, the histogram of the data is:

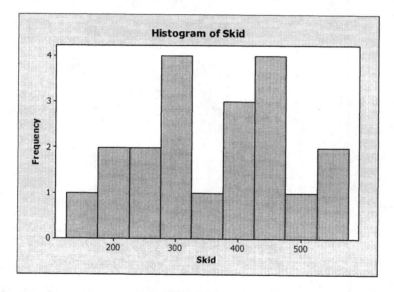

From the histogram, the data appear to be fairly mound-shaped. This indicates that the data may be normal.

Next, we look at the intervals $\bar{x} \pm s$, $\bar{x} \pm 2s$, $\bar{x} \pm 3s$. If the proportions of observations falling in each interval are approximately .68, .95, and 1.00, then the data are approximately normal. Using MINITAB, the summary statistics are:

$\bar{x} \pm s \Rightarrow 358.5 \pm 117.8 \Rightarrow (240.7,\ 476.3)$ 14 of the 20 values fall in this interval. The proportion is .70. This is very close to the .68 we would expect if the data were normal.

$\bar{x} \pm 2s \Rightarrow 358.5 \pm 2(117.8) \Rightarrow 358.5 \pm 235.6 \Rightarrow (122.9,\ 594.1)$ 20 of the 20 values fall in this interval. The proportion is 1.00. This is a larger than the .95 we would expect if the data were normal.

$\bar{x} \pm 3s \Rightarrow 358.5 \pm 3(117.8) \Rightarrow 358.5 \pm 353.4 \Rightarrow (5.1, \ 711.9)$ 20 of the 20 values fall in this interval. The proportion is 1.00. This is exactly the 1.00 we would expect if the data were normal.

From this method, it appears that the data may be normal.

Next, we look at the ratio of the IQR to s. $IQR = Q_U - Q_L = 438 - 276 = 162$.

$\dfrac{IQR}{s} = \dfrac{162}{117.8} = 1.37$ This is fairly close to the 1.3 we would expect if the data were normal. This method indicates the data may be normal.

Finally, using MINITAB, the normal probability plot is:

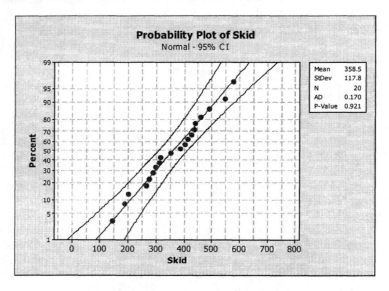

Since the data form a fairly straight line, the data may be normal.

From above, all the methods indicate the data may be normal. It appears that the assumption that the data come from a normal distribution is probably valid.

d.   No. A distance of 425 meters falls above the 95% confidence interval that was computed in part **a**. It would be very unlikely to observe a mean skidding distance of at least 425 meters.

5.35 a. The population from which the sample was drawn is the Forbes 339 Biggest Private companies.

b. Using MINITAB, the descriptive statistics are:

Descriptive Statistics: Revenue

Variable	N	N*	Mean	SE Mean	StDev	Minimum	Q1	Median	Q3	Maximum
Revenue	15	0	2.791	0.583	2.258	1.050	1.400	1.800	3.080	8.230

For confidence coefficient .98, $\alpha = .02$ and $\alpha/2 = .02/2 = .01$. From Table VI, Appendix B, with df $= n - 1 = 15 - 1 = 14$, $t_{.01} = 2.624$. The 98% confidence interval is:

$$\bar{x} \pm t_{.025}\frac{s}{\sqrt{n}} \Rightarrow 2.791 \pm 2.624\frac{2.258}{\sqrt{15}} \Rightarrow 2.791 \pm 1.530 \Rightarrow (1.261, \ 4.321)$$

c. We are 98% confident that the mean revenue is between $1.261 and $4.321 billion .

d. The population must be normally distributed in order for the procedure used in part **b** to be valid.

e. Yes. The value of $3.04 billion dollars falls in the 98% confidence interval computed in part **b**. Therefore, we should believe *Forbes'* claim.

5.37 The sample size is large enough if $\hat{p} \pm 3\sigma_{\hat{p}}$ lies within the interval (0, 1).

$$\hat{p} \pm 3\sigma_{\hat{p}} \Rightarrow \hat{p} \pm 3\sqrt{\frac{pq}{n}} \Rightarrow \hat{p} \pm 3\sqrt{\frac{\hat{p}\hat{q}}{n}}$$

a. When $n = 400$, $\hat{p} = .10$:

$$.10 \pm 3\sqrt{\frac{.10(1-.10)}{400}} \Rightarrow .10 \pm .045 \Rightarrow (.055, .145)$$

Since the interval lies completely in the interval (0, 1), the normal approximation will be adequate.

b. When $n = 50$, $\hat{p} = .10$:

$$.10 \pm 3\sqrt{\frac{.10(1-.10)}{50}} \Rightarrow .10 \pm .127 \Rightarrow (-.027, .227)$$

Since the interval does not lie completely in the interval (0, 1), the normal approximation will not be adequate.

c. When $n = 20$, $\hat{p} = .5$:

$$.5 \pm 3\sqrt{\frac{.5(1-.5)}{20}} \Rightarrow .5 \pm .335 \Rightarrow (.165, .835)$$

Since the interval lies completely in the interval $(0, 1)$, the normal approximation will be adequate.

d. When $n = 20$, $\hat{p} = .3$:

$$.3 \pm 3\sqrt{\frac{.3(1-.3)}{20}} \Rightarrow .3 \pm .307 \Rightarrow (-.007, .607)$$

Since the interval does not lie completely in the interval $(0, 1)$, the normal approximation will not be adequate.

5.39 a. The sample size is large enough if the interval $\hat{p} \pm 3\sigma_{\hat{p}}$ does not include 0 or 1.

$$\hat{p} \pm 3\sigma_{\hat{p}} \Rightarrow \hat{p} \pm 3\sqrt{\frac{pq}{n}} \Rightarrow \hat{p} \pm 3\sqrt{\frac{\hat{p}\hat{q}}{n}} \Rightarrow .46 \pm 3\sqrt{\frac{.46(1-.46)}{225}} \Rightarrow .46 \pm .0997$$
$$\Rightarrow (.3603, .5597)$$

Since the interval lies within the interval $(0, 1)$, the normal approximation will be adequate.

b. For confidence coefficient .95, $\alpha = .05$ and $\alpha/2 = .025$. From Table IV, Appendix B, $z_{.025} = 1.96$. The 95% confidence interval is:

$$\hat{p} \pm z_{.025}\sqrt{\frac{pq}{n}} \Rightarrow \hat{p} \pm 1.96\sqrt{\frac{\hat{p}\hat{q}}{n}} \Rightarrow .46 \pm 1.96\sqrt{\frac{.46(1-.46)}{225}} \Rightarrow .46 \pm .065$$
$$\Rightarrow (.395, .525)$$

c. We are 95% confident the true value of p will fall between .395 and .525.

d. "95% confidence interval" means that if repeated samples of size 225 were selected from the population and 95% confidence intervals formed, 95% of all confidence intervals will contain the true value of p.

5.41 a. The point estimate of p is $\hat{p} = \dfrac{x}{n} = \dfrac{414}{900} = .46$.

b. To see if the sample size is sufficiently large:

$$\hat{p} \pm 3\sigma_{\hat{p}} \approx \hat{p} \pm 3\sqrt{\frac{\hat{p}\hat{q}}{n}} \Rightarrow .46 \pm 3\sqrt{\frac{.46(.54)}{900}} \Rightarrow .46 \pm .050 \Rightarrow (.41, .51)$$

Since the interval is wholly contained in the interval (0, 1), we may conclude that the normal approximation is reasonable.

For confidence coefficient .90, $\alpha = .10$ and $\alpha/2 = .10/2 = .05$. From Table IV, Appendix B, $z_{.05} = 1.645$. The confidence interval is:

$$\hat{p} \pm z_{.05}\sqrt{\frac{\hat{p}\hat{q}}{n}} \Rightarrow .46 \pm 1.645\sqrt{\frac{.46(.54)}{900}} \Rightarrow .46 \pm .027 \Rightarrow (.433, \ .487)$$

c. We are 90% confident that the true proportion of contractors in the U.S. who have a company website or will have one by the end of the year is between .433 and .487.

d. The meaning of "90% confident" is that in repeated sampling, 90% of all confidence intervals constructed will contain the true proportion and 10% will not.

5.43 a. The point estimate of p is $\hat{p} = \dfrac{x}{n} = \dfrac{35}{1,165} = .030$.

b. To see if the sample size is sufficiently large:

$$\hat{p} \pm 3\sigma_{\hat{p}} \approx \hat{p} \pm 3\sqrt{\frac{\hat{p}\hat{q}}{n}} \Rightarrow .030 \pm 3\sqrt{\frac{.03(.97)}{1,165}} \Rightarrow .030 \pm .015 \Rightarrow (.015, \ .045)$$

Since the interval is wholly contained in the interval (0, 1), we may conclude that the normal approximation is reasonable.

For confidence coefficient .95, $\alpha = .05$ and $\alpha/2 = .05/2 = .025$. From Table IV, Appendix B, $z_{.025} = 1.96$. The confidence interval is:

$$\hat{p} \pm z_{.025}\sqrt{\frac{\hat{p}\hat{q}}{n}} \Rightarrow .030 \pm 1.96\sqrt{\frac{.03(.97)}{1,165}} \Rightarrow .030 \pm .0098 \Rightarrow (.0202, \ .0398)$$

c. We are 95% confident that the true proportion of drivers that use their cell phone while driving is between .0202 and .0398.

5.45 a. Since all the people surveyed were from Muncie, Indiana, the population of interest is all consumers in Muncie, Indiana.

b. The characteristic of interest in the population is the proportion of shoppers who believe that "Made in the USA" means that 100% of labor and materials are from the USA.

c. The point estimate of p is $\hat{p} = \dfrac{x}{n} = \dfrac{64}{106} = .604$.

To see if the sample size is sufficiently large:

$$\hat{p} \pm 3\sigma_{\hat{p}} \approx \hat{p} \pm 3\sqrt{\frac{\hat{p}\hat{q}}{n}} \Rightarrow .604 \pm 3\sqrt{\frac{.604(.396)}{106}} \Rightarrow .604 \pm .143 \Rightarrow (.461, \ .747)$$

Since the interval is wholly contained in the interval (0, 1), we may conclude that the normal approximation is reasonable.

For confidence coefficient .90, $\alpha = .10$ and $\alpha/2 = .10/2 = .05$. From Table IV, Appendix B, $z_{.05} = 1.645$. The confidence interval is:

$$\hat{p} \pm z_{.05}\sqrt{\frac{\hat{p}\hat{q}}{n}} \Rightarrow .604 \pm 1.645\sqrt{\frac{.604(.396)}{106}} \Rightarrow .604 \pm .078 \Rightarrow (.526, \ .682)$$

d. We are 90% confident that the true proportion of shoppers who believe that "Made in the USA" means that 100% of labor and materials are from the USA is between .526 and .682.

e. 90% confidence means that if we took repeated samples of size 106 and computed 90% confidence intervals for the true proportion shoppers who believe that "Made in the USA" means that 100% of labor and materials are from the USA, 90% of the intervals computed will contain the true proportion.

5.47 a. Of the 1000 observations, 29% said they would never give personal information to a company $\Rightarrow \hat{p} = .29$

To see if the sample size is sufficiently large:

$$\hat{p} \pm 3\sigma_{\hat{p}} \approx \hat{p} \pm 3\sqrt{\frac{\hat{p}\hat{q}}{n}} \Rightarrow .29 \pm 3\sqrt{\frac{.29(.71)}{1000}} \Rightarrow .29 \pm .043 \Rightarrow (.247, .333)$$

Since this interval is wholly contained in the interval (0, 1), we may conclude that the normal approximation is reasonable.

b. For confidence coefficient .95, $\alpha = 1 - .95 = .05$ and $\alpha/2 = .05/2 = .025$. From Table IV, Appendix B, $z_{.025} = 1.96$. The 95% confidence interval is:

$$\hat{p} \pm z_{.025}\sqrt{\frac{\hat{p}\hat{q}}{n}} \Rightarrow .29 \pm 1.96\sqrt{\frac{.29(.71)}{1000}} \Rightarrow .29 \pm .028 \Rightarrow (.262, .318)$$

We are 95% confident that the proportion of Internet users who would never give personal information to a company is between .262 and .318.

c. We must assume that the sample is a random sample from the population.

5.49 a. The point estimate of p is $\hat{p} = \frac{x}{n} = \frac{52}{60} = .867$.

b. To see if the sample size is sufficiently large:

$$\hat{p} \pm 3\sigma_{\hat{p}} \approx \hat{p} \pm 3\sqrt{\frac{\hat{p}\hat{q}}{n}} \Rightarrow .867 \pm 3\sqrt{\frac{.867(.133)}{60}} \Rightarrow .867 \pm .132 \Rightarrow (.735, \ .999)$$

Since the interval is wholly contained in the interval (0, 1), we may conclude that the normal approximation is reasonable.

For confidence coefficient .95, $\alpha = .05$ and $\alpha/2 = .05/2 = .025$. From Table IV, Appendix B, $z_{.025} = 1.96$. The confidence interval is:

$$\hat{p} \pm z_{.025}\sqrt{\frac{\hat{p}\hat{q}}{n}} \Rightarrow .867 \pm 1.96\sqrt{\frac{.867(.133)}{60}} \Rightarrow .867 \pm .085 \Rightarrow (.781, \ .953)$$

c. We are 95% confident that the true proportion of Wal-Mart stores in California that have more than 2 inaccurately priced items per 100 scanned is between .781 and .953.

d. If 99% of the California Wal-Mart stores are in compliance, then only 1% or .01 would not be. However, we found the 95% confidence interval for the proportion that are not in compliance is between .781 and .953. The value of .01 is not in this interval. Thus, it is not a likely value. This claim is not believable.

5.51 We will use a 99% confidence interval to estimate the true proportion of mailed items that are delivered on time.

First, we must compute $\hat{p}$: $\hat{p} = \dfrac{x}{n} = \dfrac{282,200}{332,000} = .85$

To see if the sample size is sufficiently large:

$$\hat{p} \pm 3\sigma_{\hat{p}} \approx \hat{p} \pm 3\sqrt{\frac{\hat{p}\hat{q}}{n}} \Rightarrow .85 \pm 3\sqrt{\frac{.85(.15)}{332,000}} \Rightarrow .85 \pm .002 \Rightarrow (.848, .852)$$

Since this interval is wholly contained in the interval (0, 1), we may conclude that the normal approximation is reasonable.

For confidence coefficient .99, $\alpha = .01$ and $\alpha/2 = .01/2 = .005$. From Table IV, Appendix B, $z_{.005} = 2.58$. The confidence interval is:

$$\hat{p} \pm z_{.005}\sqrt{\frac{pq}{n}} \approx \hat{p} \pm 2.58\sqrt{\frac{\hat{p}\hat{q}}{n}} \Rightarrow .85 \pm 2.58\sqrt{\frac{.85(.15)}{332,000}} \Rightarrow .85 \pm .002 \Rightarrow (.848, .852)$$

We are 99% confident that the true percentage of items delivered on time by the U.S. Postal Service is between 84.8% and 85.2%.

5.53 a. An estimate of σ is obtained from:

$$\text{range} \approx 4s$$

$$s \approx \frac{\text{range}}{4} = \frac{34-30}{4} = 1$$

To compute the necessary sample size, use

$$n = \frac{\left(z_{\alpha/2}\right)^2 \sigma^2}{(SE)^2} \quad \text{where } \alpha = 1 - .90 = .10 \text{ and } \alpha/2 = .05.$$

From Table IV, Appendix B, $z_{.05} = 1.645$. Thus,

$$n = \frac{(1.645)^2 (1)^2}{.2^2} = 67.65 \approx 68$$

  b. A less conservative estimate of σ is obtained from:

$$\text{range} \approx 6s$$

$$s \approx \frac{\text{range}}{6} = \frac{34-30}{6} = .6667$$

Thus, $n = \dfrac{\left(z_{\alpha/2}\right)^2 \sigma^2}{(SE)^2} = \dfrac{(1.645)^2 (.6667)^2}{.2^2} = 30.07 \approx 31$

5.55 For confidence coefficient .90, $\alpha = .10$ and $\alpha/2 = .05$. From Table IV, Appendix B, $z_{.05} = 1.645$.

We know $\hat{p}$ is in the middle of the interval, so $\hat{p} = \dfrac{.54 + .26}{2} = .4$

The confidence interval is $\hat{p} \pm z_{.05} \sqrt{\dfrac{\hat{p}\hat{q}}{n}} \Rightarrow .4 \pm 1.645 \sqrt{\dfrac{.4(.6)}{n}}$

We know $.4 - 1.645 \sqrt{\dfrac{.4(.6)}{n}} = .26$

$$\Rightarrow .4 - \frac{.8059}{\sqrt{n}} = .26$$

$$\Rightarrow .4 - .26 = \frac{.8059}{\sqrt{n}} \Rightarrow \sqrt{n} = \frac{.8059}{.14} = 5.756$$

$$\Rightarrow n = 5.756^2 = 33.1 \approx 34$$

5.57   a.   The width of a confidence interval is $2(SE) = 2z_{\alpha/2}\dfrac{\sigma}{\sqrt{n}}$

For confidence coefficient .95, $\alpha = 1 - .95 = .05$ and $\alpha/2 = .05/2 = .025$. From Table IV, Appendix B, $z_{.025} = 1.96$.

For $n = 16$,
$$W = 2z_{\alpha/2}\frac{\sigma}{\sqrt{n}} = 2(1.96)\frac{1}{\sqrt{16}} = 0.98$$

For $n = 25$,
$$W = 2z_{\alpha/2}\frac{\sigma}{\sqrt{n}} = 2(1.96)\frac{1}{\sqrt{25}} = 0.784$$

For $n = 49$,
$$W = 2z_{\alpha/2}\frac{\sigma}{\sqrt{n}} = 2(1.96)\frac{1}{\sqrt{49}} = 0.56$$

For $n = 100$,
$$W = 2z_{\alpha/2}\frac{\sigma}{\sqrt{n}} = 2(1.96)\frac{1}{\sqrt{100}} = 0.392$$

For $n = 400$,
$$W = 2z_{\alpha/2}\frac{\sigma}{\sqrt{n}} = 2(1.96)\frac{1}{\sqrt{400}} = 0.196$$

   b.

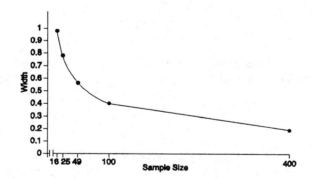

5.59   For confidence coefficient .90, $\alpha = .10$ and $\alpha/2 = .10/2 = .05$. From Table IV, Appendix B, $z_{.05} = 1.645$. Thus,

$$n = \frac{(z_{\alpha/2})^2 \sigma^2}{(SE)^2} = \frac{1.645^2 (10.9)^2}{4^2} = 20.09 \approx 21$$

Thus, we would need a sample of size 21.

5.61   For confidence coefficient .90, $\alpha = .10$ and $\alpha/2 = .10/2 = .05$. From Table IV, Appendix B, $z_{.05} = 1.645$. Since we have no estimate given for the value of p, we will use .5. The sample size is:

$$n = \frac{z_{\alpha/2}^2 pq}{(SE)^2} = \frac{1.645^2(.5)(.5)}{.02^2} = 1,691.3 \approx 1,692$$

5.63   For confidence coefficient .99, $\alpha = .01$ and $\alpha/2 = .01/2 = .005$. From Table IV, Appendix B, $z_{.005} = 2.575$. From the previous estimate, we will use $\hat{p} = .333$ to estimate p.

$$n = \frac{z_{\alpha/2}^2 pq}{(SE)^2} = \frac{2.575^2(.333)(.667)}{.01^2} = 14,727.3 \approx 14,728$$

5.65   To compute the needed sample size, use

$$n = \frac{(z_{\alpha/2})^2 \sigma^2}{(SE)^2}$$ where $\alpha = 1 - .95 = .05$ and $\alpha/2 = .05/2 = .025$.

From Table IV, Appendix B, $z_{.025} = 1.96$.

Thus, for $s = 10$, $n = \dfrac{(1.96)^2(10)^2}{3^2} = 42.68 \approx 43$

For $s = 20$, $n = \dfrac{(1.96)^2(20)^2}{3^2} = 170.74 \approx 171$

For $s = 30$, $n = \dfrac{(1.96)^2(30)^2}{3^2} = 384.16 \approx 385$

5.67   The bound is $SE = .05$. For confidence coefficient .99, $\alpha = 1 - .99 = .01$ and $\alpha/2 = .01/2 = .005$. From Table IV, Appendix B, $z_{.005} = 2.575$.

We estimate p with $= 11/27 = .407$. Thus,

$$n = \frac{(z_{\alpha/2})^2 pq}{(SE)^2} = \frac{2.575^2(.407)(.593)}{.05^2} \approx 640.1 \Rightarrow 641$$

The necessary sample size would be 641. The sample was not large enough.

5.69   a.   Percentage sampled $= \dfrac{n}{N}(100\%) = \dfrac{1000}{2500}(100\%) = 40\%$

Finite population correction factor:
$$\sqrt{\dfrac{N-n}{N}} = \sqrt{\dfrac{2500-1000}{2500}} = \sqrt{.6} = .7746$$

b.   Percentage sampled $= \dfrac{n}{N}(100\%) = \dfrac{1000}{5000}(100\%) = 20\%$

Finite population correction factor:
$$\sqrt{\dfrac{N-n}{N}} = \sqrt{\dfrac{5000-1000}{5000}} = \sqrt{.8} = .8944$$

c.   Percentage sampled $= \dfrac{n}{N}(100\%) = \dfrac{1000}{10,000}(100\%) = 10\%$

Finite population correction factor:
$$\sqrt{\dfrac{N-n}{N}} = \sqrt{\dfrac{10,000-1000}{10,000}} = \sqrt{.9} = .9487$$

d.   Percentage sampled $= \dfrac{n}{N}(100\%) = \dfrac{1000}{100,000}(100\%) = 1\%$

Finite population correction factor:
$$\sqrt{\dfrac{N-n}{N}} = \sqrt{\dfrac{100,000-1000}{100,000}} = \sqrt{.99} = .995$$

5.71   a. $\hat{\sigma}_{\bar{x}} = \dfrac{s}{\sqrt{n}}\sqrt{\dfrac{N-n}{N}} = \dfrac{50}{\sqrt{2000}}\sqrt{\dfrac{10,000-2000}{10,000}} = 1.00$

b. $\hat{\sigma}_{\bar{x}} = \dfrac{50}{\sqrt{4000}}\sqrt{\dfrac{10,000-4000}{10,000}} = .6124$

c. $\hat{\sigma}_{\bar{x}} = \dfrac{50}{\sqrt{10,000}}\sqrt{\dfrac{10,000-10,000}{10,000}} = 0$

d.   As n increases, $\sigma_{\bar{x}}$ decreases.

e.   We are computing the standard error of $\bar{x}$. If the entire population is sampled, then $\bar{x} = \mu$. There is no sampling error, so $\sigma_{\bar{x}} = 0$.

Inferences Based on a Single Sample: Estimation with Confidence Intervals   153

5.73 The approximate 95% confidence interval for p is

$$\hat{p} \pm 2\hat{\sigma}_{\hat{p}} \Rightarrow \hat{p} \pm 2\sqrt{\frac{\hat{p}(1-\hat{p})}{n}}\sqrt{\frac{N-n}{N}}$$

$$\Rightarrow .42 \pm 2\sqrt{\frac{.42(.58)}{1600}}\sqrt{\frac{6000-1600}{6000}} \Rightarrow .42 \pm .021 \Rightarrow (.399, .441)$$

5.75   a. $\bar{x} = \dfrac{\sum x}{n} = \dfrac{1081}{30} = 36.0333$

$$s^2 = \frac{\sum x^2 - \dfrac{\left(\sum x\right)^2}{n}}{n-1} = 41,747 - \frac{1081^2}{30} = 96.3782$$

$$\hat{\mu} = \bar{x} = 36.0333$$

$$\bar{x} \pm 2\hat{\sigma}_{\bar{x}} \Rightarrow \bar{x} \pm 2\frac{s}{\sqrt{n}}\sqrt{\frac{N-n}{N}}$$

$$\Rightarrow 36.0333 \pm 2\frac{\sqrt{96.3782}}{\sqrt{30}}\sqrt{\frac{300-30}{300}} \Rightarrow 36.0333 \pm 3.4008$$

$$\Rightarrow (32.6325, 39.4341)$$

b. $\hat{p} = \dfrac{x}{n} = \dfrac{21}{30} = .7$

$$\bar{x} \pm 2\hat{\sigma}_{\hat{p}} \Rightarrow \hat{p} \pm 2\sqrt{\frac{\hat{p}(1-\hat{p})}{n}}\sqrt{\frac{N-n}{N}}$$

$$\Rightarrow .7 \pm 2\sqrt{\frac{.7(.3)}{30}}\sqrt{\frac{300-30}{300}} \Rightarrow .7 \pm .159 \Rightarrow (.541, .859)$$

5.77   For $N = 251$, $n = 72$, $= .694$, the 95% confidence interval is:

$$\hat{p} \pm 2\hat{\sigma}_{\hat{p}} \Rightarrow \hat{p} \pm 2\sqrt{\frac{\hat{p}(1-\hat{p})}{n}}\sqrt{\frac{(N-n)}{N}}$$

$$\Rightarrow .694 \pm 2\sqrt{\frac{.694(.306)}{72}}\sqrt{\frac{(251-72)}{251}} \Rightarrow .694 \pm .092 \Rightarrow (.602, .786)$$

We are 95% confident that the proportion of all New Jersey's Council business members that have employees with substance abuse problems is between .602 and .786.

5.79   a.   First, we must calculate the sample mean:

$$\bar{x} = \frac{\sum_{i=1}^{15} f_i x_i}{n} = \frac{3(108) + 2(55) + 1(500) + \cdots + 19(100)}{100} = \frac{15,646}{100} = 156.46$$

The point estimate of the mean value of the parts inventory is $\bar{x} = 156.46$.

b.   The sample variance and standard deviation are:

$$s^2 = \frac{\sum_{i=1}^{15} f_i x_i^2 - \frac{\left(\sum f_i x_i\right)^2}{n}}{n-1} = \frac{3(108)^2 + 2(55)^2 + \cdots + 19(100)^2 - \frac{15,646^2}{100}}{100-1}$$

$$= \frac{6,776,336 - \frac{15,646^2}{100}}{99} = 43,720.83677$$

$$s = \sqrt{s^2} = \sqrt{43,720.83677} = 209.10$$

The estimated standard error is:

$$\hat{\sigma}_{\bar{x}} = \frac{s}{\sqrt{n}}\sqrt{\frac{N-n}{N}} = \frac{209.10}{\sqrt{100}}\sqrt{\frac{500-100}{500}} = 18.7025$$

c.   The approximate 95% confidence interval is:

$$\bar{x} \pm 2\hat{\sigma}_{\bar{x}} \Rightarrow \pm 2\left(\frac{s}{\sqrt{n}}\right)\sqrt{\frac{N-n}{N}} \Rightarrow 156.46 \pm 2(18.7025) \Rightarrow 156.46 \pm 37.405$$

$$\Rightarrow (119.055,\ 193.865)$$

We are 95% confident that the mean value of the parts inventory is between $119.06 and $193.87.

d.   Since the interval in part **c** does not include $300, the value of $300 is not a reasonable value for the mean value of the parts inventory.

5.81 $\hat{p} = \dfrac{x}{n} = \dfrac{15}{175} = .086$

The standard error of $\hat{p}$ is:

$$\hat{\sigma}_{\hat{p}} = \sqrt{\frac{\hat{p}(1-\hat{p})}{n}\left(\frac{N-n}{N}\right)} = \sqrt{\frac{.086(1-.086)}{175}\left(\frac{3000-175}{3000}\right)} = .0206$$

An approximate 95% confidence interval for p is:

$$\hat{p} \pm 2\hat{\sigma}_{\hat{p}} \Rightarrow .086 \pm 2(.0206) \Rightarrow .086 \pm .041 \Rightarrow (.045,\ .127)$$

Since .07 falls in the 95% confidence interval, it is not an uncommon value. Thus, there is no evidence that more than 7% of the corn-related products in this state have to be removed from shelves and warehouses.

5.83   a. $P(t \le t_0) = .05$ where df $= 20$

$$t_0 = -1.725$$

        b. $P(t \ge t_0) = .005$ where df $= 9$

$$t_0 = 3.250$$

        c. $P(t \le -t_0 \text{ or } t \ge t_0) = .10$ where df $= 8$ is equivalent to

$$P(t \ge t_0) = .10/2 = .05 \text{ where df} = 8$$
$$t_0 = 1.860$$

        d. $P(t \le -t_0 \text{ or } t \ge t_0) = .01$ where df $= 17$ is equivalent to

$$P(t \ge t_0) = .01/2 = .005 \text{ where df} = 17$$
$$t_0 = 2.898$$

5.85   a.   For confidence coefficient .99, $\alpha = .01$ and $\alpha/2 = .005$. From Table IV, Appendix B, $z_{.005} = 2.58$. The confidence interval is:

$$\bar{x} \pm z_{\alpha/2} \frac{s}{\sqrt{n}} \Rightarrow 32.5 \pm 2.58 \frac{30}{\sqrt{225}} \Rightarrow 32.5 \pm 5.16 \Rightarrow (27.34, 37.66)$$

        b.   The sample size is $n = \dfrac{\left(z_{\alpha/2}\right)^2 \sigma^2}{(SE)^2} = \dfrac{2.58^2 (30)^2}{.5^2} = 23,963.04 \approx 23,964$

        c.   "99% confidence" means that if repeated samples of size 225 were selected from the population and 99% confidence intervals constructed for the population mean, then 99% of all the intervals constructed will contain the population mean.

5.87   The parameters of interest for the problems are:

(1)   The question requires a categorical response. One parameter of interest might be the proportion, p, of all Americans over 18 years of age who think their health is generally very good or excellent.

(2)   A parameter of interest might be the mean number of days, μ, in the previous 30 days that all Americans over 18 years of age felt that their physical health was not good because of injury or illness.

(3)   A parameter of interest might be the mean number of days, μ, in the previous 30 days that all Americans over 18 years of age felt that their mental health was not good because of stress, depression, or problems with emotions.

(4)   A parameter of interest might be the mean number of days, μ, in the previous 30 days that all Americans over 18 years of age felt that their physical or mental health prevented them from performing their usual activities.

5.89   a.   The point estimate for the proportion of major oil spills that are caused by hull failure is:

$$\hat{p} = \frac{x}{n} = \frac{12}{50} = .24$$

b.   To see if the sample size is sufficiently large:

$$\hat{p} \pm 3\sigma_{\hat{p}} \approx \hat{p} \pm 3\sqrt{\frac{\hat{p}\hat{q}}{n}} \Rightarrow .24 \pm 3\sqrt{\frac{.24(.76)}{50}} \Rightarrow .24 \pm .181 \Rightarrow (.059, .421)$$

Since this interval is wholly contained in the interval $(0, 1)$, we may conclude that the normal approximation is reasonable.

For confidence coefficient .95, $\alpha = .05$ and $\alpha/2 = .05/2 = .025$. From Table IV, Appendix B, $z_{.025} = 1.96$. The confidence interval is:

$$\hat{p} \pm z_{.025}\sqrt{\frac{pq}{n}} \approx \pm 1.96\sqrt{\frac{\hat{p}\hat{q}}{n}} \Rightarrow .24 \pm 1.96\sqrt{\frac{.24(.76)}{50}} \Rightarrow .24 \pm .118$$

$$\Rightarrow (.122, .358)$$

We are 95% confident that the true percentage of major oil spills that are caused by hull failure is between .122 and .358.

5.91   a.   First, we must estimate the standard deviation. A conservative estimate of the standard deviation is the range divided by 4:

$$s \approx \frac{R}{4} = \frac{205,000 - 20,000}{4} = 46,250$$

For confidence coefficient .95, $\alpha = .05$ and $\alpha/2 = .05/2 = .025$. From Table IV, Appendix B, $z_{.025} = 1.96$. Thus,

$$n = \frac{(z_{\alpha/2})^2\sigma^2}{(SE)^2} = \frac{1.96^2(46,250)^2}{5,000^2} = 328.7 \approx 329$$

Thus, we would need a sample of size 329.

b.   Using $s = 19,830$, we get:

$$n = \frac{(z_{\alpha/2})^2\sigma^2}{(SE)^2} = \frac{1.96^2(19,830)^2}{5,000^2} = 60.4 \approx 61$$

Thus, we would need a sample of size 61.

c.   Since the standard deviation used in part b was based on a sample of size 2,413, it should be very reliable. Thus, we would recommend that the sample size of 61 be used. Since the estimate of the standard deviation found in part a is so much larger than the value of s in part b, the data are probably skewed to the right. A better estimate of the standard deviation might be the range divided by 6.

5.93   First we make some preliminary calculations:

$$\bar{x} = \frac{\sum x}{n} = \frac{1479.9}{8} = 184.9875$$

$$s^2 = \frac{\sum x^2 - \frac{\left(\sum x\right)^2}{n}}{n-1} = \frac{453,375.17 - \frac{1479.9^2}{8}}{8-1} = 25,658.88124$$

$$s = \sqrt{25,658.88124} = 160.1839$$

For confidence coefficient .95, $\alpha = .05$ and $\alpha/2 = .025$. From Table VI, Appendix B, with df $= n - 1 = 8 - 1 = 7$, $t_{.025} = 2.365$. The 95% confidence interval is:

$$\bar{x} \pm t_{.05}\frac{s}{\sqrt{n}} \Rightarrow 184.9875 \pm 2.365\frac{160.1839}{\sqrt{8}} \Rightarrow 184.9875 \pm 133.9384$$

$$\Rightarrow (51.0491, 318.9259)$$

We must assume that the population of private colleges' and universities' endowments are normally distributed.

5.95   There are a total of 96 channel catfish in the sample. The point estimate of p is

$$\hat{p} = \frac{x}{n} = \frac{96}{144} = .667 .$$

To see if the sample size is sufficiently large:

$$\hat{p} \pm 3\sigma_{\hat{p}} \approx \hat{p} \pm 3\sqrt{\frac{\hat{p}\hat{q}}{n}} \Rightarrow .667 \pm 3\sqrt{\frac{.667(.333)}{144}} \Rightarrow .667 \pm .118 \Rightarrow (.549, .785)$$

Since the interval is wholly contained in the interval (0, 1), we may conclude that the normal approximation is reasonable.

For confidence coefficient .90, $\alpha = .10$ and $\alpha/2 = .10/2 = .05$. From Table IV, Appendix B, $z_{.05} = 1.645$. The confidence interval is:

$$\hat{p} \pm z_{.05}\sqrt{\frac{\hat{p}\hat{q}}{n}} \Rightarrow .667 \pm 1.645\sqrt{\frac{.667(.333)}{144}} \Rightarrow .667 \pm .065 \Rightarrow (.602, .732)$$

We are 90% confident that the true proportion of channel catfish in the population is between .602 and .732.

5.97   a.   For confidence coefficient .99, $\alpha = .01$ and $\alpha/2 = .01/2 = .005$. From Table VI, Appendix B, with df $= n - 1 = 3 - 1 = 2$, $t_{.005} = 9.925$. The confidence interval is:

$$\bar{x} \pm t_{.005}\frac{s}{\sqrt{n}} \Rightarrow 49.3 \pm 9.925\frac{1.5}{\sqrt{3}} \Rightarrow 49.3 \pm 8.60 \Rightarrow (40.70, 57.90)$$

b.   We are 99% confident that the mean percentage of B(a)p removed from all soil specimens using the poison is between 40.70% and 57.90%.

c.   We must assume that the distribution of the percentages of B(a)p removed from all soil specimens using the poison is normal.

d.   Since the 99% confidence interval for the mean percent removed contains 50%, this would be a very possible value.

5.99   a.   For confidence coefficient .95, $\alpha = .05$ and $\alpha/2 = .025$. From Table IV, Appendix B, $z_{.025} = 1.96$. The confidence interval is:

$$\overline{x} \pm z_{\alpha/2}\frac{s}{\sqrt{n}}$$

Men: $7.4 \pm 1.96\dfrac{6.3}{\sqrt{159}} \Rightarrow 7.4 \pm .979 \Rightarrow (6.421, 8.379)$

We are 95% confident that the average distance to work for men in the central city is between 6.421 and 8.379 miles.

Women: $4.5 \pm 1.96\dfrac{4.2}{\sqrt{119}} \Rightarrow 4.5 \pm .755 \Rightarrow (3.745, 5.255)$

We are 95% confident that the average distance to work for women in the central city is between 3.745 and 5.255 miles.

Since the confidence intervals for men and women do not overlap, there is evidence that there is a difference in the average distance to work between men and women who live in central city residences.

b.   Men: $9.3 \pm 1.96\dfrac{7.1}{\sqrt{138}} \Rightarrow 9.3 \pm 1.185 \Rightarrow (8.115, 10.485)$

We are 95% confident that the average distance to work for men in the suburbs is between 8.115 and 10.485 miles.

Women: $6.6 \pm 1.96\dfrac{5.6}{\sqrt{93}} \Rightarrow 6.6 \pm 1.138 \Rightarrow (5.462, 7.738)$

We are 95% confident that the average distance to work for women in the suburbs is between 5.462 and 7.738 miles.

Since the confidence intervals for men and women do not overlap, there is evidence that there is a difference in the average distance to work between men and women who live in suburban residences.

5.101   a.   Of the 24 observations, 20 were 2 weeks of vacation $\Rightarrow \hat{p} = 20/24 = .833$.

For confidence coefficient .95, $\alpha = .05$ and $\alpha/2 = .05/2 = .025$. From Table IV, Appendix B, $z_{.025} = 1.96$. The confidence interval is:

$$\hat{p} \pm z_{.025}\sqrt{\frac{\hat{p}\hat{q}}{n}} \Rightarrow .833 \pm 1.96\sqrt{\frac{.833(.167)}{24}} \Rightarrow .833 \pm .149 \Rightarrow (.683, \ .982)$$

b.   To see if the sample size is sufficiently large:

$$\hat{p} \pm 3\sigma_{\hat{p}} \Rightarrow \hat{p} \pm 3\sqrt{\frac{pq}{n}} \Rightarrow \pm 3\sqrt{\frac{\hat{p}\hat{q}}{n}} \Rightarrow .833 \pm 3\sqrt{\frac{.833(.167)}{24}} \Rightarrow .833 \pm .228$$
$$\Rightarrow (.605, 1.061)$$

Since the interval does not lie within the interval (0, 1), the normal approximation will not be adequate.

c.   The bound is $SE = .02$. For confidence coefficient .95, $\alpha = .05$ and $\alpha/2 = .05/2 = .025$. From Table IV, Appendix B, $z_{.025} = 1.96$. Thus,

$$n = \frac{(z_{\alpha/2})^2 pq}{(SE)^2} = \frac{1.96^2 (.833)(.167)}{.02^2} = 1{,}336.02 \approx 1{,}337.$$

Thus, we would need a sample size of 1,337.

5.105   The bound is $SE = .1$. For confidence coefficient .99, $\alpha = 1 - .99 = .01$ and $\alpha/2 = .01/2 = .005$.

From Table IV, Appendix B, $z_{.005} = 2.575$.

We estimate p with from Exercise 5.48 which is $\hat{p} = .636$. Thus,

$$n = \frac{(z_{\alpha/2})^2 pq}{(SE)^2} = \frac{2.575^2(.636)(.364)}{.1^2}4 = 153.5 \Rightarrow 154$$

The necessary sample size would be 154.

5.107   For confidence coefficient .95, $\alpha = .05$ and $\alpha/2 = .025$. From Table IV, Appendix B, $z_{.025} = 1.96$. From Exercise 5.106, a good approximation for p is .094. Also, $SE = .02$.

The sample size is $n = \dfrac{(z_{\alpha/2})^2 pq}{(SE)^2} = \dfrac{(1.96)^2(.094)(.906)}{.02^2} = 817.9 \approx 818$

You would need to take $n = 818$ samples.

Inferences Based on a Single Sample: Tests of Hypothesis   *Chapter 6*

6.1   The null hypothesis is the "status quo" hypothesis, while the alternative hypothesis is the research hypothesis.

6.3   The "level of significance" of a test is α. This is the probability that the test statistic will fall in the rejection region when the null hypothesis is true.

6.5   The four possible results are:
   1.   Rejecting the null hypothesis when it is true. This would be a Type I error.
   2.   Accepting the null hypothesis when it is true. This would be a correct decision.
   3.   Rejecting the null hypothesis when it is false. This would be a correct decision.
   4.   Accepting the null hypothesis when it is false. This would be a Type II error.

6.7   When you reject the null hypothesis in favor of the alternative hypothesis, this does not prove the alternative hypothesis is correct. We are $100(1 - \alpha)\%$ confident that there is sufficient evidence to conclude that the alternative hypothesis is correct.

   If we were to repeatedly draw samples from the population and perform the test each time, approximately $100(1 - \alpha)\%$ of the tests performed would yield the correct decision.

6.9   Let p = student loan default rate in 2003. To see if the student loan default rate is less than .045, we test:

   H_0: $p = .045$
   H_a: $p < .045$

6.11   Let μ = mean caloric content of Virginia school lunches. To test the claim that after the testing period ended, the average caloric content dropped, we test:

   H_0: $\mu = 863$
   H_a: $\mu < 863$

6.13   a.   Since the company must give proof the drug is safe, the null hypothesis would be the drug is unsafe. The alternative hypothesis would be the drug is safe.

   b.   A Type I error would be concluding the drug is safe when it is not safe. A Type II error would be concluding the drug is not safe when it is. α is the probability of concluding the drug is safe when it is not. β is the probability of concluding the drug is not safe when it is.

   c.   In this problem, it would be more important for α to be small. We would want the probability of concluding the drug is safe when it is not to be as small as possible.

6.15 a.   A Type I error is rejecting the null hypothesis when it is true. In a murder trial, we would be concluding that the accused is guilty when, in fact, he/she is innocent.

          A Type II error is accepting the null hypothesis when it is false. In this case, we would be concluding that the accused is innocent when, in fact, he/she is guilty.

      b.   Both errors are bad. However, if an innocent person is found guilty of murder and is put to death, there is no way to correct the error. On the other hand, if a guilty person is set free, he/she could murder again.

      c.   In a jury trial, α is assumed to be smaller than β. The only way to convict the accused is for a unanimous decision of guilt. Thus, the probability of convicting an innocent person is set to be small.

      d.   In order to get a unanimous vote to convict, there has to be overwhelming evidence of guilt. The probability of getting a unanimous vote of guilt if the person is really innocent will be very small.

      e.   If a jury is predjuced against a guilty verdict, the value of α will decrease. The probability of convicting an innocent person will be even smaller if the jury if predjudiced against a guilty verdict.

      f.   If a jury is predjudiced against a guilty verdict, the value of β will increase. The probability of declaring a guilty person innocent will be larger if the jury is prejudiced against a guilty verdict.

6.17 a.

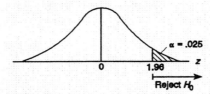

      b.

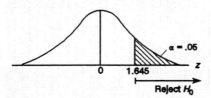

      c.

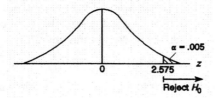

d.

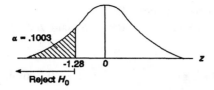

e.

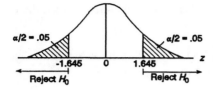

f.

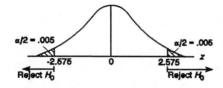

g.　$P(z > 1.96) = .025$
$P(z > 1.645) = .05$
$P(z > 2.575) = .005$
$P(z < -1.28) = .1003$
$P(z < -1.645 \text{ or } z > 1.645) = .10$
$P(z < -2.575 \text{ or } z > 2.575) = .01$

6.19　a.　H_0: $\mu = 100$
H_a: $\mu > 100$

The test statistic is $z = \dfrac{\overline{x} - \mu_0}{\sigma_{\overline{x}}} = \dfrac{\overline{x} - \mu_0}{\sigma/\sqrt{n}} = \dfrac{110 - 100}{60/\sqrt{100}} = 1.67$

The rejection region requires $\alpha = .05$ in the upper tail of the z-distribution. From Table IV, Appendix B, $z_{.05} = 1.645$. The rejection region is $z > 1.645$.

Since the observed value of the test statistic falls in the rejection region, ($z = 1.67 \not> 1.645$), H_0 is rejected. There is sufficient evidence to indicate the true population mean is greater than 100 at $\alpha = .05$.

b.　H_0: $\mu = 100$
H_a: $\mu \neq 100$

The test statistic is $z = \dfrac{\overline{x} - \mu_0}{\sigma_{\overline{x}}} = \dfrac{110 - 100}{60/\sqrt{100}} = 1.67$

The rejection region requires $\alpha/2 = .05/2 = .025$ in each tail of the z-distribution. From Table IV, Appendix B, $z_{.025} = 1.96$. The rejection region is $z < -1.96$ or $z > 1.96$.

Since the observed value of the test statistic does not fall in the rejection region, ($z = 1.67$ $\not> 1.96$), H_0 is not rejected. There is insufficient evidence to indicate μ does not equal 100 at $\alpha = .05$.

c. In part **a**, we rejected H_0 and concluded the mean was greater than 100. In part **b**, we did not reject H_0. There was insufficient evidence to conclude the mean was different from 100. Because the alternative hypothesis in part **a** is more specific than the one in **b**, it is easier to reject H_0.

6.21 a. The rejection region requires $\alpha = .01$ in the lower tail of the z-distribution. From Table IV, Appendix B, $z_{.01} = 2.33$. The rejection region is $z < -2.33$.

b. The test statistic is $z = \dfrac{\bar{x} - \mu_o}{\sigma_{\bar{x}}} = \dfrac{19.3 - 20}{11.9/\sqrt{46}} = -.40$

c. Since the observed value of the test statistics does not fall in the rejection region ($z = -.40 \not< -2.33$), H_0 is not rejected. There is insufficient evidence to indicate the true mean number of latex gloves used per week by all hospital employees is less than 20 at $\alpha = .01$.

6.23 a. The rejection region requires $\alpha = .01$ in the upper tail of the z-distribution. From Table IV, Appendix B, $z_{.01} = 2.33$. The rejection region is $z > 2.33$.

b. The test statistic is $z = \dfrac{\bar{x} - \mu_0}{\sigma_{\bar{x}}} = \dfrac{141.31 - 140}{17.77/\sqrt{100,000}} = 23.31$

c. Since the observed value of the test statistic falls in the rejection region ($z = 23.31 > 2.33$), H_0 rejected. There is sufficient evidence to indicate the mean number of semester hours of college credit taken by all first-time candidates for the CPA exam is greater than 140 hours at $\alpha = .01$.

6.25 a. To determine if the process is not operating satisfactorily, we test:

H_0: $\mu = .250$
H_a: $\mu \neq .250$

b. Using MINITAB, the descriptive statistics are:

Descriptive Statistics: Tees

Variable	N	Mean	Median	TrMean	StDev	SE Mean
Tees	40	0.25248	0.25300	0.25256	0.00223	0.00035

Variable	Minimum	Maximum	Q1	Q3
Tees	0.24700	0.25600	0.25100	0.25400

The test statistic is $z = \dfrac{\bar{x} - \mu_0}{\sigma_{\bar{x}}} = \dfrac{.25248 - .250}{.00223/\sqrt{40}} = 7.03$

The rejection region requires $\alpha/2 = .01/2 = .005$ in each tail of the z-distribution. From Table IV, Appendix B, $z_{.005} = 2.58$. The rejection region is $z < -2.58$ or $z > 2.58$.

Since the observed value of the test statistic falls in the rejection region ($z = 7.03 > 2.58$), H_0 is rejected. There is sufficient information to indicate the process is performing in an unsatisfactory manner at $\alpha = .01$.

c. α is the probability of a Type I error. A Type I error, in this case, is to say the process is unsatisfactory when, in fact, it is satisfactory. The risk, then, is to the producer since he will be spending time and money to repair a process that is not in error.

β is the probability of a Type II error. A Type II error, in this case, is to say the process is satisfactory when it, in fact, is not. This is the consumer's risk since he could unknowingly purchase a defective product.

6.27   To determine if the mean point-spread error is different from 0, we test:

H_0: $\mu = 0$
H_a: $\mu \neq 0$

The test statistic is $z = \dfrac{\bar{x} - \mu_0}{\sigma_{\bar{x}}} = \dfrac{-1.6 - 0}{13.3/\sqrt{240}} = -1.86$

The rejection region requires $\alpha/2 = .01/2 = .005$ in each tail of the z distribution. From Table IV, Appendix B, $z_{.005} = 2.575$. The rejection region is $z > 2.575$ or $z < -2.575$.

Since the observed value of the test statistic does not fall in the rejection region ($z = -1.86 \not< 2.575$), H_0 is not rejected. There is insufficient evidence to indicate that the true mean point-spread error is different from 0 at $\alpha = .01$.

6.29   a. No. Since the hypothesized value of μ_M (60,000) falls in the 95% confidence interval, it is a likely candidate for the true mean. Thus, we would not reject H_0. There is no evidence that the mean salary for males differs from $60,000.

b. To determine if the true mean salary of males with post-graduate degrees differs from $60,000, we test:

H_0: $\mu = 60,000$
H_a: $\mu \neq 60,000$

The test statistic is $z = \dfrac{\bar{x} - \mu_0}{\sigma_{\bar{x}}} = \dfrac{61,340 - 60,000}{2,185} = 0.61$

The rejection region requires $\alpha/2 = .05/2 = .025$ in each tail of the z-distribution. From Table IV, Appendix B, $z_{.025} = 1.96$. The rejection region is $z > 1.96$ or $z < -1.96$.

Since the observed value of the test statistic does not fall in the rejection region ($z = 0.61 \not> 1.96$), H_0 is not rejected. There is insufficient evidence to indicate the true mean salary of males with post-graduate degrees differs from $60,000 at $\alpha = .05$.

c. Parts a and b must agree. In both cases, a two-sided test / confidence interval is used. The z-score used in both parts is the same, as are $\bar{x}$ and $s_{\bar{x}}$.

d. No. Since the hypothesized value of μ_F (33,000) falls in the 95% confidence interval, it is a likely candidate for the true mean. Thus, we would not reject H_0. There is no evidence that the mean salary for females differs from \$33,000.

e. To determine if the true mean salary of females with post-graduate degrees differs from \$33,000, we test:

H_0: $\mu = 33,000$
H_a: $\mu \neq 33,000$

The test statistic is $z = \dfrac{\bar{x} - \mu_0}{\sigma_{\bar{x}}} = \dfrac{32,227 - 33,000}{932} = -0.83$

The rejection region requires $\alpha/2 = .05/2 = .025$ in each tail of the z-distribution. From Table IV, Appendix B, $z_{.025} = 1.96$. The rejection region is $z > 1.96$ or $z < -1.96$.

Since the observed value of the test statistic does not fall in the rejection region ($z = -0.83 \not< -1.96$), H_0 is not rejected. There is insufficient evidence to indicate the true mean salary of females with post-graduate degrees differs from \$33,000 at $\alpha = .05$.

f. Parts d and e must agree. In both cases, a two-sided test / confidence interval is used. The z-score used in both parts is the same, as are $\bar{x}$ and $s_{\bar{x}}$.

6.31 a. To determine if CEOs at all California small firms generally agree with the statement, we test:

H_0: $\mu = 3.5$
H_a: $\mu > 3.5$

The test statistic is $z = \dfrac{\bar{x} - \mu_o}{\sigma_{\bar{x}}} = \dfrac{3.85 - 3.5}{1.5/\sqrt{137}} = 2.73$

The rejection region requires $\alpha = .05$ in the upper tail of the z-distribution. From Table IV, Appendix B, $z_{.05} = 1.645$. The rejection region is $z > 1.645$.

Since the observed value of the test statistics falls in the rejection region ($z = 2.73 > 1.645$), H_0 is rejected. There is sufficient evidence to indicate CEOs at all California small firms generally agree with the statement (true mean scale score exceeds 3.5) at $\alpha = .05$.

b. Although the sample mean of 3.85 is far enough away from 3.5 to statistically conclude the population mean score is greater than 3.5, a score of 3.85 may not be practically different from 3.5 to make any difference.

c. No. Since the sample size ($n = 137$) is greater than 30, the Central Limit Theorem applies. The distribution of $\bar{x}$ is approximately normal regardless of the population distribution.

6.33   a.   Since the p-value $= .10$ is greater than $\alpha = .05$, H_0 is not rejected.

b.   Since the p-value $= .05$ is less than $\alpha = .10$, H_0 is rejected.

c.   Since the p-value $= .001$ is less than $\alpha = .01$, H_0 is rejected.

d.   Since the p-value $= .05$ is greater than $\alpha = .025$, H_0 is not rejected.

e.   Since the p-value $= .45$ is greater than $\alpha = .10$, H_0 is not rejected.

6.35 p-value $= P(z \geq 2.17) = .5 - P(0 < z < 2.17) = .5 - .4850 = .0150$

$$\text{(using Table IV, Appendix B)}$$

The probability of observing a test statistic of 2.17 or anything more unusual if the true mean is 100 is .0150. Since this probability is so small, there is evidence that the true mean is greater than 100.

6.37 p-value $= P(z \geq 2.17) + P(z \leq -2.17) = (.5 - .4850)2 = .0300$ (using Table IV, Appendix B)

6.39   The smallest value of α for which the null hypothesis would be rejected is just greater than .06.

6.41   a.   Using MINITAB and the data sampled from Exercise 5.18, we get the following:

One-Sample Z: carats-samp

```
Test of mu = 0.6 vs mu not = 0.6
The assumed sigma = 0.262

Variable            N      Mean      StDev    SE Mean
carats-samp        30    0.6910     0.2620    0.0478

Variable                95.0% CI              Z        P
carats-samp     (  0.5972,    0.7848)      1.90    0.057
```

From the printout, the p-value is $p = .057$.

b.   Since the p-value is greater than α (.057 > .05), H_0 is not rejected. There is insufficient evidence to indicate the mean number of carats per diamond is different from .6 at $\alpha = .05$.

6.43   a.   The p-value from the printout is .069.

b.   From the printout, the set of hypotheses used are:

H_0: $\mu = 6.50$
H_a: $\mu > 6.50$

Since the p-value is not small (.069), H_0 is not rejected. There is insufficient evidence to indicate the true mean full-service fee of U.S. funeral homes in 2006 exceeds $6,500 at $\alpha = .05$. This agrees with the decision in Exercise 6.28.

Inferences Based on a Single Sample: Tests of Hypothesis

6.45   a.   To determine whether Chinese smokers smoke, on average, more cigarettes a day in 2007 than in 1995, we test:

$$H_0: \ \mu = 16.5$$
$$H_a: \ \mu > 16.5$$

b.   The test statistic is $z = \dfrac{\bar{x} - \mu_0}{\sigma_{\bar{x}}} = \dfrac{17.05 - 16.5}{5.21/\sqrt{200}} = 1.49$

The observed significance level is $p = P(z \geq 1.49) = .5 - .4319 = .0681$ (using Table IV, Appendix B).

Since the observed significance level (.0681) is not less than $\alpha = .05$, H_0 is not rejected. There is insufficient evidence to indicate that Chinese smokers smoke, on average, more cigarettes a day in 2007 than in 1995 at $\alpha = .05$.

If we used $\alpha = .10$, we would reject H_0. There is sufficient evidence to indicate that Chinese smokers smoke, on average, more cigarettes a day in 2007 than in 1995 at $\alpha = .10$.

c.   The two-tailed test is inappropriate because we are interested in whether Chinese smokers, on average, smoke more cigarettes now than in 1995. This specifies only one-tail for the test.

6.47   We should use the t-distribution in testing a hypothesis about a population mean if the sample size is small, the population being sampled from is normal, and the variance of the population is unknown.

6.49   a.   The rejection region requires $\alpha/2 = .05/2 = .025$ in each tail of the t-distribution with $df = n - 1 = 14 - 1 = 13$. From Table VI, Appendix B, $t_{.025} = 2.160$. The rejection region is $t < -2.160$ or $t > 2.160$.

b.   The rejection region requires $\alpha = .01$ in the upper tail of the t-distribution with $df = n - 1 = 24 - 1 = 23$. From Table VI, Appendix B, $t_{.01} = 2.500$. The rejection region is $t > 2.500$.

c.   The rejection region requires $\alpha = .10$ in the upper tail of the t-distribution with $df = n - 1 = 9 - 1 = 8$. From Table VI, Appendix B, $t_{.10} = 1.397$. The rejection region is $t > 1.397$.

d.   The rejection region requires $\alpha = .01$ in the lower tail of the t-distribution with $df = n - 1 = 12 - 1 = 11$. From Table VI, Appendix B, $t_{.01} = 2.718$. The rejection region is $t < -2.718$.

e.   The rejection region requires $\alpha/2 = .10/2 = .05$ in each tail of the t-distribution with $df = n - 1 = 20 - 1 = 19$. From Table VI, Appendix B, $t_{.05} = 1.729$. The rejection region is $t < -1.729$ or $t > 1.729$.

f.   The rejection region requires $\alpha = .05$ in the lower tail of the t-distribution with $df = n - 1 = 4 - 1 = 3$. From Table VI, Appendix B, $t_{.05} = 2.353$. The rejection region is $t < -2.353$.

6.51   a.   We must assume that a random sample was drawn from a normal population.

       b.   The hypotheses are:

$$H_0: \ \mu = 1000$$
$$H_a: \ \mu > 1000$$

The test statistic is $t = 1.89$.

The p-value is .038.

There is evidence to reject H_0 for $\alpha > .038$. There is evidence to indicate the mean is greater than 1000 for $\alpha > .038$.

       c.   The hypotheses are:

$$H_0: \ \mu = 1000$$
$$H_a: \ \mu \neq 1000$$

The test statistic is $t = 1.89$.

The p-value is $2(.038) = .076$.

There is no evidence to reject H_0 for $\alpha = .05$. There is insufficient evidence to indicate the mean is different than 1000 for $\alpha = .05$.

There is evidence to reject H_0 for $\alpha > .076$. There is evidence to indicate the mean is different than 1000 for $\alpha > .076$.

6.53   a.   To determine if the mean surface roughness of coated interior pipe differs from 2 micrometers, we test:

$$H_0: \ \mu = 2$$
$$H_a: \ \mu \neq 2$$

       b.   From the printout, the test statistic is $t = -1.02$.

       c.   The rejection region requires $\alpha/2 = .05/2 = .025$ in each tail of the t-distribution with df $= n - 1 = 20 - 1 = 19$. From Table VI, Appendix B, $t_{.025} = 2.093$. The rejection region is $t < -2.093$ or $t > 2.093$.

       d.   Since the observed value of the test statistic does not fall in the rejection region ($t = -1.02 \not< -2.093$), H_0 is not rejected. There is insufficient evidence to indicate the true mean surface roughness of coated interior pipe differs from 2 micrometers at $\alpha = .05$.

       e.   The p-value is $p = .322$. Since the p-value is not less than $\alpha = .05$, H_0 is not rejected. There is insufficient evidence to indicate the true mean surface roughness of coated interior pipe differs from 2 micrometers at $\alpha = .05$.

Inferences Based on a Single Sample: Tests of Hypothesis

f. From Exercise 5.32, we found the 95% confidence interval for the mean surface roughness of coated interior pipe to be (1.636, 2.126). Since the hypothesized value of μ ($\mu = 2$) falls in the confidence interval, it is a likely value. We cannot reject it. The confidence interval and the test of hypothesis lead to the same conclusion because the critical values for the 2 techniques are the same.

6.55 To determine whether the true mean pouring temperature differs from the target setting, we test:

H_0: $\mu = 2{,}550$
H_a: $\mu \neq 2{,}550$

From the printout, the test statistic is $t = 1.210$ and the p-value is .257.

Since the p-value is greater than $\alpha = .01$, H_0 is not rejected. There is insufficient evidence to indicate the true mean pouring temperature is different from 2,550 degrees at $\alpha = .01$.

6.57 Using MINITAB, the descriptive statistics are:

One-Sample T: Skid

```
Test of mu = 425 vs < 425

                                        95%
                                       Upper
Variable    N     Mean     StDev  SE Mean   Bound      T      P
Skid       20  358.450   117.817   26.345  404.004  -2.53  0.010
```

To determine if the mean skidding distance is less than 425 meters, we test:

H_0: $\mu = 425$
H_a: $\mu < 425$

The test statistics is $t = \dfrac{\bar{x} - \mu_o}{s/\sqrt{n}} = \dfrac{358.45 - 425}{117.817/\sqrt{20}} = -2.53$.

The rejection region requires $\alpha = .10$ in the lower tail of the t-distribution with df $= n - 1 = 20 - 1 = 19$. From Table VI, Appendix B, $t_{.10} = 1.328$. The rejection region is $t < -1.328$.

Since the observed value of the test statistic falls in the rejection region ($t = -2.53 < -1.328$), H_0 is rejected. There is sufficient evidence to indicate the true mean skidding distance is less than 425 meters at $\alpha = .10$. There is sufficient evidence to refute the claim.

6.59   To determine if the true mean crack intensity of the Mississippi highway exceeds the AASHTO recommended maximum, we test:

$H_0: \mu = .100$

$H_a: \mu > .100$

The test statistic is $t = \dfrac{\bar{x} - \mu_0}{s/\sqrt{n}} = \dfrac{.210 - .100}{\sqrt{.011}/\sqrt{8}} = 2.97$

The rejection region requires $\alpha = .01$ in the upper tail of the t-distribution with df $= n - 1 = 8 - 1 = 7$. From Table VI, Appendix B, $t_{.01} = 2.998$. The rejection region is $t > 2.998$.

Since the observed value of the test statistic does not fall in the rejection region ($t = 2.97 \not> 2.998$), H_0 is not rejected. There is insufficient evidence to indicate that the true mean crack intensity of the Mississippi highway exceeds the AASHTO recommended maximum at $\alpha = .01$.

6.61   The sample size is large enough if the interval $p_0 \pm 3\sigma_{\hat{p}}$ is contained in the interval $(0, 1)$.

a. $p_0 \pm 3\sqrt{\dfrac{p_0 q_0}{n}} \Rightarrow .975 \pm 3\sqrt{\dfrac{(.975)(.025)}{900}} \Rightarrow .975 \pm .016 \Rightarrow (.959, .991)$

Since the interval is contained in the interval $(0, 1)$, the sample size is large enough.

b. $p_0 \pm 3\sqrt{\dfrac{p_0 q_0}{n}} \Rightarrow .01 \pm 3\sqrt{\dfrac{(.01)(.99)}{125}} \Rightarrow .01 \pm .027 \Rightarrow (-.017, .037)$

Since the interval is not contained in the interval $(0, 1)$, the sample size is not large enough.

c. $p_0 \pm 3\sqrt{\dfrac{p_0 q_0}{n}} \Rightarrow .75 \pm 3\sqrt{\dfrac{(.75)(.25)}{40}} \Rightarrow .75 \pm .205 \Rightarrow (.545, .955)$

Since the interval is contained in the interval $(0, 1)$, the sample size is large enough.

d. $p_0 \pm 3\sqrt{\dfrac{p_0 q_0}{n}} \Rightarrow .75 \pm 3\sqrt{\dfrac{(.75)(.25)}{15}} \Rightarrow .75 \pm .335 \Rightarrow (.415, 1.085)$

Since the interval is not contained in the interval $(0, 1)$, the sample size is not large enough.

e. $p_0 \pm 3\sqrt{\dfrac{p_0 q_0}{n}} \Rightarrow .62 \pm 3\sqrt{\dfrac{(.62)(.38)}{12}} \Rightarrow .62 \pm .420 \Rightarrow (.120, 1.040)$

Since the interval is not contained in the interval $(0, 1)$, the sample size is not large enough.

Inferences Based on a Single Sample: Tests of Hypothesis

6.63 a. $z = \dfrac{\hat{p} - p_0}{\sqrt{\dfrac{p_0 q_0}{n}}} = \dfrac{.83 - .9}{\sqrt{\dfrac{.9(.1)}{100}}} = -2.33$

b. The denominator in Exercise 6.62 is $\sqrt{\dfrac{.7(.3)}{100}} = .0458$ as compared to $\sqrt{\dfrac{.9(.1)}{100}} = .03$ in part **a**. Since the denominator in this problem is smaller, the absolute value of z is larger.

c. The rejection region requires $\alpha = .05$ in the lower tail of the z-distribution. From Table IV, Appendix B, $z_{.05} = 1.645$. The rejection region is $z < -1.645$.

Since the observed value of the test statistic falls in the rejection region ($z = -2.33 < -1.645$), H_0 is rejected. There is sufficient evidence to indicate the population proportion is less than .9 at $\alpha = .05$.

d. The p-value $= P(z \le -2.33) = .5 - .4901 = .0099$ (from Table IV, Appendix B). Since the p-value is less than $\alpha = .05$, H_0 is rejected.

6.65 From Exercise 5.40, $n = 50$ and since p is the proportion of consumers who do not like the snack food, $\hat{p}$ will be:

$$\hat{p} = \frac{\text{Number of 0's in sample}}{n} = \frac{29}{50} = .58$$

First, check to see if the normal approximation will be adequate:

$$p_0 \pm 3\sigma_{\hat{p}} \Rightarrow p_0 \pm 3\sqrt{\frac{pq}{n}} \approx p_0 \pm 3\sqrt{\frac{p_0 q_0}{n}} \Rightarrow .5 \pm 3\sqrt{\frac{.5(1 - .5)}{50}} \Rightarrow .5 \pm .2121$$

$$\Rightarrow (.2879, .7121)$$

Since the interval lies completely in the interval (0, 1), the normal approximation will be adequate.

a. H_0: $p = .5$
H_a: $p > .5$

The test statistic is $z = \dfrac{\hat{p} - p_0}{\sigma_{\hat{p}}} = \dfrac{\hat{p} - p_0}{\sqrt{\dfrac{p_0 q_0}{n}}} = \dfrac{.58 - .5}{\sqrt{\dfrac{.5(1 - .5)}{50}}} = 1.13$

The rejection region requires $\alpha = .10$ in the upper tail of the z-distribution. From Table IV, Appendix B, $z_{.10} = 1.28$. The rejection region is $z > 1.28$.

Since the observed value of the test statistic does not fall in the rejection region ($z = 1.13 \not> 1.28$), H_0 is not rejected. There is insufficient evidence to indicate the proportion of customers who do not like the snack food is greater than .5 at $\alpha = .10$.

b. p-value $= P(z \ge 1.13) = .5 - .3708 = .1292$

6.67   a. $\hat{p} = \dfrac{x}{n} = \dfrac{320}{616} = .519$

b.   To determine whether the value of p has changed since 1999, we test:

H_0: $p = .62$
H_a: $p \neq .62$

c.   The test statistic is $z = \dfrac{\hat{p} - p_o}{\sqrt{\dfrac{p_o q_o}{n}}} = \dfrac{.519 - .62}{\sqrt{\dfrac{.62(.38)}{616}}} = -5.16$

d.   The rejection region requires $\alpha/2 = .05/2 = .025$ in each tail of the z-distribution. From Table IV, Appendix B, $z_{.025} = 1.96$. The rejection region is $z < -1.96$ or $z > 1.96$.

e.   Since the observed value of the test statistic falls in the rejection region ($z = -5.16 < -1.96$), H_0 is rejected. There is sufficient evidence to indicate the true proportion of businesses that suffered unauthorized use of computer systems in 2006 is different than .62 at $\alpha = .05$.

f.   The p-value is

$p = P(z \le -5.16) + P(z \ge 5.16) = (.5 - .5) + (.5 - .5) = 0 + 0 = 0$
(Using Table IV, Appendix B)

Since the observed value of p is less than $\alpha = .05$, H_0 is rejected. This is the same conclusion as in part **e**.

6.69   a.   To determine whether the true proportion of toothpaste brands with the ADA seal of verifying effective decay prevention is less than .5, we test:

H_0: $p = .5$
H_a: $p < .5$

b.   From the printout, the p-value is $p = .231$.

c.   Since the observed value of p is greater than $\alpha = .10$, H_0 is not rejected. There is insufficient evidence to indicate the true proportion of toothpaste brands with the ADA seal of verifying effective decay prevention is less than .5 at $\alpha = .10$.

6.71   a.   Let p = proportion of middle-aged women who exhibit skin improvement after using the cream. For this problem, $\hat{p} = \dfrac{x}{n} = \dfrac{24}{33} = .727$.

First we check to see if the normal approximation is adequate:

$$p_0 \pm 3\sigma_{\hat{p}} \Rightarrow p_0 \pm 3\sqrt{\dfrac{p_0 q_0}{n}} \Rightarrow .6 \pm 3\sqrt{\dfrac{.6(.4)}{33}} \Rightarrow .6 \pm .256 \Rightarrow (.344, \ .856)$$

Since the interval falls completely in the interval (0, 1), the normal distribution will be adequate.

To determine if the cream will improve the skin of more than 60% of middle-aged women, we test:

H_0: $p = .60$
H_a: $p > .60$

The test statistic is $z = \dfrac{\hat{p} - p_0}{\sqrt{\dfrac{p_0 q_0}{n}}} = \dfrac{.727 - .60}{\sqrt{\dfrac{.60(.40)}{33}}} = 1.49$

The rejection region requires $\alpha = .05$ in the upper tail of the z-distribution. From Table IV, Appendix B, $z_{.05} = 1.645$. The rejection region is $z > 1.645$.

Since the observed value of the test statistic does not fall in the rejection region ($z = 1.49 \not> -1.645$), H_0 is not rejected. There is insufficient evidence to indicate the cream will improve the skin of more than 60% of middle-aged women at $\alpha = .05$.

b. The p-value is $p = P(z \geq 1.49) = (.5 - .4319) = .0681$. (Using Table IV, Appendix B.) Since the p-value is greater than $\alpha = .05$, H_0 is not rejected. There is insufficient evidence to indicate the cream will improve the skin of more than 60% of middle-aged women at $\alpha = .05$.

6.73   Let p = proportion of students choosing the three-grill display so that Grill #2 is a compromise between a more desirable and a less desirable grill.

$\hat{p} = \dfrac{x}{n} = \dfrac{85}{124} = .685$

To determine if the proportion of students choosing the three-grill display so that Grill #2 is a compromise between a more desirable and a less desirable grill is greater than .167, we test:

H_0: $p = .167$
H_a: $p > .167$

The test statistic is $z = \dfrac{\hat{p} - p_o}{\sqrt{\dfrac{p_o q_o}{n}}} = \dfrac{.685 - .167}{\sqrt{\dfrac{.167(.833)}{124}}} = 15.47$

The rejection region requires $\alpha = .05$ in the upper tail of the z-distribution. From Table IV, Appendix B, $z_{.05} = 1.645$. The rejection region is $z > 1.645$.

Since the observed value of the test statistic falls in the rejection region ($z = 15.47 > 1.645$), H_0 is rejected. There is sufficient evidence to indicate that the true proportion of students choosing the three-grill display so that Grill #2 is a compromise between a more desirable and a less desirable grill is greater than .167 at $\alpha = .05$.

6.75   To minimize the probability of a Type I error, we will select $\alpha = .01$.

First, check to see if the normal approximation is adequate:

$$p_0 \pm 3\sigma_{\hat{p}} \Rightarrow p_0 \pm 3\sqrt{\frac{p_0 q_0}{n}} \Rightarrow .5 \pm 3\sqrt{\frac{(.5)(.5)}{100}} \Rightarrow .5 \pm .15 \Rightarrow (.35, .65)$$

Since the interval falls completely in the interval (0,1), the normal distribution will be adequate.

$$\hat{p} = \frac{x}{n} = \frac{56}{100} = .56$$

To determine if more than half of all Diet Coke drinkers prefer Diet Pepsi, we test:

H_0: $p = .5$
H_a: $p > .5$

The test statistic is $z = \dfrac{\hat{p} - p_0}{\sqrt{\dfrac{p_0 q_0}{n}}} = \dfrac{.56 - .5}{\sqrt{\dfrac{.5(.5)}{100}}} = 1.20$

The rejection region requires $\alpha = .01$ in the upper tail of the z-distribution. From Table IV, Appendix B, $z_{.01} = 2.33$. The rejection region is $z > 2.33$.

Since the observed value of the test statistic does not fall in the rejection region ($z = 1.20$ $\ngtr 2.33$), H_0 is not rejected. There is insufficient evidence to indicate that more than half of all Diet Coke drinkers prefer Diet Pepsi at $\alpha = .01$.

Since H_0 was not rejected, there is no evidence that Diet Coke drinkers prefer Diet Pepsi.

6.77   a.   By the Central Limit Theorem, the sampling distribution of $\bar{x}$ is approximately normal with $\mu_{\bar{x}} = \mu = 500$ and

$$\sigma_{\bar{x}} = \frac{\sigma}{\sqrt{n}} = \frac{100}{\sqrt{25}} = 20.$$

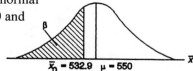

b. $\bar{x}_0 = \mu_0 + z_\alpha \sigma_{\bar{x}} = \mu_0 + z_\alpha \dfrac{\sigma}{\sqrt{n}}$ where $z_\alpha = z_{.05} = 1.645$ from Table IV, Appendix B.

Thus, $\bar{x}_0 = 500 + 1.645\dfrac{100}{\sqrt{25}} = 532.9$

c.   The sampling distribution of $\bar{x}$ is approximately normal by the Central Limit Theorem with $\mu_{\bar{x}} = \mu = 550$ and

$$\sigma_{\bar{x}} = \frac{\sigma}{\sqrt{n}} = \frac{100}{\sqrt{25}} = 20.$$

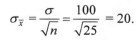

Inferences Based on a Single Sample: Tests of Hypothesis   175

d. $\beta = P(\bar{x}_0 < 532.9$ when $\mu = 550) = P\left(z < \dfrac{532.9 - 550}{100/\sqrt{25}}\right) = P(z < -.86)$

$$= .5 - .3051 = .1949$$

e. Power $= 1 - \beta = 1 - .1949 = .8051$

6.79 a. The sampling distribution of $\bar{x}$ will be approximately normal (by the Central Limit Theorem) with $\mu_{\bar{x}} = \mu = 75$ and $\sigma_{\bar{x}} = \dfrac{\sigma}{\sqrt{n}} = \dfrac{15}{\sqrt{49}} = 2.143$.

b. The sampling distribution of $\bar{x}$ will be approximately normal (by the Central Limit Theorem) with $\mu_{\bar{x}} = \mu = 70$ and $\sigma_{\bar{x}} = \dfrac{\sigma}{\sqrt{n}} = \dfrac{15}{\sqrt{49}} = 2.143$.

c. First, find $\bar{x}_0 = \mu_0 - z_\alpha \sigma_{\bar{x}} = \mu_0 - z_\alpha \dfrac{\sigma}{\sqrt{n}}$ where $z_{.10} = 1.28$ from Table IV, Appendix B.

Thus, $\bar{x}_0 = 75 - 1.28 \dfrac{15}{\sqrt{49}} = 72.257$

Now, find $\beta = P(\bar{x}_0 > 72.257$ when $\mu = 70) = P\left(z > \dfrac{72.257 - 70}{15/\sqrt{49}}\right)$

$$= P(z > 1.05) = .5 - .3531 = .1469$$

d. Power $= 1 - \beta = 1 - .1469 = .8531$

6.81 a. The sampling distribution of $\bar{x}$ will be approximately normal (by the Central Limit Theorem) with $\mu_{\bar{x}} = \mu = 30$ and $\sigma_{\bar{x}} = \dfrac{\sigma}{\sqrt{n}} = \dfrac{1.2}{\sqrt{121}} = .109$.

b. The sampling distribution of will be approximately normal (CLT) with $\mu_{\bar{x}} = \mu = 29.8$ and $\sigma_{\bar{x}} = \dfrac{\sigma}{\sqrt{n}} = \dfrac{1.2}{\sqrt{121}} = .109$.

c. First, find $\bar{x}_{0,L} = \mu_0 - z_{\alpha/2} \sigma_{\bar{x}} = \mu_0 - z_{\alpha/2} \dfrac{\sigma}{\sqrt{n}}$

where $z_{.05/2} = z_{.025} = 1.96$ from Table IV, Appendix B.

Thus, $\bar{x}_{0,L} = 30 - 1.96 \dfrac{1.2}{\sqrt{121}} = 29.79$

$$\bar{x}_{0,U} = \mu_0 + z_{\alpha/2} \sigma_{\bar{x}} = \mu_0 + z_{\alpha/2} \dfrac{\sigma}{\sqrt{n}} = 30 + 1.96 \dfrac{1.2}{\sqrt{121}} = 30.21$$

Now, find $\beta = P(29.79 < \bar{x} < 30.21$ when $\mu = 29.8)$

$$= P\left(\frac{29.79 - 29.8}{1.2/\sqrt{121}} < z < \frac{30.21 - 29.8}{1.2/\sqrt{121}}\right)$$

$$= P(-.09 < z < 3.76)$$
$$= .0359 + .5 = .5359$$

d. $\beta = P(29.79 < \bar{x} < 30.21$ when $\mu = 30.4) = P\left(\frac{29.79 - 30.4}{1.2/\sqrt{121}} < z < \frac{30.21 - 30.4}{1.2/\sqrt{121}}\right)$

$$= P(-5.59 < z < -1.74)$$
$$= .5 - .4591 = .0409$$

6.83 a. We have failed to reject H_0 when it is not true. This is a Type II error.

To compute β, first find:

$$\bar{x}_0 = \mu_0 - z_\alpha \sigma_{\bar{x}} = \mu_0 - z_\alpha \frac{\sigma}{\sqrt{n}} \text{ where } z_{.05} = 1.645 \text{ from Table IV, Appendix B.}$$

Thus, $\bar{x}_0 = 5.0 - 1.645 \frac{.01}{\sqrt{100}} = 4.998355$

Then find:

$$\beta = P(\bar{x}_0 > 4.998355 \text{ when } \mu = 4.9975) = P\left(z > \frac{4.998355 - 4.9975}{.01/\sqrt{100}}\right)$$

$$= P(z > .86) = .5 - .3051 = .1949$$

b. We have rejected H_0 when it is true. This is a Type I error. The probability of a Type I error is $\alpha = .05$.

c. A departure of .0025 below 5.0 is $\mu = 4.9975$. Using **a**, β when $\mu = 4.9975$ is .1949. The power of the test is $1 - \beta = 1 - .1949 = .8051$

6.85 First, find $\bar{x}_0$ such that $P(\bar{x} < \bar{x}_0) = .05$.

$$P(\bar{x} < \bar{x}_0) = P\left(z < \frac{\bar{x}_0 - 10}{1.2/\sqrt{48}}\right) = P(z < z_0) = .05.$$

From Table IV, Appendix B, $z_0 = -1.645$.

Thus, $z_0 = \frac{\bar{x}_0 - 10}{1.2/\sqrt{48}} \Rightarrow \bar{x}_0 = -1.645(.173) + 10 = 9.715$

The probability of a Type II error is:

$$\beta = P(\bar{x} \geq 9.715 \mid \mu = 9.5) = P\left(z \geq \frac{9.715 - 9.5}{1.2/\sqrt{48}}\right) = P(z \geq 1.24) = .5 - .3925$$

$$= .1075$$

6.87   a. $df = n - 1 = 16 - 1 = 15$; reject H_0 if $\chi^2 < 6.26214$ or $\chi^2 > 27.4884$

       b. $df = n - 1 = 23 - 1 = 22$; reject H_0 if $\chi^2 > 40.2894$

       c. $df = n - 1 = 15 - 1 = 14$; reject H_0 if $\chi^2 > 21.0642$

       d. $df = n - 1 = 13 - 1 = 12$; reject H_0 if $\chi^2 < 3.57056$

       e. $df = n - 1 = 7 - 1 = 6$; reject H_0 if $\chi^2 < 1.63539$ or $\chi^2 > 12.5916$

       f. $df = n - 1 = 25 - 1 = 24$; reject H_0 if $\chi^2 < 13.8484$

6.89   a. H_0: $\sigma^2 = 1$
            H_a: $\sigma^2 > 1$

            The test statistic is $\chi^2 = \dfrac{(n-1)s^2}{\sigma_0^2} = \dfrac{(100-1)4.84}{1} = 479.16$

            The rejection region requires $\alpha = .05$ in the upper tail of the χ^2 distribution with $df = n - 1 = 100 - 1 = 99$. From Table VII, Appendix B, $\chi^2_{.05} \approx 124.324$. The rejection region is $\chi^2 > 124.324$.

            Since the observed value of the test statistic falls in the rejection region ($\chi^2 = 479.16 > 124.324$), H_0 is rejected. There is sufficient evidence to indicate the variance is larger than 1 at $\alpha = .05$.

       b.   In part **b** of Exercise 6.88, the test statistic was $\chi^2 = 29.04$. The conclusion was to reject H_0 as it was in this problem.

6.91   a.   The rejection region requires $\alpha/2 = .01/2 = .005$ in each tail of the χ^2 distribution with $df = n - 1 = 46 - 1 = 45$. From Table VII, Appendix B, $\chi^2_{.005} \approx 73.12795$ and $\chi^2_{.995} \approx 24.3486$. The rejection region is $\chi^2 < 24.3486$ or $\chi^2 > 73.12795$.

       b.   The test statistic is $\chi^2 = \dfrac{(n-1)s^2}{\sigma_o^2} = \dfrac{(46-1)11.9^2}{100} = 63.7245$.

       c.   Since the observed value of the test statistic does not fall in the rejection region ($\chi^2 = 63.7245 \not< 24.3486$ and $\chi^2 = 63.7245 \not> 73.12795$), H_0 is not rejected. There is insufficient evidence to indicate the variance is different from 100 at $\alpha = .01$.

6.93   a.   Let σ^2 = weight variance of tees. To determine if the weight variance differs from .000004 (injection mold process is out-of-control), we test:

$$H_0: \ \sigma^2 = .000004$$
$$H_a: \ \sigma^2 \neq .000004$$

b.   Using MINITAB, the descriptive statistics are:

Descriptive Statistics: Tees

Variable	N	Mean	Median	TrMean	StDev	SE Mean
Tees	40	0.25248	0.25300	0.25256	0.00223	0.00035

Variable	Minimum	Maximum	Q1	Q3
Tees	0.24700	0.25600	0.25100	0.25400

The test statistic is $\chi^2 = \dfrac{(n-1)s^2}{\sigma_0^2} = \dfrac{(40-1)(.00223)^2}{.000004} = 48.49$

The rejection region requires $\alpha/2 = .01/2 = .005$ in each tail of the χ^2 distribution with df $= n - 1 = 40 - 1 = 39$. From Table VII, Appendix B, $\chi_{.005}^2 \approx 66.7659$ and $\chi_{.995}^2 \approx 20.7065$. The rejection region is $\chi^2 > 66.7659$ or $\chi^2 < 20.7065$.

Since the observed value of the test statistic does not fall in the rejection region ($\chi^2 = 49.49 \not> 66.7659$ and $\chi^2 = 49.49 \not< 20.7065$), H_0 is not rejected. There is insufficient evidence to indicate the injection mold process is out-of-control at $\alpha = .01$.

c.   We must assume that the distributions of the weights of tees is approximately normal. Using MINITAB, a histogram of the data is:

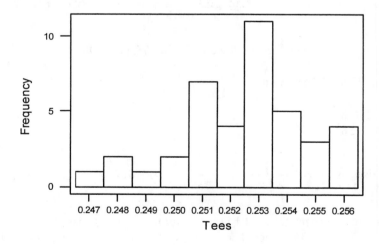

The data look fairly mound-shaped, so the assumption of normality seems to be reasonably satisfied.

6.95   To determine if the diameters of the ball bearings are more variable when produced by the new process, test:

H_0: $\sigma^2 = .00156$
H_a: $\sigma^2 > .00156$

The test statistic is $\chi^2 = \dfrac{(n-1)s^2}{\sigma_0^2} = \dfrac{99(.00211)}{.00156} = 133.90$

The rejection region requires use of the upper tail of the χ^2 distribution with df $= n - 1$ $= 100 - 1 = 99$. We will use df $= 100 \approx 99$ due to the limitations of the table. From Table VII, Appendix B, $\chi^2_{.025} = 129.561 < 133.90 < 135.807 = \chi^2_{.010}$. The p-value of the test is between .010 and .025. The decision made depends on the desired α. For $\alpha < .010$, there is not enough evidence to show that the variance in the diameters is greater than .00156; the reverse decision would be made for $\alpha \geq .025$.

6.97   a.   Since the sample mean of 3.85 is not that far from the value of 3.5, a large standard deviation would indicate that the value 3.85 is not very many standard deviations from 3.5.

b.   The rejection region requires $\alpha = .01$ in the upper tail of the z-distribution. From Table IV, Appendix B, $z_{.01} = 2.33$. The rejection region is $z > 2.33$.

The test statistic is $z = \dfrac{\overline{x} - \mu_o}{\sigma_{\overline{x}}} = \dfrac{3.85 - 3.5}{\sigma/\sqrt{137}}$

To reject H_0, $z > 2.33$. Thus, we need to find σ so $z > 2.33$.

$z = \dfrac{3.85 - 3.5}{\sigma/\sqrt{137}} > 2.33 \Rightarrow 3.85 - 3.5 > 2.33 \dfrac{\sigma}{\sqrt{137}} \Rightarrow .35 > .199065\sigma \Rightarrow 1.758 < \sigma$

Thus, the largest value of σ for which we will reject H_0 is 1.758.

c.   To determine if $\sigma < 1.758$, we test:

H_0: $\sigma^2 = 1.758^2$
H_a: $\sigma^2 < 1.758^2$

The test statistic is $\chi^2 = \dfrac{(n-1)s^2}{\sigma_o^2} = \dfrac{(137-1)1.5^2}{1.758^2} = 99.011$.

The rejection region requires $\alpha = .01$ in the lower tail of the χ^2 distribution with df $= n - 1 = 137 - 1 = 136$. Since there are no values in the table with df > 100, we will use MINITAB to compute the p-value of the test statistic.

Cumulative Distribution Function

```
Chi-Square with 136 DF

     x    P( X <= x )
99.011     0.0072496
```

Since the p-value is less than α (p-value $= 0.0072496 < \alpha = .01$), H_0 is rejected. There is sufficient evidence to indicate the standard deviation of the scores is less than 1.758 at $\alpha = .01$.

6.99   The smaller the p-value associated with a test of hypothesis, the stronger the support for the **alternative** hypothesis. The p-value is the probability of observing your test statistic or anything more unusual, given the null hypothesis is true. If this value is small, it would be very unusual to observe this test statistic if the null hypothesis were true. Thus, it would indicate the alternative hypothesis is true.

6.101   There is not a direct relationship between α and β. That is, if α is known, it does not mean β is known because β depends on the value of the parameter in the alternative hypothesis and the sample size. However, as α decreases, β increases for a fixed value of the parameter and a fixed sample size.

6.103   a. H_0: $\mu = 80$
           H_a: $\mu < 80$

The test statistic is $t = \dfrac{\bar{x} - \mu_0}{s/\sqrt{n}} = \dfrac{72.6 - 80}{\sqrt{19.4}/\sqrt{20}} = -7.51$

The rejection region requires $\alpha = .05$ in the lower tail of the t-distribution with df $= n - 1 = 20 - 1 = 19$. From Table VI, Appendix B, $t_{.05} = 1.729$. The rejection region is $t < -1.729$.

Since the observed value of the test statistic falls in the rejection region ($-7.51 < -1.729$), H_0 is rejected. There is sufficient evidence to indicate that the mean is less than 80 at $\alpha = .05$.

     b. H_0: $\mu = 80$
           H_a: $\mu \ne 80$

The test statistic is $t = \dfrac{\bar{x} - \mu_0}{s/\sqrt{n}} = \dfrac{72.6 - 80}{\sqrt{19.4}/\sqrt{20}} = -7.51$

The rejection region requires $\alpha/2 = .01/2 = .005$ in each tail of the t-distribution with df $= n - 1 = 20 - 1 = 19$. From Table VI, Appendix B, $t_{.005} = 2.861$. The rejection region is $t < -2.861$ or $t > 2.861$.

Since the observed value of the test statistic falls in the rejection region ($-7.51 < -2.861$), H_0 is rejected. There is sufficient evidence to indicate that the mean is different from 80 at $\alpha = .01$.

6.105 a. H_0: $p = .35$
H_a: $p < .35$

The test statistic is $z = \dfrac{\hat{p} - p_0}{\sqrt{\dfrac{p_0 q_0}{n}}} = \dfrac{.29 - .35}{\sqrt{\dfrac{.35(.65)}{200}}} = -1.78$

The rejection region requires $\alpha = .05$ in the lower tail of the z-distribution. From Table IV, Appendix B, $z_{.05} = 1.645$. The rejection region is $z < -1.645$.

Once the observed value of the test statistic falls in the rejection region ($z = -1.78 < -1.645$), H_0 is rejected. There is sufficient evidence to indicate $p < .35$ at $\alpha = .05$.

b. H_0: $p = .35$
H_a: $p \neq .35$

The test statistic is $z = -1.78$ (from **a**).

The rejection region requires $\alpha/2 = .05/2 = .025$ in each tail of the z-distribution. From Table IV, Appendix B, $t_{.025} = 1.96$. The rejection region is $z < -1.96$ or $z > 1.96$.

Since the observed value of the test statistic does not fall in the rejection region ($z = -1.78 \not< -1.96$), H_0 is not rejected. There is insufficient evidence to indicate p is different from .35 at $\alpha = .05$.

6.107 a. H_0: $\sigma^2 = 30$
H_a: $\sigma^2 > 30$

The test statistic is $\chi^2 = \dfrac{(n-1)s^2}{\sigma_0^2} = \dfrac{(41-1)(6.9)^2}{30} = 63.48$

The rejection region requires $\alpha = .05$ in the upper tail of the χ^2 distribution with df $= n - 1 = 40$. From Table VII, Appendix B, $\chi^2_{.05} = 55.7585$. The rejection region is $\chi^2 > 55.7585$.

Since the observed value of the test statistic falls in the rejection region ($\chi^2 = 63.48 > 55.7585$), H_0 is rejected. There is sufficient evidence to indicate the variance is larger than 30 at $\alpha = .05$.

b. H_0: $\sigma^2 = 30$
H_a: $\sigma^2 \neq 30$

The test statistic is $\chi^2 = 63.48$ (from part a).

The rejection region requires $\alpha/2 = .05/2 = .025$ in each tail of the χ^2 distribution with df $= n - 1 = 40$. From Table VII, Appendix B, $\chi^2_{.025} = 59.3417$ and $\chi^2_{.975} = 24.4331$. The rejection region is $\chi^2 < 24.4331$ or $\chi^2 > 59.3417$.

Since the observed value of the test statistic falls in the rejection region ($\chi^2 = 63.48 > 59.3417$), H_0 is rejected. There is sufficient evidence to indicate the variance is not 30 at $\alpha = .05$.

6.109   a. $\hat{p} = 15/60 = .25$

To determine if the proportion of shoppers who fail in their attempts to purchase merchandise online is less than .39, we test:

H_0: $p = .39$
H_a: $p < .39$

The test statistic is $z = \dfrac{\hat{p} - p_0}{\sqrt{\dfrac{p_0 q_0}{n}}} = \dfrac{.25 - .39}{\sqrt{\dfrac{.39(.61)}{60}}} = -2.22$

The rejection region requires $\alpha = .01$ in the lower tail of the z-distribution. From Table IV, Appendix B, $z_{.05} = 2.33$. The rejection region is $z < -2.33$.

Since the observed value of the test statistic does not fall in the rejection region ($z = -2.22 \not< -2.33$), H_0 is not rejected. There is insufficient evidence to indicate the proportion of shoppers who fail in their attempts to purchase merchandise online is less than .39 at $\alpha = .01$.

b.   The observed significance level of the test is p-value $= P(z \le -2.22) = .5 - .4868 = .0132$. Since the p-value is greater than $\alpha = .01$, H_0 is not rejected.

6.111   a.   To determine if the average high technology stock is riskier than the market as a whole, we test:

H_0: $\mu = 1$
H_a: $\mu > 1$

b.   The test statistic is $t = \dfrac{\bar{x} - \mu_0}{s/\sqrt{n}}$

The rejection region requires $\alpha = .10$ in the upper tail of the t-distribution with df $= n - 1 = 15 - 1 = 14$. From Table VI, Appendix B, $t_{.10} = 1.345$. The rejection region is $t > 1.345$.

c.   We must assume the population of beta coefficients of technology stocks is normally distributed.

d. The test statistic is $t = \dfrac{\bar{x} - \mu_0}{s/\sqrt{n}} = \dfrac{1.23 - 1}{.37/\sqrt{15}} = 2.41$

Since the observed value of the test statistic falls in the rejection region ($t = 2.41 > 1.345$), H_0 is rejected. There is sufficient evidence to indicate the mean high technology stock is riskier than the market as a whole at $\alpha = .10$.

e. From Table VI, Appendix B, with df $= n - 1 = 15 - 1 = 14$, $.01 < P(t \geq 2.41) < .025$. Thus, $.01 < p$-value $< .025$. The probability of observing this test statistic, $t = 2.41$, or anything more unusual is between .01 and .025. Since this probability is small, there is evidence to indicate the null hypothesis is false for $\alpha = .05$.

f. To determine if the variance of the stock beta values differs from .15, we test:

H_0: $\sigma^2 = .15$
H_a: $\sigma^2 \neq .15$

The test statistic is $\chi^2 = \dfrac{(n-1)s^2}{\sigma_o^2} = \dfrac{(15-1).37^2}{.15} = 12.7773$.

The rejection region requires $\alpha/2 = .05/2 = .025$ in each tail of the χ^2 distribution with df $= n - 1 = 15 - 1 = 14$. From Table VII, Appendix B, $\chi^2_{.975} = 5.62872$ and $\chi^2_{.025} = 26.1190$. The rejection region is $\chi^2 > 26.1190$ or $\chi^2 < 5.62872$.

Since the observed value of the test statistic does not fall in the rejection region ($\chi^2 = 12.7773 \not> 26.1190$ and $\chi^2 = 12.7773 \not< 5.62875$), H_0 is not rejected. There is insufficient evidence to indicate the variance of the stock beta values differs from .15 at $\alpha = .05$.

6.113 a. Let $\mu =$ mean number of offices operated by all Florida law firms. To determine if the mean is different from 5, we test:

H_0: $\mu = 5$
H_a: $\mu \neq 5$

The test statistic is $t = \dfrac{\bar{x} - \mu_0}{s/\sqrt{n}} = \dfrac{5.231 - 5}{2.847/\sqrt{26}} = 0.41$

The rejection region requires $\alpha/2 = .10/2 = .05$ in each tail of the t-distribution with df $= n - 1 = 26 - 1 = 25$. From Table VI, Appendix B, $t_{.05} = 1.708$. The rejection region is $t > 1.708$ or $t < -1.708$.

Since the observed value of the test statistic does not fall in the rejection region (t $= 0.41 \not> 1.708$), H_0 is not rejected. There is insufficient evidence to indicate the mean number of offices operated by all Florida law firms is different from 5 at $\alpha = .10$.

b. From Exercise 5.88, the 90% confidence interval is (4.277, 6.185). We are 90% confident that the true mean number of offices operated by all Florida law firms is between 4.277 and 6.185. Since the hypothesized value of the mean (5) is in the confidence interval, it is not an unusual value. It would not be rejected. Thus, the inferences in the two exercises agree.

6.115　a. The hypotheses would be:

H_0: Individual does not have the disease
H_a: Individual does have the disease

b. A Type I error would be: Conclude the individual has the disease when in fact he/she does not. This would be a false positive test.

A Type II error would be: Conclude the individual does not have the disease when in fact he/she does. This would be a false negative test.

c. If the disease is serious, either error would be grave. Arguments could be made for either error being more grave. However, I believe a Type II error would be more grave: Concluding the individual does not have the disease when he/she does. This person would not receive critical treatment, and may suffer very serious consequences. Thus, it is more important to minimize β.

6.117　a. To determine whether the true mean PTSD score of all World War II aviator POWs is less than 16, we test:

H_0: $\mu = 16$
H_a: $\mu < 16$

b. The test statistic is $z = \dfrac{\bar{x} - \mu_0}{\sigma_{\bar{x}}} = \dfrac{9 - 16}{9.32/\sqrt{33}} = -4.31$

The rejection region requires $\alpha = .10$ in the lower tail of the z-distribution. From Table IV, Appendix B, $z_{.10} = 1.28$. The rejection region is $z < -1.28$.

Since the observed value of the test statistic falls in the rejection region ($z = -4.31 < -1.28$), H_0 is rejected. There is sufficient evidence to indicate that the true mean PTSD score of all World War II aviator POWs is less than 16 at $\alpha = .10$.

The practical implications of the test are that the World War II aviator POWs have a lower level PTSD level on the average than the POWs from Vietnam.

c. The sample used in this study was a self-selected sample—only 33 of the 239 located survivors responded. Very often, self-selected respondents are not representative of the population. Here, those former POWs who are more comfortable with their lives may be more willing to respond than those who are less comfortable. Those who are less comfortable may be suffering more from PTSD than those who are more comfortable. Also, it may not be fair to compare the survivors from World War II to the survivors of Vietnam. The World War II survivors are more removed from their imprisonment than those from the Vietnam war. Also, many of the World War II POWs probably are no longer living. Again, those still alive may be the ones who are more comfortable with their lives.

6.119 a. First, check to see if n is large enough:

$$p_0 \pm 3\,\sigma_{\hat{p}} \Rightarrow p_0 \pm 3\sqrt{\frac{p_0 q_0}{n}} \Rightarrow .5 \pm 3\sqrt{\frac{.5(.5)}{250}} \Rightarrow .5 \pm .095 \Rightarrow (.405, .595)$$

Since the interval lies within the interval $(0, 1)$, the normal approximation will be adequate.

To determine if there is evidence to reject the claim that no more than half of all manufacturers are dissatisfied with their trade promotion spending, we test:

H_0: $p = .5$
H_a: $p > .5$

The test statistic is $z = \dfrac{\hat{p} - p_0}{\sqrt{\dfrac{p_0 q_0}{n}}} = \dfrac{.91 - .5}{\sqrt{\dfrac{.5(.5)}{250}}} = 12.97$

The rejection region requires $\alpha = .02$ in the upper tail of the z-distribution. From Table IV, Appendix B, $z_{.02} = 2.05$. The rejection region is $z > 2.05$.

Since the observed value of the test statistic falls in the rejection region ($z = 12.97 > 2.05$), H_0 is rejected. There is sufficient evidence to reject the claim that no more than half of all manufacturers are dissatisfied with their trade promotion spending at $\alpha = .02$.

b. The observed significance level is p-value $= P(z \geq 12.97) \approx .5 - .5 = 0$. Since this p-value is so small, H_0 will be rejected for any reasonable value of α.

c. First, we must define the rejection region in terms of .

$$\hat{p} = p_0 + z_\alpha\,\sigma_{\hat{p}} = .5 + 2.05\sqrt{\frac{.5(.5)}{250}} = .565$$

$$\beta = P(\hat{p} < .565 \mid p = .55) = P\left(z < \frac{.565 - .55}{\sqrt{\frac{.55(.45)}{250}}} \right) = P(z < .48) = .5 + .1844 = .6844$$

6.121   a.   A Type II error is concluding the percentage of shoplifters turned over to police is 50% when in fact, the percentage is higher than 50%.

   b.   First, calculate the value of $\hat{p}$ that corresponds to the border between the acceptance region and the rejection region.

   $P(\hat{p} > p_o) = P(z > z_o) = .05$.   From Table IV, Appendix B, $z_0 = 1.645$

   $\hat{p} = p_o + 1.645\sigma_{\hat{p}} = .5 + 1.645\sqrt{\dfrac{.5(.5)}{40}} = .5 + .1300 = .6300$

   $\beta = P(\hat{p} \le .6300$ when $p = .55)$

   $= P\left(z \le \dfrac{.6300 - .55}{\sqrt{\dfrac{.55(.45)}{40}}} \right) = P(z \le 1.02) = .5 + .3461 = .8461$

   c.   If n increases, the probability of a Type II error would decrease.

   First, calculate the value of $\hat{p}$ that corresponds to the border between the acceptance region and the rejection region.

   $P(\hat{p} > p_o) = P(z > z_o) = .05$.   From Table IV, Appendix B, $z_0 = 1.645$

   $\hat{p} = p_o + 1.645\sigma_{\hat{p}} = .5 + 1.645\sqrt{\dfrac{.5(.5)}{100}} = .5 + .082 = .582$

   $\beta = P(\hat{p} \le .582$ when $p = .55)$

   $= P\left(z \le \dfrac{.582 - .55}{\sqrt{\dfrac{.55(.45)}{100}}} \right) = P(z \le 0.64) = .5 + .2389 = .7389$

6.123   a.   To determine if the production process should be halted, we test:

   H_0: $\mu = 3$
   H_a: $\mu > 3$

   where μ = mean amount of PCB in the effluent.

   The test statistic is $z = \dfrac{\bar{x} - \mu_0}{\sigma_{\bar{x}}} = \dfrac{3.1 - 3}{.5/\sqrt{50}} = 1.41$

Inferences Based on a Single Sample: Tests of Hypothesis

The rejection region requires $\alpha = .01$ in the upper tail of the z-distribution. From Table IV, Appendix B, $z_{.01} = 2.33$. The rejection region is $z > 2.33$.

Since the observed value of the test statistic does not fall in the rejection region, ($z = 1.41$ $\not> 2.33$), H_0 is not rejected. There is insufficient evidence to indicate the mean amount of PCB in the effluent is more than 3 parts per million at $\alpha = .01$. Do not halt the manufacturing process.

b. As plant manager, I do not want to shut down the plant unnecessarily. Therefore, I want $\alpha = P(\text{shut down plant when } \mu = 3)$ to be small.

c. The p-value is $p = P(z \geq 1.41) = .5 - .4207 = .0793$. Since the p-value is not less than $\alpha = .01$, H_0 is not rejected.

6.125 a. No, it increases the risk of falsely rejecting H_0, i.e., closing the plant unnecessarily.

b. First, find $\bar{x}_0$ such that $P(\bar{x} > \bar{x}_0) = P(z > z_0) = .05$.

From Table IV, Appendix B, $z_0 = 1.645$

$$z = \frac{\bar{x}_0 - \mu}{\sigma / \sqrt{n}} \Rightarrow 1.645 = \frac{\bar{x}_0 - 3}{.5 / \sqrt{50}} \Rightarrow \bar{x}_0 = 3.116$$

Then, compute:

$$\beta = P(\bar{x}_0 \leq 3.116 \text{ when } \mu = 3.1) = P\left(z \leq \frac{3.116 - 3.1}{.5 / \sqrt{50}}\right) = P(z \leq .23)$$

$$= .5 + .0910 = .5910$$

Power $= 1 - \beta = 1 - .5910 = .4090$

c. The power of the test increases as α increases.

6.127 a. To determine if the product brings pain relief to headache sufferers in less than 3.5 minutes, on average, we test:

H_0: $\mu = 3.5$
H_a: $\mu < 3.5$

The test statistic is $z = \dfrac{\bar{x} - \mu_0}{\sigma_{\bar{x}}} = \dfrac{3.3 - 3.5}{1.1 / \sqrt{50}} = -1.29$

The rejection region requires $\alpha = .05$ in the lower tail of the z-distribution. From Table IV, Appendix B, $z_{.05} = 1.645$. The rejection region is $z < -1.645$.

Since the observed value of the test statistic does not fall in the rejection region ($z = -1.29 \not< -1.645$), H_0 is not rejected. There is insufficient evidence to indicate that the product brings pain relief to headache sufferers in less than 3.5 minutes, on average, at $\alpha = .05$.

b. The p-value is $p = P(z \le -1.29) = .5 - .4015 = .0985$.

c. If we are conducting a test of hypothesis where the manufacturer's claim is stated in the alternative hypothesis (H_a), then small p-values would support the manufacturer's claim. On the other hand, if we are conducting a test of hypothesis where the manufacturer's claim is stated in the null hypothesis (H_0), then large p-values would support the manufacturer's claim.

6.129 a. To determine whether the true mean rating for this instructor-related factor exceeds 4, we test:

$$H_0: \ \mu = 4$$
$$H_a: \ \mu > 4$$

The test statistic is $z = \dfrac{\overline{x} - \mu_0}{\sigma_{\overline{x}}} = \dfrac{4.7 - 4}{1.62/\sqrt{40}} = 2.73$

The rejection region requires $\alpha = .05$ in the upper tail of the z-distribution. From Table IV, Appendix B, $z_{.05} = 1.645$. The rejection region is $z > 1.645$.

Since the observed value of the test statistic falls in the rejection region ($z = 2.73 > 1.645$), H_0 is rejected. There is sufficient evidence to indicate that the true mean rating for this instructor-related factor exceeds 4 at $\alpha = .05$.

b. If the sample size is large enough, one could almost always reject H_0. Thus, we might be able to detect very small differences if the sample size is large enough. This would be statistical significance. However, even though statistical significance is found, it does not necessarily mean that there is practical significance. A statistical significance can sometimes be found between the hypothesized value of a mean and the estimated value of the mean, but, in practice, this difference would mean nothing. This would be practical significance.

c. Since the sample size is sufficiently large ($n = 40$), the Central Limit Theorem indicates that the sampling distribution of is approximately normal. Also, since the sample size is large, s is a good estimator of σ. Thus, the analysis used is appropriate.

Inferences Based on Two Samples: Confidence Intervals and Tests of Hypothesis *Chapter 7*

7.1　a.　$\mu_1 \pm 2\sigma_{\bar{x}_1} \Rightarrow \mu_1 \; 2\dfrac{\sigma_1}{\sqrt{n_1}} \Rightarrow 150 \pm 2\dfrac{\sqrt{900}}{\sqrt{100}} \Rightarrow 150 \pm 6 \Rightarrow (144, 156)$

　　　b.　$\mu_2 \pm 2\sigma_{\bar{x}_2} \Rightarrow \mu_2 \pm 2\dfrac{\sigma_2}{\sqrt{n_2}} \Rightarrow 150 \pm 2\dfrac{\sqrt{1600}}{\sqrt{100}} \Rightarrow 150 \pm 8 \Rightarrow (142, 158)$

　　　c.　$\mu_{\bar{x}_1 - \bar{x}_2} = \mu_1 - \mu_2 = 150 - 150 = 0$

　　　　　$\sigma_{\bar{x}_1 - \bar{x}_2} = \sqrt{\dfrac{\sigma_1^2}{n_1} + \dfrac{\sigma_2^2}{n_2}} = \sqrt{\dfrac{900}{100} + \dfrac{1600}{100}} = \sqrt{\dfrac{2500}{100}} = 5$

　　　d.　$(\mu_1 - \mu_2) \pm 2\sqrt{\dfrac{\sigma_1^2}{n_1} + \dfrac{\sigma_2^2}{n_2}} \Rightarrow (150 - 150) \pm 2\sqrt{\dfrac{900}{100} + \dfrac{1600}{100}} \Rightarrow 0 \pm 10 \Rightarrow (-10, 10)$

　　　e.　The variability of the difference between the sample means is greater than the variability of the individual sample means.

7.3　a.　For confidence coefficient .95, $\alpha = .05$ and $\alpha/2 = .025$. From Table IV, Appendix B, $z_{.025} = 1.96$. The confidence interval is:

$$(\bar{x}_1 - \bar{x}_2) \pm z_{.025}\sqrt{\dfrac{\sigma_1^2}{n_1} + \dfrac{\sigma_2^2}{n_2}} \Rightarrow (5{,}275 - 5{,}240) \pm 1.96\sqrt{\dfrac{150^2}{400} + \dfrac{200^2}{400}}$$

$$\Rightarrow 35 \pm 24.5 \Rightarrow (10.5, 59.5)$$

We are 95% confident that the difference between the population means is between 10.5 and 59.5.

　　　b.　The test statistic is $z = \dfrac{(\bar{x}_1 - \bar{x}_2) - (\mu_1 - \mu_2)}{\sqrt{\dfrac{\sigma_1^2}{n_1} + \dfrac{\sigma_2^2}{n_2}}} = \dfrac{(5275 - 5240) - 0}{\sqrt{\dfrac{150^2}{400} + \dfrac{200^2}{400}}} = 2.8$

The p-value of the test is $P(z \le -2.8) + P(z \ge 2.8) = 2P(z \ge 2.8) = 2(.5 - .4974)$
$$= 2(.0026) = .0052$$

Since the p-value is so small, there is evidence to reject H_0. There is evidence to indicate the two population means are different for $\alpha > .0052$.

c. The p-value would be half of the p-value in part **b**. The p-value $= P(z \geq 2.8) = .5 - .4974 = .0026$. Since the p-value is so small, there is evidence to reject H_0. There is evidence to indicate the mean for population 1 is larger than the mean for population 2 for $\alpha > .0026$.

d. The test statistic is $z = \dfrac{(\bar{x}_1 - \bar{x}_2) - (\mu_1 - \mu_2)}{\sqrt{\dfrac{\sigma_1^2}{n_1} + \dfrac{\sigma_2^2}{n_2}}} = \dfrac{(5275 - 5240) - 25}{\sqrt{\dfrac{150^2}{400} + \dfrac{200^2}{400}}} = .8$

The p-value of the test is $P(z \leq -.8) + P(z \geq .8) = 2P(z \geq .8) = 2(.5 - .2881)$
$$= 2(.2119) = .4238$$

Since the p-value is so large, there is no evidence to reject H_0. There is no evidence to indicate that the difference in the 2 population means is different from 25 for $\alpha \leq .10$.

e. We must assume that we have two independent random samples.

7.5 a. No. Both populations must be normal.

b. No. Both populations variances must be equal.

c. No. Both populations must be normal.

d. Yes.

e. No. Both populations must be normal.

7.7 Some preliminary calculations are:

$\bar{x}_1 = \dfrac{\sum x_1}{n_1} = \dfrac{11.8}{5} = 2.36$ $\quad s_1^2 = \dfrac{\sum x_1^2 - \dfrac{\left(\sum x_1\right)^2}{n_1}}{n_1 - 1} = \dfrac{30.78 - \dfrac{(11.8)^2}{5}}{5 - 1} = .733$

$\bar{x}_2 = \dfrac{\sum x_2}{n_2} = \dfrac{14.4}{4} = 3.6$ $\quad s_2^2 = \dfrac{\sum x_2^2 - \dfrac{\left(\sum x_2\right)^2}{n_2}}{n_2 - 1} = \dfrac{53.1 - \dfrac{(14.4)^2}{4}}{4 - 1} = .42$

a. $s_p^2 = \dfrac{(n_1 - 1)s_1^2 + (n_2 - 1)s_2^2}{n_1 + n_2 - 2} = \dfrac{(5-1).773 + (4-1).42}{5+4-2} = \dfrac{4.192}{7} = .5989$

b. H_0: $\mu_1 - \mu_2 = 0$
H_a: $\mu_1 - \mu_2 < 0$

The test statistic is $t = \dfrac{(\bar{x}_1 - \bar{x}_2) - D_0}{\sqrt{s_p^2 \left(\dfrac{1}{n_1} + \dfrac{1}{n_2}\right)}} = \dfrac{(2.36 - 3.6) - 0}{\sqrt{.5989\left(\dfrac{1}{5} + \dfrac{1}{4}\right)}} = \dfrac{-1.24}{.5191} = -2.39$

The rejection region *requires* $\alpha = .10$ in the lower tail of the t-distribution with df $=$ $n_1 + n_2 - 2 = 5 + 4 - 2 = 7$. From Table VI, Appendix B, $t_{.10} = 1.415$. The rejection region is $t < -1.415$.

Since the test statistic falls in the rejection region ($t = -2.39 < -1.415$), H_0 is rejected. There is sufficient evidence to indicate that $\mu_2 > \mu_1$ at $\alpha = .10$.

c. A small sample confidence interval is needed because $n_1 = 5 < 30$ and $n_2 = 4 < 30$.

For confidence coefficient .90, $\alpha = .10$ and $\alpha/2 = .05$. From Table VI, Appendix B, with df $= n_1 + n_2 - 2 = 5 + 4 - 2 = 7$, $t_{.05} = 1.895$. The 90% confidence interval for $(\mu_1 - \mu_2)$ is:

$$(\bar{x}_1 - x_2) \pm t_{.05}\sqrt{s_p^2\left(\dfrac{1}{n_1} + \dfrac{1}{n_2}\right)} \Rightarrow (2.36 - 3.6) \pm 1.895\sqrt{.5989\left(\dfrac{1}{5} + \dfrac{1}{4}\right)}$$

$$\Rightarrow -1.24 \pm .98 \Rightarrow (-2.22, -0.26)$$

d. The confidence interval in part **c** provides more information about $(\mu_1 - \mu_2)$ than the test of hypothesis in part **b**. The test in part **b** only tells us that μ_2 is greater than μ_1. However, the confidence interval estimates what the difference is between μ_1 and μ_2.

7.9   a. The p-value $= .1150$. Since the p-value is not small, there is no evidence to reject H_0 for $\alpha \le .10$. There is insufficient evidence to indicate the two population means differ for $\alpha \le .10$.

b. If the alternative hypothesis had been one-tailed, the p-value would be half of the value for the two-tailed test. Here, p-value $= .1150/2 = .0575$.

There is no evidence to reject H_0 for $\alpha = .05$. There is insufficient evidence to indicate the mean for population 1 is less than the mean for population 2 at $\alpha = .05$.

There is evidence to reject H_0 for $\alpha > .0575$. There is sufficient evidence to indicate the mean for population 1 is less than the mean for population 2 at $\alpha > .0575$.

7.11   a. $s_p^2 = \dfrac{(n_1 - 1)s_1^2 + (n_2 - 1)s_2^2}{n_1 + n_2 - 2} = \dfrac{(17-1)3.4^2 + (12-1)4.8^2}{17 + 12 - 2} = 16.237$

H_0: $(\mu_1 - \mu_2) = 0$
H_a: $(\mu_1 - \mu_2) \ne 0$

The test statistic is $t = \dfrac{(\bar{x}_1 - \bar{x}_2) - 0}{\sqrt{s_p^2\left(\dfrac{1}{n_1} + \dfrac{1}{n_2}\right)}} = \dfrac{(5.4 - 7.9) - 0}{\sqrt{16.237\left(\dfrac{1}{17} + \dfrac{1}{12}\right)}} = -1.646$

Since no α was given, we will use $\alpha = .05$. The rejection region requires $\alpha/2 = .05/2 = .025$ in each tail of the t-distribution with df $= n_1 + n_2 - 2 = 17 + 12 - 2 = 27$. From Table VI, Appendix B, $t_{.025} = 2.052$. The rejection region is $t < -2.052$ or $t > 2.052$.

Since the observed value of the test statistic does not fall in the rejection region ($t = -1.646 \not< -2.052$), H_0 is not rejected. There is insufficient evidence to indicate $\mu_1 - \mu_2$ is different from 0 at $\alpha = .05$.

b.   For confidence coefficient .95, $\alpha = .05$ and $\alpha/2 = .025$. From Table VI, Appendix B, with df $= n_1 + n_2 - 2 = 17 + 12 - 2 = 27$, $t_{.025} = 2.052$. The confidence interval is:

$$(\bar{x}_1 - \bar{x}_2) \pm t_{.025}\sqrt{s_p^2\left(\frac{1}{n_1} + \frac{1}{n_2}\right)} \text{ where } t \text{ has 27 df}$$

$$\Rightarrow (5.4 - 7.9) - 2.052\sqrt{16.237\left(\frac{1}{17} + \frac{1}{12}\right)} \Rightarrow -2.50 \pm 3.12 \Rightarrow (-5.62, 0.62)$$

7.13   a.   Let μ_1 = mean number of items recalled by those in the video only group and μ_2 = mean number of items recalled by those in the audio and video group. To determine if the mean number of items recalled by the two groups is the same, we test:

$H_o: \mu_1 - \mu_2 = 0$
$H_a: \mu_1 - \mu_2 \neq 0$

b. $s_p^2 = \dfrac{(n_1 - 1)s_1^2 + (n_2 - 1)s_2^2}{n_1 + n_2 - 2} = \dfrac{(20 - 1)1.98^2 + (20 - 1)2.13^2}{20 + 20 - 2} = 4.22865$

The test statistic is $t = \dfrac{(\bar{x}_1 - \bar{x}_2) - D_o}{\sqrt{s_p^2\left(\frac{1}{n_1} + \frac{1}{n_2}\right)}} = \dfrac{(3.70 - 3.30) - 0}{\sqrt{4.22865\left(\frac{1}{20} + \frac{1}{20}\right)}} = \dfrac{0.4}{.65028} = 0.62$

c.   The rejection region requires $\alpha/2 = .10/2 = .05$ in each tail of the t-distribution with df $= n_1 + n_2 - 2 = 20 + 20 - 2 = 38$. From Table VI, Appendix B, $t_{.05} \approx 1.684$. The rejection region is $t < -1.684$ or $t > 1.684$.

d.   Since the observed value of the test statistic does not fall in the rejection region ($t = 0.62 \not> 1.684$), H_o is not rejected. There is insufficient evidence to indicate a difference in the mean number of items recalled by the two groups at $\alpha = .10$.

e.   The p-value is $p = .542$. This is the probability of observing our test statistic or anything more unusual if H_0 is true. Since the p-value is not less than $\alpha = .10$, there is no evidence to reject H_0. There is insufficient evidence to indicate a difference in the mean number of items recalled by the two groups at $\alpha = .10$.

f. We must assume:

    1.   Both populations are normal
    2.   Random and independent samples
    3. $\sigma_1^2 = \sigma_2^2$

7.15   a.   Yes. The sample mean of the virtual-reality group is 10.67 points higher than the sample mean of the simple user interface group.

    b.   Let μ_1 = mean improvement score for the virtual-reality group and μ_2 = mean improvement score for the simple user interface group.

To determine if the mean improvement scores for the virtual-reality group is higher than that for the simple user interface group, we test:

$H_0:\ \mu_1 - \mu_2 = 0$
$H_a:\ \mu_1 - \mu_2 > 0$

The test statistic is $z = \dfrac{(\bar{x}_1 - \bar{x}_2) - D_o}{\sqrt{\left(\dfrac{\sigma_1^2}{n_1} + \dfrac{\sigma_2^2}{n_2}\right)}} = \dfrac{(43.15 - 32.48) - 0}{\sqrt{\left(\dfrac{12.57^2}{45} + \dfrac{9.26^2}{45}\right)}} = \dfrac{10.67}{2.3274} = 4.58$

The rejection region requires $\alpha = .05$ in the upper tail of the z-distribution. From Table IV, Appendix B, $z_{.05} = 1.645$. The rejection region is $z > 1.645$.

Since the observed value of the test statistic falls in the rejection region ($z = 4.58 > 1.645$), H_0 is rejected. There is sufficient evidence to indicate the mean improvement scores for the virtual-reality group is higher than that for the simple user interface group $\alpha = .05$.

7.17   a.   The descriptive statistics are:

Descriptive Statistics: Text-line, Witness-line, Intersection

Variable	N	Mean	Median	TrMean	StDev	SE Mean
Text-lin	3	0.3830	0.3740	0.3830	0.0531	0.0306
Witness-	6	0.3042	0.2955	0.3042	0.1015	0.0415
Intersec	5	0.3290	0.3190	0.3290	0.0443	0.0198

Variable	Minimum	Maximum	Q1	Q3
Text-lin	0.3350	0.4400	0.3350	0.4400
Witness-	0.1880	0.4390	0.2045	0.4075
Intersec	0.2850	0.3930	0.2900	0.3730

Let μ_1 = mean zinc measurement for the text-line, μ_2 = mean zinc measurement for the witness-line, and μ_3 = mean zinc measurement for the intersection.

$$s_p^2 = \frac{(n_1 - 1)s_1^2 + (n_3 - 1)s_3^2}{n_1 + n_3 - 2} = \frac{(3 - 1).0531^2 + (5 - 1).0443^2}{3 + 5 - 2} = .00225$$

For $\alpha = .05$, $\alpha/2 = .05/2 = .025$. Using Table VI, Appendix B, with df $= n_1 + n_2 - 2 = 3 + 5 - 2 = 6$, $t_{.025} = 2.447$. The 95% confidence interval is:

$$(\bar{x}_1 - \bar{x}_3) \pm t_{\alpha/2} \sqrt{s_p^2 \left(\frac{1}{n_1} + \frac{1}{n_3} \right)} \Rightarrow (.3830 - .3290) \pm 2.447 \sqrt{.00225 \left(\frac{1}{3} + \frac{1}{5} \right)}$$

$$\Rightarrow 0.0540 \pm .0848 \Rightarrow (-0.0308, \ 0.1388)$$

We are 95% confident that the difference in mean zinc level between text-line and intersection is between −0.0308 and 0.1388.

To determine if there is a difference in the mean zinc measurement between text-line and intersection, we test:

H_0: $\mu_1 = \mu_3$
H_a: $\mu_1 \neq \mu_3$

The test statistic is $t = \dfrac{(\bar{x}_1 - \bar{x}_3) - D_o}{\sqrt{s_p^2 \left(\dfrac{1}{n_1} + \dfrac{1}{n_3} \right)}} = \dfrac{(.3830 - .3290) - 0}{\sqrt{.00225 \left(\dfrac{1}{3} + \dfrac{1}{5} \right)}} = 1.56$

The rejection region requires $\alpha/2 = .05/2 = .025$ in each tail of the t-distribution with df $= n_1 + n_2 - 2 = 3 + 5 - 2 = 6$. From Table VI, Appendix B, $t_{.025} = 2.447$. The rejection region is $t < -2.447$ or $t > 2.447$.

Since the observed value of the test statistic does not fall in the rejection region ($t = 1.56 \not> 2.365$), H_0 is not rejected. There is insufficient evidence to indicate a difference in the mean zinc measurement between text-line and intersection at $\alpha = .05$.

b. $s_p^2 = \dfrac{(n_2 - 1)s_2^2 + (n_3 - 1)s_3^2}{n_2 + n_3 - 2} = \dfrac{(6-1).1015^2 + (5-1).0443^2}{6 + 5 - 2} = .006596$

For $\alpha = .05$, $\alpha/2 = .05/2 = .025$. Using Table VI, Appendix B, with df $= n_1 + n_2 - 2 = 6 + 5 - 2 = 9$, $t_{.025} = 2.262$. The 95% confidence interval is:

$$(\bar{x}_2 - \bar{x}_3) \pm t_{\alpha/2} \sqrt{s_p^2 \left(\frac{1}{n_2} + \frac{1}{n_3} \right)} \Rightarrow (.3042 - .3290) \pm 2.262 \sqrt{.006596 \left(\frac{1}{6} + \frac{1}{5} \right)}$$

$$\Rightarrow -.0248 \pm .1112 \Rightarrow (-.1361, \ .0864)$$

We are 95% confident that the difference in mean zinc level between witness-line and intersection is between −0.1361 and 0.0864.

To determine if the difference in mean zinc measurement between the witness-line and the intersection, we test:

H_0: $\mu_2 = \mu_3$
H_a: $\mu_2 \neq \mu_3$

The test statistic is $t = \dfrac{(\bar{x}_2 - \bar{x}_3) - D_o}{\sqrt{s_p^2 \left(\dfrac{1}{n_2} + \dfrac{1}{n_3}\right)}} = \dfrac{(.3042 - .3290) - 0}{\sqrt{.006596 \left(\dfrac{1}{6} + \dfrac{1}{5}\right)}} = -.50$

The rejection region requires $\alpha/2 = .05/2 = .025$ in each tail of the t-distribution. From Table VI, Appendix B, with df $= n_1 + n_2 - 2 = 6 + 5 - 2 = 9$, $t_{.025} = 2.262$. The rejection region is $t < -2.262$ or $t > 2.262$.

Since the observed value of the test statistic does not fall in the rejection region $(t = -.50 \not< -2.262)$, H_0 is not rejected. There is insufficient evidence to indicate a difference in mean zinc measurement between witness-line and intersection at $\alpha = .05$.

c. If we order the sample means, the largest is Text-line, the next largest is intersection and the smallest is witness-line. In parts **a** and **b**, we found that text-line is not different from the intersection and that the witness-line is not different from the intersection. However, we cannot make any decisions about the difference between the witness-line and the text-line.

d. In order for the above inferences to be valid, we must assume:

1. The three samples are randomly selected in an independent manner from the three target populations.

2. All three sampled populations have distributions that are approximately normal.

3. All three population variances are equal (i.e. $\sigma_1^2 = \sigma_2^2 = \sigma_3^2$)

7.19 a. Let $\mu_1 =$ mean ingratiatory score for managers and $\mu_2 =$ mean ingratiatory score for clerical personnel. To determine if there is a difference in ingratiatory behavior between managers and clerical personnel, we test:

H_0: $\mu_1 = \mu_2$
H_a: $\mu_1 \neq \mu_2$

b. The test statistic is $z = \dfrac{(\bar{x}_1 - \bar{x}_2) - D_0}{\sqrt{\dfrac{s_1^2}{n_1} + \dfrac{s_2^2}{n_2}}} = \dfrac{(2.41 - 1.90) - 0}{\sqrt{\dfrac{(.74)^2}{288} + \dfrac{(.59)^2}{110}}} = 7.17$

The rejection region requires $\alpha/2 = .05/2 = .025$ in each tail of the z-distribution. From Table IV, Appendix B, $z_{.025} = 1.96$. The rejection region is $z < -1.96$ or $z > 1.96$.

Since the observed value of the test statistic falls in the rejection region ($z = 7.17 > 1.96$), H_0 is rejected. There is sufficient evidence to indicate a difference in ingratiatory behavior between managers and clerical personnel at $\alpha = .05$.

c. For confidence coefficient .95, $\alpha = .05$ and $\alpha/2 = .05/2 = .025$. From Table IV, Appendix B, $z_{.025} = 1.96$. The 95% confidence interval is:

$$(\bar{x}_1 - \bar{x}_2) \pm z_{.025}\sqrt{\frac{s_1^2}{n_1} + \frac{s_2^2}{n_2}} \Rightarrow (2.41 - 1.90) \pm 1.96\sqrt{\frac{.74^2}{288} + \frac{.59^2}{110}}$$

$$\Rightarrow .51 \pm .14 \Rightarrow (.37, .65)$$

We are 95% confident that the difference in mean ingratiatory scores between managers and clerical personnel is between .37 and .65. Since this interval does not contain 0, it is consistent with the test of hypothesis which rejected the hypothesis that there was no difference in mean scores for the two groups.

7.21 a. Using MINITAB, the descriptive statistics are:

Descriptive Statistics: Purchasers, Nonpurchasers

Variable	N	Mean	Median	TrMean	StDev	SE Mean
Purchase	20	39.80	38.00	39.67	10.04	2.24
Nonpurch	20	47.20	52.00	47.56	13.62	3.05

Variable	Minimum	Maximum	Q1	Q3
Purchase	23.00	59.00	32.25	48.75
Nonpurch	22.00	66.00	33.50	58.75

$$s_p^2 = \frac{(n_1-1)s_1^2 + (n_2-1)s_2^2}{n_1 + n_2 - 2} = \frac{(20-1)10.04^2 + (20-1)13.62^2}{20 + 20 - 2} = 143.153$$

Let μ_1 = mean age of nonpurchasers and μ_2 = mean age of purchasers.

To determine if there is a difference in the mean age of purchasers and nonpurchasers, we test:

H_0: $\mu_1 - \mu_2 = 0$
H_a: $\mu_1 - \mu_2 \neq 0$

The test statistic is $t = \dfrac{(\bar{x}_1 - \bar{x}_2) - 0}{\sqrt{s_p^2\left(\dfrac{1}{n_1} + \dfrac{1}{n_2}\right)}} = \dfrac{(39.80 - 47.20) - 0}{\sqrt{143.153\left(\dfrac{1}{20} + \dfrac{1}{20}\right)}} = -1.96$

The rejection region requires $\alpha/2 = .10/2 = .05$ in each tail of the t-distribution with df = $n_1 + n_2 - 2 = 20 + 20 - 2 = 38$. From Table VI, Appendix B, $t_{.05} \approx 1.684$. The rejection region is $t < -1.684$ or t > 1.684.

Since the observed value of the test statistic falls in the rejection region ($t = -1.96 < -1.684$), H_0 is rejected. There is sufficient evidence to indicate the mean age of purchasers and nonpurchasers differ at $\alpha = .10$.

b.   The necessary assumptions are:

1.   Both sampled populations are approximately normal.
2.   The population variances are equal.
3.   The samples are randomly and independently sampled.

c.   The p-value is $P(z \le -1.96) + P(z \ge 1.96) = (.5 - .4750) + (.5 - .4750) = .05$. The probability of observing a test statistic of this value or more unusual if H_0 is true is .05. Since this value is less than $\alpha = .10$, H_0 is rejected. There is sufficient evidence to indicate there is a difference in the mean age of purchasers and nonpurchasers.

d.   For confidence coefficient .90, $\alpha = 1 - .90 = .10$ and $\alpha/2 = .10/2 = .05$. From Table VI, Appendix B, with df $= 38$, $t_{.05} \approx 1.684$. The confidence interval is:

$$(\bar{x}_2 - \bar{x}_1) \pm t_{.05}\sqrt{s_p^2\left(\frac{1}{n_1} + \frac{1}{n_2}\right)} \Rightarrow (39.8 - 47.2) \pm 1.684\sqrt{143.1684\left(\frac{1}{20} + \frac{1}{20}\right)}$$

$$\Rightarrow -7.4 \pm 6.382 \Rightarrow (-13.772, -1.028)$$

We are 90% confident that the difference in mean ages between purchasers and nonpurchasers is between -13.772 and -1.028.

7.23   a.   Let μ_1 = the mean heat rates of traditional augmented gas turbines and μ_2 = the mean heat rates of aeroderivative augmented gas turbines.

Some preliminary calculations are:

$$s_p^2 = \frac{(n_1 - 1)s_1^2 + (n_2 - 1)s_2^2}{n_1 + n_2 - 2} = \frac{(39 - 1)1279^2 + (7 - 1)2652^2}{39 + 7 - 2} = 2,371,831.409$$

To determine if there is a difference in the mean heat rates for traditional augmented gas turbines and the mean heat rates of aeroderivative augmented gas turbines, we test:

H_0: $\mu_1 - \mu_2 = 0$
H_a: $\mu_1 - \mu_2 \neq 0$

The test statistic is

$$t = \frac{(\bar{x}_1 - \bar{x}_2) - D_o}{\sqrt{s_p^2\left(\frac{1}{n_1} + \frac{1}{n_2}\right)}} = \frac{(11,544 - 12,312) - 0}{\sqrt{2,371,831.409\left(\frac{1}{39} + \frac{1}{7}\right)}} = \frac{-768}{632.1782} = -1.21$$

The rejection region requires $\alpha/2 = .05/2 = .025$ in each tail of the t-distribution with df $= n_1 + n_2 - 2 = 39 + 7 - 2 = 44$. From Table VI, Appendix B, $t_{.025} \approx 2.021$. The rejection region is $t < -2.021$ or $t > 2.021$.

Since the observed value of the test statistic does not fall in the rejection region ($t = -1.20 \nless -2.021$), H_0 is not rejected. There is insufficient evidence to indicate that there is a difference in the mean heat rates for traditional augmented gas turbines and the mean heat rates of aeroderivative augmented gas turbines at $\alpha = .05$.

b. Let $\mu_3 =$ the mean heat rates of advanced augmented gas turbines and $\mu_2 =$ the mean heat rates of aeroderivative augmented gas turbines.

Some preliminary calculations are:

$$s_p^2 = \frac{(n_3 - 1)s_3^2 + (n_2 - 1)s_2^2}{n_3 + n_2 - 2} = \frac{(21-1)639^2 + (7-1)2652^2}{21 + 7 - 2} = 1{,}937{,}117.077$$

To determine if there is a difference in the mean heat rates for traditional augmented gas turbines and the mean heat rates of aeroderivative augmented gas turbines, we test:

$H_0: \mu_3 - \mu_2 = 0$
$H_a: \mu_3 - \mu_2 \neq 0$

The test statistic is

$$t = \frac{(\bar{x}_3 - \bar{x}_2) - D_o}{\sqrt{s_p^2\left(\dfrac{1}{n_3} + \dfrac{1}{n_2}\right)}} = \frac{(9{,}764 - 12{,}312) - 0}{\sqrt{1{,}937{,}117.077\left(\dfrac{1}{21} + \dfrac{1}{7}\right)}} = \frac{-2{,}548}{607.4329} = -4.19$$

The rejection region requires $\alpha/2 = .05/2 = .025$ in each tail of the t-distribution with df $= n_1 + n_2 - 2 = 21 + 7 - 2 = 26$. From Table VI, Appendix B, $t_{.025} \approx 2.056$. The rejection region is $t < -2.056$ or $t > 2.056$.

Since the observed value of the test statistic falls in the rejection region ($t = -4.19 < -2.021$), H_0 is rejected. There is sufficient evidence to indicate that there is a difference in the mean heat rates for advanced augmented gas turbines and the mean heat rates of aeroderivative augmented gas turbines at $\alpha = .05$.

7.25 a. The rejection region requires $\alpha = .05$ in the upper tail of the t-distribution with df $= n_d - 1 = 12 - 1 = 11$. From Table VI, Appendix B, $t_{.05} = 1.796$. The rejection region is $t > 1.796$.

b. From Table VI, with df $= n_d - 1 = 24 - 1 = 23$, $t_{.10} = 1.319$. The rejection region is $t > 1.319$.

c. From Table VI, with df $= n_d - 1 = 4 - 1 = 3$, $t_{.025} = 3.182$. The rejection region is $t > 3.182$.

d. From Table VI, with df $= n_d - 1 = 8 - 1 = 7$, $t_{.01} = 2.998$. The rejection region is $t > 2.998$.

7.27 Let μ_1 = mean of population 1 and μ_2 = mean of population 2.

a. H_0: $\mu_d = 0$
H_a: $\mu_d < 0$ where $\mu_d = \mu_1 - \mu_2$

b. Some preliminary calculations are:

Pair	Population 1	Population 2	Difference, d
1	19	24	−5
2	25	27	−2
3	31	36	−5
4	52	53	−1
5	49	55	−6
6	34	34	0
7	59	66	−7
8	47	51	−4
9	17	20	−3
10	51	55	−4

$$\bar{d} = \frac{\sum_{i=1}^{n_d} d_i}{n_d} = \frac{-37}{10} = -3.7 \qquad s_d^2 = \frac{\sum_{i=1}^{n_d} d_i^2 - \frac{\left(\sum_{i=1}^{n_d} d_i\right)^2}{n_d}}{n_d - 1} = \frac{181 - \frac{(-37)^2}{10}}{10 - 1} = 4.9$$

The test statistic is $t = \dfrac{\bar{d}}{s_d / \sqrt{n_d}} = \dfrac{-3.7}{\sqrt{4.9}\Big/\sqrt{10}} = -5.29$

The rejection region requires $\alpha = .10$ in the lower tail of the t-distribution with df $= n_d - 1 = 10 - 1 = 9$. From Table VI, Appendix B, $t_{.10} = 1.383$. The rejection region is $t < -1.383$.

Since the observed value of the test statistic falls in the rejection region ($t = -5.29 < -1.383$), H_0 is rejected. There is sufficient evidence to indicate the mean of population 1 is less than the mean for population 2 at $\alpha = .10$.

c. For confidence coefficient .90, $\alpha = .10$ and $\alpha/2 = .10/2 = .05$. From Table VI, Appendix B, with df $= n_d - 1 = 10 - 1 = 9$, $t_{.05} = 1.833$. The 90% confidence interval is:

$$\bar{d} \pm t_{\alpha/2} \frac{s_d}{\sqrt{n_d}} \Rightarrow -3.7 \pm 1.833 \frac{\sqrt{4.9}}{\sqrt{10}} \Rightarrow -3.7 \pm 1.2831 \Rightarrow (-4.9831, \; -2.4169)$$

We are 90% confident that the difference in the two population means is between -4.9831 and -2.4169.

d. We must assume that the population of differences is normal, and the sample of differences is randomly selected.

7.29 a. Some preliminary calculations:

$$\bar{d} = \frac{\sum_{i=1}^{n_d} d_i}{n_d} = \frac{468}{40} = 11.7$$

$$s_d^2 = \frac{\sum_{i=1}^{n_d} d_i^2 - \frac{\left(\sum_{i=1}^{n_d} d_i\right)^2}{n_d}}{n_d - 1} = \frac{6,880 - \frac{468^2}{40}}{40 - 1} = 36.0103$$

To determine if $(\mu_1 - \mu_2) = \mu_d$ is different from 10, we test:

$H_0: \mu_d = 10$
$H_a: \mu_d \neq 10$

The test statistic is $z = \dfrac{\bar{d} - D_0}{\dfrac{s_d}{\sqrt{n_d}}} = \dfrac{11.7 - 10}{\dfrac{\sqrt{36.0103}}{\sqrt{40}}} = 1.79$

The rejection region requires $\alpha/2 = .05/2 = .025$ in each tail of the z-distribution. From Table IV, Appendix B, $z_{.025} = 1.96$. The rejection region is $z < -1.96$ or $z > 1.96$.

Since the observed value of the test statistic does not fall in the rejection region ($z = 1.79$ $\not>$ 1.96), H_0 is not rejected. There is insufficient evidence to indicate $(\mu_1 - \mu_2) = \mu_d$ is different from 10 at $\alpha = .05$.

b. The p-value is $p = P(z \leq -1.79) + P(z \geq 1.79) = (.5 - .4633) + (.5 - .4633) = .0367 + .0367 = .0734$. The probability of observing our test statistic or anything more unusual if H_0 is true is .0734. Since this p-value is not small, there is no evidence to indicate $(\mu_1 - \mu_2) = \mu_d$ is different from 10 at $\alpha = .05$.

c.	No, we do not need to assume that the population of differences is normally distributed. Because our sample size is 40, the Central Limit Theorem applies.

7.31	a.	The data should be analyzed using a paired-difference analysis because that is how the data were collected. Reaction times were collected twice from each subject, once under the random condition and once under the static condition. Since the two sets of data are not independent, they cannot be analyzed using independent samples analyses.

b.	Let μ_1 = mean reaction time under the random condition and μ_2 = mean reaction time under the static condition. Let $\mu_d = \mu_1 - \mu_2$. To determine if there is a difference in mean reaction time between the two conditions, we test:

$H_0: \ \mu_d = 0$
$H_a: \ \mu_d \neq 0$

c.	The test statistic is $t = 1.52$ with a p-value of .15. Since the p-value is not small, there is no evidence to reject H_0 for any reasonable value of α. There is insufficient evidence to indicate a difference in the mean reaction times between the two conditions. This supports the researchers' claim that visual search has no memory.

7.33	Some preliminary calculations are:

Circuit	Standard Method	Huffman-coding Method	Difference
1	.80	.78	.02
2	.80	.80	.00
3	.83	.86	-.03
4	.53	.53	.00
5	.50	.51	-.01
6	.96	.68	.28
7	.99	.82	.17
8	.98	.72	.26
9	.81	.45	.36
10	.95	.79	.16
11	.99	.77	.22

$$\bar{d} = \frac{\sum_{1}^{n_d} d_i}{n_d} = \frac{1.43}{11} = 0.13$$

$$s_d^2 = \frac{\sum_{1}^{n_d} d_i^2 - \frac{\left(\sum_{1}^{n_d} d_i\right)^2}{n_d}}{n_d - 1} = \frac{0.3799 - \frac{(1.43)^2}{11}}{11 - 1} = 0.0194$$

$$s_d = \sqrt{s_d^2} = \sqrt{0.0194} = 0.1393$$

For confidence coefficient .95, $\alpha = .05$ and $\alpha/2 = .05/2 = .025$. From Table VI, Appendix B, with df $= n_d - 1 = 11 - 1 = 10$, $t_{.025} = 2.228$. The 95% confidence interval is:

$$\bar{d} \pm t_{.025}\frac{s_d}{\sqrt{n}} \Rightarrow .13 \pm 2.228\frac{.1393}{\sqrt{11}} \Rightarrow .13 \pm .094 \Rightarrow (0.036, \quad 0.224)$$

We are 95% confident that the true difference in mean compression ratio between the standard method and the Huffman-based coding method is between 0.036 and 0.224. Since 0 is not contained in the interval, we can conclude there is a difference in mean compression ratios between the two methods. Since the values of the confidence interval are positive, we can conclude that the mean compression ratio for the Huffman-based method is smaller than the standard method.

7.35   Some preliminary calculations are:

Operator	Difference (Before - After)
1	5
2	3
3	9
4	7
5	2
6	-2
7	-1
8	11
9	0
10	5

$$\bar{d} = \frac{\sum d}{n_d} = \frac{39}{10} = 3.9$$

$$s_d^2 = \frac{\sum d^2 - \frac{\left(\sum d\right)^2}{n_E}}{n_d - 1} = \frac{319 - \frac{39^2}{10}}{10 - 1} = 18.5444$$

$$s_d = \sqrt{18.5444} = 4.3063$$

a.   To determine if the new napping policy reduced the mean number of customer complaints, we test:

H_0: $\mu_d = 0$
H_a: $\mu_d > 0$

The test statistic is $t = \dfrac{\bar{d} - 0}{\dfrac{s_d}{\sqrt{n_d}}} = \dfrac{3.9 - 0}{\dfrac{4.3063}{\sqrt{10}}} = 2.864$

The rejection region requires $\alpha = .05$ in the upper tail of the t-distribution with df $= n_d - 1$ $= 10 - 1 = 9$. From Table VI, Appendix B, $t_{.05} = 1.833$. The rejection region is $t > 1.833$.

Since the observed value of the test statistic falls in the rejection region ($t = 2.864 >$ 1.833), H_0 is rejected. There is sufficient evidence to indicate the new napping policy reduced the mean number of customer complaints at $\alpha = .05$.

b.   In order for the above test to be valid, we must assume that

1. The population of differences is normal
2. The differences are randomly selected

7.37   a.   Let μ_d = mean difference in pupil dilation between pattern 1 and pattern 2.

To determine if the pupil dilation differs for the two patterns, we test:

H_0: $\mu_d = 0$
H_a: $\mu_d \neq 0$

b.   Using MINITAB, the descriptive statistics are:

Descriptive Statistics: Pattern1, Pattern2, Diff

Variable	N	Mean	Median	TrMean	StDev	SE Mean
Pattern1	15	1.122	1.000	1.141	0.505	0.130
Pattern2	15	0.883	0.910	0.892	0.453	0.117
Diff	15	0.2393	0.2100	0.2338	0.1608	0.0415

Variable	Minimum	Maximum	Q1	Q3
Pattern1	0.150	1.850	0.850	1.460
Pattern2	0.050	1.600	0.650	1.220
Diff	-0.0400	0.5900	0.1200	0.3100

The test statistic is $t = \dfrac{\bar{d} - D_0}{\dfrac{s_d}{\sqrt{n_d}}} = \dfrac{.2393 - 0}{\dfrac{0.1608}{\sqrt{15}}} = 5.76$

Since no α is given, we will use $\alpha = .05$. The rejection region requires $\alpha/2 = .05/2 = .025$ in each tail of the t-distribution with df $= n_d - 1 = 15 - 1 = 14$. From Table VI, Appendix B, $t_{.025} = 2.145$. The rejection region is $t < -2.145$ or $t > 2.145$.

Since the observed value of the test statistic falls in the rejection region ($t = 5.76 >$ 2.145), H_0 is rejected. There is sufficient evidence to indicate that there is a difference in the mean pupil dilation between pattern 1 and pattern 2 at $\alpha = .05$.

c. The paired difference design is better. There is much variation in pupil dilation from person to person. By using the paired difference design, we can eliminate the person to person differences.

7.39   Using MINITAB, the descriptive statistics are:

Descriptive Statistics: Male, Female, Diff

```
Variable            N         Mean      Median      TrMean      StDev      SE Mean
Male               19        5.895       6.000       5.706       2.378       0.546
Female             19        5.526       5.000       5.294       2.458       0.564
Diff               19        0.368       1.000       0.294       3.515       0.806

Variable      Minimum     Maximum          Q1          Q3
Male            3.000      12.000       4.000       8.000
Female          3.000      12.000       4.000       7.000
Diff           -5.000       7.000      -3.000       3.000
```

Let μ_1 = mean number of swims by male rat pups and μ_2 = mean number of swims by female rat pups. Then $\mu_d = \mu_1 - \mu_2$. To determine if there is a difference in the mean number of swims required by male and female rat pups, we test:

H_0: $\mu_d = 0$
H_a: $\mu_d \neq 0$

The test statistic is $t = \dfrac{\bar{d} - D_o}{\dfrac{s_d}{\sqrt{n_d}}} = \dfrac{.368 - 0}{\dfrac{3.515}{\sqrt{19}}} = 0.46$

The rejection region requires $\alpha/2 = .10/2 = .05$ in each tail of the t-distribution with df $= n_d - 1$ $= 19 - 1 = 18$. From Table VI, Appendix B, $t_{.05} = 1.734$. The rejection region is $t < -1.734$ or $t > 1.734$.

Since the observed value of the test statistic does not fall in the rejection region ($t = 0.46 \not> 1.734$), H_0 is not rejected. There is insufficient evidence to indicate that there is a difference in the mean number of swims required by male and female rat pups at $\alpha = .10$.

Since the sample size is not large, we must assume that the population of differences is normally distributed and that the sample of differences is random. There is no indication that the sample differences are not from a random sample. However, because the number of swims is discrete, the differences are probably not normal.

7.41   a. From the exercise, we know that x_1 is a binomial random variable with the number of trials equal to n_1. From Chapter 7, we know that for large n, the distribution of $\hat{p}_1 = \dfrac{x_1}{n_1}$ is approximately normal. Since x_1 is simply $\hat{p}_1$ multiplied by a constant, x_1 will also have a normal distribution. Similarly, the distribution of $\hat{p}_2 = \dfrac{x_2}{n_2}$ is approximately normal, and thus, the distribution of x_2 is approximately normal.

b. The Central Limit Theorem is necessary to find the sampling distributions of $\hat{p}_1$ and $\hat{p}_2$ when n_1 and n_2 are large. Once we have established that both $\hat{p}_1$ and $\hat{p}_2$ have normal distributions, then the distribution of their difference will also be normal.

7.43 From Section 5.3, it was given that the distribution of $\hat{p}$ is approximately normal if the interval $\hat{p} \pm 3\sigma_{\hat{p}}$ does not contain 0 or 1.

a. $\sigma_{\hat{p}_1} \approx \sqrt{\dfrac{\hat{p}_1\hat{q}_1}{n_1}} = \sqrt{\dfrac{.42(.58)}{12}} = .142$ $\qquad \hat{p}_1 \pm 3\sigma_{\hat{p}_1} \Rightarrow .42 \pm 3(.142)$

$$\Rightarrow .42 \pm .426 \Rightarrow (-.006, .846)$$

$\sigma_{\hat{p}_2} \approx \sqrt{\dfrac{\hat{p}_1\hat{q}_1}{n_1}} = \sqrt{\dfrac{.57(.43)}{14}} = .132$ $\qquad \hat{p}_2 \pm 3\sigma_{\hat{p}_2} \Rightarrow .57 \pm 3(.132)$

$$\Rightarrow .57 \pm .396 \Rightarrow (.174, .966)$$

No. The interval $\hat{p}_1 \pm 3\sigma_{\hat{p}_1}$ contains 0.

b. $\sigma_{\hat{p}_1} \approx \sqrt{\dfrac{.92(.08)}{12}} = .078$ $\qquad \hat{p}_1 \pm 3\sigma_{\hat{p}_1} \Rightarrow .92 \pm 3(.078)$

$$\Rightarrow .92 \pm .234 \Rightarrow (.686, 1.154)$$

$\sigma_{\hat{p}_2} \approx \sqrt{\dfrac{.86(.14)}{14}} = .093$ $\qquad \hat{p}_2 \pm 3\sigma_{\hat{p}_2} \Rightarrow .86 \pm 3(.093)$

$$\Rightarrow .86 \pm .279 \Rightarrow (.581, 1.139)$$

No. Both intervals contain 1.

c. $\sigma_{\hat{p}_1} \approx \sqrt{\dfrac{.70(.30)}{30}} = .084$ $\qquad \hat{p}_1 \pm 3\sigma_{\hat{p}_1} \Rightarrow .70 \pm 3(.084)$

$$\Rightarrow .70 \pm .252 \Rightarrow (.448, .952)$$

$\sigma_{\hat{p}_2} \approx \sqrt{\dfrac{.73(.27)}{30}} = .081$ $\qquad \hat{p}_2 \pm 3\sigma_{\hat{p}_2} \Rightarrow .73 \pm 3(.081)$

$$\Rightarrow .73 \pm .243 \Rightarrow (.487, .973)$$

Yes. Both intervals are contained in the interval $(0, 1)$.

d. $\sigma_{\hat{p}_1} \approx \sqrt{\dfrac{.93(.07)}{100}} = .026$ $\qquad \hat{p}_1 \pm 3\sigma_{\hat{p}_1} \Rightarrow .93 \pm 3(.026)$

$$\Rightarrow .93 \pm .078 \Rightarrow (.852, 1.008)$$

$\sigma_{\hat{p}_2} \approx \sqrt{\dfrac{.97(.03)}{250}} = .011$ $\qquad \hat{p}_2 \pm 3\sigma_{\hat{p}_2} \Rightarrow .97 \pm 3(.011)$

$$\Rightarrow .97 \pm .033 \Rightarrow (.937, 1.003)$$

No. Both intervals contain 1.

e. $\sigma_{\hat{p}_1} \approx \sqrt{\dfrac{.08(.92)}{125}} = .024$

$\hat{p}_1 \pm 3\sigma_{\hat{p}_1} \Rightarrow .08 \pm 3(.024)$

$\Rightarrow .08 \pm .072 \Rightarrow (.008, .152)$

$\sigma_{\hat{p}_2} \approx \sqrt{\dfrac{.12(.88)}{200}} = .023$

$\hat{p}_1 \pm 3\sigma_{\hat{p}_1} \Rightarrow .12 \pm 3(.023)$

$\Rightarrow .12 \pm .069 \Rightarrow (.051, .189)$

Yes. Both intervals are contained in the interval (0, 1).

7.45   a. H_0: $(p_1 - p_2) = 0$
H_a: $(p_1 - p_2) \neq 0$

Will need to calculate the following:

$$\hat{p}_1 = \frac{320}{800} = .40 \qquad \hat{p}_2 = \frac{400}{800} = .50 \qquad \hat{p} = \frac{320 + 400}{800 + 800} = .45$$

The test statistic is $z = \dfrac{(\hat{p}_1 - \hat{p}_2) - 0}{\sqrt{\hat{p}\hat{q}\left(\dfrac{1}{n_1} + \dfrac{1}{n_2}\right)}} = \dfrac{(.40 - .50) - 0}{\sqrt{(.45)(.55)\left(\dfrac{1}{800} + \dfrac{1}{800}\right)}} = -4.02$

The rejection region requires $\alpha/2 = .05/2 = .025$ in each tail of the z-distribution. From Table IV, Appendix B, $z_{.025} = 1.96$. The rejection region is $z < -1.96$ or $z > 1.96$.

Since the observed value of the test statistic falls in the rejection region ($z = -4.02 < -1.96$), H_0 is rejected. There is sufficient evidence to indicate that the proportions are unequal at $\alpha = .05$.

b.   The problem is identical to part **a** until the rejection region. The rejection region requires $\alpha/2 = .01/2 = .005$ in each tail of the z-distribution. From Table IV, Appendix B, $z_{.005} = 2.58$. The rejection region is $z < -2.58$ or $z > 2.58$.

Since the observed value of the test statistic falls in the rejection region ($z = -4.02 < -2.58$), H_0 is rejected. There is sufficient evidence to indicate that the proportions are unequal at $\alpha = .01$.

c. H_0: $p_1 - p_2 = 0$
H_a: $p_1 - p_2 < 0$

Test statistic as above: $z = -4.02$

The rejection region requires $\alpha = .01$ in the lower tail of the z-distribution. From Table IV, Appendix B, $z_{.01} = 2.33$. The rejection region is $z < -2.33$.

Since the observed value of the test statistic falls in the rejection region ($z = -4.02 < -2.33$), H_0 is rejected. There is sufficient evidence to indicate that $p_1 < p_2$ at $\alpha = .01$.

Inferences Based on Two Samples: Confidence Intervals and Tests of Hypotheses

d. For confidence coefficient .90, $\alpha = .10$ and $\alpha/2 = .10/2 = .05$. From Table IV, Appendix B, $z_{.05} = 1.645$. The confidence interval is:

$$(\hat{p}_1 - \hat{p}_2) \pm z_{.05}\sqrt{\frac{\hat{p}_1\hat{q}_1}{n_1} + \frac{\hat{p}_2\hat{p}_2}{n_2}} \Rightarrow (.4 - .5) \pm (1.645)\sqrt{\frac{(.4)(.6)}{800} + \frac{(.5)(.5)}{800}}$$

$$\Rightarrow -.10 \pm .04 \Rightarrow (-.14, -.06)$$

We are 90% confident that the difference between p_1 and p_2 is between $-.14$ and $-.06$.

7.47 a. $\hat{p}_1 = \dfrac{x_1}{n_1} = \dfrac{29}{189} = .153$

b. $\hat{p}_2 = \dfrac{x_2}{n_2} = \dfrac{32}{149} = .215$

c. For confidence coefficient .90, $\alpha = .10$ and $\alpha/2 = .10/2 = .05$. From Table IV, Appendix B, $z_{.05} = 1.645$. The 90% confidence interval is:

$$(\hat{p}_1 - \hat{p}_2) \pm z_{\alpha/2}\sqrt{\frac{\hat{p}_1\hat{q}_1}{n_1} + \frac{\hat{p}_2\hat{q}_2}{n_2}} \Rightarrow (.153 - .215) \pm 1.645\sqrt{\frac{.153(.847)}{189} + \frac{.215(.785)}{149}}$$

$$\Rightarrow -.062 \pm .070 \Rightarrow (-.132, \quad .008)$$

d. We are 90% confident that the difference in the proportion of bidders who fall prey to the winner's curse between super-experienced bidders and less-experienced bidders is between $-.132$ and $.008$. Since this interval contains 0, there is no evidence to indicate that there is a difference in the proportion of bidders who fall prey to the winner's curse between super-experienced bidders and less-experienced bidders.

7.49 a. Let p_1 = proportion of employed individuals who had a routine checkup in the past year and p_2 = proportion of unemployed individuals who had a routine checkup in the past year. The researchers are interested in whether there is a difference in these two proportions, so the parameter of interest is $p_1 - p_2$.

b. To determine if there is a difference in the proportions of employed and unemployed individuals who had a routine checkup in the past year, we test:

H_0: $p_1 - p_2 = 0$
H_a: $p_1 - p_2 \neq 0$

c. Some preliminary calculations are:

$$\hat{p}_1 = \frac{x_1}{n_1} = \frac{642}{1,140} = .563 \qquad\qquad \hat{p}_2 = \frac{x_2}{n_2} = \frac{740}{1,106} = .669$$

$$\hat{p} = \frac{x_1 + x_2}{n_1 + n_2} = \frac{642 + 740}{1,140 + 1,106} = \frac{1,382}{2,246} = .615 \qquad\qquad \hat{q} = 1 - \hat{p} = 1 - .615 = .385$$

The test statistic is $z = \dfrac{(\hat{p}_1 - \hat{p}_2) - 0}{\sqrt{\hat{p}\hat{q}\left(\dfrac{1}{n_1} + \dfrac{1}{n_2}\right)}} = \dfrac{(.563 - .669) - 0}{\sqrt{.615(.385)\left(\dfrac{1}{1,140} + \dfrac{1}{1,106}\right)}} = -5.16$

d. The rejection region requires $\alpha/2 = .01/2 = .005$ in each tail of the z-distribution. From Table IV, Appendix B, $z_{.005} = 2.58$. The rejection region is $z < -2.58$ or $z > 2.58$.

e. The p-value is $P(z \leq -5.16) + P(z \geq 5.16) \approx (.5 - .5) + (.5 - .5) = 0$. This agrees with what was reported.

f. Since the observed value of the test statistic falls in the rejection region ($z = -5.16 < -2.58$), H_0 is rejected. There is sufficient evidence to indicate a difference in the proportion of employed and unemployed individuals who had routine checkups in the past year at $\alpha = .01$.

7.51 a. Let p_1 = proportion of African-American drivers searched by the LAPD and p_2 = proportion of white drivers searched by the LAPD.

Some preliminary calculations are:

$$\hat{p}_1 = \frac{x_1}{n_1} = \frac{12,016}{61,688} = .195 \qquad\qquad \hat{p}_2 = \frac{x_2}{n_2} = \frac{5,312}{106,892} = .050$$

$$\hat{p} = \frac{x_1 + x_2}{n_1 + n_2} = \frac{12,016 + 5,312}{61,688 + 106,892} = \frac{17,328}{168,580} = .103$$

To determine if the proportions of African-American and white drivers searched differs, we test:

H_0: $p_1 - p_2 = 0$
H_a: $p_1 - p_2 \neq 0$

The test statistic is $z = \dfrac{(\hat{p}_1 - \hat{p}_2) - 0}{\sqrt{\hat{p}\hat{q}\left(\dfrac{1}{n_1} + \dfrac{1}{n_2}\right)}} = \dfrac{.195 - .050}{\sqrt{.103(.897)\left(\dfrac{1}{61,688} + \dfrac{1}{106,892}\right)}} = 94.35$

The rejection region requires $\alpha/2 = .05/2 = .025$ in each tail of the z-distribution. From Table IV, Appendix B, $z_{.025} = 1.96$. The rejection region is $z < -1.96$ or $z > 1.96$.

Since the observed value of the test statistic falls in the rejection region ($z = 94.35 > 1.96$), H_0 is rejected. There is sufficient evidence to indicate the proportions of African-American drivers and white drivers searched differs at $\alpha = .05$.

b. Let p_1 = proportion of 'hits' for African-American drivers searched by the LAPD and p_2 = proportion of 'hits' for white drivers searched by the LAPD.

Some preliminary calculations are:

$$\hat{p}_1 = \frac{x_1}{n_1} = \frac{5,134}{12,016} = .427 \qquad\qquad \hat{p}_2 = \frac{x_2}{n_2} = \frac{3,006}{5,312} = .566$$

$$\hat{p} = \frac{x_1 + x_2}{n_1 + n_2} = \frac{5,134 + 3,006}{12,016 + 5,312} = \frac{8,140}{17,328} = .470$$

For confidence coefficient .95, $\alpha = .05$ and $\alpha/2 = .05/2 = .025$. From Table IV, Appendix B, $z_{.025} = 1.96$. The 95% confidence interval is:

$$(\hat{p}_1 - \hat{p}_2) \pm z_{.025}\sqrt{\frac{\hat{p}_1\hat{q}_1}{n_1} + \frac{\hat{p}_2\hat{q}_2}{n_2}} \Rightarrow (.427 - .566) \pm 1.96\sqrt{\frac{.427(.573)}{12,016} + \frac{.566(.434)}{5,312}}$$

$$\Rightarrow -.139 \pm .016 \Rightarrow (-.155, \ -.123)$$

We are 95% confident that the difference in 'hit' rates between African-American drivers and white drivers searched by the LAPD is between $-.155$ and $-.123$.

7.53   a.   Let p_1 = proportion of 9th grade boys who gambled weekly or daily in 1992 and p_2 = proportion of 9th grade boys who gambled weekly or daily in 1998. The researchers are interested in whether there is a difference in these two proportions, so the parameter of interest is $p_1 - p_2$.

Some preliminary calculations are:

$$\hat{p}_1 = \frac{x_1}{n_1} = \frac{4,684}{21,484} = .218 \qquad\qquad \hat{p}_2 = \frac{x_2}{n_2} = \frac{5,313}{23,199} = .229$$

$$\hat{p} = \frac{x_1 + x_2}{n_1 + n_2} = \frac{4,684 + 5,313}{21,484 + 23,199} = \frac{9,997}{44,683} = .224 \qquad \hat{q} = 1 - \hat{p} = 1 - .224 = .776$$

To determine if there is a difference in the proportions of 9th grade boys who gambled weekly or daily in 1992 and 1998, we test:

H_0: $p_1 - p_2 = 0$
H_a: $p_1 - p_2 \neq 0$

The test statistic is $z = \dfrac{(\hat{p}_1 - \hat{p}_2) - 0}{\sqrt{\hat{p}\hat{q}\left(\dfrac{1}{n_1} + \dfrac{1}{n_2}\right)}} = \dfrac{(.218 - .229) - 0}{\sqrt{.224(.776)\left(\dfrac{1}{21,484} + \dfrac{1}{23,199}\right)}} = -2.79$

The rejection region requires $\alpha/2 = .01/2 = .005$ in each tail of the z-distribution. From Table IV, Appendix B, $z_{.005} = 2.58$. The rejection region is $z < -2.58$ or $z > 2.58$.

Since the observed value of the test statistic falls in the rejection region ($z = -2.79 < -2.58$), H_0 is rejected. There is sufficient evidence to indicate a difference in the proportions of 9th grade boys who gambled weekly or daily in 1992 and 1998 at $\alpha = .01$.

b. Yes. If samples sizes are large enough, differences can almost always be found. Suppose we compute a 99% confidence interval. For confidence coefficient .99, $\alpha = .01$ and $\alpha/2 = .01/2 = .005$. From Table IV, Appendix B, $z_{.005} = 2.58$. The 99% confidence interval is:

$$(\hat{p}_1 - \hat{p}_2) \pm z_{\alpha/2}\sqrt{\frac{\hat{p}_1\hat{q}_1}{n_1} + \frac{\hat{p}_2\hat{q}_2}{n_2}} \Rightarrow (.218 - .229) \pm 2.58\sqrt{\frac{.218(.782)}{21,484} + \frac{.229(.771)}{23,199}}$$

$$\Rightarrow -.011 \pm .010 \Rightarrow (-.021, \ -.001)$$

We are 99% confident that the difference in the proportions of 9th grade boys who gambled weekly or daily in 1992 and 1998 is between $-.021$ and $-.001$.

7.55 To determine if there is a difference in the proportions of consumer/commercial and industrial product managers who are at least 40 years old, we could use either a test of hypothesis or a confidence interval. Since we are asked only to determine if there is a difference in the proportions, we will use a test of hypothesis.

Let p_1 = proportion of consumer/commercial product managers at least 40 years old and p_2 = proportion of industrial product managers at least 40 years old.

$$\hat{p}_1 = .40 \qquad \hat{q}_1 = 1 - \hat{p}_1 = 1 - .40 = .60$$

$$\hat{p}_2 = .54 \qquad \hat{q}_2 = 1 - \hat{p}_1 = 1 - .54 = .46$$

$$= \frac{n_1\hat{p}_1 + n_2\hat{p}_2}{n_1 + n_2} = \frac{93(.40) + 212(.54)}{93 + 212} = .497 \qquad \hat{q} = 1 - \hat{p} = 1 - .497 = .503$$

To see if the samples are sufficiently large:

$$\hat{p}_1 \pm 3\sigma_{\hat{p}_1} \Rightarrow \hat{p}_1 \pm 3\sqrt{\frac{p_1q_1}{n_1}} \Rightarrow \hat{p}_1 \pm 3\sqrt{\frac{\hat{p}_1\hat{q}_1}{n_1}} \Rightarrow .40 \pm 3\sqrt{\frac{.40(.60)}{93}}$$

$$\Rightarrow .40 \pm .152 \Rightarrow (.248, .552)$$

$$\hat{p}_2 \pm 3\sigma_{\hat{p}_2} \Rightarrow \hat{p}_2 \pm 3\sqrt{\frac{p_2q_2}{n_2}} \Rightarrow \hat{p}_2 \pm 3\sqrt{\frac{\hat{p}_2\hat{q}_2}{n_2}} \Rightarrow .54 \pm 3\sqrt{\frac{.54(.46)}{212}}$$

$$\Rightarrow .54 \pm .103 \Rightarrow (.437, .643)$$

Since both intervals lie within the interval $(0, 1)$, the normal approximation will be adequate.

To determine if there is a difference in the proportions of consumer/commercial and industrial product managers who are at least 40 years old, we test:

H_0: $p_1 - p_2 = 0$
H_a: $p_1 - p_2 \neq 0$

The test statistic is $z = \dfrac{(\hat{p}_1 - \hat{p}_2) - 0}{\sqrt{\hat{p}\hat{q}\left(\dfrac{1}{n_1} + \dfrac{1}{n_2}\right)}} = \dfrac{(.40 - .54) - 0}{\sqrt{.497(.503)\left(\dfrac{1}{93} + \dfrac{1}{212}\right)}} = -2.25$

We will use $\alpha = .05$. The rejection region requires $\alpha/2 = .05/2 = .025$ in each tail of the z-distribution. From Table IV, Appendix B, $z_{.025} = 1.96$. The rejection region is $z < -1.96$ or $z > 1.96$.

Since the observed value of the test statistic falls in the rejection region ($z = -2.25 < -1.96$), H_0 is rejected. There is sufficient evidence to indicate that there is a difference in the proportions of consumer/commercial and industrial product managers who are at least 40 years old at $\alpha = .05$.

Since the test statistic is negative, there is evidence to indicate that the industrial product managers tend to be older than the consumer/commercial product managers.

7.57 a. We will assume that the sample sizes for the men and the women will be the same. Let p_1 = proportion of women who have food cravings and p_2 = proportion of men who have food cravings.

We know that $\hat{p}_1 = .97$ and $\hat{p}_2 = .67$. If $n_1 = n_2 = n$, then

$\hat{p} = \dfrac{n\hat{p}_1 + n\hat{p}_2}{n + n} = \dfrac{n(.97) + n(.67)}{2n} = \dfrac{1.64}{2} = .82$ and $\hat{q} = 1 - \hat{p} = 1 - .82 = .18$

To determine if the proportion of women who crave food exceeds that of men, we test:

H_0: $p_1 - p_2 = 0$
H_a: $p_1 - p_2 > 0$

The test statistic would be

$z = \dfrac{(\hat{p}_1 - \hat{p}_2) - 0}{\sqrt{\hat{p}\hat{q}\left(\dfrac{1}{n} + \dfrac{1}{n}\right)}} = \dfrac{(.97 - .67) - 0}{\sqrt{.82(.18)\left(\dfrac{1}{n} + \dfrac{1}{n}\right)}} = \dfrac{.30}{\sqrt{\dfrac{.2952}{n}}}$

The rejection region requires $\alpha = .01$ in the upper tail of the z-distribution. From Table IV, Appendix B, $z_{.01} = 2.33$. The rejection region would be $z > 2.33$. Thus, to reject H_0, our test statistic must be greater than 2.33. Setting our test statistic greater than 2.33 and solving for n, we can determine the sample size:

$z = \dfrac{.30}{\sqrt{\dfrac{.2952}{n}}} = 2.33 \Rightarrow .30 = 2.33\sqrt{\dfrac{.2952}{n}} \Rightarrow .30^2 = 2.33^2 \dfrac{.2952}{n} \Rightarrow .09n = 1.6026$

$\Rightarrow n = 17.8 \approx 18$

Thus, we would need sample sizes of 18 or more from both the women and the men in order to say that the true proportions were different.

b. This study involved 1,000 McMaster University students. It is very dangerous to generalize the results of this study to the general adult population of North America. The sample of students used may not be representative of the population of interest.

7.59 $n_1 = n_2 = \dfrac{(z_{\alpha/2})^2(\sigma_1^2 + \sigma_2^2)}{(ME)^2}$

For confidence coefficient .95, $\alpha = 1 - .95 = .05$ and $\alpha/2 = .05/2 = .025$. From Table IV, Appendix B, $z_{.025} = 1.96$.

$$n_1 = n_2 = \frac{1.96^2(14+14)}{1.8^2} = 33.2 \approx 34$$

7.61 a. For confidence coefficient .99, $\alpha = 1 - .99 = .01$ and $\alpha/2 = .01/2 = .005$. From Table IV, Appendix B, $z_{.005} = 2.58$.

$$n_1 = n_2 = \frac{(z_{\alpha/2})^2(p_1 q_1 + p_2 q_2)}{(ME)^2} = \frac{2.58^2\left(.4(1-.4) + .7(1-.7)\right)}{.01^2} = \frac{2.99538}{.0001}$$
$$= 29,953.8 \approx 29,954$$

b. For confidence coefficient .90, $\alpha = 1 - .90 = .10$ and $\alpha/2 = .10/2 = .05$. From Table IV, Appendix B, $z_{.05} = 1.645$. Since we have no prior information about the proportions, we use $p_1 = p_2 = .5$ to get a conservative estimate. For a width of .05, the margin of error is .025.

$$n_1 = n_2 = \frac{(z_{\alpha/2})^2(p_1 q_1 + p_2 q_2)}{(ME)^2} = \frac{(1.645)^2\left(.5(1-.5) + .5(1-.5)\right)}{.025^2} = 2164.82 \approx 2165$$

c. From part **b**, $z_{.05} = 1.645$.

$$n_1 = n_2 = \frac{(z_{\alpha/2})^2(p_1 q_1 + p_2 q_2)}{(ME)^2} = \frac{(1.645)^2\left(.2(1-.2) + .3(1-.3)\right)}{.03^2} = \frac{1.00123}{.0009}$$
$$= 1112.48 \approx 1113$$

7.63 For confidence coefficient .90, $\alpha = .10$ and $\alpha/2 = .10/2 = .05$. From Table IV, Appendix B, $z_{.05} = 1.645$. If we assume that we do not know the return rates,

$$n_1 = n_2 = \frac{(z_{.05})^2(p_1 q_1 + p_2 q_2)}{ME^2} = \frac{1.645^2(.5(.5) + .5(.5))}{.01^2} = 13,530.1 \approx 13,531$$

7.65   For confidence coefficient .95, $\alpha = .05$ and $\alpha/2 = .025$. From Table IV, Appendix B, $z_{.025} = 1.96$.

$$n_1 = n_2 = \frac{(z_{\alpha/2})^2 (\sigma_1^2 + \sigma_2^2)}{(ME)^2} = \frac{1.96^2 (15^2 + 15^2)}{1^2} = 1728.72 \approx 1729$$

7.67   For confidence coefficient .90, $\alpha = 1 - .90 = .10$ and $\alpha = .10/2 = .05$. From Table IV, Appendix B, $z_{.05} = 1.645$. Since prior information is given about the values of p_1 and p_2, we will use these values as estimators. Thus, $p_1 = p_2 = .5$. A width of .10 means the margin of error is $.10/2 = .05$.

$$n_1 = n_2 = \frac{(z_{\alpha/2})^2 (p_1 q_1 + p_2 q_2)}{(ME)^2} = \frac{(1.645)^2 (.5(.5) + .5(.5))}{.05^2} = 541.2 \approx 542$$

7.69   a.   With $v_1 = 9$ and $v_2 = 6$, $F_{.05} = 4.10$.

b.   With $v_1 = 18$ and $v_2 = 14$, $F_{.01} \approx 3.57$. (Since $v_1 = 18$ is not given, we estimate the value between those for $v_1 = 15$ and $v_1 = 20$.)

c.   With $v_1 = 11$ and $v_2 = 4$, $F_{.025} \approx 8.805$. (Since $v_1 = 11$ is not given, we estimate the value by averaging those given for $v_1 = 10$ and $v_1 = 12$.)

d.   With $v_1 = 20$ and $v_2 = 5$, $F_{.10} = 3.21$.

7.71   a.   Reject H_0 if $F > F_{.10} = 1.74$. (From Table VIII, Appendix B, with $v_1 = 30$ and $v_2 = 20$.)

b.   Reject H_0 if $F > F_{.05} = 2.04$. (From Table IX, Appendix B, with $v_1 = 30$ and $v_2 = 20$.)

c.   Reject H_0 if $F > F_{.025} = 2.35$. (From Table X.)

d.   Reject H_0 if $F > F_{.01} = 2.78$. (From Table XI.)

7.73   a.   The rejection region requires $\alpha = .05$ in the upper tail of the F-distribution with $v_1 = n_1 - 1 = 25 - 1 = 24$ and $v_2 = n_2 - 1 = 20 - 1 = 19$. From Table IX, Appendix B, $F_{.05} = 2.11$. The rejection region is $F > 2.11$ (if $s_1^2 > s_2^2$).

b.   The rejection region requires $\alpha = .05$ in the upper tail of the F-distribution with $v_1 = n_2 - 1 = 15 - 1 = 14$ and $v_2 = n_1 - 1 = 10 - 1 = 9$. From Table IX, Appendix B, $F_{.05} \approx 3.01$. The rejection region is $F > 3.01$ (if $s_2^2 > s_1^2$).

c.   The rejection region requires $\alpha/2 = .10/2 = .05$ in the upper tail of the F-distribution. If $s_1^2 > s_2^2$, $v_1 = n_1 - 1 = 21 - 1 = 20$ and $v_2 = n_2 - 1 = 31 - 1 = 30$. From Table IX, Appendix B, $F_{.05} = 1.93$. The rejection region is $F > 1.93$. If $s_1^2 < s_2^2$, $v_1 = n_2 - 1 = 30$ and $v_2 = n_1 - 1 = 20$. From Table IX, $F_{.05} = 2.04$. The rejection region is $F > 2.04$.

d. The rejection region requires $\alpha = .01$ in the upper tail of the F-distribution with $\nu_1 = n_2 - 1 = 41 - 1 = 40$ and $\nu_2 = n_1 - 1 = 31 - 1 = 30$. From Table XI, Appendix B, $F_{.01} = 2.30$. The rejection region is $F > 2.30$ (if $s_2^2 > s_1^2$).

e. The rejection region requires $\alpha/2 = .05/2 = .025$ in the upper tail of the F-distribution. If $s_1^2 > s_2^2$, $\nu_1 = n_1 - 1 = 7 - 1 = 6$ and $\nu_2 = n_2 - 1 = 16 - 1 = 15$. From Table X, Appendix B, $F_{.025} = 3.14$. The rejection region is $F > 3.14$. If $s_1^2 < s_2^2$, $\nu_1 = n_2 - 1 = 15$ and $\nu_2 = n_1 - 1 = 6$. From Table X, Appendix B, $F_{.025} = 5.27$. The rejection region is $F > 5.27$.

7.75 a. Using MINITAB, the descriptive statistics are:

Descriptive Statistics: Sample 1, Sample 2

Variable	N	Mean	Median	TrMean	StDev	SE Mean
Sample 1	6	2.417	2.400	2.417	1.436	0.586
Sample 2	5	4.36	3.70	4.36	2.97	1.33

Variable	Minimum	Maximum	Q1	Q3
Sample 1	0.700	4.400	1.075	3.650
Sample 2	1.40	8.90	1.84	7.20

To determine if the variance for population 2 is greater than that for population 1, we test:

H_0: $\sigma_1^2 = \sigma_2^2$

H_a: $\sigma_1^2 < \sigma_2^2$

The test statistic is $F = \dfrac{s_2^2}{s_1^2} = \dfrac{2.97^2}{1.436^2} = 4.28$

The rejection region requires $\alpha = .05$ in the upper tail of the F-distribution with $\nu_1 = n_2 - 1 = 5 - 1 = 4$ and $\nu_2 = n_1 - 1 = 6 - 1 = 5$. From Table IX, Appendix B, $F_{.05} = 5.19$. The rejection region is $F > 5.19$.

Since the observed value of the test statistic does not fall in the rejection region ($F = 4.29 \not> 5.19$), H_0 is not rejected. There is insufficient evidence to indicate the variance for population 2 is greater than that for population 1 at $\alpha = .05$.

b. The p-value is $P(F \geq 4.28)$. From Tables VIII and IX, with $\nu_1 = 4$ and $\nu_2 = 5$,

$.05 < P(F \geq 4.28) < .10$

There is no evidence to reject H_0 for $\alpha < .05$ but there is evidence to reject H_0 for $\alpha = .10$.

7.77 a. To determine if σ_M^2 is less than σ_F^2, we test:

H_0: $\sigma_M^2 = \sigma_F^2$
H_a: $\sigma_M^2 < \sigma_F^2$

b. The test statistic is $F = \dfrac{\text{Larger sample variance}}{\text{Smaller sample variance}} = \dfrac{s_F^2}{s_M^2} = \dfrac{6.94^2}{6.73^2} = 1.063$

c. The rejection region requires $\alpha = .10$ in the upper tail of the F-distribution with $v_1 = n_F - 1 = 114 - 1 = 113$ and $v_2 = n_M - 1 = 127 - 1 = 126$. From Table VIII, Appendix B, $F_{.10} \approx 1.26$. The rejection region is $F > 1.26$.

d. The p-value is $P(F \geq 1.063)$. From Table VIII, Appendix B, with $v_1 = 113$ and $v_2 = 126$, $.10 < P(F \geq 1.063)$ or $p > .10$

e. Since the observed value of the test statistic does not fall in the rejection region ($F = 1.063 \ngtr 1.26$), H_0 is not rejected. There is insufficient evidence to indicate the variation in the male perception scores is less than that for females at $\alpha = .10$.

f. We must assume that we have two random and independent samples drawn from normal populations.

7.79 Using MINITAB, the descriptive statistics are:

Descriptive Statistics: Novice, Experienced

Variable	N	Mean	Median	TrMean	StDev	SE Mean
Novice	12	32.83	32.00	32.60	8.64	2.49
Experien	12	20.58	19.50	20.60	5.74	1.66

Variable	Minimum	Maximum	Q1	Q3
Novice	20.00	48.00	26.75	39.00
Experien	10.00	31.00	17.25	24.75

a. Let σ_1^2 = variance in inspection errors for novice inspectors and σ_2^2 = variance in inspection errors for experienced inspectors. Since we wish to determine if the data support the belief that the variance is lower for experienced inspectors than for novice inspectors, we test:

H_0: $\sigma_1^2 = \sigma_2^2$
H_a: $\sigma_1^2 < \sigma_2^2$

The test statistic is $F = \dfrac{\text{Larger sample variance}}{\text{Smaller sample variance}} = \dfrac{s_1^2}{s_2^2} = \dfrac{8.64^2}{5.74^2} = 2.27$

The rejection region requires $\alpha = .05$ in the upper tail of the F-distribution with $v_1 = n_1 - 1 = 12 - 1 = 11$ and $v_2 = n_2 - 1 = 12 - 1 = 11$. From Table IX, Appendix B, $F_{.05} \approx 2.82$ (using interpolation). The rejection region is $F > 2.82$.

Since the observed value of the test statistic does not fall in the rejection region ($F = 2.27$ $\not> 2.82$), H_0 is not rejected. The sample data do not support her belief at $\alpha = .05$.

b. The p-value $= P(F \geq 2.27)$ with $v_1 = 11$ and $v_2 = 11$. Checking Tables VIII, IX, X, and XI in Appendix B, we find $F_{.10} = 2.23$ and $F_{.05} = 2.82$. Since the observed value of F exceeds $F_{.10}$ but is less than $F_{.05}$, the observed significance level for the test is less than .10. So $.05 < p$-value $< .10$.

7.81 a. Let σ_1^2 = variance of the order-to-delivery times for the Persian Gulf War and σ_2^2 = variance of the order-to-delivery times for Bosnia.

Descriptive Statistics: Gulf, Bosnia

Variable	N	Mean	Median	TrMean	StDev	SE Mean
Gulf	9	25.24	27.50	25.24	10.52	3.51
Bosnia	9	7.38	6.50	7.38	3.65	1.22

Variable	Minimum	Maximum	Q1	Q3
Gulf	9.10	41.20	15.30	32.15
Bosnia	3.00	15.10	5.25	9.20

To determine if the variances of the order-to-delivery times for the Persian Gulf and Bosnia shipments are equal, we test:

$$H_0: \quad \frac{\sigma_1^2}{\sigma_2^2} = 1$$

$$H_a: \quad \frac{\sigma_1^2}{\sigma_2^2} \neq 1$$

The test statistic is $F = \dfrac{\text{Larger sample variance}}{\text{Smaller sample variance}} = \dfrac{s_1^2}{s_2^2} = \dfrac{10.52^2}{3.65^2} = 8.307$

The rejection region requires $\alpha/2 = .05/2 = .025$ in the upper tail of the F-distribution with $v_1 = n_1 - 1 = 9 - 1 = 8$ and $v_2 = n_2 - 1 = 9 - 1 = 8$. From Table X, Appendix B, $F_{.025} = 4.43$. The rejection region is $F > 4.43$.

Since the observed value of the test statistic falls in the rejection region ($F = 8.307 > 4.43$), H_0 is rejected. There is sufficient evidence to indicate the variances of the order-to-delivery times for the Persian Gulf and Bosnia shipments differ at $\alpha = .05$.

b. No. One assumption necessary for the small sample confidence interval for $(\mu_1 - \mu_2)$ is that $\sigma_1^2 = \sigma_2^2$. For this problem, there is evidence to indicate that $\sigma_1^2 \neq \sigma_2^2$.

7.83 Let σ_1^2 = variance of the mathematics achievement test scores for males and σ_2^2 = variance of the mathematics achievement test scores for females. To determine if the test scores are more variable for the males than the females, we test:

$$H_0: \ \sigma_1^2 = \sigma_2^2$$
$$H_a: \ \sigma_1^2 > \sigma_2^2$$

The test statistic is $F = \dfrac{\text{Larger sample variance}}{\text{Smaller sample variance}} = \dfrac{s_1^2}{s_2^2} = \dfrac{12.96^2}{11.85^2} = 1.196$

The rejection region requires $\alpha = .01$ in the upper tail of the F distribution with numerator df $v_1 = n_1 - 1 = 1764 - 1 = 1763$ and denominator df $v_2 = n_2 - 1 = 1739 - 1 = 1738$. From Table XI, Appendix B, $F_{.01} \approx 1.00$. The rejection region is $F > 1.00$.

Since the observed value of the test statistic falls in the rejection region ($F = 1.196 > 1.00$), H_0 is rejected. There is sufficient evidence to indicate the test scores are more variable for the males than the females at $\alpha = .01$.

7.85 a. $s_p^2 = \dfrac{(n_1 - 1)s_1^2 + (n_1 - 1)s_2^2}{n_1 + n_2 - 2} = \dfrac{11(74.2) + 13(60.5)}{12 + 14 - 2} = 66.7792$

$$H_0: \ \mu_1 - \mu_2 = 0$$
$$H_a: \ \mu_1 - \mu_2 > 0$$

The test statistic is $t = \dfrac{(\bar{x}_1 - \bar{x}_2) - 0}{\sqrt{s_p^2 \left(\dfrac{1}{n_1} + \dfrac{1}{n_2} \right)}} = \dfrac{(17.8 - 15.3) - 0}{\sqrt{66.7792 \left(\dfrac{1}{12} + \dfrac{1}{14} \right)}} = .78$

The rejection region requires $\alpha = .05$ in the upper tail of the t-distribution with df = $n_1 + n_2 - 2 = 12 + 14 - 2 = 24$. From Table VI, Appendix B, for df = 24, $t_{.05} = 1.711$. The rejection region is $t > 1.711$.

Since the observed value of the test statistic does not fall in the rejection region ($0.78 \not> 1.711$), H_0 is not rejected. There is insufficient evidence to indicate that $\mu_1 > \mu_2$ at $\alpha = .05$.

b. For confidence coefficient .99, $\alpha = .01$ and $\alpha/2 = .01/2 = .005$. From Table VI, Appendix B, with df = $n_1 + n_2 - 2 = 12 + 14 - 2 = 24$, $t_{.005} = 2.797$. The confidence interval is:

$$(\bar{x}_1 - \bar{x}_2) \pm t_{.005} \sqrt{s_p^2 \left(\dfrac{1}{n_1} + \dfrac{1}{n_2} \right)} \Rightarrow (17.8 - 15.3) \pm 2.797 \sqrt{66.7792 \left(\dfrac{1}{12} + \dfrac{1}{14} \right)}$$
$$\Rightarrow 2.50 \pm 8.99 \Rightarrow (-6.49, 11.49)$$

c. For confidence coefficient .99, $\alpha = .01$ and $\alpha/2 = .01/2 = .005$. From Table IV, Appendix B, $z_{.005} = 2.58$.

$$n_1 = n_2 = \frac{(z_{\alpha/2})\left(\sigma_1^2 + \sigma_2^2\right)}{(ME)^2} = \frac{(2.58)^2(74.2 + 60.5)}{2^2} = 224.15 \approx 225$$

7.87 a. For confidence coefficient .90, $\alpha = .10$ and $\alpha/2 = .05$. From Table IV, Appendix B, $z_{.05} = 1.645$. The confidence interval is:

$$(\bar{x}_1 - \bar{x}_2) \pm z_{.05}\sqrt{\frac{s_1^2}{n_1} + \frac{s_2^2}{n_2}} \Rightarrow (12.2 - 8.3) \pm 1.645\sqrt{\frac{2.1}{135} + \frac{3.0}{148}}$$

$$\Rightarrow 3.90 \pm .31 \Rightarrow (3.59, 4.21)$$

b. $H_0: \mu_1 - \mu_2 = 0$
$H_a: \mu_1 - \mu_2 \neq 0$

The test statistic is $z = \dfrac{(\bar{x}_1 - \bar{x}_2)}{\sqrt{\dfrac{s_1^2}{n_1} + \dfrac{s_2^2}{n_2}}} = \dfrac{(12.2 - 8.3) - 0}{\sqrt{\dfrac{2.1}{135} + \dfrac{3.0}{148}}} = 20.60$

The rejection region requires $\alpha/2 = .01/2 = .005$ in each tail of the z-distribution. From Table IV, Appendix B, $z_{.005} = 2.58$. The rejection region is $z < -2.58$ or $z > 2.58$.

Since the observed value of the test statistic falls in the rejection region ($20.60 > 2.58$), H_0 is rejected. There is sufficient evidence to indicate that $\mu_1 \neq \mu_2$ at $\alpha = .01$.

c. For confidence coefficient .90, $\alpha = .10$ and $\alpha/2 = .05$. From Table IV, Appendix B, $z_{.05} = 1.645$.

$$n_1 = n_2 = \frac{(z_{\alpha/2})\left(\sigma_1^2 + \sigma_2^2\right)}{(ME)^2} = \frac{(1.645)^2(2.1 + 3.0)}{.2^2} = 345.02 \approx 346$$

7.89 a. This is a paired difference experiment.

Pair	Difference (Pop. 1 - Pop. 2)
1	6
2	4
3	4
4	3
5	2

$$\bar{d} = \frac{\sum_{i=1}^{n_d} d_i}{n_d} = \frac{19}{5} = 3.8 \qquad s_d^2 = \frac{\sum_{i=1}^{n_d} d_i^2 - \dfrac{\left(\sum_{i=1}^{n_d} d_i\right)^2}{n_d}}{n_d - 1} = \frac{81 - \dfrac{19^2}{5}}{5 - 1} = 2.2$$

$$s_d = \sqrt{2.2} = 1.4832$$

$$H_0: \mu_d = 0$$
$$H_a: \mu_d \neq 0$$

The test statistic is $t = \dfrac{\bar{d} - 0}{s_d/\sqrt{n_d}} = \dfrac{3.8 - 0}{1.4832/\sqrt{5}} = 5.73$

The rejection region requires $\alpha/2 = .05/2 = .025$ in each tail of the t-distribution with df $= n - 1 = 5 - 1 = 4$. From Table VI, Appendix B, $t_{.025} = 2.776$. The rejection region is $t < -2.776$ or $t > 2.776$.

Since the observed value of the test statistic falls in the rejection region $(5.73 > 2.776)$, H_0 is rejected. There is sufficient evidence to indicate that the population means are different at $\alpha = .05$.

b. For confidence coefficient .95, $\alpha = .05$ and $\alpha/2 = .025$. Therefore, we would use the same t value as above, $t_{.025} = 2.776$. The confidence interval is:

$$\bar{x}_d \pm t_{\alpha/2} \frac{s_d}{\sqrt{n_d}} \Rightarrow 3.8 \pm 3.8 \pm 2.776 \frac{1.4832}{\sqrt{5}} \Rightarrow 3.8 \pm 1.84 \Rightarrow (1.96, 5.64)$$

c. The sample of differences must be randomly selected from a population of differences which has a normal distribution.

7.91 a. Let $\mu_1 =$ average size of the right temporal lobe of the brain for the short-recovery group and $\mu_2 =$ average size of the right temporal lobe of the brain for the long-recovery group.

The target parameter is $\mu_1 - \mu_2$. We must assume that the two samples are random and independent, the two populations being sampled from are approximately normal, and the two population variances are equal.

b. Let $p_1 =$ proportion of athletes who have a good self-image of their body and $p_2 =$ proportion of non-athletes who have a good self-image of their body.

The target parameter for this comparison is $p_1 - p_2$. We must assume that the two samples are random and independent and that the sample sizes are sufficiently large.

c. Let μ_1 = average weight of eggs produced by a sample of chickens on regular feed and μ_2 = average weight of eggs produced by a sample of chickens fed a diet supplemented by corn oil. Let μ_d = average difference in weight between eggs produced by the chickens on regular feed and then on a diet supplemented with corn oil.

The target parameter is μ_d. We must assume that we have a random sample of differences and that the population of differences is approximately normal.

7.93 a. Let μ_1 = mean GPA for traditional students and μ_2 = mean GPA for nontraditional students. To determine whether the mean GPAs of traditional and nontraditional students differ, we test:

$$H_0: \mu_1 - \mu_2 = 0$$
$$H_a: \mu_1 - \mu_2 \neq 0$$

b. The test statistic is $z = \dfrac{(\bar{x}_1 - \bar{x}_2) - D_0}{\sqrt{\dfrac{s_1^2}{n_1} + \dfrac{s_2^2}{n_2}}} = \dfrac{(2.9 - 3.5) - 0}{\sqrt{\dfrac{.5^2}{94} + \dfrac{.5^2}{73}}} = -7.69$

The rejection region requires $\alpha/2 = .01/2 = .005$ in each tail of the z-distribution. From Table IV, Appendix B, $z_{.005} = 2.58$. The rejection region is $z < -2.58$ or $z > 2.58$.

Since the observed value of the test statistic falls in the rejection region ($z = -7.69 < -2.58$), H_0 is rejected. There is sufficient evidence to indicate that the mean GPAs of traditional and nontraditional students differ for $\alpha = .01$.

c. We must assume that the two samples are randomly and independently selected from the populations of GPAs.

7.95 a. Let p_1 = proportion of earthquake-insured residents in Contra Costa County and p_2 = proportion of earthquake-insured residents in Los Angeles County.

$$\hat{p}_1 = \frac{x_1}{n_1} = \frac{117}{521} = .225 \qquad \hat{p}_2 = \frac{x_2}{n_2} = \frac{133}{337} = .395$$

For confidence coefficient .95, $\alpha = .05$ and $\alpha/2 = .05/2 = .025$. From Table IV, Appendix B, $z_{.025} = 1.96$. The confidence interval is:

$$(\hat{p}_2 - \hat{p}_1) \pm z_{.025} \sqrt{\frac{\hat{p}_2 \hat{q}_2}{n_2} + \frac{\hat{p}_1 \hat{q}_1}{n_1}} \Rightarrow (.395 - .225) \pm 1.96 \sqrt{\frac{.395(.605)}{337} + \frac{.225(.775)}{521}}$$
$$\Rightarrow .17 \pm .063 \Rightarrow (.107, \ .233)$$

We are 95% confident that the difference in the proportions of earthquake-insured residents between Los Angeles County and Contra Costa County is between .107 and .233.

b. Since 0 is not in the confidence interval, there is evidence to indicate the proportion of earthquake-insured residents in Los Angeles County is greater than the proportion in Contra Costa County.

7.97   a.   Let μ_1 = mean response by noontime watchers and μ_2 = mean response by non-noontime watchers. To determine if the mean response differs for noontime and non-noontime watchers, we test:

$$H_0: \ \mu_1 = \mu_2$$
$$H_a: \ \mu_1 \neq \mu_2$$

   b.   Since the p-value ($p = .02$) is less than $\alpha = .05$, H_0 is rejected. There is sufficient evidence to indicate the mean response differs for noontime and non-noontime watchers at $\alpha = .05$.

   c.   Since the p-value ($p = .02$) is greater than $\alpha = .01$, H_0 is not rejected. There is insufficient evidence to indicate the mean response differs for noontime and non-noontime watchers at $\alpha = .01$.

   d.   Since the two sample means are so close together, there appears to be no "practical" difference between the two means. Even if there is a statistically significant difference between the two means, there is no practical difference.

7.99   For confidence coefficient .90, $\alpha = .10$ and $\alpha/2 = .10/2 = .05$. From Table IV, Appendix B, $z_{.05} = 1.645$. Since we would expect the percentages in 2000 and 2003 to be fairly similar to the percentage in 1999, we will use $\hat{p}_{1999} = .92$ to estimate both p_{2000} and p_{2003}.

$$n_1 = n_2 = \frac{(z_{\alpha/2})^2 (p_1 q_1 + p_2 q_2)}{(ME)^2} = \frac{(1.645)^2 \left(.92(.08) + .92(.08)\right)}{.03^2} = 442.6 \approx 443$$

We would need to sample 443 adult Americans in each year.

7.101   Let p_1 = unemployment rate for the urban industrial community and p_2 = unemployment rate for the university community.

Some preliminary calculations are:

$$\hat{p}_1 = \frac{x_1}{n_1} = \frac{47}{525} = .0895 \qquad \hat{p}_2 = \frac{x_2}{n_2} = \frac{22}{375} = .0587$$

For confidence coefficient .95, $\alpha = 1 - .95 = .05$ and $\alpha/2 = .05/2 = .025$. From Table IV, Appendix B, $z_{.025} = 1.96$. The confidence interval is:

$$(\hat{p}_1 - \hat{p}_2) \pm z_{.025} \sqrt{\frac{\hat{p}_1 \hat{q}_1}{n_1} + \frac{\hat{p}_2 \hat{q}_2}{n_2}}$$

$$\Rightarrow (.0895 - .0587) \pm 1.96 \sqrt{\frac{.0895(.9105)}{525} + \frac{.0587(.9413)}{375}}$$

$$\Rightarrow .0308 \pm .0341 \Rightarrow (-.0033, .0649)$$

We are 95% confident the difference in unemployment rates in the two communities is between −.0033 and .0649.

7.103 a. Yes. The mean wastes for cities of industrialized countries are all greater than 2 while the mean wastes for cities of middle-income countries are all less than 1.0.

b. Using MINITAB, the descriptive statistics are:

Descriptive Statistics: Industrial, Middle

Variable	N	Mean	Median	TrMean	StDev	SE Mean
Industri	5	2.2300	2.2400	2.2300	0.0652	0.0292
Middle	7	0.6114	0.5400	0.6114	0.1729	0.0653

Variable	Minimum	Maximum	Q1	Q3
Industri	2.1500	2.3100	2.1650	2.2900
Middle	0.4600	0.8700	0.5000	0.8500

$$s_p^2 = \frac{(n_1-1)s_1^2 + (n_2-1)s_2^2}{n_1+n_2-2} = \frac{(5-1).0652^2 + (7-1).1729^2}{5+7-2} = .01964$$

Let μ_1 = mean waste for cities in industrialized countries and μ_2 = mean waste for cities in middle-income countries. To determine if the mean waste generation rates of cities in industrialized and middle-income countries differ, we test:

H_0: $\mu_1 - \mu_2 = 0$
H_a: $\mu_1 - \mu_2 \neq 0$

The test statistic is $t = \dfrac{(\bar{x}_1 - \bar{x}_2) - D_o}{\sqrt{s_p^2\left(\dfrac{1}{n_1} + \dfrac{1}{n_2}\right)}} = \dfrac{(2.2300 - .6114) - 0}{\sqrt{.01964\left(\dfrac{1}{5} + \dfrac{1}{7}\right)}} = 19.72$

The rejection region requires $\alpha/2 = .05/2 = .025$ in each tail of the t-distribution with df $= n_1 + n_2 - 2 = 5 + 7 - 2 = 10$. From Table VI, Appendix B, $t_{.025} = 2.228$. The rejection region is $t < -2.228$ or $t > 2.228$.

Since the observed value of the test statistic falls in the rejection region ($t = 19.73 > 2.228$), H_0 is rejected. There is sufficient evidence to indicate that the mean waste generation rates of cities in industrialized and middle-income countries differ at $\alpha = .05$.

c. Let σ_1^2 = variance of the solid-waste generation rates for industrialized countries and σ_2^2 = variance of the solid-waste generation rates for middle-income countries. To determine if the variances differ, we test:

H_0: $\dfrac{\sigma_1^2}{\sigma_2^2} = 1$

H_a: $\dfrac{\sigma_1^2}{\sigma_2^2} \neq 1$

The test statistic is $F = \dfrac{\text{Larger sample variance}}{\text{Smaller sample variance}} = \dfrac{s_2^2}{s_1^2} = \dfrac{.1729^2}{.0652^2} = 7.032$

The rejection region requires $\alpha/2 = .05/2 = .025$ in the upper tail of the F-distribution with $v_1 = n_2 - 1 = 7 - 1 = 6$ and $v_2 = n_1 - 1 = 5 - 1 = 4$. From Table X, Appendix B, $F_{.025} = 9.20$. The rejection region is $F > 9.20$.

Since the observed value of the test statistic does not fall in the rejection region ($F = 7.032 \not> 9.20$), H_0 is not rejected. There is insufficient evidence to indicate the variances of the solid-waste generation rates for industrialized countries and middle-income countries differ at $\alpha = .05$.

d.   The p-value is $P(F \geq 7.032)$. From Tables IX and X, with $v_1 = = 6$ and $v_2 = 4$. $.025 < P(F \geq 7.032) < .05$. Thus, the p-value us between .05 and .10.

From the test, there is insufficient evidence to indicate the variances are different at $\alpha = .05$. However, the p-value is quite close to $\alpha = .05$. If we conclude that the variances are equal, we have a chance of committing a Type II error. Without specifying a fixed alternate value for the ratio of the variances, we cannot compute the probability of committing a Type II error, β. If we would inflate the value of α, (say to the value of .25 or higher), then we know that the value of σ will decrease. If we still do not reject H_0 with the inflated value of α, then we can have confidence that the variances are equal. In this problem, however, the p-value is quite small. Thus, the assumption of equal variances is questionable and the two-sample t-test might not be appropriate.

7.105   Let $\mu_1 =$ mean length of commercial in 1992 and $\mu_2 =$ length of commercial in 1998. To determine if a trend exists over a 6-year period (change in mean length), we test:

H_0: $\mu_1 = \mu_2$
H_a: $\mu_1 \neq \mu_2$

The test statistic is $z = \dfrac{(\bar{x}_1 - \bar{x}_2) - 0}{\sqrt{\left(\dfrac{s_1^2}{n_1} + \dfrac{s_2^2}{n_2}\right)}} = \dfrac{(24.52 - 24.21) - 0}{\sqrt{\dfrac{7.32^2}{105} + \dfrac{8.21^2}{106}}} = 0.29$

No α level was given, so we will use $\alpha = .05$. The rejection region requires $\alpha/2 = .05/2 = .025$ in each tail of the z-distribution. From Table IV, Appendix B, $z_{.025} = 1.96$. The rejection region is $z < -1.96$ or $z > 1.96$.

Since the observed value of the test statistic does not fall in the rejection region ($z = 0.29 \not> 1.96$), H_0 is not rejected. There is insufficient evidence to indicate a trend exists over a 6-year period (change in mean length) at $\alpha = .05$.

7.107 a. $\mu_d = \dfrac{\sum_{i=1}^{51} d_i}{51} = \dfrac{1,701}{51} = 33.35$

b. We do not need to estimate anything – we know the parameter's value.

c. Using MINITAB, the descriptive statistics are:

Descriptive Statistics: SAT1990, SAT2005, DIFF

Variable	N	N*	Mean	SE Mean	StDev	Minimum	Q1	Median	Q3
SAT1990	51	0	1043.7	8.33	59.5	942.0	993.0	1034.0	1089.0
SAT2005	51	0	1077.0	9.51	67.9	968.0	1018.0	1056.0	1127.0
DIFF	51	0	33.35	3.30	23.59	-2.00	18.00	32.00	42.00

Variable	Maximum
SAT1990	1172.0
SAT2005	1204.0
DIFF	111.00

Let μ_1 = mean SAT score in 2005 and μ_2 = mean SAT score in 1999. Then $\mu_d = \mu_1 - \mu_2$. To determine if the true mean SAT score in 2005 differs from that in 1999, we test:

$H_0:\ \mu_d = 0$
$H_a:\ \mu_d \neq 0$

The test statistic is $z = \dfrac{\bar{d} - D_o}{\dfrac{s_d}{\sqrt{n_d}}} = \dfrac{33.35 - 0}{\dfrac{23.59}{\sqrt{51}}} = 10.10$

The rejection region requires $\alpha/2 = .10/2 = .05$ in each tail of the z-distribution. From Table IV, Appendix B, $z_{.05} = 1.645$. The rejection region is $z < -1.645$ or $z > 1.645$.

Since the observed value of the test statistic falls in the rejection region ($z = 10.10 > 1.645$), H_0 is rejected. There is sufficient evidence to indicate the true mean SAT score in 2005 is different than that in 1999 at $\alpha = .10$.

7.109 For probability .95, $\alpha = 1 - .95 = .05$ and $\alpha/2 = .05/2 = .025$. From Table IV, Appendix B, $z_{.025} = 1.96$. Since we have no prior information about the proportions, we use $p_1 = p_2 = .5$ to get a conservative estimate.

$$n_1 = n_2 = \dfrac{(z_{\alpha/2})^2 (p_1 q_1 + p_2 q_2)}{(ME)^2} = \dfrac{(1.96)^2 (.5(1-.5) + .5(1-.5))}{.02^2} = \dfrac{1.9208}{.0004} = 4,802$$

7.111 a. Let p_1 = death rate of Operation Crossroads sailors and p_2 = death rate of a comparable group of sailors. The parameter of interest for this problem is $p_1 - p_2$, or the difference in the death rates for the two groups.

b. "The increase was not statistically significant" means that even though the sample death rate of Operation Crossroads sailors is 4.6% higher than the sample death rate of a comparable group of sailors, we could not reject the null hypothesis that there is no difference in the death rates of the two groups of soldiers. For the given samples sizes, the test statistic did not fall in the rejection region.

7.113 Attitude towards the Advertisement:

The p-value = .091. There is no evidence to reject H_0 for $\alpha = .05$. There is no evidence to indicate the first ad will be more effective when shown to males for $\alpha = .05$. There is evidence to reject H_0 for $\alpha = .10$. There is evidence to indicate the first ad will be more effective when shown to males for $\alpha = .10$.

Attitude toward Brand of Soft Drink:

The p-value = .032. There is evidence to reject H_0 for $\alpha > .032$. There is evidence to indicate the first ad will be more effective when shown to males for $\alpha > .032$.

Intention to Purchase the Soft Drink:

The p-value = .050. There is no evidence to reject H_0 for $\alpha = .05$. There is no evidence to indicate the first ad will be more effective when shown to males for $\alpha = .05$. There is evidence to reject H_0 for $\alpha > .050$. There is evidence to indicate the first ad will be more effective when shown to males for $\alpha > .050$.

No, I do not agree with the author's hypothesis. The results agree with the author's hypothesis for only the attitude toward the advertisement id using $\alpha = .05$. If we want to use $\alpha = .10$, then the author's hypotheses are all supported.

7.115 Some preliminary calculations are:

Working Days	Difference (Design 1 - Design 2)
8/16	−53
8/17	−271
8/18	−206
8/19	−266
8/20	−213
8/23	−183
8/24	−118
8/25	−87

$$\bar{d} = \frac{\sum d}{n_d} = \frac{-1,397}{8} = -174.625$$

$$s_d^2 = \frac{\sum d^2 - \frac{\left(\sum d\right)^2}{n_d}}{n_d - 1} = \frac{289,793 - \frac{(-1,397)^2}{8}}{8 - 1} = 6,548.839$$

$$s_d = \sqrt{s_d^2} = \sqrt{6,548.839} = 80.925$$

To determine if Design 2 is superior to Design 1, we test:

H_0: $\mu_d = 0$
H_a: $\mu_d < 0$

The test statistic is $t = \dfrac{\overline{d} - \mu_o}{s_d/\sqrt{n_d}} = \dfrac{-174.625 - 0}{80.925/\sqrt{8}} = -6.103$

Since no α value was given, we will use $\alpha = .05$. The rejection region requires $\alpha = .05$ in the lower tail of the t-distribution with df $= n_d - 1 = 8 - 1 = 7$. From Table VI, Appendix B, $t_{.05} = 1.895$. The rejection region is $t < -1.895$.

Since the observed value of the test statistic falls in the rejection region ($t = -6.103 < -1.895$), H_0 is rejected. There is sufficient evidence to indicate Design 2 is superior to Design 1 at $\alpha = .05$.

Design of Experiments and Analysis of Variance — Chapter 8

8.1 Since only one factor is utilized, the treatments are the four levels (A, B, C, D) of the qualitative factor.

8.3 One has no control over the levels of the factors in an observational experiment. One does have control of the levels of the factors in a designed experiment.

8.5 a. This is an observational experiment. The economist has no control over the factor levels or unemployment rates.

b. This is a designed experiment. The manager chooses only three different incentive programs to compare, and randomly assigns an incentive program to each of nine plants.

c. This is an observational experiment. Even though the marketer chooses the publication, he has no control over who responds to the ads.

d. This is an observational experiment. The load on the facility's generators is only observed, not controlled.

e. This is an observational experiment. One has no control over the distance of the haul, the goods hauled, or the price of diesel fuel.

8.7 a. The response variable is the age when the tumor was first detected.

b. The experimental units are the smokers.

c. There is one factor in this problem: screening method.

d. There are 2 treatments in this problem, corresponding to the 2 levels of the factor. The treatments are CT and chest X-ray.

8.9 a. There are 2 factors in this problem, each with 2 levels. Thus, there are a total of $2 \times 2 = 4$ treatments.

b. The 4 treatments are: (Within-store, home), (Within-store, in store), (Between-store, home), and (Between-store, in store).

8.11 a. The experimental units for this study are the students in the introductory psychology class.

b. The study is a designed experiment because the students are randomly assigned to a particular study group.

c. There are 2 factors in this problem: Class standing and study group.

d. Class standing has 3 levels: Low, Medium, and High. Study group has 2 levels: practice test and review.

e. There are a total of $3 \times 2 = 6$ treatments. They are: (Low, Review), (Low, Practice exam), (Medium, Review), (Medium, Practice exam), (High, Review), and (High, Practice exam).

f. The response variable is the final exam score.

8.13 a. The dependent variable is the dissolution time.

b. There are 3 factors in this experiment: Binding agent, binding concentration, and relative density. Binding agent has 2 levels – khaya gum and PVP. Binding concentration has 2 levels – .5% and 4.0%. Relative density has 2 levels – high and low.

c. There could be a total of $2 \times 2 \times 2 = 8$ treatments for this experiment. They are:

khaya gum, .5%, high   PVP, .5%, high
khaya gum, .5%, low   PVP, .5%, low
khaya gum, 4.0%, high   PVP, 4.0%, high
khaya gum, 4.0%, low   PVP, 4.0%, low

8.15 a. $P(F \le 3.48) = 1 - .05 = .95$ using Table IX, Appendix B, with $v_1 = 5$ and $v_2 = 9$

b. $P(F > 3.09) = .01$ using Table XI, Appendix B, with $v_1 = 15$ and $v_2 = 20$

c. $P(F > 2.40) = .05$ using Table IX, Appendix B, with $v_1 = 15$ and $v_2 = 15$

d. $P(F \le 1.83) = 1 - .10 = .90$ using Table VIII, Appendix B, with $v_1 = 8$ and $v_2 = 40$

8.17 For each dot diagram, we want to test:

$H_0: \mu_1 = \mu_2$
$H_a: \mu_1 \ne \mu_2$

From Exercise 8.16,

Diagram #1	Diagram #2
$\bar{x}_1 = 9$	$\bar{x}_1 = 9$
$\bar{x}_2 = 14$	$\bar{x}_2 = 14$
$s_1^2 = 2$	$s_1^2 = 14.4$
$s_2^2 = 2$	$s_2^2 = 14.4$

a.

Diagram #1	Diagram #2
$s_p^2 = \dfrac{s_1^2 + s_2^2}{2}$	$s_p^2 = \dfrac{s_1^2 + s_2^2}{2}$
$= \dfrac{2+2}{2} = 2 \ \ (n_1 = n_2)$	$= \dfrac{14.4 + 14.4}{2} = 14.4 \ \ (n_1 = n_2)$
In Exercise 8.16, MSE $= 2$	In Exercise 8.16, MSE $= 14.4$

The pooled variance for the two-sample t-test is the same as the MSE for the F-test.

b.

Diagram #1	Diagram #2
$t = \dfrac{\bar{x}_1 - \bar{x}_2}{\sqrt{s_p^2\left(\dfrac{1}{n_1} + \dfrac{1}{n_2}\right)}} = \dfrac{9 - 14}{\sqrt{2\left(\dfrac{1}{6} + \dfrac{1}{6}\right)}}$	$t = \dfrac{\bar{x}_1 - \bar{x}_2}{\sqrt{s_p^2\left(\dfrac{1}{n_1} + \dfrac{1}{n_2}\right)}} = \dfrac{9 - 14}{\sqrt{14.4\left(\dfrac{1}{6} + \dfrac{1}{6}\right)}}$
$= -6.12$	$= -2.28$
In Exercise 8.16, $F = 37.5$	In Exercise 8.16, $F = 5.21$

The test statistic for the F-test is the square of the test statistic for the t-test.

c.

Diagram #1	Diagram #2
For the t-test, the rejection region requires $\alpha/2 = .05/2 = .025$ in each tail of the t-distribution with df $= n_1 + n_2 - 2 = 6 + 6 - 2 = 10$. From Table VI, Appendix B, $t_{.025} = 2.228$.	For the t-test, the rejection region is the same as Diagram #1 since we are using the same α, n_1, and n_2 for both tests.

The rejection region is $t < -2.228$ or $t > 2.228$.

In Exercise 8.16, the rejection region for both diagrams using the F-test is $F > 4.96$.

The tabled F value equals the square of the tabled t value.

d.

Diagram #1	Diagram #2
For the t-test, since the test statistic falls in the rejection region ($t = -6.12 < -2.228$), we would reject H_0. In Exercise 8.16, using the F-test, we rejected H_0.	For the t-test, since the test statistic falls in the rejection region ($t = -2.28 < -2.228$), we would reject H_0. In Exercise 8.16, using the F-test, we rejected H_0.

e. Assumptions for the t-test:

1. Both populations have relative frequency distributions that are approximately normal.
2. The two population variances are equal.
3. Samples are selected randomly and independently from the populations.

Assumptions for the F-test:

1. Both population probability distributions are normal.
2. The two population variances are equal.
3. Samples are selected randomly and independently from the respective populations.

The assumptions are the same for both tests.

8.19 For all parts, the hypotheses are:

H_0: $\mu_1 = \mu_2 = \mu_3 = \mu_4 = \mu_5 = \mu_6$
H_a: At least two treatment means differ

The rejection region for all parts is the same.

The rejection region requires $\alpha = .10$ in the upper tail of the F-distribution with $v_1 = k - 1 = 6 - 1 = 5$ and $v_2 = n - k = 36 - 6 = 30$. From Table VIII, Appendix B, $F_{.10} = 2.05$. The rejection region is $F > 2.05$.

a. $SST = .2(500) = 100$ $\qquad$ $SSE = SS(Total) - SST = 500 - 100 = 400$

$MST = \dfrac{SST}{k-1} = \dfrac{100}{6-1} = 20$ $\qquad$ $MSE = \dfrac{SSE}{n-k} = \dfrac{400}{36-6} = 13.333$

$F = \dfrac{MST}{MSE} = \dfrac{20}{13.333} = 1.5$

Since the observed value of the test statistic does not fall in the rejection region ($F = 1.5 \not> 2.05$), H_0 is not rejected. There is insufficient evidence to indicate differences among the treatment means at $\alpha = .10$.

b. $SST = .5(500) = 250$ $\qquad$ $SSE = SS(Total) - SST = 500 - 250 = 250$

$MST = \dfrac{SST}{k-1} = \dfrac{250}{6-1} = 50$ $\quad MSE = \dfrac{SSE}{n-k} = \dfrac{250}{36-6} = 8.333$

$F = \dfrac{MST}{MSE} = \dfrac{50}{8.333} = 6$

Since the observed value of the test statistic falls in the rejection region ($F = 6 > 2.05$), H_0 is rejected. There is sufficient evidence to indicate differences among the treatment means at $\alpha = .10$.

c. $SST = .8(500) = 400$ $\quad\quad\quad SSE = SS(Total) - SST = 500 - 400 = 100$

$$MST = \frac{SST}{k-1} = \frac{400}{6-1} = 80 \quad MSE = \frac{SSE}{n-k} = \frac{100}{36-6} = 3.333$$

$$F = \frac{MST}{MSE} = \frac{80}{3.333} = 24$$

Since the observed value of the test statistic falls in the rejection region ($F = 24 > 2.05$), H_0 is rejected. There is sufficient evidence to indicate differences among the treatment means at $\alpha = .10$.

d. The F-ratio increases as the treatment sum of squares increases.

8.21 a. Some preliminary calculations are:

$$CM = \frac{\left(\sum y_i\right)^2}{n} = \frac{37.1^2}{12} = 114.701$$

$$SS(Total) = \sum y_i^2 - CM = 145.89 - 114.701 = 31.189$$

$$SST = \sum \frac{T_i^2}{n_i} - CM = \frac{16.9^2}{5} + \frac{16.0^2}{4} + \frac{4.2^2}{3} - 114.701$$

$$= 127.002 - 114.701 = 12.301$$

$$SSE = SS(Total) - SST = 31.189 - 12.301 = 18.888$$

$$MST = \frac{SST}{k-1} = \frac{12.301}{3-1} = 6.1505 \quad\quad MSE = \frac{SSE}{n-k} = \frac{18.888}{12-3} = 2.0987$$

$$F = \frac{MST}{MSE} = \frac{6.1505}{2.0987} = 2.931$$

Source	df	SS	MS	F
Treatments	2	12.301	6.1505	2.931
Error	9	18.888	2.0987	
Total	11	31.189		

b. $H_0: \; \mu_1 = \mu_2 = \mu_3$
$H_a:$ At least two treatment means differ

The test statistic is $F = 2.931$.

The rejection region requires $\alpha = .01$ in the upper tail of the F-distribution with $v_1 = k - 1 = 3 - 1 = 2$ and $v_2 = n - k = 12 - 3 = 9$. From Table XI, Appendix B, $F_{.01} = 8.02$. The rejection region is $F > 8.02$.

Since the observed value of the test statistic does not fall in the rejection region ($F = 2.931 \not> 8.02$), H_0 is not rejected. There is insufficient evidence to indicate a difference in the treatment means at $\alpha = .01$.

8.23   a.   The experimental units in the study are the 324 adults who participated in the experiment.

   b.   The dependent variable for this study is the recall score.

   c.   There is one factor in this study and it is the type of TV program. It has 3 levels, and thus, there are 3 treatments. The 3 levels or treatments are: TV program with violent content, TV program with a sex content, and TV program with neither a sex nor a violent content.

   d.   The summary statistics are based only on a sample from the entire population. If other samples were selected, the summary statistics could change.

   e.   The test statistic is $F = 20.45$ and the p-value $= 0.000$.

   f.   Since the observed value of the p-value ($p = 0.000$) is less than $\alpha = .01$, H_0 is rejected. There is sufficient evidence to indicate a difference in mean recall among the different types of TV programming.

8.25   a.   To determine if the mean ages of all powerful American women differ among four groups based on position within the firm, we test:

   H_0: $\mu_1 = \mu_2 = \mu_3 = \mu_4$
   H_a: At least two means differ

   b.   The means at the bottom of the output are sample means. These sample means are actually observed values of random variables. Even if we took a second sample from within each treatment, the new sample means will probably differ from the first sample means. Thus, simply comparing the sample means is not valid. Within each of the treatments, there is variation among the observations. In order to determine if the three population means differ, we must compare the variation within the treatments to the variation between the treatments.

   c.   From the printout, the test statistic is $F = 2.5004$ and the p-value is $p = 0.071175$. Since the p-value (.071175) is less than $\alpha = .10$, H_0 is rejected. There is sufficient evidence to indicate a difference in mean age among the four groups based on position within the firm at $\alpha = .10$.

d.   Using MINITAB, histograms for the four groups are:

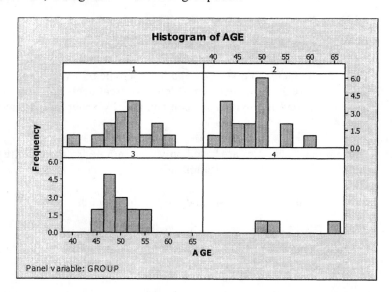

Except for group 4, each of the other 3 graphs looks fairly mound-shaped.   Group 4 has only 3 observations, so it is very difficult to judge normality. The assumption of normality looks to be valid.

Using MINITAB, the box plots for the 4 groups are:

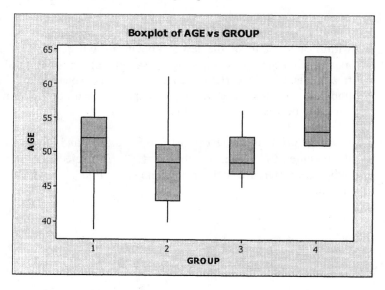

The spreads of the 4 groups do not appear to be the same. The spread of group 3 appears to be much smaller than the other 3 groups. Thus, the assumption of equal variances is probably not met.

8.27   To determine if a driver's propensity to engage in road rage is related to his/her income, we test:

H_0: $\mu_1 = \mu_2 = \mu_3$
H_a: At least two means differ

The test statistic is $F = 3.90$ and the p-value is $p < .01$. Since the p-value is so small, H_0 is rejected. There is sufficient evidence to indicate a driver's propensity to engage in road rage is related to his/her income for $\alpha > .01$. Since the sample means increase as the income increases, it appears that road rage increases as income increases.

8.29   a.   Using MINITAB, the ANOVA table is:

One-way ANOVA: Length versus Species

```
Analysis of Variance for Length
Source      DF       SS        MS       F        P
Species      2     3533.1    1766.5   76.88    0.000
Error      141     3239.9      23.0
Total      143     6772.9
                                    Individual 95% CIs For Mean
                                    Based on Pooled StDev
Level       N      Mean      StDev   -+---------+---------+---------+-----
CHANNELC    96    44.729     4.581                                   (-*)
LARGEMOU    12    26.542     4.480    (---*----)
SMALLMOU    36    43.125     5.413                                (--*--)
                                    -+---------+---------+---------+-----
Pooled StDev =     4.794            24.0      30.0      36.0      42.0
```

To determine if differences exist in the mean lengths among the 3 fish species, we test:

H_0: $\mu_1 = \mu_2 = \mu_3$
H_a: At least two means differ

The test statistic is $F = 76.88$ and the p-value is $p = 0.000$.

Since the p-value (0.000) is less than $\alpha = .05$, H_0 is rejected. There is sufficient evidence to indicate differences exist in the mean lengths among the 3 fish species at $\alpha = .05$.

b.   Using MINITAB, the output is:

One-way ANOVA: Weight versus Species

```
Analysis of Variance for Weight
Source      DF       SS         MS       F        P
Species      2     5884467   2942233   28.83    0.000
Error      141    14391071    102064
Total      143    20275537
                                    Individual 95% CIs For Mean
                                    Based on Pooled StDev
Level       N      Mean      StDev   ------+---------+---------+---------+
CHANNELC    96     987.3     262.7                       (-*-)
LARGEMOU    12     629.0     324.8      (-----*-----)
SMALLMOU    36    1356.4     436.7                              (--*---)
                                    ------+---------+---------+---------+
Pooled StDev =     319.5              600       900      1200      1500
```

To determine if differences exist in the mean weights among the 3 fish species, we test:

H_0: $\mu_1 = \mu_2 = \mu_3$
H_a: At least two means differ

The test statistic is $F = 28.83$ and the p-value is $p = 0.000$.

Since the p-value (0.000) is less than $\alpha = .05$, H_0 is rejected. There is sufficient evidence to indicate differences exist in the mean weights among the 3 fish species at $\alpha = .05$.

c. Using MINITAB, the output is:

One-way ANOVA: DDT versus Species

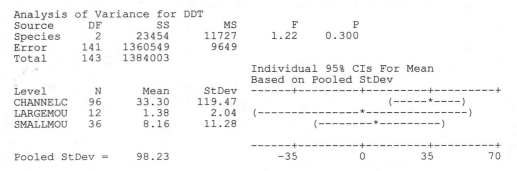

```
Analysis of Variance for DDT
Source      DF        SS         MS         F         P
Species      2      23454      11727      1.22     0.300
Error      141    1360549       9649
Total      143    1384003
                                        Individual 95% CIs For Mean
                                        Based on Pooled StDev
Level        N       Mean      StDev    ------+---------+---------+---------+
CHANNELC    96      33.30     119.47                         (-----*----)
LARGEMOU    12       1.38       2.04    (---------------*---------------)
SMALLMOU    36       8.16      11.28              (--------*---------)

                                        ------+---------+---------+---------+
Pooled StDev =      98.23                  -35         0        35        70
```

To determine if differences exist in the mean DDT levels among the 3 fish species, we test:

H_0: $\mu_1 = \mu_2 = \mu_3$
H_a: At least two means differ

The test statistic is $F = 1.22$ and the p-value is $p = 0.300$.

Since the p-value (0.300) is greater than $\alpha = .05$, H_0 is not rejected. There is insufficient evidence to indicate differences exist in the mean DDT levels among the 3 fish species at $\alpha = .05$.

d. Using MINITAB, the stem-and-leaf plots for the 3 fish species are:

Stem-and-Leaf Display: Length

```
Stem-and-leaf of Length    Species = 1    N = 96
Leaf Unit = 1.0

      1     2 9
      2     3 2
     11     3 556667899
     42     4 00000111111222222223333334444444
    (42)    4 55555555556666666777777777788888888899999
     12     5 000011111122
```

```
Stem-and-leaf of Length    Species = 2    N  = 12
Leaf Unit = 1.0

    1     1 7
    3     2 33
   (7)    2 5566889
    2     3 0
    1     3 6

Stem-and-leaf of Length    Species = 3    N  = 36
Leaf Unit = 1.0

    4     3 2234
   11     3 5668888
   16     4 13344
  (19)    4 5666666666777788899
    1     5 2
```

All three of the plots look somewhat mound-shaped, so the assumption of normality of fish lengths appears to be valid.

Stem-and-Leaf Display: Weight

```
Stem-and-leaf of Weight    Species = 1    N  = 96
Leaf Unit = 100

    1     0 3
    7     0 445555
   19     0 666667777777
  (34)    0 88888888888888889999999999999999999
   43     1 0000000000000001111111111111
   16     1 22222223333
    5     1 44
    3     1 677

Stem-and-leaf of Weight    Species = 2    N  = 12
Leaf Unit = 100

    1     0 1
    3     0 33
   (4)    0 4555
    5     0 777
    2     0 8
    1     1
    1     1
    1     1 4

Stem-and-leaf of Weight    Species = 3    N  = 36
Leaf Unit = 100

    3     0 555
    5     0 66
    8     0 889
   11     1 111
   16     1 22233
   (9)    1 444444445
   11     1 66777777
    3     1
    3     2 00
    1     2 3
```

All three of the plots look somewhat mound-shaped, so the assumption of normality of fish weights appears to be valid.

Stem-and-Leaf Display: DDT

```
Stem-and-leaf of DDT        Species = 1    N  = 96
Leaf Unit = 10

  (90)    0000000000000000000000000000000000000000000000000001111111111111111+
   6      1  3458
   2      2
   2      3  6
   1      4
   1      5
   1      6
   1      7
   1      8
   1      9
   1     10
   1     11  0

Stem-and-leaf of DDT        Species = 2    N  = 12
Leaf Unit = 10

  (12)    0  000000000000

Stem-and-leaf of DDT        Species = 3    N  = 36
Leaf Unit = 10

  (36)    0  000000000000000000000000000111112344
```

The plots do not look mound-shaped, so the assumption of normality of fish DDT levels may not be valid.

Using MINITAB, the box plots of the data are:

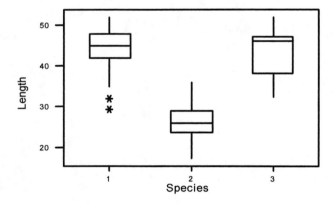

The spreads of the 3 species of fish appear to be about the same. The assumption of common variance in the fish lengths appears to be valid.

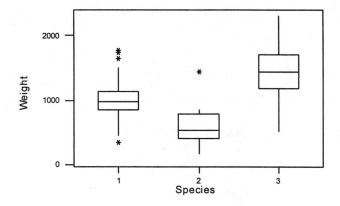

The spreads of the 3 species of fish appear to be about the same. The assumption of common variance in the fish weights appears to be valid.

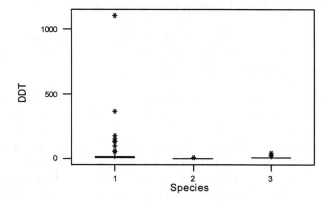

The spreads of the 3 species of fish do not appear to be the same. The assumption of common variance in the fish DDT levels does not appear to be valid.

10.31   a.   To determine if the mean level of trust differs among the six treatments, we test:

H_0: $\mu_1 = \mu_2 = \mu_3 = \mu_4 = \mu_5 = \mu_6$
H_a: At least one μ_i differs

b.   The test statistic is $F = 2.21$.

The rejection region requires α in the upper tail of the F-distribution with $v_1 = k - 1 = 6 - 1 = 5$ and $v_2 = n - k = 237 - 6 = 231$. From Table IX, Appendix B, $F_{.05} \approx 2.21$. The rejection region is $F > 2.21$.

Since the observed value of the test statistic does not fall in the rejection region ($F = 2.21$ $\not> 2.21$), H_0 is not rejected. There is insufficient evidence to indicate that at least two mean trusts differ at $\alpha = .05$.

c.   We must assume that all six samples are drawn from normal populations, the six population variances are the same, and that the samples are independent.

d. I would classify this experiment as designed. Each subject was randomly assigned to receive one of the six scenarios.

8.33 The number of pairwise comparisons is equal to $k(k-1)/2$.

    a. For $k = 3$, the number of comparisons is $3(3-1)/2 = 3$.

    b. For $k = 5$, the number of comparisons is $5(5-1)/2 = 10$.

    c. For $k = 4$, the number of comparisons is $4(4-1)/2 = 6$.

    d. For $k = 10$, the number of comparisons is $10(10-1)/2 = 45$.

8.35 A comparisonwise error rate is the error rate (or the probability of declaring the means different when, in fact, they are not different) for each individual comparison. That is, if each comparison is run using $\alpha = .05$, then the comparisonwise error rate is .05.

8.37 The mean response for Division I coaches is significantly higher than the mean responses for the Division II and Division III coaches. There is no difference in the mean responses between Division II and Division III coaches.

8.39   a. Tukey's multiple comparison method is preferred over other methods because it controls experimental error at the chosen α level. It is more powerful than the other methods.

    b. From the confidence interval comparing large-cap and medium-cap mutual funds, we find that 0 is in the interval. Thus, 0 is not an unusual value for the difference in the mean rates of return between large-cap and medium-cap mutual funds. This means we would not reject H_0. There is insufficient evidence of a difference in mean rates of return between large-cap and medium-cap mutual funds at $\alpha = .05$.

    c. From the confidence interval comparing large-cap and small-cap mutual funds, we find that 0 is not in the interval. Thus, 0 is an unusual value for the difference in the mean rates of return between large-cap and small-cap mutual funds. This means we would reject H_0. There is sufficient evidence of a difference in mean rates of return between large-cap and small-cap mutual funds at $\alpha = .05$.

    d. From the confidence interval comparing medium-cap and small-cap mutual funds, we find that 0 is in the interval. Thus, 0 is not an unusual value for the difference in the mean rates of return between medium-cap and small-cap mutual funds. This means we would not reject H_0. There is insufficient evidence of a difference in mean rates of return between medium-cap and small-cap mutual funds at $\alpha = .05$.

    e. From the above, the mean rate of return for large-cap mutual funds is the largest, followed by medium-cap, followed by small-cap mutual funds. The mean rate of return for large-cap funds is significantly larger than that for small-cap funds. No other differences exist.

    f. We are 95% confident of this decision.

8.41   a.   There are a combination of 3 things taken 2 at a time or 3 pair-wise comparisons.

b.   The confidence interval for the comparison of the S and V groups is: (-0.923, 0.183). We are 95% confident that the difference in the mean recall scores between Sexual and Violent content programs is between –0.923 and 0.183. Since 0 is in this interval, there is no evidence to indicate a difference in the mean recall scores between the Sexual and Violent content programs.

c.   The confidence interval for the comparison of the N and V groups is: (0.530, 1.636). We are 95% confident that the difference in the mean recall scores between Neutral and Violent content programs is between 0.530 and 1.636. Since 0 is not in this interval, there is evidence to indicate a difference in the mean recall scores between the Neutral and Violent content programs.

The confidence interval for the comparison of the N and S groups is: (0.901, 2.007). We are 95% confident that the difference in the mean recall scores between Neutral and Sexual content programs is between 0.901 and 2.007. Since 0 is not in this interval, there is evidence to indicate a difference in the mean recall scores between the Neutral and Sexual content programs.

From the comparisons above, both the Violent and Sexual content programs had lower mean recall scores than the Neutral programs. There was no difference in the mean recall scores between the Violent and Sexual content programs. Thus, either the Neutral content program had the largest mean recall score.

d.   Yes. We found that the mean recall score for those watching the Neutral program was significantly larger than the mean recall scores of the other two groups.

8.43   From Exercise 8.29, we found that there were differences in the mean lengths among the 3 fish species and differences in the mean weight among the 3 fish species. There were no differences in the mean DDT levels among the 3 fish species.

Length:

From Exercise 8.29, the mean lengths of the 3 species of fish are:

Channel catfish   44.729
Largemouth bass   26.542
Smallmouth buffalofish   43.125

Using MINITAB, the Tukey confidence intervals are:

```
Tukey's pairwise comparisons

    Family error rate = 0.0500
Individual error rate = 0.0192

Critical value = 3.35
```

```
Intervals for (column level mean) - (row level mean)

                    1                2

        2        14.711
                 21.664

        3        -0.615          -20.368
                  3.823          -12.798
```

The confidence interval for the difference in mean length between channel catfish and largemouth bass is (14.711, 21.664). Since 0 is not in this interval, there is sufficient evidence of a difference in mean length between channel catfish and largemouth bass.

The confidence interval for the difference in mean length between channel catfish and smallmouth buffalofish is (−0.615, 3.823). Since 0 is in this interval, there is insufficient evidence of a difference in mean length between channel catfish and smallmouth buffalofish.

The confidence interval for the difference in mean length between largemouth bass and smallmouth buffalofish is (−20.368, −12.798). Since 0 is not in this interval, there is sufficient evidence of a difference in mean length between largemouth bass and smallmouth buffalofish.

In summary, the mean length of largemouth bass is significantly shorter than the mean lengths of channel catfish and smallmouth buffalofish. No other differences exist.

Weight:

From Exercise 8.29, the mean weights of the 3 species of fish are:

Channel catfish   987.3
Largemouth bass   629.0
Smallmouth buffalofish   1,356.4

Using MINITAB, the Tukey confidence intervals are:

```
Tukey's pairwise comparisons

    Family error rate = 0.0500
Individual error rate = 0.0192

Critical value = 3.35

Intervals for (column level mean) - (row level mean)

                    1                2

        2           127
                    590

        3          -517             -980
                   -221             -475
```

The confidence interval for the difference in mean weight between channel catfish and largemouth bass is (127, 590). Since 0 is not in this interval, there is sufficient evidence of a difference in mean weight between channel catfish and largemouth bass.

The confidence interval for the difference in mean weight between channel catfish and smallmouth buffalofish is (−517, −221). Since 0 is not in this interval, there is sufficient evidence of a difference in mean weight between channel catfish and smallmouth buffalofish.

The confidence interval for the difference in mean weight between largemouth bass and smallmouth buffalofish is (−980, −475). Since 0 is not in this interval, there is sufficient evidence of a difference in mean weight between largemouth bass and smallmouth buffalofish.

In summary, the mean weight of largemouth bass is significantly less than the mean weights of channel catfish and smallmouth buffalofish. The mean weight of channel catfish is significantly less than the mean weight of smallmouth buffalofish.

8.45   The mean level of trust for the "no close" technique is significantly higher than that for the "assumed close" and the "either-or" techniques. The mean level of trust for the "impending event" technique is significantly higher than that for the "either-or" technique. No other significant differences exist.

8.47   a.   Treatment $df = k - 1 = 3 - 1 = 2$
              Block $df = b - 1 = 3 - 1 = 2$
              Error $df = n - k - b + 1 = 9\ 3 - 3 + 1 = 4$
              Total $df = n - 1 = 9 - 1 = 8$

$$SSB = \sum_{i=1}^{b} \frac{B_i^2}{k} - CM \text{ from Appendix B}$$

$$\text{where } CM = \frac{\left(\sum x_i\right)^2}{n} = \frac{49^2}{9} = 266.7778$$

$$SSB = \frac{17^2}{3} + \frac{15^2}{3} + \frac{17^2}{3} - 266.7778 = .8889$$

$$SSE = SS(Total) - SST - SSB = 30.2222 - 21.5555 - .8889 = 7.7778$$

$$MST = \frac{SST}{k-1} = \frac{21.5555}{2} = 10.7778 \quad MSB = \frac{SSB}{b-1} = \frac{.8889}{2} = .4445$$

$$MSE = \frac{SSE}{n-k-b+1} = \frac{7.7778}{4} = 1.9445$$

$$F_T = \frac{MST}{MSE} = \frac{10.7778}{1.9445} = 5.54 \qquad F_B = \frac{MSB}{MSE} = \frac{.4445}{1.9445} = .23$$

The ANOVA table is:

Source	df	SS	MS	F
Treatment	2	21.5555	10.7778	5.54
Block	2	.8889	.4445	.23
Error	4	7.7778	1.9445	
Total	8	30.2222		

b. H_0: $\mu_1 = \mu_2 = \mu_3$ vs H_a: At least two treatment means differ c.	The test statistic is $F = \dfrac{\text{MST}}{\text{MSE}} = 5.54$

d.	A Type I error would be concluding at least two treatment means differ when they do not.

A Type II error would be concluding all the treatment means are the same when at least two differ.

e.	The rejection region requires $\alpha = .05$ in the upper tail of the F distribution with $v_1 = k - 1 = 3 - 1 = 2$ and $v_2 = n - k - b + 1 = 9 - 3 - 3 + 1 = 4$. From Table IX, Appendix A, $F_{.05} = 6.94$. The rejection region is $F > 6.94$.

Since the observed value of the test statistic does not fall in the rejection region ($F = 5.54 \not> 6.94$), H_0 is not rejected. There is insufficient evidence to indicate at least two of the treatment means differ at $\alpha = .05$.

8.49	a.	$\text{SST} = .2(500) = 100 \qquad\qquad\qquad \text{SSB} = .3(500) = 150$
$\text{SSE} = \text{SS(Total)} - \text{SST} - \text{SSB} = 500 - 100 - 150 = 250$

$$\text{MST} = \frac{\text{SST}}{k-1} = \frac{100}{4-1} = 33.3333 \qquad \text{MSB} = \frac{\text{SSB}}{b-1} = \frac{150}{9-1} = 18.75$$

$$\text{MSE} = \frac{\text{SSE}}{n-k-b+1} = \frac{250}{36-4-9+1} = \frac{250}{4} = 10.4167$$

$$F_{\text{T}} = \frac{\text{MST}}{\text{MSE}} = \frac{33.3333}{10.4167} = 3.20 \qquad F_{\text{B}} = \frac{\text{MSB}}{\text{MSE}} = \frac{18.75}{10.4167} = 1.80$$

To determine if differences exist among the treatment means, we test:

H_0: $\mu_1 = \mu_2 = \mu_3 = \mu_4 = \mu_5$
H_a: At least two treatment means differ

The test statistic is $F = 3.20$.

The rejection region requires $\alpha = .05$ in the upper tail of the F distribution with $v_1 = k - 1 = 4 - 1 = 3$ and $v_2 = n - k - b + 1 = 36 - 4 - 9 + 1 = 24$. From Table IX, Appendix B, $F_{.05} = 3.01$. The rejection region is $F > 3.01$.

Since the observed value of the test statistic falls in the rejection region ($F = 3.20 > 3.01$), H_0 is rejected. There is sufficient evidence to indicate differences among the treatment means at $\alpha = .05$.

To determine if differences exist among the block means, we test:

H_0: $\mu_1 = \mu_2 = \cdots = \mu_9$
H_a: At least two block means differ

The test statistic is $F = 1.80$.

The rejection region requires $\alpha = .05$ in the upper tail of the F distribution with $v_1 = b - 1 = 9 - 1 = 8$ and $v_2 = n - b - k + 1 = 36 - 9 - 4 + 1 = 24$. From Table IX, Appendix B, $F_{.05} = 2.36$. The rejection region is $F > 2.36$.

Since the observed value of the test statistic does not fall in the rejection region ($F = 1.80 \not> 2.36$), H_0 is not rejected. There is insufficient evidence to indicate differences among the block means at $\alpha = .05$.

b. $\text{SST} = .5(500) = 250$ $\qquad\qquad$ $\text{SS}B = .2(500) = 100$

$\text{SSE} = \text{SS(Total)} - \text{SST} - \text{SS}B = 500 - 250 - 100 = 150$

$$\text{MST} = \frac{\text{SST}}{k-1} = \frac{250}{4-1} = 83.3333 \qquad \text{MSB} = \frac{\text{SS}B}{b-1} = \frac{100}{9-1} = 12.5$$

$$\text{MSE} = \frac{\text{SSE}}{n-k-b+1} = \frac{150}{36-4-9+1} = 6.25$$

$$F_\text{T} = \frac{\text{MST}}{\text{MSE}} = \frac{83.3333}{6.25} = 13.33 \qquad F_\text{B} = \frac{\text{MSB}}{\text{MSE}} = \frac{12.5}{6.25} = 2$$

To determine if differences exist among the treatment means, we test:

H_0: $\mu_1 = \mu_2 = \mu_3 = \mu_4$
H_a: At least two treatment means differ

The test statistic is $F = 13.33$.

The rejection region is $F > 3.01$ (same as above).

Since the observed value of the test statistic falls in the rejection region ($F = 13.33 > 3.01$), H_0 is rejected. There is sufficient evidence to indicate differences exist among the treatment means at $\alpha = .05$.

To determine if differences exist among the block means, we test:

H_0: $\mu_1 = \mu_2 = \cdots = \mu_9$
H_a: At least two block means differ

The test statistic is $F = 2.00$.

The rejection region is $F > 2.36$ (same as above).

Since the observed value of the test statistic does not fall in the rejection region ($F = 2.00 \not> 2.36$), H_0 is not rejected. There is insufficient evidence to indicate differences exist among the block means at $\alpha = .05$.

c. $\text{SST} = .2(500) = 100$ $\qquad\qquad$ $\text{SS}B = .5(500) = 250$

$\text{SSE} = \text{SS(Total)} - \text{SST} - \text{SS}B = 500 - 100 - 250 = 150$

$$\text{MST} = \frac{\text{SST}}{k-1} = \frac{100}{4-1} = 33.3333 \qquad \text{MSB} = \frac{\text{SS}B}{b-1} = \frac{250}{9-1} = 31.25$$

$$\text{MSE} = \frac{\text{SSE}}{n-k-b+1} = \frac{150}{36-4-9+1} = 6.25$$

$$F_\text{T} = \frac{\text{MST}}{\text{MSE}} = \frac{33.3333}{6.25} = 5.33 \qquad F_\text{B} = \frac{\text{MSB}}{\text{MSE}} = \frac{31.25}{6.25} = 5.00$$

To determine if differences exist among the treatment means, we test:

H_0: $\mu_1 = \mu_2 = \mu_3 = \mu_4$
H_a: At least two treatment means differ

The test statistic is $F = 5.33$.
The rejection region is $F > 3.01$ (same as above).

Since the observed value of the test statistic falls in the rejection region ($F = 5.33 > 3.01$), H_0 is rejected. There is sufficient evidence to indicate differences exist among the treatment means at $\alpha = .05$.

To determine if differences exist among the block means, we test:

H_0: $\mu_1 = \mu_2 = \cdots = \mu_9$
H_a: At least two block means differ

The test statistic is $F = 5.00$.

The rejection region is $F > 2.36$ (same as above).

Since the observed value of the test statistic falls in the rejection region ($F = 5.00 > 2.36$), H_0 is rejected. There is sufficient evidence to indicate differences exist among the block means at $\alpha = .05$.

d.　　$SST = .4(500) = 200$　　　　　　$SSB = .4(500) = 200$
　　　$SSE = SS(Total) - SST - SSB = 500 - 200 - 200 = 100$

$$MST = \frac{SST}{k-1} = \frac{200}{4-1} = 66.6667 \qquad MSB = \frac{SSB}{b-1} = \frac{200}{9-1} = 25$$

$$MSE = \frac{SSE}{n-k-b+1} = \frac{100}{36-4-9+1} = 4.1667$$

$$F_T = \frac{MST}{MSE} = \frac{66.6667}{4.1667} = 16.0 \qquad F_B = \frac{MSB}{MSE} = \frac{25}{4.1667} = 6.00$$

To determine if differences exist among the treatment means, we test:

H_0: $\mu_1 = \mu_2 = \mu_3 = \mu_4$
H_a: At least two treatment means differ

The test statistic is $F = 16.0$.

The rejection region is $F > 3.01$ (same as above).

Since the observed value of the test statistic falls in the rejection region ($F = 16.0 > 3.01$), H_0 is rejected. There is sufficient evidence to indicate differences among the treatment means at $\alpha = .05$.

To determine if differences exist among the block means, we test:

H_0: $\mu_1 = \mu_2 = \cdots = \mu_9$
H_a: At least two block means differ

The test statistic is $F = 6.00$.

The rejection region is $F > 2.36$ (same as above).

Since the observed value of the test statistic falls in the rejection region ($F = 6.00 > 2.36$), H_0 is rejected. There is sufficient evidence to indicate differences exist among the block means at $\alpha = .05$.

e. $\text{SST} = .2(500) = 100$ $\text{SSB} = .2(500) = 100$
    $\text{SSE} = \text{SS(Total)} - \text{SST} - \text{SSB} = 500 - 100 - 100 = 300$

$$\text{MST} = \frac{\text{SST}}{k-1} = \frac{100}{4-1} = 33.3333 \qquad \text{MSB} = \frac{\text{SSB}}{b-1} = \frac{100}{9-1} = 12.5$$

$$\text{MSE} = \frac{\text{SSE}}{n-k-b+1} = \frac{300}{36-4-9+1} = 12.5$$

$$F_T = \frac{\text{MST}}{\text{MSE}} = \frac{33.3333}{12.5} = 2.67 \qquad F_B = \frac{\text{MSB}}{\text{MSE}} = \frac{12.5}{12.5} = 1.00$$

To determine if differences exist among the treatment means, we test:

H_0: $\mu_1 = \mu_2 = \mu_3 = \mu_4$
H_a: At least two treatment means differ

The test statistic is $F = 2.67$.

The rejection region is $F > 3.01$ (same as above).

Since the observed value of the test statistic does not fall in the rejection region ($F = 2.67 \not> 3.01$), H_0 is not rejected. There is insufficient evidence to indicate differences exist among the treatment means at $\alpha = .05$.

To determine if differences exist among the block means, we test:

H_0: $\mu_1 = \mu_2 = \cdots = \mu_9$
H_a: At least two block means differ

The test statistic is $F = 1.00$.

The rejection region is $F > 2.36$ (same as above).

Since the observed value of the test statistic does not fall in the rejection region ($F = 1.00 \not> 2.36$), H_0 is not rejected. There is insufficient evidence to indicate differences among the block means at $\alpha = .05$.

8.51   a.   The time of the year (month) could affect the number of rigs running, so a randomized complete block design was used to "block" out the month to month variation.

        b.   There are 3 treatments in this experiment. They are the three states – California, Utah, and Alaska.

        c.   There are 3 blocks in this experiment – the three months selected: November 2000, October 2001, and November 2001.

        d.   To determine if there is a difference in the mean number of rigs running among the three states, we test:

              H_0: $\mu_1 = \mu_2 = \mu_3$

        e.   From the printout, the test statistic is $F = 38.07$ and the p-value is $p = 0.002$. Since the p-value is so small, we would reject H_0 for any value of $\alpha > .002$. There is sufficient evidence to indicate a difference in the mean number of oil rigs running among the three states.

        f.   From the SPSS printout, there is no significant difference in the mean number of oil rigs running in Alaska and Utah. However, both of these states have a significantly smaller number of rigs running than does California. Thus, California has the largest mean number of oil rigs running.

8.53   a.   The experimenters expected there to be much variation in the number of participants from week to week (more participants at the beginning and fewer as time goes on). Thus, by blocking on weeks, this extraneous source of variation can be controlled.

        b.   df(Week) = $b - 1 = 6 - 1 = 5$

              MS(Prompt) = $\dfrac{SST}{df} = \dfrac{1185.0}{4} = 296.25$

              F(Prompt) = $\dfrac{MST}{MSE} = \dfrac{296.25}{7.43} = 39.87$

              The ANOVA table is:

Source	df	SS	MS	F	p
Prompt	4	1185.0	296.25	39.87	0.0001
Week	5	386.4	77.28	10.40	0.0001
Error	20	148.6	7.43		
Total	29	1720.0			

        c.   To determine if a difference exists in the mean number of walkers per week among the five walker groups, we test:

              H_0: $\mu_1 = \mu_2 = \mu_3 = \mu_4 = \mu_5$
              H_a: At least two treatment means differ

              where μ_i represents the mean number of walkers in group i.

The test statistic is $F = 39.87$.

The rejection region requires $\alpha = .05$ in the upper tail of the F distribution with $v_1 = k - 1 = 5 - 1 = 4$ and $v_2 = n - k - b + 1 = 30 - 4 - 6 + 1 = 20$. From Table IX, Appendix B, $F_{.05} = 2.69$. The rejection region is $F > 2.69$.

Since the observed value of the test statistic falls in the rejection region ($F = 39.87 > 2.69$), H_0 is rejected. There is sufficient evidence to indicate differences exist among the mean number of walkers per week among the 5 walker groups at $\alpha = .05$.

d. The following conclusions are drawn:

The mean number of walkers per week in the "Frequent/High" group is significantly higher than the mean number of walkers per week in the "Infrequent/Low" group, the "Infrequent/High" group, and the "Control" group. The mean number of walkers per week in the "Frequent/Low" group is significantly higher than the mean number of walkers per week in the "Infrequent/Low" group, the "Infrequent/High" group, and the "Control" group. The mean number of walkers per week in the "Infrequent/Low" group is significantly higher than the mean number of walkers per week in the "Control" group. The mean number of walkers per week in the "Infrequent/High" group is significantly higher than the mean number of walkers per week in the "Control group.

e. In order for the above inferences to be valid, the following assumptions must hold:

1) The probability distributions of observations corresponding to all block-treatment conditions are normal.
2) The variances of all the probability distributions are equal.

8.55 Using MINITAB, the ANOVA table is:

Two-way ANOVA: Rate versus Week, Day

```
Analysis of Variance for Rate
Source      DF        SS        MS        F         P
Week         8     575.2      71.9      6.10     0.000
Day          4      94.2      23.5      2.00     0.118
Error       32     376.9      11.8
Total       44    1046.4

                      Individual 95% CI
Day          Mean   -+---------+---------+---------+---------+
1             8.8                        (--------*---------)
2             4.6    (--------*---------)
3             5.8        (--------*--------)
4             5.4    (--------*---------)
5             6.4          (---------*--------)
                    -+---------+---------+---------+---------+
                    2.5       5.0       7.5      10.0      12.5
```

To determine if there is a difference in mean rate of absenteeism among the 5 days of the week, we test:

H_0: $\mu_1 = \mu_2 = \mu_3 = \mu_4 = \mu_5$
H_a: At least two treatment means differ

The test statistic is $F = 2.00$.

Since no α was given, we will select $\alpha = .05$. The rejection region requires $\alpha = .05$ in the upper tail of the F distribution with $v_1 = k - 1 = 5 - 1 = 4$ and $v_2 = n - k - b + 1 = 45 - 5 - 9 + 1 = 32$. From Table IX, Appendix B, $F_{.05, 4, 32} \approx 2.69$. The rejection region is $F > 2.69$. Since the observed value of the test statistic does not fall in the rejection region ($F = 2.00 \not> 2.69$), H_0 is not rejected. There is insufficient evidence to indicate a difference in mean rate of absenteeism among the 5 days of the week at $\alpha = .05$.

To test for the effectiveness of blocking, we test:

H_0: All block means are the same
H_a: At least two block means differ

The test statistic is $F = 6.10$.

The rejection region requires $\alpha = .05$ in the upper tail of the F distribution with $v_1 = b - 1 = 9 - 1 = 8$ and $v_2 = n - k - b + 1 = 45 - 5 - 9 + 1 = 32$. From Table IX, Appendix B, $F_{.05, 8, 32} \approx 2.27$. The rejection region is $F > 2.27$.

Since the observed value of the test statistic falls in the rejection region ($F = 6.10 > 2.27$), H_0 is rejected. There is sufficient evidence to indicate blocking was effective at $\alpha = .05$.

8.57   Using MINITAB, the ANOVA table is:

Two-way ANOVA: Corrosion versus Time, System

```
Source   DF      SS        MS        F        P
Time      2   63.1050   31.5525   337.06   0.000
System    3    9.5833    3.1944    34.12   0.000
Error     6    0.5617    0.0936
Total    11   73.2500

S = 0.3060    R-Sq = 99.23%    R-Sq(adj) = 98.59%


                       Individual 95% CIs For Mean Based on
                       Pooled StDev
System     Mean    ------+---------+---------+---------+---
1         9.0667        (----*-----)
2         9.7333              (-----*----)
3        11.0667                              (----*-----)
4         8.7333    (----*-----)
                    ------+---------+---------+---------+---
                        8.80      9.60     10.40     11.20
```

To determine if there is a difference in mean corrosion rates among the 4 systems, we test:

H_0: $\mu_1 = \mu_2 = \mu_3 = \mu_4$
H_a: At least two treatment means differ

The test statistic is $F = 34.12$.

Since no α level was given, we will select $\alpha = .05$. The rejection region requires $\alpha = .05$ in the upper tail of the F distribution with $v_1 = k - 1 = 4 - 1 = 3$ and $v_2 = n - k - b + 1 = 12 - 4 - 3 + 1 = 6$. From Table IX, Appendix B, $F_{.05, 3, 6} = 4.76$. The rejection region is $F > 4.76$.

Since the observed value of the test statistic falls in the rejection region ($F = 34.12 > 4.76$), H_0 is rejected. There is sufficient evidence to indicate a difference in mean corrosion rates among the 4 systems at $\alpha = .05$.

Using SAS, Tukey's multiple comparison results are:

```
Tukey's Studentized Range (HSD) Test for CORROSION

NOTE: This test controls the Type I experimentwise error rate, but it generally has a higher
      Type II error rate than REGWQ.

              Alpha                                        0.05
              Error Degrees of Freedom                        6
              Error Mean Square                        0.093611
              Critical Value of Studentized Range       4.89559
              Minimum Significant Difference             0.8648


          Means with the same letter are not significantly different.

          Tukey Grouping         Mean     N    SYSTEM

                      A       11.0667     3     3

                      B        9.7333     3     2
                      B
              C       B        9.0667     3     1
              C
              C                8.7333     3     4
```

The mean corrosion rate for system 3 is significantly larger than all of the other mean corrosion rates. The mean corrosion rate of system 2 is significantly larger than the mean for system 4. If we want the system (epoxy coating) with the lowest corrosion rate, we would pick either system 1 or system 4. There is no significant difference between these two groups and they are in the lowest corrosion rate group.

8.59   a.   The ANOVA table is:

Source	df	SS	MS	F
A	2	.8	.4000	3.69
B	3	5.3	1.7667	16.31
AB	6	9.6	1.6000	14.77
Error	12	1.3	.1083	
Total	23	17.0		

df for A is $a - 1 = 3 - 1 = 2$
    df for $B = b - 1 = 4 - 1 = 3$
df for AB is $(a - 1)(b - 1) = 2(3) = 6$
    df for Error is $n - ab = 24 - 3(4) = 12$
df for Total is $n - 1 = 24 - 1 = 23$

$$SSE = SS(\text{Total}) - SSA - SSB - SSAB = 17.0 - .8 - 5.3 - 9.6 = 1.3$$

$$MSA = \frac{SSA}{a-1} = \frac{.8}{3-1} = .40 \quad MSB = \frac{SSB}{b-1} = \frac{5.3}{4-1} = 1.7667$$

$$MSAB = \frac{SSAB}{(a-1)(b-1)} = \frac{9.6}{(3-1)(4-1)} = 1.60$$

$$MSE = \frac{SSE}{n-ab} = \frac{1.3}{24-3(4)} = .1083$$

$$F_A = \frac{MSA}{MSE} = \frac{.4000}{.1083} = 3.69 \qquad F_B = \frac{MSB}{MSE} = \frac{1.7667}{.1083} = 16.31$$

$$F_{AB} = \frac{MSAB}{MSE} = \frac{1.6000}{.1083} = 14.77$$

b. Sum of Squares for Treatment $= SSA + SSB + SSAB = .8 = 5.3 + 2.6 = 15.7$

$$MST = \frac{SST}{ab-1} = \frac{15.7}{3(4)-1} = 1.4273 \qquad\qquad F_T = \frac{MST}{MSE} = \frac{1.4273}{.1083} = 13.18$$

To determine if the treatment means differ, we test:

$H_0: \mu_1 = \mu_2 = \cdots = \mu_{12}$
$H_a:$ At least two treatments means differ

The test statistic is $F = 13.18$.

The rejection region requires $\alpha = .05$ in the upper tail of the F-distribution with $v_1 = ab - 1 = 3(4) - 1 = 11$ and $v_2 = n - ab = 24 - 3(4) = 12$. From Table IX, Appendix B, $F_{.05} \approx 2.75$. The rejection region is $F > 2.75$.

Since the observed value of the test statistic falls in the rejection region ($F = 13.18 > 2.75$), H_0 is rejected. There is sufficient evidence to indicate the treatment means differ at $\alpha = .05$.

c. Yes. We need to partition the Treatment Sum of Squares into the Main Effects and Interaction Sum of Squares. Then we test whether factors A and B interact. Depending on the conclusion of the test for interaction, we either test for main effects or compare the treatment means.

d. Two factors are said to interact if the effect of one factor on the dependent variable is not the same at different levels of the second factor. If the factors interact, then tests for main effects are not necessary. We need to compare the treatment means for one factor at each level of the second.

e. To determine if the factors interact, we test:

H_0: Factors A and B do not interact to affect the response mean
H_a: Factors A and B do interact to affect the response mean

The test statistic is $F = \dfrac{MSAB}{MSE} = 14.77$

The rejection region requires $\alpha = .05$ in the upper tail of the F-distribution with $v_1 = (a-1)(b-1) = (3-1)(4-1) = 6$ and $v_2 = n - ab = 24 - 3(4) = 12$. From Table IX, Appendix B, $F_{.05} = 3.00$. The rejection region is $F > 3.00$.

Since the observed value of the test statistic falls in the rejection region ($F = 14.77 > 3.00$), H_0 is rejected. There is sufficient evidence to indicate the two factors interact to affect the response mean at $\alpha = .05$.

f. No. Testing for main effects is not warranted because interaction is present. Instead, we compare the treatment means of one factor at each level of the second factor.

8.61 a. The treatments for this experiment consist of a level for factor A and a level for factor B. There are six treatments—$(1, 1)$, $(1, 2)$, $(1, 3)$, $(2, 1)$, $(2, 2)$, and $(2, 3)$ where the first number represents the level of factor A and the second number represents the level of factor B.

The treatment means appear to be different because the sample means are quite different. The factors appear to interact because the lines are not parallel.

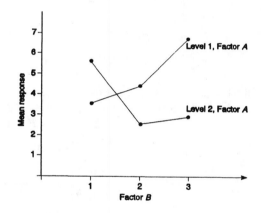

b. $SST = SSA + SSB + SSAB = 4.4408 + 4.1267 + 18.0667 = 26.5742$

$MST = \dfrac{SST}{ab-1} = \dfrac{26.5742}{2(3)-1} = 5.315$ $F_T = \dfrac{MST}{MSE} = \dfrac{5.315}{.246} = 21.62$

To determine whether the treatment means differ, we test:

H_0: $\mu_1 = \mu_2 = \mu_3 = \mu_4 = \mu_5 = \mu_6$
H_a: At least two treatment means differ

The test statistic is $F = \dfrac{MST}{MSE} = 21.62$

The rejection region requires $\alpha = .05$ in the upper tail of the F-distribution with $v_1 = ab - 1 = 2(3) - 1 = 5$ and $v_2 = n - ab = 12 - 2(3) = 6$. From Table IX, Appendix B, $F_{.05} = 4.39$. The rejection region is $F > 4.39$.

Since the observed value of the test statistic falls in the rejection region ($F = 21.62 > 4.39$), H_0 is rejected. There is sufficient evidence to indicate that the treatment means differ at $\alpha = .05$. This supports the plot in **a**.

c. Yes. Since there are differences among the treatment means, we test for interaction. To determine whether the factors A and B interact, we test:

H_0: Factors A and B do not interact to affect the mean response
H_a: Factors A and B do interact to affect the mean response

The test statistic is $F = \dfrac{\text{MSAB}}{\text{MSE}} = \dfrac{9.0033}{.24583} = 36.62$

The rejection region requires $\alpha = .05$ in the upper tail of the F-distribution with $v_1 = (a - 1)(b - 1) = (2 - 1)(3 - 1) = 2$ and $v_2 = n - ab = 12 - 2(3) = 6$. From Table IX, Appendix B, $F_{.05} = 5.14$. The rejection region is $F > 5.14$.

Since the observed value of the test statistic falls in the rejection region ($F = 36.62 > 5.14$), H_0 is rejected. There is sufficient evidence to indicate that factors A and B interact to affect the response mean at $\alpha = .05$.

d. No. Because interaction is present, the tests for main effects are not warranted.

e. The results of the tests in parts **b** and **c** support the visual interpretation in part **a**.

8.63 a. $\text{SS}A = .2(1000) = 200$, $\text{SS}B = .1(1000) = 100$, $\text{SS}AB = .1(1000) = 100$
$\text{SSE} = \text{SS(Total)} - \text{SS}A - \text{SS}B - \text{SS}AB = 1000 - 200 - 100 - 100 = 600$
$\text{SST} = \text{SS}A + \text{SS}B + \text{SS}AB = 200 + 100 + 100 = 400$

$\text{MS}A = \dfrac{\text{SS}A}{a-1} = \dfrac{200}{3-1} = 100$ $\qquad$ $\text{MS}B = \dfrac{\text{SS}B}{b-1} = \dfrac{100}{3-1} = 50$

$\text{MS}AB = \dfrac{\text{SS}AB}{(a-1)(b-1)} = \dfrac{100}{(3-1)(3-1)} = 25$

$\text{MSE} = \dfrac{\text{SSE}}{n-ab} = \dfrac{600}{27-3(3)} = 33.333$ $\qquad$ $\text{MST} = \dfrac{\text{SST}}{ab-1} = \dfrac{400}{3(3)-1} = 50$

$F_A = \dfrac{\text{MS}A}{\text{MSE}} = \dfrac{100}{33.333} = 3.00$ $\qquad$ $F_B = \dfrac{\text{MS}B}{\text{MSE}} = \dfrac{50}{33.333} = 1.50$

$F_{AB} = \dfrac{\text{MS}AB}{\text{MSE}} = \dfrac{25}{33.333} = .75$ $\qquad$ $F_T = \dfrac{\text{MST}}{\text{MSE}} = \dfrac{50}{33.333} = 1.50$

Source	df	SS	MS	F
A	2	200	100	3.00
B	2	100	50	1.50
AB	4	100	25	.75
Error	18	600	33.333	
Total	26	1000		

To determine whether the treatment means differ, we test:

H_0: $\mu_1 = \mu_2 = \cdots = \mu_9$
H_a: At least two treatment means differ

The test statistic is $F = \dfrac{\text{MST}}{\text{MSE}} = 1.50$

Suppose $\alpha = .05$. The rejection region requires $\alpha = .05$ in the upper tail of the F-distribution with $v_1 = ab - 1 = 3(3) - 1 = 8$ and $v_2 = n - ab = 27 - 3(3) = 18$. From Table IX, Appendix B, $F_{.05} = 2.51$. The rejection region is $F > 2.51$.

Since the observed value of the test statistic does not fall in the rejection region ($F = 1.50 \not> 2.51$), H_0 is not rejected. There is insufficient evidence to indicate the treatment means differ at $\alpha = .05$. Since there are no treatment mean differences, we have nothing more to do.

b. $\text{SS}A = .1(1000) = 100$, $\text{SS}B = .1(1000) = 100$, $\text{SS}AB = .5(1000) = 500$
$\text{SSE} = \text{SS(Total)} - \text{SS}A - \text{SS}B - \text{SS}AB = 1000 - 100 - 100 - 500 = 300$
$\text{SST} = \text{SS}A + \text{SS}B + \text{SS}AB = 100 + 100 + 500 = 700$

$$\text{MS}A = \frac{\text{SS}A}{a-1} = \frac{100}{3-1} = 50 \qquad\qquad \text{MS}B = \frac{\text{SS}B}{b-1} = \frac{100}{3-1} = 50$$

$$\text{MS}AB = \frac{\text{SS}AB}{(a-1)(b-1)} = \frac{500}{(3-1)(3-1)} = 125$$

$$\text{MSE} = \frac{\text{SSE}}{n-ab} = \frac{300}{27-3(3)} = 16.667 \qquad \text{MST} = \frac{\text{SST}}{ab-1} = \frac{700}{9-1} = 87.5$$

$$F_A = \frac{\text{MS}A}{\text{MSE}} = \frac{50}{16.667} = 3.00 \qquad\qquad F_B = \frac{\text{MS}B}{\text{MSE}} = \frac{50}{16.667} = 3.00$$

$$F_{AB} = \frac{\text{MS}AB}{\text{MSE}} = \frac{125}{16.667} = 7.50 \qquad\qquad F_T = \frac{\text{MST}}{\text{MSE}} = \frac{87.5}{16.667} = 5.25$$

Source	df	SS	MS	F
A	2	100	50	3.00
B	2	100	50	3.00
AB	4	500	125	7.50
Error	18	300	16.667	
Total	26	1000		

To determine if the treatment means differ, we test:

H_0: $\mu_1 = \mu_2 = \cdots = \mu_9$
H_a: At least two treatment means differ

The test statistic is $F = \dfrac{MST}{MSE} = 5.25$

The rejection region requires $\alpha = .05$ in the upper tail of the F-distribution with $\nu_1 = ab - 1 = 3(3) - 1 = 8$ and $\nu_2 = n - ab = 27 - 3(3) = 18$. From Table IX, Appendix B, $F_{.05} = 2.51$. The rejection region is $F > 2.51$.

Since the observed value of the test statistic falls in the rejection region ($F = 5.25 > 2.51$), H_0 is rejected. There is sufficient evidence to indicate the treatment means differ at $\alpha = .05$.

Since the treatment means differ, we next test for interaction between factors A and B. To determine if factors A and B interact, we test:

H_0: Factors A and B do not interact to affect the mean response
H_a: Factors A and B do interact to affect the mean response

The test statistic is $F = \dfrac{MSAB}{MSE} = 7.50$

The rejection region requires $\alpha = .05$ in the upper tail of the F-distribution with $\nu_1 = (a - 1)(b - 1) = (3 - 1)(3 - 1) = 4$ and $\nu_2 = n - ab = 27 - 3(3) = 18$. From Table IX, Appendix B, $F_{.05} = 2.93$. The rejection region is $F > 2.93$.

Since the observed value of the test statistic falls in the rejection region ($F = 7.50 > 2.93$), H_0 is rejected. There is sufficient evidence to indicate the factors A and B interact at $\alpha = .05$. Since interaction is present, no tests for main effects are necessary.

c. $SSA = .4(1000) = 400$, $SSB = .1(1000) = 100$, $SSAB = .2(1000) = 200$
$SSE = SS(Total) - SSA - SSB - SSAB = 1000 - 400 - 100 - 200 = 300$
$SST = SSA + SSB + SSAB = 400 + 100 + 200 = 700$

$$MSA = \frac{SSA}{a-1} = \frac{400}{3-1} = 50 \qquad\qquad MSB = \frac{SSB}{b-1} = \frac{100}{3-1} = 50$$

$$MSAB = \frac{SSAB}{(a-1)(b-1)} = \frac{200}{(3-1)(3-1)} = 50$$

$$MSE = \frac{SSE}{n-ab} = \frac{300}{27-3(3)} = 16.667 \qquad MST = \frac{SST}{ab-1} = \frac{700}{3(3)-1} = 87.5$$

$$F_A = \frac{MSA}{MSE} = \frac{200}{16.667} = 12.00 \qquad F_B = \frac{MSB}{MSE} = \frac{50}{16.667} = 3.00$$

$$F_{AB} = \frac{MSAB}{MSE} = \frac{50}{16.667} = 3.00 \qquad F_T = \frac{MST}{MSE} = \frac{87.5}{16.667} = 5.25$$

Source	df	SS	MS	F
A	2	400	200	12.00
B	2	100	50	3.00
AB	4	200	50	3.00
Error	18	300	16.667	
Total	26	1000		

To determine if the treatment means differ, we test:

H_0: $\mu_1 = \mu_2 = \cdots = \mu_9$
H_a: At least two treatment means differ

The test statistic is $F = \dfrac{\text{MST}}{\text{MSE}} = 5.25$

The rejection region requires $\alpha = .05$ in the upper tail of the F-distribution with $v_1 = ab - 1 = 3(3) - 1 = 8$ and $v_2 = n - ab = 27 - 3(3) = 18$. From Table IX, Appendix B, $F_{.05} = 2.51$. The rejection region is $F > 2.51$.

Since the observed value of the test statistic falls in the rejection region ($F = 5.25 > 2.51$), H_0 is rejected. There is sufficient evidence to indicate the treatment means differ at $\alpha = .05$.

Since the treatment means differ, we next test for interaction between factors A and B. To determine if factors A and B interact, we test:

H_0: Factors A and B do not interact to affect the mean response
H_a: Factors A and B do interact to affect the mean response

The test statistic is $F = \dfrac{\text{MSAB}}{\text{MSE}} = 3.00$

The rejection region requires $\alpha = .05$ in the upper tail of the F-distribution with $v_1 = (a - 1)(b - 1) = (3 - 1)(3 - 1) = 4$ and $v_2 = n - ab = 27 - 3(3) = 18$. From Table IX, Appendix B, $F_{.05} = 2.93$. The rejection region is $F > 2.93$.

Since the observed value of the test statistic falls in the rejection region ($F = 3.00 > 2.93$), H_0 is rejected. There is sufficient evidence to indicate the factors A and B interact at $\alpha = .05$. Since interaction is present, no tests for main effects are necessary.

d. $SSA = .4(1000) = 400$, $SSB = .4(1000) = 400$, $SSAB = .1(1000) = 100$
$SSE = SS(\text{Total}) - SSA - SSB - SSAB = 1000 - 400 - 400 - 100 = 100$
$SST = SSA + SSB + SSAB = 400 + 400 + 100 = 900$

$$MSA = \frac{SSA}{a-1} = \frac{400}{3-1} = 200 \qquad\qquad MSB = \frac{SSB}{b-1} = \frac{400}{3-1} = 200$$

$$MSAB = \frac{SSAB}{(a-1)(b-1)} = \frac{100}{(3-1)(3-1)} = 25$$

$$MSE = \frac{SSE}{n-ab} = \frac{100}{27-3(3)} = 5.556 \qquad\qquad MST = \frac{SST}{ab-1} = \frac{900}{3(3)-1} = 112.5$$

$$F_A = \frac{MSA}{MSE} = \frac{200}{5.556} = 36.00 \qquad\qquad F_B = \frac{MSB}{MSE} = \frac{200}{5.556} = 36.00$$

$$F_{AB} = \frac{MSAB}{MSE} = \frac{25}{5.556} = 4.50 \qquad\qquad F_T = \frac{MST}{MSE} = \frac{112.5}{5.556} = 20.25$$

Source	df	SS	MS	F
A	2	400	200	36.00
B	2	400	200	36.00
AB	4	100	25	4.50
Error	18	100	5.556	
Total	26	1000		

To determine if the treatment means differ, we test:

H_0: $\mu_1 = \mu_2 = \cdots = \mu_9$
H_a: At least two treatment means differ

The test statistic is $F = \dfrac{MST}{MSE} = 20.25$

The rejection region requires $\alpha = .05$ in the upper tail of the F-distribution with $v_1 = ab - 1 = 3(3) - 1 = 8$ and $v_2 = n - ab = 27 - 3(3) = 18$. From Table IX, Appendix B, $F_{.05} = 2.51$. The rejection region is $F > 2.51$.

Since the observed value of the test statistic falls in the rejection region ($F = 20.25 > 2.51$), H_0 is rejected. There is sufficient evidence to indicate the treatment means differ at $\alpha = .05$.

Since the treatment means differ, we next test for interaction between factors A and B. To determine if factors A and B interact, we test:

H_0: Factors A and B do not interact to affect the mean response
H_a: Factors A and B do interact to affect the mean response

The test statistic is $F = \dfrac{MSAB}{MSE} = 4.50$

The rejection region requires $\alpha = .05$ in the upper tail of the F-distribution with $v_1 = (a - 1)(b - 1) = (3 - 1)(3 - 1) = 4$ and $v_2 = n - ab = 27 - 3(3) = 18$. From Table IX, Appendix B, $F_{.05} = 2.93$. The rejection region is $F > 2.93$.

Since the observed value of the test statistic falls in the rejection region ($F = 4.50 > 2.93$), H_0 is rejected. There is sufficient evidence to indicate the factors A and B interact at $\alpha = .05$. Since interaction is present, no tests for main effects are necessary.

8.65   a.   This is a complete 6×6 factorial design.

       b.   There are 2 factors – Coagulant and pH level. There are 6 levels of coagulant: 5, 10, 20, 50, 100, and 200 mg / liter. There are 6 levels of pH: 4.0, 5.0, 6.0, 7.0, 8.0, and 9.0.

There are 6 x 6 = 36 treatments. In the pairs, let the coagulant level be the first number and pH level the second. The 36 treatments are:

(5, 4.0)   (5, 5.0)   (5, 6.0)   (5, 7.0)   (5, 8.0)   (5, 9.0)
(10, 4.0)   (10, 5.0)   (10, 6.0)   (10, 7.0)   (10, 8.0)   (10, 9.0)
(20, 4.0)   (20, 5.0)   (20, 6.0)   (20, 7.0)   (20, 8.0)   (20, 9.0)
(50, 4.0)   (50, 5.0)   (50, 6.0)   (50, 7.0)   (50, 8.0)   (50, 9.0)
(100, 4.0)   (100, 5.0)   (100, 6.0)   (100, 7.0)   (100, 8.0)   (100, 9.0)
(200, 4.0)   (200, 5.0)   (200, 6.0)   (200, 7.0)   (200, 8.0)   (200, 9.0)

8.67 a. This is a complete 2 × 2 factorial design. The 2 factors are Color and Question. There are two levels of color – Blue and Red. There are two levels of question – difficult and simple.

b. There is a significant interaction between color and question. The effect of color on the mean score is different at each level of question.

c. Using MINITAB, the graph is:

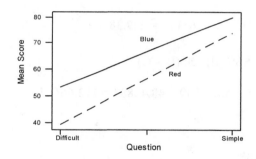

Since the lines are not parallel, it indicates that there is significant interaction between color and question.

8.69 a. A 6 × 5 factorial design was used for this experiment. There are 6 cylinders and 5 batches.

b. The two factors are cylinders with 6 levels and batches with 5 levels.

c. There are a total of $a \times b = 6 \times 5 = 30$ treatments.

d. $\sum x_i = 1 + 1 + 2 + \ldots + 2 = 145$

$$CM = \frac{\left(\sum x_i\right)^2}{n} = \frac{(145)^2}{90} = 233.61111$$

$$SS(\text{Batch}) = \frac{\sum A_i^2}{br} - CM = \frac{12^2}{6(3)} + \frac{24^2}{6(3)} + \frac{57^2}{6(3)} + \frac{24^2}{6(3)} + \frac{28^2}{6(3)} - 233.61111$$

$$= 296.05556 - 233.61111 = 62.44445$$

$$SS(\text{Cyl}) = \frac{\sum B_i^2}{br} - CM = \frac{46^2}{5(3)} + \frac{14^2}{5(3)} + \frac{31^2}{5(3)} + \frac{14^2}{5(3)} + \frac{14^2}{5(3)} + \frac{26^2}{5(3)} - 233.61111$$

$$= 289.4 - 233.61111 = 55.78889$$

$$SS(B \times C) = \frac{\sum\sum AB_{ij}^2}{r} - SS(\text{Batch}) - SS(\text{Cyl}) - CM$$

$$= \frac{4^2}{3} + \frac{1^2}{3} + \frac{3^2}{3} + \cdots + \frac{6^2}{3} - 62.44445 - 55.78889 - 233.61111$$

$$= \frac{1201}{3} - 62.44445 - 55.78889 - 233.61111 = 48.48888$$

$$SSTot = \sum\sum x_{ij}^2 - CM = 513 - 233.61111 = 279.38889$$

$$SSE = SSTot - SS(\text{Batch}) - SS(\text{Cyl}) - SS(B \times C)$$

$$= 279.38889 - 62.44445 - 55.78889 - 48.48888 = 112.66667$$

$$MS(\text{Batch}) = \; = 15.6111$$

$$MS(\text{Cyl}) = \frac{SS(\text{Cyl})}{b-1} = \frac{55.78889}{6-1} = 11.1578$$

$$MS(B \times C) = \frac{SS(B \times C)}{(a-1)(b-1)} = \frac{48.48888}{(5-1)(6-1)} = 2.4244$$

$$MSE = \frac{SSE}{n-ab} = \frac{112.66667}{90-5(6)} = 1.8778$$

$$F_B = \frac{MS(\text{Batch})}{MSE} = \frac{15.6111}{1.8778} = 8.31 \qquad F_C = \frac{MS(\text{Cyl})}{MSE} = \frac{11.1578}{1.8778} = 5.94$$

$$F_{B \times C} = \frac{MS(B \times C)}{MSE} = \frac{2.4244}{1.8778} = 1.29$$

The ANOVA Table is:

Source	df	SS	MS	F
Batch	4	62.44444	15.6111	8.31
Cyl	5	55.78889	11.1578	5.94
B × C	20	48.48888	2.4244	1.29
Error	60	112.66667	1.8778	
Total	89	279.38889		

$$\text{SST} = \text{SS(Batch)} + \text{SS(Cyl)} + \text{SS}(B \times C) = 62.44444 + 55.788889 + 48.48888$$

$$= 166.72221$$

$$\text{MST} = \frac{\text{SST}}{ab-1} = \frac{166.72221}{5(6)-1} = 5.749 \qquad F_T = \frac{\text{MST}}{\text{MSE}} = 3.06$$

To determine if differences exist among the treatment means, we test:

H_0: $\mu_1 = \mu_2 = \mu_3 = \ldots = \mu_{30}$
H_a: At least two means differ

The test statistic is $F_T = 3.06$.

Since no α is given, we will use $\alpha = .05$. The rejection region requires $\alpha = .05$ in the upper tail of the F distribution with $v_1 = ab - 1 = 5(6) - 1 = 29$ and $v_2 = n - ab = 90 - 5(6) = 60$. From Table IX, Appendix B, $F_{.05} \approx 1.65$. The rejection region is $F > 1.65$.

Since the observed value of the test statistic falls in the rejection region ($F = 3.06 > 1.65$), H_0 is rejected. There is sufficient evidence to indicate differences exist among the treatment means at $\alpha = .05$.

e. If batch and cylinder interact to affect the mean weight, this means that the effect of batch on mean weight depends on the level of cylinder. Batch 1 may have the highest mean weight on cylinder 2, but Batch 4 may have the highest mean weight on cylinder 6.

f. To determine if Batch and Cylinder interact to affect mean weight, we test:

H_0: Batch and Cylinder do not interact
H_a: Batch and Cylinder interact

The test statistic is $F = \dfrac{\text{MS}(B \times C)}{\text{MSE}} = 1.29$

The rejection region requires $\alpha = .05$ in the upper tail of the F distribution with $v_1 = (a - 1)(b - 1) = (5 - 1)(6 - 1) = 20$ and $v_2 = n - ab = 90 - 5(6) = 60$. From Table IX, Appendix B, $F_{.05} = 1.75$. The rejection region is $F > 1.75$.

Since the observed value of the test statistic does not fall in the rejection region ($F = 1.29$ $\not> 1.75$), H_0 is not rejected. There is insufficient evidence to indicate Batch and Cylinder interact to affect the mean weight at $\alpha = .05$.

g. Since we did not find any evidence of interaction in part **f**, we will test for the main effects.

To determine if the mean weights differ among the batches, we test:

H_0: $\mu_1 = \mu_2 = \mu_3 = \mu_4 = \mu_5$
H_a: At least two means differ

The test statistic is $F_B = 8.31$.

The rejection region requires $\alpha = .05$ in the upper tail of the F distribution with $v_1 = a - 1$ $= 5 - 1 = 4$ and $v_2 = n - ab = 90 - 5(6) = 60$. From Table IX, Appendix B, $F_{.05} = 2.53$. The rejection region is $F > 2.53$.

Since the observed value of the test statistic falls in the rejection region ($F = 8.31 > 2.53$), H_0 is rejected. There is sufficient evidence to indicate differences exist among the batches at $\alpha = .05$.

To determine if the mean weights differ among the cylinders, we test:

H_0: $\mu_1 = \mu_2 = \mu_3 = \mu_4 = \mu_5 = \mu_6$
H_a: At least two means differ

The test statistic is $F_C = 5.94$.

The rejection region requires $\alpha = .05$ in the upper tail of the F distribution with $v_1 = b - 1$ $= 6 - 1 = 5$ and $v_2 = n - ab = 90 - 5(6) = 60$. From Table IX, Appendix B, $F_{.05} \approx 2.37$. The rejection region is $F > 2.37$.

Since the observed value of the test statistic falls in the rejection region ($F = 5.94 > 2.37$), H_0 is rejected. There is sufficient evidence to indicate differences exist among the cylinders at $\alpha = .05$.

8.71   Yes. Using MINITAB, a plot of the data is:

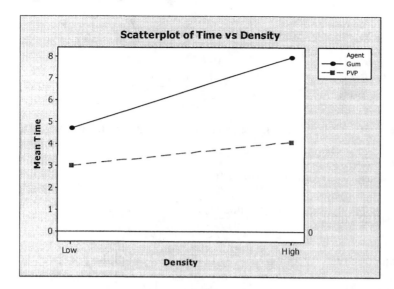

Since the lines are not parallel, this indicates interaction is present. The increase in mean time when density is increased from low to high for PVP is not as great as the increase in mean time when density is increased from low to high for GUM.

8.73   In a completely randomized design, independent random selection of treatments to be assigned to experimental units is required. In a randomized block design, the experimental units are first grouped into blocks such that within the blocks the experimental units are homogeneous and between the blocks the experimental units are heterogeneous.

8.75   When the overall level of significance of a multiple comparisons procedure is α, the level of significance for each comparison is less than α.

8.77   a.   SS(Treatment) = SS(Total) – SS(Block) – SSE = 22.31 – 10.688 - .288 = 11.334

$$MS(Treatment) \;=\; \frac{SS(Treatment)}{k\ -\ 1} = \frac{11.334}{4-1} = 3.778, \quad df = k-1 = 4-1 = 3$$

$$MS(Block) \;=\; \frac{SS(Block)}{b\ -\ 1} = \frac{10.688}{5-1} = 2.672, \ \ df = b-1 = 5-1 = 4$$

$$MSE \;=\; \frac{SSE}{n-k-b\ +\ 1} = \frac{.288}{20-4-5+1} = .024, \ \ df = n-k-b+1 = 20-4-5+1 = 12$$

$$Treatment\ F \;=\; \frac{MS(Treatment)}{MSE} = \frac{3.778}{.024} = 157.42$$

$$Block\ F \;=\; \frac{MS(Block)}{MSE} = \frac{2.672}{.024} = 111.33$$

Design of Experiments and Analysis of Variance   263

The ANOVA Table is:

Source	df	SS	MS	F
Treatment	3	11.334	3.778	157.42
Block	4	10.688	2.672	111.33
Error	12	0.288	0.024	
Total	19	22.310		

b. To determine if there is a difference among the treatment means, we test:

H_0: $\mu_A = \mu_B = \mu_C = \mu_D$
H_a: At least two treatment means differ

The test statistic is $F = \dfrac{MS(Treatment)}{MSE} = 157.42$

The rejection region requires $\alpha = .05$ in the upper tail of the F distribution with $v_1 = k - 1 = 4 - 1 = 3$ and $v_2 = n - k - b + 1 = 20 - 4 - 5 + 1 = 12$. From Table IX, Appendix B, $F_{.05} = 3.49$. The rejection region is $F > 3.49$.

Since the observed value of the test statistic falls in the rejection region ($F = 157.42 > 3.49$), H_0 is rejected. There is sufficient evidence to indicate a difference among the treatment means at $\alpha = .05$.

c. Since there is evidence of differences among the treatment means, we need to compare the treatment means. The number of pairwise comparisons is $\dfrac{k(k-1)}{2} = \dfrac{4(4-1)}{2} = 6$.

d. To determine if there are difference among the block means, we test:

H_0: All block means are the same
H_a: At least two block means differ

The test statistic is $F = \dfrac{MS(Block)}{MSE} = 111.33$

The rejection region requires $\alpha = .05$ in the upper tail of the F distribution with $v_1 = b - 1 = 5 - 1 = 4$ and $v_2 = n - k - b + 1 = 20 - 4 - 5 + 1 = 12$. From Table IX, Appendix B, $F_{.05} = 3.26$. The rejection region is $F > 3.26$.

Since the observed value of the test statistic falls in the rejection region ($F = 111.33 > 3.26$), H_0 is rejected. There is sufficient evidence that the block means differ at $\alpha = .05$.

8.79 a. The data are collected as a completely randomized design because five boxes of each size were randomly selected and tested.

b. Yes. The confidence intervals surrounding each of the means do not overlap. This would indicate that there is a difference in the means for the two sizes.

c. No. Several of the confidence intervals overlap. This would indicate that the mean compression strengths of the sizes that have intervals that overlap are not significantly different.

8.81 a. The experimental design used in this example was a randomized block design.

b. The experimental units in this problem are the electronic commerce and internet-based companies. The response variable is the rate of return for the stock of the companies. The treatments are the 4 categories of companies: e-companies, internet software and service, internet hardware, and internet communication. The blocks are the 4 age categories: 1 year-old, 2 year-old, 3 year-old, and 4 year-old.

8.83 a. To determine if leadership style affects behavior of subordinates, we test:

H_0: All four treatment means are the same
H_a: At least two treatment means differ

The test statistic is $F = 30.4$.

The rejection region requires $\alpha = .05$ in the upper tail of the F-distribution with $v_1 = ab - 1 = 2(2) - 1 = 3$ and $v_2 = n - ab = 257 - 2(2) = 253$. From Table IX, Appendix B, $F_{.05} \approx 2.60$. The rejection region is $F > 2.60$.

Since the observed value of the test statistic falls in the rejection region ($F = 30.4 > 2.60$), H_0 is rejected. There is sufficient evidence to indicate that leadership style affects behavior of subordinates at $\alpha = .05$.

b. From the table, the mean response for High control, low consideration is significantly higher than for any other treatment. The mean response for Low control, low consideration is significantly higher than that for High control, high consideration and for Low control, high consideration. No other significant differences exist.

c. The assumptions for Bonferroni's method are the same as those for the ANOVA. Thus, we must assume that:

i. The populations sampled from are normal.
ii. The population variances are the same.
iii. The samples are independent.

8.85 a. Some preliminary calculations are:

$$CM = \frac{\left(\sum x_i\right)^2}{n} = \frac{2939^2}{48} = 179,952.5208$$

$$SS(Total) = \sum x_i^2 - CM = 317,093 - 179,952.5208 = 137,140.4792$$

$$SST = \sum \frac{T_i^2}{n_i} - CM = \frac{766^2}{10} + \frac{851^2}{12} + \frac{669^2}{14} + \frac{653^2}{12} - 179,952.5208$$

$$= 186,528.4095 - 179,952.5208 = 6,575.8887$$

$$SSE = SS(Total) - SST = 137,140.4792 - 6,575.8887 = 130,564.5905$$

$$MST = \frac{SST}{k-1} = \frac{6,575.8887}{4-1} = 2,191.9629$$

$$MSE = \frac{SSE}{n-k} = \frac{130,564.5905}{48-4} = 2,967.3771$$

$$F = \frac{MST}{MSE} = \frac{2,191.9629}{2,967.3771} = .739$$

Source	df	SS	MS	F
Treatments	3	6,575.8887	2,191.9629	.739
Error	44	130,564.5905	2,967.3771	
Total	47	137,140.4792		

To determine if differences exist among the mean spillage amounts for the four accident causes, we test:

H_0: $\mu_1 = \mu_2 = \mu_3 = \mu_4$
H_a: At least two means differ

The test statistic is $F = .739$.

The rejection region requires $\alpha = .01$ in the upper tail of the F-distribution with $v_1 = k - 1$ = 4 – 1 = 3 and $v_2 = n - k = 48 - 4 = 44$. From Table XI, Appendix B, $F_{.01} \approx 4.31$. The rejection region is $F > 4.31$.

Since the observed value of the test statistic does not fall in the rejection region (F = .739 $\not>$ 4.31), H_0 is not rejected. There is insufficient evidence to indicate differences exist among the mean spillage amounts for the four accident causes at $\alpha = .01$.

Using MINITAB, the stem-and-leaf plots for the 4 treatments are:

Stem-and-Leaf Display: Spillage

```
Stem-and-leaf of Spillage   Cause = 1      N  = 10
Leaf Unit = 10

      3      0 333
     (3)     0 444
      4      0 6
      3      0 9
      2      1
      2      1 2
      1      1
      1      1
      1      1
      1      2
      1      2
      1      2 5

Stem-and-leaf of Spillage   Cause = 2      N  = 12
Leaf Unit = 10

      4      0 2333
     (4)     0 4455
      4      0 7
      3      0 8
      2      1
      2      1 3
      1      1
      1      1
      1      1
      1      2
      1      2 3

Stem-and-leaf of Spillage   Cause = 3      N  = 14
Leaf Unit = 10

     (8)     0 22233333
      6      0 445
      3      0 6
      2      0 9
      1      1
      1      1 2

Stem-and-leaf of Spillage   Cause = 4      N  = 12
Leaf Unit = 10

     (8)     0 22233333
      4      0 44
      2      0
      2      0
      2      1 0
      1      1
      1      1
      1      1
      1      1
      1      2
      1      2 2
```

None of the plots look mound-shaped. However, the data do not need to be exactly normal for the ANOVA to yield valid results.

The box plots for the four groups are:

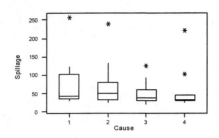

The spreads of the four groups do not appear to be the same. The spread of the third group (grounding) is smaller than the spreads of the other three groups. Thus, the assumption of equal variances is probably not met.

b. Since the conclusion for the test in part **a** was 'Do not reject H_o, no follow-up analyses are needed.

8.87 a. The quality of the steel ingot.

b. There are two factors: temperature and pressure. They are quantitative factors since they are numerical.

c. The treatments are the $3 \times 5 = 15$ factor-level combinations of temperature and pressure.

d. The steel ingots are the experimental units.

8.89 a. A completely randomized design was used. There are five treatments. They are the five different educational levels.

b. To determine if the mean concern ratings differ for at least two education levels, we test:

H_0: $\mu_1 = \mu_2 = \mu_3 = \mu_4 = \mu_5$
H_a: At least two treatment means differ

where μ_i represents the mean concern rating of the ith education level.

The test statistic is $F = 3.298$.

The rejection region requires $\alpha = .05$ in the upper tail of the F-distribution with $v_1 = p - 1 = 5 - 1 = 4$ and $v_2 = n - p = 315 - 5 = 310$. From Table IX, Appendix B, $F_{.05} \approx 2.37$. The rejection region is $F > 2.37$.

Since the observed value of the test statistic falls in the rejection region ($F = 3.298 > 2.37$), H_0 is rejected. There is sufficient evidence to indicate a difference in the mean concern ratings among the 5 education levels at $\alpha = .05$.

c. The mean concern rating for those with post-graduate education is significantly greater than the mean concern rating for the four other education level groups. There are no other significant differences.

8.91 a. The experiment is completely randomized. The response is the attitude test score after 1 month. The two factors are scheduling (2 levels) and payment (2 levels). Both factors are qualitative. There are $2 \times 2 = 4$ different treatments, where each treatment consists of a level of each factor, A_1B_1, A_1B_2, A_2B_1, and A_2B_2. The experimental units are the workers.

b. To determine if the treatment means differ, we test:

H_0: $\mu_1 = \mu_2 = \mu_3 = \mu_4$
H_a: At least one treatment mean differs

The test statistic is $F = \dfrac{MST}{MSE} = 12.29$

The rejection region requires $\alpha = .05$ in the upper tail of the F-distribution with $v_1 = ab - 1 = 2(2) - 1 = 3$ and $v_2 = n - ab = 16 - 2(2) = 12$. From Table IX, Appendix B, $F_{.05} = 3.49$. The rejection region is $F > 3.49$.

Since the observed value of the test statistic falls in the rejection region ($F = 12.29 > 3.49$), H_0 is rejected. There is sufficient evidence to indicate the treatment means differ at $\alpha = .05$.

c. To determine if the factors interact, we test:

H_0: Factor A and factor B do not interact to affect the response mean
H_a: Factors A and B do interact to affect the response mean

The test statistic is $F = \dfrac{MSAB}{MSE} = .02$

The rejection region requires $\alpha = .05$ in the upper tail of the F-distribution with $v_1 = (a - 1)(b - 1) = (2 - 1)(2 - 1) = 1$ and $v_2 = n - ab = 16 - 2(2) = 12$. From Table IX, Appendix B, $F_{.05} = 4.75$. The rejection region is $F > 4.75$.

Since the observed value of the test statistic does not fall in the rejection region ($F = .02 \not> 4.75$), H_0 is not rejected. There is insufficient evidence to indicate the factors interact at $\alpha = 05$.

To determine if the mean attitude test scores differ for the two types of scheduling, we test:

H_0: $\mu_1 = \mu_2$
H_a: $\mu_1 \neq \mu_2$

The test statistic is $F = \dfrac{MS(Schedule)}{MSE} = 7.37$

The rejection region requires $\alpha = .05$ in the upper tail of the F-distribution with $v_1 = (a - 1) = 2 - 1 = 1$ and $v_2 = n - ab = 16 - 2(2) = 12$. From Table IX, Appendix B, $F_{.05} = 4.75$. The rejection region is $F > 4.75$.

Since the observed value of the test statistic falls in the rejection region ($F = 7.37 > 4.75$), H_0 is rejected. There is sufficient evidence to indicate the mean attitude test scores differ for the two types of scheduling at $\alpha = .05$.

To determine if the mean attitude test scores differ for the two types of payments, we test:

H_0: $\mu_1 = \mu_2$
H_a: $\mu_1 \neq \mu_2$

The test statistic is $F = \dfrac{MS(\text{Payment})}{MSE} = 29.47$

The rejection region requires $\alpha = .05$ in the upper tail of the F-distribution with $v_1 = b - 1 = 2 - 1 = 1$ and $v_2 = n - ab = 16 - 2(2) = 12$. From Table IX, Appendix B, $F_{.05} = 4.75$. The rejection region is $F > 4.75$.

Since the observed value of the test statistic falls in the rejection region ($F = 29.47 > 4.75$), H_0 is rejected. There is sufficient evidence to indicate the mean attitude test scores differ for the two types of payment at $\alpha = .05$.

Since the mean attitude test scores for 8–5 is $558/8 = 69.75$ and the mean for worker-modified schedules is $634/8 = 79.25$, the mean attitude test scores for those on worker-modified schedules is significantly higher than for those on 8–5 schedules.
Since the mean attitude test scores for those on hourly rate is $520/8 = 65$ and the mean for those on hourly and piece rate is $672/8 = 84$, the mean attitude test scores for those on hourly and piece rate is significantly higher than for those on hourly rate.

d. The necessary assumptions are:

1. The probability distributions for each schedule-payment combination is normal.
2. The variances for each distribution are equal.
3. The samples are random and independent.

8.93 a. This is a 2 × 2 factorial experiment.

b. The two factors are the tent type (treated or untreated) and location (inside or outside). There are 2 × 2 = 4 treatments. The four treatments are (treated, inside), (treated, outside), (untreated, inside), and (untreated, outside).

c. The response variable is the number of mosquito bites received in a 20 minute interval.

d. There is sufficient evidence to indicate interaction is present. This indicates that the effect of the tent type on the number of mosquito bites depends on whether the person is inside or outside.

8.95 Using MINITAB, the ANOVA Table is:

General Linear Model: Rating versus Prep, Standing

```
Factor      Type Levels Values
Prep        fixed     2 PRACTICE REVIEW
Standing    fixed     3 HI  LOW MED

Analysis of Variance for Rating, using Adjusted SS for Tests

Source            DF    Seq SS    Adj SS    Adj MS       F      P
Prep               1    54.735    54.735    54.735   14.40  0.000
Standing           2    16.500    16.500     8.250    2.17  0.118
Prep*Standing      2    13.470    13.470     6.735    1.77  0.174
Error            126   478.955   478.955     3.801
Total            131   563.659

Tukey 95.0% Simultaneous Confidence Intervals
Response Variable Rating
All Pairwise Comparisons among Levels of Prep


Prep = PRACTICE subtracted from:

Prep          Lower    Center    Upper  ---+---------+---------+---------+---
REVIEW       -1.960    -1.288  -0.6162   (-----------*----------)
                                        ---+---------+---------+---------+---
                                         -1.80     -1.20     -0.60      0.00
```

First, we must test for treatment effects.

SST = SS(Prep) + SS(Stand) + SS(PxS) = 54.735 + 16.500 + 13.470 = 84.705.

The df = 1 + 2 + 2 = 5.

$$MST = \frac{SST}{ab-1} = \frac{84.705}{2(3)-1} = 16.941 \qquad F = \frac{MST}{MSE} = \frac{16.941}{3.801} = 4.46$$

To determine if there are differences in mean ratings among the 6 treatments, we test:

H_0: All treatment means are the same
H_a: At least two treatment means differ

The test statistic is $F = 4.46$.

Since no α was given, we will use $\alpha = .05$. The rejection region requires $\alpha = .05$ in the upper tail of the F distribution with $v_1 = ab - 1 = 2(3) - 1 = 5$ and $v_2 = n - ab = 132 - 2(3) = 126$. From Table IX, Appendix B, $F_{.05} \approx 2.29$. The rejection region is $F > 2.29$.

Since the observed value of the test statistic falls in the rejection region ($F = 4.46 > 2.29$), H_0 is rejected. There is sufficient evidence that differences exist among the treatment means at $\alpha = .05$. Since differences exist, we now test for the interaction effect between Preparation and Class Standing.

To determine if Preparation and Class Standing interact, we test:

H_0: Preparation and Class Standing do not interact
H_a: Preparation and Class Standing do interact

The test statistic is $F = 1.77$ and p $= .174$

Since the p-value is greater than α ($p = .174 > .05$), H_0 is not rejected. There is insufficient evidence that Preparation and Class Standing interact at $\alpha = .05$. Since the interaction does not exist, we test for the main effects of Preparation and Class standing.

To determine if there are differences in the mean rating between the three levels of Class standing, we test:

H_0: $\mu_L = \mu_M = \mu_H$
H_a: At least 2 means differ

The test statistics is $F = 2.17$ and $p = 0.118$.

Since the p-value is greater than α ($p = .118 > .05$), H_0 is not rejected. There is insufficient evidence that the mean ratings differ among the 3 levels of Class Standing at $\alpha = .05$.

To determine if there are differences in the mean rating between the two levels of Preparation, we test:

H_0: $\mu_P = \mu_S$
H_a: $\mu_P \neq \mu_S$

The test statistics is $F = 14.40$ and $p = 0.000$.

Since the p-value is less than α ($p = 0.000 < .05$), H_0 is rejected. There is sufficient evidence that the mean ratings differ between the two levels of preparation at $\alpha = .05$.

There are only 2 levels of Preparation. The mean rating for Practice is higher than the mean rating Review.

Categorical Data Analysis

Chapter 9

9.1   a.   The rejection region requires $\alpha = .05$ in the upper tail of the χ^2 distribution with df = $k - 1 = 3 - 1 = 2$. From Table VII, Appendix B, $\chi^2_{.05} = 5.99147$. The rejection region is $\chi^2 > 5.99147$.

        b.   The rejection region requires $\alpha = .10$ in the upper tail of the χ^2 distribution with df = $k - 1 = 5 - 1 = 4$. From Table VII, Appendix B, $\chi^2_{.10} = 7.77944$. The rejection region is $\chi^2 > 7.77944$.

        c.   The rejection region requires $\alpha = .01$ in the upper tail of the χ^2 distribution with df = $k - 1 = 4 - 1 = 3$. From Table VII, Appendix B, $\chi^2_{.01} = 11.3449$. The rejection region is $\chi^2 > 11.3449$.

9.3   The sample size n will be large enough so that, for every cell, the expected cell count, $E(n_i)$, will be equal to 5 or more.

9.5   Some preliminary calculations are:

        If the probabilities are the same, $p_{1,0} = p_{2,0} = p_{3,0} = p_{4,0} = .25$

$$E(n_1) = np_{1,0} = 205(.25) = 51.25$$
$$E(n_2) = E(n_3) = E(n_4) = 205(.25) = 51.25$$

        a.   To determine if the multinomial probabilities differ, we test:

        H_0: $p_1 = p_2 = p_3 = p_4 = .25$
        H_a: At least one of the probabilities differs from .25

        The test statistic is $\chi^2 = \sum \dfrac{[n_i - E(n_i)]^2}{E(n_i)}$

$$= \frac{(43 - 51.25)^2}{51.25} + \frac{(56 - 51.25)^2}{51.25} + \frac{(59 - 51.25)^2}{51.25} + \frac{(47 - 51.25)^2}{51.25} = 3.293$$

        The rejection region requires $\alpha = .05$ in the upper tail of the χ^2 distribution with df = $k - 1 = 4 - 1 = 3$. From Table VII, Appendix B, $\chi^2_{.05} = 7.81473$. The rejection region is $\chi^2 > 7.81473$.

        Since the observed value of the test statistic does not fall in the rejection region ($\chi^2 = 3.293 \ngtr 7.81473$), H_0 is not rejected. There is insufficient evidence to indicate the multinomial probabilities differ at $\alpha = .05$.

b.   The Type I error is concluding the multinomial probabilities differ when, in fact, they do not.

The Type II error is concluding the multinomial probabilities are equal, when, in fact, they are not.

c.   For confidence coefficient .95, $\alpha = .05$ and $\alpha/2 = .05/2 = .025$. From Table IV, Appendix B, $z_{.025} = 1.96$.

$\hat{p}_3 = 59/205 = .288$

The confidence interval is:

$$\hat{p}_3 \pm z_{.025}\sqrt{\frac{\hat{p}\hat{q}}{n}} \Rightarrow .288 \pm 1.96\sqrt{\frac{.288(.712)}{205}} \Rightarrow .288 \pm .062 \Rightarrow (.226, .350)$$

9.7   a.   The qualitative variable in this exercise is what "Made in the USA" means. There are 4 levels or categories for this variable: 100% of labor and materials are produced in the US, 75-99% of labor and materials are produced in the US, 50-74% of labor and materials are produced in the US, and less than 50% of labor and materials are produced in the US.

b.   The consumer advocate group hypothesized that $p_1 = \frac{1}{2} = .50$, $p_2 = \frac{1}{4} = .25$, $p_3 = 1/5 = .20$, and $p_4 = .05$.

c.   To determine if the consumer advocate group's claim is correct, we test:

H_0: $p_1 = .5$, $p_2 = .25$, $p_3 = .20$, and $p_4 = .05$
H_a: At least one of the proportions differs from their hypothesized values

d.   Some preliminary calculations are:

$n = 64 + 20 + 18 + 4 = 106$.

$E(n_1) = np_{1,0} = 106(.50) = 53$; $E(n_2) = np_{2,0} = 106(.25) = 26.5$;
$E(n_3) = np_{3,0} = 106(.20) = 21.2$; $E(p_4) = np_{4,0} = 106(.05) = 5.3$

$$\chi^2 = \sum \frac{[n_i - E(n_i)]^2}{E(n_i)} = \frac{(64-53)^2}{53} + \frac{(20-26.5)^2}{26.5} + \frac{(18-21.2)^2}{21.2} + \frac{(4-5.3)^2}{5.3} = 4.679$$

e.   The rejection region requires $\alpha = .10$ in the upper tail of the χ^2 distribution with df $= k - 1 = 4 - 1 = 3$. From Table VII, Appendix B, $\chi^2_{.10} = 6.25139$. The rejection region is $\chi^2 > 6.25139$.

f.   Since the observed value of the test statistic does not fall in the rejection region ($\chi^2 = 4.679 \not> 6.25139$), H_0 is not rejected. There is insufficient evidence to indicate the consumer advocate group's claim is incorrect at $\alpha = .10$.

g. $\hat{p}_1 = \dfrac{n_1}{n} = \dfrac{64}{106} = .604$

For confidence coefficient .90, $\alpha = 1 - .90 = .10$ and $\alpha/2 = .10/2 = .05$. From Table IV, Appendix B, $z_{.05} = 1.645$. The 90% confidence interval is:

$$\hat{p}_1 \pm z_{.05}\sqrt{\dfrac{\hat{p}_1(1-\hat{p}_1)}{n}} \Rightarrow .604 \pm 1.645\sqrt{\dfrac{.604(.396)}{106}} \Rightarrow .604 \pm .078 \Rightarrow (.526, \ .682)$$

We are 90% confident that the proportion of all consumers who believe "Made in the USA" means "100%" of labor and material are produced in the US is between .526 and .682.

9.9   a.   Since there are 10 income groups, we would expect 10% or $1,072(.10) = 107.2$ givers in each of the income categories.

       b.   The null hypothesis for testing whether the true proportions of charitable givers in each income group are the same is:

H_0: $p_1 = p_2 = \ldots = p_{10} = .10$

       c.   Some preliminary calculations are:

$E(n_1) = E(n_2) = \ldots = E(n_{10}) = np_{1,0} = 1,072(.10) = 170.2$

$$\chi^2 = \sum \dfrac{[n_i - E(n_i)]^2}{E(n_i)} = \dfrac{(42 - 107.2)^2}{107.2} + \dfrac{(93 - 107.2)^2}{107.2} + \ldots + \dfrac{(127 - 107.2)^2}{107.2} = 93.149$$

       d.   The rejection region requires $\alpha = .10$ in the upper tail of the χ^2 distribution with df $= k - 1 = 10 - 1 = 9$. From Table VII, Appendix B, $\chi^2_{.10} = 14.6837$. The rejection region is $\chi^2 > 14.6837$.

       e.   Since the observed value of the test statistic falls in the rejection region ($\chi^2 = 93.149 > 14.6837$), H_0 is rejected. There is sufficient evidence to indicate that the true proportions of charitable givers in each income group are not all the same at $\alpha = .10$.

9.11   a.   To determine if the opinions are not evenly divided on the issue of national health insurance, we test:

H_0: $p_1 = p_2 = p_3 = 1/3$
H_a: At least one p_i differs from its hypothesized value.

The test statistic is $\chi^2 = 87.74$ (from the printout)

Categorical Data Analysis

The observed p-value is $p = .0000$. Since the observed p-value is less than α ($p = .0000 < \alpha = .01$), H_0 is rejected. There is sufficient evidence to indicate the opinions are not evenly divided on the issue of national health insurance at $\alpha = .01$.

b. Let $p_1 =$ proportion of heads of household in the U.S. population that favor national health insurance. Some preliminary calculations are:

$$\hat{p}_1 = \frac{n_1}{n} = \frac{234}{434} = .539$$

For confidence coefficient .95, $\alpha = .05$ and $\alpha/2 = .05/2 = .025$. From Table IV, Appendix B, $z_{.025} = 1.96$. The 95% confidence interval is:

$$\hat{p}_1 \pm z_{.025}\sqrt{\frac{\hat{p}_1(1-\hat{p}_1)}{n}} \Rightarrow .539 \pm 1.96\sqrt{\frac{.539(1-.539)}{434}}$$
$$\Rightarrow .539 \pm .047 \Rightarrow (.492, .586)$$

We are 95% confident that the true proportion of heads of household in the U.S. population that favor national health insurance is between .492 and .586.

9.13   Some preliminary calculations are:

$$E(n_1) = E(n_2) = E(n_3) = E(n_4) = np_{1,0} = 83(.25) = 20.75$$

To determine if there are differences in the percentage of incidents in the four cause categories, we test:

H_0: $p_1 = p_2 = p_3 = p_4 = .25$
H_a: At least one p_i differs from its hypothesized value

The test statistic is

$$\chi^2 = \sum \frac{\left[n_i - E(n_i)\right]^2}{E(n_i)} = \frac{(27-20.75)^2}{20.75} + \frac{(24-20.75)^2}{20.75} + \frac{(22-20.75)^2}{20.75} + \frac{(10-20.75)^2}{20.75}$$
$$= 8.036$$

The rejection region requires $\alpha = .05$ in the upper tail of the χ^2 distribution with df $= k - 1 = 4 - 1 = 3$. From Table VII, Appendix B, $\chi^2_{.05} = 7.81473$. The rejection region is $\chi^2 > 7.81473$.

Since the observed value of the test statistic falls in the rejection region ($\chi^2 = 80.36 > 7.81473$), H_0 is rejected. There is sufficient evidence to indicate there are differences in the percentages of incidents in the four cause categories at $\alpha = .05$.

9.15   To determine if the number of overweight trucks per week is distributed over the 7 days of the week in direct proportion to the volume of truck traffic, we test:

H_0: $p_1 = .191, p_2 = .198, p_3 = .187, p_4 = .180, p_5 = .155, p_6 = .043, p_7 = .046$
H_a: At least one of the probabilities differs from the hypothesized value

$E(n_1) = np_{1,0} = 414(.191) = 79.074$
$E(n_2) = np_{2,0} = 414(.198) = 81.972$
$E(n_3) = np_{3,0} = 414(.187) = 77.418$
$E(n_4) = np_{4,0} = 414(.180) = 74.520$
$E(n_5) = np_{5,0} = 414(.155) = 64.170$
$E(n_6) = np_{6,0} = 414(.043) = 17.802$
$E(n_7) = np_{7,0} = 414(.046) = 19.044$

The test statistic is $\chi^2 = \sum \dfrac{[n_i - E(n_i)]^2}{E(n_i)} = \dfrac{(90 - 79.074)^2}{79.074} + \dfrac{(82 - 81.972)^2}{81.972}$

$+ \dfrac{(72 - 77.418)^2}{77.418} + \dfrac{(70 - 74.520)^2}{74.520} + \dfrac{(51 - 64.170)^2}{64.170} + \dfrac{(18 - 17.802)^2}{17.802}$

$+ \dfrac{(31 - 19.044)^2}{19.044} = 12.374$

The rejection region requires $\alpha = .05$ in the upper tail of the χ^2 distribution with df = $k - 1 = 7 - 1 = 6$. From Table VII, Appendix B, $\chi^2_{.05} = 12.5916$. The rejection region is $\chi^2 > 12.5916$.

Since the observed value of the test statistic does not fall in the rejection region ($\chi^2 = 12.374$ $\not> 12.5916$), H_0 is not rejected. There is insufficient evidence to indicate the number of overweight trucks per week is distributed over the 7 days of the week is not in direct proportion to the volume of truck traffic at $\alpha = .05$.

9.17   a. H_0:   The row and column classifications are independent
              H_a: The row and column classifications are dependent

       b.   The test statistic is $\chi^2 = \sum \dfrac{[n_{ij} - E_{ij}]^2}{E_{ij}}$

            The rejection region requires $\alpha = .01$ in the upper tail of the χ^2 distribution with df = $(r - 1)(c - 1) = (2 - 1)(3 - 1) = 2$. From Table VII, Appendix B, $\chi^2_{.01} = 9.21034$. The rejection region is $\chi^2 > 9.21034$.

c. The expected cell counts are:

$$E_{11} = \frac{R_1 C_1}{n} = \frac{96(25)}{167} = 14.37 \qquad E_{21} = \frac{R_2 C_1}{n} = \frac{71(25)}{167} = 10.63$$

$$E_{12} = \frac{R_1 C_2}{n} = \frac{96(64)}{167} = 36.79 \qquad E_{22} = \frac{R_2 C_2}{n} = \frac{71(64)}{167} = 27.21$$

$$E_{13} = \frac{R_1 C_3}{n} = \frac{96(78)}{167} = 44.84 \qquad E_{23} = \frac{R_2 C_3}{n} = \frac{71(78)}{167} = 33.16$$

d. The test statistic is $\chi^2 = \sum \frac{[n_{ij} - E_{ij}]^2}{E_{ij}}$

$$= \frac{(9-14.37)^2}{14.37} + \frac{(34-36.79)^2}{36.79} + \frac{(53-44.84)^2}{44.84} + \frac{(16-10.63)^2}{10.63}$$

$$+ \frac{(30-27.21)^2}{27.21} + \frac{(25-33.16)^2}{33.16} = 8.71$$

Since the observed value of the test statistic does not fall in the rejection region ($\chi^2 = 8.71 \not> 9.21034$), H_0 is not rejected. There is insufficient evidence to indicate the row and column classifications are dependent at $\alpha = .01$.

9.19 Some preliminary calculations are:

$$E_{11} = \frac{R_1 C_1}{n} = \frac{154(134)}{439} = 47.007 \qquad E_{21} = \frac{186(134)}{439} = 56.774$$

$$E_{12} = \frac{154(163)}{439} = 57.180 \qquad E_{22} = \frac{186(163)}{439} = 69.062$$

$$E_{13} = \frac{154(142)}{439} = 49.813 \qquad E_{23} = \frac{186(142)}{439} = 60.164$$

$$E_{31} = \frac{99(134)}{439} = 30.219 \qquad E_{33} = \frac{99(142)}{439} = 32.023$$

$$E_{32} = \frac{99(163)}{439} = 36.759$$

To determine if the row and column classifications are dependent, we test:

H_0: The row and column classifications are independent
H_a: The row and column classifications are dependent

The test statistic is $\chi^2 = \sum \frac{[n_{ij} - E_{ij}]^2}{E_{ij}}$

$$= \frac{(40 - 47.007)^2}{47.007} + \frac{(72 - 57.180)^2}{57.180} + \frac{(42 - 49.813)^2}{49.813} + \frac{(63 - 56.774)^2}{56.774}$$

$$+ \frac{(53 - 69.062)^2}{69.062} + \frac{(70 - 60.164)^2}{60.164} + \frac{(31 - 30.219)^2}{30.219}$$

$$+ \frac{(38 - 36.759)^2}{36.759} + \frac{(30 - 32.023)^2}{32.023} = 12.36$$

The rejection region requires $\alpha = .05$ in the upper tail of the χ^2 distribution with df = $(r - 1)(c - 1) = (3 - 1)(3 - 1) = 4$. From Table VII, Appendix B, $\chi^2_{.05} = 9.48773$. The rejection region is $\chi^2 > 9.48773$.

Since the observed value of the test statistic falls in the rejection region ($\chi^2 = 12.36 > 9.48773$), H_0 is rejected. There is sufficient evidence to indicate the row and column classification are dependent at $\alpha = .05$.

9.21   a.   Let p_1 = proportion of abstainers with congestive heart failure. Then

$$\hat{p}_1 = \frac{n_1}{n} = \frac{146}{896} = .163$$

b.   Let p_2 = proportion of moderate drinkers with congestive heart failure. Then

$$\hat{p}_2 = \frac{n_2}{n} = \frac{106}{696} = .152$$

c.   Let p_3 = proportion of heavy drinkers with congestive heart failure. Then

$$\hat{p}_3 = \frac{n_3}{n} = \frac{29}{321} = .090$$

d.   The three sample proportions found in parts a, b, and c appear to be different. It appears that the proportion of AMI patients with congestive heart failure depends on alcohol consumption.

e.   To determine if the proportion of AMI patients with congestive heart failure depends on alcohol consumption, we test:

H_0:   The proportion of AMI patients with congestive heart failure is independent of alcohol consumption

f. H_a: The proportion of AMI patients with congestive heart failure depends on alcohol consumption

The test statistics is $\chi^2 = 10.197$, $p = .006$

Since the p-value (.006) is less than $\alpha = .05$, H_0 is rejected. There is sufficient evidence to indicate that the proportion of AMI patients with congestive heart failure depends on alcohol consumption at $\alpha = .05$.

9.23 a. To compare the two proportions, we could use either a test of hypothesis or a confidence interval. I will use a 95% confidence interval.

Some preliminary calculations are:

$$\hat{p}_{M1} = \frac{x_{M1}}{n_M} = \frac{29}{103} = .282 \qquad \hat{p}_{F1} = \frac{x_{F1}}{n_F} = \frac{89}{174} = .511$$

For confidence coefficient .95, $\alpha = .05$ and $\alpha/2 = .05/2 = .025$. From Table IV, Appendix B, $z_{.025} = 1.96$. The 95% confidence interval is:

$$\left(\hat{p}_{M1} - \hat{p}_{F1}\right) \pm z_{.025} \sqrt{\frac{\hat{p}_{M1}\hat{q}_{M1}}{n_M} + \frac{\hat{p}_{F1}\hat{q}_{F1}}{n_F}} \Rightarrow (.282 - .511) \pm 1.96 \sqrt{\frac{.282(.718)}{103} + \frac{.511(.489)}{174}}$$

$$\Rightarrow -.229 \pm .114 \Rightarrow (-.343, \quad -.115)$$

We are 95% confident that the difference in the proportions of male and female professionals who believe their salaries are too low is between $-.343$ and -.115. Since 0 is not in this interval, there is evidence that the two proportions are different.

b. Some preliminary calculations are:

$$\hat{p}_{M2} = \frac{x_{M2}}{n_M} = \frac{58}{103} = .563 \qquad \hat{p}_{F2} = \frac{x_{F2}}{n_F} = \frac{64}{174} = .368$$

For confidence coefficient .95, $\alpha = .05$ and $\alpha/2 = .05/2 = .025$. From Table IV, Appendix B, $z_{.025} = 1.96$. The 95% confidence interval is:

$$\left(\hat{p}_{M2} - \hat{p}_{F2}\right) \pm z_{.025} \sqrt{\frac{\hat{p}_{M2}\hat{q}_{M2}}{n_M} + \frac{\hat{p}_{F2}\hat{q}_{F2}}{n_F}} \Rightarrow (.563 - .368) \pm 1.96 \sqrt{\frac{.563(.437)}{103} + \frac{.368(.632)}{174}}$$

$$\Rightarrow .195 \pm .120 \Rightarrow (.075, \quad .315)$$

We are 95% confident that the difference in the proportions of male and female professionals who believe their salaries are equitable/fair is between .075 and .315. Since 0 is not in this interval, there is evidence that the two proportions are different.

c. Some preliminary calculations are:

$$\hat{p}_{M3} = \frac{x_{M3}}{n_M} = \frac{16}{103} = .155 \qquad \hat{p}_{F3} = \frac{x_{F3}}{n_F} = \frac{21}{174} = .121$$

For confidence coefficient .95, $\alpha = .05$ and $\alpha/2 = .05/2 = .025$. From Table IV, Appendix B, $z_{.025} = 1.96$. The 95% confidence interval is:

$$\left(\hat{p}_{M3} - \hat{p}_{F3}\right) \pm z_{.025}\sqrt{\frac{\hat{p}_{M3}\hat{q}_{M3}}{n_M} + \frac{\hat{p}_{F3}\hat{q}_{F3}}{n_F}} \Rightarrow (.155 - .121) \pm 1.96\sqrt{\frac{.155(.845)}{103} + \frac{.121(.879)}{174}}$$

$$\Rightarrow .034 \pm .085 \Rightarrow (-.051, \ .119)$$

We are 95% confident that the difference in the proportions of male and female professionals who believe they are well paid is between $-.051$ and $.119$.
Since 0 is in this interval, there is no evidence that the two proportions are different.

d.   Yes. Since there were differences between the proportions of males and females on 2 of the 3 levels, there is evidence that the opinions of males and females are different.

e.   Some preliminary calculations are:

$$E_{11} = \frac{R_1 C_1}{n} = \frac{118(103)}{277} = 43.877 \qquad\qquad E_{12} = \frac{R_1 C_2}{n} = \frac{118(174)}{277} = 74.123$$

$$E_{21} = \frac{R_2 C_1}{n} = \frac{122(103)}{277} = 45.365 \qquad\qquad E_{22} = \frac{R_2 C_2}{n} = \frac{122(174)}{277} = 76.635$$

$$E_{31} = \frac{R_3 C_1}{n} = \frac{37(103)}{277} = 13.758 \qquad\qquad E_{33} = \frac{R_3 C_3}{n} = \frac{37(174)}{277} = 23.242$$

To determine if the opinion on the fairness of a travel professional's salary differ for males and females, we test:

H_0: Opinion and Gender are independent
H_a: Opinion and Gender are dependent

The test statistic is

$$\chi^2 = \sum\sum \frac{\left[n_{ij} - E_{ij}\right]^2}{E_{ij}} = \frac{(29 - 43.877)^2}{43.877} + \frac{(89 - 74.123)^2}{74.123} + \frac{(58 - 45.365)^2}{45.365}$$

$$+ \frac{(64 - 76.635)^2}{76.635} + \frac{(16 - 13.758)^2}{13.758} + \frac{(21 - 23.242)^2}{23.242} = 14.214$$

The rejection region requires $\alpha = .10$ in the upper tail of the χ^2 distribution with df $= (r-1)(c-1) = (3-1)(2-1) = 2$. From Table VII, Appendix B, $\chi^2_{.10} = 4.60517$. The rejection region is $\chi^2 > 4.60517$.

Since the observed value of the test statistic falls in the rejection region ($\chi^2 = 14.214 > 4.60517$), H_0 is rejected. There is sufficient evidence to indicate that the opinion on the fairness of a travel professional's salary differ for males and females at $\alpha = .10$.

f. For confidence coefficient .90, $\alpha = .10$ and $\alpha/2 = .10/2 = .05$. From Table IV, Appendix B, $z_{.05} = 1.645$. The 90% confidence interval is:

$$\left(\hat{p}_{M1} - \hat{p}_{F1}\right) \pm z_{.05}\sqrt{\frac{\hat{p}_{M1}\hat{q}_{M1}}{n_M} + \frac{\hat{p}_{F1}\hat{q}_{F1}}{n_F}} \Rightarrow (.282 - .511) \pm 1.645\sqrt{\frac{.282(.718)}{103} + \frac{.511(.489)}{174}}$$

$$\Rightarrow -.229 \pm .096 \Rightarrow (-.325, \ -.133)$$

We are 90% confident that the difference in the proportions of male and female professionals who believe their salaries are too low is between -.325 and -.133. Since 0 is not in this interval, there is evidence that the two proportions are different.

9.25   To determine if Defect and Pred_EVG are dependent, we test:

H_0: Defect and Pred_EVG are independent
H_a: Defect and Pred_EVG are dependent

The test statistic is $\chi^2 = 1.188$.

Since no α level was given, we will use $\alpha = .05$. The rejection region requires $\alpha = .05$ in the upper tail of the χ^2 distribution with df $= (r-1)(c-1) = (2-1)(2-1) = 1$. From Table VII, Appendix B, $\chi^2_{.05} = 3.84146$. The rejection region is $\chi^2 > 3.84146$.

Since the observed value of the test statistic does not fall in the rejection region ($\chi^2 = 1.188 > 3.84146$), H_0 is not rejected. There is insufficient evidence to indicate that Defect and Pred_EVG are dependent at $\alpha = .05$. If Defect and Pred_EVG are independent, then the Pred_EVG is no better predicting defects than just guessing. I would not recommend the essential complexity algorithm be used as a predictor of defective software modules.

9.27   Some preliminary calculations:

$$E_{11} = \frac{R_1 C_1}{n} = \frac{2,359(1,712)}{5,026} = 803.543 \qquad E_{12} = \frac{R_1 C_2}{n} = \frac{2,359(3,314)}{5,026} = 1,555.457$$

$$E_{21} = \frac{R_2 C_1}{n} = \frac{2,667(1,712)}{5,026} = 908.457 \qquad E_{22} = \frac{R_2 C_2}{n} = \frac{2,667(3,314)}{5,026} = 1,758.543$$

To determine if travelers who use the Internet to search for travel information are likely to be people who are college educated, we test:

H_0: Education and use of Internet for travel information are independent
H_a: Education and use of Internet for travel information are dependent

The test statistic is $\chi^2 = \sum\sum \dfrac{[n_{ij} - E_{ij}]^2}{E_{ij}}$

$$= \frac{(1,072 - 803.543)^2}{803.543} + \frac{(1,287 - 1,555.457)^2}{1,555.457} + \frac{(640 - 908.547)^2}{908.457} + \frac{(2,027 - 1,758.543)^2}{1,758.543}$$

$$= 256.336$$

The rejection region requires $\alpha = .05$ in the upper tail of the χ^2 distribution with df $= (r-1)(c-1) = (2-1)(2-1) = 1$. From Table VII, Appendix B, $\chi^2_{.05} = 3.84146$. The rejection region is $\chi^2 > 3.84146$.

Since the observed value of the test statistic falls in the rejection region
($\chi^2 = 256.336 > 3.814146$), H_0 is rejected. There is sufficient evidence to indicate that travelers who use the Internet to search for travel information and level of education are dependent at
$\alpha = .05$. Since the proportion of college educated who use the Internet to search for travel information ($1072/2359 = .45$) is greater than the proportion of less than college educated ($640/2667 = .24$), the conclusion supports the researchers claim that travelers who use the Internet to search for travel information are likely to be people who are college educated.

The necessary assumptions are
1. The k observed counts are a random sample from the populations of interest.
2. The sample size, n, will be large enough so that, for every cell, the expected count, E_{ij}, will be equal to 5 or more.

9.29   Some preliminary calculations are:

$$E_{11} = \frac{R_1 C_1}{n} = \frac{32(32)}{96} = 10.667 \qquad E_{12} = \frac{R_1 C_2}{n} = \frac{32(64)}{96} = 21.333$$

$$E_{21} = \frac{R_2 C_1}{n} = \frac{32(32)}{96} = 10.667 \qquad E_{22} = \frac{R_2 C_2}{n} = \frac{32(64)}{96} = 21.333$$

$$E_{31} = \frac{R_3 C_1}{n} = \frac{32(32)}{96} = 10.667 \qquad E_{32} = \frac{R_3 C_2}{n} = \frac{32(64)}{96} = 21.333$$

To determine if the proportion of subjects who selected menus consistent with the theory depends on goal condition, we test:

H_0: Goal condition and Consistent with theory are independent
H_a: Goal condition and Consistent with theory are dependent

The test statistic is

$$\chi^2 = \sum\sum \frac{\left[n_{ij} - E_{ij} \right]^2}{E_{ij}} = \frac{(15 - 10.667)^2}{10.667} + \frac{(17 - 21.333)^2}{21.333} + \frac{(14 - 10.667)^2}{10.667} + \frac{(18 - 21.333)^2}{21.333}$$
$$+ \frac{(3 - 10.667)^2}{10.667} + \frac{(29 - 21.333)^2}{21.333} = 12.469$$

The rejection region requires $\alpha = .01$ in the upper tail of the χ^2 distribution with df $= (r - 1)(c - 1) = (3 - 1)(2 - 1) = 2$. From Table VII, Appendix B, $\chi^2_{.01} = 9.21034$. The rejection region is $\chi^2 > 9.21034$.

Since the observed value of the test statistic falls in the rejection region
($\chi^2 = 12.469 > 9.21034$), H_0 is rejected. There is sufficient evidence to indicate that the proportion of subjects who selected menus consistent with the theory depends on goal condition at $\alpha = .01$.

9.31   a.   To determine if the vaccine is effective in treating the MN strain of HIV, we test:

H_0: Vaccine status and MN strain are independent
H_a: Vaccine status and MN strain are dependent

The test statistic is $\chi^2 = 4.411$ (from the printout)

The p-value is .036. Since the p-value is less than $\alpha = .05$, H_0 is rejected. There is sufficient evidence to indicate that the vaccine is effective in treating the MN strain of HIV at $\alpha = .05$.

b.   We must assume that we have a random sample from the population of interest. We cannot really check this assumption. The second assumption is that all expected cell counts will be 5 or more. In this case, since there are only 7 observations in the second row, there is no way that the expected cell counts in that row will both be 5 or more (the sum of the expected cell counts in the row must sum to the observed row total).

c. $$\frac{\binom{7}{2}\binom{31}{22}}{\binom{38}{24}} = \frac{\frac{7!}{2!(7-2)!}\frac{31!}{22!(31-22)!}}{\frac{38!}{24!(38-24)!}} = \frac{\frac{7\cdot6\cdots1}{2\cdot5\cdot4\cdot3\cdot2\cdot1}\frac{31\cdot30\cdots1}{22\cdot21\cdots1\cdot9\cdot8\cdots1}}{\frac{38\cdot37\cdots1}{24\cdot23\cdots1\cdot14\cdot13\cdots1}} = .04378$$

d.   Table 1:

$$\frac{\binom{7}{1}\binom{31}{23}}{\binom{38}{24}} = \frac{\frac{7!}{1!(7-1)!}\frac{31!}{23!(31-23)!}}{\frac{38!}{24!(38-24)!}} = \frac{\frac{7\cdot6\cdots1}{1\cdot6\cdot5\cdot4\cdot3\cdot2\cdot1}\frac{31\cdot30\cdots1}{23\cdot22\cdots1\cdot8\cdot7\cdots1}}{\frac{38\cdot37\cdots1}{24\cdot23\cdots1\cdot14\cdot13\cdots1}} = .00571$$

Table 2:

$$\frac{\binom{7}{0}\binom{31}{24}}{\binom{38}{24}} = \frac{\frac{7!}{0!(7-0)!}\frac{31!}{24!(31-24)!}}{\frac{38!}{24!(38-24)!}} = \frac{\frac{7\cdot6\cdots1}{1\cdot7\cdot6\cdot5\cdot4\cdot3\cdot2\cdot1}\frac{31\cdot30\cdots1}{24\cdot23\cdots1\cdot7\cdot6\cdots1}}{\frac{38\cdot37\cdots1}{24\cdot23\cdots1\cdot14\cdot13\cdots1}} = .00027$$

e.   The p-value is .04378 + .00571 + .00027 = .04976. Since the p-value is less than $\alpha = .05$, H_0 is rejected. There is sufficient evidence to indicate that the vaccine is effective in treating the MN strain of HIV at $\alpha = .05$.

9.33   a.   Some preliminary calculations are:
If all the categories are equally likely,

$$p_{1,0} = p_{2,0} = p_{3,0} = p_{4,0} = p_{5,0} = .2$$

$$E(n_1) = E(n_2) = E(n_3) = E(n_4) = E(n_5) = np_{1,0} = 150(.2) = 30$$

To determine if the categories are not equally likely, we test:

H_0: $p_1 = p_2 = p_3 = p_4 = p_5 = .2$
H_a: At least one probability is different from .2

The test statistic is $\chi^2 = \sum \dfrac{[n_i - E(n_i)]^2}{E(n_i)}$

$$= \frac{(28-30)^2}{30} + \frac{(35-30)^2}{30} + \frac{(33-30)^2}{30} + \frac{(25-30)^2}{30} + \frac{(29-30)^2}{30} = 2.133$$

The rejection region requires $\alpha = .10$ in the upper tail of the χ^2 distribution with df $= k - 1 = 5 - 1 = 4$. From Table VII, Appendix B, $\chi^2_{.10} = 7.77944$. The rejection region is $\chi^2 > 7.77944$.

Since the observed value of the test statistic does not fall in the rejection region ($\chi^2 = 2.133 \not> 7.77944$), H_0 is not rejected. There is insufficient evidence to indicate the categories are not equally likely at $\alpha = .10$.

b. $\hat{p}_2 = \dfrac{35}{150} = .233$

For confidence coefficient .90, $\alpha = .10$ and $\alpha/2 = .05$. From Table IV, Appendix B, $z_{.05} = 1.645$. The confidence interval is:

$$\hat{p}_2 \pm z_{.05} \sqrt{\frac{\hat{p}_2 \hat{q}_2}{n_2}} \Rightarrow .233 \pm 1.645 \sqrt{\frac{.233(.767)}{150}} \Rightarrow .233 \pm .057 \Rightarrow (.176, .290)$$

9.35   a.   To determine if the opinions of Internet users are evenly divided among the four categories, we test:

H_0: $p_1 = p_2 = p_3 = p_4 = .25$
H_a: At least one $p_i \neq .25$, for $i = 1, 2, 3, 4$

b.   Some preliminary calculations are:

$E(n_1) = np_{1,0} = 328(.25) = 82$
$E(n_2) = E(n_3) = E(n_4) = 328(.25) = 82$

Categorical Data Analysis

The test statistic is $\chi^2 = \sum \dfrac{[n_i - E(n_i)]^2}{E(n_i)}$

$$= \frac{(59-82)^2}{82} + \frac{(108-82)^2}{82} + \frac{(82-82)^2}{82} + \frac{(79-82)^2}{82} = 14.805$$

The rejection region requires $\alpha = .05$ in the upper tail of the χ^2 distribution with df $= k - 1 = 4 - 1 = 3$. From Table VII, Appendix B, $\chi^2_{.05} = 7.81473$. The rejection region is $\chi^2 > 7.81473$.

Since the observed value of the test statistic falls in the rejection region ($\chi^2 = 14.805 > 7.81473$), H_0 is rejected. There is sufficient evidence to indicate that the opinions of Internet users are not evenly divided among the four categories at $\alpha = .05$.

c. A Type I error would be to conclude that the opinions of Internet users are not evenly divided among the four categories when, in fact, they are evenly divided.

A Type II error would be to conclude that the opinions of Internet users are evenly divided among the four categories when, in fact, they are not evenly divided.

d. We must assume that:

1. A multinomial experiment was conducted. This is generally satisfied by taking a random sample from the population of interest.
2. The sample size n will be large enough so that, for every cell, the expected cell count, $E(n_i)$, will be equal to 5 or more.

9.37 a. The sample proportion of injured Hispanic children who were not wearing seatbelts during the accident is:

$\hat{p} = 283/314 = .901$

b. The sample proportion of injured non-Hispanic white children who were not wearing seatbelts during the accident is:

$\hat{p} = 330/478 = .690$

c. Since the proportion of injured Hispanic children who were not wearing seatbelts during the accident (.901) is .211 higher than the proportion of injured non-Hispanic white children who were not wearing seatbelts during the accident (.690), the proportions probably differ.

d. Some preliminary calculations are:

$$E_{11} = \frac{R_1 C_1}{n} = \frac{179(314)}{792} = 70.97 \qquad E_{12} = \frac{R_1 C_2}{n} = \frac{179(478)}{792} = 108.03$$

$$E_{21} = \frac{R_2 C_1}{n} = \frac{613(314)}{792} = 243.03 \qquad E_{22} = \frac{R_2 C_2}{n} = \frac{613(478)}{792} = 369.97$$

To determine whether seatbelt usage in motor vehicle accidents depends on ethnic status in the San Diego County Regionalized Trauma System, we test:

H_0: Seatbelt usage in motor vehicle accidents and ethnic status in the San Diego County Regionalized Trauma System are independent

H_a: Seatbelt usage in motor vehicle accidents and ethnic status in the San Diego County Regionalized Trauma System are dependent

The test statistic is $\chi^2 = \sum \dfrac{[n_{ij} - E_{ij}]^2}{E_{ij}}$

$$= \frac{(31 - 70.97)^2}{70.97} + \frac{(148 - 108.03)^2}{108.03} + \frac{(283 - 243.03)^2}{243.03} + \frac{(330 - 369.97)^2}{369.97} = 48.191$$

The rejection region requires $\alpha = .01$ in the upper tail of the χ^2 distribution with df = $(r - 1)(c - 1) = (2 - 1)(2 - 1) = 1$. From Table VII, Appendix B, $\chi^2_{.01} = 6.63490$. The rejection region is $\chi^2 > 6.63490$.

ince the observed value of the test statistic falls in the rejection region ($\chi^2 = 48.191 > 6.63490$), H_0 is rejected. There is sufficient evidence to indicate seatbelt usage in motor vehicle accidents depends on ethnic status in the San Diego County Regionalized Trauma System at $\alpha = .01$.

e. For confidence coefficient .99, $\alpha = .01$ and $\alpha/2 = .01/2 = .005$. From Table IV, Appendix B, $z_{.005} = 2.58$. The confidence interval is:

$$(\hat{p}_1 - \hat{p}_2) \pm z_{.005} \sqrt{\frac{\hat{p}_1 \hat{q}_1}{n_1} + \frac{\hat{p}_2 \hat{q}_2}{n_2}} \Rightarrow (.901 - .690) \pm 2.58 \sqrt{\frac{.901(.099)}{314} + \frac{.690(.310)}{478}}$$

$$\Rightarrow .211 \pm .070 \Rightarrow (.141, .281)$$

We are 99% confident that the difference in the proportion of injured Hispanic children who were not wearing seatbelts and the proportion of injured non-Hispanic white children who were not wearing seatbelts is between .141 and .281.

9.39   a.   Some preliminary calculations:

$$E(n_1) = np_{1,0} = 306(1/3) = 102$$
$$E(n_2) = np_{2,0} = 306(1/3) = 102$$
$$E(n_3) = np_{3,0} = 306(1/3) = 102$$

To determine if the percentages in the three frequency of use response categories differ for computer spreadsheets, we test:

H_0: $p_1 = p_2 = p_3 = 1/3$
H_a: At least one p_i differs from 1/2, $i = 1, 2, 3$

The test statistic is $\chi^2 = \sum \dfrac{[n_i - E(n_i)]^2}{E(n_i)} = \dfrac{(58-102)^2}{102} + \dfrac{(67-102)^2}{102} + \dfrac{(181-102)^2}{102}$

$$= 92.176$$

The rejection region requires $\alpha = .01$ in the upper tail of the χ^2 distribution with df $= k - 1$ $= 3 - 1 = 2$. From Table VII, Appendix B, $\chi^2_{.01} = 9.21034$. The rejection region is $\chi^2 > 9.21034$.

Since the observed value of the test statistic falls in the rejection region ($\chi^2 = 92.176 > 9.21034$), H_0 is rejected. There is sufficient evidence to indicate that at least one of the percentages in the three frequency of use response categories differs for computer spreadsheets at $\alpha = .01$.

b.   Some preliminary calculations:

$$E(n_1) = np_{1,0} = 306(1/3) = 102$$
$$E(n_2) = np_{2,0} = 306(1/3) = 102$$
$$E(n_3) = np_{3,0} = 306(1/3) = 102$$

To determine if the percentages in the three frequency of use response categories differ for word processing, we test:

H_0: $p_1 = p_2 = p_3 = 1/3$
H_a: At least one p_i differs from 1/2, $i = 1, 2, 3$

The test statistic is $\chi^2 = \sum \dfrac{[n_i - E(n_i)]^2}{E(n_i)} = \dfrac{(168-102)^2}{102} + \dfrac{(61-102)^2}{102} + \dfrac{(77-102)^2}{102}$

$$= 65.314$$

The rejection region is $\chi^2 > 9.21034$ from (part **a**).

Since the observed value of the test statistic falls in the rejection region ($\chi^2 = 65.314 > 9.21034$), H_0 is rejected. There is sufficient evidence to indicate that at least one of the percentages in the three frequency of use response categories differs for word processing at $\alpha = .01$.

c. Some preliminary calculations:

$$E(n_1) = np_{1,0} = 306(1/3) = 102$$
$$E(n_2) = np_{2,0} = 306(1/3) = 102$$
$$E(n_3) = np_{3,0} = 306(1/3) = 102$$

To determine if the percentages in the three frequency of use response categories differ for statistical software, we test:

H_0: $p_1 = p_2 = p_3 = 1/3$
H_a: At least one p_i differs from 1/2, $i = 1, 2, 3$

The test statistic is $\chi^2 = \sum \dfrac{[n_i - E(n_i)]^2}{E(n_i)} = \dfrac{(37-102)^2}{102} + \dfrac{(82-102)^2}{102} + \dfrac{(187-102)^2}{102}$

$$= 116.176$$

The rejection region is $\chi^2 > 9.21034$ from (part **a**).

Since the observed value of the test statistic falls in the rejection region ($\chi^2 = 116.176 > 9.21034$), H_0 is rejected. There is sufficient evidence to indicate that at least one of the percentages in the three frequency of use response categories differs for statistical software at $\alpha = .01$.

d. For confidence coefficient .99, $\alpha = .01$ and $\alpha/2 = .01/2 = .005$. From Table IV, Appendix B, $z_{.005} = 2.58$.

$$\hat{p}_3 = 181/306 = .59$$

The confidence interval is:

$$\hat{p} \pm z_{.005}\sqrt{\dfrac{\hat{p}\hat{q}}{n}} \Rightarrow .59 \pm 2.58\sqrt{\dfrac{.59(.41)}{306}} \Rightarrow .59 \pm .07 \Rightarrow (.52, .66)$$

We are 99% confident that the true percentage of faculty who never use computer spreadsheets in the classroom is between 52% and 66%.

9.41 Some preliminary calculations are:

$$E(n_1) = E(n_2) = E(n_3) = E(n_4) = E(n_5) = np_{1,0} = 95(.20) = 19$$

To determine if the true percentages of ADEs in the five "cause" categories are different, we test:

H_0: $p_1 = p_2 = p_3 = p_4 = p_5 = .2$
H_a: At least one proportion differs from .2

The test statistic is

$$\chi^2 = \sum \frac{[n_i - E(n_i)]^2}{E(n_i)} = \frac{(29-19)^2}{19} + \frac{(17-19)^2}{19} + \frac{(17-19)^2}{19} + \frac{(17-19)^2}{19} + \frac{(17-19)^2}{19} = 16$$

The rejection region requires $\alpha = .10$ in the upper tail of the χ^2 distribution with df $= k - 1 = 5 - 1 = 4$. From Table VII, Appendix B, $\chi^2_{.10} = 7.77944$. The rejection region is $\chi^2 > 7.77944$.

Since the observed value of the test statistic falls in the rejection region ($\chi^2 = 16 > 7.77944$), H_0 is rejected. There is sufficient evidence to indicate that the true percentages of ADEs in the five "cause" categories are different at $\alpha = .10$.

9.43   a.   The contingency table is:

		Committee		
		Acceptable	Rejected	Totals
Inspector	Acceptable	101	23	124
	Rejected	10	19	29
	Totals	111	42	153

b.   Yes. To plot the percentages, first convert frequencies to percentages by dividing the numbers in each column by the column total and multiplying by 100. Also, divide the row totals by the overall total and multiply by 100.

		Acceptable	Rejected	Totals
Inspector	Acceptable	$\frac{101}{111} \cdot 100 = 90.99\%$	$\frac{23}{42} \cdot 100 = 54.76\%$	$\frac{124}{153} \cdot 100 = 81.05\%$
	Rejected	$\frac{10}{111} \cdot 100 = 9.01\%$	$\frac{19}{42} \cdot 100 = 45.23\%$	$\frac{29}{153} \cdot 100 = 18.95\%$

Using MINITAB, the graph of the data is:

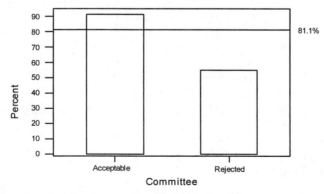

From the plot, it appears there is a relationship.

c. Some preliminary calculations are:

$$E_{11} = \frac{R_1 C_1}{n_1} = \frac{124(111)}{153} = 89.691 \qquad E_{12} = \frac{R_1 C_2}{n_1} = \frac{124(42)}{153} = 34.039$$

$$E_{21} = \frac{R_2 C_1}{n_1} = \frac{29(111)}{153} = 21.039 \qquad E_{22} = \frac{R_2 C_2}{n_1} = \frac{29(42)}{153} = 7.961$$

To determine if the inspector's classifications and the committee's classifications are related, we test:

H_0: The inspector's and committee's classification are independent
H_a: The inspector's and committee's classifications are dependent

The test statistic is $\chi^2 = \sum\sum \dfrac{\left[n_{ij} - E_{ij}\right]^2}{E_{ij}}$

$$= \frac{(101 - 89.961)^2}{89.961} + \frac{(23 - 34.039)^2}{34.039} + \frac{(10 - 21.039)^2}{21.039} + \frac{(19 - 7.961)^2}{7.961}$$

$$= 26.034$$

The rejection region requires $\alpha = .05$ in the upper tail of the χ^2 distribution with df = $(r-1)(c-1) = (2-1)(2-1) = 1$. From Table VII, Appendix B, $\chi^2_{.05} = 3.84146$. The rejection region is $\chi^2 > 3.84146$.

Since the observed value of the test statistic falls in the rejection region ($\chi^2 = 26.034 > 3.84146$), H_0 is rejected. There is sufficient evidence to indicate the inspector's and committee's classifications are related at $\alpha = .05$. This indicates that the inspector and committee tend to make the same decisions.

9.45 a. Some preliminary calculations are:

$E(n_1) = np_{1,0} = 19,115(.2010) = 3,842.115$
$E(n_2) = np_{2,0} = 19,115(.1010) = 1,930.615$
$E(n_3) = np_{3,0} = 19,115(.0542) = 1,036.033$
$E(n_4) = np_{4,0} = 19,115(.1601) = 3,060.3115$
$E(n_5) = np_{5,0} = 19,115(.2865) = 5,476.4475$
$E(n_6) = np_{6,0} = 19,115(.1238) = 2,366.437$
$E(n_7) = np_{7,0} = 19,115(.0732) = 1,399.218$

To determine if there is evidence to conclude that the purchases of the household panel is representative of the population of households, we test:

H_0: $p_1 = .201, p_2 = .101, p_3 = .0542, p_4 = .1601, p_5 = .2865, p_6 = .1238, p_7 = .0732$
H_a: At least one p_i does not equal its hypothesized value

The test statistic is $\chi^2 = \sum \dfrac{[n_i - E(n_i)]^2}{E(n_i)}$

$$= \frac{(3,165 - 3,842.115)^2}{3,842.115} + \frac{(1,892 - 1,930.615)^2}{1,930.615} + \frac{(726 - 1,036.033)^2}{1,036.033}$$

$$+ \frac{(4,079 - 3,060.3115)^2}{3,060.3115} + \frac{(6,206 - 5,476.4475)^2}{5,476.4475} + \frac{(1,627 - 2,366.437)^2}{2,366.437}$$

$$+ \frac{(1,420 - 1,399.218)^2}{1,399.218} = 880.521$$

The rejection region requires $\alpha = .05$ in the upper tail of the χ^2 distribution with df $= k - 1 = 7 - 1 = 6$. From Table VII, Appendix B, $\chi^2_{.05} = 12.5916$. The rejection region is $\chi^2 > 12.5916$.

Since the observed value of the test statistic falls in the rejection region ($\chi^2 = 880.521 > 12.5916$), H_0 is rejected. There is sufficient evidence to indicate that the purchases of the household panel is not representative of the population of households at $\alpha = .05$.

b. We must assume that:

1. A multinomial experiment was conducted. This is generally satisfied by taking a random sample from the population of interest.
2. The sample size n will be large enough so that, for every cell, the expected cell count, $E(n_i)$, will be equal to 5 or more.

c. From Table VII, Appendix B, with df $= 6$, the p-value $= P(\chi^2 > 880.521) < .005$.

9.47   The contingency table is:

Ebert Rating	Roeper Rating		Totals
	Down	Up	
Down	50	28	78
Up	32	108	140
Totals	82	136	218

Some preliminary calculations are:

$$E_{11} = \frac{R_1 C_1}{n} = \frac{78(82)}{218} = 29.339 \qquad E_{12} = \frac{R_1 C_2}{n} = \frac{78(136)}{218} = 48.661$$

$$E_{21} = \frac{R_2 C_1}{n} = \frac{140(82)}{218} = 52.661 \qquad E_{22} = \frac{R_2 C_2}{n} = \frac{140(136)}{218} = 87.339$$

To determine if the movie reviews of the two critics are independent, we test:

H_0: Movie reviews of the two critics are independent
H_a: Movie reviews of the two critics are dependent

The test statistic is

$$\chi^2 = \sum\sum \frac{\left[n_{ij} - E_{ij}\right]^2}{E_{ij}}$$

$$= \frac{(50 - 29.339)^2}{29.339} + \frac{(28 - 48.661)^2}{48.661} + \frac{(32 - 52.661)^2}{52.661} + \frac{(108 - 87.339)^2}{87.339}$$

$$= 36.316$$

The rejection region requires $\alpha = .05$ in the upper tail of the χ^2 distribution with df $= (r - 1)(c - 1) = (2 - 1)(2 - 1) = 1$. From Table VII, Appendix B, $\chi^2_{.05} = 3.84146$. The rejection region is $\chi^2 > 3.84146$.

Since the observed value of the test statistic falls in the rejection region ($\chi^2 = 36.316 > 3.84146$), H_0 is rejected. There is sufficient evidence to indicate that the movie reviews of the two critics are dependent at $\alpha = .05$. In other words, Roeper and Ebert agree more often than expected if their reviews were independent.

9.49   a. $\chi^2 = \sum \frac{[n_i - E(n_i)]^2}{E(n_i)}$

$$= \frac{(26 - 23)^2}{23} + \frac{(146 - 136)^2}{136} + \frac{(361 - 341)^2}{341} + \frac{(143 - 136)^2}{136} + \frac{(13 - 23)^2}{23}$$

$$= 9.647$$

b.   From Table VII, Appendix B, with df $= 5$, $\chi^2_{.05} = 11.0705$

c.   No. $\chi^2 = 9.647 \not> 11.0705$. Do not reject H_0. There is insufficient evidence to indicate the salary distribution is nonnormal for $\alpha = .05$.

d.   The p-value $= P(\chi^2 \geq 9.647)$.

Using Table VII, Appendix B, with df $= 5$,

$$.05 < P(\chi^2 \geq 9.647) < .10.$$

10.1   a. 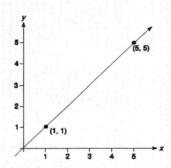   b.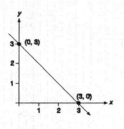

c. 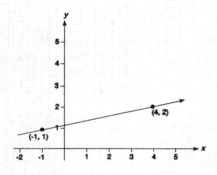   d.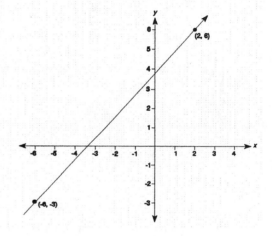

10.3   The two equations are:

$$4 = \beta_0 + \beta_1(-2) \text{ and } 6 = \beta_0 + \beta_1(4)$$

Subtracting the first equation from the second, we get

$$6 = \beta_0 + 4\beta_1$$
$$-(4 = \beta_0 - 2\beta_1)$$
$$\overline{\quad\quad\quad\quad\quad}$$
$$2 = \quad 6\beta_1 \ \Rightarrow \beta_1 = \frac{1}{3}$$

Substituting $\beta_1 = \dfrac{1}{3}$ into the first equation, we get:

$$4 = \beta_0 + \frac{1}{3}(-2) \Rightarrow \beta_0 = 4 + \frac{2}{3} = \frac{14}{3}$$

The equation for the line is $y = \dfrac{14}{3} = \dfrac{1}{3}x$.

10.5   To graph a line, we need two points. Pick two values for x, and find the corresponding y values by substituting the values of x into the equation.

a.   Let $x = 0 \Rightarrow y = 4 + (0) = 4$
      and $x = 2 \Rightarrow y = 4 + (2) = 6$

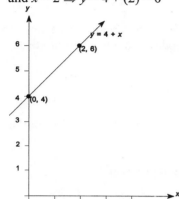

b.   Let $x = 0 \Rightarrow y = 5 - 2(0) = 5$
      and $x = 2 \Rightarrow y = 5 - 2(2) = 1$

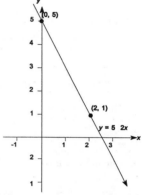

c.   Let $x = 0 \Rightarrow y = -4 + 3(0) = -4$ and $x = 2$
      $\Rightarrow y = -4 + 3(2) = 2$

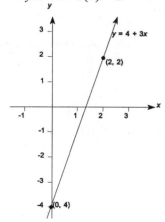

d.   Let $x = 0 \Rightarrow y = -2(0) = 0$
      and $x = 2 \Rightarrow y = -2(2) = -4$

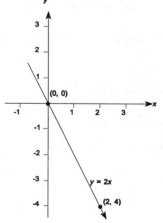

Simple Linear Regression

e.   Let $x = 0 \Rightarrow y = 0$
and $x = 2 \Rightarrow y = 2$

f.   Let $x = 0 \Rightarrow y = .5 + 1.5(0) = .5$
and $x = 2 \Rightarrow y = .5 + 1.5(2) = 3.5$

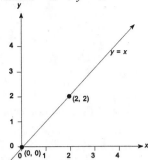

10.7   A deterministic model does not allow for random error or variation, whereas a probabilistic model does. An example where a deterministic model would be appropriate is:

Let y = cost of a 2 × 4 piece of lumber and
   x = length (in feet)

The model would be $y = \beta_1 x$. There should be no variation in price for the same length of wood.

An example where a probabilistic model would be appropriate is:

Let y = sales per month of a commodity and
   x = amount of money spent advertising

The model would be $y = \beta_0 + \beta_1 x + \varepsilon$. The sales per month will probably vary even if the amount of money spent on advertising remains the same.

10.9   No. The random error component, ε, allows the values of the variable to fall above or below the line.

10.11   From Exercise 10.10, $\hat{\beta}_0 = 7.10$ and $\hat{\beta}_1 = -.78$.

The fitted line is $\hat{y} = 7.10 - .78x$. To obtain values for , we substitute values of x into the equation and solve for $\hat{y}$.

a.

x	y	$\hat{y} = 7.10 - .78x$	$(y - \hat{y})$	$(y - \hat{y})^2$
7	2	1.64	.36	.1296
4	4	3.98	.02	.0004
6	2	2.42	−.42	.1764
2	5	5.54	−.54	.2916
1	7	6.32	.68	.4624
1	6	6.32	−.32	.1024
3	5	4.76	.24	.0576
			$\sum(y - \hat{y}) = 0.02$	SSE $= \sum(y - \hat{y})^2 = 1.2204$

b.

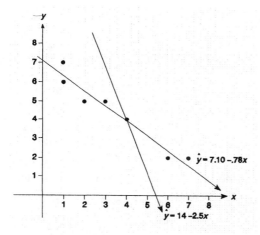

c.

x	y	$\hat{y} = 14 - 2.5x$	$(y - \hat{y})$	$(y - \hat{y})^2$
7	2	−3.5	5.5	30.25
4	4	4	0	0
6	2	−1	3	9
2	5	9	−4	16
1	7	11.5	−4.5	20.25
1	6	11.5	−5.5	30.25
3	5	6.5	−1.5	2.25
			$\sum(y - \hat{y}) = -7$	SSE $= 108.00$

10.13 a.

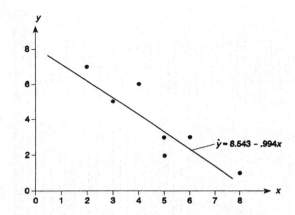

b.   Looking at the scattergram, x and y appear to have a negative linear relationship.

c.   From the printout, $\hat{\beta}_1 = -.9939$ and $\hat{\beta}_0 = 8.543$

d.   The least squares line is $\hat{y} = 8.543 - .994x$. The line is plotted in part **a**. It appears to fit the data well.

10.15 a.   The straight-line model would be: $y = \beta_o + \beta_1 x + \varepsilon$

b.   From the printout, the least squares line is: $\hat{y} = -43.308 + 1.073x$.

c.   Since range of observed values for the 1990 SAT scores (x) does not include 0, the y-intercept has no meaning.

d.   The slope of the line is β_1. In terms of this problem, β_1 is the change in the mean 2005 SAT score for each additional point increase in the 1990 SAT score. This interpretation is meaningful for values of x within the observed range. The observed range of x is 942 to 1,172.

10.17 a.   Some preliminary calculations are:

$$\sum x = 5.45 \qquad\qquad \sum y = 239 \qquad\qquad \sum xy = 237.1$$

$$\sum x^2 = 5.5075 \qquad\qquad \sum y^2 = 10,255$$

$$\bar{x} = \frac{\sum x}{n} = \frac{5.45}{6} = .908333333 \qquad\qquad \bar{y} = \frac{\sum y}{n} = \frac{239}{6} = 39.83333333$$

$$SS_{xy} = \sum xy - \frac{\left(\sum x\right)\left(\sum y\right)}{n} = 237.1 - \frac{5.45(239)}{6}$$
$$= 237.1 - 217.09166667 = 20.0083333$$

$$SS_{xx} = \sum x^2 - \frac{\left(\sum x\right)^2}{n} = 5.5075 - \frac{(5.45)^2}{6} = 5.5075 - 4.950416667 = .5570833333$$

$$\hat{\beta}_1 = \frac{SS_{xy}}{SS_{xx}} = \frac{20.0083333}{.5570833333} = 35.91623038 \approx 35.916$$

$$\hat{\beta}_0 = \bar{y} - \hat{\beta}_1 \bar{x} = 39.8333333 - 35.91623038(.90833333) = 7.20942408 \approx 7.209$$

$$\hat{y} = 7.209 + 35.916x$$

b.   Since 0 is not in the observed range of x (Surface Area to Volume), $\hat{\beta}_0$ has not meaning. $\hat{\beta}_1 = 35.916$. For each unit change in Surface Area to Volume, the mean Drug Release Rate is estimated to increase by 35.916.

c.   For $x = .50$, $\hat{y} = 7.209 + 35.916(.50) = 25.167$

d.   The reliability of the estimate in part c is in question. The value of x, .50, is outside the observed range of x. We have no idea what the relationship between y and x is outside the observed range.

10.19   a.   A proposed model is $E(y) = \beta_0 + \beta_1 x$.

b.   (Note: There are 3 observations that have missing values on the Net Worth variable. Thus, only 47 observations are used.) Some preliminary calculations are:

$$\sum x = 337,059 \qquad \sum y = 34,290 \qquad \sum xy = 593,034,746$$

$$\sum x^2 = 12,725,850,505 \qquad \sum y^2 = 102,624,918$$

$$\bar{x} = \frac{\sum x}{n} = \frac{337,059}{47} = 7,171.468085 \qquad \bar{y} = \frac{\sum y}{n} = \frac{34,290}{47} = 729.5744681$$

$$SS_{xy} = \sum xy - \frac{\left(\sum x\right)\left(\sum y\right)}{n} = 593,034,746 - \frac{337,059(34,290)}{47}$$
$$= 593,034,746 - 245,909,640.6 = 347,124,105.4$$

$$SS_{xx} = \sum x^2 - \frac{\left(\sum x\right)^2}{n} = 12,725,850,505 - \frac{(337,059)^2}{47}$$
$$= 12,725,850,505 - 2,417,207,861 = 10,308,642,644$$

$$\hat{\beta}_1 = \frac{SS_{xy}}{SS_{xx}} = \frac{347,124,105.4}{10,308,642,644} = 0.033673212 \approx 0.0337$$

$$\hat{\beta}_o = \bar{y} - \hat{\beta}_1\bar{x} = 729.5744681 - (0.033673212)(7171.468085)$$
$$= 488.0881029 \approx 488.0881$$

The fitted regression line is: $\hat{y} = 488.0881 + 0.0337x$

c. Using MINITAB, the fitted regression line is:

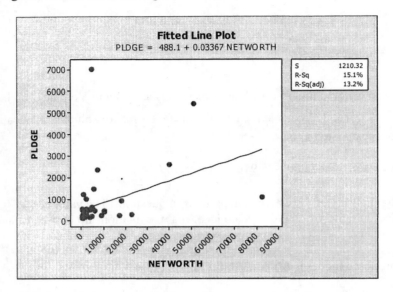

There does not appear to be a very much of a relationship between Net Worth and Amount Pledged. There is a very weak positive linear relationship between Net Worth and Amount Pledged.

d. $\hat{\beta}_o = 488.0881$. Since 0 is not in the range of observed values of Net Worth, the y-intercept has no meaning.

$\hat{\beta}_1 = 0.0337$. For each additional million dollars of Net Worth, the mean Amount Pledged is estimated to increase by .0337 million dollars.

10.21 a. It appears as salary increases, the retaliation index decreases.

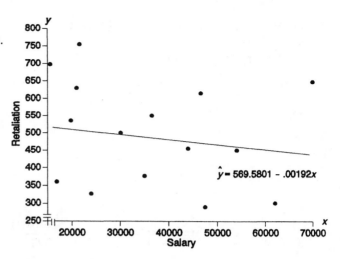

b. $\sum x = 544,100 \qquad \sum y = 7,497 \qquad \sum xy = 263,977,000$
$\sum x^2 = 23,876,290,000$

$\bar{x} = \dfrac{\sum x}{n} = \dfrac{544,100}{15} = 36,273.333 \quad \bar{y} = \dfrac{\sum y}{n} = \dfrac{7,497}{15} = 499.8$

$SS_{xy} = \sum xy - \dfrac{(\sum x)(\sum y)}{n} = 263,977,000 - \dfrac{(544,100)(7,497)}{15}$
$= 263,977,000 - 271,941,180 = -7,964,180$

$SS_{xx} = \sum x^2 - \dfrac{(\sum x)^2}{n} = 23,876,290,000 - \dfrac{(544,100)^2}{15}$
$= 23,876,290,000 - 19,736,320,670 = 4,139,969,330$

$\hat{\beta}_1 = \dfrac{SS_{xy}}{SS_{xx}} = \dfrac{-7,964,180}{4,139,969,330} = -.001923729 \approx -.00192$

$\hat{\beta}_0 = \bar{y} - \hat{\beta}_1\bar{x} = 499.8 - (-.001923729)(36,273.333)$
$= 499.8 + 69.78007144 = 569.5800714 \approx 569.5801$
$\hat{y} = 569.5801 - .00192x$

c. The least squares line supports the answer because the line has a negative slope.

d. $\hat{\beta}_0 = 569.5801$ This has no meaning because $x = 0$ is not in the observed range.

e. $\hat{\beta}_1 = -.00192$ When the salary increases by \$1, the mean retaliation index is estimated to decrease by .00192. This is meaningful for the range of x from \$16,900 to \$70,000.

10.23   We will fit the model $E(y) = \beta_o + \beta_1 x$.

Some preliminary calculations are:

$$\sum x = 526 \qquad\qquad \sum y = 60.1 \qquad\qquad \sum xy = 586.95$$

$$\sum x^2 = 18,936 \qquad\qquad \sum y^2 = 262.2708$$

$$\bar{x} = \frac{\sum x}{n} = \frac{526}{23} = 22.86956522 \qquad\qquad \bar{y} = \frac{\sum y}{n} = \frac{60.1}{23} = 2.613043478$$

$$SS_{xy} = \sum xy - \frac{(\sum x)(\sum y)}{n} = 586.95 - \frac{526(60.1)}{23}$$
$$= 586.95 - 1,374.46087 = -787.51087$$

$$SS_{xx} = \sum x^2 - \frac{(\sum x)^2}{n} = 18,936 - \frac{(526)^2}{23}$$
$$= 18,936 - 12,029.3913 = 6906.6087$$

$$\hat{\beta}_1 = \frac{SS_{xy}}{SS_{xx}} = \frac{-787.51087}{6906.6087} = -0.114022801 \approx -0.114$$

$$\hat{\beta}_o = \bar{y} - \hat{\beta}_1\bar{x} = 2.613043478 - (-0.114022801)(22.86956522) = 5.220695365 \approx 5.221$$

The fitted regression line is: $\hat{y} = 5.221 - 0.114x$

Since the estimate of the coefficient of the time variable is negative, it indicates that the spill tends to diminish as time increases. It is estimated that for each minute of time, the mean mass will diminish by .114 pounds.

Using MINITAB, the fitted regression line is:

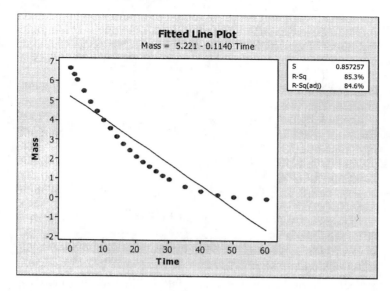

We can see that as time increases, the mass decreases. However, it appears that the mass decreases at a non-constant rate. A curvilinear line might be a better fit.

10.25   a. $s^2 = \dfrac{SSE}{n-2} = \dfrac{8.34}{26-2} = .3475$

   b.   We would expect most of the observations to be within $2s$ of the least squares line. This is:
   $$2s = 2\sqrt{.3475} \approx 1.179$$

10.27 $SSE = SS_{yy} - \hat{\beta}_1 SS_{xy}$

   where $SS_{yy} = \sum y_i^2 - \dfrac{\left(\sum y_i\right)^2}{n}$

   For Exercise 10.10,
   $$\sum y_i^2 = 159 \qquad\qquad \sum y_i = 31$$
   $$SS_{yy} = 159 - \frac{31^2}{7} = 159 - 137.2857143 = 21.7142857$$
   $$SS_{xy} = -26.2857143 \qquad \hat{\beta}_1 = -.779661017$$

   Therefore, $SSE = 21.7142857 - (-.779661017)(-26.2857143) = 1.22033896 \approx 1.2203$

   $$s^2 = \frac{SSE}{n-2} = \frac{1.22033896}{7-2} = .244067792, \; s = \sqrt{.244067792} = .4960$$

   We would expect most of the observations to fall within $2s$ or $2(.4940)$ or $.988$ units of the least squares prediction line.

Simple Linear Regression

303

For Exercise 10.13,

$$\sum x = 33 \quad \sum y = 27 \quad \sum xy = 104 \quad \sum x^2 = 179 \quad \sum y^2 = 133$$

$$SS_{xy} = \sum xy - \frac{\left(\sum x\right)\left(\sum y\right)}{n} = 104 - \frac{(23)(27)}{7} = 104 - 127.2857143 = -23.2857143$$

$$SS_{xx} = \sum x^2 - \frac{\left(\sum x\right)^2}{n} = 179 - \frac{(33)^2}{7} = 179 - 155.5714286 = 23.4285714$$

$$SS_{yy} = \sum y^2 - \frac{\left(\sum y\right)^2}{n} = 133 - \frac{(27)^2}{7} = 133 - 104.1428571 = 28.8571429$$

$$\hat{\beta}_1 = \frac{SS_{xy}}{SS_{xx}} = \frac{-23.2857143}{23.4285714} = -.99390244$$

$$SSE = SS_{yy} - \hat{\beta}_1 SS_{xy} = 28.8571429 - (.99390244)(-23.2857143)$$
$$= 28.8571429 - 23.14372824 = 5.71341466$$

$$s^2 = \frac{SSE}{n-2} = \frac{5.71341466}{7-2} = 1.142682932 \quad s = \sqrt{1.142682932} = 1.0690$$

We would expect most of the observations to fall within $2s$ or $2(1.0690)$ or 2.1380 units of the least squares prediction line.

10.29   a.   From the printout, SSE = 26,877.46, s^2 = MSE = 548.520, and s = 23.420.

   b. s = 23.420. We would expect approximately 95% of the observed values of y (2005 SAT Score) to fall within $2s$ or $2(23.42) = 46.84$ units of their least squares predicted values.

10.31   a.   From Exercise 10.18, $SS_{xy} = -130.44167$, $\hat{\beta}_1 = -.002310625$, $\sum y = 135.8$, and $\sum y^2 = 769.72$.

$$SS_{yy} = \sum y^2 - \frac{\left(\sum y\right)^2}{n} = 769.72 - \frac{(135.8)^2}{24}$$
$$= 769.72 - 768.4016667 = 1.3183333$$

$$SSE = SS_{yy} - \hat{\beta}_1 SS_{xy} = 1.3183333 - (-.002310625)(-130.44167) = 1.016931516$$

$$s^2 = MSE = \frac{SSE}{n-2} = \frac{1.016931516}{24-2} = 0.046224159 \quad \text{and}$$

$$s = \sqrt{0.046224159} = 0.214998$$

   b. s^2 is measured in square units. It is very difficult to explain something measured in square units.

   c. s = 0.2150. We would expect approximately 95% of the observed values of y (sweetness index) to fall within $2s$ or $2(0.2150) = 0.43$ units of their least squares predicted values.

10.33 a. From Exercise 10.20, $SS_{xy} = -3,881.9986$, $\sum y = 3,781.1$, $\sum y^2 = 651,612.45$,
and $\hat{\beta}_1 = -0.305444503$.

$$SS_{yy} = \sum y^2 - \frac{\left(\sum y\right)^2}{n} = 651,612.45 - \frac{(3,781.1)^2}{22}$$
$$= 651,612.45 - 649,850.7823 = 1,761.6677$$

$$SSE = SS_{yy} - \hat{\beta}_1 SS_{xy} = 1,761.6677 - (-.305444503(-3,882.3686)) = 575.8195525$$

$$s^2 = MSE = \frac{SSE}{n-2} = \frac{575.8195525}{22-2} = 28.79097763 \quad \text{and} \quad s = \sqrt{28.79097763} = 5.3657$$

$s = 5.3657$. We would expect approximately 95% of the observed values of y
(FCAT-Math scores) to fall within $2s$ or $2(5.3657) = 10.7314$ units of their least
squares predicted values.

b. From Exercise 10.20, $SS_{xy} = -3,442.16$, $\sum y = 3,764.2$, $\sum y^2 = 645,221.16$,
and $\hat{\beta}_1 = -0.270811187$.

$$SS_{yy} = \sum y^2 - \frac{\left(\sum y\right)^2}{n} = 645,221.16 - \frac{(3,764.2)^2}{22}$$
$$= 645,221.16 - 644,054.62 = 1,166.54$$

$$SSE = SS_{yy} - \hat{\beta}_1 SS_{xy} = 1,166.54 - (-.270811187(-3,442.16)) = 234.3645646$$

$$s^2 = MSE = \frac{SSE}{n-2} = \frac{234.3645646}{22-2} = 11.71822823 \quad \text{and} \quad s = \sqrt{11.71822823} = 3.4232$$

$s = 3.4232$. We would expect approximately 95% of the observed values of y
(FCAT-Reading scores) to fall within $2s$ or $2(3.4232) = 6.8464$ units of their least
squares predicted values.

c. The sample standard deviation for predicting FCAT-Math scores is $s = 5.3657$. The
sample standard deviation for predicting FCAT-Reading scores is $s = 3.4232$. Since the
standard deviation for predicting FCAT-Reading scores is smaller than the standard
deviation for predicting FCAT-Math scores, we can more accurately predict the FCAT-
Reading scores.

10.35 a.   For confidence coefficient .95, $\alpha = 1 - .95 = .05$ and $\alpha/2 = .05/2 = .025$. From Table VI, Appendix B, with df $= n - 2 = 12 - 2 = 10$, $t_{.025} = 2.228$.

The 95% confidence interval for β_1 is:

$$\hat{\beta}_1 \pm t_{.025}\, s_{\hat{\beta}_1} \quad \text{where} \quad s_{\hat{\beta}_1} = \frac{s}{\sqrt{SS_{xx}}} = \frac{3}{\sqrt{35}} = .5071$$

$$\Rightarrow 31 \pm 2.228(.5071) \Rightarrow 31 \pm 1.13 \Rightarrow (29.87,\ 32.13)$$

For confidence coefficient .90, $\alpha = 1 - .90 = .10$ and $\alpha/2 = .10/2 = .05$. From Table VI, Appendix B, with df $= 10$, $t_{.05} = 1.812$.

The 90% confidence interval for β_1 is:

$$\hat{\beta}_1 \pm t_{.05}\, s_{\hat{\beta}_1} \Rightarrow 31 \pm 1.812(.5071) \Rightarrow 31 \pm .92 \Rightarrow (30.08,\ 31.92)$$

b. $s^2 = \dfrac{SSE}{n-2} = \dfrac{1960}{18-2} = 122.5,\ s = \sqrt{s^2} = 11.0680$

For confidence coefficient, .95, $\alpha = 1 - .95 = .05$ and $\alpha/2 = .05/2 = .025$. From Table VI, Appendix B, with df $= n - 2 = 18 - 2 = 16$, $t_{.025} = 2.120$. The 95% confidence interval for β_1 is:

$$\hat{\beta}_1 \pm t_{.025}\, s_{\hat{\beta}_1} \quad \text{where} \quad s_{\hat{\beta}_1} = \frac{s}{\sqrt{SS_{xx}}} = \frac{11.0680}{\sqrt{30}} = 2.0207$$

$$\Rightarrow 64 \pm 2.120(2.0207) \Rightarrow 64 \pm 4.28 \Rightarrow (59.72,\ 68.28)$$

For confidence coefficient .90, $\alpha = 1 - .90 = .10$ and $\alpha/2 = .10/2 = .05$. From Table VI, Appendix B, with df $= 16$, $t_{.05} = 1.746$.

The 90% confidence interval for β_1 is:

$$\hat{\beta}_1 \pm t_{.05}\, s_{\hat{\beta}_1} \Rightarrow 64 \pm 1.746(2.0207) \Rightarrow 64 \pm 3.53 \Rightarrow (60.47,\ 67.53)$$

c. $s^2 = \dfrac{SSE}{n-2} = \dfrac{146}{24-2} = 6.6364,\ s = \sqrt{s^2} = 2.5761$

For confidence coefficient .95, $\alpha = 1 - .95 = .05$ and $\alpha/2 = .05/2 = .025$. From Table VI, Appendix B, with df $= n - 2 = 24 - 2 = 22$, $t_{.025} = 2.074$. The 95% confidence interval for β_1 is:

$$\hat{\beta}_1 \pm t_{.025}\, s_{\hat{\beta}_1} \quad \text{where} \quad s_{\hat{\beta}_1} = \frac{s}{\sqrt{SS_{xx}}} = \frac{2.5761}{\sqrt{64}} = .3220$$

$$\Rightarrow -8.4 \pm 2.074(.322) \Rightarrow -8.4 \pm .67 \Rightarrow (-9.07,\ -7.73)$$

For confidence coefficient .90, $\alpha = 1 - .90 = .10$ and $\alpha/2 = .10/2 = .05$. From Table VI, Appendix B, with df $= 22$, $t_{.05} = 1.717$.

The 90% confidence interval for β_1 is:

$$\hat{\beta}_1 \pm t_{.05} s_{\hat{\beta}_1} \Rightarrow -8.4 \pm 1.717(.322) \Rightarrow -8.4 \pm .55 \Rightarrow (-8.95, -7.85)$$

10.37   From Exercise 10.36 $= .8214$, $s = 1.1922$, $SS_{xx} = 28$, and $n = 7$.

For confidence coefficient .80, $\alpha = 1 - .80 = .20$ and $\alpha/2 = .20/2 = .10$. From Table VI, Appendix B, with df $= n - 2 = 7 - 2 = 5$, $t_{.10} = 1.476$. The 80% confidence interval for β_1 is:

$$\hat{\beta}_1 \pm t_{.025} s_{\hat{\beta}_1} \text{ where } s_{\hat{\beta}_1} = \frac{s}{\sqrt{SS_{xx}}} = \frac{1.1922}{\sqrt{28}} = .2253$$

$$\Rightarrow .8214 \pm 1.476(.2253) \Rightarrow .8214 \pm .3325 \Rightarrow (.4889, 1.1539)$$

For confidence coefficient .98, $\alpha = 1 - .98 = .02$ and $\alpha/2 = .02/2 = .01$. From Table VI, Appendix B, with df $= 5$, $t_{.01} = 3.365$.

The 98% confidence interval for β_1 is:

$$\hat{\beta}_1 \pm t_{.01} s_{\hat{\beta}_1} \Rightarrow .8214 \pm 3.365(.2253) \Rightarrow .8214 \pm .7581 \Rightarrow (.0633, 1.5795)$$

10.39   a.   To determine if a positive linear relationship exists between the number of carats and the asking price, we test:

H_0: $\beta_1 = 0$
H_a: $\beta_1 > 0$

b.   From the printout, the p-value is $p = 0.000$. However, for a one-tailed test, the p-value is $0.000/2 = 0.000$. Since the p-value is less than $\alpha = .01$, H_0 is rejected. There is sufficient evidence to indicate a positive linear relationship exists between the number of carats and the asking price at $\alpha = .01$.

c.   For confidence coefficient .99, $\alpha = .01$ and $\alpha/2 = .01/2 = .005$. From Table IV, Appendix B, $z_{.005} = 2.58$. The confidence interval is:

$$\hat{\beta}_1 \pm z_{.005} s_{\hat{\beta}_1} \Rightarrow 11,598.9 \pm 2.58(230.1) \Rightarrow 11,598.9 \pm 593.658 \Rightarrow (11,005.242, \ 12,192.558)$$

We are 99% confident that for each additional carat, the mean asking price will increase from between $11,005.24 and $12,192.56

10.41   First, we must compute s^2. From Exercise 10.17, $SS_{xy} = 20.00833333$,

$SS_{xx} = 0.5570833333$, $\sum y = 239$, $\sum y^2 = 10,255$, and $\hat{\beta}_1 = 35.91623038$.

$$SS_{yy} = \sum y^2 - \frac{\left(\sum y\right)^2}{n} = 10,255 - \frac{(239)^2}{6}$$
$$= 10,255 - 9,520.1666667 = 734.8333333$$

$$SSE = SS_{yy} - \hat{\beta}_1 SS_{xy} = 734.83333333 - (35.91623038)(20.008333333) = 16.2094236$$

$$s^2 = MSE = \frac{SSE}{n-2} = \frac{16.2094326}{6-2} = 4.0523559 \text{ and } s = \sqrt{4.0523559} = 2.0130$$

$$s_{\hat{\beta}_1} = \frac{\sqrt{MSE}}{\sqrt{SS_{xx}}} = \frac{\sqrt{4.0523559}}{\sqrt{0.55708333}} = 2.6971$$

For confidence coefficient .90, $\alpha = .10$ and $\alpha/2 = .10/2 = .05$. From Table VI, Appendix B, with df $= n - 2 = 6 - 2 = 4$, $t_{.05} = 2.132$. The 90% confidence interval is:

$$\hat{\beta}_1 \pm t_{.05} s_{\hat{\beta}_1} \Rightarrow 35.916 \pm 2.132(2.6971) \Rightarrow 35.916 \pm 5.7502 \Rightarrow (30.1658, \ 41.6662)$$

We are 90% confident that for each additional unit increase in Surface Area to Volume, the increase in the Drug release rate is between 30.1658 and 41.6662.

10.43   Some preliminary calculations are:

$$\sum x = 301,713 \qquad\qquad \sum y = 811 \qquad\qquad \sum xy = 27,261,248$$

$$\sum x^2 = 10,707,042,109 \qquad\qquad \sum y^2 = 73,235$$

$$\bar{x} = \frac{\sum x}{n} = \frac{301,713}{9} = 33,523.66667 \qquad\qquad \bar{y} = \frac{\sum y}{n} = \frac{811}{9} = 90.1111111$$

$$SS_{xy} = \sum xy - \frac{\left(\sum x\right)\left(\sum y\right)}{n} = 27,261,248 - \frac{301,713(811)}{9}$$
$$= 27,261,248 - 27,187,693.67 = 73,554.33$$

$$SS_{xx} = \sum x^2 - \frac{\left(\sum x\right)^2}{n} = 10,707,042,109 - \frac{(301,713)^2}{9}$$
$$= 10,707,042,109 - 10,114,526,041 = 592,516,068$$

$$SS_{yy} = \sum y^2 - \frac{\left(\sum y\right)^2}{n} = 73,235 - \frac{(811)^2}{9}$$
$$= 73,235 - 73,080.111111 = 154.88889$$

$$\hat{\beta}_1 = \frac{SS_{xy}}{SS_{xx}} = \frac{73,554.33}{592,516,068} = 0.000124138 \approx 0.0001241$$

$$SSE = SS_{yy} - \hat{\beta}_1 SS_{xy} = 154.888889 - (.000124138)(73,554.33) = 145.7580026$$

$$s^2 = MSE = \frac{SSE}{n-2} = \frac{145.7580026}{9-2} = 20.8225718 \quad \text{and} \quad s = \sqrt{20.8225718} = 4.5632$$

$$s_{\hat{\beta}_1} = \frac{\sqrt{MSE}}{\sqrt{SS_{xx}}} = \frac{\sqrt{20.8225718}}{\sqrt{592,516,068}} = 0.0001875$$

To determine if there is a positive linear relationship between the percentage of graduates with job offers and tuition costs, we test:

H_0: $\beta_1 = 0$
H_a: $\beta_1 > 0$

The test statistic is $t = \dfrac{\hat{\beta}_1 - 0}{s_{\hat{\beta}_1}} = \dfrac{.0001243}{.0001875} = .66$

The rejection region requires $\alpha = .10$ in the upper tail of the t-distribution with df = $n - 2 = 9 - 2 = 7$. From Table VI, Appendix B, $t_{.10} = 1.415$. The rejection region is $t > 1.415$.

Since the observed value of the test statistic does not fall in the rejection region ($t = .66 \not> 1.415$), H_0 is not rejected. There is insufficient evidence to indicate a positive linear relationship between the percentage of graduates with job offers and tuition costs at $\alpha = .10$.

10.45   a.   Using MINITAB, the scattergram of the data is:

If the players' rankings remained the same, then the scattergram would be a straight line with a slope of 1. If the claim is true, then the scattergram would reveal points that would lie above this imaginary line. From the plot, there appears to be more points above this line than below it, which would support the claim.

b. $\quad \sum x = 541 \qquad \sum y = 851 \qquad \sum xy = 32{,}145 \qquad \sum x^2 = 25{,}401$

$$\bar{x} - \frac{\sum x}{n} = \frac{541}{22} = 24.59090909 \qquad \bar{y} - \frac{\sum y}{n} = \frac{851}{22} = 38.68181818$$

$$SS_{xy} = \sum xy - \frac{\left(\sum x\right)\left(\sum y\right)}{n} \, 32{,}145 - \frac{541(851)}{22}$$
$$= 32{,}145 - 20{,}926.86364 = 11{,}218.13636$$

$$SS_{xx} = \sum x^2 - \frac{\left(\sum x\right)^2}{n} = 25{,}401 - \frac{541^2}{22}$$
$$= 25{,}401 - 13{,}303.68182 = 12{,}097.31818$$

$$SS_{yy} = \sum y^2 - \frac{\left(\sum y\right)^2}{n} = 77{,}931 - \frac{851^2}{22}$$
$$= 77{,}931 - 32{,}918.22727 = 45{,}012.77273$$

$$\hat{\beta}_1 = \frac{SS_{xy}}{SS_{xx}} = \frac{11{,}218.13636}{12{,}097.31818} = .927324237 \approx .927$$

$$\hat{\beta}_0 = \bar{y} - \hat{\beta}_1 \bar{x} = 38.68181818 - .927324237(24.59090909) = 15.87807217 \approx 15.878$$

The fitted model is: $\hat{y} = 15.878 + .927x$

c. $\quad SSE = SS_{yy} - \hat{\beta}_1 SS_{xy} = 45{,}012.77273 - .927324237(11{,}218.13636)$

$= 45{,}012.77273 - 10{,}402.84974 = 34{,}609.92299$

$$s^2 = \frac{SSE}{n-2} = \frac{34{,}609.92299}{22-2} = 1730.49615 \quad s = \sqrt{s^2} = \sqrt{1{,}730.49615} = 41.5992$$

To determine if the model contributes information for predicting players' rankings on their first anniversary, we test:

$H_0: \beta_1 = 0$
$H_a: \beta_1 \neq 0$

The test statistic is $t = \dfrac{\hat{\beta}_1 - 0}{s_{\hat{\beta}_1}} = \dfrac{.927 - 0}{\dfrac{41.5992}{\sqrt{12,097.31818}}} = 2.451$

The rejection region requires $\alpha/2 = .05/2 = .025$ in each tail of the t-distribution with df $= n - 2 = 22 - 2 = 20$. From Table VI, Appendix B, $t_{.025} = 2.086$. The rejection region is $t < -2.086$ or $t > 2.086$.

Since the observed value of the test statistic falls in the rejection region ($t = 2.451 > 2.086$), H_0 is rejected. There is sufficient evidence to indicate the model contributes information for predicting players' rankings on their first anniversary at $\alpha = .05$.

d. If there were no changes whatsoever in the rankings of the sample players after getting married, the true value of β_0 would be 0 and the true value of β_1 would be 1.

10.47 a. There appears to be a somewhat positive linear relationship.

b. If there was very little snowfall in an area, then the erosion will not be typical. Thus, it seems reasonable to remove these data points.

c. For confidence level .90, $\alpha = .10$ and $\alpha/2 = .10/2 = .05$. From Table VI, Appendix B, with df $= n - 2 = 47 - 2 = 45$, $t_{.05} \approx 1.684$. The confidence interval is:

$$\hat{\beta}_1 \pm t_{.05}\, s_{\hat{\beta}_1} \Rightarrow 1.39 \pm 1.684(.06) \Rightarrow 1.39 \pm .101 \Rightarrow (1.289, 1.491)$$

d. We are 90% confident that the change in the mean McCool winter-adjusted rainfall erosivity index for each one unit change in the once-in-5-year snowmelt runoff amount is between 1.289 and 1.491.

10.49 From Exercise 10.21,

$SS_{xx} = 4,362,209,330 \qquad \hat{\beta}_1 = -.002186456$

$SS_{xy} = -9,537,780$

$\sum y_i = 7497 \qquad\qquad \sum y_i^2 = 4,061,063$

$SS_{yy} = \sum y_i^2 - \dfrac{\left(\sum y_i\right)^2}{n} = 4,061,063 - \dfrac{7497^2}{15} = 314,062.4$

$SSE = SS_{yy} - \hat{\beta}_1\, SS_{xy} = 314,062.4 - (-.002186456)(-9,537,780) = 293,208.4637$

$s^2 = \dfrac{SSE}{n-2} = \dfrac{293,208.4637}{15-2} = 22,554.49721 \qquad s = \sqrt{22,554.49721} = 150.1815$

To determine if extent of retaliation is related to whistle blower's power, we test:

H_0: $\beta_1 = 0$
H_a: $\beta_1 \neq 0$

The test statistic is $t = \dfrac{\hat{\beta}_1 - 0}{s_{\hat{\beta}_1}} = \dfrac{-.0022}{\dfrac{150.1815}{\sqrt{4,362,209,330}}} = -.96$

The rejection region requires $\alpha/2 = .05/2 = .025$ in each tail of the t-distribution with df $= n - 2 = 15 - 2 = 13$. From Table VI, Appendix B, $t_{.025} = 2.160$. The rejection region is $t > 2.160$ or $t < -2.160$.

Since the observed value of the test statistic does not fall in the rejection region ($t = -.96 \nless -2.160$), H_0 is not rejected. There is insufficient evidence to indicate the extent of retaliation is related to the whistle blower's power at $\alpha = .05$. This agrees with Near and Miceli.

10.51   a.   If $r = .7$, there is a positive relationship between x and y. As x increases, y tends to increase. The slope is positive.

b.   If $r = -.7$, there is a negative relationship between x and y. As x increases, y tends to decrease. The slope is negative.

c.   If $r = 0$, there is a 0 slope. There is no relationship between x and y.

d.   If $r^2 = .64$, then r is either .8 or $-.8$. The relationship between x and y could be either positive or negative.

10.53   a.   From Exercises 10.10 and 10.27,
$$r^2 = 1 - \frac{SSE}{SS_{yy}} = 1 - \frac{1.22033896}{21.7142857} = 1 - .0562 = .9438$$

94.38% of the total sample variability around the sample mean response is explained by the linear relationship between y and x.

b.   From Exercises 10.13 and 10.27,
$$r^2 = 1 - \frac{SSE}{SS_{yy}} = 1 - \frac{5.71341466}{28.8571429} = .8020$$

80.20% of the total sample variability around the sample mean response is explained by the linear relationship between y and x.

10.55   a.   The value of r is .70. Since this number is fairly large, there is a moderately strong positive linear relationship between self-knowledge skill level and goal-setting ability.

b.   Since the p-value is so small ($p = .001$), there is evidence to reject H_0. There is sufficient evidence to indicate a significant positive linear relationship between self-knowledge skill level and goal-setting ability for any value of $\alpha > .001$.

c. $r^2 = .70^2 = .49$. 49% of the total sample variability around the sample mean goal-setting ability is explained by the linear relationship between self-knowledge skill level and goal-setting ability.

10.57 Some preliminary calculations are:

$$\sum x = 6{,}167 \qquad \sum x^2 = 1{,}641{,}115 \qquad \sum xy = 34{,}764.5 \qquad \sum y = 135.8$$
$$\sum y^2 = 769.72$$

$$SS_{xy} = \sum xy - \frac{\sum x \sum y}{n} = 34{,}764.5 - \frac{6167(135.8)}{24} = -130.44167$$

$$SS_{xx} = \sum x^2 - \frac{\left(\sum x\right)^2}{n} = 1{,}641{,}115 - \frac{(6{,}167)^2}{24} = 56{,}452.95833$$

$$SS_{yy} = \sum y^2 - \frac{\left(\sum y\right)^2}{n} = 769.72 - \frac{135.8^2}{24} = 1.3183333$$

$$\hat{\beta}_1 = \frac{SS_{xy}}{SS_{xx}} = \frac{-130.44167}{56{,}452.95833} = -0.002310625$$

$$SSE = SS_{yy} - \hat{\beta}_1 SS_{xy} = 1.3183333 - (-0.002310625)(-130.44167) = 1.016931516$$

$$r^2 = \frac{SS_{yy} - SSE}{SS_{yy}} = \frac{1.3183333 - 1.016931516}{1.3183333} = .2286$$

22.86% of the total sample variability around the sample mean sweetness index is explained by the linear relationship between the sweetness index and the amount of water soluble pectin.

$$r = -\sqrt{.2286} = -.478 \quad \text{(The value of r is negative because } \hat{\beta}_1 \text{ is negative.)}$$

Since this value is not close to one, there is a rather weak negative linear relationship between the sweetness index and the amount of water soluble pectin.

10.59   a.   Since $r = .41$, there is a fairly weak positive linear relationship between height and average earnings from 1985-2000 for those whose occupation is in Sales.

b. $r^2 = .41^2 = .1681$. Since $r^2 = .1681$, 16.81% of the total sample variability around the sample mean average earnings from 1985-2000 for those who are in Sales is explained by the linear relationship between average earnings and height.

c.   To determine whether average earnings and height are positively correlated for those in Sales, we test:

$$H_0: \ \rho = 0$$
$$H_a: \ \rho > 0$$

d. $t = \dfrac{r\sqrt{n-2}}{\sqrt{1-r^2}} = \dfrac{.41\sqrt{117-2}}{\sqrt{1-.41^2}} = 4.82$

e. The rejection region requires $\alpha = .01$ in the upper tail of the t-distribution with df $= n - 2 = 117 - 2 = 115$. From Table VI, Appendix B, $t_{.01} \approx 2.358$. The rejection region is $t > 2.358$.

Since the observed value of the test statistic falls in the rejection region ($t = 4.82 > 2.358$), H_0 is rejected. There is sufficient evidence to indicate the average earnings and height for those in Sales are positively correlated at $\alpha = .01$.

f. Suppose we pick managers.

Since $r = .35$, there is a fairly weak positive linear relationship between height and average earnings from 1985-2000 for those whose occupation is Managers.

$r^2 = .35^2 = .1225$. Since $r^2 = .1225$, 12.25% of the total sample variability around the sample mean average earnings from 1985-2000 for Managers is explained by the linear relationship between average earnings and height.

To determine whether average earnings and height are positively correlated for Managers, we test:

H_0: $\rho = 0$
H_a: $\rho > 0$

$t = \dfrac{r\sqrt{n-2}}{\sqrt{1-r^2}} = \dfrac{.35\sqrt{455-2}}{\sqrt{1-.35^2}} = 7.95$

The rejection region requires $\alpha = .01$ in the upper tail of the t-distribution with df $= n - 2 = 455 - 2 = 453$. From Table VI, Appendix B, $t_{.01} \approx 2.326$. The rejection region is $t > 2.326$.

Since the observed value of the test statistic falls in the rejection region ($t = 7.95 > 2.326$), H_0 is rejected. There is sufficient evidence to indicate the average earnings and height for Managers are positively correlated at $\alpha = .01$.

10.61 From Exercise 10.43, $SS_{xy} = 73{,}554.33$, $SS_{xx} = 592{,}516{,}068$, $SS_{yy} = 154.888889$, $\hat{\beta}_1 = 0.000124138 \approx 0.0001241$, $\sum y = 811$ and $\sum x = 301{,}713$

$r = \dfrac{SS_{xy}}{\sqrt{SS_{xx}}\sqrt{SS_{yy}}} = \dfrac{73{,}554.33}{\sqrt{592{,}516{,}068}\sqrt{154.888889}} = .243$

There is a weak positive linear relationship between the percentage of graduates with job offers and the tuition cost.

$r^2 = .243^2 = .059$ Approximately 5.9% of the variability in the percentage of graduates with job offers around the sample mean is explained by the linear relationship between percentage of graduates with job offers and tuition cost.

$$\hat{\beta}_o = \bar{y} - \hat{\beta}_1\bar{x} = \frac{811}{9} - (0.000124138)(\frac{301,713}{9}) = 85.94955018 \approx 85.9496$$

The fitted regression line is: $\hat{y} = 85.9496 + .0001241x$.

10.63 a. The correlation between Australia and the U.S. is .48. There is a moderately weak positive linear relationship between the returns on stocks of Australia and the U.S.

c. These correlation coefficients are measuring the strength of the linear relationship between the returns on stocks of a country and the U.S. The actual relationship could be something other than linear.

10.65 a. From the printout, $r = .570$.

b. Since the coefficient of correlation is close to .5, there is a weak positive linear relationship between the agreement of American managers and Asian managers. Since the coefficient of correlation is not very close to 1, this indicates that there is a trend in views between American managers and Asian managers, but it is not very strong. Thus, the attitudes of these two groups are only somewhat similar.

c. Some preliminary calculations:

$$\sum x = 195 \quad \sum x^2 = 8,425 \quad \sum xy = 14,700 \quad \sum y = 355 \quad \sum y^2 = 26,125$$

$$SS_{xy} = \sum xy - \frac{(\sum x)(\sum y)}{n} = 14,700 - \frac{195(355)}{5} = 855$$

$$SS_{xx} = \sum x^2 - \frac{(\sum x)^2}{n} = 8,425 - \frac{195^2}{5} = 820$$

$$SS_{yy} = \sum y^2 - \frac{(\sum y)^2}{n} = 26,125 - \frac{355^2}{5} = 920$$

$$r = \frac{SS_{xy}}{\sqrt{SS_{xx}SS_{yy}}} = \frac{855}{\sqrt{820(920)}} = .9844$$

The coefficient of correlation is .9844. There is a very strong positive linear relationship between views of American and Asian managers. Even though the coefficient of correlation is close to one, the values of the Asian managers are approximately 30 points higher in each case than the values of the American managers.

10.67   **a, b.** The scattergram is:

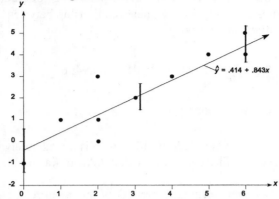

c. $SSE = SS_{yy} - \hat{\beta}_1 SS_{xy} = 33.6 - .84318766(32.8) = 5.94344473$

$$s^2 = \frac{SSE}{n-2} = \frac{5.94344473}{10-2} = .742930591 \qquad s = \sqrt{.742930591} = .8619$$

$$\bar{x} = \frac{31}{10} = 3.1$$

The form of the confidence interval is $\hat{y} \pm t_{\alpha/2} s \sqrt{\dfrac{1}{n} + \dfrac{\left(x_p - \bar{x}\right)^2}{SS_{xx}}}$

For $x_p = 6$, $\hat{y} = -.414 + .843(6) = 4.644$

For confidence coefficient .95, $\alpha = .05$ and $\alpha/2 = .025$. From Table VI, Appendix B, with df $= n - 2 = 10 - 2 = 8$, $t_{.025} = 2.306$. The confidence interval is:

$$4.644 \pm 2.306(.8619)\sqrt{\frac{1}{10} + \frac{(6-3.1)^2}{38.9}} \Rightarrow 4.644 \pm 1.118 \Rightarrow (3.526, 5.762)$$

d.   For $x_p = 3.2$, $\hat{y} = -.414 + .843(3.2) = 2.284$

The confidence interval is:

$$2.284 \pm 2.306(.8619)\sqrt{\frac{1}{10} + \frac{(3.2-3.1)^2}{38.9}} \Rightarrow 2.284 \pm .629 \Rightarrow (1.655, 2.913)$$

For $x_p = 0$, $\hat{y} = -.414 + .843(0) = -.414$

The confidence interval is:

$$-.414 \pm 2.306(.8619)\sqrt{\frac{1}{10} + \frac{(0-3.1)^2}{38.9}} \Rightarrow -.414 \pm 1.717 \Rightarrow (-1.585, .757)$$

e.   The width of the confidence interval for the mean value of y depends on the distance x_p is from $\bar{x}$. The width of the interval for $x_p = 3.2$ is the smallest because 3.2 is the closest to $\bar{x} = 3.1$. The width of the interval for $x_p = 0$ is the widest because 0 is the farthest from $\bar{x} = 3.1$.

10.69　a.　$\hat{\beta}_1 = \dfrac{SS_{xy}}{SS_{xx}} = \dfrac{28}{32} = .875$

$\hat{\beta}_0 - \bar{y} - \hat{\beta}_1 \bar{x} = 4 - .875(3) = 1.375$

The least squares line is $\hat{y} = 1.375 + .875x$.

b.　The least squares line is:

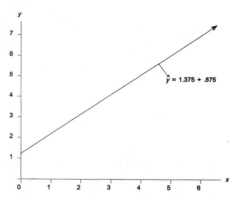

c.　$SSE = SS_{yy} - \hat{\beta}_1 SS_{xy} = 26 - .875(28) = 1.5$

d.　$s^2 = \dfrac{SSE}{n-2} = \dfrac{1.5}{10-2} = .1875$

e.　$s = \sqrt{.1875} = .4330$

The form of the confidence interval is $\hat{y} \pm t_{\alpha/2}\, s\sqrt{\dfrac{1}{n} + \dfrac{\left(x_p - \bar{x}\right)^2}{SS_{xx}}}$

For $x_p = 2.5$, $\hat{y} = 1.375 + .875(2.5) = 3.5625$

For confidence coefficient .95, $\alpha = .05$ and $\alpha/2 = .025$. From Table VI, Appendix B, with df $= n - 2 = 10 - 2 = 8$, $t_{.025} = 2.306$. The confidence interval is:

$$3.5625 \pm 2.306(.4330)\sqrt{\dfrac{1}{10} + \dfrac{(2.5-3)^2}{32}} \Rightarrow 3.5625 \pm .3279 \Rightarrow (3.2346, 3.8904)$$

f.　The form of the prediction interval is $\hat{y} \pm t_{\alpha/2}\, s\sqrt{1 + \dfrac{1}{n} + \dfrac{\left(x_p - \bar{x}\right)^2}{SS_{xx}}}$

For $x_p = 4$, $\hat{y} = 1.375 + .875(4) = 4.875$

For confidence coefficient .95, $\alpha = .05$ and $\alpha/2 = .025$. From Table VI, Appendix B, with df $= n - 2 = 10 - 2 = 8$, $t_{.025} = 2.306$. The prediction interval is:

$$3.875 \pm 2.306(.4330)\sqrt{1 + \dfrac{1}{10} + \dfrac{(4-3)^2}{32}} \Rightarrow 3.875 \pm 1.062 \Rightarrow (2.813, 4.937)$$

10.71   From the printout, the 90% prediction interval is (19.9715, 30.3636). We are 90% confident that the actual value of the drug release rate is between 19.9715 and 30.3636 when the surface area to volume ratio is .50.

10.73   a.   Using MINITAB, the prediction interval for the actual value and confidence interval for the mean are:

```
Predicted Values for New Observations

New
Obs    Fit   SE Fit      99% CI          99% PI
 1    3.510   0.196   (2.955, 4.066)   (1.020, 6.000)

Values of Predictors for New Observations

New
Obs   Time
 1    15.0
```

The 99% confidence interval for the mean mass of all spills with an elapsed time of 15 minutes is (2.955, 4.066). We are 99% confident that the mean mass of the spill will be between 2.995 and 4.066 when the elapsed time is 15 minutes.

   b.   The 99% prediction interval for the actual mass of a spill with an elapsed time of 15 minutes is (1.020, 6.000). We are 99% confident that the actual mass of the spill will be between 1.020 and 6.000 when the elapsed time is 15 minutes.

   c.   The prediction interval for the actual value is larger than the confidence interval for the mean. This will always be true. The prediction interval for the actual value contains 2 errors. First, we must locate the true mean of the distribution. Once this mean is located, the actual values of the variables can still vary around this mean. There is variance in locating the mean and then variance of the actual observations around the mean.

10.75   a.   Using MINITAB, the results of the regression analysis are:

Regression Analysis: QuitRate versus AvgWage

```
The regression equation is
QuitRate = 4.86 - 0.347 AvgWage

Predictor        Coef     SE Coef         T         P
Constant       4.8615      0.5201      9.35     0.000
AvgWage       -0.34655     0.05866    -5.91     0.000

S = 0.4862      R-Sq = 72.9%      R-Sq(adj) = 70.8%

Analysis of Variance

Source            DF          SS         MS         F         P
Regression         1      8.2507     8.2507     34.90     0.000
Residual Error    13      3.0733     0.2364
Total             14     11.3240
```

To determine if the average hourly wage rate contributes information to predict quit rates, we test:

H_0: $\beta_1 = 0$
H_a: $\beta_1 \neq 0$

The test statistic is $t = \dfrac{\hat{\beta}_1 - 0}{s_{\hat{\beta}_1}} = -5.91$ (from printout).

The rejection region requires $\alpha/2 = .05/2 = .025$ in each tail of the t-distribution with df $= n - 2 = 15 - 2 = 13$. From Table VI, Appendix B, $t_{.025} = 2.160$. The rejection region is $t < -2.160$ or $t > 2.160$.

Since the observed value of the test statistic falls in the rejection region ($t = -5.91 < -2.160$), H_0 is rejected. There is sufficient evidence to indicate that the average hourly wage rate contributes information to predict quit ratio at $\alpha = .05$.

Since the slope is negative ($\hat{\beta}_1 = -.3466$), the model suggests that x and y have a negative relationship. As the average hourly wage rate increases, the quit rate tends to decrease.

b.   Some preliminary calculations are:

$$\sum x = 129.05 \qquad \sum x^2 = 1{,}179 \qquad \bar{x} = \frac{\sum x}{n} = \frac{129.05}{15} = 8.6033$$

$$\hat{y} = 4.8615 - 0.34655(9) = 1.743$$

$$SS_{xx} = \sum x^2 - \frac{\left(\sum x\right)^2}{n} = 1{,}179 - \frac{(129.05)^2}{15} = 68.739833$$

For confidence level .95, $\alpha = .05$ and $\alpha/2 = .05/2 = .025$. From Table VI, Appendix B, with df $= n - 2 = 15 - 2 = 13$, $t_{.025} = 2.160$. The 95% prediction interval is:

$$\hat{y} \pm t_{\alpha/2} s \sqrt{1 + \frac{1}{n} + \frac{\left(x_p - \bar{x}\right)^2}{SS_{xx}}} \Rightarrow 1.743 \pm 2.160(.4862)\sqrt{1 + \frac{1}{15} + \frac{(9 - 8.6033)^2}{68.739833}}$$

$$\Rightarrow 1.743 \pm 1.086 \Rightarrow (0.657, \quad 2.829)$$

We are 95% confident that the actual quit rate when the average hourly wage is \$9.00 is between 0.657 and 2.829.

c.   The 95% confidence interval is:

$$\hat{y} \pm t_{\alpha/2} s \sqrt{\frac{1}{n} + \frac{\left(x_p - \bar{x}\right)^2}{SS_{xx}}} \Rightarrow 1.743 \pm 2.160(.4862)\sqrt{\frac{1}{15} + \frac{(9 - 8.6033)^2}{68.739833}}$$

$$\Rightarrow 1.743 \pm 0.276 \Rightarrow (1.467, \quad 2.019)$$

We are 95% confident that the mean quit rate when the average hourly wage is \$9.00 is between 1.467 and 2.019.

10.77   a. $\hat{\beta}_1 = \dfrac{SS_{xy}}{SS_{xx}} = \dfrac{-88}{55} = -1.6, \ \hat{\beta}_0 = \bar{y} - \hat{\beta}_1 \bar{x} = 35 - (-1.6)(1.3) = 37.08$

The least squares line is $\hat{y} = 37.08 - 1.6x$.

b.

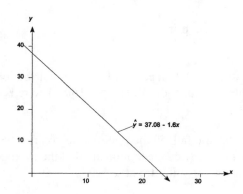

c. $SSE = SS_{yy} - \hat{\beta}_1 \, SS_{xy} = 198 - (-1.6)(-88) = 57.2$

d. $s^2 = \dfrac{SSE}{n-2} = \dfrac{57.2}{15-2} = 4.4$

e.   For confidence coefficient .90, $\alpha = 1 - .90 = .10$ and $\alpha/2 = .10/2 = .05$. From Table VI, Appendix B, with df $= n - 2 = 15 - 2 = 13$, $t_{.05} = 1.771$. The 90% confidence interval for β_1 is:

$$\hat{y} \pm t_{\alpha/2} \dfrac{s}{\sqrt{SS_{xx}}} \Rightarrow -1.6 \pm 1.771 \dfrac{\sqrt{4.4}}{\sqrt{55}} \Rightarrow -1.6 \pm .501 \Rightarrow (-2.101, -1.099)$$

We are 90% confident the change in the mean value of y for each unit change in x is between -2.101 and -1.099.

f.   For $x_p = 15$, $\hat{y} = 37.08 - 1.6(15) = 13.08$

The 90% confidence interval is:

$$\hat{y} \pm t_{\alpha/2} \, s \sqrt{\dfrac{1}{n} + \dfrac{(x_p - \bar{x})^2}{SS_{xx}}} \Rightarrow 13.08 \pm 1.771 \left(\sqrt{4.4}\right) \sqrt{\dfrac{1}{15} + \dfrac{(15 - 1.3)^2}{55}}$$

$$\Rightarrow 13.08 \pm 6.929 \Rightarrow (6.151, 20.009)$$

g.   The 90% prediction interval is:

$$\hat{y} \pm t_{\alpha/2} \, s \sqrt{\dfrac{1}{n} + \dfrac{(x_p - \bar{x})^2}{SS_{xx}}} \Rightarrow 13.08 \pm 1.771 \left(\sqrt{4.4}\right) \sqrt{\dfrac{1}{15} + \dfrac{(15 - 1.3)^2}{55}}$$

$$\Rightarrow 13.08 \pm 7.862 \Rightarrow (5.218, 20.942)$$

10.79 a.

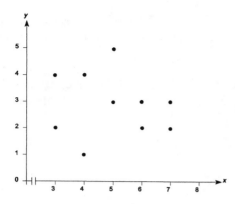

b. Some preliminary calculations are:

$$\sum x = 50 \qquad \sum x^2 = 270 \qquad \sum xy = 143$$

$$\sum y = 29 \qquad \sum y^2 = 97$$

$$SS_{xy} = \sum xy - \frac{\sum x \sum y}{n} = 143 - \frac{50(29)}{10} = -2$$

$$SS_{xx} = \sum x^2 - \frac{\left(\sum x\right)^2}{n} = 270 - \frac{50^2}{10} = 20$$

$$SS_{yy} = \sum y^2 - \frac{\left(\sum y\right)^2}{n} = 97 - \frac{29^2}{10} = 12.9$$

$$r = \frac{SS_{xy}}{\sqrt{SS_{xx}SS_{yy}}} = \frac{-2}{\sqrt{20(12.9)}} = -.1245$$

$$r^2 = (-.1245)^2 = .0155$$

c. Some preliminary calculations are:

$$\hat{\beta}_1 = \frac{SS_{xy}}{SS_{xx}} = \frac{-2}{20} = -.1$$

$$SSE = SS_{yy} - \hat{\beta}_1 SS_{xy} = 12.9 - (-.1)(-2) = 12.7$$

$$s^2 = \frac{SSE}{n-2} = \frac{12.7}{10-2} = 1.5875 \quad s = \sqrt{1.5875} = 1.25996$$

To determine if x and y are linearly correlated, we test:

H_0: $\beta_1 = 0$
H_a: $\beta_1 \neq 0$

The test statistic is $t = \dfrac{\hat{\beta}_1 - 0}{\dfrac{s}{\sqrt{SS_{xx}}}} = \dfrac{-.1 - 0}{\dfrac{1.25996}{\sqrt{20}}} = -.35$

The rejection requires $\alpha/2 = .10/2 = .05$ in the each tail of the t-distribution with df $= n - 2 = 10 - 2 = 8$. From Table VI, Appendix B, $t_{.05} = 1.86$. The rejection region is $t > 1.86$ or $t < -1.86$.

Since the observed value of the test statistic does not fall in the rejection region ($t = -.35$ $\nless -1.86$), H_0 is not rejected. There is insufficient evidence to indicate that x and y are linearly correlated at $\alpha = .10$.

10.81   a.   Using MINITAB, the plot of the data is:

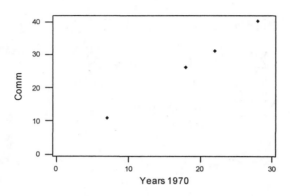

Yes, there is a trend. As the number of years since 1970 increases, the total commercials increase.

   b.   Some preliminary calculations are:

$$\sum x = 75 \qquad \sum x^2 = 1,641 \qquad \sum xy = 2,347 \qquad \sum y = 108 \qquad \sum y^2 = 3,358$$

$$SS_{xy} = \sum xy - \frac{\sum x \sum y}{n} = 2,347 - \frac{75(108)}{4} = 322$$

$$SS_{xx} = \sum x^2 - \frac{\left(\sum x\right)^2}{n} = 1,641 - \frac{75^2}{4} = 234.75$$

$$SS_{yy} = \sum y^2 - \frac{\left(\sum y\right)^2}{n} = 3,358 - \frac{108^2}{4} = 442$$

$$\hat{\beta}_1 = \frac{SS_{xy}}{SS_{xx}} = \frac{322}{234.75} = 1.371671991 \approx 1.372$$

$$\hat{\beta}_0 = \bar{y} - \hat{\beta}_1 \bar{x} = \frac{108}{4} - 1.371671991 \frac{75}{4} = 1.281150175 \approx 1.281$$

The least squares prediction equation is: $\hat{y} = 1.281 + 1.372x$

c.   For each additional year since 1970, the mean rate of total commercials per hour increases by an estimated 1.372.

d.   Since 0 is not in the observed range of values for years since 1970, the y-intercept has no meaning.

e.   Using MINITAB, the plot of the data is:

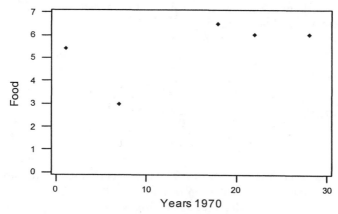

Yes, there is a trend. As the number of years since 1970 increases, the food ads per hour tend to increase.

Some preliminary calculations are:

$$\sum x = 76 \qquad \sum x^2 = 1,642 \qquad \sum xy = 443.4 \qquad \sum y = 26.9 \qquad \sum y^2 = 152.41$$

$$SS_{xy} = \sum xy - \frac{\sum x \sum y}{n} = 443.4 - \frac{76(26.9)}{5} = 34.52$$

$$SS_{xx} = \sum x^2 - \frac{\left(\sum x\right)^2}{n} = 1,642 - \frac{76^2}{5} = 486.8$$

$$SS_{yy} = \sum y^2 - \frac{\left(\sum y\right)^2}{n} = 152.41 - \frac{26.9^2}{5} = 7.688$$

$$\hat{\beta}_1 = \frac{SS_{xy}}{SS_{xx}} = \frac{34.52}{486.8} = 0.070912078 \approx 0.0709$$

$$\hat{\beta}_0 = \bar{y} - \hat{\beta}_1 \bar{x} = \frac{26.9}{5} - 0.070912078 \frac{76}{5} = 4.302136402 \approx 4.302$$

The least squares prediction equation is: $\hat{y} = 4.302 + 0.0709x$

For each additional year since 1970, the mean rate of food ads per hour increases by an estimated 0.0709.

Since 0 is not in the observed range of values for years since 1970, the y-intercept has no meaning.

f. From part **b** above, $SS_{xx} = 234.75$, $SS_{xy} = 322$, $SS_{yy} = 442$, and $\hat{\beta}_1 = 1.371671991$.

$$SSE = SS_{yy} - \hat{\beta}_1 SS_{xy} = 442 - (1.371671991)(322) = 0.3216189$$

$$s^2 = MSE = \frac{SSE}{n-2} = \frac{0.3216189}{4-2} = 0.16080945 \text{ and } s = \sqrt{0.16080945} = 0.4010$$

To determine if there is a linear relationship between years since 1970 and the rate of total commercials per hour, we test:

H_0: $\beta_1 = 0$
H_a: $\beta_1 \neq 0$

The test statistics is $t = \dfrac{\hat{\beta}_1 - 0}{s_{\hat{\beta}_1}} = \dfrac{1.372 - 0}{\dfrac{.4010}{\sqrt{234.75}}} = 52.43$

Since no α was given, we will use $\alpha = .05$. The rejection region requires $\alpha/2 = .05/2 = .025$ in each tail of the t-distribution with df $= n - 2 = 4 - 2 = 2$. From Table VI, Appendix B, $t_{.025} = 4.303$. The rejection region is $t > 4.303$ or $t < -4.303$. Since the observed value of the test statistic falls in the rejection region ($t = 52.43 > 4.303$), H_0 is rejected. There is sufficient evidence to indicate a significant linear relationship between years since 1970 and the rate of total commercials per hour at $\alpha = .05$.

A 95% confidence interval for β is

$$\hat{\beta}_1 \pm t_{.025} s_{\hat{\beta}_1} \Rightarrow 1.372 \pm 4.303 \frac{.4010}{\sqrt{234.75}} \Rightarrow 1.372 \pm .113 \Rightarrow (1.259, \ 1.485)$$

Since 1.4 is in this interval, it is a likely candidate for the true value of β. Thus, we agree with the statement that "the hourly rate for total commercials is increasing significantly by 1.4 commercials per hour each year.

g. From part **e** above, $SS_{xx} = 486.8$, $SS_{xy} = 34.52$, $SS_{yy} = 7.688$, and $\hat{\beta}_1 = 0.070912078$.

$$SSE = SS_{yy} - \hat{\beta}_1 SS_{xy} = 7.688 - (0.070912078)(34.52) = 5.240115067$$

$$s^2 = MSE = \frac{SSE}{n-2} = \frac{5.240115067}{5-2} = 1.746705022 \text{ and } s = \sqrt{1.746705022} = 1.322$$

To determine if there is a linear relationship between years since 1970 and the rate of food advertisements per hour, we test:

H_0: $\beta_1 = 0$
H_a: $\beta_1 \neq 0$

The test statistics is $t = \dfrac{\hat{\beta}_1 - 0}{s_{\hat{\beta}_1}} = \dfrac{0.0709 - 0}{\dfrac{1.322}{\sqrt{486.8}}} = 1.18$

Since no α was given, we will use $\alpha = .05$. The rejection region requires $\alpha/2 = .05/2 = .025$ in each tail of the t-distribution with df $= n - 2 = 5 - 2 = 3$. From Table VI, Appendix B, $t_{.025} = 3.182$. The rejection region is $t > 3.182$ or $t < -3.182$.

Since the observed value of the test statistic does not fall in the rejection region ($t = 1.18 \not> 3.182$), H_0 is not rejected. There is insufficient evidence to indicate a significant linear relationship between years since 1970 and the rate of food commercials per hour at $\alpha = .05$.

Thus, we do agree with the statement that "the hourly rate for food commercials is not changing over time in a statistically significant fashion."

h. $\bar{x} = \dfrac{\sum x}{n} = \dfrac{75}{4} = 18.75$ For year 2005, the years since 1970 is $x = 35$.

$\hat{y} = 1.281 + 1.372(35) = 49.301$

For confidence level .95, $\alpha = .05$ and $\alpha/2 = .05/2 = .025$. From Table VI, Appendix B, with df $= n - 2 = 4 - 2 = 2$, $t_{.025} = 4.303$. The 95% prediction interval is:

$$\hat{y} \pm t_{\alpha/2} s \sqrt{1 + \dfrac{1}{n} + \dfrac{(x_p - \bar{x})^2}{SS_{xx}}} \Rightarrow 49.301 \pm 4.303(.4010) \sqrt{1 + \dfrac{1}{4} + \dfrac{(35 - 18.75)^2}{234.75}}$$

$$\Rightarrow 49.301 \pm 2.659 \Rightarrow (46.642, \quad 51.960)$$

i. We are 95% confident that the actual rate of total number of prime-time TV commercials per hour in 2005 will be between 46.642 and 51.960.

j. The inference in part i may not be valid because we are predicting a value of y for a value of x outside the observed range. We cannot be sure that the relationship between x and y will remain the same outside the observed range.

10.83   a.   To determine if x and y are linearly related, we test:

H_0: $\beta_1 = 0$
H_a: $\beta_1 \neq 0$

The test statistic is $t = 4.98$.

The p-value is .001. Since the p-value is less than $\alpha = .01$, H_0 is rejected at $\alpha = .01$. There is sufficient evidence to indicate that x and y are linearly related.

   b.   Since the model is adequate, it is reasonable to use it to predict values of y.

For $x = 3$, $\hat{y} = .202 + .135x = .202 + .135(3) = .607$. This value is meaningful only if $x = 3$ is within the observed range.

   c. $r = .679$. Because this value is near .5, there is a moderate positive linear relationship between the fraction of documents retrieved using Medline and the number of terms in the search query.

   d. $r^2 = .679^2 = .461$. 46.1% of the total sample variability around the sample mean fraction of documents retrieved using Medline is explained by the linear relationship between the fraction of documents retrieved using Medline and the number of terms in the search query.

10.85   a.   Using MINITAB, the regression analysis is:

Regression Analysis: Index versus Interactions

```
The regression equation is
Index = 44.1 + 0.237 Interactions

Predictor        Coef      SE Coef           T          P
Constant       44.130        9.362        4.71      0.000
Interact       0.2366        0.1865        1.27      0.222

S = 19.40        R-Sq = 8.6%       R-Sq(adj) = 3.3%

Analysis of Variance

Source          DF           SS           MS          F          P
Regression       1        606.0        606.0       1.61      0.222
Residual Error  17       6400.6        376.5
Total           18       7006.6
```

For confidence coefficient .90, $\alpha = 1 - .90 = .10$ and $\alpha/2 = .10/2 = .05$. From Table VI, Appendix B, $t_{.05} = 1.740$ with df $= n - 2 = 19 - 2 = 17$.

The prediction interval is:

$$\hat{y} \pm t_{\alpha/2}\, s \sqrt{1 + \frac{1}{n} + \frac{(x_p - \bar{x})^2}{SS_{xx}}} \quad \text{where } \hat{y} = 44.13 + .2366(55) = 57.143$$

$$\Rightarrow 57.143 \pm 1.74(19.40)\sqrt{1 + \frac{1}{19} + \frac{(55 - 44.1579)^2}{10,824.5263}} \Rightarrow 57.143 \pm 34.818$$

$$\Rightarrow (22.325, 91.961)$$

b. The number of interactions with outsiders in the study went from 10 to 82. The value 110 is not within this interval. We do not know if the relationship between x and y is the same outside the observed range. Also, the farther x_p lies from the larger will be the error of prediction. The prediction interval for a particular value of y will be very wide when $x_p = 110$.

c. The prediction interval for a manager's success index will be narrowest when the number of contacts with people outside her work unit is $\bar{x} = 44.1579$ (44).

10.87 Using MINITAB, the regression analysis is:

Regression Analysis: Value versus Age

```
The regression equation is
Value = - 92.5 + 8.35 Age

Predictor        Coef      SE Coef          T          P
Constant       -92.46        79.29      -1.17      0.249
Age             8.347         2.570       3.25      0.002

S = 286.5       R-Sq = 18.0%      R-Sq(adj) = 16.3%

Analysis of Variance

Source            DF           SS          MS          F          P
Regression         1       865746      865746      10.55      0.002
Residual Error    48      3939797       82079
Total             49      4805542
```

The fitted regression line is: $\hat{y} = -92.46 + 8.347x$

A scattergram of the data is:

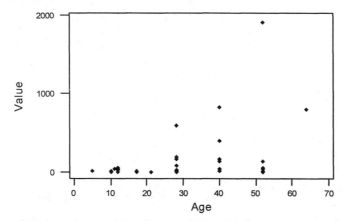

It appears that there is a positive linear relationship between age and market value, but it does not appear to be very strong.

To determine if age and market value are linearly related, we test:

H_0: $\beta_1 = 0$
H_0: $\beta_1 \neq 0$

From the printout, the test statistic is $t = 3.25$.

The p-value is $p = .002$. Since the p-value is so small, we will reject H_0. There is sufficient evidence to indicate a linear relationship between age and market value at $\alpha > .002$.

$r^2 = .18$. 18% of the total sample variability around the sample mean market value is explained by the linear relationship between market value and age.

10.89 a.

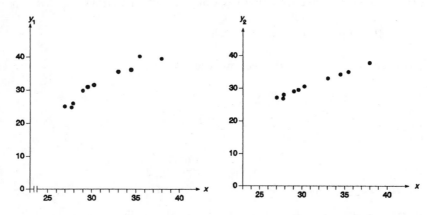

b. It appears that the weigh-in-motion reading after calibration adjustment is more highly correlated with the static weight of trucks than prior to calibration adjustment. The scattergram is closer to a straight line.

c. Some preliminary calculations are:

$$\sum x = 312.8 \qquad \sum y = 9911.42 \qquad \sum xy_1 = 10,201.41$$

$$\sum y_1 = 320.2 \qquad \sum y_1^2 = 10,543.68 \qquad n = 10$$

$$\sum y_2 = 311.2 \qquad \sum y_2^2 = 9809.52 \qquad \sum xy_2 = 9859.84$$

$$SS_{xy_1} = \sum xy_1 - \frac{\sum x \sum y_1}{n} = 10,201.41 - \frac{312.8(320.2)}{10} = 185.554$$

$$SS_{xx} = \sum x^2 - \frac{\left(\sum x\right)^2}{n} = 9911.42 - \frac{312.8^2}{10} = 127.036$$

$$SS_{y_1 y_1} = \sum y_1^2 - \frac{\left(\sum y_1\right)^2}{n} = 10,543.68 - \frac{320.2^2}{10} = 290.876$$

$$SS_{xy_2} = \sum xy_2 - \frac{\sum x \sum y_2}{n} = 9859.84 - \frac{312.8(311.2)}{10} = 125.504$$

$$SS_{y_2 y_2} = \sum y_2^2 - \frac{\left(\sum y_2\right)^2}{n} = 9809.52 - \frac{311.2^2}{10} = 124.976$$

$$r_1 = \frac{SS_{xy_1}}{\sqrt{SS_{xx} SS_{y_1 y_1}}} = \frac{185.554}{\sqrt{127.036(290.876)}} = .9653$$

$$r_2 = \frac{SS_{xy_2}}{\sqrt{SS_{xx} SS_{y_2 y_2}}} = \frac{125.504}{\sqrt{127.036(124.976)}} = .9960$$

$r_1 = .9563$ implies the static weight of trucks and weigh-in-motion prior to calibration adjustment have a strong positive linear relationship.

$r_2 = .996$ implies the static weight of trucks and weigh-in-motion after calibration adjustment have a stronger positive linear relationship.

The closer r is to 1 indicates the more accurate the weigh-in-motion readings are.

d. Yes. If the weigh-in-motion readings were all exactly the same distance below (or above) the actual readings, r would be 1.

10.91 a. Using MINITAB, the results of fitting the regression line are:

Regression Analysis: Offices versus Lawyers

```
The regression equation is
Offices = 2.78 + 0.0170 Lawyers


Predictor       Coef    SE Coef        T       P
Constant      2.7803     0.7522     3.70   0.001
Lawyers     0.016958   0.004219     4.02   0.001


S = 2.24627    R-Sq = 40.2%    R-Sq(adj) = 37.7%


Analysis of Variance

Source            DF        SS        MS        F       P
Regression         1    81.518    81.518    16.16   0.001
Residual Error    24   121.097     5.046
Total             25   202.615


Unusual Observations

Obs   Lawyers   Offices      Fit   SE Fit   Residual   St Resid
  1       529    11.000   11.751    1.681     -0.751     -0.50 X
 14       100    12.000    4.476    0.479      7.524      3.43R

R denotes an observation with a large standardized residual.
X denotes an observation whose X value gives it large influence.
```

The least squares regression lie is: $\hat{y} = 2.7803 + 0.01696x$.

b. To determine if there is a significant linear relationship between the number of law offices and the number of lawyers, we test:

H_0: $\beta = 0$
H_a: $\beta \neq 0$

From the printout, the test statistic is $t = 4.02$ and the p-value is $p = 0.001$. Since the p-value is very small, we would reject H_0 for any reasonable value of α. There is sufficient evidence to indicate that there is a linear relationship between the number of law offices and the number of lawyers at any value of $\alpha > 0.001$.

From the printout, the value of r^2 is R-Sq = 40.2%. Thus, 40.2% of the total sample variability around the sample mean number of law offices is explained by the linear relationship between the number of law offices and the number of lawyers. Thus, there is a significant linear relationship between the number of law offices and the number of lawyers, but less than half of the variability is being explained by the model. This model may not be real good for predicting the number of law offices based on the number of lawyers.

c. For $x = 300$, $\hat{y} = 2.7803 + 0.01696(300) = 7.8683$. Thus, if a firm has 300 lawyers, they build 8 law offices.

10.93 Using MINITAB, the two regression analyses are:

Regression Analysis

The regression equation is
Ind.Costs = 301 + 10.3 Mach-Hours

Predictor	Coef	StDev	T	P
Constant	301.0	229.8	1.31	0.219
Mach-Hou	10.312	3.124	3.30	0.008

S = 170.5   R-Sq = 52.1%   R-Sq(adj) = 47.4%

Analysis of Variance

Source	DF	SS	MS	F	P
Regression	1	316874	316874	10.90	0.008
Residual Error	10	290824	29082		
Total	11	607698			

Regression Analysis

The regression equation is
Ind.Costs = 745 + 7.72 Direct-Hours

Predictor	Coef	StDev	T	P
Constant	744.7	217.6	3.42	0.007
Direct-H	7.716	5.396	1.43	0.183

S = 224.6   R-Sq = 17.0%   R-Sq(adj) = 8.7%

Analysis of Variance

Source	DF	SS	MS	F	P
Regression	1	103187	103187	2.05	0.183
Residual Error	10	504511	50451		
Total	11	607698			

Unusual Observations

Obs	Direct-H	Ind.Cost	Fit	StDev Fit	Residual	St Resid
9	70.0	1316.0	1284.8	181.9	31.2	0.24 X

X denotes an observation whose X value gives it large influence.

From these two cost functions, the model containing Machine-Hours should be used to predict Indirect Manufacturing Labor Costs. There is a significant linear relationship between Indirect Manufacturing Labor Costs and Machine-Hours $(t = 3.30, p = 0.008)$. There is not a significant linear relationship between Indirect Manufacturing Labor Costs and Direct Manufacturing Labor-Hours $(t = 1.43, p = 0.183)$. The r^2 for the first model is .521 while the r^2 for the second model is .170. In addition, the standard deviation for the first model is 170.5 while the standard deviation for the second model is 224.6. All of these lead to the better model as the model containing Machine-Hours as the independent variable.

Multiple Regression and Model Building

Chapter 11

11.1   a. $E(y) = \beta_0 + \beta_1 x_1 + \beta_2 x_2$

b. $E(y) = \beta_0 + \beta_1 x_1 + \beta_2 x_2 + \beta_3 x_3 + \beta_4 x_4$

c. $E(y) = \beta_0 + \beta_1 x_1 + \beta_2 x_2 + \beta_3 x_3 + \beta_4 x_4 + \beta_5 x_5$

11.3   a.   We are given $\hat{\beta}_2 = 2.7$, $s_{\hat{\beta}_1} = 1.86$, and $n = 30$.

$$H_0: \ \beta_2 = 0$$
$$H_a: \ \beta_2 \neq 0$$

The test statistic is $t = \dfrac{\hat{\beta}_2 - 0}{s_{\hat{\beta}_2}} = \dfrac{2.7}{1.86} = 1.45$

The rejection region requires $\alpha/2 = .05/2 = .025$ in each tail of the t distribution with df $= n - (k + 1) = 30 - (3 + 1) = 26$. From Table VI, Appendix B, $t_{.025} = 2.056$. The rejection region is $t < -2.056$ or $t > 2.056$.

Since the observed value of the test statistic does not fall in the rejection region ($t = 1.45 \not> 2.056$), H_0 is not rejected. There is insufficient evidence to indicate $\beta_2 \neq 0$ at $\alpha = .05$.

b.   We are given $\beta_3 = .93$, $s_{\hat{\beta}_3} = .29$, and $n = 30$.

Test $H_0: \ \beta_3 = 0$
          $H_a: \ \beta_3 \neq 0$

The test statistic is $t = \dfrac{\hat{\beta}_3 - 0}{s_{\hat{\beta}_3}} = \dfrac{.93}{.29} = 3.21$

The rejection region is the same as part **a**, $t < -2.056$ or $t > 2.056$.

Since the observed value of the test statistic falls in the rejection region ($t = 3.21 > 2.056$), H_0 is rejected. There is sufficient evidence to indicate $\beta_3 \neq 0$ at $\alpha = .05$.

c. $\hat{\beta}_3$ has a smaller estimated standard error than $\hat{\beta}_2$. Therefore, the test statistic is larger for $\hat{\beta}_3$ even though $\hat{\beta}_3$ is smaller than $\hat{\beta}_2$.

11.5 The number of degrees of freedom available for estimating σ^2 is $n - (k + 1)$ where k is the number of independent variables in the regression model. Each additional independent variable placed in the model causes a corresponding decrease in the degrees of freedom.

11.7 a. Yes. Since $R^2 = .92$ is close to 1, this indicates the model provides a good fit. Without knowledge of the units of the dependent variable, the value of SSE cannot be used to determine how well the model fits.

b. H_0: $\beta_1 = \beta_2 = \cdots = \beta_5 = 0$
H_a: At least one of the parameters is not 0

The test statistic is $F = \dfrac{R^2 / k}{(1 - R^2)/[n - (k + 1)]} = \dfrac{.92/5}{(1 - .92)/[30 - (5 + 1)]} = 55.2$

The rejection region requires $\alpha = .05$ in the upper tail of the F distribution with $v_1 = k = 5$ and $v_2 = n - (k + 1) = 30 - (5 + 1) = 24$. From Table IX, Appendix B, $F_{.05} = 2.62$. The rejection region is $F > 2.62$.

Since the observed value of the test statistic falls in the rejection region ($F = 55.2 > 2.62$), H_0 is rejected. There is sufficient evidence to indicate the model is useful in predicting y at $\alpha = .05$.

11.9 a. The least squares prediction equation is: $\hat{y} = 1.81231 + 0.10875x_1 + 0.00017x_2$

b. $\hat{\beta}_o = 1.81231$. Since $x_1 = 0$ and $x_2 = 0$ are not in the observed range, $\hat{\beta}_o$ has no meaning.

$\hat{\beta}_1 = 0.10875$. For each additional mile of roadway length, the mean number of crashes per three years is estimated to increase by .10875 when average annual daily traffic is held constant.

$\hat{\beta}_2 = 0.00017$. For each additional unit increase in average annual daily traffic, the mean number of crashes per three years is estimated to increase by .00017 when miles of roadway length is held constant.

c. For confidence coefficient .99, $\alpha = .01$ and $\alpha/2 = .01/2 = .005$. From Table VI, Appendix B, with df $= n - (k + 1) = 100 - (2 + 1) = 97$, $t_{.005} \approx 2.63$. The 99% confidence interval is:

$$\hat{\beta}_1 \pm t_{.005} s_{\hat{\beta}_1} \Rightarrow 0.10875 \pm 2.63(0.03166) \Rightarrow 0.10875 \pm 0.08327$$

$$\Rightarrow (0.02548,\ 0.19202)$$

We are 99% confident that the increase in the mean number of crashes per three years will be between 0.02548 and 0.19202 for each additional mile of roadway length, holding average annual daily traffic constant.

d. The 99% confidence interval is:

$$\hat{\beta}_2 \pm t_{.005} s_{\hat{\beta}_2} \Rightarrow 0.00017 \pm 2.63(0.00003) \Rightarrow 0.00017 \pm 0.00008$$

$$\Rightarrow (0.00009, \ 0.00025)$$

We are 99% confident that the increase in the mean number of crashes per three years will be between 0.00009 and 0.00025 for each additional unit increase in average annual daily traffic, holding mile of roadway length constant.

e. The least squares prediction equation is: $\hat{y} = 1.20785 + 0.06343x_1 + 0.00056x_2$

$\hat{\beta}_o = 1.20785$. Since $x_1 = 0$ and $x_2 = 0$ are not in the observed range, $\hat{\beta}_o$ has no meaning.

$\hat{\beta}_1 = 0.06343$. For each additional mile of roadway length, the mean number of crashes per three years is estimated to increase by 0.06343 when average annual daily traffic is held constant.

$\hat{\beta}_2 = 0.00056$. For each additional unit increase in average annual daily traffic, the mean number of crashes per three years is estimated to increase by 0.00056 when miles of roadway length is held constant.

The 99% confidence interval is:

$$\hat{\beta}_1 \pm t_{.005} s_{\hat{\beta}_1} \Rightarrow 0.06343 \pm 2.63(0.01809) \Rightarrow 0.06343 \pm 0.04758$$

$$\Rightarrow (0.01585, \ 0.11101)$$

We are 99% confident that the increase in the mean number of crashes per three years will be between 0.01585 and 0.11101 for each additional mile of roadway length, holding average annual daily traffic constant.

The 99% confidence interval is:

$$\hat{\beta}_2 \pm t_{.005} s_{\hat{\beta}_2} \Rightarrow 0.00056 \pm 2.63(0.00012) \Rightarrow 0.00056 \pm 0.00032$$

$$\Rightarrow (0.00024, \ 0.00088)$$

We are 99% confident that the increase in the mean number of crashes per three years will be between 0.00024 and 0.00088 for each additional unit increase in average annual daily traffic, holding mile of roadway length constant.

11.11 a. The first order model would be

$$y = \beta_0 + \beta_1 x_1 + \beta_2 x_2 + \beta_3 x_3 + \beta_4 x_4 + \varepsilon$$

b.   Since the p-value is less than α $(p = .005 < .01)$, H_0 is rejected. There is sufficient evidence to indicate that there is a negative linear relationship between change from routine and the number of years played golf, holding number of rounds of golf per year, total number of golf vacations, and average golf score constant.

c.   The statement would be correct if the independent variables are not correlated. However, if the independent variables are correlated, then this interpretation would not necessarily hold.

d.   To determine if the overall first-order regression model is adequate, we test:

$$H_0: \; \beta_1 = \beta_2 = \beta_3 = \beta_4 = 0$$

e.   For all dependent variables, the rejection region requires $\alpha = .01$ in the upper tail of the F-distribution with $v_1 = k = 4$ and $v_2 = n - (k + 1) = 393 - (4 + 1) = 388$. From Table XI, Appendix B, $F_{.01} \approx 3.32$. The rejection region is $F > 3.32$. Using MINITAB, the exact $F_{.01, \, 4, \, 388}$ is 3.67. The true rejection region is $F > 3.67$.

f.   For **Thrill**: Since the observed value of the test statistic falls in the rejection region $(F = 5.56 > 3.67)$, H_0 is rejected. There is sufficient evidence to indicate at least one of the 4 independent variables is linearly related to Thrill at $\alpha = .01$.

       For **Change from Routine**: Since the observed value of the test statistic does not fall in the rejection region $(F = 3.02 \not> 3.67)$, H_0 is not rejected. There is insufficient evidence to indicate at least one of the 4 independent variables is linearly related to Change from Routine at $\alpha = .01$.

       For **Surprise**: Since the observed value of the test statistic does not fall in the rejection region $(F = 3.33 \not> 3.67)$, H_0 is not rejected. There is insufficient evidence to indicate at least one of the 4 independent variables is linearly related to Surprise at $\alpha = .01$.

g.   For Thrill: Since the p-value is less than α $(p < .001 < .01)$, H_0 is rejected. There is sufficient evidence to indicate that at least one of the independent variables is linearly related to Thrill at $\alpha = .01$.

       For Change from Routine: Since the p-value is not less than α $(p = .018 > .01)$, H_0 is not rejected. There is insufficient evidence to indicate that at least one of the independent variables is linearly related to Change from Routine at $\alpha = .01$.

       For Surprise: Since the p-value is not less than α $(p = .011 > .01)$, H_0 is not rejected. There is insufficient evidence to indicate that at least one of the independent variables is linearly related to Surprise at $\alpha = .01$.

h.   For Thrill: $R^2 = .055$. 5.5% of the total variability around the mean thrill values can be explained by the model containing the 4 independent variables: $x_1 =$ number of rounds of golf per year, $x_2 =$ total number of golf vacations taken, $x_3 =$ number of years played golf, and $x_4 =$ average golf score.

For Change from Routine: $R^2 = .030$. 3.0% of the total variability around the mean change from routine values can be explained by the model containing the 4 independent variables: x_1 = number of rounds of golf per year, x_2 = total number of golf vacations taken, x_3 = number of years played golf, and x_4 = average golf score.

For Surprise: $R^2 = .023$. 2.3% of the total variability around the mean surprise values can be explained by the model containing the 4 independent variables: x_1 = number of rounds of golf per year, x_2 = total number of golf vacations taken, x_3 = number of years played golf, and x_4 = average golf score.

11.13   a.   The least squares prediction equation is:

$\hat{\beta}_1 = .110$. For each unit increase in total country population, the mean urban/rural rating is estimated to increase by .110, holding all other variables constant.

$\hat{\beta}_2 = .065$. For each unit increase in population density, the mean urban/rural rating is estimated to increase by .065, holding all other variables constant.

$\hat{\beta}_3 = .540$. For each unit increase in population concentration, the mean urban/rural rating is estimated to increase by .540, holding all other variables constant.

$\hat{\beta}_4 = -.009$. For each unit increase in population growth, the mean urban/rural rating is estimated to decrease by .009, holding all other variables constant.

$\hat{\beta}_5 = -.150$. For each unit increase in proportion of county land in farms, the mean urban/rural rating is estimated to decrease by .150, holding all other variables constant.

$\hat{\beta}_6 = -.027$. For each unit increase in 5-year change in agricultural land base, the mean urban/rural rating is estimated to decrease by .027, holding all other variables constant.

b.   To determine the overall adequacy of the model, we test:

$$H_0: \beta_1 = \beta_2 = \beta_3 = \beta_4 = \beta_5 = \beta_6 = 0$$

c.   The alternative hypothesis is:

$$H_a: \text{At least one } \beta_i \neq 0$$

The test statistic is $F = 32.47$ and the p-value is $p < .001$.

Since the p-value is less than α ($p < .001 < .01$), H_0 is rejected. There is sufficient evidence to indicate the model is adequate for the prediction of the rating of the "home" counties at $\alpha = .01$.

d. $R^2 = .44$. 44% of the total variability around the "home" county ratings is explained by the model containing the variables: total county population, population density, population concentration, population growth, proportion of county land in farms, and 5-year change in agricultural land base.

$R^2_{adj} = .43$. 43% of the total variability around the "home" county ratings is explained by the model containing the variables: total county population, population density, population concentration, population growth, proportion of county land in farms, and 5-year change in agricultural land base, adjusting for the sample size and the number of independent variables.

e. To determine if population growth contributes to the model, we test:

H_0: $\beta_4 = 0$

f. The alternative hypothesis is:

H_a: $\beta_4 \neq 0$

The p-value is $p = .860$. Since the p-value is not less than α ($p = .860 > .01$), H_0 is not rejected. There is insufficient evidence to indicate population growth contributes to the prediction of urban/rural rating at $\alpha = .01$.

11.15 a. The first-order model is: $E(y) = \beta_0 + \beta_1 x_1 + \beta_2 x_2$

b. Using MINITAB, the results of fitting the model are:

Regression Analysis: Earnings versus Age, Hours

```
The regression equation is
Earnings = - 20 + 13.4 Age + 244 Hours

Predictor     Coef    SE Coef      T       P
Constant     -20.4      652.7   -0.03   0.976
Age         13.350      7.672    1.74   0.107
Hours       243.71      63.51    3.84   0.002


S = 547.737    R-Sq = 58.2%    R-Sq(adj) = 51.3%


Analysis of Variance

Source            DF        SS        MS      F      P
Regression         2   5018232   2509116   8.36  0.005
Residual Error    12   3600196    300016
Total             14   8618428

Source    DF    Seq SS
Age        1    600498
Hours      1   4417734


Unusual Observations

Obs    Age   Earnings    Fit   SE Fit   Residual   St Resid
  4   18.0       1552   2657      205      -1105      -2.18R

R denotes an observation with a large standardized residual.
```

The least squares prediction equation is: $\hat{y} = -20.4 + 13.350x_1 + 243.71x_2$

c. $\hat{\beta}_0 = -20.4$. This has no meaning since $x_1 = 0$ and $x_2 = 0$ are not in the observed range.

$\hat{\beta}_1 = 13.350$. For each additional year of age, the mean annual earnings is predicted to increase by \$13.350, holding hours worked per day constant.

$\hat{\beta}_2 = 243.71$. For each additional hour worked per day, the mean annual earnings is predicted to increase by \$243.71, holding age constant.

d. To determine if age is a useful predictor of annual earnings, we test:

$H_0: \beta_1 = 0$
$H_a: \beta_1 \neq 0$

The test statistic is $t = 1.74$.

The p-value is $p = .107$. Since the p-value is greater than $\alpha = .01$ ($p = .107 > \alpha = .01$), H_0 is not rejected. There is insufficient evidence to indicate that age is a useful predictor of annual earnings, adjusted for hours worked per day, at $\alpha = .01$.

e. For confidence coefficient .95, $\alpha = .05$ and $\alpha/2 = .05/2 = .025$. From Table VI, Appendix B, with df $= n - (k + 1) = 15 - (2 + 1) = 12$, $t_{.025} = 2.179$. The 95% confidence interval is:

$$\hat{\beta}_2 \pm t_{.005} s_{\hat{\beta}_2} \Rightarrow 243.71 \pm 2.179(63.51) \Rightarrow 243.71 \pm 138.388$$
$$\Rightarrow (105.322, \quad 382.098)$$

We are 95% confident that the change in the mean annual earnings for each additional hour worked per day will be somewhere between \$105.322 and \$382.098, holding age constant.

f. From the printout, $R^2 = R\text{-Sq} = 58.2\%$. 58.2% of the total sample variance of annual earnings is explained by the model containing age and hours worked per day.

g. $R^2_a = R\text{-Sq(adj)} = 51.3\%$. 51.3% of the total sample variance of annual earnings is explained by the model containing age and hours worked per day, adjusted for the sample size and the number of parameters in the model.

h. To determine if at least one of the variables is useful in predicting the annual earnings, we test:

$H_0: \beta_1 = \beta_2 = 0$
$H_a:$ At least 1 $\beta_i \neq 0$

The test statistic is $F = 8.36$ and the p-value is $p = .005$. Since the p-value is less than $\alpha = .01$ ($p = .005 < .01$), H_0 is rejected. There is sufficient evidence to indicate at least one of the variables is useful in predicting the annual earnings at $\alpha = .01$.

11.17 a. The 1st-order model is $E(y) = \beta_0 + \beta_1 x_1 + \beta_2 x_2 + \beta_3 x_3 + \beta_4 x_4 + \beta_5 x_5$.

b. Using MINITAB, the results are:

Regression Analysis: HEATRATE versus RPM, INLET-TEMP, ...

```
The regression equation is
HEATRATE = 13614 + 0.0888 RPM - 9.20 INLET-TEMP + 14.4 EXH-TEMP + 0.4 CPRATIO
         - 0.848 AIRFLOW
```

Predictor	Coef	SE Coef	T	P
Constant	13614.5	870.0	15.65	0.000
RPM	0.08879	0.01391	6.38	0.000
INLET-TEMP	-9.201	1.499	-6.14	0.000
EXH-TEMP	14.394	3.461	4.16	0.000
CPRATIO	0.35	29.56	0.01	0.991
AIRFLOW	-0.8480	0.4421	-1.92	0.060

```
S = 458.828   R-Sq = 92.4%   R-Sq(adj) = 91.7%
```

Analysis of Variance

Source	DF	SS	MS	F	P
Regression	5	155055273	31011055	147.30	0.000
Residual Error	61	12841935	210524		
Total	66	167897208			

Source	DF	Seq SS
RPM	1	119598530
INLET-TEMP	1	26893467
EXH-TEMP	1	7784225
CPRATIO	1	4623
AIRFLOW	1	774427

Unusual Observations

Obs	RPM	HEATRATE	Fit	SE Fit	Residual	St Resid
11	18000	14628.0	13214.0	117.9	1414.0	3.19R
32	14950	10656.0	11663.0	132.5	-1007.0	-2.29R
36	4473	13523.0	12489.5	195.1	1033.5	2.49R
47	7280	11588.0	10533.0	154.7	1055.0	2.44R
61	33000	16243.0	15758.0	246.5	485.0	1.25 X
64	3600	8714.0	8415.2	340.9	298.8	0.97 X

```
R denotes an observation with a large standardized residual.
X denotes an observation whose X value gives it large influence.
```

The least squares prediction equation is:

$$\hat{y} = 13,614.5 + 0.0888x_1 - 9.201x_2 + 14.394x_3 + 0.35x_4 - 0.848x_5$$

c. $\hat{\beta}_o = 13,614.5$. Since 0 is not within the range of all the independent variables, this value has no meaning.

$\hat{\beta}_1 = 0.0888$. For each unit increase in RPM, the mean heat rate is estimated to increase by .0888, holding all the other 4 variables constant.

$\hat{\beta}_2 = -9.201$. For each unit increase in inlet temperature, the mean heat rate is estimated to decrease by 9.201, holding all the other 4 variables constant.

$\hat{\beta}_3 = 14.394$. For each unit increase in exhaust temperature, the mean heat rate is estimated to increase by 14.394, holding all the other 4 variables   constant.

$\hat{\beta}_4 = 0.35$. For each unit increase in cycle pressure ratio, the mean heat rate is estimated to increase by 0.35, holding all the other 4 variables constant.

$\hat{\beta}_5 = -0.8480$. For each unit increase in air flow rate, the mean heat rate is estimated to decrease by .848, holding all the other 4 variables constant.

d.   From the printout, $s = 458.828$. We would expect to see most of the heat rate values within $2s$ or $2(458.828) = 917.656$ units of the least squares line.

e.   To determine if at least one of the variables is useful in predicting the heat rate values, we test:

H_0: $\beta_1 = \beta_2 = \beta_3 = \beta_4 = \beta_5 = 0$
H_a: At least 1 $\beta_i \neq 0$

The test statistic is $F = 147.30$ and the p-value is $p = .000$. Since the p-value is less than $\alpha = .01$ $(p = .000 < .01)$, H_0 is rejected. There is sufficient evidence to indicate at least one of the variables is useful in predicting the heat rate values at $\alpha = .01$.

f. $R^2_a = R\text{-Sq(adj)} = 91.7\%$. 91.7% of the total sample variance of the heat rate values is explained by the model containing the 5 independent variables.

g.   To determine if there is evidence to indicate heat rate is linearly related to inlet temperature, we test:

H_0: $\beta_2 = 0$
H_a: $\beta_2 \neq 0$

The test statistic is $t = -6.14$ and the p-value is $p = 0.000$. Since the p-value is less than $\alpha = .01$ $(p = .000 < .01)$, H_0 is rejected. There is sufficient evidence to indicate heat rate is linearly related to inlet temperature at $\alpha = .01$.

11.19 a. $E(y) = \beta_0 + \beta_1x_1 + \beta_2x_2 + \beta_3x_3 + \beta_4x_4 + \beta_5x_5 + \beta_6x_6 + \beta_7x_7$

  b.   Using MINITAB, the output is:

```
The regression equation is y = 0.998 - 0.0224 x1 + 0.156x2 - 0.0172x3
 - 0.00953x4 + 0.421x5 + 0.417x6 - 0.155x7


Predictor         Coef        StDev            T            P
Constant        0.9981       0.2475         4.03        0.002
x1            -0.022429     0.005039        -4.45        0.001
x2             0.15571       0.07429         2.10        0.060
x3            -0.01719       0.01186        -1.45        0.175
x4            -0.009527      0.009619       -0.99        0.343
x5             0.4214        0.1008          4.18        0.002
x6             0.4171        0.4377          0.95        0.361
x7            -0.1552        0.1486         -1.04        0.319


S = 0.4365          R-Sq = 77.1%       R-Sq(adj) = 62.5%

   Analysis of Variance

Source            DF          SS          MS          F          P
Regression         7       7.9578      1.1368       5.29      0.007
Residual Error    11       2.3632      0.2148
Total             18      10.3210

Source     DF      Seq SS
x1          1      1.4016
x2          1      1.9263
x3          1      0.1171
x4          1      0.0446
x5          1      4.0771
x6          1      0.1565
x7          1      0.2345

Unusual Observations

Obs        x1          y       Fit StDev Fit  Residual  St Resid
14        80.0      0.120    -0.628    0.328     0.748     2.28R

R denotes an observation with a large standardized residual.
```

The least squares model is $\hat{y} = .9981 - .0224x_1 + .1557x_2 - .0172x_3 - .0095x_4 + .4214x_5 + .4171x_6 - .1552x_7$

  c. $\hat{\beta}_0 = .9981 =$ the estimate of the y-intercept.

$\hat{\beta}_1 = -.0224$. We estimate that the mean voltage will decrease by .0224 kw/cm, for each additional increase of 1% of x_1, the disperse phase volume (with all other variables held constant).

$\hat{\beta}_2 = .1557$. We estimate that the mean voltage will increase by .1557 kw/cm for each additional increase of 1% of x_2, the salinity (with all other variables held constant).

$\hat{\beta}_3 = -.0172$. We estimate the the mean voltage will decrease by .0172 kw/cm for each additional increase of 1 degree of x_3, the temperature in Celsius (with all other variables held constant).

$\hat{\beta}_4 = -.0095$. We estimate that the mean voltage will decrease by .0095 kw/cm for each additional increase of 1 hour of x_4, the time delay (with all other variables held constant).

$\hat{\beta}_5 = .4214$. We estimate that the mean voltage will increase by .4214 kw/cm for each additional increase of 1% of x_5, surfiant concentration (with all other variables held constant).

$\hat{\beta}_6 = .4171$. We estimate that the mean voltage will increase by .4171 kw/cm for each additional increase of 1 unit of x_6, span: Triton (with all other variables held constant).

$\hat{\beta}_7 = -.1552$. We estimate that the mean voltage will decrease by .1552 kw/cm for each additional increase of 1% of x_7, the solid particles (with all other variables held constant).

d.   To determine if at least one of the variables is useful in predicting voltage, we test:

H_0: $\beta_1 = \beta_2 = \beta_3 = \beta_4 = \beta_5 = \beta_6 = \beta_7 = 0$
H_a: At least 1 $\beta_i \neq 0$

The test statistic is $F = 5.29$ and the p-value is $p = .007$. Since the p-value is less than $\alpha = .10$ ($p = .007 < .10$), H_0 is rejected. There is sufficient evidence to indicate at least one of the 7 variables is useful in predicting voltage at $\alpha = .10$.

11.21   a. $R^2 = .362$. 36.2% of the variability in the AC scores can be explained by the model containing the variables self-esteem score, optimism score, and group cohesion score.

b.   To test the utility of the model, we test:

H_0: $\beta_1 = \beta_2 = \beta_3 = 0$
H_a: At least one $\beta_i \neq 0$, $i = 1, 2, 3$

The test statistic is:

$$F = \frac{R^2 / k}{(1 - R^2)/[n - (k+1)]} = \frac{.362/3}{(1-.362)/[31-(3+1)]} = 5.11$$

The rejection region requires $\alpha = .05$ in the upper tail of the F distribution with $v_1 = k = 3$ and $v_2 = n - (k + 1) = 31 - (3 + 1) = 27$. From Table IX, Appendix B, $F_{.05} = 2.96$. The rejection region is $F > 2.96$.

Since the observed value of the test statistic falls in the rejection region ($F = 5.11 > 2.96$), H_0 is rejected. There is sufficient evidence that the model is useful in predicting AC score at $\alpha = .05$.

11.23 a. **Model 1:**

H_0: $\beta_1 = 0$
H_a: $\beta_1 \neq 0$

The test statistic is $t = \dfrac{\hat{\beta}_1 - 0}{s_{\hat{\beta}_1}} = \dfrac{.0354}{.0137} = 2.58$.

Since no α was given, we will use $\alpha = .05$. The rejection region requires $\alpha/2 = .05/2 = .025$ in each tail of the t distribution. From Table VI, Appendix B, with df $= n - (k + 1) = 12 - (1 + 1) = 10$, $t_{.025} = 2.228$. The rejection region is $t < -2.228$ or $t > 2.228$.

Since the observed value of the test statistic falls in the rejection region ($t = 2.58 > 2.228$), H_0 is rejected. There is sufficient evidence to indicate that there is a linear relationship between vintage and the logarithm of price.

Model 2:

H_0: $\beta_1 = 0$
H_a: $\beta_1 \neq 0$

The test statistic is $t = \dfrac{\hat{\beta}_1 - 0}{s_{\hat{\beta}_1}} = \dfrac{.0238}{.00717} = 3.32$

Since no α was given, we will use $\alpha = .05$. The rejection region requires $\alpha/2 = .05/2 = .025$ in each tail of the t distribution. From Table VI, Appendix B, with df $= n - (k + 1) = 12 - (4 + 1) = 7$, $t_{.025} = 2.365$. The rejection region is $t < -2.365$ or $t > 2.365$.

Since the observed value of the test statistic falls in the rejection region ($t = 3.32 > 2.365$), H_0 is rejected. There is sufficient evidence to indicate that there is a linear relationship between vintage and the logarithm of price, adjusting for all other variables.

H_0: $\beta_2 = 0$
H_a: $\beta_2 \neq 0$

The test statistic is $t = \dfrac{\hat{\beta}_2 - 0}{s_{\hat{\beta}_2}} = \dfrac{.616}{.0952} = 6.47$

The rejection region is $t < -2.365$ or $t > 2.365$.

Since the observed value of the test statistic falls in the rejection region ($t = 6.47 > 2.365$), H_0 is rejected. There is sufficient evidence to indicate that there is a linear relationship between average growing season temperature and the logarithm of price, adjusting for all other variables.

H_0: $\beta_3 = 0$

H_a: $\beta_3 \neq 0$

The test statistic is $t = \dfrac{\hat{\beta}_3 - 0}{s_{\hat{\beta}_3}} = \dfrac{-.00386}{.00081} = -4.77$

The rejection region is $t < -2.365$ or $t > 2.365$.

Since the observed value of the test statistic falls in the rejection region ($t = -4.77 < -2.365$), H_0 is rejected. There is sufficient evidence to indicate that there is a linear relationship between Sept./ Aug. rainfall and the logarithm of price, adjusting for all other variables.

H_0: $\beta_4 = 0$

H_a: $\beta_4 \neq 0$

The test statistic is $t = \dfrac{\hat{\beta}_4 - 0}{s_{\hat{\beta}_4}} = \dfrac{.0001173}{.000482} = 0.24$.

The rejection region is $t < -2.365$ or $t > 2.365$.

Since the observed value of the test statistic does not fall in the rejection region ($t = 0.24 \not> 2.365$), H_0 is not rejected. There is insufficient evidence to indicate that there is a linear relationship between rainfall in months preceding vintage and the logarithm of price, adjusting for all other variables.

Model 3:

H_0: $\beta_1 = 0$

H_a: $\beta_1 \neq 0$

The test statistic is $t = \dfrac{\hat{\beta}_1 - 0}{s_{\hat{\beta}_1}} = \dfrac{.0240}{.00747} = 3.21$

Since no α was given, we will use $\alpha = .05$. The rejection region requires $\alpha/2 = .05/2 = .025$ in each tail of the t distribution. From Table VI, Appendix B, with df $= n - (k + 1) = 12 - (5 + 1) + 7$, $t_{.025} = 2.447$. The rejection region is $t < -2.447$ or $t > 2.447$.

Since the observed value of the test statistic falls in the rejection region ($t = 3.21 > 2.447$), H_0 is rejected. There is sufficient evidence to indicate that there is a linear relationship between vintage and the logarithm of price, adjusting for all other variables.

H_0: $\beta_2 = 0$

H_a: $\beta_2 \neq 0$

The test statistic is $t = \dfrac{\hat{\beta}_2 - 0}{s_{\hat{\beta}_2}} = \dfrac{.608}{.116} = 5.24$.

The rejection region is $t < -2.447$ or $t > 2.447$.

Since the observed value of the test statistic falls in the rejection region ($t = 5.24 > 2.447$), H_0 is rejected. There is sufficient evidence to indicate that there is a linear relationship between average growing season temperature and the logarithm of price, adjusting for all other variables.

H_0: $\beta_3 = 0$
H_a: $\beta_3 \neq 0$

The test statistic is $t = \dfrac{\hat{\beta}_3 - 0}{s_{\hat{\beta}_3}} = \dfrac{-.00380}{.00095} = -4.00$

The rejection region is $t < -2.447$ or $t > -2.447$.

Since the observed value of the test statistic falls in the rejection region ($t = -4.00 < -2.447$), H_0 is rejected. There is sufficient evidence to indicate that there is a linear relationship between Sept./Aug. rainfall and the logarithm of price, adjusting for all other variables.

H_0: $\beta_4 = 0$
H_a: $\beta_4 \neq 0$

The test statistic is $t = \dfrac{\hat{\beta}_4 - 0}{s_{\hat{\beta}_4}} = \dfrac{.00115}{.000505} = 2.28$

The rejection region is $t < -2.447$ or $t > 2.447$.

Since the observed value of the test statistic does not fall in the rejection region ($t = 2.28 \not> 2.365$), H_0 is not rejected. There is insufficient evidence to indicate that there is a linear relationship between rainfall in months preceding vintage and the logarithm of price, adjusting for all other variables.

H_0: $\beta_5 = 0$
H_a: $\beta_5 \neq 0$

The test statistic is $t = \dfrac{\hat{\beta}_5 - 0}{s_{\hat{\beta}_5}} = \dfrac{.00765}{.0565} = 0.14$.

The rejection region is $t < -2.447$ or $t > 2.447$.

Since the observed value of the test statistic does not fall in the rejection region ($t = 0.14 \not> 2.365$), H_0 is not rejected. There is insufficient evidence to indicate that there is a linear relationship between average September temperature and the logarithm of price, adjusting for all other variables.

b.   **Model 1:**

$\hat{\beta}_1 = .0354$, $e^{.0354} - 1 = .036$

We estimate that the mean price will increase by 3.6% for each additional increase of unit of x_1, vintage year.

Model 2:

$\hat{\beta}_1 = .0238$, $e^{.0238} - 1 = .024$

We estimate that the mean price will increase by 2.4% for each additional increase of 1 unit of x_1, vintage year (with all other variables held constant).

$\hat{\beta}_2 = .616$, $e^{.616} - 1 = .852$

We estimate that the mean price will increase by 85.2% for each additional increase of 1 unit of x_2, average growing season temperature °C (with all other variables held constant).

$\hat{\beta}_3 = -.00386$, $e^{.00386} - 1 = -.004$

We estimate that the mean price will decrease by .4% for each additional increase of 1 unit of x_3, Sept./Aug. rainfall in cm (with all other variables held constant).

$\hat{\beta}_4 = .0001173$, $e^{.0001173} - 1 = .0001$

We estimate that the mean price will increase by .01% for each additional increase of 1 unit of x_4, rainfall in months preceding vintage in cm (with all other variables held constant).

Model 3:

$\hat{\beta}_1 = .0240$, $e^{.0240} - 1 = .024$

We estimate that the mean price will increase by 2.4% for each additional increase of 1 unit of x_1, vintage. year (with all other variables held constant).

$\hat{\beta}_2 = .608$, $e^{.608} - 1 = .837$

We estimate that the mean price will increase by 83.7% for each additional increase of 1 unit of x_2, average growing season temperatures in °C (with all other variables held constant).

$\hat{\beta}_3 = -.00380$, $e^{.00380} - 1 = -.004$

We estimate that the mean price will decrease by .4% for each additional increase of 1 unit of x_3, Sept./Aug. rainfall in cm, (with all other variables held constant).

$\hat{\beta}_4 = .00115$, $e^{.00115} - 1 = .001$

We estimate that the average mean price will increase by .1% for each additional increase of 1 unit of x_4, rainfall in months preceding vintage in cm (with all other variables held constant).

$\hat{\beta}_5 = .00765$, $e^{.00765} - 1 = .008$

We estimate that the average mean price will increase by .8% for each additional increase of 1 unit of x_5, average Sept. temperature in °C (with all other variables held constant).

c.   I would recommend model 2. Model 1 has only 1 independent variable in the model and it is significant at $\alpha = .05$. The R^2 for this model is $R^2 = .212$ and $s = .575$. Model 2 has 4 independent variables in the model and all terms are significant at $\alpha = .05$ except one. This one variable is significant at $\alpha = .10$. This model has $R^2 = .828$ and $s = .287$. Comparing model 2 to model 1, the R^2 for model 2 is much larger than that for model 1 and the estimate of the standard deviation is much smaller. Model 3 contains all of the independent variables that model 2 has plus one additional variable. This additional variable is not significant at $\alpha = .10$. In addition, the R^2 for this new model $= .828$, the same as for model 2. However, the estimate of the standard deviation of model 3 is now larger than that of model 2. This indicates that model 2 is better than model 3.

11.25   a.   The 95% prediction interval is (1,759.7, 4,275.4). We are 95% confident that the true actual annual earnings for a vendor who is 45 years old and who works 10 hours per day is between $1,759.7 and $4,275.4.

b.   The 95% confidence interval is (2,620.3, 3,414.9). We are 95% confident that the true mean annual earnings for vendors who are 45 years old and who work 10 hours per day is between $2,620.3 and $3,414.9.

c.   Yes. The prediction interval for the ACTUAL value of y is always wider than the confidence interval for the MEAN value of y.

11.27   a.   The 95% prediction interval is (11,599.6, 13,665.5). We are 95% confident that the actual heat rate will be between 11,599.6 and 13.665.5 when the RPM is 7,500, the inlet temperature is 1,000, the exhaust temperature is 525, the cycle pressure ratio is 13.5 and the air flow rate is 10.

b.   The 95% confidence interval is (12,157.9, 13,107.1). We are 95% confident that the mean heat rate will be between 12,157.9 and 13,107.1 when the RPM is 7,500, the inlet temperature is 1,000, the exhaust temperature is 525, the cycle pressure ratio is 13.5 and the air flow rate is 10.

c.   Yes. The confidence interval for the mean will always be smaller than the prediction interval for the actual value. This is because there are 2 error terms involved in predicting an actual value and only one error term involved in estimating the mean. First, we have the error in locating the mean of the distribution. Once the mean is located, the actual value can still vary around the mean, thus, the second error. There is only one error term involved when estimating the mean, which is the error in locating the mean.

11.29 a. From MINITAB, the output is:

Regression Analysis: WeightChg versus Digest, Fiber

```
The regression equation is
WeightChg = 12.2 - 0.0265 Digest - 0.458 Fiber

Predictor        Coef     SE Coef        T        P
Constant       12.180       4.402     2.77    0.009
Digest       -0.02654     0.05349    -0.50    0.623
Fiber         -0.4578      0.1283    -3.57    0.001

S = 3.519      R-Sq = 52.9%     R-Sq(adj) = 50.5%


Analysis of Variance

Source            DF          SS         MS        F        P
Regression         2      542.03     271.02    21.88    0.000
Residual Error    39      483.08      12.39
Total             41     1025.12

Source           DF      Seq SS
Digest            1      384.24
Fiber             1      157.79

Predicted Values for New Observations

New Obs     Fit    SE Fit         95.0% CI            95.0% PI
1        -1.687     0.866   ( -3.439,   0.065)  ( -9.019,   5.644)

Values of Predictors for New Observations

New Obs   Digest    Fiber
1           5.00     30.0
```

The confidence interval is (−3.439, .065)
With 95% confidence, we can conclude that the mean gosling weight change for all goslings with properties $x_1 = 5\%$ and $x_2 = 30\%$ will fall between −3.439% and .065%.

b. The prediction interval is (−9.019, 5.644). With 95% confidence, we can conclude that the weight change for an individual gosling with $x_1 = 5\%$ and $x_2 = 30\%$ will fall between −9.019% and 5.644%.

11.31 a. From MINITAB, the output is:

Regression Analysis: Man-Hours versus Capacity, Pressure, Type, Drum

```
The regression equation is
Man-Hours = - 3783 + 0.00875 Capacity + 1.93 Pressure + 3444 Type + 2093 Drum

Predictor        Coef     SE Coef        T        P
Constant        -3783        1205    -3.14    0.004
Capacity    0.0087490   0.0009035     9.68    0.000
Pressure       1.9265      0.6489     2.97    0.006
Type           3444.3       911.7     3.78    0.001
Drum           2093.4       305.6     6.85    0.000

S = 894.6      R-Sq = 90.3%     R-Sq(adj) = 89.0%
```

```
Analysis of Variance

Source              DF        SS          MS        F        P
Regression          4     230854854    57713714    72.11    0.000
Residual Error     31      24809761      800315
Total              35     255664615

Source         DF      Seq SS
Capacity        1    175007141
Pressure        1       490357
Type            1     17813091
Drum            1     37544266

Predicted Values for New Observations

New Obs    Fit     SE Fit         95.0% CI              95.0% PI
1         1936       239     (   1449,    2424)   (      48,    3825)

Values of Predictors for New Observations

New Obs  Capacity  Pressure     Type      Drum
1          150000       500     1.00  0.000000
```

The fitted regression line is:

$$\hat{y} = -3,793 + 0.00875x_1 + 1.9265x_2 + 3,444.3x_3 + 2,053.4x_4$$

b. To determine if the model is useful for predicting the number of man-hours needed, we test:

H_0: $\beta_1 = \beta_2 = \beta_3 = \beta_4 = 0$
H_a: At least one $\beta_i \neq 0$, $i = 1, 2, 3, 4$

The test statistic is $F = 72.11$ with p-value $= .000$. Since the p-value is less than $\alpha = .01$, we can reject H_0. There is sufficient evidence that the model is useful for predicting man-hours at $\alpha = .01$.

c. The confidence interval is (1449, 2424).

With 95% confidence, we can conclude that the mean number of man-hours for all boilers with characteristics $x_1 = 150,000$, $x_2 = 500$, $x_3 = 1$, $x_4 = 0$ will fall between 1449 hours and 2424 hours.

11.33 a. The response surface is a twisted surface in three-dimensional space.

b. For $x_1 = 0$, $E(y) = 3 + 0 + 2x_2 - 0x_2 = 3 + 2x_2$
For $x_1 = 1$, $E(y) = 3 + 1 + 2x_2 - 1x_2 = 4 + x_2$
For $x_1 = 2$, $E(y) = 3 + 2 + 2x_2 - 2x_2 = 5$

The plot of the lines is

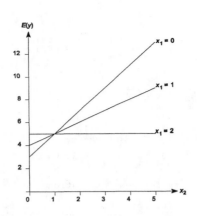

c.   The lines are not parallel because interaction between x_1 and x_2 is present. Interaction between x_1 and x_2 means that the effect of x_2 on y depends on what level x_1 takes on.

d.   For $x_1 = 0$, as x_2 increases from 0 to 5, $E(y)$ increases from 3 to 13.
      For $x_1 = 1$, as x_2 increases from 0 to 5, $E(y)$ increases from 4 to 9.
      For $x_1 = 2$, as x_2 increases from 0 to 5, $E(y) = 5$.

e.   For $x_1 = 2$ and $x_2 = 4$, $E(y) = 5$
      For $x_1 = 0$ and $x_2 = 5$, $E(y) = 13$

      Thus, $E(y)$ changes from 5 to 13.

11.35   a.   The prediction equation is:

$$\hat{y} = -2.55 + 3.82x_1 + 2.63x_2 - 1.29x_1x_2$$

b.   The response surface is a twisted plane, since the equation contains an interaction term.

c.   For $x_2 = 1$, $= -2.55 + 3.82x_1 + 2.63(1) - 1.29x_1(1)$
                        $= .08 + 2.53x_1$
      For $x_2 = 3$, $= -2.55 + 3.82x_1 + 2.63(3) - 1.29x_1(3)$
                        $= 5.34 - .05x_1$
      For $x_2 = 5$, $= -2.55 + 3.82x_1 + 2.63(5) - 1.29x_1(5)$
                        $= 10.6 - 2.63x_1$

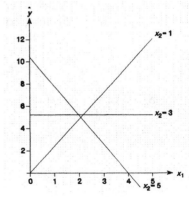

d.   If x_1 and x_2 interact, the effect of x_1 on $\hat{y}$ is different at different levels of x_2. When $x_2 = 1$, as x_1 increases, $\hat{y}$ also increases. When $x_2 = 5$, as x_1 increases, $\hat{y}$ decreases.

e.   The hypotheses are:

$$H_0:\ \beta_3 = 0$$
$$H_a:\ \beta_3 \ne 0$$

f. The test statistic is $t = \dfrac{\hat{\beta}_3}{s_{\hat{\beta}_3}} = \dfrac{-1.285}{.159} = -8.06$

The rejection region requires $\alpha/2 = .01/2 = .005$ in each tail of the t distribution with df $= n - (k + 1) = 15 - (3 + 1) = 11$. From Table VI, Appendix B, $t_{.005} = 3.106$. The rejection region is $t < -3.106$ or $t > 3.106$.

Since the observed value of the test statistic falls in the rejection region ($t = -8.06 < -3.106$), H_0 is rejected. There is sufficient evidence to indicate that x_1 and x_2 interact at $\alpha = .01$.

11.37 a. A regression model incorporating interaction between x_1 and x_2 would be:

$$E(y) = \beta_o + \beta_1 x_1 + \beta_2 x_2 + \beta_3 x_1 x_2$$

b. If the slope of the relationship between number of defects (y) and turntable speed (x_1) is steeper for lower values of cutting blade speed, then the interaction term must be negative. As the value of cutting speed increases, the steepness gets smaller, thus, the interaction term must get smaller.

11.39 a. Using MINITAB, the results of fitting the interaction model are:

Regression Analysis: Earnings versus Age, Hours, A_H

```
The regression equation is
Earnings = 1042 - 13.2 Age + 103 Hours + 3.62 A_H


Predictor     Coef   SE Coef      T      P
Constant      1042      1304   0.80  0.441
Age         -13.24     29.23  -0.45  0.659
Hours        103.3     162.0   0.64  0.537
A_H          3.621     3.840   0.94  0.366


S = 550.289    R-Sq = 61.4%    R-Sq(adj) = 50.8%


Analysis of Variance

Source           DF        SS       MS      F      P
Regression        3   5287427  1762476   5.82  0.012
Residual Error   11   3331000   302818
Total            14   8618428


Source   DF     Seq SS
Age       1     600498
Hours     1    4417734
A_H       1     269196
```

The least squares prediction equation is:

$$\hat{y} = 1042 - 13.24 x_1 + 103.3 x_2 + 3.621 x_1 x_2$$

b. When $x_2 = 10$, the least squares line is:

$$\hat{y} = 1042 - 13.24x_1 + 103.3(10) + 3.621x_1(10)$$
$$= 1042 + 1033 - 13.24x_1 + 36.21x_1 = 2075 + 22.97x_1$$

The estimated slope relating annual earnings to age is 22.97. When hours worked is equal to 10, for each additional year of age, the mean annual earnings is estimated to increase by 22.97.

c. When $x_1 = 40$, the least squares line is:

$$\hat{y} = 1042 - 13.24(40) + 103.3x_2 + 3.621(40)x_2$$
$$= 1042 - 529.6 + 103.3x_2 + 144.84x_2 = 512.4 + 248.14x_2$$

The estimated slope relating annual earnings to hours worked is 248.14. When age is equal to 40, for each additional hour worked, the mean annual earnings is estimated to increase by 248.14.

d. To determine if age and hours worked interact, we test:

H_0: $\beta_3 = 0$

e. From the printout, the test statistic for the test for interaction is $t = 0.94$ and the p-value is $p = .366$.

f. Since the p-value is so large ($p = .366$), H_0 is not rejected. There is insufficient evidence to indicate age and hours worked interact to affect annual earnings.

11.41   a. The model that incorporates the researchers' theories is:

$$E(y) = \beta_0 + \beta_1 x_2 + \beta_2 x_3 + \beta_3 x_5 + \beta_4 x_2 x_5 + \beta_5 x_3 x_5$$

b. Using MINITAB, the results of fitting the model are:

Regression Analysis: HEATRATE versus INLET-TEMP, EXH-TEMP, ...

```
The regression equation is
HEATRATE = 13945 - 15.1 INLET-TEMP + 28.8 EXH-TEMP - 0.69 AIRFLOW
           + 0.0228 IT_AFR - 0.0543 ET_AFR


Predictor        Coef    SE Coef        T      P
Constant        13945       1044    13.35  0.000
INLET-TEMP   -15.1379     0.7775   -19.47  0.000
EXH-TEMP      28.843       2.304    12.52  0.000
AIRFLOW       -0.689       3.628    -0.19  0.850
IT_AFR       0.022770   0.002999     7.59  0.000
ET_AFR       -0.05430    0.01053    -5.16  0.000


S = 425.072    R-Sq = 93.4%    R-Sq(adj) = 92.9%
```

```
Analysis of Variance

Source             DF        SS          MS        F       P
Regression          5    156875371    31375074   173.64   0.000
Residual Error     61     11021838      180686
Total              66    167897208
```

The least squares prediction equation is:

$$\hat{y} = 13{,}945 - 15.1379x_2 + 28.843x_3 - 0.689x_5 + 0.02277x_2x_5 - 0.0543x_3x_5$$

c. To determine if inlet temperature and air flow rate interact to affect heat rate, we test:

H_0: $\beta_4 = 0$
H_a: $\beta_4 \neq 0$

The test statistic is $t = 7.59$ with a p-value of $p = 0.000$. Since the p-value is less than $\alpha = .05$, H_0 is rejected. There is sufficient evidence to indicate that inlet temperature and air flow rate interact to affect heat rate.

d. To determine if exhaust temperature and air flow rate interact to affect heat rate, we test:

H_0: $\beta_5 = 0$
H_a: $\beta_5 \neq 0$

The test statistic is $t = -5.16$ with a p-value of $p = 0.000$. Since the p-value is less than $\alpha = .05$, H_0 is rejected. There is sufficient evidence to indicate that exhaust temperature and air flow rate interact to affect heat rate.

e. Since the interaction of inlet temperature and air flow rate is significant, it means that the effect of inlet temperature on the heat rate depends on the level of air flow rate. Also, since the interaction of exhaust temperature and air flow rate is significant, it means that the effect of exhaust temperature on the heat rate also depends on the level of air flow rate

11.43 a. By including the interaction terms, it implies that the relationship between voltage and volume fraction of the disperse phase depends on the levels of salinity and surfactant concentration.

A possible sketch of the relationship is:

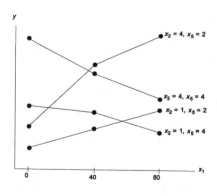

Multiple Regression and Model Building

b.   From MINITAB, the output is:

Regression Analysis: Voltage versus x1, x2, x5, x1x2, x1x5

```
The regression equation is
Voltage = 0.906 - 0.0228 x1 + 0.305 x2 + 0.275 x5 - 0.00280 x1x2
+ 0.00158 x1x5

Predictor         Coef      SE Coef            T          P
Constant        0.9057       0.2855         3.17      0.007
x1           -0.022753      0.008318        -2.74      0.017
x2             0.3047        0.2366         1.29      0.220
x5             0.2747        0.2270         1.21      0.248
x1x2         -0.002804      0.003790        -0.74      0.473
x1x5          0.001579      0.003947         0.40      0.696

S = 0.5047      R-Sq = 67.9%      R-Sq(adj) = 55.6%

Analysis of Variance

Source            DF           SS           MS          F          P
Regression         5       7.0103       1.4021       5.51      0.006
Residual Error    13       3.3107       0.2547
Total             18      10.3210

Source     DF      Seq SS
x1          1      1.4016
x2          1      1.9263
x5          1      3.5422
x1x2        1      0.0994
x1x5        1      0.0408
```

The fitted regression line is:

$$\hat{y} = .906 - .023x_1 + .305x_2 + .275x_5 - .003x_1x_2 + .002x_1x_5$$

To determine if the model is useful, we test:

H_0: $\beta_1 = \beta_2 = \beta_3 = \beta_4 = \beta_5 = 0$
H_a: At least one $\beta_i \neq 0$, for $i = 1, 2, ..., 5$

The test statistic is $F = 5.51$.

Since no α was given, $\alpha = .05$ will be used. The rejection region requires $\alpha = .05$ in the upper tail of the F-distribution with $v_1 = k = 5$ and $v_2 = n - (k + 1) = 19 - (5 + 1) = 13$. From Table VIII, Appendix B, $F_{.05} = 3.03$. The rejection region is $F > 3.03$.

Since the observed value of the test statistic falls in the rejection region ($F = 5.51 > 3.03$), H_0 is rejected. There is sufficient evidence to indicate the model is useful for predicting voltage at $\alpha = .05$.

$R^2 = .679$. Thus, 67.9% of the sample variation of voltage is explained by the model containing the three independent variables and two interaction terms.

The estimate of the standard deviation is $s = .5047$.

Comparing this model to that fit in Exercise 11.19, the model in Exercise 11.19 appears to fit the data better. The model in Exercise 11.19 has a higher R^2 (.771 vs .679) and a smaller estimate of the standard deviation (.4365 vs .5047).

c. $\hat{\beta}_0 = .906$.   This is simply the estimate of the y-intercept.

$\hat{\beta}_1 = -.023$.   For each unit increase in disperse phase volume, we estimate that the mean voltage will decrease by .023 units, holding salinity and surfactant concentration at 0.

$\hat{\beta}_2 = .305$.   For each unit increase in salinity, we estimate that the mean voltage will increase by .305 units, holding disperse phase volume and surfactant concentration at 0.

$\hat{\beta}_3 = .275$.   For each unit increase in surfactant concentration, we estimate that the mean voltage will increase by .275 units, holding disperse phase volume and salinity at 0.

$\hat{\beta}_4 = -.003$.   This estimates the difference in the slope of the relationship between voltage and disperse phase volume for each unit increase in salinity, holding surfactant concentration constant.

$\hat{\beta}_5 = .002$.   This estimates the difference in the slope of the relationship between voltage and disperse phase volume for each unit increase in surfactant concentration, holding salinity constant.

11.45   a. $E(y) = \beta_0 + \beta_1 x + \beta_2 x^2$

b. $E(y) = \beta_0 + \beta_1 x_1 + \beta_2 x_2 + \beta_3 x_1^2 + \beta_4 x_2^2 + \beta_5 x_1 x_2$

c. $E(y) = \beta_0 + \beta_1 x_1 + \beta_2 x_2 + \beta_3 x_3 + \beta_4 x_1^2 + \beta_5 x_2^2 + \beta_6 x_3^2 + \beta_7 x_1 x_2 + \beta_8 x_1 x_3 + \beta_9 x_2 x_3$

11.47   a.   To determine if the model contributes information for predicting y, we test:

H_0: $\beta_1 = \beta_2 = 0$
H_a: At least one $\beta_i \neq 0$, $i = 1, 2$

The test statistic is $F = \dfrac{R^2 / k}{(1 - R^2)/[n - (k + 1)]} = \dfrac{.91/2}{(1 - .91)/[20 - (2 + 1)]} = 85.94$

The rejection region requires $\alpha = .05$ in the upper tail of the F distribution, with $v_1 = k = 2$, and $v_2 = n - (k + 1) = 20 - (2 + 1) = 17$. From Table IX, Appendix B, $F_{.05} = 3.59$. The rejection region is $F > 3.59$.

Since the observed value of the test statistic falls in the rejection region ($F = 85.94 > 3.59$), H_0 is rejected. There is sufficient evidence that the model contributes information for predicting y at $\alpha = .05$.

b.	To determine if upward curvature exists, we test:

$$H_0: \ \beta_2 = 0$$
$$H_a: \ \beta_2 > 0$$

c.	To determine if downward curvature exists, we test:

$$H_0: \ \beta_2 = 0$$
$$H_a: \ \beta_2 < 0$$

11.49	a.	To determine if at least one of the parameters is nonzero, we test:

$$H_0: \ \beta_1 = \beta_2 = \beta_3 = \beta_4 = \beta_5 = 0$$
$$H_a: \ \text{At least one } \beta_i \neq 0, \ i = 1, 2, 3, 4, 5$$

The test statistic is $F = 25.93$, with p-value $= 0.000$. Since the p-value is less than $\alpha = .05$, H_0 is rejected. There is sufficient evidence to indicate that at least one of the parameters $\beta_1, \beta_2, \beta_3, \beta_4$, and β_5 is nonzero at $\alpha = .05$.

b.	$H_0: \ \beta_4 = 0$
$H_a: \ \beta_4 \neq 0$

The test statistic is $t = -10.74$ with p-value $= 0.000$. Since the p-value is less than $\alpha = .01$, H_0 is rejected. There is sufficient evidence to indicate that $\beta_4 \neq 0$ at $\alpha = .01$.

c.	$H_0: \ \beta_5 = 0$
$H_a: \ \beta_5 \neq 0$

The test statistic is $t = .60$ with p-value $= .550$. Since the p-value is greater than $\alpha = .01$, H_0 is not rejected. There is insufficient evidence to indicate that $\beta_5 \neq 0$ at $\alpha = .01$.

d.	Graphs may vary.

11.51	a.

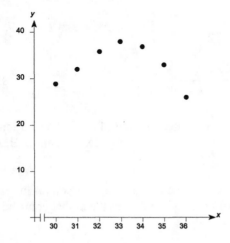

b. If information were available only for $x = 30, 31, 32$, and 33, we would suggest a first-order model where $\beta_1 > 0$. If information was available only for $x = 33, 34, 35$, and 36, we would again suggest a first-order model where $\beta_1 < 0$. If all the information was available, we would suggest a second-order model.

11.53 a. $E(y) = \beta_0 + \beta_1 x_1 + \beta_2 x_2 + \beta_3 x_1 x_2 + \beta_4 x_1^2 + \beta_5 x_2^2$

b. $\beta_4 x_1^2$ and $\beta_5 x_2^2$

11.55 a. From MINITAB, the output is:

Regression Analysis: Time versus Exp, Exp-sq

```
The regression equation is
Time = 20.1 - 0.671 Exp + 0.00953 Exp-sq

Predictor        Coef      SE Coef          T        P
Constant      20.0911       0.7247      27.72    0.000
Exp           -0.6705       0.1547      -4.33    0.001
Exp-sq       0.009535     0.006326       1.51    0.158

S = 1.091       R-Sq = 91.6%      R-Sq(adj) = 90.2%

Analysis of Variance

Source            DF          SS          MS        F        P
Regression         2     156.119      78.060    65.59    0.000
Residual Error    12      14.281       1.190
Total             14     170.400

Source            DF      Seq SS
Exp                1     153.416
Exp-sq             1       2.704
```

$\hat{y} = 20.0911 - .6705x + .0095x^2$

b. It appears that the relationship between time to assemble and months of experience is fairly linear. It is possible the quadratic term is significant, but not likely.

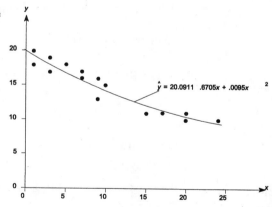

c. H_0: $\beta_2 = 0$
H_a: $\beta_2 \neq 0$

The test statistic is $t = \dfrac{\hat{\beta}_2 - 0}{s_{\hat{\beta}_2}} = \dfrac{.0095 - 0}{.00632580} = 1.51$

The rejection region requires $\alpha/2 = .01/2 = .005$ in each tail of the t-distribution with df $= n - (k + 1) = 15 - (2 + 1) = 12$. From Table VI, Appendix B, $t_{.005} = 3.055$. The rejection region is $t < -3.055$ or $t > 3.055$.

Since the observed value of the test statistic does not fall in the rejection region ($t = 1.51 \not> 3.055$), H_0 is not rejected. There is insufficient evidence to indicate $\beta_2 \neq 0$ at $\alpha = .01$.

d. Some preliminary calculations are:

$$\sum x = 151 \qquad \sum x^2 = 2295 \qquad \sum xy = 1890$$
$$\sum y = 222 \qquad \sum y^2 = 3456$$

$$SS_{xy} = \sum xy - \frac{\sum x \sum y}{n} = 1890 - \frac{151(225)}{15} = -344.8$$

$$SS_{xx} = \sum x^2 - \frac{(\sum x)^2}{n} = 2295 - \frac{151^2}{15} = 774.9333333$$

$$SS_{yy} = \sum y^2 - \frac{(\sum y)^2}{n} = 3456 - \frac{222^2}{15} = 170.4$$

$$\hat{\beta}_0 = \frac{SS_{xy}}{SS_{xx}} = \frac{-344.8}{774.933333} = -.4449415 \approx -.445$$

$$\hat{\beta}_0 = \bar{y} - \hat{\beta}_0 \bar{x} = \frac{222}{15} - (-.4449415)\left(\frac{151}{15}\right) = 19.27907777 = 19.279$$

The reduced fitted model is $\hat{y} = 19.279 - .445x$.

e. β_1 = change in mean time to complete task for each additional month of experience.

Some preliminary calculations are:

$$SSE = SS_{yy} - \hat{\beta}_1 SS_{xy} = 170.4 - (-.4449415)(-344.8) = 16.9841708$$

$$s^2 = \frac{SSE}{n-2} = \frac{16.9841708}{15-2} = 1.30647, \; s = \sqrt{1.30647} = 1.143$$

For confidence coefficient .90, $\alpha = .10$ and $\alpha/2 = .05$. From Table VI, Appendix B, with df $= n - (k + 1) = 15 - (1 + 1) = 13$, $t_{.05} = 1.771$. The confidence interval is:

$$\hat{\beta}_1 \pm t_{.05} \, s_{\hat{\beta}_1} \Rightarrow -.445 \pm 1.771\left(\frac{1.143}{\sqrt{774.93333}}\right) \Rightarrow -.445 \pm .0727 \Rightarrow (-.5177, -.3723)$$

11.57 The model would be $E(y) = \beta_0 + \beta_1 x + \beta_2 x^2$. Since the value of y is expected to increase and then decrease as x gets larger, β_2 will be negative. A sketch of the model would be:

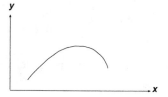

11.59 Let $x = \begin{cases} 1 & \text{if qualitative variable assumes 2nd level} \\ 0 & \text{otherwise} \end{cases}$

The model is $E(y) = \beta_0 + \beta_1 x$

β_0 = mean value of y when the qualitative variable assumes the first level
β_1 = difference in the mean values of y between levels 2 and 1 of the qualitative variable

11.61 a. Level 1 implies $x_1 = x_2 = x_3 = 0$. $\hat{y} = 10.2$
Level 2 implies $x_1 = 1$ and $x_2 = x_3 = 0$. $\hat{y} = 10.2 - 4(1) = 6.2$
Level 3 implies $x_2 = 1$ and $x_1 = x_3 = 0$. $\hat{y} = 10.2 + 12(1) = 22.2$
Level 4 implies $x_3 = 1$ and $x_1 = x_2 = 0$. $\hat{y} = 10.2 + 2(1) = 12.2$

b. The hypotheses are:

H_0: $\beta_1 = \beta_2 = \beta_3 = 0$
H_a: At least one $\beta_i \neq 0$, $i = 1, 2, 3$

11.63 a. Let $x = \begin{cases} 1 & \text{if Developer} \\ 0 & \text{otherwise} \end{cases}$

Then the model would be: $E(y) = \beta_0 + \beta_1 x$

β_0 = mean accuracy for the Project Leader

β_1 = difference in mean accuracy between the Developer and the Project Leader

b. Let $x_1 = \begin{cases} 1 & \text{if Low} \\ 0 & \text{otherwise} \end{cases}$ Let $x_2 = \begin{cases} 1 & \text{if Medium} \\ 0 & \text{otherwise} \end{cases}$

Then the model would be: $E(y) = \beta_0 + \beta_1 x_1 + \beta_2 x_2$

β_0 = mean accuracy for the High task complexity

β_1 = difference in mean accuracy between Low and High task complexity

β_2 = difference in mean accuracy between Medium and High task complexity

c. Let $x = \begin{cases} 1 & \text{if Fixed price} \\ 0 & \text{otherwise} \end{cases}$

Then the model would be: $E(y) = \beta_0 + \beta_1 x$

β_0 = mean accuracy for the Hourly rate

β_1 = difference in mean accuracy between the Fixed price and the Hourly rate

d. Let $x_1 = \begin{cases} 1 & \text{if Time-of-delivery} \\ 0 & \text{otherwise} \end{cases}$ $\qquad$ Let $x_2 = \begin{cases} 1 & \text{if Cost} \\ 0 & \text{otherwise} \end{cases}$

Then the model would be: $E(y) = \beta_0 + \beta_1 x_1 + \beta_2 x_2$

β_0 = mean accuracy for the Quality

β_1 = difference in mean accuracy between Time-of-delivery and Quality

β_2 = difference in mean accuracy between Cost and Quality

11.65 a. $R_{adj}^2 = .76$. 76% of the total sample variation of SAT-Math scores is explained by the regression model including score on PSAT and whether the student was coached or not, adjusting for the sample size and the number of independent variables in the model.

b. For confidence level .95, $\alpha = .05$ and $\alpha/2 = .05/2 = .025$. From Table VI, Appendix B, with df $= n - (k + 1) = 3,492 - (2 + 1) = 3,489$, $t_{.025} = 1.96$. The 95% confidence interval is:

$$\hat{\beta}_2 \pm t_{\alpha/2} s_{\hat{\beta}_2} \Rightarrow 19 \pm 1.96(3) \Rightarrow 19 \pm 5.88 \Rightarrow (13.12, \ 24.88)$$

We are 95% confident that the mean SAT-Math score for those who were coached was anywhere from 13.12 to 24.88 points higher than the mean for those who were not coached, holding PSAT scores constant.

c. Since 0 is not contained in the confidence interval for β_2, we can conclude that the coaching effect was present. Those who received coaching scored higher on the SAT-Math than those who did not, holding PSAT scores constant.

11.67 a. Let $x_1 = \begin{cases} 1 & \text{if Group V} \\ 0 & \text{otherwise} \end{cases}$ $\qquad$ Let $x_2 = \begin{cases} 1 & \text{if Group S} \\ 0 & \text{otherwise} \end{cases}$

The model would be: $E(y) = \beta_0 + \beta_1 x_1 + \beta_2 x_2$

b. Using MINITAB, the results are:

Regression Analysis: Recall versus x1, x2

```
The regression equation is
Recall = 3.17 - 1.08 x1 - 1.45 x2


Predictor      Coef   SE Coef       T       P
Constant     3.1667    0.1670   18.96   0.000
x1          -1.0833    0.2362   -4.59   0.000
x2          -1.4537    0.2362   -6.15   0.000


S = 1.73596   R-Sq = 11.3%   R-Sq(adj) = 10.7%


Analysis of Variance

Source            DF        SS      MS       F       P
Regression         2   123.265  61.633   20.45   0.000
Residual Error   321   967.352   3.014
Total            323  1090.617


Source  DF    Seq SS
x1       1     9.150
x2       1   114.116
```

The least squares prediction equation is: $\hat{y} = 3.1667 - 1.0833x_1 - 1.4537x_2$.

c. To determine if the overall model is useful, we test:

H_0: $\beta_1 = \beta_2 = 0$
H_a: At least one $\beta_i \neq 0$

The test statistic is $F = 20.45$ and the p-value is $p = 0.000$. Since the p-value is less than $\alpha = .01$, H_0 is rejected. There is sufficient evidence to indicate the model is useful in predicting brand recall at $\alpha = .01$.

From Exercise 8.23, the test statistic was $F = 20.45$ and the p-value was $p = 0.000$. These are identical to those above. The model is useful in predicting recall. This is the same as the conclusion that there is a difference in mean recall among the 3 groups.

d. With the dummy variable coding in part **a**, β_0 is the mean recall for group N. Thus, the estimated mean recall for Group N is 3.1667 or 3.17. β_1 is the difference in mean recall between Group V and Group N. Thus, the mean recall for Group V is $\beta_0 + \beta_1$ and is estimated to be $3.1667 - 1.0833 = 2.0834$ or 2.08. β_2 is the difference in mean recall between Group S and Group N. Thus, the mean recall for Group S is $\beta_0 + \beta_2$ and is estimated to be $3.1667 - 1.4537 = 1.7130$ or 1.71.

11.69   a.   Let $x_1 = 1$ if Lotion/cream
                   0 otherwise

b.   From MINITAB, the output is:

```
Regression Analysis: Cost/Use versus Type

The regression equation is
Cost/Use = 0.778 + 0.109 Type

Predictor        Coef      SE Coef          T          P
Constant       0.7775       0.2975       2.61      0.023
Type           0.1092       0.4545       0.24      0.814

S = 0.8415      R-Sq = 0.5%      R-Sq(adj) = 0.0%

Analysis of Variance

Source             DF          SS          MS          F          P
Regression          1      0.0409      0.0409       0.06      0.814
Residual Error     12      8.4973      0.7081
Total              13      8.5381
```

The fitted model is: $\hat{y} = 0.7775 + .1092x_1$

c.   To determine whether repellent type is a useful predictor of cost-per-use, we test:

$H_0: \beta_1 = 0$

d.   The alternative hypothesis is

$H_a: \beta_1 \neq 0$

The test statistic is $t = 0.24$ and the p-value is $p = 0.814$.

Since the p-value is greater than α ($p = .814 > .10$), H_0 is not rejected. There is insufficient evidence to indicate that repellent type is a useful predictor of cost-per-use at $\alpha = .10$.

e.   The dummy variable will be defined the same way and the model will look the same (just the dependent variable will be different).

From MINITAB, the output is:

Regression Analysis: MaxProt versus Type

```
The regression equation is
MaxProt = 7.56 - 1.65 Type

Predictor          Coef       SE Coef          T           P
Constant          7.563         2.339       3.23       0.007
Type             -1.646         3.574      -0.46       0.653

S = 6.617         R-Sq = 1.7%        R-Sq(adj) = 0.0%

Analysis of Variance

Source            DF            SS          MS          F          P
Regression         1          9.29        9.29       0.21      0.653
Residual Error    12        525.43       43.79
Total             13        534.71
```

The fitted model is: $\hat{y} = 7.563 - 1.646x_1$

To determine whether repellent type is a useful predictor of cost-per-use, we test:

H_0: $\beta_1 = 0$
H_a: $\beta_1 \neq 0$

The test statistic is $t = -0.46$ and the p-value is $p = 0.653$.

Since the p-value is greater than α ($p = .653 > .10$), H_0 is not rejected. There is insufficient evidence to indicate that repellent type is a useful predictor of maximum number of hours of protection at $\alpha = .10$.

11.71   a. $E(y) = \beta_0 + \beta_1 x_1 + \beta_2 x_2 + \beta_3 x_3$

where $x_1 = \begin{cases} 1 & \text{if franchise is cleaning} \\ 0 & \text{otherwise} \end{cases}$

$x_2 = \begin{cases} 1 & \text{if franchise is accounting/consulting} \\ 0 & \text{otherwise} \end{cases}$

$x_3 = \begin{cases} 1 & \text{if franchise is hospitality} \\ 0 & \text{otherwise} \end{cases}$

b.   By definition, β_0 = mean number of new franchises for the food industry. Thus,

$$\hat{\beta}_0 = \bar{x}_F = \frac{\sum x_F}{n_F} = \frac{1524}{7} = \frac{1524}{7} = 217.7$$

By definition, β_1 = difference in the mean number of new franchises between the cleaning industry and the food industry. Thus,

$$\hat{\beta}_1 = \bar{x}_C - \bar{x}_F = \frac{\sum x_C}{n_C} - \bar{x}_F = \frac{1473}{5} = -217.7 = 294.6 - 217.7 = 76.9$$

By definition, β_2 = difference in the mean number of new franchises between the accounting/consulting industry and the food industry. Thus,

$$\hat{\beta}_2 = \bar{x}_A - \bar{x}_F = \frac{\sum x_A}{n_A} - \bar{x}_F = \frac{228}{4} - 217.7 = 57 - 217.7 = -160.7$$

By definition, β_3 = difference in the mean number of new franchises between the hospitality industry and the food industry. Thus,

$$\hat{\beta}_3 = \bar{x}_H - \bar{x}_F = \frac{\sum x_H}{n_H} - \bar{x}_F = \frac{424}{3} = -217.7 = 141.333 - 217.7 = -76.367$$

c. Using MINITAB, the printout is:

```
The regression equation is
y = 218 + 77x1 - 161x2 - 76x3


Predictor        Coef         StDev            T              P
Constant       217.71         72.06         3.02          0.009
x1              76.9         111.6          0.69          0.501
x2            -160.7         119.5         -1.34          0.199
x3             -76.4         131.6         -0.58          0.570


S = 190.6         R-Sq = 20.2%       R-Sq(adj) = 4.2%

Analysis of Variance

Source            DF       SS        MS       F       P
Regression         3    137864     45955    1.26    0.322
Residual Error    15    545199     36347
Total             18    683063

Source     DF     Seq SS
x1          1      71358
x2          1      54254
x3          1      12252
Unusual Observations

Obs      x1         y      Fit  StDev Fit  Residual  St Resid
8      0.00     744.0    217.7       72.1     526.3     2.98R

R denotes an observation with a large standardized residual
```

The fitted model is $\hat{y} = 217.7 + 76.9x_1 - 160.7x_2 - 76.4x_3$

To determine if there are differences in the mean number of franchises for the four franchise types, we test:

H_0: $\beta_1 = \beta_2 = \beta_3 = 0$
H_a: At least one $\beta_i \neq 0$, $i = 1, 2, 3$

The test statistic is $F = 1.26$ with p-value $= .322$. Since the p-value is so large, there is insufficient evidence to indicate there are differences in the mean number of franchises for the four franchise types at $\alpha < .322$.

11.73 a. The complete second-order model is $E(y) = \beta_0 + \beta_1x_1 + \beta_2 x_1^2$

b. The new model is $E(y) = \beta_0 + \beta_1x_1 + \beta_2 x_1^2 + \beta_3x_2 + \beta_4x_3$

where $x_2 = \begin{cases} 1 \text{ if level 2} \\ 0 \text{ otherwise} \end{cases}$ $x_3 = \begin{cases} 1 \text{ if level 3} \\ 0 \text{ otherwise} \end{cases}$

c. The model with the interaction terms is:

$E(y) = \beta_0 + \beta_1x_1 + \beta_2 x_1^2 + \beta_3x_2 + \beta_4x_3 + \beta_5x_1x_2 + \beta_6x_1x_3 + \beta_7x_1^2x_2 + \beta_8x_1^2x_3$

d. The response curves will have the same shape if none of the interaction terms are present or if $\beta_5 = \beta_6 = \beta_7 = \beta_8 = 0$.

e. The response curves will be parallel lines if the interaction terms as well as the second-order terms are absent or if $\beta_2 = \beta_5 = \beta_6 = \beta_7 = \beta_8 = 0$.

f. The response curves will be identical if no terms involving the qualitative variable are present or $\beta_3 = \beta_4 = \beta_5 = \beta_6 = \beta_7 = \beta_8 = 0$.

11.75 a. For $x_2 = 0$ and $x_3 = 0$, $\hat{y} = 48.8 - 3.4x_1 + .07x_1^2$

For $x_2 = 1$ and $x_3 = 0$, $\hat{y} = 48.8 - 3.4x_1 + .07x_1^2 - 2.4(1) + 3.7x_1(1) - .02x_1^2(1)$
$= 46.4 + 0.3x_1 + .05x_1^2$

For $x_2 = 0$ and $x_3 = 1$, $\hat{y} = 48.8 - 3.4x_1 + .07x_1^2 - 7.5(1) + 2.7x_1(1) - .04x_1^2(1)$
$= 41.3 - 0.7x_1 + 0.03x_1^2$

b. The plots of the lines are:

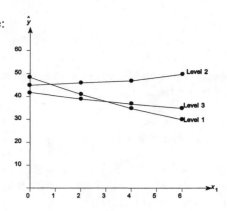

11.77 a. Let $x_1 = \begin{cases} 1 & \text{if Channel catfish} \\ 0 & \text{otherwise} \end{cases}$ $\qquad$ $x_2 = \begin{cases} 1 & \text{if Largemouth bass} \\ 0 & \text{otherwise} \end{cases}$

b. Let x_3 = weight. The model would be: $E(y) = \beta_0 + \beta_1 x_1 + \beta_2 x_2 + \beta_3 x_3$

c. The model would be: $E(y) = \beta_0 + \beta_1 x_1 + \beta_2 x_2 + \beta_3 x_3 + \beta_4 x_1 x_3 + \beta_4 x_2 x_3$

d. From MINITAB, the output is:

Regression Analysis: DDT versus x1, x2, Weight

```
The regression equation is
DDT = 3.1 + 26.5 x1 - 4.1 x2 + 0.0037 Weight

Predictor         Coef      SE Coef          T          P
Constant          3.13        38.89       0.08      0.936
x1               26.51        21.52       1.23      0.220
x2               -4.09        37.91      -0.11      0.914
Weight         0.00371      0.02598       0.14      0.887

S = 98.57       R-Sq = 1.7%       R-Sq(adj) = 0.0%

Analysis of Variance

Source             DF          SS         MS          F          P
Regression          3       23652       7884       0.81      0.490
Residual Error    140     1360351       9717
Total             143     1384003

Source    DF      Seq SS
x1         1       23041
x2         1         414
Weight     1         198
```

The least squares prediction equation is: $\hat{y} = 3.1 + 26.5 x_1 - 4.1 x_2 + 0.0037 x_3$

e. $\hat{\beta}_3 = 0.0037$. For each additional gram of weight, the mean level of DDT is expected to increase by 0.0037 units, holding species constant.

f.   From MINITAB, the output is:

Regression Analysis: DDT versus x1, x2, Weight, x1Weight, x2Weight

```
The regression equation is
DDT = 3.5 + 25.6 x1 - 3.5 x2 + 0.0034 Weight + 0.0008 x1Weight
      - 0.0013 x2Weight

Predictor          Coef      SE Coef          T        P
Constant           3.50        54.69       0.06    0.949
x1                25.59        67.52       0.38    0.705
x2                -3.47        84.70      -0.04    0.967
Weight          0.00344      0.03843       0.09    0.929
x1Weight        0.00082      0.05459       0.02    0.988
x2Weight       -0.00129      0.09987      -0.01    0.990

S = 99.29       R-Sq = 1.7%       R-Sq(adj) = 0.0%

Analysis of Variance

Source             DF           SS         MS        F        P
Regression          5        23657       4731     0.48    0.791
Residual Error    138      1360346       9858
Total             143      1384003

Source           DF      Seq SS
x1                1       23041
x2                1         414
Weight            1         198
x1Weight          1           4
x2Weight          1           2
```

The least squares prediction equation is:

$$\hat{y} = 3.5 + 26.5x_1 - 3.5x_2 + 0.0034x_3 + 0.008x_1x_3 - .0013x_2x_3$$

g.   For Channel catfish, $x_1 = 1$ and $x_2 = 0$. The least squares line is

$$\hat{y} = 3.5 + 26.5(1) + 0.0034x_3 + 0.008(1)x_3 = 30.0 + .0114x_3$$

The estimated slope is .0114.

11.79   a.   For obese smokers, $x_2 = 0$. The equation of the hypothesized line relating mean REE to time after smoking for obese smokers is:

$$E(y) = \beta_0 + \beta_1 x_1 + \beta_2(0) + \beta_3 x_1(0) = \beta_0 + \beta_1 x_1$$

The slope of the line is β_1.

b.   For normal weight smokers, $x_2 = 1$. The equation of the hypothesized line relating mean REE to time after smoking for normal smokers is:

$$E(y) = \beta_0 + \beta_1 x_1 + \beta_2(1) + \beta_3 x_1(1) = (\beta_0 + \beta_2) + (\beta_1 + \beta_3)x_1$$

The slope of the line is $\beta_1 + \beta_3$.

c.   The reported p-value is .044. Since the p-value is small, there is evidence to indicate that interaction between time and weight is present for $\alpha > .044$.

11.81   a.   Let x_1 = sales volume

$$x_2 = \begin{cases} 1 \text{ if NW} \\ 0 \text{ if not} \end{cases} \qquad x_3 = \begin{cases} 1 \text{ if S} \\ 0 \text{ if not} \end{cases}$$

$$x_4 = \begin{cases} 1 \text{ if W} \\ 0 \text{ if not} \end{cases}$$

The complete second order model for the sales price of a single-family home is:

$$E(y) = \beta_0 + \beta_1 x_1 + \beta_2 x_1^2 + \beta_3 x_2 + \beta_4 x_3 + \beta_5 x_4 + \beta_6 x_1 x_2 + \beta_7 x_1 x_3 + \beta_8 x_1 x_4$$
$$+ \beta_9 x_1^2 x_2 + \beta_{10} x_1^2 x_3 + \beta_{11} x_1^2 x_4$$

b.   For the West, $x_2 = 0$, $x_3 = 0$, and $x_4 = 1$. The equation would be:

$$E(y) = \beta_0 + \beta_1 x_1 + \beta_2 x_1^2 + \beta_3(0) + \beta_4(0) + \beta_5(0) + \beta_6 x_1(0) + \beta_7 x_1(0)$$
$$+ \beta_8 x_1(0) + \beta_9 x_1^2(0) + \beta_{10} x_1^2(0) + \beta_{11} x_1^2(0)$$

$$= \beta_0 + \beta_1 x_1 + \beta_2 x_1^2 + \beta_5 + \beta_8 x_1 + \beta_{11} x_1^2$$

$$= \beta_0 + \beta_5 + \beta_1 x_1 + \beta_8 x_1 + \beta_2 x_1^2 + \beta_{11} x_1^2$$
$$= (\beta_0 + \beta_5) + (\beta_1 + \beta_8) x_1 + (\beta_2 + \beta_{11}) x_1^2$$

c.   For the Northwest, $x_2 = 1$, $x_3 = 0$, and $x_4 = 0$. The equation would be:

$$E(y) = \beta_0 + \beta_1 x_1 + \beta_2 x_1^2 + \beta_3(1) + \beta_4(0) + \beta_5(0) + \beta_6 x_1(1) + \beta_7 x_1(0)$$
$$+ \beta_8 x_1(0) + \beta_9 x_1^2(1) + \beta_{10} x_1^2(0) + \beta_{11} x_1^2(0)$$

$$= \beta_0 + \beta_1 x_1 + \beta_2 x_1^2 + \beta_3 + \beta_6 x_1 + \beta_9 x_1^2$$

$$= \beta_0 + \beta_3 + \beta_1 x_1 + \beta_6 x_1 + \beta_2 x_1^2 + \beta_9 x_1^2$$
$$= (\beta_0 + \beta_3) + (\beta_1 + \beta_6) x_1 + (\beta_2 + \beta_9) x_1^2$$

d.   The parameters β_3, β_4, and β_5 allow for the y-intercepts of the 4 regions to be different. The parameters β_6, β_7, and β_8 allow for the peaks of the curves to be a different values of sales volume (x_1) for the four regions. The parameters β_9, β_{10}, and β_{11} allow for the shapes of the curves to be different for the four regions. Thus, all the parameters from β_3 through β_{11} allow for differences in mean sales prices among the four regions.

e. Using MINITAB, the printout is:

Regression Analysis: Price versus X1, X1SQ, ...

The regression equation is
Price = 1904740 - 70.4 X1 + 0.000721 X1SQ + 159661 X2 + 5291908 X3 + 3663319 X4
        + 22.2 X1X2 - 23.9 X1X3 - 37 X1X4 - 0.000421 X1SQX2 - 0.000404 X1SQX3
        - 0.000181 X1SQX4

Predictor	Coef	SE Coef	T	P
Constant	1904740	1984278	0.96	0.351
X1	-70.44	72.09	-0.98	0.343
X1SQ	0.0007211	0.0006515	1.11	0.285
X2	159661	2069265	0.08	0.939
X3	5291908	4812586	1.10	0.288
X4	3663319	4478880	0.82	0.425
X1X2	22.25	73.74	0.30	0.767
X1X3	-23.86	92.09	-0.26	0.799
X1X4	-37.2	103.0	-0.36	0.723
X1SQX2	-0.0004210	0.0006589	-0.64	0.532
X1SQX3	-0.0004044	0.0006777	-0.60	0.559
X1SQX4	-0.0001810	0.0007333	-0.25	0.808

S = 24365.8   R-Sq = 85.0%   R-Sq(adj) = 74.6%

Analysis of Variance

Source	DF	SS	MS	F	P
Regression	11	53633628997	4875784454	8.21	0.000
Residual Error	16	9499097458	593693591		
Total	27	63132726455			

Source	DF	Seq SS
X1	1	3591326
X1SQ	1	64275360
X2	1	11338642654
X3	1	10081000583
X4	1	241539024
X1X2	1	18258475317
X1X3	1	5579187440
X1X4	1	7566169810
X1SQX2	1	138146367
X1SQX3	1	326425228
X1SQX4	1	36175888

Unusual Observations

Obs	X1	Price	Fit	SE Fit	Residual	St Resid
2	61025	235900	291659	18746	-55759	-3.58R
5	60324	345300	279697	15712	65603	3.52R
7	61025	240855	241084	24360	-229	-0.42 X

R denotes an observation with a large standardized residual.
X denotes an observation whose X value gives it large influence.

To determine if the model is useful for predicting sales price, we test:

H_0: $\beta_1 = \beta_2 = \ldots = \beta_{11} = 0$
H_a: At least one of the coefficients is nonzero

The test statistic is $F = \dfrac{\text{MS(Model)}}{\text{MSE}} = 8.21$

The p-value is $p = .000$. Since the p-value is less than $\alpha = .01$ ($p = .000 < .01$), H_0 is rejected. There is sufficient evidence to indicate the model is useful in predicting sales price at $\alpha = .01$.

11.83   a.   Let $x_2 = \begin{cases} 1 & \text{if Developing} \\ 0 & \text{otherwise} \end{cases}$

The model would be:

$$E(y) = \beta_0 + \beta_1 x_1 + \beta_2 x_2 + \beta_3 x_1 x_2$$

       b.   Using MINITAB, the plot of the data is:

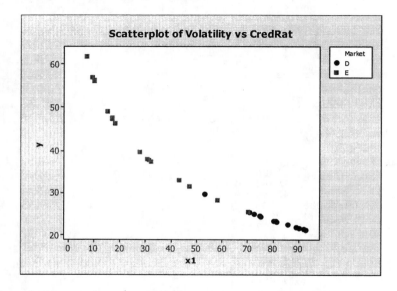

From the plot, it appears that the model is appropriate. The two lines appear to have different slopes.

c. Using MINITAB, the output is:

Regression Analysis: y versus x1, x2, x1x2

```
The regression equation is
y = 58.8 - 0.557 x1 - 18.7 x2 + 0.354 x1x2


Predictor        Coef  SE Coef        T       P
Constant       58.786    1.217    48.30   0.000
x1           -0.55743  0.03669   -15.19   0.000
x2            -18.718    5.572    -3.36    0.002
x1x2          0.35368  0.07615    4.64    0.000


S = 2.66123   R-Sq = 96.1%   R-Sq(adj) = 95.7%


Analysis of Variance

Source          DF       SS      MS        F       P
Regression       3   4596.5  1532.2   216.34   0.000
Residual Error  26    184.1     7.1
Total           29   4780.6


Source   DF   Seq SS
x1        1   4388.0
x2        1     55.7
x1x2      1    152.8
```

The fitted regression model is:

$$\hat{y} = 58.786 - .557x_1 - 18.718x_2 + .354x_1x_2$$

For the emerging countries, $x_2 = 0$. The fitted model is:

$$\hat{y} = 58.786 - .557x_1 - 18.718(0) + .354x_1(0) = 58.786 - .557x_1$$

For the developed countries, $x_2 = 1$. The fitted model is:

$$\hat{y} = 58.786 - .557x_1 - 18.718(1) + .354x_1(1) = 40.068 - .203x_1$$

d.   The plot of the fitted lines is:

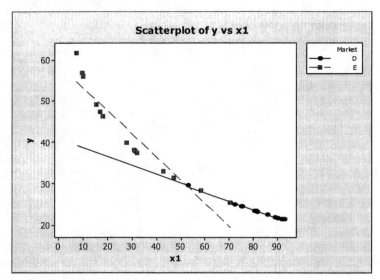

e.   To determine if the slope of the linear relationship between volatility and credit rating depends on market type, we test:

H_0: $\beta_3 = 0$
H_a: $\beta_3 \neq 0$

The test statistic is $t = 4.64$.

The p-value is 0.000. Since the p-value is less than $\alpha = .01$, H_0 is rejected. There is sufficient evidence to indicate that the slope of the linear relationship between volatility and credit rating depends on market type at $\alpha = .01$.

11.85   The models in parts **a** and **b** are nested:

The complete model is $E(y) = \beta_0 + \beta_1 x_1 + \beta_2 x_2$
The reduced model is $E(y) = \beta_0 + \beta_1 x_1$

The models in parts **a** and **d** are nested.

The complete model is $E(y) = \beta_0 + \beta_1 x_1 + \beta_2 x_2 + \beta_3 x_1 x_2$
The reduced model is $E(y) = \beta_0 + \beta_1 x_1 + \beta_2 x_2$

The models in parts **a** and **e** are nested.

The complete model is $E(y) = \beta_0 + \beta_1 x_1 + \beta_2 x_2 + \beta_3 x_1 x_2 + \beta_4 x_1^2 + \beta_5 x_2^2$
The reduced model is $E(y) = \beta_0 + \beta_1 x_1 + \beta_2 x_2$

The models in parts **b** and **c** are nested.

The complete model is $E(y) = \beta_0 + \beta_1x_1 + \beta_2x_1^2$
The reduced model is $E(y) = \beta_0 + \beta_1x_1$

The models in parts **b** and **d** are nested.

The complete model is $E(y) = \beta_0 + \beta_1x_1 + \beta_2x_2 + \beta_3x_1x_2$
The reduced model is $E(y) = \beta_0 + \beta_1x_1$

The models in parts **b** and **e** are nested.

The complete model is $E(y) = \beta_0 + \beta_1x_1 + \beta_2x_2 + \beta_3x_1x_2 + \beta_4x_1^2 + \beta_5x_2^2$
The reduced model is $E(y) = \beta_0 + \beta_1x_1$

The models in parts **c** and **e** are nested.

The complete model is $E(y) = \beta_0 + \beta_1x_1 + \beta_2x_2 + \beta_3x_1x_2 + \beta_4x_1^2 + \beta_5x_2^2$
The reduced model is $E(y) = \beta_0 + \beta_1x_1 + \beta_2x_1^2$

The models in parts **d** and **e** are nested.

The complete model is $E(y) = \beta_0 + \beta_1x_1 + \beta_2x_2 + \beta_3x_1x_2 + \beta_4x_1^2 + \beta_5x_2^2$
The reduced model is $E(y) = \beta_0 + \beta_1x_1 + \beta_2x_2 + \beta_3x_1x_2$

11.87 a. Including β_0, there are five β parameters in the complete model and three in the reduced model.

b. The hypotheses are:

H_0: $\beta_3 = \beta_4 = 0$
H_a: At least one $\beta_i \neq 0$, $i = 3, 4$

c. The test statistic is $F = \dfrac{(SSE_R - SSE_C)/(k - g)}{SSE_C/[n - (k+1)]}$

$$= \frac{(160.44 - 152.66)/(4 - 2)}{152.66/[20 - (4+1)]} = \frac{3.89}{10.1773} = .38$$

The rejection region requires $\alpha = .05$ in the upper tail of the F distribution with numerator df $= k - g = 4 - 2 = 2$ and denominator df $= n - (k+1) = 20 - (4+1) = 15$. From Table IX, Appendix B, $F_{.05} = 3.68$. The rejection region is $F > 3.68$.

Since the observed value of the test statistic does not fall in the rejection region ($F = .38$ $\ngtr$ 3.68), H_0 is not rejected. There is insufficient evidence to indicate the complete model is better than the reduced model at $\alpha = .05$.

11.89   a.   Let x_1 = cycle speed and x_2 = cycle pressure ratio. A complete second order model is:

$$E(y) = \beta_0 + \beta_1 x_1 + \beta_2 x_2 + \beta_3 x_1^2 + \beta_4 x_2^2 + \beta_5 x_1 x_2$$

   b.   To determine whether the curvature terms in the complete 2nd–order model are useful for predicting heat rate, we test:

H_o: $\beta_3 = \beta_4 = \beta_5 = 0$
H_a: At least one of the parameters β_3, β_4, β_5 differs from 0

   c.   The complete model is: $E(y) = \beta_0 + \beta_1 x_1 + \beta_2 x_2 + \beta_3 x_1^2 + \beta_4 x_2^2 + \beta_5 x_1 x_2$

   The reduced model is: $E(y) = \beta_0 + \beta_1 x_1 + \beta_2 x_2$

   d.   From the printout, $SSE_R = 25{,}310{,}639$, $SSE_C = 19{,}370{,}350$, and $MSE_C = 317{,}547$.

   e.   The test statistic is:

$$F = \frac{(SSE_R - SSE_C)/(k-g)}{SSE_C/[n-(k+1)]} = \frac{(25{,}310{,}639 - 19{,}370{,}350)/(5-2)}{19{,}370{,}350/[67-(5+1)]} = 6.236$$

   f.   The rejection region requires $\alpha = .10$ in the upper tail of the F-distribution with $v_1 = k - g = 5 - 2 = 3$ and $v_2 = n - (k+1) = 67 - (5+1) = 61$. From Table VIII, Appendix B, $F_{.10} = 2.18$. The rejection region is $F > 2.18$.

   g.   Since the observed value of the test statistic falls in the rejection region ($F = 6.236 > 2.18$), H_0 is rejected. There is sufficient evidence to indicate at least one of the curvature terms in the complete 2nd–order model are useful for predicting heat rate at $\alpha = .10$.

11.91   a.   The hypothesized equation for $E(y)$ is:

$$E(y) = \beta_0 + \beta_1 x_1 + \beta_2 x_2 + \beta_3 x_3 + \beta_4 x_4 + \beta_5 x_5 + \beta_6 x_6 + \beta_7 x_7 + \beta_8 x_8 + \beta_9 x_9 + \beta_{10} x_{10}$$

   b.   To determine if the initial model is sufficient, we test:

H_0: $\beta_3 = \beta_4 = \ldots = \beta_{10} = 0$
H_a: At least one $\beta_i \neq 0$ $i = 3, 4, \ldots, 10$

   c.   Since the F was significant, we reject H_0 at $\alpha = .05$. There is sufficient evidence to indicate that at least one of the additional variables (student ethnicity, socio-economic status, school performance, number of math courses taken in high school and overall GPA in the math courses) contributes to the prediction of the SAT-math score.

d. R^2_{adj} = .79. 79% of the sample variability of SAT-math scores is explained by the model containing the 10 independent variables, adjusted for the sample size and the number of variables.

e. For confidence coefficient .95, α = .05 and $\alpha/2$ = .05/2 = .025. From Table VI, Appendix B, with df = $n - (k + 1)$ = 3,492 − (10 + 1) = 3,481, $t_{.025}$ = 1.96. The confidence interval is:

$$\hat{\beta}_2 \pm t_{\alpha/2}s_{\hat{\beta}_2} \Rightarrow 14 \pm 1.96(3) \Rightarrow 14 \pm 5.88 \Rightarrow (8.12, \ 19.88)$$

We are 95% confident that the mean SAT-Math score for those who were coached was anywhere from 8.12 to 19.88 points higher than the mean for those who were not coached, holding all other variables constant.

f. Yes. The value of $\hat{\beta}_2$ decreased from 19 to 14 when the additional variables were added to the model. Thus, the increase from coaching is not as great.

g. Te new model including all the interaction terms is:

$$E(y) = \beta_0 + \beta_1 x_1 + \beta_2 x_2 + \beta_3 x_3 + \beta_4 x_4 + \beta_5 x_5 + \beta_6 x_6 + \beta_7 x_7 + \beta_8 x_8 + \beta_9 x_9 + \beta_{10} x_{10}$$
$$+ \beta_{11} x_1 x_2 + \beta_{12} x_3 x_2 + \beta_{13} x_4 x_2 + \beta_{14} x_5 x_2 + \beta_{15} x_6 x_2 + \beta_{16} x_7 x_2 + \beta_{17} x_8 x_2$$
$$+ \beta_{18} x_9 x_2 + \beta_{19} x_{10} x_2$$

h. To determine if the model with the interaction terms is better in predicting SAT-Math scores, we test:

H_0: $\beta_{11} = \beta_{12} = ... = \beta_{19} = 0$
H_a: At least one $\beta_i \neq 0$ i = 11, 12, ..., 19

We would fit the complete model above. We would then compare it to the fitted model from part a (Reduced model). The test statistic would be:

$$F = \frac{(SSE_R - SSE_C)/(k - g)}{SSE_C /[n - (k + 1)]}$$

11.93 a. The model would be:

$$E(y) = \beta_0 + \beta_1 x_1 + \beta_2 x_2 + \beta_3 x_3$$

b. The model including the interaction terms is:

$$E(y) = \beta_0 + \beta_1 x_1 + \beta_2 x_2 + \beta_3 x_3 + \beta_4 x_1 x_2 + \beta_5 x_1 x_3$$

c. For AL, $x_2 = x_3 = 0$. The model would be:

$$E(y) = \beta_0 + \beta_1 x_1 + \beta_2(0) + \beta_3(0) + \beta_4 x_1(0) + \beta_5 x_1(0) = \beta_0 + \beta_1 x_1$$

The slope of the line is β_1.

For TDS-3A, $x_2 = 1$ and $x_3 = 0$. The model would be:

$$E(y) = \beta_0 + \beta_1 x_1 + \beta_2(1) + \beta_3(0) + \beta_4 x_1(1) + \beta_5 x_1(0) = (\beta_0 + \beta_2) + (\beta_1 + \beta_4)x_1$$

The slope of the line is $\beta_1 + \beta_4$.

For FE, $x_2 = 0$ and $x_3 = 1$. The model would be:

$$E(y) = \beta_0 + \beta_1 x_1 + \beta_2(0) + \beta_3(1) + \beta_4 x_1(0) + \beta_5 x_1(1) = (\beta_0 + \beta_3) + (\beta_1 + \beta_5)x_1$$

The slope of the line is $\beta_1 + \beta_5$.

d. To test for the presence of temperature-waste type interaction, we would fit the complete model listed in part **b** and the reduced model found in part **a**. The hypotheses would be:

H_0: $\beta_4 = \beta_5 = 0$
H_a: At least one $\beta_i \neq 0$, for $i = 4, 5$

The test statistic would be $F = F = \dfrac{(SSE_R - SSE_C)/(k-g)}{SSE_C /[n-(k+1)]}$ where $k = 5$, $q = 3$, SSE_R is

the SSE for the reduced model, and SSE_C is the SSE for the complete model.

11.95   a.   Using MINITAB, the output from fitting a complete second-order model is:

```
* NOTE *        X1 is highly correlated with other  predictor variables
* NOTE *        X2 is highly correlated with other  predictor variables
* NOTE *      X1X2 is highly correlated with other  predictor variables

The regression equation is
Y = 172788 - 10739 X1 - 499 X2 - 20.2 X1X2 + 198 X1SQ + 14.7 X2SQ


Predictor        Coef      Stdev     t-ratio        p
Constant       172788      97785        1.77    0.084
X1             -10739       2789       -3.85    0.000
X2               -499       1444       -0.35    0.731
X1X2           -20.20      21.36       -0.95    0.350
X1SQ           197.57      22.60        8.74    0.000
X2SQ           14.678      8.819        1.66    0.103


s = 13132      R-sq = 95.9%      R-sq(adj) = 95.5%

Analysis of Variance

SOURCE        DF           SS           MS           F         p
Regression     5  1.70956E+11  34191134720      198.27     0.000
Error         42   7242915328    172450368
Total         47  1.78199E+11

SOURCE        DF       SEQ SS
X1             1  1.56067E+11
X2             1     13214024
X1X2           1   1686339840
X1SQ           1  12711371776
X2SQ           1    477704384

Unusual Observations
Obs.      X1           Y      Fit Stdev.Fit   Residual    St.Resid
 14     62.9      203288   235455      6002     -32167      -2.75R
 22     45.4       27105    58567      3603     -31462      -2.49R
 34     28.2       28722    15156     11311      13566       2.03RX
 43     64.3      230329   248054      8790     -17725      -1.82 X
 47     63.9      212309   240469      4904     -28160      -2.31R

R denotes an obs. with a large st. resid.
X denotes an obs. whose X value gives it large influence.
```

b. To test the hypothesis H_0: $\beta_4 = \beta_5 = 0$, we must fit the reduced model

$$E(y) = \beta_0 + \beta_1 x_1 + \beta_2 x_2 + \beta_3 x_1 x_2$$

Using MINITAB, the output from fitting the reduced model is:

```
* NOTE *      X1X2 is highly correlated with other  predictor variables

The regression equation is
Y = - 476768 + 11458 X1 + 3404 X2 - 64.4 X1X2

Predictor          Coef        Stdev     t-ratio          p
Constant        -476768       100852       -4.73      0.000
X1                11458         1874        6.11      0.000
X2                 3404         1814        1.88      0.067
X1X2             -64.35        33.77       -1.91      0.063

s = 21549        R-sq = 88.5%      R-sq(adj) = 87.8%

Analysis of Variance

SOURCE          DF          SS            MS          F          p
Regression       3 1.57767E+11 52588867584      113.25      0.000
Error           44 20431990784    464363424
Total           47 1.78199E+11

SOURCE          DF      SEQ SS
X1               1 1.56067E+11
X2               1    13214024
X1X2             1  1686339840

Unusual Observations
Obs.        X1          Y      Fit Stdev.Fit   Residual    St.Resid
 34       28.2      28722    -59713    11922      88435      4.93RX
 38       66.5     290411    250350     9553      40061      2.07R
 43       64.3     230329    202899    11574      27430      1.51 X

R denotes an obs. with a large st. resid.
X denotes an obs. whose X value gives it large influence.
```

The test is:

H_0: $\beta_4 = \beta_5 = 0$
H_a: At least one $\beta_i \neq 0$, for $i = 4, 5$

The test statistic is $F = \dfrac{(SSE_R - SSE_C)/(k - g)}{SSE_C /[n - (k + 1)]}$

$$= \frac{(20,431,990,784 - 7,242,915,328)/(5 - 3)}{7,242,915,328/[48 - (5 + 1)]} = 38.24$$

The rejection region requires $\alpha = .05$ in the upper tail of the F-distribution with $v_1 = k - g = 5 - 3 = 2$ and $v_2 = n - (k + 1) = 48 - (5 + 1) = 42$. From Table IX, Appendix B, $F_{.05} \approx 3.23$. The rejection region is $F > 3.23$.

Since the observed value of the test statistic falls in the rejection region ($F = 38.24 > 3.23$), H_0 is rejected. There is sufficient evidence to indicate that at least one of the quadratic terms contributes to the prediction of monthly collision claims at $\alpha = .05$.

c. From part **b**, we know at least one of the quadratic terms is significant. From part **a**, it appears that none of the terms involving x_2 may be significant.

Thus, we will fit the model with just x_1 and x_1^2. The MINITAB output is:

```
The regression equation is
Y = 185160 - 11580 X1 + 196 X1SQ

Predictor          Coef        Stdev     t-ratio        p
Constant         185160        54791        3.38    0.002
X1               -11580         2182       -5.31    0.000
X1SQ             195.54        21.64        9.04    0.000

s = 13219        R-sq = 95.6%       R-sq(adj) = 95.4%

Analysis of Variance

SOURCE          DF           SS          MS          F        p
Regression       2  1.70335E+11  85167357952     487.36    0.000
Error           45   7863868416    174752624
Total           47  1.78199E+11

SOURCE          DF      SEQ SS
X1               1  1.56067E+11
X1SQ             1  14267676672

Unusual Observations
Obs.       X1          Y     Fit  Stdev.Fit  Residual   St.Resid
 10      35.8      28957   21200       5825      7757      0.65 X
 14      62.9     203288  230397       4044    -27109     -2.15R
 22      45.4      27105   62456       2856    -35351     -2.74R
 34      28.2      28722   14099      11344     14623      2.15RX
 38      66.5     290411  279798       6189     10613      0.91 X
 47      63.9     212309  243611       4570    -31302     -2.52R

R denotes an obs. with a large st. resid.
X denotes an obs. whose X value gives it large influence.
```

To see if any of the terms involving x_2 are significant, we test:

H_0: $\beta_2 = \beta_3 = \beta_5 = 0$
H_a: At least one $\beta_i \neq 0$, for $i = 2, 3, 5$

The test statistic is $F = \dfrac{(\text{SSE}_R - \text{SSE}_C)/(k - g)}{\text{SSE}_C/[n - (k+1)]}$

$$= \frac{(7,863,868,416 - 7,242,915,328)/(5 - 2)}{7,242,915,328/[48 - (5+1)]} = 1.20$$

The rejection region requires $\alpha = .05$ in the upper tail of the F-distribution with $v_1 = k - g = 5 - 2 = 3$ and $v_2 = n - (k+1) = 48 - (5+1) = 42$. From Table IX, Appendix B, $F_{.05} \approx 2.84$. The rejection region is $F > 2.84$

Since the observed value of the test statistic does not fall in the rejection region ($F = 1.20$ $\not> 2.84$), H_0 is not rejected. There is insufficient evidence to indicate that any of the terms involving x_2 contribute to the model at $\alpha = .05$.

Thus, it appears that the best model is $E(y) = \beta_0 + \beta_1 x_1 + \beta_2 x_1^2$. The model does not support the analyst's claim. In the model above, the estimate for β_2 is positive. This would indicate that the higher claims are for both the young and the old. Also, there is no evidence to support the claim that there are more claims when the temperature goes down.

11.97   a.   In Step 1, all one-variable models are fit to the data. These models are of the form:

$E(y) = \beta_0 + \beta_1 x_i$

Since there are 7 independent variables, 7 models are fit. (Note: There are actually only 6 independent variables. One of the qualitative variables has three levels and thus two dummy variables. Some statistical packages will allow one to bunch these two variables together so that they are either both in or both out. In this answer, we are assuming that each x_i stands by itself.

   b.   In Step 2, all two-varirable models are fit to the data, where the variable selected in Step 1, say x_1, is one of the variables. These models are of the form:

$E(y) = \beta_0 + \beta_1 x_1 + \beta_2 x_i$

Since there are 6 independent variables remaining, 6 models are fit.

   c.   In Step 3, all three-variable models are fit to the data, where the variables selected in Step 2, say x_1 and x_2, are two of the variables. These models are of the form:

$E(y) = \beta_0 + \beta_1 x_1 + \beta_2 x_2 + \beta_3 x_i$

Since there are 5 independent variables remaining, 5 models are fit.

   d.   The procedure stops adding independent variables when none of the remaining variables, when added to the model, have a p-value less than some predetermined value. This predetermined value is usually $\alpha = .05$.

e.   Two major drawbacks to using the final stepwise model as the "best" model are:
       (1)   An extremely large number of single β parameter t-tests have been conducted.
             Thus, the probability is very high that one or more errors have been made in
             including or excluding variables.

       (2)   Often the variables selected to be included in a stepwise regression do not include
             the high-order terms. Consequently, we may have initially omitted several
             important terms from the model.

11.99 a.   From the printout, the three variables that should be included in the model are: ST-
              DEPTH, TGRSWT, and TI. They are all entered into the model using stepwise
              regression and all are retained.

       b.   No. There may be other independent variables that were not included.

       c.   The model is $E(y) = \beta_0 + \beta_1 x_4 + \beta_2 x_5 + \beta_3 x_6 + \beta_4 x_4 x_5 + \beta_5 x_4 x_6 + \beta_6 x_5 x_6$

       d.   He would test H_0: $\beta_4 = \beta_5 = \beta_6 = 0$ versus
                                       H_a: At least one $\beta_i \neq 0$, $i = 4, 5, 6$

              He would fit the first-order model and record SSE_R. He would then fit the model with
              the interaction terms and record SSE_C.

              The test statistic is $F = \dfrac{(SSE_R - SSE_C)/(k - g)}{SSE_C /[n - (k + 1)]}$

       e.   To improve the model, the marine biologist could try to find other independent variables
              that affect y, the log of the number of marine animals present, or higher order terms of
              the already identified independent variables.

11.101 Yes. x_2 and x_4 are highly correlated (.93), as well as x_4 and x_5 (.86). When highly correlated
       independent variables are present in a regression model, the results can be confusing. The
       researcher may want to include only one of the variables.

11.103 Variables that are highly correlated with each other are x_4 and x_5 ($r = -.84$). When highly
       correlated independent variables are present in a regression model, the results can be
       confusing. Possible problems include:

       1.   Global test indicates at least one independent variable is useful in the prediction of y, but
              none of the individual tests for the independent variables is significant.

       2.   The signs of the estimated beta coefficients are opposite from what is expected.

11.105 a.   The normal probability plot should be used to check for normal errors. The points in this plot are fairly close to the straight line, so the assumption of normality appears to be satisfied.

b.   The graph of the residuals versus the fitted values should be used to check for unequal variances. The spread of the residuals appears to be fairly constant in this graph. It appears that the assumption of equal variances is satisfied.

11.107 From MINITAB, the output and residual plots are:

Regression Analysis: Acid versus Oxidant

```
The regression equation is
Acid = - 0.024 + 0.0196 Oxidant

Predictor          Coef      SE Coef           T          P
Constant        -0.0237       0.2458       -0.10      0.924
Oxidant        0.019579     0.004737        4.13      0.001

S = 0.3759        R-Sq = 50.1%      R-Sq(adj) = 47.2%

Analysis of Variance

Source             DF          SS          MS          F          P
Regression          1      2.4136      2.4136      17.08      0.001
Residual Error     17      2.4023      0.1413
Total              18      4.8160
```

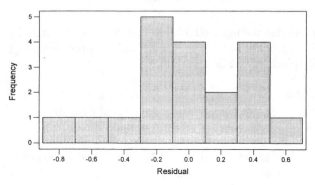

Histogram of the Residuals
(response is Acid)

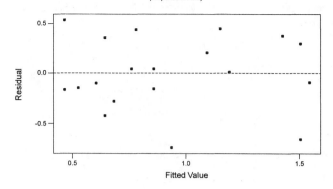

Residuals Versus the Fitted Values
(response is Acid)

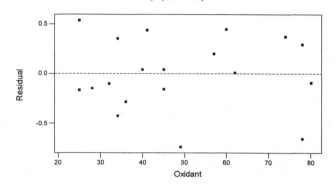

Residuals Versus Oxidant
(response is Acid)

First, we plot the residuals versus the independent variable, oxidant. From the plot, there is no systematic trend. Thus, the linear model appears to be appropriate. In addition, there is no cone shape, indicating the residuals have constant variance. From the printout, the standard deviation is .3759 (s). Two standard deviations is 2(.3759) = .7518. Three standard deviations is 3(.3759) = 1.1277. No residual is more than two standard deviations from 0, indicating that there are no outliers. The histogram of the residuals is somewhat mound-shaped, so it appears that the residuals are approximately normally distributed.

11.109 Using MINITAB, the results of the regression are:

Regression Analysis: HEATRATE versus RPM, CPRATIO, RPM*CPR

```
The regression equation is
HEATRATE = 12065 + 0.170 RPM - 146 CPRATIO - 0.00242 RPM*CPR


Predictor        Coef    SE Coef        T      P
Constant      12065.5      418.5    28.83  0.000
RPM           0.16969    0.03467     4.89  0.000
CPRATIO       -146.07      26.66    -5.48  0.000
RPM*CPR      -0.002425   0.003120    -0.78  0.440


S = 633.842    R-Sq = 84.9%    R-Sq(adj) = 84.2%


Analysis of Variance

Source            DF          SS         MS       F      P
Regression         3   142586570   47528857  118.30  0.000
Residual Error    63    25310639     401756
Total             66   167897208


Source     DF      Seq SS
RPM         1   119598530
CPRATIO     1    22745478
RPM*CPR     1      242561


Unusual Observations

Obs     RPM   HEATRATE       Fit   SE Fit   Residual   St Resid
 11   18000    14628.0   12710.6    165.1     1917.4      3.13R
 28   22516    14796.0   14561.9    277.9      234.1      0.41 X
 36    4473    13523.0   11428.0    171.5     2095.0      3.43R
 61   33000    16243.0   16105.3    410.2      137.7      0.28 X
 62   30000    14628.0   15296.4    288.7     -668.4     -1.18 X
 64    3600     8714.0    7258.6    427.1     1455.4      3.11RX

R denotes an observation with a large standardized residual.
X denotes an observation whose X value gives it large influence.
```

The residual plots are:

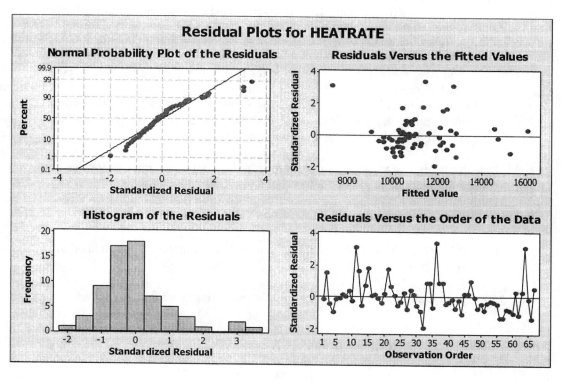

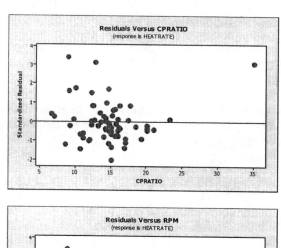

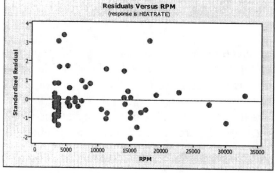

From the normal probability plot, the points do not fall on a straight line, indicating the residuals are not normal. The histogram of the residuals indicates the residuals are skewed to the right, which also indicates that the residuals are not normal. The plot of the residuals versus yhat indicates that there are potentially 3 outliers with standardized residuals of 3 or more. The variance appears to be constant. On the graph of the residuals versus RPM, the spread of the residuals appears to decrease as the value of RPM increases. This indicates the variance may not be constant for RPMs. Since the assumptions of normality and constant variance appear to be violated, we could consider transforming the data. We should also check the outlying observations to see if there are any errors connected with these observations.

11.111 In multiple regression, as in simple regression, the confidence interval for the mean value of y is narrower than the prediction interval of a particular value of y.

11.113 a. The least squares equation is $\hat{y} = 90.1 - 1.836x_1 + .285x_2$

b. $R^2 = .916$. About 91.6% of the sample variability in the y's is explained by the model $E(y) = \beta_0 + \beta_1 x_1 + \beta_2 x_2$

c. To determine if the model is useful for predicting y, we test:

H_0: $\beta_1 = \beta_2 = 0$
H_a: At least one $\beta_i \neq 0$, $i = 1, 2$

The test statistic is $F = \dfrac{MSR}{MSE} = \dfrac{7400}{114} = 64.91$

The rejection region requires $\alpha = .05$ in the upper tail of the F distribution with $v_1 = k = 2$ and $v_2 = n - (k + 1) = 15 - (2 + 1) = 12$. From Table IX, Appendix B, $F_{.05} = 3.89$. The rejection region is $F > 3.89$.

Since the observed value of the test statistic falls in the rejection region ($F = 64.91 > 3.89$), H_0 is rejected. There is sufficient evidence to indicate the model is useful for predicting y at $\alpha = .05$.

d. H_0: $\beta_1 = 0$
H_a: $\beta_1 \neq 0$

The test statistic is $t = \dfrac{\hat{\beta}_1}{s_{\hat{\beta}_1}} = \dfrac{-1.836}{.367} = -5.01$

The rejection region requires $\alpha/2 = .05/2 = .025$ in each tail of the t distribution with df = $n - (k + 1) = 15 - (2 + 1) = 12$. From Table VI, Appendix B, $t_{.025} = 2.179$. The rejection region is $t < -2.179$ or $t > 2.179$.

Since the observed value of the test statistic falls in the rejection region ($t = -5.01 < -2.179$), H_0 is rejected. There is sufficient evidence to indicate β_1 is not 0 at $\alpha = .05$.

e.   The standard deviation is $\sqrt{MSE} = \sqrt{114} = 10.677$. We would expect about 95% of the observations to fall within $2(10.677) = 21.354$ units of the fitted regression line.

11.115 The model-building step is the key to the success or failure of a regression analysis. If the model is a good model, we will have a good predictive model for the dependent variable y. If the model is not a good model, the predictive ability will not be of much use.

11.117 $E(y) = \beta_0 + \beta_1 x_1 + \beta_2 x_2 + \beta_3 x_3$

where $x_1 = \begin{cases} 1, \text{ if level 2} \\ 0, \text{ otherwise} \end{cases}$ $x_2 = \begin{cases} 1, \text{ if level 3} \\ 0, \text{ otherwise} \end{cases}$ $x_3 = \begin{cases} 1, \text{ if level 4} \\ 0, \text{ otherwise} \end{cases}$

11.119 The stepwise regression method is used to try to find the best model to describe a process. It is a screening procedure that tries to select a small subset of independent variables from a large set of independent variables that will adequately predict the dependent variable. This method is useful in that it can eliminate some unimportant independent variables from consideration.

11.121 Even though SSE = 0, we cannot estimate σ^2 because there are no degrees of freedom corresponding to error. With three data points, there are only two degrees of freedom available. The degrees of freedom corresponding to the model is $k = 2$ and the degrees of freedom corresponding to error is $n - (k + 1) = 3 - (2 + 1) = 0$. Without an estimate for σ^2, no inferences can be made.

11.123 a.   The type of juice extractor is qualitative.
          The size of the orange is quantitative.

b.   The model is $E(y) = \beta_0 + \beta_1 x_1 + \beta_2 x_2$

      where $x_1 = $ diameter of orange

               $x_2 = \begin{cases} 1 \text{ if Brand B} \\ 0 \text{ if not} \end{cases}$

c.   To allow the lines to differ, the interaction term is added:

           $E(y) = \beta_0 + \beta_1 x_1 + \beta_2 x_2 + \beta_3 x_1 x_2$

d.   For part **b**:

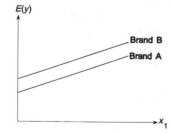

For part c:

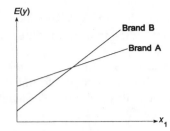

e. To determine whether the model in part **c** provides more information for predicting yield than does the model in part **b**, we test:

H_0: $\beta_3 = 0$
H_a: $\beta_3 \neq 0$

f. The test statistic would be $F = \dfrac{(SSE_R - SSE_C)/(k-g)}{SSE_C/[n-(k+1)]}$

To compute SSE_R: The model in part **b** is fit and SSE_R is the sum of squares for error.

To compute SSE_C: The model in part **c** is fit and SSE_C is the sum of squares for error.

$k - g$ = number of parameters in H_0 which is 1
$n - (k + 1)$ = degrees of freedom for error in the complete model

11.125 a. To determine if crime prevalence is positively related to density, we test:

H_0: $\beta_1 = 0$
H_a: $\beta_1 > 0$

The test statistic is $t = 3.88$.

The p-value is $p < .01/2 = .005$. Since the p-value is so small, there is strong evidence to indicate that the crime prevalence is positively related to density for $\alpha > .005$.

b. No. The tests are not independent of each other. If we conduct a series of t-tests to determine whether the independent variables are contributing to the predictive relationship, we would very likely make one or more errors in deciding which terms to retain in the model and which to exclude.

c. To test the utility of the model, we test:

H_0: $\beta_1 = \beta_2 = \beta_3 = \cdots = \beta_{18} = 0$
H_a: At least one $\beta_i \neq 0$, $i = 1, 2, 3, \dots, 18$

The test statistic is:

$$F = \frac{R^2/k}{(1-R^2)/[n-(k+1)]} = \frac{.411/18}{(1-.411)/[313-(18+1)]} = 11.397$$

The rejection region requires $\alpha = .05$ in the upper tail of the F distribution with $v_1 = k = 18$ and $v_2 = n - (k+1) = 313 - (18+1) = 294$. From Table IX, Appendix B, $F_{.05} \approx 1.57$. The rejection region is $F > 1.57$.

Since the observed value of the test statistic falls in the rejection region ($F = 11.397 > 1.57$), H_0 is rejected. There is sufficient evidence that the model is useful in predicting crime prevalence at $\alpha = .05$.

11.127 a.   The first order model for $E(y)$ as a function of the first five independent variables is:

$$E(y) = \beta_0 + \beta_1 x_1 + \beta_2 x_2 + \beta_3 x_3 + \beta_4 x_4 + \beta_5 x_5$$

b.   To test the utility of the model, we test:

H_0: $\beta_1 = \beta_2 = \beta_3 = \beta_4 = \beta_5 = 0$
H_a: At least one $\beta_i \neq 0$, $i = 1, 2, 3, 4, 5$

The test statistic is $F = 34.47$.

The p-value is $p < .001$. Since the p-value is so small, there is sufficient evidence to indicate the model is useful for predicting GSI at $\alpha > .001$.

$R^2 = .469$.   46.9% of the variability in the GSI scores is explained by the model including the first five independent variables.

c.   The first order model for $E(y)$ as a function of all seven independent variables is:

$$E(y) = \beta_0 + \beta_1 x_1 + \beta_2 x_2 + \beta_3 x_3 + \beta_4 x_4 + \beta_5 x_5 + \beta_6 x_6 + \beta_7 x_7$$

d. $R^2 = .603$ 60.3% of the variability in the GSI scores is explained by the model including the first seven independent variables.

e.   Since the p-values associated with the variables DES and PDEQ-SR are both less than .001, there is evidence that both variables contribute to the prediction of GSI, adjusted for all the other variables already in the model for $\alpha > .001$.

11.129 The correlation coefficient between Importance and Replace is .2682. This correlation coefficient is fairly small and would not indicate a problem with multicollinearity between Importance and Replace. The correlation coefficient between Importance and Support is .6991. This correlation coefficient is fairly large and would indicate a potential problem with multicollinearity between Importance and Support. Probably only one of these variables should be included in the regression model. The correlation coefficient between Replace and Support is −.0531. This correlation coefficient is very small and would not indicate a problem with multicollinearity between Replace and Support. Thus, the model could probably include Replace and one of the variables Support or Importance.

11.131 a. $\hat{\beta}_0 = 39.05 =$ the estimate of the y-intercept

$\hat{\beta}_1 = -5.41$. We estimate that the mean operating margin will decrease by 5.41% for each additional increase of 1 unit of x_1, the state population divided by the total number of inns in the state (with all other variables held constant).

$\hat{\beta}_2 = 5.86$. We estimate that the mean operating margin will increase by 5.86% for each additional increase of 1 unit of x_2, the room rate (with all other variables held constant).

$\hat{\beta}_3 = -3.09$. We estimate that the mean operating margin will decrease by 3.09% for each additional increase of 1 unit of x_3, the square root of the median income of the area (with all other variables held constant).

$\hat{\beta}_4 = 1.75$. We estimate that the mean operating margin will increase by 1.75% for each additional increase of 1 unit of x_4, the number of college students within four miles of the inn (with all other variables held constant).

b. $R^2 = .51$. 51% of the variability in the operating margins can be explained by the model containing these four independent variables.

c.   To determine if the model is adequate, we test:

H_0: $\beta_1 = \beta_2 = \beta_3 = \beta_4 = 0$
H_a: At least one $\beta_i \neq 0$, $i = 1, 2, 3, 4$

The test statistic is

$$F = \frac{R^2 k}{(1-R^2)/[n-(k+1)]} = \frac{.51/4}{(1-.51)/[57-(4+1)]} = 13.53$$

The rejection region requires $\alpha = .05$ in the upper tail of the F distribution with $v_1 = k = 4$ and $v_2 = n - (k+1) = 57 - (4+1) = 52$. From Table IX, Appendix B, $F_{.05} \approx 2.61$. The rejection region is $F > 2.61$.

Since the observed value of the test statistic falls in the rejection region ($F = 13.53 > 2.61$), H_0 is rejected. There is sufficient evidence that the model is useful in predicting operating margins at $\alpha = .05$.

11.133 a.   Not necessarily. If Nickel was highly correlated to several other variables, then it might be better to keep Nickel and drop some of the other highly correlated variables.

b.   Using stepwise regression is a good start for selecting the best set of predictor variables. However, one should use caution when looking at the model selected using stepwise regression. Sometimes important variables are not selected to be entered into the model. Also, many t-tests have been run, thus inflating the Type I and Type II error rates. One must also consider using higher order terms in the model and interaction terms.

c. No, further exploration should be used. One should consider using higher order terms for the variables (i.e. squared terms) and also interaction terms.

11.135 a. Using MINITAB, the scattergram is:

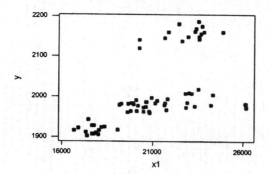

b. Let $x_2 = \begin{cases} 1 \text{ if } 1-35W \\ 0 \text{ if not} \end{cases}$

The complete second-order model would be

$$E(y) = \beta_0 + \beta_1 x_1 + \beta_2 x_1^2 + \beta_3 x_2 + \beta_4 x_1 x_2 + \beta_5 x_1^2 x_2$$

c. Using MINITAB, the printout is:

Regression Analysis

```
   The regression equation is
 y = 776 + 0.104 x1 -0.000002 x1sq + 232 x2 - 0.0091 x1x2
         +0.000000 x1sqx2


Predictor          Coef        StDev          T         P
Constant          776.4        144.5       5.37     0.000
x1              0.10418      0.01388       7.50     0.000
x1sq        -0.00000223   0.00000033      -6.73     0.000
x2                  232         1094       0.21     0.833
x1x2           -0.00914      0.09829      -0.09     0.926
x1sqx2       0.00000027   0.00000220       0.12     0.903


 S = 15.58       R-Sq = 97.2%      R-Sq(adj) = 97.0%
```

```
Analysis of Variance

Source           DF          SS         MS        F        P
Regression        5      555741     111148   457.73    0.000
Residual Error   66       16027        243
Total            71      571767


Source           DF      Seq SS
x1                1      254676
x1sq              1       21495
x2                1      279383
x1x2              1         183
x1sqx2            1           4

Unusual Observations
Obs      x1       y      Fit  StDev Fit  Residual  St Resid
 27   19062  1917.64  1953.27     2.51    -35.63    -2.32R
 48   26148  1982.02  1978.23     9.10      3.79     0.30 X
 53   26166  1972.92  1978.01     9.15     -5.09    -0.40 X
 55   20250  2120.00  2130.56    10.57    -10.56    -0.92 X
 56   20251  2140.00  2130.57    10.57      9.43     0.82 X
 63   24885  2160.02  2161.81    12.67     -1.79    -0.20 X
```

R denotes an observation with a large standardized residual
X denotes an observation whose X value gives it large influence.

The fitted model is
$$\hat{y} = 776 + .104x_1 - .000002x_1^2 + 232x_2 - .0091x_1x_2 + .00000027x_1^2x_2 .$$

To determine if the curvilinear relationship is different at the two locations, we test:

$H_0: \beta_3 = \beta_4 = \beta_5 = 0$
$H_0:$ At least one of the coefficients is nonzero
In order to test this hypothesis, we must fit the reduced model

$$E(y) = \beta_0 + \beta_1x_1 + \beta_2x_1{}^2$$

Using MINITAB, the printout from fitting the reduced model is:

Regression Analysis

```
The regression equation is
y = 197 + 0.149 x1 -0.000003 x1sq
```

Predictor	Coef	StDev	T	P
Constant	197.5	578.9	0.34	0.734
x1	0.14921	0.05551	2.69	0.009
x1sq	-0.00000295	0.00000132	-2.24	0.028

```
S = 65.45        R-Sq = 48.3%        R-Sq(adj) = 46.8%
```

Analysis of Variance

Source	DF	SS	MS	F	P
Regression	2	276171	138085	32.23	0.000
Residual Error	69	295597	4284		
Total	71	571767			

Source	DF	Seq SS
x1	1	254676
x1sq	1	21495

Unusual Observations

Obs	x1	y	Fit	StDev Fit	Residual	St Resid
30	16691	1916.13	1865.11	23.39	51.02	·0.83 X
48	26148	1982.02	2079.68	33.08	-97.66	-1.73 X
53	26166	1972.92	2079.59	33.31	-106.67	-1.89 X
56	20251	2140.00	2007.88	10.43	132.12	2.04R

```
R denotes an observation with a large standardized residual
X denotes an observation whose X value gives it large influence.
```

The fitted regression line is $\hat{y} = 197 + .149x_1 - .000003x_1^2$

To determine if the curvilinear relationship is different at the two locations, we test:

H_0: $\beta_3 = \beta_4 = \beta_5 = 0$
H_a: At least one of the coefficients is nonzero

The test statistic is $F = \dfrac{(\text{SSE}_R - \text{SSE}_C)/(k-g)}{\text{SSE}_C /[n-(k+1)]} = \dfrac{(295{,}597 - 16{,}027)/(5-2)}{16{,}027 /[72 - (5+2)]}$

$= 383.76$

Since no α was given we will use $\alpha = .05$. The rejection region requires $\alpha = .05$ in the upper tail of the F-distribution with $v_1 = (k-g) = (5-2) = 3$ and $v_2 = n - (k+1) = 72 - (5+1) = 66$. From Table IX, Appendix B, $F_{.05} \approx 2.76$. The rejection region is $F > 2.76$.

Since the observed value of the test statistic falls in the rejection region ($F = 383.76 > 2.76$), H_0 is rejected. There is sufficient evidence to indicate the curvilinear relationship is different at the two locations at $\alpha = .05$.

d. Using MINITAB, the plot of the residual versus x_1 is:

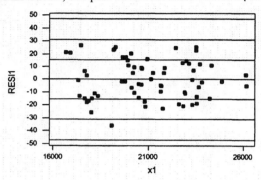

From this plot, we notice that there is only one point more than 2 standard deviations from the mean and no points that are more than 3 standard deviations from the mean. Thus, there do not appear to be any outliers. There is no curve to the residuals, so we have the appropriate model.

A stem-and-leaf display of the residuals is:

```
Character Stem-and-Leaf Display

Stem-and-leaf of RESI1     N  = 72
Leaf Unit = 1.0

     1    -3 5
     1    -3
     2    -2 5
     5    -2 210
    13    -1 99877755
    23    -1 4443221100
    29    -0 996655
   (10)   -0 4432111000
    33     0 03344
    28     0 5678899
    21     1 11222244
    13     1 577
    10     2 0012334
     3     2 556
```

The stem-and-leaf display looks fairly mound-shaped, so it appears that the assumption of normality is valid.

A plot of the residuals versus the fitted values is:

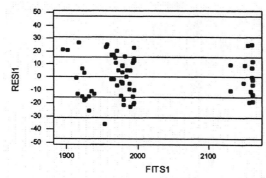

From this plot, there is no cone-shape. Thus, it appears that the assumption of constant variance is valid.

11.137 a.   The model is:

$$E(y) = \beta_0 + \beta_1 x_1 + \beta_2 x_2 + \beta_3 x_3$$

where y = market share

$$x_1 = \begin{cases} 1 \text{ if VH} \\ 0 \text{ otherwise} \end{cases} \qquad x_2 = \begin{cases} 1 \text{ if H} \\ 0 \text{ otherwise} \end{cases} \qquad x_3 = \begin{cases} 1 \text{ if M} \\ 0 \text{ otherwise} \end{cases}$$

We assume that the error terms (ε_i) or y's are normally distributed at each exposure level, with a common variance. Also, we assume the ε_i's have a mean of 0 and are independent.

b.   No interaction terms were included because we have only one independent variable, exposure level. Even though we have 3 x_i's in the model, they are dummy variables and correspond to different levels of the one independent variable.

c.   Using MINITAB, the output is:

Regression Analysis: y versus x1, x2, x3

```
The regression equation is
y = 10.2 + 0.500 x1 + 2.02 x2 + 0.683 x3

Predictor        Coef      SE Coef           T          P
Constant      10.2333       0.1084       94.41      0.000
x1             0.5000       0.1533        3.26      0.004
x2             2.0167       0.1533       13.16      0.000
x3             0.6833       0.1533        4.46      0.000

S = 0.2655      R-Sq = 90.4%      R-Sq(adj) = 89.0%
```

Multiple Regression and Model Building

```
Analysis of Variance

Source              DF          SS          MS        F         P
Regression           3     13.3433      4.4478     63.09     0.000
Residual Error      20      1.4100      0.0705
Total               23     14.7533

Source        DF        Seq SS
x1             1        0.7200
x2             1       11.2225
x3             1        1.4008
```

The fitted model is $\hat{y} = 10.2 + .5x_1 + 2.02x_2 + .683x_3$

$$x_1 = \begin{cases} 1 \text{ if VH} \\ 0 \text{ otherwise} \end{cases}$$

$$x_2 = \begin{cases} 1 \text{ if H} \\ 0 \text{ otherwise} \end{cases}$$

$$x_3 = \begin{cases} 1 \text{ if M} \\ 0 \text{ otherwise} \end{cases}$$

d. To determine if the firm's expected market share differs for different levels of advertising exposure, we test:

H_0: $\beta_1 = \beta_2 = \beta_3 = 0$
H_a: At least one $\beta_i \neq 0$, $i = 1, 2, 3$

The test statistic is $F = 63.09$.

The rejection region requires $\alpha = .05$ in the upper tail of the F-distribution with $v_1 = k = 3$ and $v_2 = n - (k + 1) = 24 - (3 + 1) = 20$. From Table IX, Appendix B, $F_{.05} = 3.10$. The rejection region is $F > 3.10$.

Since the observed value of the test statistic falls in the rejection region ($F = 63.09 > 3.10$), H_0 is rejected. There is sufficient evidence to indicate the firm's expected market share differs for different levels of advertising exposure at $\alpha = .05$.

11.139 a. $\hat{\beta}_0 = -105$ has no meaning because $x_3 = 0$ is not in the observable range. $\hat{\beta}_0$ is simply the y-intercept.

$\hat{\beta}_1 = 25$. The estimated difference in mean attendance between weekends and weekdays is 25, temperature and weather constant.

$\hat{\beta}_2 = 100$. The estimated difference in mean attendance between sunny and overcast days is 100, type of day (weekend or weekday) and temperature constant.

$\hat{\beta}_3 = 10$. The estimated change in mean attendance for each additional degree of temperature is 10, type of day (weekend or weekday) and weather (sunny or overcast) held constant.

b. To determine if the model is useful for predicting daily attendance, we test:

H_0: $\beta_1 = \beta_2 = \beta_3 = 0$
H_a: At least one $\beta_i \neq 0$, $i = 1, 2, 3$

The test statistic is $F = \dfrac{R^2/k}{(1-R^2)/[n-(k+1)]} = \dfrac{.65/3}{(1-.65)/[30-(3+1)]} = 16.10$

The rejection region requires $\alpha = .05$ in the upper tail of the F distribution with numerator df $= k = 3$ and denominator df $= n - (k+1) = 30 - (3+1) = 26$. From Table IX, Appendix B, $F_{.05} \approx 2.98$. The rejection region is $F > 2.98$.

Since the observed value of the test statistic falls in the rejection region ($F = 16.10 > 2.98$), H_0 is rejected. There is sufficient evidence to indicate the model is useful for predicting daily attendance at $\alpha = .05$.

c. To determine if mean attendance increases on weekends, we test:

H_0: $\beta_1 = 0$
H_a: $\beta_1 > 0$

The test statistic is $t = \dfrac{\hat{\beta}_1}{s_{\hat{\beta}_1}} = \dfrac{25-0}{10} = 2.5$

The rejection region requires $\alpha = .10$ in the upper tail of the t distribution with df $= n - (k+1) = 30 - (3+1) = 26$. From Table VI, Appendix B, $t_{.10} = 1.315$. The rejection region is $t > 1.315$.

Since the observed value of the test statistic falls in the rejection region ($t = 2.5 > 1.315$), H_0 is rejected. There is sufficient evidence to indicate the mean attendance increases on weekends at $\alpha = .10$.

d. Sunny $\Rightarrow x_2 = 1$, Weekday $\Rightarrow x_1 = 0$, Temperature $95° \Rightarrow x_3 = 95°$
$= -105 + 25(0) + 100(1) + 10(95) = 945$

e. We are 90% confident that the actual attendance for sunny weekdays with a temperature of 95° is between 645 and 1245.

11.141 a. $E(y) = \beta_0 + \beta_1 x_1 + \beta_2 x_6 + \beta_3 x_7$

where $x_6 = \begin{cases} 1 \text{ if condition is good} \\ 0 \text{ otherwise} \end{cases}$

$x_7 = \begin{cases} 1 \text{ if condition is fair} \\ 0 \text{ otherwise} \end{cases}$

b. The model specified in part **a** seems appropriate. The points for E, F, and G cluster around three parallel lines.

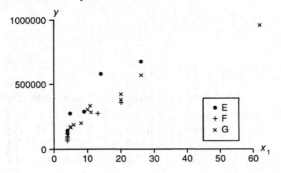

c. Using MINITAB, the output is

```
The regression equation is
y = 188875 + 15617 x1 - 103046 x6 - 152487 x7

Predictor          Coef        StDev            T          P
Constant         188875        28588         6.61      0.000
x1                15617         1066        14.66      0.000
x6              -103046        31784        -3.24      0.004
x7              -152487        39157        -3.89      0.001

S = 64624        R-Sq = 91.8%     R-Sq(adj) = 90.7%

Analysis of Variance

Source             DF            SS           MS          F        P

Regression          3    9.86170E+11   3.28723E+11      78.71    0.000
Residual Error     21    87700442851    4176211564
Total              24    1.07387E+12

Source      DF          SeqSS
x1           1    9.15776E+11
x6           1     7061463149
x7           1    63332198206

Unusual Observations
Obs     x1        y         Fit     StDev Fit     Residual     St Resid
 10   62.0   950000     1054078        53911      -104078      -2.92RX
 23   14.0   573200      407512        26670       165688       2.81R

R denotes an observation with a large standardized residual
X denotes an observation whose X value gives it large influence.
```

The fitted model is $\hat{y} = 188{,}875 + 15{,}617x_1 - 103{,}046x_6 - 152{,}487x_7$

For excellent condition, $\hat{y} = 188{,}875 + 15{,}617x_1$
For good condition, $\hat{y} = 85{,}829 + 15{,}617x_1$
For fair condition, $\hat{y} = 36{,}388 + 15{,}617x_1$

d.

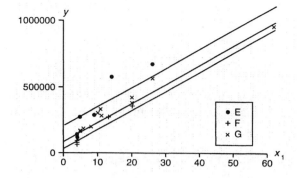

e. We must first fit a reduced model with just x_1, number of apartments. Using MINITAB, the output is:

```
The regression equation is
y = 101786 + 15525 x1

Predictor          Coef         StDev              T          P
Constant         101786         23291           4.37      0.000
x1                15525          1345          11.54      0.000

S = 82908        R-Sq = 85.3%      R-Sq(adj) = 84.6%

Analysis of Variance

Source            DF            SS             MS          F          P
Regression         1    9.15776E+11    9.15776E+11     133.23      0.000
Residual Error    23    1.58094E+11     6873656705
Total             24    1.07387E+12

Unusual Observations
Obs      x1          y           Fit     StDev Fit     Residual     St Resid
  4    26.0     676200        505433         24930       170757        2.16R
 10    62.0     950000       1064353         69058      -114353       -2.49RX
 23    14.0     573200        319140         16765       254060        3.13R

R denotes an observation with a large standardized residual
X denotes an observation whose X value gives it large influence.
```

The fitted model is $\hat{y} = 101{,}786 + 15{,}525x_1$.

To determine if the relationship between sale price and number of units differs depending on the physical condition of the apartments, we test:

H_0: $\beta_2 = \beta_3 = 0$
H_a: At least one $\beta_i \neq 0$, $i = 2, 3$

The test statistic is:

$$F = \frac{(SSE_R - SSE_C)/(k-g)}{SSE_C/[n-(k+1)]} = \frac{(1.58094 \times 10^{11} - 87,700,442,851)/2}{4,176,211,564} = 8.43$$

The rejection region requires $\alpha = .05$ in the upper tail of the F distribution with $v_1 = k - g$ $= 3 - 1 = 2$ and $v_2 = n - (k+1) = 25 - (3+1) = 21$. From Table IX, Appendix B, $F_{.05} =$ 3.47. The rejection region is $F > 3.47$.

Since the observed value of the test statistic falls in the rejection region ($F = 8.43 >$ 3.47), H_0 is rejected. There is evidence to indicate that the relationship between sale price and number of units differs depending on the physical condition of the apartments at $\alpha = .05$.

f.   We will look for high pairwise correlations.

```
        x1       x2       x3      x4      x5      x6
x2   -0.014
x3    0.800  -0.188
x4    0.224  -0.363   0.166
x5    0.878   0.027   0.673  0.089
x6    0.175  -0.447   0.271  0.112   0.020
x7   -0.128   0.392  -0.118  0.050  -0.238  -0.564
```

When highly correlated independent variables are present in a regression model, the results are confusing. The researchers may only want to include one of the variables. This may be the case for the variables: x_1 and x_3, x_1 and x_5, x_3 and x_5

g.   Use the following plots to check the assumptions on $\in$.

residuals vs x_1
residuals vs x_2
residuals vs x_3
residuals vs x_4
residuals vs x_5
resisduals vs predicted values
frequency distribution of the standardized residuals.

From the plots of the residuals, there do not appear to be any outliers - no standardized residuals are larger than 2.38 in magnitude. In all the plots of the residuals vs x_i, there is no trend that would indicate non-constant variance (no funnel shape). In addition, there is no U or upside-down U shape that would indicate that any of the variables should be squared. In the histogram of the residuals, the plot is fairly mound-shaped, which would indicate the residuals are approximately normally distributed. All of the assumptions appear to be met.

Residuals Versus x_1
(response is y)

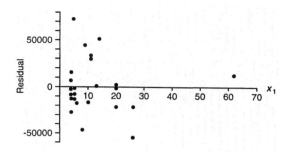

Residuals Versus x_2
(response is y)

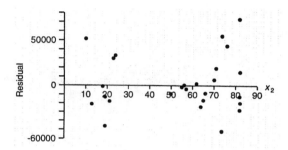

Residuals Versus x_3
(response is y)

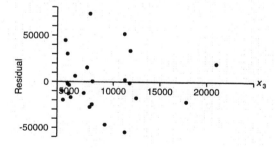

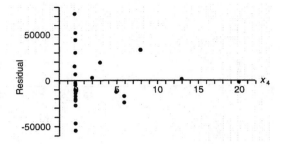

Residuals Versus x_4
(response is y)

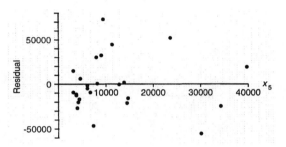

Residuals Versus x_5
(response is y)

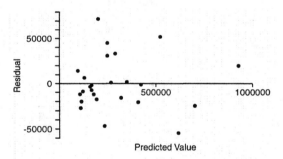

Residuals Versus the Predicted Values
(response is y)

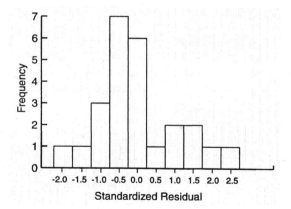

Histogram of the Residuals
(response is y)

11.143 a.   To determine whether the complete model contributes information for the prediction of y, we test:

H_0: $\beta_1 = \beta_2 = \beta_3 = \beta_4 = \beta_5 = 0$
H_a: At least one of the β's is not 0, $i = 1, 2, 3, 4, 5$

b. $$\text{MSR} = \frac{\text{SS(Model)}}{k} = \frac{4,911.56}{5} = 982.31$$

$$\text{MSE} = \frac{\text{SSE}}{n - (k+1)} = \frac{1,830.44}{40 - (5+1)} = 53.84$$

The test statistic is $F = \dfrac{\text{MSR}}{\text{MSE}} = \dfrac{982.31}{53.84} = 18.24$

The rejection region requires $\alpha = .05$ in the upper tail of the F distribution with numerator df $= k = 5$ and denominator df $= n - (k + 1) = 40 - (5 + 1) = 34$. From Table IX, Appendix B, $F_{.05} \approx 2.53$. The rejection region is $F > 2.53$.

Since the observed value of the test statistic falls in the rejection region ($F = 18.24 > 2.53$), H_0 is rejected. There is sufficient evidence to indicate that the complete model contributes information for the prediction of y at $\alpha = .05$.

c.   To determine whether a second-order model contributes more information than a first-order model for the prediction of y, we test:

H_0: $\beta_3 = \beta_4 = \beta_5 = 0$
H_a: At least one $\beta_i \neq 0$, $i = 3, 4, 5$

d. The test statistic is $F = \dfrac{(SSE_R - SSE_C)/(k-g)}{SSE_C/[n-(k+1)]} = \dfrac{(3197.16 - 1830.44)/(5-2)}{1830.44/(40-(5+1))}$

$$= \frac{455.5733}{53.8365} = 8.46$$

The rejection region requires $\alpha = .05$ in the upper tail of the F distribution with numerator df $= k - g = 3$ and denominator df $= n - (k + 1) = 40 - (5 + 1) = 34$. From Table IX, Appendix B, $F_{.05} \approx 2.92$. The rejection region is $F > 2.92$.

Since the observed value of the test statistic falls in the rejection region ($F = 8.46 > 2.92$), H_0 is rejected. There is sufficient evidence to indicate the second-order model contributes more information than a first-order model for the prediction of y at $\alpha = .05$.

e. The second-order model, based on the test result in part **d**.

11.145 First, we will fit the simple linear regression model: $E(y) = \beta_o + \beta_1 x_1 + \beta_2 x_2$
Using MINITAB, the results are:

Regression Analysis: y versus x1, x2

```
The regression equation is
y = - 1.57 + 0.0257 x1 + 0.0336 x2

Predictor       Coef      SE Coef          T          P
Constant      -1.5705      0.4937      -3.18      0.003
x1           0.025732     0.004024       6.40      0.000
x2           0.033615     0.004928       6.82      0.000

S = 0.4023      R-Sq = 68.1%      R-Sq(adj) = 66.4%

Analysis of Variance

Source            DF           SS          MS          F          P
Regression         2      12.7859      6.3930      39.51      0.000
Residual Error    37       5.9876      0.1618
Total             39      18.7735

Source            DF      Seq SS
x1                 1      5.2549
x2                 1      7.5311

Unusual Observations
Obs        x1           y          Fit      SE Fit     Residual     St Resid
  4       100      1.5400       2.6498      0.1699      -1.1098       -3.04R
 32        39      1.2200       2.1558      0.1483      -0.9358       -2.50R

R denotes an observation with a large standardized residual
```

To determine if the model is useful in the prediction of y (GPA), we test:

H_0: $\beta_1 = \beta_2 = 0$
H_a: At least one $\beta_i \neq 0$, $i = 1, 2$

The test statistic is $F = 39.51$ and the p-value is $p = 0.000$. Since the p-value is so small, H_0 is rejected for any reasonable value of α. There is sufficient evidence to indicate at least one of the variables Verbal score or Mathematics score is useful in predicting GPA.

To determine if Verbal score is useful in predicting GPA, controlling for Mathematics score, we test:

H_0: $\beta_1 = 0$
H_a: $\beta_1 \neq 0$

The test statistic is $t = 6.40$ and the p-value is $p = 0.000$. Since the p-value is so small, H_0 is rejected for any reasonable value of α. There is sufficient evidence to indicate Verbal score is useful in predicting GPA, controlling for Mathematics score.

To determine if Mathematics score is useful in predicting GPA, controlling for Verbal score, we test:

H_0: $\beta_2 = 0$
H_a: $\beta_2 \neq 0$

The test statistic is $t = 6.82$ and the p-value is $p = 0.000$. Since the p-value is so small, H_0 is rejected for any reasonable value of α. There is sufficient evidence to indicate Mathematics score is useful in predicting GPA, controlling for Verbal score.

Thus, both terms in the model are significant. The R-squared value is $R^2 = .681$.

This indicates that 68.1% of the sample variance of the GPA's is explained by the model.

Now, we need to check the residuals. From MINITAB, the plots are:

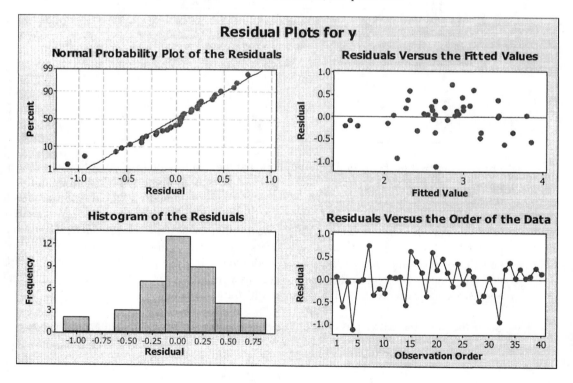

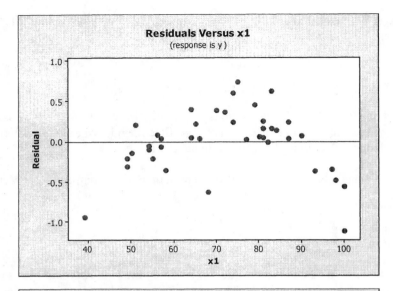

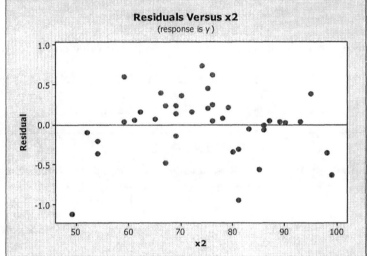

From the normal probability plot, it appears that the assumption of normality is valid. The points are very close to a straight line except for the first 2 points. The histogram of the residuals implies that the residuals are slightly skewed to the left. I would still consider the assumption to be valid. The plot of the residuals versus y-hat indicates a random spread of the residuals between the two bands. This indicates that the assumption of equal variances is probably valid. The plot of the residuals versus x_1 indicates that the relationship between GPA and Verbal score may not be linear, but quadratic because the points form a somewhat upside down U shape. The plot of the residuals versus x_2 indicates that the relationship between GPA and Mathematics score may or may not be quadratic.

Since the plots indicate a possible 2nd order model and the R^2 value is not real large, we will fit a complete 2nd order model:

$$E(y) = \beta_o + \beta_1 x_1 + \beta_2 x_2 + \beta_3 x_1^2 + \beta_4 x_2^2 + \beta_5 x_1 x_2$$

Using MINITAB, the results are:

Regression Analysis: y versus x1, x2, x1sq, x2sq, x1x2

```
The regression equation is
y = - 9.92 + 0.167 x1 + 0.138 x2 - 0.00111 x1sq - 0.000843 x2sq + 0.000241 x1x2


Predictor          Coef    SE Coef       T      P
Constant         -9.917      1.354   -7.32  0.000
x1              0.16681    0.02124    7.85  0.000
x2              0.13760    0.02673    5.15  0.000
x1sq         -0.0011082  0.0001173   -9.45  0.000
x2sq         -0.0008433  0.0001594   -5.29  0.000
x1x2          0.0002411  0.0001440    1.67  0.103


S = 0.187142   R-Sq = 93.7%   R-Sq(adj) = 92.7%


Analysis of Variance

Source            DF       SS      MS       F      P
Regression         5  17.5827  3.5165  100.41  0.000
Residual Error    34   1.1908  0.0350
Total             39  18.7735


Source   DF   Seq SS
x1        1   5.2549
x2        1   7.5311
x1sq      1   3.6434
x2sq      1   1.0552
x1x2      1   0.0982


Unusual Observations

Obs   x1      y     Fit  SE Fit  Residual  St Resid
  2   68  2.8900  3.2820  0.1002   -0.3920    -2.48R
  4  100  1.5400  1.5806  0.1404   -0.0406    -0.33 X
 34   70  3.8200  3.3940  0.0753    0.4260     2.49R

R denotes an observation with a large standardized residual.
X denotes an observation whose X value gives it large influence.
```

To determine if the interaction between Verbal score and Mathematics score is useful in the prediction of y (GPA), we test:

$$H_0: \ \beta_5 = 0$$
$$H_a: \ \beta_5 \neq 0$$

The test statistic is $t = 1.67$ and the p-value is $p = 0.103$. Since the p-value is not small, H_0 is not rejected for any value of $\alpha < .10$. There is insufficient evidence to indicate the interaction between Verbal score and Mathematics score is useful in predicting GPA.

Now, we will fit a model without the interaction term, but including the squared terms:

$$E(y) = \beta_o + \beta_1 x_1 + \beta_2 x_2 + \beta_3 x_1^2 + \beta_4 x_2^2$$

Using MINITAB, the results are:

Regression Analysis: y versus x1, x2, x1sq, x2sq

```
The regression equation is
y = - 11.5 + 0.189 x1 + 0.159 x2 - 0.00114 x1sq - 0.000871 x2sq


Predictor          Coef     SE Coef         T      P
Constant        -11.458       1.019    -11.24  0.000
x1              0.18887     0.01709     11.05  0.000
x2              0.15874     0.02417      6.57  0.000
x1sq         -0.0011412   0.0001186     -9.62  0.000
x2sq         -0.0008705   0.0001626     -5.35  0.000


S = 0.191905    R-Sq = 93.1%    R-Sq(adj) = 92.3%


Analysis of Variance

Source             DF        SS        MS       F      P
Regression          4   17.4845    4.3711  118.69  0.000
Residual Error     35    1.2890    0.0368
Total              39   18.7735


Source   DF   Seq SS
x1        1   5.2549
x2        1   7.5311
x1sq      1   3.6434
x2sq      1   1.0552


Unusual Observations

Obs    x1      y      Fit   SE Fit   Residual   St Resid
  2    68   2.8900   3.2921   0.1025   -0.4021     -2.48R
  4   100   1.5400   1.7059   0.1219   -0.1659     -1.12 X
 32    39   1.2200   1.3190   0.1240   -0.0990     -0.68 X
 34    70   3.8200   3.3954   0.0772    0.4246      2.42R

R denotes an observation with a large standardized residual.
X denotes an observation whose X value gives it large influence.
```

To determine if the relationship between Verbal score and GPA is quadratic, controlling for Mathematics score, we test:

$$H_0: \ \beta_3 = 0$$
$$H_a: \ \beta_3 \neq 0$$

The test statistic is $t = -9.62$ and the p-value is $p = 0.000$. Since the p-value is so small, H_0 is rejected for any reasonable value of α. There is sufficient evidence to indicate the relationship between Verbal score and GPA is quadratic, controlling for Mathematics score.

To determine if the relationship between Verbal score and GPA is quadratic, controlling for Mathematics score, we test:

$$H_0: \ \beta_4 = 0$$
$$H_a: \ \beta_4 \neq 0$$

The test statistic is $t = -5.35$ and the p-value is $p = 0.000$. Since the p-value is so small, H_0 is rejected for any reasonable value of α. There is sufficient evidence to indicate the relationship between Mathematics score and GPA is quadratic, controlling for Verbal score.

Thus, both quadratic terms in the model are significant. The R-squared value is $R^2 = .913$. This indicates that 91.3% of the sample variance of the GPA's is explained by the model.

Now, we need to check the residuals. From MINITAB, the plots are:

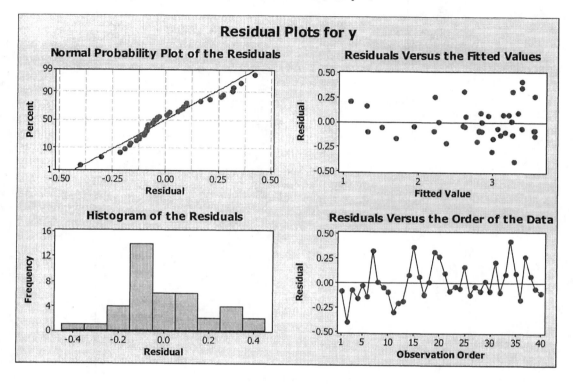

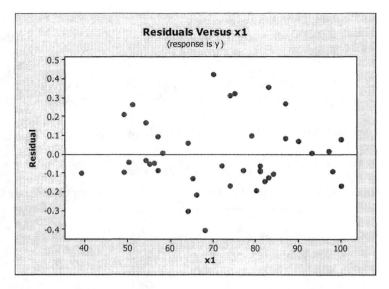

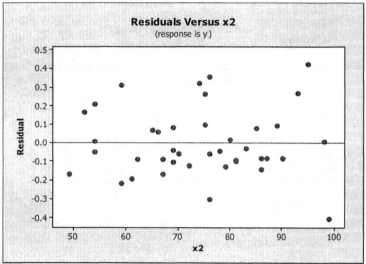

From the normal probability plot, it appears that the assumption of normality is valid. The points are very close to a straight line. The histogram of the residuals also implies that the residuals are approximately normal. The plot of the residuals versus y-hat indicates a random spread of the residuals between the two bands. This indicates that the assumption of equal variances is probably valid. The plot of the residuals versus x_1 indicates a random spread of the residuals between the two bands. This indicates that the order of x_1 (2nd) is appropriate. The plot of the residuals versus x_2 indicates a random spread of the residuals between the two bands. This indicates that the order of x_2 (2nd) is appropriate.

The model appears to be pretty good. All terms in the model are significant, the residual analysis indicates the assumptions are met and the R-squared value is fairly close to 1.

Methods for Quality Improvement

Chapter 12

12.1   A control chart is a time series plot of individual measurements or means of a quality variable to which a centerline and two other horizontal lines called control limits have been added. The center line represents the mean of the process when the process is in a state of statistical control. The upper control limit and the lower control limit are positioned so that when the process is in control the probability of an individual measurement or mean falling outside the limits is very small. A control chart is used to determine if a process is in control (only common causes of variation present) or not (both common and special causes of variation present). This information helps us to determine when to take action to find and remove special causes of variation and when to leave the process alone.

12.3   When a control chart is first constructed, it is not known whether the process is in control or not. If the process is found not to be in control, then the centerline and control limits should not be used to monitor the process in the future.

12.5   Even if all the points of an $\bar{x}$-chart fall within the control limits, the process may be out of control. Nonrandom patterns may exist among the plotted points that are within the control limits, but are very unlikely if the process is in control. Examples include six points in a row steadily increasing or decreasing and 14 points in a row alternating up and down.

12.7
Rule 1:   One point beyond Zone A: No points are beyond Zone A.

Rule 2:   Nine points in a row in Zone C or beyond: No sequence of nine points are in Zone C (on one side of the centerline) or beyond.

Rule 3:   Six points in a row steadily increasing or decreasing: No sequence of six points steadily increase or decrease.

Rule 4:   Fourteen points in a row alternating up and down: This pattern does not exist.

Rule 5:   Two out of three points in Zone A or beyond: There are no groups of three consecutive points that have two or more in Zone A or beyond.

Rule 6:   Four out of five points in a row in Zone B or beyond: Points 18 through 21 are all in Zone B or beyond. This indicates the process is out of control.

Thus, rule 6 indicates this process is out of control.

12.9   Using Table XII, Appendix B:

     a.   With $n = 3$, $A_2 = 1.023$

     b.   With $n = 10$, $A_2 = 0.308$

     c.   With $n = 22$, $A_2 = 0.167$

12.11   a.   For each sample, we compute $\bar{x}_1 = \dfrac{\sum x}{n}$ and R = range = largest measurement - smallest measurement. The results are listed in the table:

Sample No.	$\bar{x}_1$	R	Sample No.	$\bar{x}_2$	R
1	20.225	1.8	11	21.225	3.2
2	19.750	2.8	12	20.475	0.9
3	20.425	3.8	13	19.650	2.6
4	19.725	2.5	14	19.075	4.0
5	20.550	3.7	15	19.400	2.2
6	19.900	5.0	16	20.700	4.3
7	21.325	5.5	17	19.850	3.6
8	19.625	3.5	18	20.200	2.5
9	19.350	2.5	19	20.425	2.2
10	20.550	4.1	20	19.900	5.5

b. $\bar{\bar{x}} = \dfrac{\bar{x}_1 + \bar{x}_2 + \cdots \bar{x}_{20}}{k} = \dfrac{402.325}{20} = 20.11625$

$\bar{R} = \dfrac{R_1 + R_2 + \cdots R_{20}}{k} = \dfrac{66.2}{20} = 3.31$

c. $Centerline = \bar{\bar{x}} = 20.116$

From Table XII, Appendix B, with $n = 4$, $A_2 = .729$.

$Upper\ control\ limit = \bar{\bar{x}} + A_2\bar{R} = 20.116 + .729(3.31) = 22.529$
$Lower\ control\ limit = \bar{\bar{x}} - A_2\bar{R} = 20.116 - .729(3.31) = 17.703$

d. $Upper\ A\text{-}B\ boundary = \bar{\bar{x}} + \dfrac{2}{3}(A_2\bar{R}) = 20.116 + \dfrac{2}{3}(.729)(3.31) = 21.725$

$Lower\ A\text{-}B\ boundary = \bar{\bar{x}} - \dfrac{2}{3}(A_2\bar{R}) = 20.116 - \dfrac{2}{3}(.729)(3.31) = 18.507$

$Upper\ B\text{-}C\ boundary = \bar{\bar{x}} + \dfrac{1}{3}(A_2\bar{R}) = 20.116 + \dfrac{1}{3}(.729)(3.31) = 20.920$

$Lower\ B\text{-}C\ boundary = \bar{\bar{x}} - \dfrac{1}{3}(A_2\bar{R}) = 20.116 - \dfrac{1}{3}(.729)(3.31) = 19.312$

e.   The $\bar{x}$-chart is:

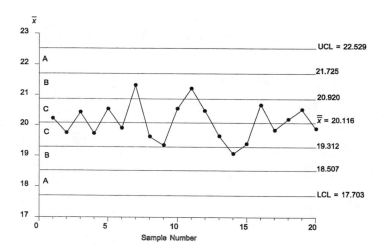

Rule 1:   One point beyond Zone A: No points are beyond Zone A.
Rule 2:   Nine points in a row in Zone C or beyond: No sequence of nine points are in Zone C (on one side of the centerline) or beyond.
Rule 3:   Six points in a row steadily increasing or decreasing: No sequence of six points steadily increase or decrease.
Rule 4:   Fourteen points in a row alternating up and down: This pattern does not exist.
Rule 5:   Two out of three points in Zone A or beyond: There are no groups of three consecutive points that have two or more in Zone A or beyond.
Rule 6:   Four out of five points in a row in Zone B or beyond: No sequence of five points has four or more in Zone B or beyond.

The process appears to be in control.

12.13   a. $\bar{\bar{x}} = \dfrac{\bar{x}_1 + \bar{x}_2 + \cdots + \bar{x}_{20}}{k} = \dfrac{479.942}{20} = 23.9971$

$\bar{R} = \dfrac{R_1 + R_2 \cdots + R_{20}}{k} = \dfrac{3.63}{20} = .1815$

$Centerline = \bar{\bar{x}} = 23.9971$

From Table XII, Appendix B, with $n = 5$, $A_2 = .577$.

$Upper\ control\ limit = \bar{\bar{x}} + A_2 = 23.9971 + .577(.1815) = 24.102$
$Lower\ control\ limit = \bar{\bar{x}} - A_2 = 23.9971 - .577(.1815) = 23.892$

$Upper\ \text{A-B}\ boundary = \bar{\bar{x}} + \dfrac{2}{3}(A_2\bar{R}) = 23.9971 + \dfrac{2}{3}(.577)(.1815) = 24.067$

$Lower\ \text{A-B}\ boundary = \bar{\bar{x}} - \dfrac{2}{3}(A_2\bar{R}) = 23.9971 - \dfrac{2}{3}(.577)(.1815) = 23.927$

$Upper\ \text{B-C}\ boundary = \bar{\bar{x}} + \dfrac{1}{3}(A_2\bar{R}) = 23.9971 + \dfrac{1}{3}(.577)(.1815) = 24.032$

Lower B-C *boundary* $= \bar{\bar{x}} - \dfrac{1}{3}(A_2\bar{R}) = 23.9971 - \dfrac{1}{3}(.577)(.1815) = 23.962$

The $\bar{x}$-chart is:

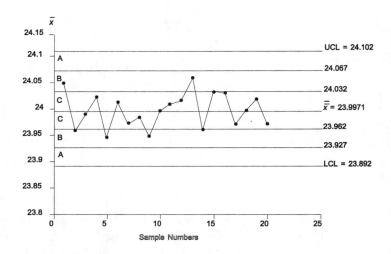

b.   To determine if the process is in or out of control, we check the six rules:

Rule 1:   One point beyond Zone A: No points are beyond Zone A.
Rule 2:   Nine points in a row in Zone C or beyond: No sequence of nine points are in Zone C (on one side of the centerline) or beyond.
Rule 3:   Six points in a row steadily increasing or decreasing: No sequence of six points steadily increase or decrease.
Rule 4:   Fourteen points in a row alternating up and down: This pattern does not exist.
Rule 5:   Two out of three points in Zone A or beyond: There are no groups of three consecutive points that have two or more in Zone A or beyond.
Rule 6:   Four out of five points in a row in Zone B or beyond: No sequence of five points has four or more in Zone B or beyond.

The process appears to be in control.

c.   Since the process is in control, these limits should be used to monitor future process output.

d.   The rational subgrouping strategy used by K-Company will facilitate the identification of process variation caused by differences in the two shifts. All observations within one sample are from the same shift. The shift change is at 3:00 P.M. The samples are selected at 8:00 A.M., 11:00 A.M., 2:00 P.M., 5:00 P.M., and 8:00 P.M. No samples will contain observations from both shifts.

12.15 a. First, we must compute the range for each sample. The range = R = largest measurement – smallest measurement. The results are listed in the table:

Sample No.	R	Sample No.	R	Sample No.	R
1	2.0	25	4.6	49	4.0
2	2.1	26	3.0	50	4.9
3	1.8	27	3.4	51	3.8
4	1.6	28	2.3	52	4.6
5	3.1	29	2.2	53	7.1
6	3.1	30	3.3	54	4.6
7	4.2	31	3.6	55	2.2
8	3.6	32	4.2	56	3.6
9	4.6	33	2.4	57	2.6
10	2.6	34	4.5	58	2.0
11	3.5	35	5.6	59	1.5
12	5.3	36	4.9	60	6.0
13	5.5	37	10.2	61	5.7
14	5.6	38	5.5	62	5.6
15	4.6	39	4.7	63	2.3
16	3.0	40	4.7	64	2.3
17	4.6	41	3.6	65	2.6
18	4.5	42	3.0	66	3.8
19	4.8	43	2.2	67	2.8
20	5.4	44	3.3	68	2.2
21	5.5	45	3.2	69	4.2
22	3.8	46	0.8	70	2.6
23	3.6	47	4.2	71	1.0
24	2.5	48	5.6	72	1.9

$$\bar{\bar{x}} = \frac{\bar{x}_1 + \bar{x}_2 + \cdots + \bar{x}_{72}}{k} = \frac{3537.3}{72} = 49.129$$

$$\bar{R} = \frac{R_1 + R_1 + \cdots + R_{72}}{k} = \frac{268.8}{72} = 3.733$$

Centerline = $\bar{\bar{x}}$ = 49.13

From Table XII, Appendix B, with $n = 6$, $A_2 = .483$.

Upper control limit = $\bar{\bar{x}}$ + $A_2\bar{R}$ = 49.129 + .483(3.733) = 50.932
Lower control limit = $\bar{\bar{x}}$ + $A_2\bar{R}$ = 49.129 – .483(3.733) = 47.326

Upper A–B boundary = $\bar{\bar{x}}$ + $\frac{2}{3}(A_2\bar{R})$ = 49.129 + $\frac{2}{3}$(.483)(3.733) = 50.331

Lower A–B boundary = $\bar{\bar{x}}$ + $\frac{2}{3}(A_2\bar{R})$ = 49.129 – $\frac{2}{3}$(.483)(3.733) = 47.927

$$\text{Upper B–C boundary} = \overline{\overline{x}} + \frac{1}{3}(A_2\overline{R}) = 49.129 + \frac{1}{3}(.483)(3.733) = 49.730$$

$$\text{Lower B–C boundary} = \overline{\overline{x}} - \frac{1}{3}(A_2\overline{R}) = 49.129 - \frac{1}{3}(.483)(3.733) = 48.528$$

The $\overline{x}$-chart is:

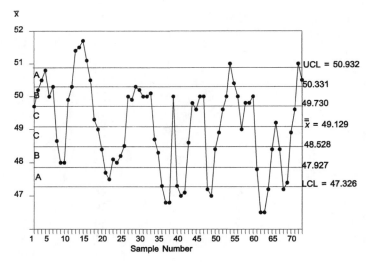

b.   To determine if the process is in or out of control, we check the six rules:

Rule 1:   One point beyond Zone A: There are a total of 17 points beyond Zone A.

Rule 2:   Nine points in a row in Zone C or beyond: No sequence of nine points are in Zone C (on one side of the centerline) or beyond.

Rule 3:   Six points in a row steadily increasing or decreasing: There is one sequence of seven points that are steadily increasing—Points 15 through 21.

Rule 4:   Fourteen points in a row alternating up and down: This pattern does not exist.

Rule 5:   Two out of three points in Zone A or beyond: There are four groups of at least three points in Zone A or beyond—Points 12–16, Points 35–37, Points 39–41, and Points 60–63.

Rule 6:   Four out of five points in a row in Zone B or beyond: There are four groups of points that satisfy this rule—Points 10–16, Points 19–24, Points 26–32, and Points 60–64.

The process appears to be out of control. Rules 1, 3, 5, and 6 indicate that the process is out of control.

c.   No. The problem does not give the times of the shifts. However, suppose we let the first shift be from 6:00 A.M. to 2:00 P.M., the second shift be from 2:00 P.M. to 10:00 P.M., and the third shift be from 10:00 P.M. to 6:00 A.M. If this is the case, the major problems are during the second shift.

12.17   a. $\overline{\overline{x}} = \dfrac{\overline{x}_1 + \overline{x}_2 + \cdots + \overline{x}_{20}}{k} = \dfrac{1,052.933333}{20} = 52.6467$

$\overline{R} = \dfrac{R_1 + R_2 + \cdots + R_{20}}{k} = \dfrac{15.1}{20} = .755$

$Centerline = \bar{\bar{x}} = 52.6467$

From Table XII, Appendix B, with $n = 3$, $A_2 = 1.023$

$Upper\ control\ limit = \bar{\bar{x}} + A_2\bar{R} = 52.6467 + 1.023(.755) = 53.419$

$Lower\ control\ limit = \bar{\bar{x}} - A_2\bar{R} = 52.6467 - 1.023(.755) = 51.874$

$Upper\ A - B\ boundary = \bar{\bar{x}} + \frac{2}{3}(A_2\bar{R}) = 52.6467 + \frac{2}{3}(1.023)(.755) = 53.162$

$Lower\ A - B\ boundary = \bar{\bar{x}} - \frac{2}{3}(A_2\bar{R}) = 52.6467 - \frac{2}{3}(1.023)(.755) = 52.132$

$Upper\ B - C\ boundary = \bar{\bar{x}} + \frac{1}{3}(A_2\bar{R}) = 52.6467 + \frac{1}{3}(1.023)(.755) = 52.904$

$Lower\ B - C\ boundary = \bar{\bar{x}} - \frac{1}{3}(A_2\bar{R}) = 52.6467 - \frac{1}{3}(1.023)(.755) = 52.389$

The $\bar{x}$-chart is:

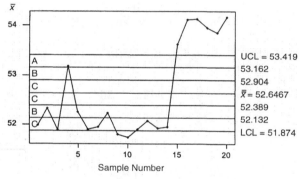

b. To determine if the process is in or out of control, we check the six rules:

Rule 1:   One point beyond Zone A: Eight points are beyond Zone A.
Rule 2:   Nine points in a row in Zone C or beyond: Data points 5 through 14 (10 points) are in Zone C (on one side of the centerline) or beyond.
Rule 3:   Six points in a row steadily increasing or decreasing: No sequence of six points steadily increase or decrease.
Rule 4:   Fourteen points in a row alternating up and down: This pattern does not exist.
Rule 5:   Two out of three points in Zone A or beyond: There are several sets of three consecutive points that have two points in Zone A or beyond.
Rule 6:   Four out of five points in a row in Zone B or beyond: There are several sets of five points where four or more are in Zone B or beyond.

Special causes of variation appear to be present. The process appears to be out of control. Rules 1, 2, 5, and 6 indicate the process is out of control.

c. Processes that are out of control exhibit variation that is the result of both common causes and special causes of variation. Common causes affect all output of the process. Special causes typically affect only local areas or operations within a process.

d. Since the process is out of control, the control limits and centerline should not be used to monitor future output.

12.19 The control limits of the -chart are a function of and reflect the variation in the process. If the variation were unstable (i.e., out of control), the control limits would not be constant. Under these circumstances, the fixed control limits of the -chart would have little meaning. We use the R-chart to determine whether the variation of the process is stable. If it is, the -chart is meaningful. Thus, we interpret the R-chart prior to the -chart.

12.21 a. From Exercise 12.10, $\bar{R} = \dfrac{R_1 + R_2 + \cdots + R_{25}}{k} = \dfrac{198.7}{25} = 7.948$

$Centerline = \bar{R} = 7.948$

From Table XII, Appendix B, with $n = 5$, $D_4 = 2.114$ and $D_3 = 0$.

$Upper\ control\ limit = \bar{R}D_4 = 7.948(2.114) = 16.802$

Since $D_3 = 0$, the lower control limit is negative and is not included on the chart.

b. From Table XII, Appendix B, with $n = 5$, $d_2 = 2.326$, and $d_3 = .864$.

$Upper\ A\text{--}B\ boundary = \bar{R} + 2d_3\dfrac{\bar{R}}{d_2} = 7.948 + 2(.864)\dfrac{7.948}{2.326} = 13.853$

$Lower\ A\text{--}B\ boundary = \bar{R} - 2d_3\dfrac{\bar{R}}{d_2} = 7.948 - 2(.864)\dfrac{7.948}{2.326} = 2.043$

$Upper\ B\text{--}C\ boundary = \bar{R} + d_3\dfrac{\bar{R}}{d_2} = 7.948 + (.864)\dfrac{7.948}{2.326} = 10.900$

$Lower\ B\text{--}C\ boundary = \bar{R} - d_3\dfrac{\bar{R}}{d_2} = 7.948 - (.864)\dfrac{7.948}{2.326} = 4.996$

c.   The R-chart is:

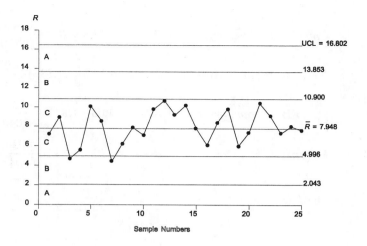

To determine if the process is in or out of control, we check the four rules:

Rule 1:   One point beyond Zone A: No points are beyond Zone A.
Rule 2:   Nine points in a row in Zone C or beyond: No sequence of nine points are in Zone C (on one side of the centerline) or beyond.
Rule 3:   Six points in a row steadily increasing or decreasing: No sequence of six points steadily increase or decrease.
Rule 4:   Fourteen points in a row alternating up and down: This pattern does not exist.

The process appears to be in control.

12.23   First, we construct an R-chart.

$$\bar{R} = \frac{R_1 + R_2 + \cdots + R_{20}}{k} = \frac{80.6}{20} = 4.03$$

$Centerline = \bar{R} = 4.03$

From Table XII, Appendix B, with $n = 7$, $D_4 = 1.924$ and $D_3 = .076$.

$Upper\ control\ limit = \bar{R}D_4 = 4.03(1.924) = 7.754$
$Lower\ control\ limit = \bar{R}D_3 = 4.03(0.076) = 0.306$

From Table XII, Appendix B, with $n = 7$, $d_2 = 2.704$ and $d_3 = .833$.

$$Upper\ \text{A–B}\ boundary = \bar{R} + 2d_3\frac{\bar{R}}{d_2} = 4.03 + 2(.833)\frac{4.03}{2.704} = 6.513$$

$$Lower\ \text{A–B}\ boundary = \bar{R} - 2d_3\frac{\bar{R}}{d_2} = 4.03 - 2(.833)\frac{4.03}{2.704} = 1.547$$

$$Upper\ \text{B–C}\ boundary = \bar{R} + d_3\frac{\bar{R}}{d_2} = 4.03 + (.833)\frac{4.03}{2.704} = 5.271$$

$$Lower\ \text{B–C}\ boundary = \bar{R} - d_3\frac{\bar{R}}{d_2} = 4.03 - (.833)\frac{4.03}{2.704} = 2.789$$

The R-chart is:

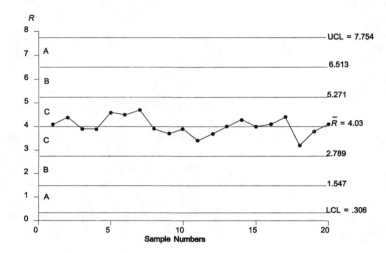

To determine if the process is in or out of control, we check the four rules:

Rule 1: One point beyond Zone A: No points are beyond Zone A.

Rule 2: Nine points in a row in Zone C or beyond: No sequence of nine points are in Zone C (on one side of the centerline) or beyond.

Rule 3: Six points in a row steadily increasing or decreasing: No sequence of six points steadily increase or decrease.

Rule 4: Fourteen points in a row alternating up and down: This pattern does not exist.

The process appears to be in control. Since the process variation is in control, it is appropriate to construct the $\bar{x}$-chart.

To construct an $\bar{x}$-chart, we first calculate the following:

$$\bar{\bar{x}} = \frac{\bar{x}_1 + \bar{x}_2 + \cdots + \bar{x}_{20}}{k} = \frac{434.56}{20} = 21.728$$

$$\bar{R} = \frac{R_1 + R_2 + \cdots R_{20}}{k} = \frac{80.6}{20} = 4.03$$

$$Centerline = \bar{\bar{x}} = 21.728$$

From Table XII, Appendix B, with $n = 7$, $A_2 = .419$.

Upper control limit $= \bar{\bar{x}} + A_2\bar{R} = 21.728 + .419(4.03) = 23.417$
Lower control limit $= \bar{\bar{x}} - A_2\bar{R} = 21.728 - .419(4.03) = 20.039$

Upper A-B *boundary* $= \bar{\bar{x}} + \dfrac{2}{3}(A_2\bar{R}) = 21.728 + \dfrac{2}{3}(.419)(4.03) = 22.854$

Lower A-B *boundary* $= \bar{\bar{x}} - \dfrac{2}{3}(A_2\bar{R}) = 21.728 - \dfrac{2}{3}(.419)(4.03) = 20.602$

Upper B-C *boundary* $= \bar{\bar{x}} + \dfrac{1}{3}(A_2\bar{R}) = 21.728 + \dfrac{1}{3}(.419)(4.03) = 22.291$

Lower B-C *boundary* $= \bar{\bar{x}} - \dfrac{1}{3}(A_2\bar{R}) = 21.728 - \dfrac{1}{3}(.419)(4.03) = 21.165$

The $\bar{x}$-chart is:

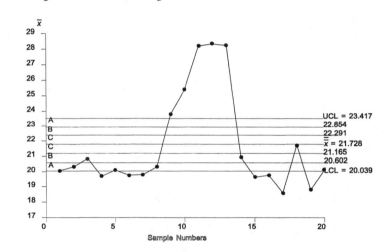

To determine if the process is in or out of control, we check the six rules:

Rule 1: One point beyond Zone A: There are 12 points beyond Zone A. This indicates the process is out of control.

Rule 2: Nine points in a row in Zone C or beyond: No sequence of nine points are in Zone C (on one side of the centerline) or beyond.

Rule 3: Six points in a row steadily increasing or decreasing: Points 6 through 12 steadily increase. This indicates the process is out of control.

Rule 4: Fourteen points in a row alternating up and down: This pattern does not exist.

Rule 5: Two out of three points in Zone A or beyond: There are several groups of three consecutive points that have two or more in Zone A or beyond. This indicates the process is out of control.

Rule 6: Four out of five points in a row in Zone B or beyond: Several sequences of five points have four or more in Zone B or beyond. This indicates the process is out of control.

Rules 1, 3, 5, and 6 indicate that the process is out of control.

12.25 a. Yes. Because all five observations in each sample were selected from the same dispenser, the rational subgrouping will enable the company to detect variation in fill caused by differences in the carbon dioxide dispensers.

b. For each sample, we compute the range = R = largest measurement - smallest measurement. The results are listed in the table:

Sample No.	R	Sample No.	R
1	.05	13	.05
2	.06	14	.04
3	.06	15	.05
4	.05	16	.05
5	.07	17	.06
6	.07	18	.06
7	.09	19	.05
8	.08	20	.08
9	.08	21	.08
10	.11	22	.12
11	.14	23	.12
12	.14	24	.15

$$\bar{R} = \frac{R_1 + R_2 + \cdots R_{24}}{k} = \frac{1.91}{24} = .0796$$

Centerline = $\bar{R}$ = .0796

From Table XII, Appendix B, with $n = 5$, $D_4 = 2.114$, and $D_3 = 0$.

Upper control limit = $\bar{R}D_4$ = .0796(2.114) = .168

Since $D_3 = 0$, the lower control limit is negative and is not included on the chart.

From Table XII, Appendix B, with $n = 5$, $d_2 = 2.326$, and $d_3 = .864$.

Upper A–B *boundary* = $\bar{R} + 2d_3\dfrac{\bar{R}}{d_2}$ = .0796 + 2(.864)$\dfrac{.0796}{2.326}$ = .139

Lower A–B *boundary* = $\bar{R} - 2d_3\dfrac{\bar{R}}{d_2}$ = .0796 − 2(.864)$\dfrac{.0796}{2.326}$ = .020

Upper B–C *boundary* = $\bar{R} + d_3\dfrac{\bar{R}}{d_2}$ = .0796 + (.864)$\dfrac{.0796}{2.326}$ = .109

Lower B–C *boundary* = $\bar{R} - d_3\dfrac{\bar{R}}{d_2}$ = .0796 − (.864)$\dfrac{.0796}{2.326}$ = .050

The *R*-chart is:

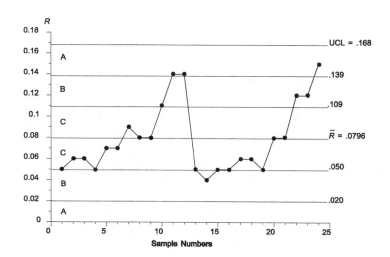

c. To determine if the process is in or out of control, we check the four rules:

    Rule 1:   One point beyond Zone A: No points are beyond Zone A.

    Rule 2:   Nine points in a row in Zone C or beyond: No sequence of nine points are in Zone C (on one side of the centerline) or beyond.

    Rule 3:   Six points in a row steadily increasing or decreasing: No sequence of six points steadily increase or decrease.

    Rule 4:   Fourteen points in a row alternating up and down: This pattern does not exist.

The process appears to be in control.

d. Since the process variation is in control, the *R*-chart should be used to monitor future process output.

e. The $\bar{x}$-chart should be constructed. The control limits of the $\bar{x}$-chart depend on the variation of the process. (In particular, they are constructed using $\bar{R}$.) If the variation of the process is in control, the control limits of the $\bar{x}$-chart are meaningful.

12.27   a.   From Table XII, Appendix B, with $n = 6$, $D_3 = .000$ and $D_4 = 2.004$.

$\bar{R} = 3.733$ (from Exercise 12.15).

Upper control limit $= \bar{R}D_4 = 3.733(2.004) = 7.481$

Since $D_3 = 0$, the lower control limit is negative and is not included on the chart.

From Table XII, Appendix B, with $n = 6$, $d_2 = 2.534$, and $d_3 = .848$.

Upper A–B *boundary* $= \bar{R} + 2d_3 \dfrac{\bar{R}}{d_2} = 3.733 + 2(.848)\dfrac{3.733}{2.534} = 6.231$

$$Lower\ A\text{–}B\ boundary = \bar{R} - 2d_3\frac{\bar{R}}{d_2} = 3.733 - 2(.848)\frac{3.733}{2.534} = 1.235$$

$$Upper\ B\text{–}C\ boundary = \bar{R} + d_3\frac{\bar{R}}{d_2} = 3.733 + (.848)\frac{3.733}{2.534} = 4.982$$

$$Lower\ B\text{–}C\ boundary = \bar{R} - d_3\frac{\bar{R}}{d_2} = 3.733 - (.848)\frac{3.733}{2.534} = 2.484$$

The *R*-chart is:

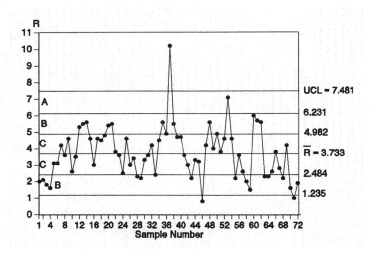

b.   To determine if the process is in control, we check the four rules.

> Rule 1: One point beyond Zone A: There is 1 point beyond Zone A.
>
> Rule 2: Nine points in a row in Zone C or beyond: No sequence of nine points are in Zone C (on one side of the centerline) or beyond.
>
> Rule 3: Six points in a row steadily increasing or decreasing: This pattern is not present.
>
> Rule 4: Fourteen points in a row alternating up and down: This pattern does not exist.

Rule 1 indicates that the process is out of control. The process is unstable.

c.   Yes. The process variation is not under control.

12.29   a. $\bar{R} = \dfrac{R_1 + R_2 + \cdots + R_{25}}{k} = \dfrac{2.5 + 1.5 + \cdots + 2.0}{25} = \dfrac{52}{25} = 2.08$

Centerline $= \bar{R} = 2.08$

From Table XII, Appendix B, with $n = 5$, $D_4 = 2.114$ and $D_3 = 0$.

Upper control limit $= \bar{R}D_4 = 2.08(2.114) = 4.397$

Since $D_3 = 0$, the lower control limit is negative and is not included on the chart.

From Table XII, Appendix B, with $n = 5$, $d_2 = 2.326$ and $d_3 = 0.864$.

$$\text{Upper } A - B \text{ boundary} = \bar{R} + 2d_3\frac{\bar{R}}{d_2} = 2.08 + 2(.864)\frac{2.08}{2.326} = 3.625$$

$$\text{Lower } A - B \text{ boundary} = \bar{R} - 2d_3\frac{\bar{R}}{d_2} = 2.08 - 2(.864)\frac{2.08}{2.326} = .535$$

$$\text{Upper } B - C \text{ boundary} = \bar{R} + d_3\frac{\bar{R}}{d_2} = 2.08 + (.864)\frac{2.08}{2.326} = 2.853$$

$$\text{Lower } B - C \text{ boundary} = \bar{R} - d_3\frac{\bar{R}}{d_2} = 2.08 - (.864)\frac{2.08}{2.326} = 1.307$$

The R-chart is:

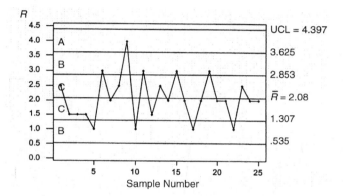

To determine if the process is in or out of control, we check the four rules:

Rule 1: One point beyond Zone A: No points are beyond Zone A.
Rule 2: Nine points in a row in Zone C or beyond: No sequence of nine points are in Zone C (on one side of the centerline) or beyond.
Rule 3: Six points in a row steadily increasing or decreasing: No sequence of six points steadily increase or decrease.
Rule 4: Fourteen points in a row alternating up and down: This pattern does not exist.

The process appears to be in control since none of the out-of-control signals are observed. No special causes of variation appear to be present.

b. Since the process appears to be under control, it is appropriate to construct an $\bar{x}$-chart for the data.

c. $$\bar{R} = \frac{R_1 + R_2 + \cdots + R_{25}}{k} = \frac{2.5 + 0.0 + \cdots + 2.5}{25} = \frac{42.5}{25} = 1.7$$

$$Centerline = \bar{R} = 1.7$$

From Table XII, Appendix B, with $n = 5$, $D_4 = 2.114$ and $D_3 = 0$.

$$Upper\ control\ limit = \bar{R}D_4 = 1.7(2.114) = 3.594$$

Since $D_3 = 0$, the lower control limit is negative and is not included on the chart.

From Table XII, Appendix B, with $n = 5$, $d_2 = 2.326$ and $d_3 = 0.864$.

$$Upper\ A-B\ boundary = \bar{R} + 2d_3\frac{\bar{R}}{d_2} = 1.7 + 2(.864)\frac{1.7}{2.326} = 2.963$$

$$Lower\ A-B\ boundary = \bar{R} - 2d_3\frac{\bar{R}}{d_2} = 1.7 - 2(.864)\frac{1.7}{2.326} = .437$$

$$Upper\ B-C\ boundary = \bar{R} + d_3\frac{\bar{R}}{d_2} = 1.7 + (.864)\frac{1.7}{2.326} = 2.331$$

$$Lower\ B-C\ boundary = \bar{R} - d_3\frac{\bar{R}}{d_2} = 1.7 - (.864)\frac{1.7}{2.326} = 1.069$$

The R chart is:

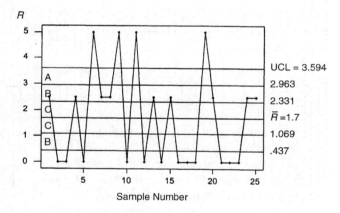

To determine if the process is in or out of control, we check the four rules:

Rule 1: One point beyond Zone A: Four points are beyond Zone A.
Rule 2: Nine points in a row in Zone C or beyond: No sequence of nine points are in Zone C (on one side of the centerline) or beyond.
Rule 3: Six points in a row steadily increasing or decreasing: No sequence of six points steadily increase or decrease.
Rule 4: Fourteen points in a row alternating up and down: This pattern does not exist.

The process appears to be out of control. Rule 1 indicates the process is out of control. Since this process is out of control, it is not appropriate to construct an x-chart for the data.

d. We get two different answers as to whether this process is in control, depending on the accuracy of the data. When the data were measured to an accuracy of .5 gram, the process appears to be in control. However, when the data were measured to an accuracy of only 2.5 grams, the process appears to be out of control. The same data were used for each chart – just measured to different accuracies.

12.31 The sample size is determined as follows:

$$n > \frac{9(1-p_0)}{p_0} = \frac{9(1-.08)}{.08} = 103.5 \approx 104$$

12.33 a. We must first calculate . To do this, it is necessary to find the total number of defectives in all the samples. To find the number of defectives per sample, we multiple the proportion by the sample size, 150. The number of defectives per sample are shown in the table:

Sample No.	p	No. Defectives	Sample No.	p	No. Defectives
1	.03	4.5	11	.07	10.5
2	.05	7.5	12	.04	6.0
3	.10	15.0	13	.06	9.0
4	.02	3.0	14	.05	7.5
5	.08	12.0	15	.07	10.5
6	.09	13.5	16	.06	9.0
7	.08	12.0	17	.07	10.5
8	.05	7.5	18	.02	3.0
9	.07	10.5	19	.05	7.5
10	.06	9.0	20	.03	4.5

Note: There cannot be a fraction of a defective. The proportions presented in the exercise have been rounded off. I have used the fractions to minimize the roundoff error.

To get the total number of defectives, sum the number of defectives for all 20 samples. The sum is 172.5. To get the total number of units sampled, multiply the sample size by the number of samples: 150(20) = 3000.

$$\bar{p} = \frac{\text{Total defective in all samples}}{\text{Total units sampled}} = \frac{172.5}{3000} = .0575$$

$Centerline = \bar{p} = .0575$

$$Upper\ control\ limit = \bar{p} + 3\sqrt{\frac{\bar{p}(1-\bar{p})}{n}} = .0575 + 3\sqrt{\frac{.0575(.9425)}{150}} = .1145$$

$$Lower\ control\ limit = \bar{p} - 3\sqrt{\frac{\bar{p}(1-\bar{p})}{n}} = .0575 - 3\sqrt{\frac{.0575(.9425)}{150}} = .0005$$

b. $Upper$ A–B $boundary = \bar{p} + 2\sqrt{\dfrac{\bar{p}(1-\bar{p})}{n}} = .0575 + 2\sqrt{\dfrac{.0575(.9425)}{150}} = .0955$

$Lower$ A-B $boundary = \bar{p} - 2\sqrt{\dfrac{\bar{p}(1-\bar{p})}{n}} = .0575 - 2\sqrt{\dfrac{.0575(.9425)}{150}} = .0195$

$Upper$ B-C $boundary = \bar{p} + \sqrt{\dfrac{\bar{p}(1-\bar{p})}{n}} = .0575 + \sqrt{\dfrac{.0575(.9425)}{150}} = .0765$

$Lower$ B-C $boundary = \bar{p} - \sqrt{\dfrac{\bar{p}(1-\bar{p})}{n}} = .0575 - \sqrt{\dfrac{.0575(.9425)}{150}} = .0385$

c. The p-chart is:

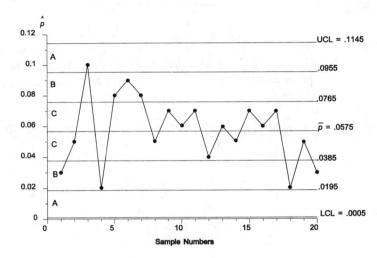

d. To determine if the process is in or out of control, we check the four rules:

Rule 1: One point beyond Zone A: No points are beyond Zone A.

Rule 2: Nine points in a row in Zone C or beyond: No sequence of nine points are in Zone C (on one side of the centerline) or beyond.

Rule 3: Six points in a row steadily increasing or decreasing: No sequence of six points steadily increase or decrease.

Rule 4: Fourteen points in a row alternating up and down: Points 7 through 20 alternate up and down. This indicates the process is out of control.

Rule 4 indicates that the process is out of control.

e. Since the process is out of control, the centerline and control limits should not be used to monitor future process output. The centerline and control limits are intended to represent the behavior of the process when it is under control.

12.35   a.   Yes. The minimum sample size necessary so the lower control limit is not negative is:

$$n > \frac{9(1-p_0)}{p_0}$$

From the data, $p_0 \approx .01$

Thus, $n > \dfrac{9(1-.01)}{.01} = 891$. Our sample size was 1000.

b. $Upper\ control\ limit = \bar{p} + 3\sqrt{\dfrac{\bar{p}(1-\bar{p})}{n}} = .0105 + 3\sqrt{\dfrac{.0105(.9895)}{1000}} = .0202$

$Lower\ control\ limit = \bar{p} - 3\sqrt{\dfrac{\bar{p}(1-\bar{p})}{n}} = .0105 - 3\sqrt{\dfrac{.0105(.9895)}{1000}} = .0008$

c.   To determine if special causes are present, we must complete the p-chart.

$Upper\ A - B\ boundary = \bar{p} + 2\sqrt{\dfrac{\bar{p}(1-\bar{p})}{n}} = .0105 + 2\sqrt{\dfrac{.0105(.9895)}{1000}} = .0169$

$Lower\ A - B\ boundary = \bar{p} - 2\sqrt{\dfrac{\bar{p}(1-\bar{p})}{n}} = .0105 - 2\sqrt{\dfrac{.0105(.9895)}{1000}} = .0041$

$Upper\ B - C\ boundary = \bar{p} + \sqrt{\dfrac{\bar{p}(1-\bar{p})}{n}} = .0105 + \sqrt{\dfrac{.0105(.9895)}{1000}} = .0137$

$Lower\ B - C\ boundary = \bar{p} - \sqrt{\dfrac{\bar{p}(1-\bar{p})}{n}} = .0105 - \sqrt{\dfrac{.0105(.9895)}{1000}} = .0073$

To determine if the process is in control, we check the four rules.

Rule 1:   One point beyond Zone A: No points are beyond Zone A.
Rule 2:   Nine points in a row in Zone C or beyond: There are not nine points in a row in Zone C (on one side of the centerline) or beyond.
Rule 3:   Six points in a row steadily increasing or decreasing: No sequence of six points steadily increase or decrease.
Rule 4:   Fourteen points in a row alternating up and down: This pattern does not exist.

It appears that the process is in control.

d.   The rational subgrouping strategy says that samples should be chosen so that it gives the maximum chance for the measurements in each sample to be similar and so that it gives the maximum chance for the samples to differ. By selecting 1000 consecutive chips each time, this gives the maximum chance for the measurements in the sample to be similar. By selecting the samples every other day, there is a relatively large chance that the samples differ.

Methods for Quality Improvement

12.37   a.   To compute the proportion of defectives in each sample, divide the number of defectives by the number in the sample, 100:

$$\hat{p} = \frac{\text{No. of defectives}}{\text{No. in sample}}$$

The sample proportions are listed in the table:

Sample No.	$\hat{p}$	Sample No.	$\hat{p}$
1	.02	16	.02
2	.04	17	.03
3	.10	18	.07
4	.04	19	.03
5	.01	20	.02
6	.01	21	.03
7	.13	22	.07
8	.09	23	.04
9	.11	24	.03
10	.00	25	.02
11	.03	26	.02
12	.04	27	.00
13	.02	28	.01
14	.02	29	.03
15	.08	30	.04

To get the total number of defectives, sum the number of defectives for all 30 samples. The sum is 120. To get the total number of units sampled, multiply the sample size by the number of samples: $100(30) = 3000$.

$$\bar{p} = \frac{\text{Total defective in all samples}}{\text{Total units sampled}} = \frac{120}{3000} = .04$$

The centerline is $\bar{p} = .04$

$$Upper\ control\ limit = \bar{p} + 3\sqrt{\frac{\bar{p}(1-\bar{p})}{n}} = .04 + 3\sqrt{\frac{.04(1-.04)}{100}} = .099$$

$$Lower\ control\ limit = \bar{p} - 3\sqrt{\frac{\bar{p}(1-\bar{p})}{n}} = .04 - 3\sqrt{\frac{.04(1-.04)}{100}} = -.019$$

$$Upper\ A\text{–}B\ boundary = \bar{p} + 2\sqrt{\frac{\bar{p}(1-\bar{p})}{n}} = .04 + 2\sqrt{\frac{.04(1-.04)}{100}} = .079$$

$$Lower\ A\text{–}B\ boundary = \bar{p} - 2\sqrt{\frac{\bar{p}(1-\bar{p})}{n}} = .04 - 2\sqrt{\frac{.04(1-.04)}{100}} = .001$$

$$Upper\ B\text{–}C\ boundary = \bar{p} + \sqrt{\frac{\bar{p}(1-\bar{p})}{n}} = .04 + \sqrt{\frac{.04(1-.04)}{100}} = .060$$

$$Lower\ B\text{–}C\ boundary = \sqrt{\frac{\bar{p}(1-\bar{p})}{n}} = .04 - \sqrt{\frac{.04(1-.04)}{100}} = .020$$

The *p*-chart is:

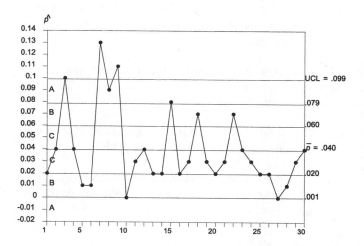

b. To determine if the process is in or out of control, we check the four rules for the *p*-chart.

Rule 1: One point beyond Zone A: There are 3 points beyond Zone A—points 2, 7, and 9.

Rule 2: Nine points in a row in Zone C or beyond: No sequence of nine points are in Zone C (on one side of the centerline) or beyond.

Rule 3: Six points in a row steadily increasing or decreasing: This pattern is not present.

Rule 4: Fourteen points in a row alternating up and down: This pattern does not exist.

The process does not appear to be in control. Rule 1 indicates that the process is out of control.

c. No. Since the process is not in control, then these control limits are meaningless.

12.39 A capability analysis is a methodology used to help determine when common cause variation is unacceptably high. If a process is not in statistical control, then both common causes and special causes of variation exist. It would not be possible to determine if the common cause variation is too high because it could not be separated from special cause variation.

12.41 One way to assess the capability of a process is to construct a frequency distribution or stem-and-leaf display for a large sample of individual measurements from the process. Then, the specification limits and the target value for the output variable are added to the graph. This is called a capability analysis diagram. A second way to assess the capability of a process is to quantify capability. The most direct way to quantify capability is to count the number of items that fall outside the specification limits in the capability analysis diagram and report the percentage of such items in the sample. Also, one can construct a capability index. This is the ratio of the difference in the specification spread and the difference in the process spread. This measure is called C_P. If C_P is less than 1, then the process is not capable.

12.43 a. $C_P = 1.00$. For this value, the specification spread is equal to the process spread. This indicates that the process is capable. Approximately 2.7 units per 1,000 will be unacceptable.

b. $C_P = 1.33$. For this value, the specification spread is greater than the process spread. This indicates that the process is capable. Approximately 63 units per 1,000,000 will be unacceptable.

c. $C_P = 0.50$. For this value, the specification spread is less than the process spread. This indicates that the process is not capable.

d. $C_P = 2.00$. For this value, the specification spread is greater than the process spread. This indicates that the process is capable. Approximately 2 units per billion will be unacceptable.

12.45 The process spread is 6σ.

a. For $\sigma = 21$, the process spread is $6(21) = 126$

b. For $\sigma = 5.2$, the process spread is $6(5.2) = 31.2$

c. For $s = 110.06$, the process spread is estimated by $6(110.06) = 660.36$

d. For $s = .0024$, the process spread is estimated by $6(.0024) = .0144$

12.47 We know that $C_P = \dfrac{\text{USL} - \text{LSL}}{6\sigma}$

Thus, if $C_P = 2$, then $2 = \dfrac{\text{USL} - \text{LSL}}{6\sigma} \Rightarrow 12\sigma = \text{USL} - \text{LSL}$. The process mean is halfway between the USL and the LSL. Since the specification spread covers 12σ, then the USL must be $12\sigma/2 = 6\sigma$ from the process mean.

12.49 a. A capability analysis diagram is:

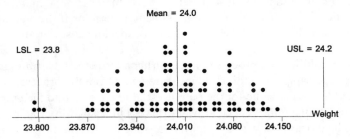

b. From the sample, $\bar{x} = 23.997$ and $s = .077$.

$$C_P = \frac{\text{USL - LSL}}{6\sigma} \approx \frac{24.2 - 23.8}{6(.077)} = \frac{.4}{.462} = .866$$

Since the C_P value is less than 1, the process is not capable.

12.51   a.   The capability analysis diagram is:

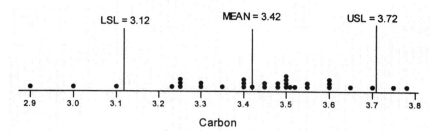

b.   Two observations are above the upper specification limit and three observations are below the lower specification limit. Thus, the proportion of measurements that fall outside the specifications is $5 / 33 = .152$.

c.   From the sample, $\bar{x} = 3.43$ and $s = 0.1982$.

$$C_p = \frac{USL - LSL}{6\sigma} = \frac{3.72 - 3.12}{6(.1982)} = \frac{.6}{1.1892} = .505$$

Since the C_p value is less than 1, the process is not capable.

12.53   A system is a collection or arrangement of interacting components that has an on-going purpose or mission. A system receives inputs from its environment, transforms those inputs to outputs, and delivers those outputs to its environment.

12.57   Yes. Even though the output may all fall within the specification limits, the process may still be out of control.

12.61   If a process is in control and remains in control, its future will be like its past. It is predictable in that its output will stay within certain limits. If a process is out of control, there is no way of knowing what the future pattern of output from the process may look like.

12.63   Control limits are a function of the natural variability of the process. The position of the limits is a function of the size of the process standard deviation. Specification limits are boundary points that define the acceptable values for an output variable of a particular product or service. They are determined by customers, management, and/or product designers. Specification limits may be either two-sided, with upper and lower limits, or one-sided with either an upper or lower limit. Specification limits are not dependent on the process in any way. The process may not be able to meet the specification limits even when it is under statistical control.

12.65   The C_P statistic is used to assess capability if the process is stable (in control) and if the process is centered on the target value.

12.67 a. The centerline is:

$$\overline{x} = \frac{\sum x}{n} = \frac{96}{15} = 6.4$$

The time series plot is:

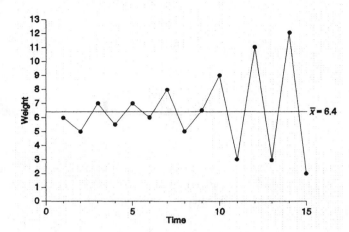

b. The type of variation best described by the pattern in this plot is increasing variance. The spread of the measurements increases with the passing of time.

12.69 To determine if the process is in or out of control, we check the six rules:

Rule 1: One point beyond Zone A: No points are beyond Zone A.

Rule 2: Nine points in a row in Zone C or beyond: Points 8 through 16 are in Zone C (on one side of the centerline) or beyond. This indicates the process is out of control.

Rule 3: Six points in a row steadily increasing or decreasing: No sequence of six points steadily increase or decrease.

Rule 4: Fourteen points in a row alternating up and down: This pattern does not exist.

Rule 5: Two out of three points in Zone A or beyond: No group of three consecutive points have two or more in Zone A or beyond.

Rule 6: Four out of five points in a row in Zone B or beyond: No sequence of five points has four or more in Zone B or beyond.

Rule 2 indicates that the process is out of control. A special cause of variation appears to be present.

12.71   a.   To compute the range, subtract the larger score minus the smaller score. The ranges for the samples are listed in the table:

Sample No.	R	$\bar{x}$	Sample No.	R	$\bar{x}$
1	4	343.0	11	5	357.5
2	3	329.5	12	10	330.0
3	12	349.0	13	2	349.0
4	1	351.5	14	1	336.5
5	12	354.0	15	16	337.0
6	6	339.0	16	7	354.5
7	3	329.5	17	1	352.5
8	0	344.0	18	6	337.0
9	25	346.5	19	6	338.0
10	15	353.5	20	13	351.5

The centerline is $\bar{R} = \dfrac{\sum R}{k} = \dfrac{148}{20} = 7.4$

From Table XII, Appendix B, with $n = 2$, $D_3 = 0$, and $D_4 = 3.267$.

Upper control limit $= \bar{R}D_4 = 7.4(3.267) = 24.1758$

Since $D_3 = 0$, the lower control limit is negative and is not included on the chart.

From Table XII, Appendix B, with $n = 2$, $d_2 = 1.128$, and $d_3 = .853$.

Upper A–B boundary $= \bar{R} + 2d_3\dfrac{\bar{R}}{d_2} = 7.4 + 2(.853)\dfrac{(7.4)}{1.128} = 18.5918$

Lower A–B boundary $= \bar{R} - 2d_3\dfrac{\bar{R}}{d_2} = 7.4 - 2(.853)\dfrac{(7.4)}{1.128} = -3.7918$

Upper B–C boundary $= \bar{R} + d_3\dfrac{\bar{R}}{d_2} = 7.4 + (.853)\dfrac{(7.4)}{1.128} = 12.9959$

Lower B–C boundary $= \bar{R} - d_3\dfrac{\bar{R}}{d_2} = 7.4 - (.853)\dfrac{(7.4)}{1.128} = 1.8041$

The *R*-chart is:

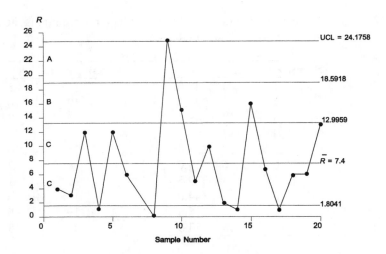

To determine if the process is in control, we check the four rules.

Rule 1: One point beyond Zone A: Point 9 is beyond Zone A. This indicates the process is out of control.

Rule 2: Nine points in a row in Zone C or beyond: There are not nine points in a row in Zone C (on one side of the centerline) or beyond.

Rule 3: Six points in a row steadily increasing or decreasing: No sequence of six points steadily increase or decrease.

Rule 4: Fourteen points in a row alternating up and down: This pattern does not exist.

Rule 1 indicates that the process is out of control. We should not use this to construct the $\bar{x}$-chart.

b. We will construct the $\bar{x}$-chart even though the *R*-chart indicates the variation is out of control. First, compute the mean for each sample by adding the 2 observations and dividing by 2. These values are in the table in part **a**.

The centerline is $\bar{\bar{x}} = \dfrac{\sum \bar{x}}{k} = \dfrac{6883}{20} = 344.15$

From Table XII, Appendix B, with $n = 2$, $A_2 = 1.880$.

$\bar{\bar{x}} = 344.15$ and $\bar{R} = 7.4$

Upper control limit $= \bar{\bar{x}} + A_2 = 344.15 + 1.88(7.4) = 358.062$

Lower control limit $= \bar{\bar{x}} - A_2 = 344.15 - 1.88(7.4) = 330.238$

Upper A–B *boundary* $= \bar{\bar{x}} + \dfrac{2}{3}(A_2 \bar{R}) = 344.15 + \dfrac{2}{3}(1.88)(7.4) = 353.425$

Lower A–B *boundary* $= \bar{\bar{x}} - \dfrac{2}{3}(A_2 \bar{R}) = 344.15 - \dfrac{2}{3}(1.88)(7.4) = 334.875$

$$\text{Upper B–C boundary} = \bar{\bar{x}} + \frac{1}{3}(A_2\bar{R}) = 344.15 + \frac{1}{3}(1.88)(7.4) = 348.787$$

$$\text{Lower B–C boundary} = \bar{\bar{x}} - \frac{1}{3}(A_2\bar{R}) = 344.15 - \frac{1}{3}(1.88)(7.4) = 339.513$$

The $\bar{x}$-chart is:

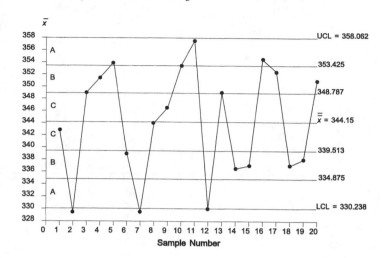

To determine if the process is in control, we check the six rules.

Rule 1: One point beyond Zone A: Points 2 and 7 are beyond Zone A. This indicates the process is out of control.

Rule 2: Nine points in a row in Zone C or beyond: There are nine points (Points 9 through 17) in a row in Zone C (on one side of the centerline) or beyond. This indicates that the process is out of control.

Rule 3: Six points in a row steadily increasing or decreasing: No sequence of six points steadily increase or decrease.

Rule 4: Fourteen points in a row alternating up and down: This pattern does not exist.

Rule 5: Two out of three points in Zone A or beyond: Points 10 and 11 are in Zone 3 or beyond. This indicates that the process is out of control.

Rule 6: Four out of five points in a row in Zone B or beyond: No sequence of five points has four or more in Zone B or beyond.

Rules 1 and 5 indicate the process is out of control. The $\bar{x}$-chart should not be used to monitor the process.

c. These control limits should not be used to monitor future output because both processes are out of control. One or more special causes of variation are affecting the process variation and process mean. These should be identified and eliminated in order to bring the processes into control.

d. Of the 40 patients sampled, 10 received care that did not conform to the hospital's requirement. The proportion is 10/40 = .25.

12.73   a.   For each sample, we compute $\bar{x} = \dfrac{\sum x}{n}$ and $R = $ range = largest measurement - smallest measurement. The results are listed in the table:

Sample No.	$\bar{x}$	R	Sample No.	$\bar{x}$	R
1	4.36	7.1	11	3.32	4.8
2	5.10	7.7	12	4.02	4.8
3	4.52	5.0	13	5.24	7.8
4	3.42	5.8	14	3.58	3.9
5	2.62	6.2	15	3.48	5.5
6	3.94	3.9	16	5.00	3.0
7	2.34	5.3	17	3.68	6.2
8	3.26	3.2	18	2.68	3.9
9	4.06	8.0	19	3.66	4.4
10	4.96	7.1	20	4.10	5.5

$$\bar{\bar{x}} = \frac{\bar{x}_1 + \bar{x}_2 + \cdots + \bar{x}_{20}}{k} = \frac{77.24}{20} = 3.867$$

$$\bar{R} = \frac{R_1 + R_2 + \cdots + R_{20}}{k} = \frac{109.1}{20} = 5.455$$

First, we construct an R-chart.

Centerline $= \bar{R} = 5.455$

From Table XII, Appendix B, with $n = 5$, $D_4 = 2.114$, and $D_3 = 0$.

Upper control limit $= \bar{R}D_4 = 5.455(2.114) = 11.532$

Since $D_3 = 0$, the lower control limit is negative and is not included on the chart.

Upper A–B *boundary* $= \bar{R} + 2d_3\dfrac{\bar{R}}{d_2} = 5.455 + 2(.864)\dfrac{(5.455)}{2.326} = 9.508$

Lower A–B *boundary* $= \bar{R} - 2d_3\dfrac{\bar{R}}{d_2} = 5.455 - 2(.864)\dfrac{(5.455)}{2.326} = 1.402$

Upper B–C *boundary* $= \bar{R} + d_3\dfrac{\bar{R}}{d_2} = 5.455 + (.864)\dfrac{(5.455)}{2.326} = 7.481$

Lower B–C *boundary* $= \bar{R} - d_3\dfrac{\bar{R}}{d_2} = 5.455 - (.864)\dfrac{(5.455)}{2.326} = 3.429$

The *R*-chart is:

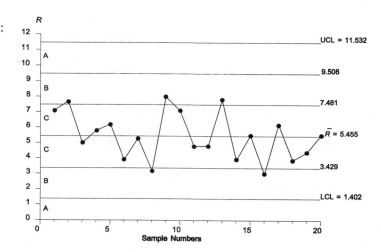

b. To determine if the process is in or out of control, we check the four rules:

Rule 1: One point beyond Zone A: No points are beyond Zone A.
Rule 2: Nine points in a row in Zone C or beyond: No sequence of nine points are in Zone C (on one side of the centerline) or beyond.
Rule 3: Six points in a row steadily increasing or decreasing: No sequence of six points steadily increase or decrease.
Rule 4: Fourteen points in a row alternating up and down: This pattern does not exist.

The process appears to be in control. Since the process variation is in control, it is appropriate to construct the $\bar{x}$-chart.

c. In order for the -chart to be valid, the process variation must be in control. The *R*-chart checks to see if the process variation is in control. For more details, see the answer to Exercise 12.19.

d. To construct an $\bar{x}$-chart, we first calculate the following:

$$\bar{\bar{x}} = \frac{\bar{x}_1 + \bar{x}_2 + \cdots + \bar{x}_{20}}{k} = \frac{77.24}{20} = 3.867$$

$$\bar{R} = \frac{R_1 + R_2 + \cdots + R_{20}}{k} = \frac{109.1}{20} = 5.455$$

Centerline $= \bar{\bar{x}} = 3.867$

From Table XII, Appendix B, with $n = 5$, $A_2 = .577$.

Upper control limit $= \bar{\bar{x}} + A_2\bar{R} = 3.867 + .577(5.455) = 7.015$
Lower control limit $= \bar{\bar{x}} - A_2\bar{R} = 3.867 - .577(5.455) = .719$

$$\text{Upper A–B boundary} = \overline{\overline{x}} + \frac{2}{3}(A_2\overline{R}) = 3.867 + \frac{2}{3}(.577)(5.455) = 5.965$$

$$\text{Lower A–B boundary} = \overline{\overline{x}} - \frac{2}{3}(A_2\overline{R}) = 3.867 - \frac{2}{3}(.577)(5.455) = 1.769$$

$$\text{Upper B–C boundary} = \overline{\overline{x}} + \frac{1}{3}(A_2\overline{R}) = 3.867 + \frac{1}{3}(.577)(5.455) = 4.916$$

$$\text{Lower B–C boundary} = \overline{\overline{x}} - \frac{1}{3}(A_2\overline{R}) = 3.867 - \frac{1}{3}(.577)(5.455) = 2.818$$

The $\overline{x}$-chart is:

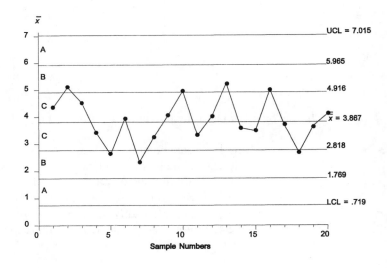

e. To determine if the process is in or out of control, we check the six rules:

Rule 1: One point beyond Zone A: No points are beyond Zone A.

Rule 2: Nine points in a row in Zone C or beyond: No sequence of nine points are in Zone C (on one side of the centerline) or beyond.

Rule 3: Six points in a row steadily increasing or decreasing: No sequence of six points steadily increases or decreases.

Rule 4: Fourteen points in a row alternating up and down: This pattern does not exist.

Rule 5: Two out of three points in Zone A or beyond: There are no groups of three consecutive points that have two or more in Zone A or beyond.

Rule 6: Four out of five points in a row in Zone B or beyond: No sequence of five points has four or more in Zone B or beyond.

The process appears to be in control.

f. Since both the R-chart and the $\overline{x}$-chart are in control, these control limits should be used to monitor future process output.

12.75 a.   The sample size is determined by the following:

$$n > \frac{9(1-p_0)}{p_0} = \frac{9(1-.06)}{.06} = 141$$

The minimum sample size is 141. Since the sample size of 150 was used, it is large enough.

b.   To compute the proportion of defectives in each sample, divide the number of defectives by the number in the sample, 150:

$$\hat{p} = \frac{No. of\ defectives}{No.\ in\ sample}$$

The sample proportions are listed in the table:

Sample No.	$\hat{p}$	Sample No.	$\hat{p}$
1	.060	11	.047
2	.073	12	.040
3	.080	13	.080
4	.053	14	.067
5	.067	15	.073
6	.040	16	.047
7	.087	17	.040
8	.060	18	.080
9	.073	19	.093
10	.033	20	.067

To get the total number of defectives, sum the number of defectives for all 20 samples. The sum is 189. To get the total number of units sampled, multiply the sample size by the number of samples: 150(20) = 3000.

$$\bar{p} = \frac{Total\ defectives\ in\ all\ samples}{Total\ units\ sampled} = \frac{189}{3000} = .063$$

Centerline $= \bar{p} = .063$

Upper control limit $= \bar{p} + 3\sqrt{\frac{\bar{p}(1-\bar{p})}{n}} = .063 + 3\sqrt{\frac{.063(.937)}{150}} = .123$

Lower control limit $= \bar{p} - 3\sqrt{\frac{\bar{p}(1-\bar{p})}{n}} = .063 - 3\sqrt{\frac{.063(.937)}{150}} = .003$

Upper A-B boundary $= \bar{p} + 2\sqrt{\frac{\bar{p}(1-\bar{p})}{n}} = .063 + 2\sqrt{\frac{.063(.937)}{150}} = .103$

Lower A-B boundary $= \bar{p} - 2\sqrt{\frac{\bar{p}(1-\bar{p})}{n}} = .063 - 2\sqrt{\frac{.063(.937)}{150}} = .023$

Methods for Quality Improvement

$$\text{Upper B-C } boundary = \bar{p} + \sqrt{\frac{\bar{p}(1-\bar{p})}{n}} = .063 + \sqrt{\frac{.063(.937)}{150}} = .083$$

$$\text{Lower B-C } boundary = \bar{p} - \sqrt{\frac{\bar{p}(1-\bar{p})}{n}} = .063 - \sqrt{\frac{.063(.937)}{150}} = .043$$

The *p*-chart is:

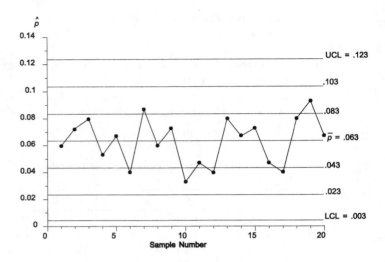

c. To determine if the process is in or out of control, we check the four rules.

     Rule 1:   One point beyond Zone A: No points are beyond Zone A.

     Rule 2:   Nine points in a row in Zone C or beyond: No sequence of nine points are in Zone C (on one side of the centerline) or beyond.

     Rule 3:   Six points in a row steadily increasing or decreasing: No sequence of six points steadily increase or decrease.

     Rule 4:   Fourteen points in a row alternating up and down: Points 2 through 16 alternate up and down. This indicates the process is out of control.

Rule 4 indicates the process is out of control. Special causes of variation appear to be present.

e. Since the process is out of control, the control limits should not be used to monitor future process output. It would not be appropriate to evaluate whether the process is in control using control limits determined during a period when the process was out of control.

Time Series: Descriptive Analyses, Models, and Forecasting

Chapter 13

13.1 To calculate a simple index number, first obtain the prices or quantities over a time period and select a base year. For each time period, the index number is the number at that time period divided by the value at the base period multiplied by 100.

13.3 A Laspeyres index uses the purchase quantity at the base period as the weights for all other time periods. A Paasche index uses the purchase quantity at each time period as the weight for that time period. The weights at the specified time period are also used with the base period to find the index.

13.5 a. To find Laspeyres index, we use the quantities for the base period as the weights. We multiply the quantity for quarter 1 times the prices for quarters 1 and 4 for each product (A, B, or C). We then sum the products for both time periods. Finally, we divide the sum for quarter 4 by the sum for quarter 1. The sum of the products for quarter 1 is $100(3.25) + 20(1.75) + 50(8.00) = 325 + 35 + 400 = 760$. The sum of the products for quarter 4 is $100(4.25) + 20(1.00) + 50(10.50) = 425 + 20 + 525 = 970$. Laspeyres index is $(970 / 760) \times 100 = 127.63$.

b. To find Paasche index, we use the quantities for all time periods as weights. We multiple the quantity for each quarter and each product by the corresponding price. We then sum these products for the base period quarter 2 and the quarter for which we want to compute Paasche's index (quarter 4). The sum for quarter 2 is $200(3.50) + 25(1.25) + 35(9.35) = 700 + 31.25 + 327.25 = 1058.5$. The sum of the products for quarter 4 is $300(4.25) + 100(1.00) + 20(10.50) = 1275 + 100 + 210 = 1585$. Paasche's index is $(1585 / 1058.5) \times 100 = 149.74$.

13.7. a. To compute the simple index, divide each U.S. Beer Production value by the 1980 value, 194, and then multiply by 100.

Year	Simple Index		Year	Simple Index	
1980	$(194/194) \times 100 =$	100.00	1993	$(202/194) \times 100 =$	104.12
1981	$(194/194) \times 100 =$	100.00	1994	$(203/194) \times 100 =$	104.64
1982	$(196/194) \times 100 =$	101.03	1995	$(200/194) \times 100 =$	103.09
1983	$(196/194) \times 100 =$	101.03	1996	$(200/194) \times 100 =$	103.09
1984	$(193/194) \times 100 =$	99.48	1997	$(199/194) \times 100 =$	102.58
1985	$(194/194) \times 100 =$	100.00	1998	$(198/194) \times 100 =$	102.06
1986	$(197/194) \times 100 =$	101.55	1999	$(198/194) \times 100 =$	102.06
1987	$(195/194) \times 100 =$	100.52	2000	$(200/194) \times 100 =$	103.09
1988	$(197/194) \times 100 =$	101.55	2001	$(199/194) \times 100 =$	102.58
1989	$(199/194) \times 100 =$	102.58	2002	$(200/194) \times 100 =$	103.09
1990	$(202/194) \times 100 =$	104.12	2003	$(195/194) \times 100 =$	100.52
1991	$(204/194) \times 100 =$	105.15	2004	$(197/194) \times 100 =$	101.55
1992	$(201/194) \times 100 =$	103.61	2005	$(195/194) \times 100 =$	100.52

The index value for 2005 is 100.52. Thus, the beer production in 2005 increased by 100.52 − 100 = .52% over the beer production in the base year of 1980.

b. This is a quantity index because the numbers collected were the number of barrels produced rather than the price.

c. To compute the simple index, divide each U.S. Beer Production value by the 1991 value, 204, and then multiply by 100.

Year	Simple Index		Year	Simple Index	
1980	(194/204) × 100 =	95.10	1993	(202/204) × 100 =	99.02
1981	(194/204) × 100 =	95.10	1994	(203/204) × 100 =	99.51
1982	(196/204) × 100 =	96.08	1995	(200/204) × 100 =	98.04
1983	(196/204) × 100 =	96.08	1996	(200/204) × 100 =	98.04
1984	(193/204) × 100 =	94.61	1997	(199/204) × 100 =	97.55
1985	(194/204) × 100 =	95.10	1998	(198/204) × 100 =	97.06
1986	(197/204) × 100 =	96.57	1999	(198/204) × 100 =	97.06
1987	(195/204) × 100 =	95.59	2000	(200/204) × 100 =	98.04
1988	(197/204) × 100 =	96.57	2001	(199/204) × 100 =	97.55
1989	(199/204) × 100 =	97.55	2002	(200/204) × 100 =	98.04
1990	(202/204) × 100 =	99.02	2003	(195/204) × 100 =	95.59
1991	(204/204) × 100 =	100.00	2004	(197/204) × 100 =	96.57
1992	(201/204) × 100 =	98.53	2005	(195/204) × 100 =	95.59

The plots of the two simple indices are:

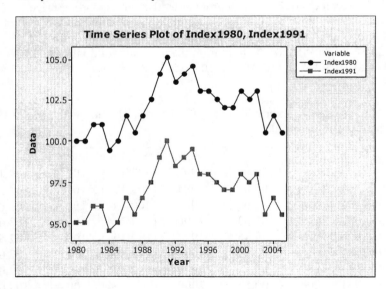

The two plots have the same shape, just at different levels. For both, there is a fairly steep increase in the indices from 1987 to 1991. After 1991, there is a steady decrease in the indices.

13.9   a.   To compute the simple index, divide each natural gas price by the 1980 value, 3.68, and then multiply by 100.

Year	Simple Index	
1980	$(3.68/3.68) \times 100 =$	100.00
1990	$(5.80/3.68) \times 100 =$	157.61
1991	$(5.82/3.68) \times 100 =$	158.15
1992	$(5.89/3.68) \times 100 =$	160.05
1993	$(6.16/3.68) \times 100 =$	167.39
1994	$(6.41/3.68) \times 100 =$	174.18
1995	$(6.06/3.68) \times 100 =$	164.67
1996	$(6.34/3.68) \times 100 =$	172.28
1997	$(6.94/3.68) \times 100 =$	188.59
1998	$(6.82/3.68) \times 100 =$	185.33
1999	$(6.69/3.68) \times 100 =$	181.79
2000	$(7.71/3.68) \times 100 =$	209.51
2001	$(9.63/3.68) \times 100 =$	261.68
2002	$(7.91/3.68) \times 100 =$	214.95
2003	$(9.52/3.68) \times 100 =$	258.70
2004	$(10.74/3.68) \times 100 =$	291.85

The plot of the index is:

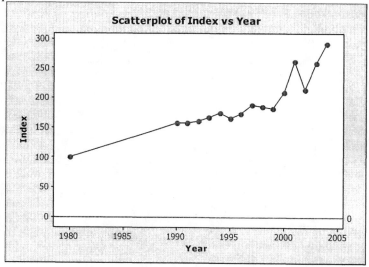

b.   From 1980 to 1990 there was an increase in the price of natural gas. From 1990 to 2000, there was again a general increase in the price of natural gas with a couple of small dips. From 2000 to 2004, the price was very volatile, with sharp increases from 2000 to 2001, a sharp decrease from 2001 to 2002, and a sharp increase from 2002 to 2004.

c.   The index constructed is a price index since it is based on the price of natural gas.

13.11   a.   To compute the simple composite index, first sum the three values (durables, nondurables, and services) for every time period. Then, divide each sum by the sum in 1970, 646.5, and then multiply by 100. The simple composite index for 1970 is:

Year	Sum	Simple Composite Index-1970	Simple Composite Index-1980
1960	332.5	51.43	19.02
1965	444.6	68.77	25.43
1970	646.5	100.00	36.98
1975	1,024.8	158.52	58.62
1980	1,748.1	270.39	100.00
1985	2,667.4	412.59	152.59
1990	3,761.2	581.78	215.16
1995	4,969.0	768.60	284.26
2000	6,683.7	1,033.83	382.35
2003	8,229.9	1,272.99	470.80

b.   To update the 1970 index to the 1980 index, divide the 1970 index values by the 1970 index value for 1980, 270.39, and then multiply by 100. The 1980 simple composite index is also listed in the table in part **a**.

c.   The graph of the two indices is:

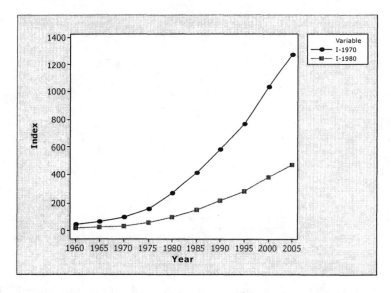

Changing the base year from 1970 to 1980 flattens out the graph. Also, the spread of the values for the 1980 index is much smaller than the spread of the values in the 1970 index.

13.13 a. To compute the simple index for the average hourly earnings for manufacturing workers, divide the hourly earnings for each year by the hourly earnings for the base year, 4.83, and multiply by 100. To compute the simple index for the average hourly earnings for transportation and public utilities workers, divide the hourly earnings for each year by the hourly earnings for the base year, 5.88, and multiply by 100. The two indices are:

Year	Manufacturing Index	Transportation/Utilities Index
1975	100.00	100.00
1980	150.52	150.85
1985	197.52	193.88
1990	224.22	220.58
1995	256.11	242.01
2000	297.72	275.85

b. The two plots are:

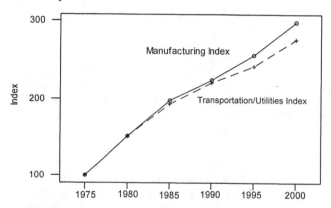

The simple earnings indices are very similar. From 1975 to 2000, the hourly earnings have increased 175.85% for the transportation and public utilities workers and 197.72% for the manufacturing workers.

c. To compute the simple composite index for the hourly earnings, sum the earnings for the three industries for each time period. Then divide the sum at each year by the sum at the base year, 15.43, and multiply by 100. To compute the simple composite index for weekly hours, sum the weekly hours for the three industries for each time period. Then divide the sum at each year by the sum at the base year, 117.8, and multiply by 100. The two composite indices are:

Year	Earnings	Hours	Earnings Index	Hours Index
1975	15.43	117.80	100.00	100.00
1980	23.09	117.70	149.64	99.92
1985	30.09	118.40	195.01	100.51
1990	34.59	117.80	224.17	100.00
1995	39.03	119.40	252.95	101.36
2000	45.80	119.70	296.82	101.61

Time Series: Descriptive Analyses, Models, and Forecasting

d. The plots of the two composite indices are:

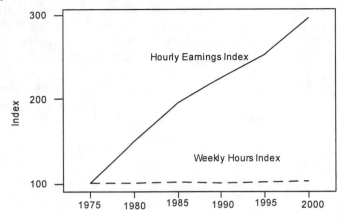

The composite earnings index increased 196.82% from 1975 to 2000. However, the composite weekly hours has increased only 1.61% from 1975 to 2000.

13.15   The smaller the value of w, the smoother the series. With $w = .2$, the current value receives a weight of .2 while the previous exponentially smoothed value receives a weight of .8. With $w = .8$, the current value receives a weight of .8 while the previous exponentially smoothed value receives a weight of .2. The smaller the value of w, the less chance the series can be affected by large jumps.

13.17   a. The exponentially smoothed beer production for the first period is equal to the beer production for that period. For the rest of the time periods, the exponentially smoothed beer production is found by multiplying the beer production of that time period by $w = .2$ and adding to that $(1 - .2)$ times the exponentially smoothed value above it. The exponentially smoothed value for the second period is $.2(194) + (1 - .2)(194) = 194$.

The rest of the values are shown in the following table.

Year	Beer Production	Exponentially Smoothed Production $w = .2$	Exponentially Smoothed Production $w = .8$
1980	194	194.0	194.0
1981	194	194.0	194.0
1982	196	194.4	195.6
1983	196	194.7	195.9
1984	193	194.4	193.6
1985	194	194.3	193.9
1986	197	194.8	196.4
1987	195	194.9	195.3
1988	197	195.3	196.7
1989	199	196.0	198.5
1990	202	197.2	201.3
1991	204	198.6	203.5
1992	201	199.1	201.5
1993	202	199.7	201.9
1994	203	200.3	202.8
1995	200	200.3	200.6
1996	200	200.2	200.1
1997	199	200.0	199.2
1998	198	199.6	198.2
1999	198	199.3	198.0
2000	200	199.4	199.6
2001	199	199.3	199.1
2002	200	199.5	199.8
2003	195	198.6	196.0
2004	197	198.3	196.8
2005	195	197.6	195.4

b.   The exponentially smoothed beer production for the first period is equal to the beer production for that period. For the rest of the time periods, the exponentially smoothed beer production is found by multiplying .8 times the beer production of that time period and adding to that $(1 - .8)$ times the value of the exponentially smoothed beer production figure of the previous time period. The exponentially smoothed beer production for the second time period is $.8(194) + (1 - .8)(194) = 194$. The rest of the values are shown in the table in part **a**.

c.   The plot of the two series is:

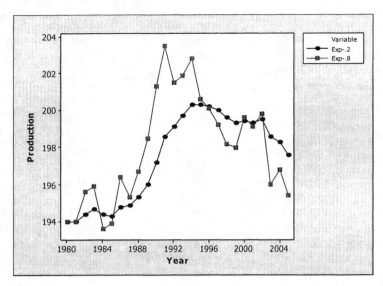

The exponentially smoothed series with $w = .2$ is smoother than the series with $w = .8$. Thus, the series with $w = .2$ best portrays the long-term trend.

13.19   a.   The exponentially smoothed gold price for the first period is equal to the gold price for that period. For the rest of the time periods, the exponentially smoothed gold price is found by multiplying the price for the time period by $w = .8$ and adding to that $(1 - .8)$ times the exponentially smoothed value from the previous time period. The wxponentially smoothed value for the second time period is $.8(448) + (1 - .8)(368) = 432.0$. The rest of the values are shown below.

Year	Price	$w = .8$ Exponentially Smoothed Price
1986	368	368.00
1987	448	432.00
1988	438	436.80
1989	383	393.76
1990	385	386.75
1991	363	367.75
1992	345	349.55
1993	361	358.71
1994	387	381.34
1995	385	384.27
1996	389	388.05
1997	333	344.01
1998	294	304.00
1999	278	283.20
2000	279	279.84
2001	273	274.37
2002	310	302.87
2003	363	350.97
2004	409	397.39
2005	444	434.68

b. The plot of the two series is:

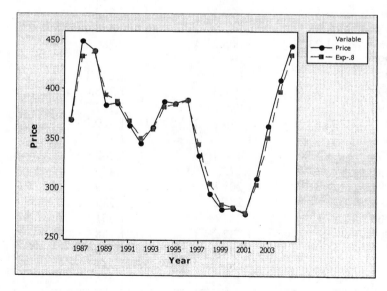

The exponentially smooth series with $w = .8$ is almost the same as the original series.

13.21   a.   The exponentially smoothed imports for the first period is equal to the imports that period. For the rest of the time periods, the exponentially smoothed imports is found by multiplying $w = .1$ times the imports for that time period and adding to that $(1 - .1)$ times the value of the exponentially smoothed imports figure of the previous time period. The exponentially smoothed imports for the second time period is $.1(1171) + (1 - .1)(926) = 950.5$. The rest of the values are shown in the table.

The same procedure is followed for $w = .9$. The exponentially smoothed imports/exports for the second time period is $.9(1171) + (1 - .9)(926) = 1,146.5$. The rest of the values are shown in the table.

Year	Imports	Exponentially Smoothed Series $w = .1$	Exponentially Smoothed Series $w = .9$
1974	926	926.0	926.0
1975	1,171	950.5	1,146.5
1976	1,663	1,021.8	1,611.4
1977	2,058	1,125.4	2,013.3
1978	1,892	1,202.0	1,904.1
1979	1,866	1,268.4	1,869.8
1980	1,414	1,283.0	1,459.6
1981	1,067	1,261.4	1,106.3
1982	633	1,198.6	680.3
1983	540	1,132.7	554.0
1984	553	1,074.7	553.1
1985	479	1,015.2	486.4
1986	771	990.7	742.5
1987	876	979.3	862.7
1988	987	980.0	974.6
1989	1,232	1,005.2	1,206.3
1990	1,282	1,032.9	1,274.4
1991	1,233	1,052.9	1,237.1
1992	1,247	1,072.3	1,246.0
1993	1,339	1,099.0	1,329.7
1994	1,307	1,119.8	1,309.3
1995	1,303	1,138.1	1,303.6
1996	1,258	1,150.1	1,262.6
1997	1,378	1,172.9	1,366.5
1998	1,522	1,207.8	1,506.4
1999	1,543	1,241.3	1,539.3
2000	1,664	1,283.6	1,651.5
2001	1,770	1,332.2	1,758.2
2002	1,490	1,348.0	1,516.8
2003	1,671	1,380.3	1,655.6
2004	1,833	1,425.6	1,815.3

b.   The plot of the three series is:

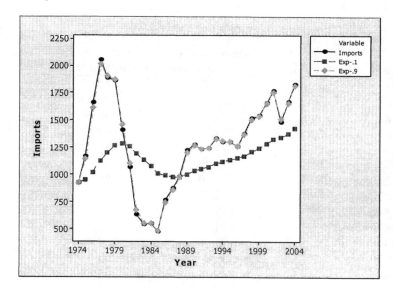

The exponentially smoothed series with w = .9 looks more like the original series. The closer w is to 1 the closer the exponentially smoothed curve looks like the original.

13.23   If w is small (near 0), one will obtain a smooth, slowly changing series of forecasts. If w is large (near 1), one will obtain more rapidly changing forecasts that depend mostly on the current values of the series.

13.25   a.   We first compute the exponentially smoothed values $E_1, E_2, \ldots, E_t$ for years $1980 - 2002$.

$E_1 = Y_1 = 194$

For $w = .3$, $E_2 = wY_2 + (1 - w)E_1 = .3(194) + (1 - .3)(194) = 194$
$\quad\quad\quad\quad E_3 = wY_3 + (1 - w)E_2 = .3(196) + (1 - .3)(194) = 194.6$

The rest of the values appear in the table.

For $w = .7$, $E_2 = wY_2 + (1 - w)E_1 = .7(194) + (1 - .7)(194) = 194$
$\quad\quad\quad\quad E_3 = wY_3 + (1 - w)E_2 = .7(196) + (1 - .7)(194) = 195.4$

The rest of the values appear in the table.

Year	Beer Production	$w = .3$ Exponentially Smoothed Value	$w = .7$ Exponentially Smoothed Value
1980	194	194.00	194.00
1981	194	194.00	194.00
1982	196	194.60	195.40
1983	196	195.02	195.82
1984	193	194.41	193.85
1985	194	194.29	193.95
1986	197	195.10	196.09
1987	196	195.37	196.03
1988	197	195.86	196.71
1989	199	196.80	198.31
1990	202	198.36	200.89
1991	204	200.05	203.07
1992	201	200.34	201.62
1993	202	200.84	201.89
1994	203	201.49	202.67
1995	200	201.04	200.80
1996	200	200.73	200.24
1997	199	200.21	199.37
1998	198	199.55	198.41
1999	198	199.08	198.12
2000	200	199.36	199.44
2001	199	199.25	199.13
2002	200	199.48	199.74
2003	195		
2004	197		
2005	195		

To forecast using exponentially smoothed values, we use the following:

For $w = .3$:
$$F_{2003} = F_{t+1} = E_t = 199.48$$
$$F_{2004} = F_{t+2} = F_{t+1} = 199.48$$
$$F_{2005} = F_{t+3} = F_{t+1} = 199.48$$

For $w = .7$:
$$F_{2003} = F_{t+1} = E_t = 199.74$$
$$F_{2004} = F_{t+2} = F_{t+1} = 199.74$$
$$F_{2005} = F_{t+3} = F_{t+1} = 199.74$$

b. We first compute the Holt-Winters values for the years 1980-2002.

With $w = .7$ and $v = .3$,

$$E_2 = Y_2 = 194$$

$E_3 = wY_3 + (1 - w)(E_2 + T_2) = .7(196) + (1 - .7)(194 + 0) = 195.4.$

$T_2 = Y_2 - Y_1 = 194 - 194 = 0$
$T_3 = v(E_3 - E_2) + (1 - v)T_2 = .3(195.4 - 194) + (1 - .3)0 = .42$

The rest of the E_t's and T_t's appear in the table that follows.

With $w = .3$ and $v = .7$,

$E_2 = Y_2 = 194$
$E_3 = wY_3 + (1 - w)(E_2 + T_2) = .3(196) + (1 - .3)(194 + 0) = 194.6.$

$T_2 = Y_2 - Y_1 = 194 - 194 = 0$
$T_3 = v(E_3 - E_2) + (1 - v)T_2 = .7(194.6 - 194) + (1 - .7)0 = .42$

The rest of the E_t's and T_t's appear in the table that follows.

Year	Beer Production	E_t $w=.7$ $v=.3$	T_t $w=.7$ $v=.3$	E_t $w=.3$ $v=.7$	T_t $w=.3$ $v=.7$
1980	194				
1981	194	194.00	0.00	194.00	0.00
1982	196	195.40	0.42	194.60	0.42
1983	196	195.95	0.46	195.31	0.63
1984	193	194.02	-0.26	195.06	0.01
1985	194	193.93	-0.21	194.75	-0.22
1986	197	196.02	0.48	195.27	0.30
1987	196	196.15	0.38	195.70	0.39
1988	197	196.86	0.48	196.37	0.58
1989	199	198.50	0.83	197.56	1.01
1990	202	201.20	1.39	199.60	1.73
1991	204	203.58	1.68	202.14	2.29
1992	201	202.28	0.79	203.40	1.57
1993	202	202.32	0.57	204.08	0.95
1994	203	202.97	0.59	204.42	0.52
1995	200	201.07	-0.16	203.46	-0.52
1996	200	200.27	-0.35	202.06	-1.13
1997	199	199.28	-0.54	200.35	-1.54
1998	198	198.22	-0.70	198.57	-1.71
1999	198	197.86	-0.60	197.20	-1.47
2000	200	199.18	-0.02	197.01	-0.57
2001	199	199.05	-0.05	197.21	-0.04
2002	200	199.70	0.16	198.02	0.56
2003	195				
2004	197				
2005	195				

To forecast using the Holt-Winters Model:

For $w = .7$ and $v = .3$,

$$F_{2003} = F_{t+1} = E_t + T_t = 199.70 + .16 = 199.86$$

$$F_{2004} = F_{t+2} = E_t + 2T_t = 199.70 + 2(.16) = 200.02$$
$$F_{2005} = F_{t+3} = E_t + 3T_t = 199.70 + 3(.16) = 200.18$$

For $w = .3$ and $v = .7$,

$$F_{2003} = F_{t+1} = E_t + T_t = 198.02 + .56 = 198.58$$

$$F_{2004} = F_{t+2} = E_t + 2T_t = 198.02 + 2(.56) = 199.14$$
$$F_{2005} = F_{t+3} = E_t + 3T_t = 198.02 + 3(.56) = 199.70$$

13.27 a. Using MINITAB, the time series plot is:

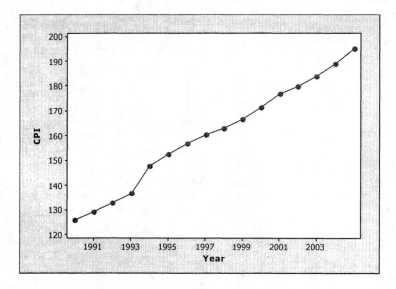

     b. To compute the exponentially smoothed values, we follow these steps:

$$E_1 = Y_1 = 125.8$$

$$E_2 = wY_2 + (1-w)E_1 = .4(129.1) + (1-.4)(125.8) = 127.12$$
$$E_3 = wY_3 + (1-w)E_2 = .4(132.8) + (1-.4)(127.12) = 129.39$$

The rest of the values are computed in a similar manner and are listed in the table:

Year	CPI	Exponentially Smoothed $w = .4$
1990	125.8	125.80
1991	129.1	127.12
1992	132.8	129.39
1993	136.8	132.36
1994	147.8	138.53
1995	152.4	144.08
1996	156.9	149.21
1997	160.5	153.72
1998	163.0	157.43
1999	166.6	161.10
2000	171.5	165.26
2001	177.1	170.00
2002	179.9	173.96
2003	184.0	177.97
2004	188.9	182.34
2005	195.3	187.53

Using MINITAB, the plot is:

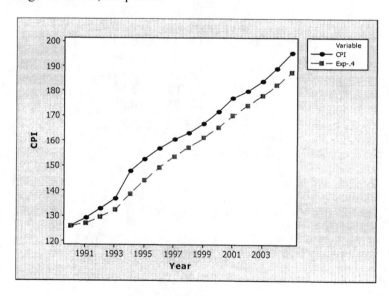

To forecast using exponentially smoothed values, we use the following:

$$F_{2006} = F_{t+1} = E_t = 187.53$$

c.   We first compute the Holt-Winters values for the years 1990-2005.

With $w = .4$ and $v = .5$,

$E_2 = Y_2 = 129.1$
$E_3 = wY_3 + (1 - w)(E_2 + T_2) = .4(132.8) + (1 - .4)(129.1 + 3.3) = 132.56.$

$T_2 = Y_2 - Y_1 = 129.1 - 125.8 = 3.3$
$T_3 = v(E_3 - E_2) + (1 - v)T_2 = .5(132.56 - 129.1) + (1 - .5)(3.3) = 3.38$

The rest of the E_t's and T_t's appear in the table that follows.

Year	CPI	E_t $w = .4$ $v = .5$	T_t $w = .4$ $v = .5$
1990	125.8		
1991	129.1	129.10	3.30
1992	132.8	132.56	3.38
1993	136.8	136.28	3.55
1994	147.8	143.02	5.14
1995	152.4	149.86	5.99
1996	156.9	156.27	6.20
1997	160.5	161.68	5.81
1998	163.0	165.69	4.91
1999	166.6	169.00	4.11
2000	171.5	172.47	3.79
2001	177.1	176.59	3.96
2002	179.9	180.29	3.83
2003	184.0	184.07	3.80
2004	188.9	188.28	4.01
2005	195.3	193.50	4.61

To forecast using the Holt-Winters Model:

For $w = .4$ and $v = .5$,

$F_{2006} = F_{t+1} = E_t + T_t = 193.50 + 4.61 = 198.11$

13.29 a.   To compute the exponentially smoothed values, we follow these steps:

$E_t = Y_1 = 1,286.4$

For $w = .7$,

$E_2 = wY_2 + (1 - w)E_1 = .7(1,372.7) + (1 - .7)(1,286.4) = 1,346.8$
$E_3 = wY_3 + (1 - w)E_2 = .7(1,282.7) + (1 - .7)(1,346.8) = 1,301.9$

The rest of the values are computed in a similar manner and are listed in the table:

Year	Quarter	S&P 500	Exponentially Smoothed w = .7	Exponentially Smoothed w = .3
1999	1	1286.4	1286.4	1286.4
	2	1372.7	1346.8	1312.3
	3	1282.7	1301.9	1303.4
	4	1469.2	1419.0	1353.1
2000	1	1498.6	1474.7	1396.8
	2	1454.6	1460.6	1414.1
	3	1436.5	1443.7	1420.8
	4	1320.3	1357.3	1390.7
2001	1	1160.3	1219.4	1321.6
	2	1224.4	1222.9	1292.4
	3	1040.9	1095.5	1217.0
	4	1148.1	1132.3	1196.3
2002	1	1147.4	1142.9	1181.6
	2	989.8	1035.7	1124.1
	3	815.3	881.4	1031.4
	4	879.8	880.3	986.0
2003	1	848.2	857.8	944.6
	2	974.5	939.5	953.6
	3	996	979.0	966.3
	4	1111.9	1072.0	1010.0
2004	1	1126.2	1110.0	1044.9
	2	1140.8	1131.5	1073.6
	3	1114.6	1119.7	1085.9
	4	1211.9	1184.2	1123.7
2005	1	1180.6	1181.7	1140.8
	2	1191.3	1188.4	1155.9
	3	1228.8	1216.7	1177.8
	4	1248.3	1238.8	1198.9
2006	1	1294.9		
	2	1270.2		
	3	1335.8		

The forecasts using the exponentially smoothed values with $w = .7$ are:

$$F_{2006,1} = F_{t+1} = E_t = 1{,}238.8$$
$$F_{2006,2} = F_{t+2} = F_{t+1} = 1{,}238.8$$
$$F_{2006,3} = F_{t+3} = F_{t+1} = 1{,}238.8$$

b. To compute the exponentially smoothed values, we follow these steps:

$$E_t = Y_1 = 1{,}286.4$$

For $w = .3$,

$$E_2 = wY_2 + (1 - w)E_1 = .3(1{,}372.7) + (1 - .3)(1{,}286.4) = 1{,}312.3$$
$$E_3 = wY_3 + (1 - w)E_2 = .3(1{,}282.7) + (1 - .3)(1{,}312.3) = 1{,}303.4$$

The rest of the values are computed in a similar manner and are listed in the table above.

The forecasts using the exponentially smoothed values with w = .3 are:

$$F_{2006,1} = F_{t+1} = E_t = 1,198.9$$
$$F_{2006,2} = F_{t+2} = F_{t+1} = 1,198.9$$
$$F_{2006,3} = F_{t+3} = F_{t+1} = 1,198.9$$

13.31 a.   We first compute the exponentially smoothed values $E_1, E_2, \ldots, E_t$ for 1998 through 2005.

$$E_1 = Y_1 = 304.9$$

For $w = .5$,

$$E_2 = wY_2 + (1 - w)E_1 = .5(297.4) + (1 - .5)(304.9) = 301.15$$
$$E_3 = wY_3 + (1 - w)E_2 = .5(301.0) + (1 - .5)(301.15) = 301.08$$

The rest of the values are found in the table:

Year	Month	Gold Price	Exponentially Smoothed $w=.5$	Holt-Winters E_t $w=.5$	T_t $v=.5$
1998	Jan	304.9	304.90		
	Feb	297.4	301.15	297.40	-7.50
	Mar	301.0	301.08	295.45	-4.72
	Apr	310.7	305.89	300.71	0.27
	May	293.6	299.74	297.29	-1.58
	Jun	296.3	298.02	296.01	-1.43
	Jul	288.9	293.46	291.74	-2.85
	Aug	273.4	283.43	281.14	-6.72
	Sep	293.9	288.67	284.16	-1.85
	Oct	294.0	291.33	288.15	1.07
	Nov	294.7	293.02	291.96	2.44
	Dec	287.8	290.41	291.10	0.79
1999	Jan	285.4	287.90	288.64	-0.83
	Feb	287.1	287.50	287.46	-1.01
	Mar	279.5	283.50	282.97	-2.75
	Apr	286.6	285.05	283.41	-1.15
	May	269.0	277.03	275.63	-4.47
	Jun	262.6	269.81	266.88	-6.61
	Jul	255.6	262.71	257.94	-7.78
	Aug	254.8	258.75	252.48	-6.62
	Sep	307.5	283.13	276.68	8.79
	Oct	299.1	291.11	292.29	12.20
	Nov	291.4	291.26	297.94	8.93
	Dec	290.3	290.78	298.59	4.78
2000	Jan	284.3	287.54	293.84	0.02
	Feb	299.9	293.72	296.88	1.53

	Mar	286.4	290.06	292.40	-1.47
	Apr	279.9	284.98	285.42	-4.23
	May	275.3	280.14	278.24	-5.70
	Jun	285.7	282.92	279.12	-2.41
	Jul	281.6	282.26	279.15	-1.19
	Aug	274.5	278.38	276.23	-2.06
	Sep	273.7	276.04	273.94	-2.17
	Oct	270.0	273.02	270.88	-2.62
	Nov	266.0	269.51	267.13	-3.18
	Dec	271.5	270.50	267.73	-1.30
2001	Jan	265.5	268.00	265.97	-1.53
	Feb	261.9	264.95	263.17	-2.16
	Mar	263.0	263.98	262.00	-1.66
	Apr	260.5	262.24	260.42	-1.62
	May	272.4	267.32	265.60	1.78
	Jun	270.2	268.76	268.79	2.48
	Jul	267.5	268.13	269.39	1.54
	Aug	272.4	270.26	271.66	1.91
	Sep	283.4	276.83	278.49	4.37
	Oct	283.1	279.97	282.98	4.43
	Nov	276.2	278.08	281.80	1.63
	Dec	275.9	276.99	279.66	-0.26
2002	Jan	281.7	279.35	280.55	0.32
	Feb	295.5	287.42	288.19	3.97
	Mar	294.0	290.71	293.08	4.43
	Apr	302.7	296.71	300.11	5.73
	May	314.5	305.60	310.17	7.90
	Jun	321.2	313.40	319.63	8.68
	Jul	313.3	313.35	320.81	4.93
	Aug	310.3	311.83	318.02	1.07
	Sep	319.2	315.51	319.14	1.10
	Oct	316.6	316.06	318.42	0.19
	Nov	319.2	317.63	318.90	0.34
	Dec	333.4	325.51	326.32	3.88
2003	Jan	356.9	341.21	343.55	10.55
	Feb	359.0	350.10	356.55	11.78
	Mar	340.6	345.35	354.46	4.85
	Apr	328.2	336.78	343.75	-2.93
	May	355.7	346.24	348.26	0.79
	Jun	356.5	351.37	352.77	2.65
	Jul	351.0	351.18	353.21	1.54
	Aug	359.8	355.49	357.28	2.81
	Sep	378.9	367.20	369.49	7.51
	Oct	378.9	373.05	377.95	7.98
	Nov	389.9	381.47	387.92	8.98
	Dec	407.6	394.54	402.25	11.65
2004	Jan	414.0	404.27	413.95	11.68
	Feb	405.3	404.78	415.46	6.60
	Mar	406.7	405.74	414.38	2.76
	Apr	403.0	404.37	410.07	-0.78

	May	383.4	393.89	396.34	-7.25
	Jun	392.0	392.94	390.55	-6.52
	Jul	398.1	395.52	391.06	-3.00
	Aug	400.5	398.01	394.28	0.11
	Sep	405.3	401.66	399.84	2.83
	Oct	420.5	411.08	411.59	7.29
	Nov	439.4	425.24	429.14	12.42
	Dec	441.7	433.47	441.63	12.46
2005	Jan	424.2	428.83	439.14	4.98
	Feb	423.4	426.12	433.76	-0.20
	Mar	434.2	430.16	433.88	-0.04
	Apr	428.9	429.53	431.37	-1.28
	May	421.9	425.71	426.00	-3.32
	Jun	430.7	428.21	426.69	-1.32
	Jul	424.5	426.35	424.93	-1.54
	Aug	437.9	432.13	430.65	2.09
	Sep	456.0	444.06	444.37	7.91
	Oct	469.9	456.98	461.09	12.31
	Nov	476.7	466.84	475.05	13.14
	Dec	509.8	488.32	498.99	18.54

To forecast the monthly prices for 2005 using the data through December 2004:

$$F_{t+1} = E_t \qquad F_{t+1} = F_{t+i} = E_t \text{ for } i = 2, 3, \ldots$$
$$F_{t+1} = E_{\text{Dec},2004} = 433.47$$

Year	Month	Forecast
2005	Jan	433.47
	Feb	433.47
	Mar	433.47
	Apr	433.47
	May	433.47
	Jun	433.47
	Jul	433.47
	Aug	433.47
	Sep	433.47
	Oct	433.47
	Nov	433.47
	Dec	433.47

b. To compute the one-step-ahead forecasts for 2005, we use $F_{t+1} = E_t$, where E_t is recomputed each time period (month). The forecasts are obtained from the table in part **a**.

Year	Month	Forecast
2005	Jan	433.47
	Feb	428.83
	Mar	426.12
	Apr	430.16
	May	429.53
	Jun	425.71
	Jul	428.21
	Aug	426.35
	Sep	432.13
	Oct	444.06
	Nov	456.98
	Dec	466.84

c. First, we compute the Holt-Winters values for the years 1998-2005.

With $w = .5$ and $v = .5$,

$E_2 = Y_2 = 297.4$
$E_3 = wY_3 + (1 - w)(E_2 + T_2) = .5(301.0) + (1 - .5)(297.4 - 7.5) = 295.45.$

$T_2 = Y_2 - Y_1 = 297.4 - 304.9 = -7.5$
$T_3 = v(E_3 - E_2) + (1 - v)T_2 = .5(295.45 - 297.4) + (1 - .5)(-7.5) = -4.72$

The rest of the E_t's and T_t's appear in the table in part a.

To forecast the monthly prices for 2005 using the data through December 2004:

$F_{t+1} = E_t + T_t = 441.63 + 12.46 = 454.09$
$F_{t+2} = E_t + 2T_t = 441.63 + 2(12.46) = 466.55$

The rest of the forecasts appear in the table:

Year	Month	Forecast
2005	Jan	454.09
	Feb	466.55
	Mar	479.01
	Apr	491.47
	May	503.93
	Jun	516.39
	Jul	528.85
	Aug	541.31
	Sep	553.77
	Oct	566.23
	Nov	578.69
	Dec	591.15

To compute the one-step-ahead forecasts for 2005, we use $F_{t+1} = E_t + T_t$ where E_t and T_t are recomputed each time period. The forecasts are obtained from the table in part **a**.

$$F_{Jan,2005} = E_{Dec, 2004} + T_{Dec, 2004} = 441.63 + 12.46 = 454.09$$
$$F_{Feb,2005} = E_{Jan, 2005} + T_{Jan, 2005} = 439.14 + 4.98 = 444.12$$

The rest of the values appear in the table:

Year	Month	Forecast
2005	Jan	454.09
	Feb	444.12
	Mar	433.57
	Apr	433.84
	May	430.10
	Jun	422.67
	Jul	425.37
	Aug	423.40
	Sep	432.74
	Oct	452.27
	Nov	473.40
	Dec	488.19

13.33   a.   From Exercise 13.25b, the Holt-Winters forecasts for 2003-2005 using $w = .3$ and $v = .7$ are:

$$F_{2003} = 198.58$$
$$F_{2004} = 199.14$$
$$F_{2005} = 199.70$$

The errors are the differences between the actual values and the predicted values. Thus, the errors are:

$$Y_{2003} - F_{2003} = 195 - 198.58 = -3.58$$
$$Y_{2004} - F_{2004} = 197 - 199.14 = -2.14$$
$$Y_{2005} - F_{2005} = 195 - 199.70 = -4.70$$

   b.   From Exercise 13.25b, the Holt-Winters forecasts for 2003-2005 using $w = .7$ and $v = .3$ are:

$$F_{2003} = 199.86$$
$$F_{2004} = 200.02$$
$$F_{2005} = 200.18$$

The errors are:

$$Y_{2003} - F_{2003} = 195 - 199.86 = -4.86$$
$$Y_{2004} - F_{2004} = 197 - 200.02 = -3.02$$
$$Y_{2005} - F_{2005} = 195 - 200.18 = -5.18$$

c.   For the Holt-Winters forecasts with $w = .3$ and $v = .7$,

$$\text{MAD} = \frac{\sum_{i=1}^{m} |Y_t - F_t|}{m} = \frac{|195 - 198.58| + |197 - 199.14| + |195 - 199.70|}{3} = \frac{10.42}{3} = 3.47$$

$$\text{MAPE} = \left[\frac{\sum_{i=1}^{m} \frac{|(Y_t - F_t)|}{Y_t}}{m} \right] 100 = \left[\frac{\left[\frac{|195 - 198.58|}{195} + \frac{|197 - 199.14|}{197} + \frac{|195 - 199.70|}{195} \right]}{3} \right] 100$$

$$= \left[\frac{.0533}{3} \right] 100 = 1.7775$$

$$\text{RMSE} = \sqrt{\frac{\sum_{i=1}^{m} (Y_t - F_t)^2}{m}} = \sqrt{\frac{(195 - 198.58)^2 + (197 - 199.14)^2 + (195 - 199.70)^2}{3}}$$

$$= \sqrt{\frac{39.486}{3}} = 3.628$$

d.   For the Holt-Winters forecasts with $w = .7$ and $v = .3$,

$$\text{MAD} = \frac{\sum_{i=1}^{m} |Y_t - F_t|}{m} = \frac{|195 - 199.86| + |197 - 200.02| + |195 - 200.18|}{3} = \frac{13.06}{3} = 4.35$$

$$\text{MAPE} = \left[\frac{\sum_{i=1}^{m} \frac{|(Y_t - F_t)|}{Y_t}}{m} \right] 100 = \left[\frac{\left[\frac{|195 - 199.86|}{195} + \frac{|197 - 200.02|}{197} + \frac{|195 - 200.18|}{195} \right]}{3} \right] 100$$

$$= \left[\frac{.0668}{3} \right] 100 = 2.227$$

$$\text{RMSE} = \sqrt{\frac{\sum_{i=1}^{m} (Y_t - F_t)^2}{m}} = \sqrt{\frac{(195 - 199.86)^2 + (197 - 200.02)^2 + (195 - 200.18)^2}{3}}$$

$$= \sqrt{\frac{59.5724}{3}} = 4.456$$

13.35   a.   From Exercise 13.30, the forecasts for the 3 quarters of 2006 using the Holt-Winters forecasts with w = .3 and v = .5 are:

$$F_{2006,1} = 1{,}228.54$$
$$F_{2006,2} = 1{,}227.12$$
$$F_{2006,3} = 1{,}225.70$$

$$MAD = \frac{\sum\limits_{i=1}^{m} |Y_t - F_t|}{m} = \frac{|1294.9 - 1228.54| + |1270.2 - 1227.12| + |1335.8 - 1225.70|}{3}$$

$$= \frac{219.54}{3} = 73.18$$

$$MAPE = \left[\frac{\sum\limits_{i=1}^{m} \left| \dfrac{(Y_t - F_t)}{Y_t} \right|}{m} \right] 100$$

$$= \left[\frac{\left| \dfrac{1294.9 - 1228.54}{1294.9} \right| + \left| \dfrac{1270.2 - 1227.12}{1270.2} \right| + \left| \dfrac{1335.8 - 1225.70}{1335.8} \right|}{3} \right] 100$$

$$= \left[\frac{.1676}{3} \right] 100 = 5.586$$

$$RMSE = \sqrt{\frac{\sum\limits_{i=1}^{m} (Y_t - F_t)^2}{m}}$$

$$= \sqrt{\frac{(1294.9 - 1228.54)^2 + (1270.2 - 1227.12)^2 + (1335.8 - 1225.70)^2}{3}}$$

$$= \sqrt{\frac{18{,}381.546}{3}} = 78.276$$

   b.   From Exercise 13.30, the forecasts for the 3 quarters of 2006 using the Holt-Winters forecasts with w = .7 and v = .5 are:

$$F_{2006,1} = 1{,}266.12$$
$$F_{2006,2} = 1{,}286.64$$
$$F_{2006,3} = 1{,}307.16$$

$$MAD = \frac{\sum\limits_{i=1}^{m}|Y_t - F_t|}{m}$$

$$= \frac{|1294.9 - 1266.12| + |1270.2 - 1286.64| + |1335.8 - 1307.16|}{3}$$

$$= \frac{73.86}{3} = 24.62$$

$$MAPE = \left[\frac{\sum\limits_{i=1}^{m}\left|\frac{(Y_t - F_t)}{Y_t}\right|}{m} \right] 100$$

$$= \left[\frac{\left|\frac{1294.9 - 1266.12}{1294.9}\right| + \left|\frac{1270.2 - 1286.64}{1270.2}\right| + \left|\frac{1335.8 - 1307.16}{1335.8}\right|}{3} \right] 100$$

$$= \left[\frac{.0566}{3} \right] 100 = 1.887$$

$$RMSE = \sqrt{\frac{\sum\limits_{i=1}^{m}(Y_t - F_t)^2}{m}}$$

$$= \sqrt{\frac{(1294.9 - 1266.12)^2 + (1270.2 - 1286.64)^2 + (1335.8 - 1307.16)^2}{3}}$$

$$= \sqrt{\frac{1918.8116}{3}} = 25.290$$

c.   For all three measures of error, the Holt-Winters series with $w = .7$ and $v = .5$ is smaller than the Holt-Winters series with $w = .3$ and $v = .5$. Thus, the more accurate series would be the Holt-Winters series with $w = .7$ and $v = .5$.

13.37   a.   To compute the exponentially smoothed values, we follow these steps:

$E_1 = Y_t = 58,305$

$E_2 = wY_2 + (1 - w)E_1 = .8(57,916) + (1 - .8)(58,305) = 57,993.8$
$E_3 = wY_3 + (1 - w)E_2 = .8(57,951) + (1 - .8)(57,993.8) = 57,959.6$

The rest of the values are computed in a similar manner and are listed in the table:

Year	Enroll	Exponentially Smoothed $w = .8$	Et $w = .8$ $v = .7$	Tt $w = .8$ $v = .7$
1980	58,305	58,305.0		
1981	57,916	57,993.8	57,916.0	-389.0
1982	57,951	57,959.6	57,866.2	-151.6
1983	57,432	57,537.5	57,488.5	-309.8
1984	57,150	57,227.5	57,155.7	-325.9
1985	57,226	57,226.3	57,146.8	-104.1
1986	57,709	57,612.5	57,575.7	269.1
1987	58,254	58,125.7	58,172.2	498.2
1988	58,485	58,413.1	58,522.1	394.4
1989	59,436	59,231.4	59,332.1	685.3
1990	60,267	60,059.9	60,217.1	825.1
1991	61,605	61,296.0	61,492.4	1140.3
1992	62,686	62,408.0	62,675.3	1170.1
1993	63,241	63,074.4	63,361.9	831.6
1994	63,986	63,803.7	64,027.5	715.4
1995	64,764	64,571.9	64,759.8	727.2
1996	65,743	65,508.8	65,691.8	870.6
1997	66,470	66,277.8	66,488.5	818.8
1998	66,983	66,842.0	67,047.9	637.2
1999	67,667	67,502.0	67,670.6	627.1
2000	68,146	68,017.2	68,176.3	542.1
2001	69,936			
2002	71,215			
2003	71,442			
2004	71,688			
2005	72,075			

The forecasts for 2001-2005 using the exponential smoothing series with w = .8 are:

$$F_{2001} = F_{t+1} = E_t = 68,017.2$$
$$F_{2002} = F_{t+2} = F_{t+1} = 68,017.2$$
$$F_{2003} = F_{t+3} = F_{t+1} = 68,017.2$$
$$F_{2004} = F_{t+4} = F_{t+1} = 68,017.2$$
$$F_{2005} = F_{t+5} = F_{t+1} = 68,017.2$$

b. To compute the Holt-Winters values with $w = .8$ and $v = .7$:

$E_2 = Y_2 = 57,916$
$E_3 = wY_3 + (1 - w)(E_2 + T_2) = .8(57,951) + (1 - .8)(57,916 + (-389)) = 57,866.2$

$T_2 = Y_2 - Y_1 = 57,916 - 58,305 = -389$
$T_3 = v(E_3 - E_2) + (1 - v)T_2 = .7(57,866.2 - 57,916) + (1 - .7)(-389) = -151.6$

The rest of the E_t's and T_t's appear in the table in part a.

The forecasts for 2001-2005 using the Holt-Winters series with $w = .8$ and $v = .7$ are:

$$F_{2001} = F_{t+1} = E_t + T_t = 68,176.3 + 542.1 = 68,718.4$$
$$F_{2002} = F_{t+2} = E_t + 2T_t = 68,176.3 + 2(542.1) = 69,260.5$$
$$F_{2003} = F_{t+3} = E_t + 3T_t = 68,176.3 + 3(542.1) = 69,802.6$$
$$F_{2004} = F_{t+4} = E_t + 4T_t = 68,176.3 + 4(542.1) = 70,344.7$$
$$F_{2005} = F_{t+5} = E_t + 5T_t = 68,176.3 + 5(542.1) = 70,886.8$$

c. For the exponential smoothing forecasts with $w = .8$:

$$MAD = \frac{\sum_{i=1}^{m} |Y_t - F_t|}{m}$$

$$= \frac{|69,936 - 68,017.2| + |71,215 - 68,017.2| + \cdots + |72,075 - 68,017.2|}{5} = \frac{16,270}{5} = 3,254$$

$$MAPE = \left[\frac{\sum_{i=1}^{m} \left| \frac{(Y_t - F_t)}{Y_t} \right|}{m} \right] 100$$

$$= \left[\frac{\left| \frac{69,936 - 68,017.2}{69,936} \right| + \left| \frac{71,215 - 68,017.2}{71,215} \right| + \cdots + \left| \frac{72,075 - 68,017.2}{72,075} \right|}{5} \right] 100$$

$$= \left[\frac{.2278}{5} \right] 100 = 4.556$$

$$RMSE = \sqrt{\frac{\sum_{i=1}^{m} (Y_t - F_t)^2}{m}}$$

$$= \sqrt{\frac{(69,936 - 68,017.2)^2 + (71,215 - 68,017.2)^2 + \cdots + (72,075 - 68,017.2)^2}{5}}$$

$$= \sqrt{\frac{55,577,486.8}{5}} = 3,333.991$$

For the Holt-Winters forecasts with $w = .8$ and $v = .7$:

$$\text{MAD} = \frac{\sum_{i=1}^{m} |Y_t - F_t|}{m}$$

$$= \frac{|69,936 - 68,718.4| + |71,215 - 69,260.5| + \cdots + |72,075 - 70,886.8|}{5}$$

$$= \frac{7,343}{5} = 1,468.6$$

$$\text{MAPE} = \left[\frac{\sum_{i=1}^{m} \left| \frac{(Y_t - F_t)}{Y_t} \right|}{m} \right] 100$$

$$= \left[\frac{\left| \frac{69,936 - 68,718.4}{69,936} \right| + \left| \frac{71,215 - 69,260.5}{71,215} \right| + \cdots + \left| \frac{72,075 - 70,886.8}{72,075} \right|}{5} \right] 100$$

$$= \left[\frac{.1030}{5} \right] 100 = 2.061$$

$$\text{RMSE} = \sqrt{\frac{\sum_{i=1}^{m} (Y_t - F_t)^2}{m}}$$

$$= \sqrt{\frac{(69,936 - 68,718.4)^2 + (71,215 - 69,260.5)^2 + \cdots + (72,075 - 70,886.8)^2}{5}}$$

$$= \sqrt{\frac{11,206,526.5}{5}} = 1,497.099$$

For all three measures of forecast errors, the Holt-Winters forecasts have smaller errors. Thus, the Holt-Winters forecasts are better.

13.39 a.   Let $x_1 = \begin{cases} 1 \text{ if quarter 1} \\ 0 \text{ otherwise} \end{cases}$ $x_2 = \begin{cases} 1 \text{ if quarter 2} \\ 0 \text{ otherwise} \end{cases}$ $x_3 = \begin{cases} 1 \text{ if quarter 3} \\ 0 \text{ otherwise} \end{cases}$

$t = \text{time} = 1, 2, \ldots, 40$

The model is $Y_t = \beta_0 + \beta_1 t + \beta_2 x_1 + \beta_3 x_2 + \beta_4 x_3 + \varepsilon$.

b.   Using MINITAB, the output is:

Regression Analysis: Y versus T, X1, X2, X3

```
The regression equation is
Y = 11.5 + 0.510 T - 3.95 X1 - 2.09 X2 - 4.52 X3

Predictor        Coef       SE Coef          T          P
Constant      11.4933        0.2420      47.49      0.000
T            0.509848      0.007607      67.02      0.000
X1            -3.9505        0.2483     -15.91      0.000
X2            -2.0903        0.2477      -8.44      0.000
X3            -4.5202        0.2473     -18.28      0.000

S = 0.5528      R-Sq = 99.3%      R-Sq(adj) = 99.2%

Analysis of Variance

Source           DF           SS         MS          F          P
Regression        4      1558.79     389.70    1275.44      0.000
Residual Error   35        10.69       0.31
Total            39      1569.48

Source     DF      Seq SS
T           1     1433.96
X1          1       22.56
X2          1        0.21
X3          1      102.06
```

The fitted model is $\hat{Y}_t = 11.4933 + .5098t - 3.9505x_1 - 2.0903x_2 - 4.5202x_3$.

To determine if the model is adequate, we test:

H_0: $\beta_1 = \beta_2 = \beta_3 = \beta_4 = 0$
H_a: At least one $\beta_i \neq 0$, $i = 1, 2, 3, 4$

The test statistic is $F = 1275.44$.

The rejection region requires $\alpha = .05$ in the upper tail of the F-distribution with numerator df $= k = 4$ and denominator df $= n - (k + 1) = 40 - (4 + 1) = 35$. From Table VIII, Appendix B, $F_{.05} \approx 2.69$. The rejection region is $F > 2.69$.

Since the observed value of the test statistic falls in the rejection region ($F = 1275.44 > 2.69$), H_0 is rejected. There is sufficient evidence to indicate the model is useful at $\alpha = .05$.

c. From MINITAB, the predicted values and prediction intervals are:

Predicted Values for New Observations

```
New Obs      Fit      SE Fit       95.0% CI              95.0% PI
1        28.4467      0.2420   ( 27.9554, 28.9379)  ( 27.2217, 29.6716)
```

Values of Predictors for New Observations

```
New Obs            T        X1        X2        X3
1               41.0      1.00  0.000000  0.000000
```

Predicted Values for New Observations

```
New Obs      Fit      SE Fit       95.0% CI              95.0% PI
1        30.8167      0.2420   ( 30.3254, 31.3079)  ( 29.5917, 32.0416)
```

Values of Predictors for New Observations

```
New Obs            T        X1        X2        X3
1               42.0  0.000000      1.00  0.000000
```

Predicted Values for New Observations

```
New Obs      Fit      SE Fit       95.0% CI              95.0% PI
1        28.8967      0.2420   ( 28.4054, 29.3879)  ( 27.6717, 30.1216)
```

Values of Predictors for New Observations

```
New Obs            T        X1        X2        X3
1               43.0  0.000000  0.000000      1.00
```

Predicted Values for New Observations

```
New Obs      Fit      SE Fit       95.0% CI              95.0% PI
1        33.9267      0.2420   ( 33.4354, 34.4179)  ( 32.7017, 35.1516)
```

Values of Predictors for New Observations

```
New Obs            T        X1        X2        X3
1               44.0  0.000000  0.000000  0.000000
```

From the above output, the predicted values and 95% prediction intervals are:

For year = 11, quarter = 1, $\hat{y} = 28.4467$ and the 95% PI is (27.2217, 29.6716)
For year = 11, quarter = 2, $\hat{y} = 30.8167$ and the 95% PI is (29.5917, 32.0416)
For year = 11, quarter = 3, $\hat{y} = 28.8967$ and the 95% PI is (27.6717, 30.1216)
For year = 11, quarter = 4, $\hat{y} = 33.9267$ and the 95% PI is (32.7017, 35.1516)

13.41　a.　Using MINITAB, the results are:

Regression Analysis: Interest versus t

```
The regression equation is
Interest = 15.5 - 0.417 t


Predictor        Coef  SE Coef        T      P
Constant      15.5242   0.4499    34.50  0.000
t            -0.41731  0.03027   -13.79  0.000


S = 1.09125    R-Sq = 89.2%    R-Sq(adj) = 88.7%


Analysis of Variance

Source            DF       SS      MS       F      P
Regression         1   226.39  226.39  190.11  0.000
Residual Error    23    27.39    1.19
Total             24   253.78


Unusual Observations

Obs     t   Interest      Fit  SE Fit  Residual  St Resid
  3   3.0    16.830   14.272   0.373     2.558     2.49R

R denotes an observation with a large standardized residual.


Predicted Values for New Observations

New
Obs    Fit  SE Fit        95% CI             95% PI
  1  3.840   0.504  (2.798, 4.882)   (1.353, 6.326)


Values of Predictors for New Observations

New
Obs     t
  1  28.0
```

The fitted model is: $\hat{Y}_t = 15.5242 - .41731t$

b.　For 2007, $t = 28$. The forecast for the average interest rate in 2007 is
$$\hat{Y}_{28} = 15.5242 - .41731(28) = 3.840$$

From the printout, the 95% prediction interval is (1.353, 6.326).

13.43 a. Using MINITAB, the results are:

Regression Analysis: Policies versus t

```
The regression equation is
Policies = 385 - 0.363 t


Predictor      Coef  SE Coef       T      P
Constant    385.326    5.280   72.98  0.000
t            -0.3632   0.2632   -1.38  0.177


S = 15.0555   R-Sq = 5.6%   R-Sq(adj) = 2.7%


Analysis of Variance

Source           DF      SS      MS      F      P
Regression        1   431.6   431.6   1.90  0.177
Residual Error   32  7253.3   226.7
Total            33  7685.0


Unusual Observations

Obs     t  Policies      Fit  SE Fit  Residual  St Resid
  1   1.0    355.00   384.96    5.05    -29.96    -2.11R

R denotes an observation with a large standardized residual.
```

Predicted Values for New Observations

```
New
Obs     Fit  SE Fit         95% CI              95% PI
  1  372.61    5.28  (361.86, 383.37)  (340.12, 405.11)


Values of Predictors for New Observations

New
Obs     t
  1  35.0
```

Predicted Values for New Observations

```
New
Obs     Fit  SE Fit         95% CI              95% PI
  1  372.25    5.51  (361.03, 383.48)  (339.59, 404.91)


Values of Predictors for New Observations

New
Obs     t
  1  36.0
```

The fitted model is: $\hat{Y}_t = 385.326 - .3632t$

b.   From the printout, the forecasted values for 2004 and 2005 ($t = 35$ and $t = 36$) are:

2004: 372.61
2005: 372.25

c.   From the printout, the 95% prediction intervals for 2004 and 2005 are:

2004: (340.12, 405.11)
2005: (339.59, 404.91)

13.45   Autocorrelation is the correlation between time series residuals at different points in time.

13.47   a.   For $\alpha = .05$, the rejection region is $d < d_{L,\alpha} = d_{L,.05} = 1.10$. The value of $d_{L,.05}$ is found in Table XIII, Appendix B, with $k = 2$, $n = 20$, and $\alpha = .05$.

Since the test statistic does not fall in the rejection region ($d = 1.1 \not< 1.10$), H_0 is not rejected.

b.   For $\alpha = .01$, the rejection region is $d < d_{L,\alpha} = d_{L,.01} = .86$. The value of $d_{L,.01}$ is found in Table XIV, Appendix B, with $k = 2$, $n = 20$, and $\alpha = .01$.

Since the test statistic does not fall in the rejection region ($d = 1.1 \not< .86$), H_0 is not rejected.

c.   For $\alpha = .05$, the rejection region is $d < d_{L,\alpha} = d_{L,.05} = 1.44$. The value of $d_{L,.05}$ is found in Table XIII, Appendix B, with $k = 5$, $n = 65$, and $\alpha = .05$.

Since the test statistic falls in the rejection region ($d = .95 < 1.44$), H_0 is rejected.

d.   For $\alpha = .01$, the rejection region is $d < d_{L,\alpha} = d_{L,.01} = 1.15$. The value of $d_{L,.01}$ is found in Table XIV, Appendix B, with $k = 1$, $n = 31$, and $\alpha = .01$.

Since the test statistic does not fall in the rejection region ($d = 1.35 \not< 1.15$), H_0 is not rejected.

13.49   a.   For Bank 1, $R^2 = .914$. 91.4% of the sample variation of the deposit shares of Bank 1 is explained by the model containing expenditures on promotion-related activities, expenditures on service-related activities, and expenditures on distribution-related activities.

For Bank 2, $R^2 = .721$. 72.1% of the sample variation of the deposit shares of Bank 2 is explained by the model containing expenditures on promotion-related activities, expenditures on service-related activities, and expenditures on distribution-related activities.

For Bank 3, $R^2 = .926$. 92.6% of the sample variation of the deposit shares of Bank 3 is explained by the model containing expenditures on promotion-related activities, expenditures on service-related activities, and expenditures on distribution-related activities.

For Bank 4, $R^2 = .827$. 82.7% of the sample variation of the deposit shares of Bank 4 is explained by the model containing expenditures on promotion-related activities, expenditures on service-related activities, and expenditures on distribution-related activities.

For Bank 5, $R^2 = .270$. 27.0% of the sample variation of the deposit shares of Bank 5 is explained by the model containing expenditures on promotion-related activities, expenditures on service-related activities, and expenditures on distribution-related activities.

For Bank 6, $R^2 = .616$. 61.6% of the sample variation of the deposit shares of Bank 6 is explained by the model containing expenditures on promotion-related activities, expenditures on service-related activities, and expenditures on distribution-related activities.

For Bank 7, $R^2 = .962$. 96.2% of the sample variation of the deposit shares of Bank 7 is explained by the model containing expenditures on promotion-related activities, expenditures on service-related activities, and expenditures on distribution-related activities.

For Bank 8, $R^2 = .495$. 49.5% of the sample variation of the deposit shares of Bank 8 is explained by the model containing expenditures on promotion-related activities, expenditures on service-related activities, and expenditures on distribution-related activities.

For Bank 9, $R^2 = .500$. 50.0% of the sample variation of the deposit shares of Bank 9 is explained by the model containing expenditures on promotion-related activities, expenditures on service-related activities, and expenditures on distribution-related activities.

b. For all banks, to determine if the model is adequate, we test:

H_0: $\beta_1 = \beta_2 = \beta_3 = 0$
H_a: At least 1 $\beta_i \neq 0$ $i = 1, 2, 3$

For Bank 1, the p-value is $p = .000$. Since the p-value is less than $\alpha = .01$, H_0 is rejected. There is sufficient evidence to indicate the model is adequate at $\alpha = .01$.

For Bank 2, the p-value is $p = .004$. Since the p-value is less than $\alpha = .01$, H_0 is rejected. There is sufficient evidence to indicate the model is adequate at $\alpha = .01$.

For Bank 3, the p-value is $p = .000$. Since the p-value is less than $\alpha = .01$, H_0 is rejected. There is sufficient evidence to indicate the model is adequate at $\alpha = .01$.

For Bank 4, the p-value is $p = .000$. Since the p-value is less than $\alpha = .01$, H_0 is rejected. There is sufficient evidence to indicate the model is adequate at $\alpha = .01$.

For Bank 5, the p-value is $p = .155$. Since the p-value is not less than $\alpha = .01$, H_0 is not rejected. There is insufficient evidence to indicate the model is adequate at $\alpha = .01$.

For Bank 6, the p-value is $p = .012$. Since the p-value is not less than $\alpha = .01$, H_0 is not rejected. There is insufficient evidence to indicate the model is adequate at $\alpha = .01$.

For Bank 7, the p-value is $p = .000$. Since the p-value is less than $\alpha = .01$, H_0 is rejected. There is sufficient evidence to indicate the model is adequate at $\alpha = .01$.

For Bank 8, the p-value is $p = .014$. Since the p-value is not less than $\alpha = .01$, H_0 is not rejected. There is insufficient evidence to indicate the model is adequate at $\alpha = .01$.

For Bank 9, the p-value is $p = .011$. Since the p-value is not less than $\alpha = .01$, H_0 is not rejected. There is insufficient evidence to indicate the model is adequate at $\alpha = .01$.

c. To determine if positive autocorrelation is present, we test:

H_0: No positive first-order autocorrelation
H_a: Positive first-order autocorrelation of residuals

The test statistics is d.

For $\alpha = .01$, the rejection region is $d < d_{L,\, \alpha/2} = d_{L,.01} = .77$. The value $d_{L,.01}$ is found in Table XIV, Appendix B, with $k = 3$, $n = 20$, and $\alpha = .01$.

For Bank 1, $d = 1.3$. Since the observed value of the test statistic does not fall in the rejection region ($d = 1.3 \not< .77$), H_0 is not rejected. There is insufficient evidence to indicate the time series residuals are positively autocorrelated at $\alpha = .01$.

For Bank 2, $d = 3.4$. Since the observed value of the test statistic does not fall in the rejection region ($d = 3.4 \not< .77$), H_0 is not rejected. There is insufficient evidence to indicate the time series residuals are positively autocorrelated at $\alpha = .01$.

For Bank 3, $d = 2.7$. Since the observed value of the test statistic does not fall in the rejection region ($d = 2.7 \not< .77$), H_0 is not rejected. There is insufficient evidence to indicate the time series residuals are positively autocorrelated at $\alpha = .01$.

For Bank 4, $d = 1.9$. Since the observed value of the test statistic does not fall in the rejection region ($d = 1.9 \not< .77$), H_0 is not rejected. There is insufficient evidence to indicate the time series residuals are positively autocorrelated at $\alpha = .01$.

For Bank 5, $d = .85$. Since the observed value of the test statistic does not fall in the rejection region ($d = .85 \not< .77$), H_0 is not rejected. There is insufficient evidence to indicate the time series residuals are positively autocorrelated at $\alpha = .01$.

For Bank 6, $d = 1.8$. Since the observed value of the test statistic does not fall in the rejection region ($d = 1.8 \not< .77$), H_0 is not rejected. There is insufficient evidence to indicate the time series residuals are positively autocorrelated at $\alpha = .01$.

For Bank 7, $d = 2.5$. Since the observed value of the test statistic does not fall in the rejection region ($d = 2.5 \not< .77$), H_0 is not rejected. There is insufficient evidence to indicate the time series residuals are positively autocorrelated at $\alpha = .01$.

For Bank 8, $d = 2.3$. Since the observed value of the test statistic does not fall in the rejection region ($d = 2.3 \not< .77$), H_0 is not rejected. There is insufficient evidence to indicate the time series residuals are positively autocorrelated at $\alpha = .01$.

For Bank 9, $d = 1.1$. Since the observed value of the test statistic does not fall in the rejection region ($d = 1.1 \not< .77$), H_0 is not rejected. There is insufficient evidence to indicate the time series residuals are positively autocorrelated at $\alpha = .01$.

13.51   a.   Using MINITAB, the plot of the residuals against t is:

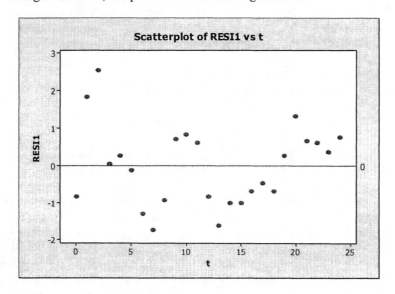

Since there appear to be groups of consecutive positive and groups of consecutive negative residuals, the data appear to be autocorrelated.

b.   Using MINITAB, the output is:

Regression Analysis: Interest versus t

```
The regression equation is
Interest = 15.1 - 0.417 t


Predictor        Coef   SE Coef        T       P
Constant      15.1069    0.4237    35.65   0.000
t            -0.41731   0.03027   -13.79   0.000


S = 1.09125     R-Sq = 89.2%    R-Sq(adj) = 88.7%


Analysis of Variance

Source          DF        SS       MS        F       P
Regression       1    226.39   226.39   190.11   0.000
Residual Error  23     27.39     1.19
Total           24    253.78


Unusual Observations

Obs    t   Interest      Fit   SE Fit   Residual   St Resid
 3   2.0    16.830   14.272    0.373      2.558      2.49R

R denotes an observation with a large standardized residual.


Durbin-Watson statistic = 0.904633
```

To determine if positive autocorrelation is present, we test:

H_0: No first-order autocorrelation
H_a: Positive first-order autocorrelation of residuals

The test statistics is $d = .9046$.

For $\alpha = .05$, the rejection region is $d < d_{L, \alpha} = d_{L,.05} = 1.29$. The value $d_{L,.05}$ is found in Table XIII, Appendix B, with $k = 1$, $n = 25$, and $\alpha = .05$.

Since the observed value of the test statistic falls in the rejection region ($d = .9046 < 1.29$), H_0 is rejected. There is sufficient evidence to indicate the time series residuals are positively autocorrelated at $\alpha = .05$.

c.   Since the error terms do not appear to be independent, the validity of the test for model adequacy is in question.

13.53 a. To determine if the overall model contributes information for the prediction of future spot exchange rates for the British pound, we test:

H_0: $\beta_1 = 0$
H_a: $\beta_1 = 0$

The test statistic is

$$F = \frac{R^2/k}{(1-R^2)/[n-(k+1)]} = \frac{.957/1}{(1-.957)/[81-(1+1)]} = 1758.21$$

The rejection region requires $\alpha = .05$ in the upper tail of the F distribution with $v_1 = k = 1$ and $v_2 = n - (1+1) = 81 - (1+1) = 79$. From Table IX, Appendix B, $F_{.05} \approx 3.96$. The rejection region is $F > 3.96$.

Since the observed value of the test statistic falls in the rejection region ($F = 1758.21 > 3.96$), H_0 is rejected. There is sufficient evidence to indicate the overall model contributes information for the prediction of future spot exchange rates for the British pound at $\alpha = .05$.

b. The value of s is .025. Almost all of the observations will fall within $\pm 2s$ or $\pm 2(.025)$ or $\pm .05$ of their least squares predicted values.

$R^2 = .957$. 95.7% of the sample variation in the future spot exchange rates for the British pound values are explained by the model containing the forward exchange rate.

c. To determine if positive autocorrelation is present, we test:

H_0: No first-order autocorrelation
H_a: Positive first-order autocorrelation of residuals

The test statistics is $d = 0.962$

For $\alpha = .05$, the rejection region is $d < d_{L, \alpha} = d_{L,.05} = 1.61$. The value $d_{L,.05}$ is found in Table XIII, Appendix B, with $k = 1$, $n = 81$, and $\alpha = .05$.

Since the observed value of the test statistic falls in the rejection region ($d = 0.962 < 1.61$, H_0 is rejected. There is sufficient evidence to indicate the time series residuals are positively autocorrelated at $\alpha = .05$.

d. No. Since the error terms do not appear to be independent, the validity of the test for model adequacy is in question.

13.55   a.   The simple composite index is found by summing the three steel prices, dividing by 85.49, the sum for the base period, 1995, and multiplying by 100. The values appear in the table.

Year	Cold Finished Price	Hot Rolled Price	Galvanized Price	Price Total	Index
1995	25.70	25.32	34.47	85.49	100.0
2000	23.08	15.67	21.38	60.13	70.3
2001	22.76	11.71	16.41	50.88	59.5
2002	23.26	16.46	22.00	61.72	72.2
2003	25.15	14.80	20.08	60.03	70.2
2004	38.67	30.84	36.69	106.20	124.2

The index decreases from 1995 through 2001, increases in 2002, and then increases significantly to above the 1995 level in 2004.

b.   This is a price index because it is based on the price of steel rather than quantity.

c.   In order to compute the Laspeyres index, we need quantities of steel for the base year 1995. To compute the Paasche index, we need quantities of steel for each of the years.

13.57   a.   Using MINITAB, the output is:

```
Regression Analysis: Daily Visits versus t

The regression equation is
Daily Visits = 38.2 + 7.32 t

Predictor       Coef     SE Coef          T        P
Constant      38.171       4.420       8.64    0.000
t             7.3192      0.7123      10.27    0.000

S = 6.470      R-Sq = 93.0%      R-Sq(adj) = 92.1%

Analysis of Variance

Source          DF          SS          MS         F        P
Regression       1      4419.5      4419.5    105.57    0.000
Residual Error   8       334.9        41.9
Total            9      4754.4

Predicted Values for New Observations

New Obs      Fit      SE Fit          95.0% CI                 95.0% PI
1         118.68        4.42  ( 108.49,  128.87)  (  100.61,   136.75)

Values of Predictors for New Observations

New Obs           t
1              11.0
```

Time Series: Descriptive Analyses, Models, and Forecasting

```
New Obs     Fit      SE Fit        95.0% CI              95.0% PI
1          126.00     5.06    ( 114.33,  137.67)   ( 107.06,  144.94)
```

Values of Predictors for New Observations

```
New Obs         t
1             12.0
```

Predicted Values for New Observations

```
New Obs     Fit      SE Fit        95.0% CI              95.0% PI
1          133.32     5.72    ( 120.13,  146.51)   ( 113.40,  153.24)
```

Values of Predictors for New Observations

```
New Obs         t
1             13.0
```

The fitted regression line is: $\hat{Y}_t = 38.171 + 7.319t$

The forecasts for the next 3 years are:

$$\hat{Y}_{11} = 38.171 + 7.319(11) = 118.680$$
$$\hat{Y}_{12} = 38.171 + 7.319(12) = 125.999$$
$$\hat{Y}_{13} = 38.171 + 7.319(13) = 133.318$$

b. From the printout, the 95% prediction intervals for the 3 years are:

> Year 11:   (100.61, 136.75)
> Year 12:   (107.06, 144.94)
> Year 13:   (113.40, 153.24)

c. There are basically two problems with using simple linear regression for predicting time series data. First, we must predict values of the time series for values of time outside the observed range. We observe data for time periods 1, 2, ..., t and use the regression model to predict values of the time series for $t + 1$, $t + 2$, ... The second problem is that simple linear regression does not allow for any cyclical effects such as seasonal trends.

d. We could use an exponentially smoothed series to forecast patient visits or we could use a Holt-Winters series to forecast patient visits.

13.59 a. To compute the Holt-Winters series, we use:

$E_2 = Y_2 = 16.54$

$E_3 = wY_3 + (1 - w)(E_2 + T_2)$

$\quad = .3(16.83) + (1 - .3)(16.54 + 2.24)$

$\quad = 18.20$

$T_2 = Y_2 - Y_1 = 16.54 - 14.30 = 2.24$

$T_3 = v(E_3 - E_2) + (1 - v)T_2$

$\quad = .7(18.20 - 16.54) + (1 - .7)(2.24)$

$\quad = 1.83$

The rest of the values appear in the table:

Year	Interest	Holt-Winters $w = .3$ E_t	$v = .7$ T_t
1980	14.30		
1981	16.54	16.54	2.24
1982	16.83	18.20	1.83
1983	13.92	18.19	0.55
1984	13.71	17.23	−0.51
1985	12.91	15.58	−1.31
1986	11.33	13.39	−1.93
1987	10.46	11.16	−2.14
1988	10.86	9.57	−1.75
1989	12.07	9.10	−0.86
1990	11.78	9.30	−0.12
1991	11.14	9.77	0.29
1992	9.29	9.83	0.13
1993	8.09	9.40	−0.26
1994	8.28	8.88	−0.44
1995	7.86	8.27	−0.56
1996	7.76	7.72	−0.55
1997	7.57	7.29	−0.47
1998	6.92	6.85	−0.45
1999	7.46	6.72	−0.22
2000	8.08	6.97	0.11
2001	7.01	7.06	0.09
2002	6.56	6.97	−0.03
2003	5.89	6.63	−0.25
2004	5.86	6.22	−0.36

The forecasts for 2005-2007 using the Holt-Winters series with $w = .3$ and $v = .7$ are:

$$F_{2005} = F_{t+1} = E_t + T_t = 6.22 + (−.36) = 5.86$$
$$F_{2006} = F_{t+2} = E_t + 2T_t = 6.22 + 2(−.36) = 5.50$$
$$F_{2007} = F_{t+3} = E_t + 3T_t = 6.22 + 3(−.36) = 5.14$$

From Exercise 13.41, the forecasts for 2005-2007 are:

2005: $\hat{Y}_{26} = 15.5242 − .41731(26) = 4.674$

2006: $\hat{Y}_{27} = 15.5242 − .41731(27) = 4.257$

2007: $\hat{Y}_{28} = 15.5242 − .41731(28) = 3.840$

The forecasts from the Holt-Winters series are larger than those of the regression forecasts.

13.61 a. Using MINITAB, the printout from fitting the model $E(Y_t) = \beta_0 + \beta_1 t$ is:

Regression Analysis: Price versus t

```
The regression equation is
Price = 47.2 - 0.065 t


Predictor       Coef   SE Coef       T       P
Constant      47.237     4.553   10.37   0.000
t            -0.0651    0.2842   -0.23   0.821


S = 11.5021    R-Sq = 0.2%    R-Sq(adj) = 0.0%


Analysis of Variance

Source          DF       SS      MS      F       P
Regression       1      7.0     7.0   0.05   0.821
Residual Error  25   3307.4   132.3
Total           26   3314.4


Durbin-Watson statistic = 1.90195
```

Predicted Values for New Observations

```
New
Obs    Fit   SE Fit        95% CI            95% PI
  1  45.41     4.55   (36.04, 54.79)   (19.94, 70.89)
```

```
Values of Predictors for New Observations

New
Obs      t
  1   28.0
```

Predicted Values for New Observations

```
New
Obs    Fit   SE Fit        95% CI            95% PI
  1  45.35     4.80   (35.46, 55.24)   (19.68, 71.02)
```

```
Values of Predictors for New Observations

New
Obs      t
  1   29.0
```

The fitted model is $\hat{Y}_t = 47.237 - .0651t$.

b.   The plot of the data is:

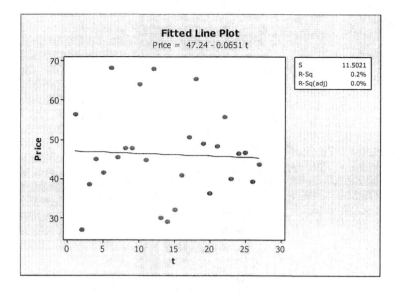

Fitted Line Plot
Price = 47.24 − 0.0651 t

S	11.5021
R-Sq	0.2%
R-Sq(adj)	0.0%

c.   From the printout in part a,

$$F_{2007} = 45.41$$
$$F_{2008} = 45.35$$

d.   Also from the printout in part a, the 95% prediction intervals are:

2007: (19.94, 70.89)   We are 95% confident that the actual closing price for 2007 will be between 19.94 and 70.89.

2008: (19.68, 71.02)   We are 95% confident that the actual closing price for 2008 will be between 19.68 and 71.02.

e.   To determine if autocorrelation is present, we test:

H_0: Autocorrelation is not present
H_a: Autocorrelation is present

The test statistic is $d = 1.90$.

Since α is not given, we will use $\alpha = .10$. The rejection region is $d < d_{L,\alpha/2} = d_{L,.05} = 1.32$ or $4 - d < d_{L,.05} = 1.32$, where $d_{L,.05}$ is from Table XIII, Appendix B, for $k = 1$, $n = 27$, and $\alpha = .10$.

Since the observed value of the test statistic does not fall in the rejection region ($d = 1.90$ $\not< 1.32$), H_0 is not rejected. There is insufficient evidence to indicate that autocorrelation is present at $\alpha = .10$.

13.63 To compute the Holt-Winters values for the years 2001-2005:

With $w = .5$ and $v = .5$,

$E_2 = Y_2 = 9,906$
$E_3 = wY_3 + (1 - w)(E_2 + T_2) = .5(9,871) + (1 - .5)(9,906 + 30) = 9,903.5.$

$T_2 = Y_2 - Y_1 = 9,906 - 9,876 = 30$
$T_3 = v(E_3 - E_2) + (1 - v)T_2 = .5(9,903.5 - 9,906) + (1 - .5)(30) = 13.75$

The rest of the values appear in the table:

Year	Quarter	GDP	E_t $w = .5$ $v = .5$	T_t $w = .5$ $v = .5$
2001	I	9,876		
	II	9,906	9,906.00	30.00
	III	9,871	9,903.50	13.75
	IV	9,910	9,913.63	11.94
2002	I	9,977	9,951.28	24.80
	II	10,032	10,004.04	38.78
	III	10,091	10,066.91	50.82
	IV	10,096	10,106.87	45.39
2003	I	10,139	10,145.63	42.08
	II	10,230	10,208.85	52.65
	III	10,411	10,336.25	90.02
	IV	10,503	10,464.64	109.21
2004	I	10,612	10,592.92	118.74
	II	10,704	10,707.83	116.83
	III	10,809	10,816.83	112.91
	IV	10,897	10,913.37	104.73
2005	I	10,999	11,008.55	99.95
	II	11,089	11,098.75	95.08
	III	11,202	11,197.91	97.12
	IV	11,248	11,271.52	85.36

The forecasts for the four quarters of 2006 are:

$F_{2006,1} = F_{t+1} = E_t + T_t = 11,271.52 + 85.36 = 11,356.88$
$F_{2006,2} = F_{t+2} = E_t + 2T_t = 11,271.52 + 2(85.36) = 11,442.24$
$F_{2006,3} = F_{t+3} = E_t + 3T_t = 11,271.52 + 3(85.36) = 11,527.60$
$F_{2006,4} = F_{t+4} = E_t + 4T_t = 11,271.52 + 4(85.36) = 11,612.96$

13.67 a. Real income 1990 $= \dfrac{\$50,000}{125.8} \times 100 = \$39,745.63$

Real income 2005 $= \dfrac{\$95,000}{195.3} \times 100 = \$48,643.11$

The real income for 2005 was greater than that for 1990. Since the real income in 2005 is greater than that in 1990, you would be able to buy more in 2005 than in 1990.

b. Let x = monetary income in 2005.

Then $\dfrac{x}{195.3} = \dfrac{\$20,000}{125.8}$

Solving for x, we get $x = \$31,049.28$.

Nonparametric Statistics

Chapter 14

14.1   The sign test is preferred to the t-test when the population from which the sample is selected is not normal.

14.3   a. $P(x \geq 7) = 1 - P(x \leq 6) = 1 - .965 = .035$

     b. $P(x \geq 5) = 1 - P(x \leq 4) = 1 - .637 = .363$

     c. $P(x \geq 8) = 1 - P(x \leq 7) = 1 - .996 = .004$

     d. $P(x \geq 10) = 1 - P(x \leq 9) = 1 - .849 = .151$

          $\mu = np = 15(.5) = 7.5$ and $\sigma = \sqrt{npq} = \sqrt{15(.5)(.5)} = 1.9365$

$$P(x \geq 10) \approx P\left(z \geq \frac{(10 - .5) - 7.5}{1.9365}\right) = P(z \geq 1.03) = .5 - .3485 = .1515$$

     e. $P(x \geq 15) = 1 - P(x \leq 14) = 1 - .788 = .212$

          $\mu = np = 25(.5) = 12.5$ and $\sigma = \sqrt{npq} = \sqrt{25(.5)(.5)} = 2.5$

$$P(x \geq 15) \approx P\left(z \geq \frac{(15 - .5) - 12.5}{2.5}\right) = P(z \geq .80) = .5 - .2881 = .2119$$

14.5   To determine if the median is greater than 75, we test:

$H_0: \eta = 75$
$H_a: \eta > 75$

The test statistic is $S =$ number of measurements greater than $75 = 17$.

The p-value $= P(x \geq 17)$ where x is a binomial random variable with $n = 25$ and $p = .5$. From Table II,

$$p\text{-value} = P(x \geq 17) = 1 - P(x \leq 16) = 1 - .946 = .054$$

Since the p-value $= .054 < \alpha = .10$, H_0 is rejected. There is sufficient evidence to indicate the median is greater than 75 at $\alpha = .10$.

We must assume the sample was randomly selected from a continuous probability distribution.

Note: Since $n \geq 10$, we could use the large-sample approximation.

14.7   a.   To determine if the median income of graduates of the MBA program was more than $96,000 in 2006, we test:

H_0: $\eta = 96,000$
H_a: $\eta > 96,000$

b.   The test statistic is $S = \{$Number of observations greater than 96,000$\} = 9$.

The p-value $= P(x \geq 9)$ where x is a binomial random variable with $n = 15$ and $p = .5$. From Table II,

$$p\text{-value} = P(x \geq 9) = 1 - P(x \leq 8) = 1 \ .696 = .304.$$

Since the p-value $= .304 > \alpha = .05$, H_0 is not rejected. There is insufficient evidence to indicate the median income of graduates of the MBA program was more than $96,000 in 2006 at $\alpha = .05$.

c.   We must assume only that the sample is selected randomly from a continuous probability distribution.

14.9   a.   To calculate the median, we first arrange the data in order from the smallest to the largest:

22, 28, 32, 33, 39, 41, 43, 43, 45, 47, 50, 54, 54, 59, 62

Since n is odd, the median is the middle number, which is 43.

b.   To determine if the median age of the terminated workers exceeds the entire company's median age, we test:

H_0: $\eta = 37$
H_a: $\eta > 37$

c.   The test statistic is $S =$ number of measurements greater than $37 = 11$.

The p-value $= P(x \geq 11)$ where x is a binomial random variable with $n = 15$ and $p = .5$. From Table II, Appendix B,

$$p\text{-value} = P(x \geq 11) = 1 - P(x \leq 10) = 1 - .941 = .059.$$

Since no α value was given, we will use $\alpha = .05$. Since the p-value $= .059 > \alpha = .05$, H_0 is not rejected. There is insufficient evidence to indicate that the median age of the terminated workers exceeds the entire company's median age at $\alpha = .05$.

(Note: If $\alpha = .10$ was used, the conclusion would be to reject H_0.)

Using MINITAB, the results are:

Sign Test for Median: Age

```
Sign test of median = 37.00 versus   >   37.00

            N   Below  Equal  Above        P     Median
Age        15     4      0     11     0.0592     45.00
```

From the printout, the p-value is .0592. Again, using $\alpha = .05$, we would not reject H_0.

d. Since the conclusion using $\alpha = .10$ is to reject H_0 and conclude that there is sufficient evidence to indicate that the median age of the terminated workers exceeds the entire company's median age, we would advise the company to reevaluate its planned RIF. With the proposed sample, there is evidence that the company is discriminating with respect to age.

14.11 a. In order for the inference to be valid, we must assume that the population we are sampling from is normal. From the sample data, it appears that the data are not from a normal distribution, but rather from a distribution that is skewed to the right.

b. To determine if the median 5-year revenue growth rate is less than 5,000%, we test:

H_0: $\eta = 5,000$
H_a: $\eta < 5,000$

c. The test statistic is $S = \{$Number of observations less than $5,000\} = 10$.

The p-value $= P(x \geq 10)$ where x is a binomial random variable with $n = 12$ and $p = .5$.

$$p - \text{value} = P(x \geq 10) = P(x = 10) + P(x = 11) + P(x = 12)$$

$$= \binom{12}{10}.5^{10}(.5)^{12-10} + \binom{12}{11}.5^{11}(.5)^{12-11} + \binom{12}{12}.5^{12}(.5)^{12-12}$$

$$= \frac{12!}{10!2!}.5^{10}(.5)^2 + \frac{12!}{11!1!}.5^{11}(.5)^1 + \frac{12!}{12!0!}.5^{12}(.5)^0$$

$$= .0161 + .0029 + .0002 = .0192$$

Since the p-value $= .0192 < \alpha = .05$, H_0 is rejected. There is sufficient evidence to indicate the median 5-year revenue growth is less than 5,000% at $\alpha = .05$.

14.13 a. The test statistic is T_2, the rank sum of population 2 (because $n_2 < n_1$).

The rejection region is $T_2 \leq 35$ or $T_2 \geq 67$, from Table XV, Appendix B, with $n_1 = 10$, $n_2 = 6$, and $\alpha = .10$.

b. The test statistic is T_1, the rank sum of population 1 (because $n_1 < n_2$).

The rejection region is $T_1 \geq 43$, from Table XV, Appendix B, with $n_1 = 5$, $n_2 = 7$, and $\alpha = .05$.

c. The test statistic is T_2, the rank sum of population 2 (because $n_2 < n_1$).

The rejection region is $T_2 \geq 93$, from Table XV, Appendix B, with $n_1 = 9$, $n_2 = 8$, and $\alpha = .025$.

d. Since $n_1 = n_2 = 15$, the test statistic is:

$$z = \frac{T_1 - \dfrac{n_1(n_1 + n_2 + 1)}{2}}{\sqrt{\dfrac{n_1 n_2(n_1 + n_2 + 1)}{12}}}$$

The rejection region is $z < -z_{\alpha/2}$ or $z > z_{\alpha/2}$. For $\alpha = .05$ and $\alpha/2 = .05/2 = .025$, $z_{.025} = 1.96$ from Table IV, Appendix B. The rejection region is $z < -1.96$ or $z > 1.96$.

14.15 a. The hypotheses are:

H_0: Two sampled populations have identical distributions
H_a: The probability distribution for population A is shifted to the left of that for B

b. First, we rank all the data:

A		B	
Observation	Rank	Observation	Rank
37	8	65	13
40	9	35	6.5
33	3.5	47	11
29	2	52	12
42	10		
33	3.5		
35	6.5		
28	1		
34	5		
$T_A = 48.5$		$T_B = 42.5$	

The test statistic is $T_B = 42.5$ because $n_B < n_A$.

The rejection region is $T_B \geq 39$ from Table XV, Appendix B, with $n_A = 9$, $n_B = 4$ and $\alpha = .05$.

Since the observed value of the test statistic falls in the rejection region ($T_B = 42.5 \geq 39$), H_0 is rejected. There is sufficient evidence to indicate the distribution for population B is shifted to the right of the distribution for population A at $\alpha = .05$.

14.17 a. The ranks of the data are:

Old Design	Rank	New Design	Rank
210	9	216	16.5
212	13.5	217	18.5
211	11	162	4
211	11	137	1
190	7	219	20
213	15	216	16.5
212	13.5	179	6
211	11	153	3
164	5	152	2
209	8	217	18.5
	$T_1=104$		$T_2=106$

b. The sum of the ranks are $T_1 = 104$.

c. The sum of the ranks are $T_2 = 106$.

d. Since $n_1 = n_2 = 10$, either T_1 or T_2 can be used. We will pick $T_1 = 104$.

e. To determine if the distributions of bursting strengths differ for the two designs, we test:

H_0: The two sampled populations have identical probability distributions

H_a: The probability distribution of the new design is located to the right or left of that for the old design.

The test statistic is $T_1 = 104$.

The null hypothesis will be rejected if $T_1 \le T_L$ or $T_1 \ge T_U$ where T_L and T_U correspond to $\alpha = .05$ (two-tailed) and $n_1 = n_2 = 10$. From Table XV, Appendix B, $T_L = 79$ and $T_U = 131$.

Reject H_0 if $T_1 \le 79$ or $T_1 \ge 131$.

Since $T_1 = 104 \not\le 79$ and $T_1 = 104 \not\ge 131$, H_0 is not rejected. There is insufficient evidence to indicate the distributions of bursting strengths differ for the two designs at $\alpha = .05$.

14.19 a. Since the data are not normal, we will use the Wilcoxon Rank Sum test. There is some concern with this test as there are many ties in the data. One of the assumptions for the Wilcoxon Rank Sum test is that the data are continuous, with relatively few ties.

b. To determine if the scores of those in the CMC group tend to be lower than the scores of those in the FTF group, we test:

H_0: The two sampled populations have identical probability distributions

H_a: The probability distribution of the FTF is located to the right of that for the CMC group.

c. Since $n_1 = n_2 = 24$, the large sample test statistic must be used. The rejection region requires $\alpha = .10$ in the lower tail of the z distribution. From Table IV, Appendix B, $z_{.10} = 1.28$. The rejection region is $z < -1.28$.

d. Some preliminary calculations are:

CMC	Rank	FTF	Rank
4	34.5	5	47
3	13.5	4	34.5
3	13.5	4	34.5
4	34.5	4	34.5
3	13.5	3	13.5
3	13.5	3	13.5
3	13.5	3	13.5
3	13.5	4	34.5
4	34.5	3	13.5
4	34.5	3.	13.5
3	13.5	3	13.5
4	34.5	3	13.5
3	13.5	4	34.5
3	13.5	4	34.5
2	2	4	34.5
4	34.5	4	34.5
2	2	4	34.5
4	34.5	3	13.5
5	47	3	13.5
4	34.5	3	13.5
4	34.5	4	34.5
4	34.5	4	34.5
5	47	2	2
3	13.5	4	34.5
	$T_1 = 578$		$T_2 = 598$

The test statistic is

$$z = \frac{T_1 - \dfrac{n_1(n_1 + n_2 + 1)}{2}}{\sqrt{\dfrac{n_1 n_2(n_1 + n_2 + 1)}{12}}} = \frac{578 - \dfrac{24(24 + 24 + 1)}{2}}{\sqrt{\dfrac{24(24)(24 + 24 + 1)}{12}}} = \frac{-10}{48.4974} = -.206$$

Nonparametric Statistics

Since the observed value of the test statistic does not fall in the rejection region ($z = -.206 \not< -1.28$), H_0 is not rejected. There is insufficient evidence to indicate the scores of those in the CMC group tend to be lower than the scores of those in the FTF group at $\alpha = .10$.

14.21   a.   In order for the t-test to be valid, the data must come from normal distributions with equal variances. For this exercise, the data may not come from normal distributions and the variances may not be equal.

b.   Some preliminary calculations:

Text-line		Intersection	
Score	**Rank**	**Score**	**Rank**
.335	4	.393	7
.374	6	.353	5
.440	8	.285	1
		.295	2
		.319	3
$T_1 = 18$		$T_2 = 18$	

To determine if the distribution of zinc measurements for the text-line is different from the distribution of zinc measurements for the intersection, we test:

H_0:   The two sampled distributions have identical distributions
H_a: The probability distribution for text-line is shifted to the right or left of that for intersection

The test statistic is $T_1 = 18$.

The rejection region is $T_1 \geq 21$ or $T_1 \leq 6$, from Table XV, Appendix B, with $n_1 = 3$, $n_2 = 5$, and $\alpha = .05$.

Since the observed value of the test statistic does not fall in the rejection region ($T_1 = 18 \not\geq 21$ and $T_1 = 18 \not\leq 6$), H_0 is not rejected. There is insufficient evidence to indicate the distribution of zinc measurements for the text-line is different from the distribution of zinc measurements for the intersection at $\alpha = .05$.

c.	Some preliminary calculations:

Witness-line		Intersection	
Score	**Rank**	**Score**	**Rank**
.210	2	.393	9
.262	3	.353	8
.188	1	.285	4
.329	7	.295	5
.439	11	.319	6
.397	10		
$T_1 = 34$		$T_2 = 32$	

To determine if the distribution of zinc measurements for the witness-line is different from the distribution of zinc measurements for the intersection, we test:

H_0: The two sampled distributions have identical distributions
H_a: The probability distribution for witness-line is shifted to the right or left of that for intersection

The test statistic is $T_2 = 32$.

The rejection region is $T_2 \geq 41$ or $T_2 \leq 19$, from Table XV, Appendix B, with $n_1 = 6$, $n_2 = 5$, and $\alpha = .05$.

Since the observed value of the test statistic does not fall in the rejection region ($T_2 = 32 \ngeq 41$ and $T_2 = 32 \nleq 19$), H_0 is not rejected. There is insufficient evidence to indicate the distribution of zinc measurements for the witness-line is different from the distribution of zinc measurements for the intersection at $\alpha = .05$.

d.	From parts b and c, we found that there was no difference in the distributions between the Text-line and Intersection. This is the same as saying there is no difference in the medians of the two groups. We also found that there was no difference in the distributions between the Witness-line and Intersection. This is the same as saying there is no difference in the medians of the two groups. We cannot say anything about whether the distributions of Witness-line and Text-line differ. This is the same as saying there is no information as to whether the medians of these two groups differ.

Nonparametric Statistics

14.23 a.   Some preliminary calculations are:

Twin Blades		Single Blades	
Observation	Rank	Observation	Rank
8	7	10	9.5
17	16	6	3.5
9	8	3	1
11	11	7	5.5
15	15	13	13
10	9.5	14	14
6	3.5	5	2
12	12	7	5.5
	$T_1 = 82$		$T_2 = 54$

To determine if twin-blade razors give more shaves than single-blade razors, we test:

H_0: The two sampled populations have identical probability distributions
H_a: The probability distribution for the twin-blade razors is shifted to the right of that for single-blade razors

The test statistic is $T_1 = 82$.

The rejection region is $T_1 \geq 84$ from Table XV, Appendix B, with $n_1 = n_2 = 8$ and $\alpha = .05$.

Since the observed value of the test statistic does not fall in the rejection region ($T_1 = 82 \ngeq 84$), H_0 is not rejected. There is insufficient evidence to indicate the twin-blade razors give more shaves than single-blade razors at $\alpha = .05$.

b.   No. It might have been better to pair the observations—have each subject shave with each type of blade. This could eliminate variability from shaver to shaver.

c.   The necessary assumptions are:

1.   The two samples are random and independent.
2.   The two probability distributions sampled from are continuous.

The last assumption is not true because the number of shaves is discrete, not continuous. However the numbers are fairly spread out, so the assumption is not critical.

14.25 a. For the unpaired t-test to compare the means of two population percentages, the
assumption that may be violated is the assumption of equal population variances.

b.

U.S. Plants		Japanese Plants	
Observation	Rank	Observation	Rank
7.11	9	3.52	4
6.06	7	2.02	2
8.00	10	4.91	6
6.87	8	3.22	3
4.77	5	1.92	1
	$T_1 = 39$		$T_2 = 16$

To determine if the distribution of American plants is shifted to the right of that for
Japanese plants, we test:

H_0: The two sampled population have identical probability distributions
H_a: The probability distribution for American plants is shifted to the right of that
for Japanese plants

The test statistic is $T_1 = 39$.

The rejection region is $T_1 \geq 36$ from Table XV, Appendix B, with $n_1 = n_2 = 5$, and
$\alpha = .05$.

Since the observed value of the test statistic falls in the rejection region ($T_1 = 39 \geq 36$),
H_0 is rejected. There is sufficient evidence to indicate the probability distribution for
U.S. plants is shifted to the right of that for Japanese plants at $\alpha = .05$.

This result agrees with that from Exercise 7.16.

14.27 a. The hypotheses are:

H_0: The two sampled populations have identical probability distributions
H_a: The probability distributions for population A is shifted to the right of that for
population B

b.   Some preliminary calculations are:

| Treatment | | Difference | Rank of Absolute |
A	B	A - B	Difference
54	45	9	5
60	45	15	10
98	87	11	7
43	31	12	9
82	71	11	7
77	75	2	2.5
74	63	11	7
29	30	−1	1
63	59	4	4
80	82	−2	2.5
			$T_- = 3.5$

The test statistic is $T_- = 3.5$

The rejection region is $T_- \leq 8$, from Table XVI, Appendix B, with $n = 10$ and $\alpha = .025$.

Since the observed value of the test statistic falls in the rejection region ($T_- = 3.5 \leq 8$), H_0 is rejected. There is sufficient evidence to indicate the responses for A tend to be larger than those for B at $\alpha = .025$.

14.29   a. H_0:   The two sampled populations have identical probability distributions
H_a: The probability distribution for population 1 is located to the right of that for population 2

b.   The test statistic is:

$$z = \frac{T_+ - \dfrac{n(n+1)}{4}}{\sqrt{\dfrac{n(n+1)(2n+1)}{24}}} = \frac{354 - \dfrac{30(30+1)}{4}}{\sqrt{\dfrac{30(30+1)(60+1)}{24}}} = \frac{121.5}{48.6184} = 2.499$$

The rejection region requires $\alpha = .05$ in the upper tail of the z-distribution. From Table IV, Appendix B, $z = 1.645$. The rejection region is $z > 1.645$.

Since the observed value of the test statistic falls in the rejection region ($z = 2.499 > 1.645$), H_0 is rejected. There is sufficient evidence to indicate population 1 is located to the right of that for population 2 at $\alpha = .05$.

c.   The p-value $= P(z \geq 2.499) = .5 - .4938 = .0062$ (using Table IV, Appendix B).

d.   The necessary assumptions are:

1.   The sample of differences is randomly selected from the population of differences.
2.   The probability distribution from which the sample of paired differences is drawn is continuous.

14.31 a. The differences between the scores for first and the third sessions are probably not normally distributed. Thus, a paired t-test probably will not be appropriate. The nonparametric Wilcoxan signed ranks test will be more appropriate.

b. To determine if the relational intimacy scores for the CMC group will tend to be higher at the third meeting than at the first meeting, we test:

H_0: The two sampled populations have identical probability distributions.

H_a: The probability distribution at the third session for the CMC group is shifted to the right of that at the first session.

c. Since no α was given, we will use $\alpha = .05$. The rejection region is $T_- \leq T_0$ where T_0 corresponds to $\alpha = .05$ (one-tailed) and $n = 24$. From Table XVI, Appendix B, $T_0 = 92$. The rejection region is $T_- \leq 92$.

d. To determine if the relational intimacy scores for the FTF group will be different at the third meeting than at the first meeting, we test:

H_0: The two sampled populations have identical probability distributions.

H_a: The probability distribution at the third session for the FTF group is shifted to the right or left of that at the first session.

e. Since no α was given, we will use $\alpha = .05$. The rejection region is $T \leq T_0$ where T_0 corresponds to $\alpha = .05$ (two-tailed) and $n = 24$. T is the smaller of T_- and T_+. From Table XVI, Appendix B, $T_0 = 81$. The rejection region is $T_- \leq 81$.

14.33

Operator	Before Policy	After Policy	Difference	Rank of Absolute Difference
1	10	5	5	5.5
2	3	0	3	4
3	16	7	9	8
4	11	4	7	7
5	8	6	2	2.5
6	2	4	-2	2.5
7	1	2	-1	1
8	14	3	11	9
9	5	5	0	(eliminated)
10	6	1	5	5.5

Negative rank sum $T_- = 3.5$
Positive rank sum $T_+ = 41.5$

Nonparametric Statistics

To determine if the distributions of the number of complaints differs for the two time periods, we test:

H_0: The distributions of the number of complaints for the two years are the same

H_a: The distribution of the number of complaints after the policy change is shifted to the right or left of the distribution before the policy change.

The test statistic is $T_- = 3.5$.

Since no α is given we will use $\alpha = .05$. The null hypothesis will be rejected if $T_- \le T_o$ where T_o corresponds to $\alpha = .05$ (two-tailed) and $n = 9$. From Table XVI, Appendix B, $T_o = 6$.

Reject H_0 if $T_- \le 6$.

Since the observed value of the test statistic falls in the rejection region ($T_- = 3.5 \le 6$), H_0 is rejected. There is sufficient evidence to indicate the distributions of the complaints are different for the two years at $\alpha = .05$.

14.35 a. Some preliminary calculations are:

Circuit	Standard Method	Huffman-coding Method	Difference S-H	Rank of Absolute Differences
1	0.80	0.78	0.02	2
2	0.80	0.80	0.00	(eliminated)
3	0.83	0.86	-0.03	3
4	0.53	0.53	0.00	(eliminated)
5	0.50	0.51	-0.01	1
6	0.96	0.68	0.28	8
7	0.99	0.82	0.17	5
8	0.98	0.72	0.26	7
9	0.81	0.45	0.36	9
10	0.95	0.79	0.16	4
11	0.99	0.77	0.22	6
				$T_- = 4$

To determine if the Huffman-coding method yields a smaller mean compression ratio, we test:

H_0: The two sampled populations have identical probability distributions.

H_a: The probability distribution of the Standard Method is shifted to the right of that for the Huffman-coding Method.

The test statistic is $T_- = 4$.

The rejection region is $T_- \le 8$, from Table XVI, Appendix B, with $n = 9$ and $\alpha = .05$ (one-tailed).

Since the observed value of the test statistic falls in the rejection region ($T- = 4 \leq 8$), H_0 is rejected. There is sufficient evidence to indicate the Huffman-coding method yields a smaller mean compression ratio at $\alpha = .05$

b. In Exercise 7.33, we concluded that the Huffman-coding method yields a smaller mean compression ratio than the standard method which is the same as the conclusion above.

14.37 The χ^2 distribution provides an appropriate characterization of the sampling distribution of H if the p sample sizes exceed 5.

14.39 a. A completely randomized design was used.

b. The hypotheses are:
  H_0: The three probability distributions are identical
  H_a: At least two of the three probability distributions differ in location

c. The rejection region requires $\alpha = .01$ in the upper tail of the χ^2 distribution with df $= p - 1 = 3 - 1 = 2$. From Table VII, Appendix B, $\chi^2_{.01} = 9.21034$. The rejection region is $H > 9.21034$.

d. Some preliminary calculations are:

I Observation	Rank	II Observation	Rank	III Observation	Rank
66	13	19	2	75	14.5
23	3	31	6	96	19
55	10	16	1	102	21
88	18	29	4	75	14.5
58	11	30	5	98	20
62	12	33	7	78	16
79	17	40	8		
49	9				
	$R_A = 93$		$R_B = 33$		$R_C = 105$

The test statistic is:

$$H = \frac{12}{n(n+1)} \sum \frac{R_j^2}{n_j} - 3(n + 1)$$

$$= \frac{12}{21(21+1)} \left[\frac{93^2}{8} + \frac{33^2}{7} + \frac{105^2}{6} \right] - 3(21+1) = 79.85 - 66 = 13.85$$

Since the observed value of the test statistic falls in the rejection region ($H = 13.85 > 9.21034$), H_0 is rejected. There is sufficient evidence to indicate at least two of the three probability distributions differ in location at $\alpha = .01$.

14.41   a.   To determine if the distributions of recalls differ among the three groups, we test:

H_0: The three probability distributions are identical

H_a: At least two of the three probability distributions differ in location

b.   The test statistic is $H = 36.04$ and the p-value is $p = 0.000$.

c.   Since the p-value is less than α ($p = 0.000 < \alpha = .01$), H_0 is rejected. There is sufficient evidence to indicate that at least two of the distributions of recalls differ in location at $\alpha = .01$.

14.43   a.   Some preliminary calculations are:

Growth		Blend		Value	
Rate	Rank	Rate	Rank	Rate	Rank
11.5	13	2.5	3	10.7	12
8.6	10	6.2	7	6.0	6
5.5	5	12.9	14	3.2	4
9.2	11	1.0	1	13.2	15
2.2	2	7.9	9	6.6	8
	$R_1 = 41$		$R_2 = 34$		$R_3 = 45$

To determine if the rate-of-return distributions differ among the three types of mutual funds, we test:

H_0: The three probability distributions are identical
H_a: At least two of the three rate-of-return distributions differ

The test statistic is:

$$H = \frac{12}{n(n+1)} \sum \frac{R_j^2}{n_j} - 3(n+1)$$

$$= \frac{12}{15(15+1)} \left[\frac{41^2}{5} + \frac{34^2}{5} + \frac{45^2}{5} \right] - 3(15+1) = 0.62$$

The rejection region requires $\alpha = .05$ in the upper tail of the χ^2 distribution with degrees of freedom $= p - 1 = 3 - 1 = 2$. From Table VII, Appendix B, $\chi_{.05}^2 = 5.99147$. The rejection region is $H > 5.99147$.

Since the observed value of the test statistic does not fall in the rejection region ($H = 0.62 \ngtr 5.99147$), H_0 is not rejected. There is insufficient evidence to indicate the rate-of-return distributions differ among the three types of mutual funds at $\alpha = .05$.

b. The necessary assumptions are:

1. The three samples are random and independent.
2. There are five or more measurements in each sample.
3. The three probability distributions from which the samples are drawn are continuous.

c. A Type I error would be concluding at least two of the rate-of-return distributions differ when they do not.

A Type II error would be concluding the three rate-of-return distributions are identical when they are not.

d. The F-test could be used if the three distributions were normal with equal variances.

14.45 a.

Aerospace/Defense		Electrice Utilities		Retailing		Chemical	
Ratio	Rank	Ratio	Rank	Ratio	Rank	Ratio	Rank
45.3	9	56.4	15	62.2	18	22.6	1
37.0	4	59.9	17	31.2	2	47.2	11
64.6	21	58.6	16	75.6	23	44.2	8
40.6	5	46.9	10	48.8	13	67.0	22
63.9	20	49.8	14	42.1	7	47.6	12
63.3	19	41.7	6				
		36.5	3				
$R_1 = 78$		$R_2 = 81$		$R_3 = 63$		$R_4 = 54$	

To determine if the debt/capital ratio distributions differ among the four industries, we test:

H_0: The four probability distributions are identical
H_a: At least two of the four debt/capital ratio distributions differ

The test statistic is:

$$H = \frac{12}{n(n+1)} \sum \frac{R_j^2}{n_j} - 3(n+1)$$

$$= \frac{12}{23(23+1)} \left[\frac{78^2}{6} + \frac{81^2}{7} + \frac{63^2}{5} + \frac{54^2}{5} \right] - 3(23+1) = 0.354$$

The rejection region requires $\alpha = .05$ in the upper tail of the χ^2 distribution with degrees of freedom $= p - 1 = 4 - 1 = 3$. From Table VII, Appendix B, $\chi^2_{.05} = 7.81473$. The rejection region is $H > 7.81473$.

Since the observed value of the test statistic does not fall in the rejection region ($H = 0.354 \not> 7.81473$), H_0 is not rejected. There is insufficient evidence to indicate the debt/capital ratio distributions differ among the four types of industries at $\alpha = .05$

b. Since we concluded there was insufficient evidence of differences among the four industry populations, we do not need to make pairwise comparisons. However, if differences were found, then we should compare all pairs of distributions using the Wilcoxon rank sum test. If c comparisons are made, then each comparison would use α^* = α/c as the level of significance.

14.47 a. The number of blocks, b, is 6.

b. H_0: The probability distributions for the four treatments are identical
H_a: At least two of the probability distributions differ in location

c. The test statistic is $F_r = \dfrac{12}{bp(p+1)} \sum R_j^2 - 3b(p+1)$

$= \dfrac{12}{6(4)(4+1)} [11^2 + 21^2 + 21^2 + 7^2] - 3(6)(4+1) = 105.2 - 90 = 15.2$

The rejection region requires $\alpha = .10$ in the upper tail of the χ^2 distribution with df = $p - 1 = 4 - 1 = 3$. From Table VII, Appendix B, $\chi_{.10}^2 = 6.25139$. The rejection region is $F_r > 6.25139$.

Since the observed value of the test statistic falls in the rejection region ($F_r = 15.2 > 6.25139$), reject H_0. There is sufficient evidence to indicate a difference in the location of at least two of the four treatments at $\alpha = .10$.

d. The p-value = $P(F_r \geq 15.2) = P(\chi^2 \geq 15.2)$. With 3 degrees of freedom, $F_r = 15.2$ falls above $\chi_{.005}^2$; therefore, p-value < .005.

e. The means are:

$$\overline{R}_A = \frac{R_A}{b} = \frac{11}{6} = 1.833 \qquad\qquad \overline{R}_B = \frac{R_B}{b} = \frac{21}{6} = 3.5$$

$$\overline{R}_C = \frac{R_C}{b} = \frac{21}{6} = 3.5 \qquad\qquad \overline{R}_D = \frac{R_D}{b} = \frac{7}{6} = 1.167$$

$$\overline{R} = \frac{1}{2}(p+1) = \frac{1}{2}(4+1) = 2.5$$

$$F_r = \frac{12}{p(p+1)} \sum b(\overline{R}_j - \overline{R})^2$$

$$= \frac{12}{(4)(4+1)} [6(1.833 - 2.5)^2 + 6(3.5 - 2.5)^2 + 6(3.5 - 2.5)^2 + 6(1.167 - 2.5)^2]$$

$$= .6[25.3307] = 15.2$$

14.49 $R_1 = 16$ $R_2 = 7$ $R_3 = 23$ $R_4 = 14$

To determine if at least two of the treatment probability distributions differ in location, we test:

H_0: The probability distributions of the four treatments are identical
H_a: At least two of the probability distributions differ in location

The test statistic is $F_r = \dfrac{12}{bp(p+1)} \sum R_j^2 - 3b(p+1)$

$$= \dfrac{12}{6(4)(4+1)} [16^2 + 7^2 + 23^2 + 14^2] - 3(6)(4+1) = 103 - 90 = 13$$

The rejection region requires $\alpha = .05$ in the upper tail of the χ^2 distribution with df $= p - 1 - 4 - 1 = 3$. From Table VII, Appendix B, $\chi^2_{.05} = 7.84173$. The rejection region is $F_r > 7.81473$.

Since the observed value of the test statistic falls in the rejection region ($F_r = 13 > 7.81473$), reject H_0. There is sufficient evidence to indicate a difference in the location for at least two of the probability distributions at $\alpha = .05$.

14.51   a.   From the printout, the rank sums are: $R_1 = 27.0$, $R_2 = 32.5$, $R_3 = 29.0$, and $R_4 = 31.5$.

b. $F_r = \dfrac{12}{bp(p+1)} \sum R_j^2 - 3b(p+1) = \dfrac{12}{12(4)(4+1)} (27^2 + 32.5^2 + 29^2 + 31.5^2) - 3(12)(4+1) = .925$

c.   From the printout, $F_r = S = .93$ and the p-value is $p = .819$.

d.   To determine if the atlas theme ranking distributions of the four groups differ, we test:

H_0: The probability distributions of the atlas theme rankings are the same for the four groups
H_a: The probability distributions of the atlas theme rankings differ in location

The test statistic is $F_r = .925$ and the p-value is $p = .819$. Since the p-value is so large, there is no evidence to reject H_0 for any reasonable value of α. There is insufficient evidence to indicate that the atlas theme ranking distributions of the four groups differ.

Nonparametric Statistics

14.53   Some preliminary calculations are:

Student	Rank Live Plant	Rank Plant Photo	Rank No Plant
1	1	2	3
2	2	3	1
3	3	2	1
4	1	2	3
5	2	3	1
6	3	2	1
7	2	1	3
8	1	3	2
9	2	1	3
10	2	1	3
	$R_1 = 19$	$R_2 = 20$	$R_3 = 21$

To determine if the students' finger temperatures depend on the experimental conditions, we test:

H_0: The probability distributions of finger temperatures are the same for the three conditions

H_a: At least two probability distributions of finger temperatures differ in location

The test statistic is $F_r = \dfrac{12}{bp(p+1)} \sum R_j^2 - 3b(p+1)$

$$= \dfrac{12}{10(3)(3+1)} (19^2 + 20^2 + 21^2) - 3(10)(3+1) = 0.2$$

Since no α was given, we will use $\alpha = .05$. The rejection region requires $\alpha = .05$ in the upper tail of the χ^2 distribution with df $= p - 1 = 3 - 1 = 2$. From Table VII, Appendix B, $\chi^2_{.05} = 5.99147$. The rejection region is $F_r > 5.99147$.

Since the observed value of the test statistic does not fall in the rejection region ($F_r = 0.2 \Uparrow$ 5.99147), H_0 is not rejected. There is insufficient evidence to indicate that the students' finger temperatures depend on the experimental conditions at $\alpha = .05$.

Because the value of the test statistic is so small, H_0 would not be rejected for any reasonable value of α.

14.55   Some preliminary calculations are:

Metal	I	Rank	II	Rank	III	Rank
1	4.6	2	4.2	1	4.9	3
2	7.2	3	6.4	1	7.0	2
3	3.4	1.5	3.5	3	3.4	1.5
4	6.2	3	5.3	1	5.9	2
5	8.4	3	6.8	1	7.8	2
6	5.6	2	4.8	1	5.7	3
7	3.7	1.5	3.7	1.5	4.1	3
8	6.1	1	6.2	2	6.4	3
9	4.9	3	4.1	1	4.2	2
10	5.2	3	5.0	1	5.1	2
		$R_1 = 23$		$R_2 = 13.5$		$R_3 = 23.5$

To determine if there is a difference in the probability distributions of the amounts of corrosion among the three types of sealers, we test:

H_0:   The probability distributions of corrosion amounts are identical for the three types of sealers

H_a: At least two of the probability distributions differ in location

The test statistic is $F_r = \dfrac{12}{bp(p+1)} \sum R_j^2 - 3b(p+1)$

$= \dfrac{12}{10(3)(3+1)} [23^2 + 13.5^2 + 23.5^2] - 3(10)(3+1) = 126.35 - 120 = 6.35$

The rejection region requires $\alpha = .05$ in the upper tail of the χ^2 distribution with df $= p - 1$ $= 3 - 1 = 2$. From Table VII, Appendix B, $\chi_{.05}^2 = 5.99147$. The rejection region is $F_r > 5.99147$.

Since the observed value of the test statistic falls in the rejection region ($F_r = 6.35 > 5.99147$), reject H_0. There is sufficient evidence to indicate a difference in the probability distributions among the three types of sealers at $\alpha = .05$.

14.57   a.   For $n = 22$, $P(r_s > .508) = .01$

b.   For $n = 28$, $P(r_s > .448) = .01$

c.   For $n = 10$, $P(r_s \leq .648) = 1 - .025 = .975$

d.   For $n = 8$, $P(r_s < -.738 \text{ or } r_s > .738) = 2(.025) = .05$

14.59 Since there are no ties, we will use the shortcut formula.

a. Some preliminary calculations are:

x Rank (u_i)	y Rank (v_i)	$d_i = u_i - v_i$	d_i^2
3	2	1	1
5	4	1	1
2	5	−3	9
1	1	0	0
4	3	1	1
			Total = 12

$$r_s = 1 - \frac{6\sum d_i^2}{n(n^2 - 1)} = 1 - \frac{6(12)}{5(5^2 - 1)} = 1 - .6 = .4$$

b.

x Rank (u_i)	y Rank (v_i)	$d_i = u_i - v_i$	d_i^2
2	3	−1	1
3	4	−1	1
4	2	2	4
5	1	4	16
1	5	−4	16
			Total = 38

$$r_s = 1 - \frac{6\sum d_i^2}{n(n^2 - 1)} = 1 - \frac{6(38)}{5(5^2 - 1)} = 1 - 1.9 = -.9$$

c.

x Rank (u_i)	y Rank (v_i)	$d_i = u_i - v_i$	d_i^2
1	2	−1	1
4	1	3	9
2	3	−1	1
3	4	−1	1
			Total = 12

$$r_s = 1 - \frac{6\sum d_i^2}{n(n^2 - 1)} = 1 - \frac{6(12)}{4(4^2 - 1)} = 1 - 1.2 = -.2$$

d.

x Rank (u_i)	y Rank (v_i)	$d_i = u_i - v_i$	d_i^2
2	1	1	1
5	3	2	4
4	5	−1	1
3	2	1	1
1	4	−3	9
			Total = 16

$$r_s = 1 - \frac{6\sum d_i^2}{n(n^2-1)} = 1 - \frac{6(16)}{5(5^2-1)} = 1 - .8 = .2$$

14.61   a.   The ranks of the 2 values appear in the table:

Brick	Apparent Porosity	Rank, u	Pore Diameter	Rank, v	Difference d_i	d_i^2
A	18.8	5	12.0	5	0	0
B	18.3	4	9.7	3	1	1
C	16.3	2	7.3	2	0	0
D	6.9	1	5.3	1	0	0
E	17.1	3	10.9	4	-1	1
F	20.4	6	16.8	6	0	0
						$\sum d_i^2 = 2$

b. $r_s = 1 - \dfrac{6\sum d_i^2}{n(n^2-1)} = 1 - \dfrac{6(2)}{6(6^2-1)} = 1 - .0571 = .9429$

c.   To determine if apparent porosity and mean pore diameter are positively correlated, we test:

H_0: $\rho_s = 0$
H_a: $\rho_s > 0$

The test statistic is $r_s = .9429$.

Reject H_0 if $r_s > r_{s,\alpha}$ where $\alpha = .01$ and $n = 6$. From Table XVII, Appendix B, $r_{s,.01} = .943$. Reject H_0 if $r_s > .943$.

Since the observed value of the test statistic does not fall in the rejection region ($r_s = .9429 \not> .943$), H_0 is not rejected. There is insufficient evidence to indicate the apparent porosity and mean pore diameter are positively correlated at $\alpha = .01$.

14.63 a. **Navigability**: $r_s = .179$. Since this value is close to 0, there is a very weak positive correlation between the ranks of organizational internet use and the ranks of navigability.

Transactions: $r_s = .334$. Since this value is relatively close to 0, there is a weak positive correlation between the ranks of organizational internet use and the ranks of transactions.

Locatability: $r_s = .590$. Since this value is about half way between 0 and 1, there is a moderate positive correlation between the ranks of organizational internet use and the ranks of locatability.

Information Richness: $r_s = -.115$. Since this value is close to 0, there is a very weak negative correlation between the ranks of organizational internet use and the ranks of information richness.

Number of files: $r_s = .114$. Since this value is close to 0, there is a very weak positive correlation between the ranks of organizational internet use and the ranks of number of files.

b. For each indicator, we will test:

$$H_o: \rho_s = 0$$
$$H_a: \rho_s \neq 0$$

Navigability: p-value $= .148$. Since the p-value is greater than $\alpha = .10$, H_0 is not rejected. There is insufficient evidence to indicate a positive correlation between organizational internet use and navigability.

Transactions: p-value $= .023$. Since the p-value is less than $\alpha = .10$, H_0 is rejected. There is sufficient evidence to indicate a positive correlation between organizational internet use and transactions.

Locatability: p-value $= .000$. Since the p-value is less than $\alpha = .10$, H_0 is rejected. There is sufficient evidence to indicate a positive correlation between organizational internet use and locatability.

Information Richness: p-value $= .252$. Since the p-value is greater than $\alpha = .10$, H_0 is not rejected. There is insufficient evidence to indicate a positive correlation between organizational internet use and information richness.

Number of files: p-value $= .255$. Since the p-value is greater than $\alpha = .10$, H_0 is not rejected. There is insufficient evidence to indicate a positive correlation between organizational internet use and number of files.

14.65 **Method I and Method II**: $r_s = .189$. Since this value is close to 0, there is a very weak positive correlation between the ranks of Method I and the ranks of Method II.

Method I and Method III: $r_s = .592$. Since this value is about half way between 0 and 1, there is a moderate positive correlation between the ranks of Method I and the ranks of Method III.

Method I and Method IV: $r_s = .340$. Since this value is fairly close to 0, there is a weak positive correlation between the ranks of Method I and the ranks of Method IV.

Method II and Method III: $r_s = .205$. Since this value is close to 0, there is a very weak positive correlation between the ranks of Method II and the ranks of Method III.

Method II and Method IV: $r_s = .324$. Since this value is fairly close to 0, there is a weak positive correlation between the ranks of Method II and the ranks of Method IV.

Method III and Method IV: $r_s = .314$. Since this value is fairly close to 0, there is a weak positive correlation between the ranks of Method III and the ranks of Method IV.

14.67   Some preliminary calculations are:

Company	1999 Rank	Rank u_i	2000 Rank	Rank v_i	$d_i = u_i - v_i$	d_i^2
1	1	1	1	1	0	0
2	14	6	6	3	3	9
3	10	5	8	5	0	0
4	15	7	9	6	1	1
5	21	10	13	7	3	9
6	6	3	14	8	−5	25
7	2	2	16	9	−7	49
8	24	11	24	11	0	0
9	19	9	27	12	−3	9
10	29	14	35	13	1	1
11	26	12	39	14	−2	4
12	37	15	41	15	0	0
13	28	13	19	10	3	9
14	8	4	4	2	2	4
15	17	8	7	4	4	16
						$\sum d_i^2 = 136$

$$r_s = 1 - \frac{6 \sum d_i^2}{n(n^2 - 1)} = 1 - \frac{6(136)}{15(15^2 - 1)} = 1 - .243 = .757$$

To determine if the 1999 and 2000 reputation ranks are positively correlated, we test:

H_0: $\rho_s = 0$
H_a: $\rho_s > 0$

The test statistic is $r_s = .757$.

Reject H_0 if $r_s > r_{s,\alpha}$ where $\alpha = .05$ and $n = 15$.

Reject H_0 if $r_s > .441$ (From Table XVII, Appendix B)

Since the observed value of the test statistic falls in the rejection region ($r_s = .757 > .441$), H_0 is rejected. There is sufficient evidence to indicate that the 1999 and 2000 reputation ranks are positively correlated at $\alpha = .05$.

14.69   a.   Some preliminary calculations are:

Pair	X	Rank u_i	Y	Rank v_i	u_i^2	v_i^2	$u_i v_i$
1	19	5	12	5	25	25	25
2	27	7	19	8	49	64	56
3	15	2	7	1	4	1	2
4	35	9	25	9	81	81	81
5	13	1	11	4	1	16	4
6	29	8	10	2.5	64	6.25	20
7	16	3.5	16	6	12.25	36	21
8	22	6	10	2.5	36	6.25	15
9	16	3.5	18	7	12.25	49	24.5
	$\sum u_i = 45$		$\sum v_i = 45$		$\sum u_i^2 = 284.5$	$\sum v_i^2 = 284.5$	$\sum u_i v_i = 248.5$

$$SS_{uv} = \sum u_i v_i - \frac{\sum u_i v_i}{n} = 248.5 - \frac{45(45)}{9} = 23.5$$

$$SS_{uu} = \sum u_i^2 - \frac{\left(\sum u_i\right)^2}{n} = 284.5 - \frac{45^2}{9} = 59.5$$

$$SS_{vv} = \sum v_i^2 - \frac{\left(\sum v_i\right)^2}{n} = 284.5 - \frac{45^2}{9} = 59.5$$

To determine if the Spearman rank correlation differs from 0, we test:

$H_0: \rho_s = 0$
$H_a: \rho_s \neq 0$

The test statistic is $r_s = \dfrac{SS_{uv}}{\sqrt{SS_{uu} SS_{vv}}} = \dfrac{23.5}{\sqrt{59.5(59.5)}} = .40$

Reject H_0 if $r_s < -r_{s,\alpha/2}$ or if $r_s > r_{s,\alpha/2}$ where $\alpha/2 = .025$ and $n = 9$:

Reject H_0 if $r_s < -.683$ or if $r_s > .683$ (from Table XVII, Appendix B)

Since the observed value of the test statistic does not fall in the rejection region ($r_s = .40 \not> .683$), H_0 is not rejected. There is insufficient evidence to indicate that Spearman's rank correlation between x and y is significantly different from 0 at $\alpha = .05$.

b. Use the Wilcoxon signed rank test. Some preliminary calculations are:

Pair	X	Y	Difference	Rank of Absolute Difference
1	19	12	7	3
2	27	19	8	4.5
3	15	7	8	4.5
4	35	25	10	6
5	13	11	2	1.5
6	29	10	19	8
7	16	16	0	(eliminated)
8	22	10	12	7
9	16	18	-2	1.5
				$T_- = 1.5$

To determine if the probability distribution of x is shifted to the right of that for y, we test:

H_0: The probability distributions are identical for the two variables
H_a: The probability distribution of x is shifted to the right of the probability distribution of y

The test statistic is $T = T_- = 1.5$.
Reject H_0 if $T \leq T_0$ where T_0 is based on $\alpha = .05$ and $n = 8$ (one-tailed):

Reject H_0 if $T \leq 6$ (from Table XVI, Appendix B).

Since the observed value of the test statistic falls in the rejection region ($T = 1.5 \leq 6$), reject H_0 at $\alpha = .05$. There is sufficient evidence to conclude that the probability distribution of x is shifted to the right of that for y.

14.71 Some preliminary calculations are:

Block	1	Rank	2	Rank	3	Rank	4	Rank	5	Rank
1	75	4	65	1	74	3	80	5	69	2
2	77	3	69	1	78	4	80	5	72	2
3	70	4	63	1.5	69	3	75	5	63	1.5
4	80	3.5	69	1	80	3.5	86	5	77	2
		$R_1 = 14.5$		$R_2 = 4.5$		$R_3 = 13.5$		$R_4 = 20$		$R_5 = 7.5$

To determine whether at least two of the treatment probability distributions differ in location, use Friedman F_r test.

H_0: The five treatments have identical probability distributions
H_a: At least two of the populations have probability distributions that differ in location

The test statistic is $F_r = \dfrac{12}{bp(p+1)} \sum R_j^2 - 3b(p+1)$

$$= \frac{12}{4(5)(6)} [(14.5)^2 + (4.5)^2 + (13.5)^2 + (20)^2 + (7.5)^2] - 3(4)(6) = 14.9$$

The rejection region requires $\alpha = .05$ in the upper tail of the χ^2 distribution with df = $p - 1$ = 5 – 1 = 4. From Table VII, Appendix B, $\chi^2_{.05} = 9.48773$. The rejection region is $F_r > 9.48773$.

Since the observed value of the test statistic falls in the rejection region ($F_r = 14.9 > 9.48773$), H_0 is rejected. There is sufficient evidence to indicate that at least two of the treatment means differ in location at $\alpha = .05$.

14.73   Some preliminary calculations are:

Type A	Rank	Type B	Rank
95	1	110	6
122	10	102	4
102	3	115	8
99	2	112	7
108	5	120	9
$T_A = 21$		$T_B = 34$	

To determine if print type A is easier to read, we test:

H_0:   The two sampled populations have identical probability distributions
H_a: The probability distribution for print type A is shifted to the left of that for print type B

The test statistic is $T_A = 21$.

The rejection region is $T_A \le 19$ form Table XV, Appendix B, with $n_A = 5$ and $n_B = 5$, and $\alpha = .05$.

Since the observed value of the test statistic does not fall in the rejection region ($T_A = 21 \not\le 19$), H_0 is not rejected. There is insufficient evidence to indicate print type A is easier to read at $\alpha = .05$.

14.75   a. $H = \dfrac{12}{n(n+1)} \sum \dfrac{R_j^2}{n_j} - 3(n+1)$

$= \dfrac{12}{217(217+1)} \left[\dfrac{1804^2}{11} + \dfrac{6398^2}{49} + \dfrac{7328^2}{62} + \dfrac{4075^2}{39} + \dfrac{2660^2}{35} + \dfrac{1388^2}{21} \right] - 3(217+1)$

$= 35.23$

b.   The rejection region requires $\alpha = .01$ in the upper tail of the χ^2 distribution with df = $p - 1 = 6 - 1 = 5$. From Table VII, Appendix B, $\chi^2_{.01} = 15.0863$. The rejection region is $H > 15.0863$.

c. To determine if the biting rates for the six wind speed conditions differ, we test:

H_0: The probability distributions of the number of bites are the same for the six wind speed conditions

H_a: At least two of the six probability distributions differ in location

Since the observed value of the test statistic falls in the rejection region ($H = 35.23 > 15.0863$), H_0 is rejected. There is sufficient evidence to indicate that the biting rates for the six wind speed conditions differ at $\alpha = .01$.

d. The p-value is $p < .01$. Since the p-value is less than $\alpha = .01$, H_0 is rejected. This supports the inference in part c.

14.77 a and b. The ranks of the x and y values are:

Year	Years since 1970		Food ads	
	x	Rank, u_i	y	Rank, v_i
1971	1	1	5.4	2
1977	7	2	3	1
1988	18	3	6.5	5
1992	22	4	6	3.5
1998	28	5	6	3.5

c.
$$SS_{uv} = \sum uv - \frac{\left(\sum u\right)\left(\sum v\right)}{n} = 50.5 - \frac{15(15)}{5} = 5.5$$

$$SS_{uu} = \sum u^2 - \frac{\left(\sum u\right)^2}{n} = 55 - \frac{15^2}{5} = 10$$

$$SS_{vv} = \sum v^2 - \frac{\left(\sum v\right)^2}{n} = 54.5 - \frac{15^2}{5} = 9.5$$

$$r_s = \frac{SS_{uv}}{\sqrt{SS_{uu}SS_{vv}}} = \frac{5.5}{\sqrt{10(9.5)}} = 0.564$$

d. Since the value of r_s is not close to 1 or -1, there is a moderate positive relationship between the number of years since 1970 (x) and the rate of food ads per hour (y).

The rejection region requires $\alpha/2 = .10/2 = .05$ in each tail. From Table XVII, Appendix B, $r_{s,.05} = .900$, with $n = 5$. The rejection region is $r_s > .900$ or $r_s < -.900$.

e. Since the observed value of the test statistic does not fall in the rejection region ($r_s = .564 \ngtr .900$), H_0 is not rejected. There is insufficient evidence to indicate the number of years since 1970 and rate of food ads are correlated at $\alpha = .10$.

Nonparametric Statistics

14.79   a.   This is a paired difference problem.

   b.   To determine if the problem-solving performance of video teleconferencing groups is superior to face-to-face groups, we test:

   H_0:   The two sampled populations have identical probability distributions
   H_a: The probability distribution for population A (face-to-face) is shifted to the left of that for population B (video teleconferencing)

   c.   Some preliminary calculations:

Group	Face-To-Face	Video Teleconferencing	Difference	Rank of Absolute Difference
1	65	75	−10	7.5
2	82	80	2	1
3	54	60	−6	6
4	69	65	4	2.5
5	40	55	−15	9
6	85	90	−5	4.5
7	98	98	0	(eliminated)
8	35	40	−5	4.5
9	85	89	−4	2.5
10	70	80	−10	7.5

Negative rank sum $T_- = 41.5$

Positive rank sum $T_+ = 3.5$

The test statistic is $T_+ = 3.5$.

The null hypothesis will be rejected if $T_+ \leq T_0$ where T_0 corresponds to $\alpha = .05$ (one-tailed) and $n = 9$. From Table XVI, Appendix B, $T_0 = 8$.

   Reject H_0 if $T_+ \leq 8$.

ince the observed value of the test statistic falls in the rejection region ($T_+ = 3.5 \leq 8$), H_0 is rejected. There is sufficient evidence to indicate that problem-solving performance of video teleconferencing groups is superior to that of groups that interact face-to-face at $\alpha = .05$.

   d.   p-value $= P(T_+ \leq 3.5)$ where $n = 9$ and the test is one-tailed. Using Table XVI, locate the appropriate column for n, then find the values in that column that include the test statistic (in this case, 6 and 3). Then read the α level corresponding to these values. Thus,

      $.01 < p$-value $< .025$

14.81 The appropriate test for paired samples is the Wilcoxon signed rank test. Some preliminary calculations are:

Subject	Aspirin	Drug	Difference	Rank of Absolute Difference
1	15	7	8	6
2	20	14	6	3.5
3	12	13	−1	1
4	20	11	9	7
5	17	10	7	5
6	14	16	−2	2
7	17	11	6	3.5
				$T_- = 3.0$
				$T_+ = 25.0$

To determine if the probability distribution of the times required to obtain relief with aspirin is shifted to the right of the probability distribution of the times required to obtain relief with the drug, we test:

H_0: The probability distributions of length of time required for pain relief are identical for aspirin and the new drug

H_a: The probability distribution of the length of time required for pain relief with aspirin is shifted to the right of that for the new drug

The test statistic is $T_- = 3$.

Reject H_0 if $T_- \le T_0$ where $\alpha = .05$ (one-tailed) and $n = 7$:

Reject H_0 if $T_- \le 4$ (from Table XVI, Appendix B).

Since $T_- = 3 \le 4$, reject H_0. There is sufficient evidence to indicate the probability distribution of time required to obtain relief with aspirin is shifted to the right of that for the new drug at $\alpha = .05$.

14.83 Some preliminary calculations:

Low-Income	Rank	Middle-Income	Rank
.60	11.5	.87	14
.52	7	.85	13
.55	9	.54	8
.60	11.5	.46	1
.50	3.5	.50	3.5
.51	6	.50	3.5
.50	3.5	.56	10
$T_1 = 52$		$T_2 = 53$	

a. We could use the Wilcoxon Rank Sum Test for independent samples.

Nonparametric Statistics

b. To determine if the distribution for the low-income countries is shifted to the right or left of the distribution for middle-income countries, we test:

H_0: The two sampled populations have identical probability distributions
H_a: The probability distribution for the low-income countries is shifted to the right or left of that for the middle-income countries

c. The null hypothesis will be rejected if $T_2 \leq T_L$ or $T_2 \geq T_U$, where $\alpha = .05$ (two-tailed), and $n_1 = n_2 = 7$. From Table XV, Appendix B, $T_L = 37$ and $T_U = 68$.

Reject H_0 if $T_2 \leq 37$ or $T_2 \geq 68$.

d. The test statistic is $T_2 = 53$.

Since $T_2 = 53 \not\geq 68$, H_0 is not rejected. There is insufficient evidence to indicate that the distribution for low-income countries is shifted to the right or left of the distribution for middle-income countries at $\alpha = .05$.

14.85 Some preliminary calculations are:

Before		After	
Observation	Rank	Observation	Rank
10	19	4	5.5
5	8.5	3	3.5
3	3.5	8	16.5
6	12	5	8.5
7	14.5	6	12
11	20	4	5.5
8	16.5	2	2
9	18	5	8.5
6	12	7	14.5
5	8.5	1	1
$T_{Before} = 132.5$		$T_{After} = 77.5$	

To determine if the situation has improved under the new policy, we test:

H_0: The two sampled population probability distributions are identical
H_a: The probability distribution associated with after the policy was instituted is shifted to the left of that before

The test statistic is $T_{Before} = 132.5$.

The rejection region is $T_{Before} \geq 127$ from Table XV, Appendix B, with $n_A = n_B = 10$ and $\alpha = .05$.

Since the observed value of the test statistic falls in the rejection region ($T_{Before} = 132.5 \geq 127$), H_0 is rejected. There is sufficient evidence to indicate the situation has improved under the new policy at $\alpha = .05$.

14.87 Since the data are already ranked, it is clear that:

$$R_1 = 19.0 \quad R_2 = 21.5 \quad R_3 = 27.5 \quad R_4 = 32.0$$

To determine if the probability distributions of ratings differ for at least two of the items, we test:

H_0: The probability distributions of responses are identical for the four aspects
H_a: At least two of the probability distributions differ in location

The test statistic is $F_r = \dfrac{12}{bp(p+1)} \sum R_j^2 - 3b(p+1)$

$$= \frac{12}{10(4)(4+1)}[19.0^2 + 21.5^2 + 27.5^2 + 32.0^2] - 3(10)(4+1)$$

$$= 156.21 - 150 = 6.21$$

The rejection region requires $\alpha = .05$ in the upper tail of the χ^2 distribution with df $=$ $p - 1 = 4 - 1 = 3$. From Table VII, Appendix B, $\chi^2_{.05} = 7.81473$. The rejection region is $F_r > 7.81473$.

Since the observed value of the test statistic does not fall in the rejection region ($F_r = 6.21 \not>$ 7.81473), do not reject H_0. There is insufficient evidence to conclude that at least two of the items negotiated differ at $\alpha = .05$.

14.89 Some preliminary calculations are:

Category	Crisis Intervention Rating	Rank, u_i	Clarity Rating	Rank, v_i	d_i	d_i^2
Psychosis	1.31	3	1.33	3	0	0
Drug/alcohol abuse	1.33	4	1.29	1	3	9
Depression/anxiety	1.48	5	1.59	4	1	1
Emphasis on acuteness	1.76	6	2.50	8	-2	4
Insistence on "short-term" response	2.48	7	3.22	9	-2	4
Suicide	1.13	2	1.32	2	0	0
Family problems	2.59	8	2.30	6	2	4
Violence/harm	1.06	1	1.86	5	-4	16
Miscellaneous	2.60	9	2.33	7	2	4
Nondefinition	3.57	10	3.57	10	0	0
						$\sum d_i^2 = 42$

To determine if there is a positive relationship between the mean crisis intervention and mean clarity ratings, we test:

H_0: $\rho_s = 0$
H_a: $\rho_s > 0$

The test statistic is $r_s = 1 - \dfrac{6 \sum d_i^2}{n(n^2 - 1)} = 1 - \dfrac{6(42)}{10(10^2 - 1)} = .255$

Reject H_0 if $r_s > r_{s,\alpha}$ where $\alpha = .05$ and $n = 10$:

Reject H_0 if $r_s > .564$ (using Table XVII, Appendix B).

Since the observed value of the test statistic does not fall in the rejection region ($r_s = .255$ $\ngtr .564$), H_0 is not rejected. There is insufficient evidence to indicate that there is a positive relationship between the mean crisis intervention and mean clarity ratings at $\alpha = .05$.